Healing Capitalism

HEALING CAPITALISM

Five Years in the Life of Business, Finance and Corporate Responsibility

JEM BENDELL AND **IAN DOYLE**

Greenleaf
PUBLISHING

© 2014 Greenleaf Publishing Limited

Published by Greenleaf Publishing Limited
Aizlewood's Mill
Nursery Street
Sheffield S3 8GG
UK
www.greenleaf-publishing.com

Cover by LaliAbril.com
Printed in the UK on environmentally friendly, acid-free paper
from managed forests by CPI Group (UK) Ltd, Croydon

British Library Cataloguing in Publication Data:
A catalogue record for this book is available from the British Library.

ISBN-13: 978-1-906093-91-4 [paperback]
ISBN-13: 978-1-907643-92-7 [paperback]
ISBN-13: 978-1-909493-21-6 [PDF ebook]
ISBN-13: 978-1-78353-046-5 [ePub ebook]

Contents

Introduction
Why do we need to heal capitalism?

Jem Bendell

Recurring financial crises and growing protests over economic policies now punctuate the headlines. Personal crises, over debt or job insecurity, punctuate our conversations with friends and family. Typical strategies for economic recovery delay an inevitable reckoning with the limits of our capacity to service debts and the limits of the natural world to service humanity. Capitalism seems sick, or at least this version of it. Even the traditionally conservative arena of management academia has noticed that all is not well. In 2013, the Academy of Management's Annual Meeting chose as its topic 'Capitalism in Question'. It was an ambitious choice of topic, given that revolution is not a research theme usually entertained by business schools. The convenors explained that 'the recent economic and financial crises, austerity, and unemployment, and the emergence of many economic, social, and environmental protest movements around the world have put back on the agenda some big questions . . .'[1] The well-known management academic Michael Porter warned that 'the capitalist system is under siege. In recent years business increasingly has been viewed as a major cause of social, environmental, and economic problems.'[2]

How does our practice, research and teaching in the fields of corporate social responsibility (CSR), sustainable business, social enterprise or responsible investment (RI) relate to these crises? If we think it is time to try to heal capitalism itself, are we acting as an anti-inflammatory, a placebo, or a potential cure? Some people in this space prefer not to address such issues and instead focus on the growing field of CSR practice and research, and the increasing (yet relatively limited) examples of social enterprise and 'shared value' partnerships. Many prefer to articulate the commercial reasons or 'business case' for voluntary action on social, environmental and governance problems, rather than express or explore their role as a participant in social change. However, others consider themselves to be working within a social movement to transform business and finance. It was to give voice to this movement-mentality, and explore what it might mean for future practice and research, that I wrote *The Corporate Responsibility Movement* in 2009, which compiled five years of analysis in World Reviews from the *Journal of Corporate Citizenship*. In the subsequent years of writing World Reviews, my co-author Ian Doyle and I looked for trends that we considered had potential for systemic change (for instance, see 'From bail-outs to better capitalism', page 194; 'The end of financial triumphalism', page 197; 'Beyond the Western financial crisis', page 202).

Despite the enthusiasm of many for CSR and RI, as they spread around the world, we did not see a major change in the outcomes of business practice during the five years we chronicle in our book, and this raises serious questions about the efficacy of voluntary business action in achieving needed changes in society. Initiatives on green consumption are insignificant in comparison to the growth of consumerism worldwide. Technical improvements in efficiency do little to address overall demands on the biosphere. Steps to improve factory conditions in one region or supply chain do little to address the downward pressure on prices and labour rights in international supply chains. The growing number of investors seeking to back enterprises that contribute to social and environmental progress is laudable, but does nothing to address the way the financial sector extracts vast wealth from the real economy, encourages short-termism and constrains the policy options of any government today. Voluntary action may achieve some progress but rarely leads to voluntary restrictions on the growth of one's business or the requirements of an economic system that only maintains sufficient job opportunities and investment if the economy is 'growing'. The social and economic benefits from being so connected online do not outweigh the fundamental risk of alliances between authorities and global corporations that monitor all our expressed thoughts and activities. To extend the metaphor of sickness and healing, the majority of activity within the CSR and RI fields is dealing with acute symptoms of a sick system in an allopathic medical way, rather than treating the chronic condition in a holistic way, which would reduce the causes of distress. As I noted in my book *Terms for Endearment* near the start of this contemporary era of CSR, 'the reality we need to remind ourselves of is one where not everything that is right to do pays, and not everything that pays is right to do'.[3]

Such doubts are now heard at the highest levels in business. The joint United Nations and Accenture study of chief executive officers (CEOs) of the 1,000 largest firms found a growing awareness of the need for, and inability to generate, systemic change. That 93% of CEOs agreed that sustainability is key to their business shows how awareness is now widespread. However, only 32% of CEOs believed the global economy is on track to meet the demands of a growing population, with only 33% agreeing that business is making sufficient efforts to address global sustainability challenges. Therefore, 83% said government needs to better create an enabling environment for future business action.[4] Simply put, CEOs are beginning to understand how their voluntary responsibility within the market is not fixing critical problems such as climate change.

Given the limitations of CSR in meeting global challenges, what should professionals, researchers and educators do? We must look deeper into our own sectors and how they contribute to systemic problems, and could contribute to systemic solutions. Some in this field are doing just that and creating new alliances that seek systemic change, which I chronicled in my last book, *Evolving Partnerships*.[5] Bold and practical initiatives for change can be helped by having unusual conversations with those outside our normal professional community, such as critics who are rarely heard by business or within business schools. Learning together openly, we may discover a more systemic agenda for our work, and begin the process of healing capitalism.

CSR and RI fields are full of 'positive thinkers', lauding achievements for a specific forest, community, group of employees or some charismatic entrepreneurs. Yet positivity can be wishful and dishonest. The scale of the predicament demands we be honest about what is working and what is not. Faced with limited progress, some have argued that we move beyond CSR, but have really been proposing nothing more than the continuation of voluntary business initiatives with new labels, such as 'shared value' or 'sustainable enterprise'. In my case, after 15 years working in this field as a practitioner and academic, a simple rebranding of my activity would not be enough to rekindle my enthusiasm! I had invested a lot of my passion, thinking and youth in front of a laptop. I had worked on CSR in over 20 countries, helped to form major international alliances like the Marine Stewardship Council, produced over 100 publications on the topic, and created Masters courses at five universities. So the possibility that this might have been a waste of time was a bit troubling. In 2009 I took time out to explore new ways of creating social change. I moved to India and rented a house on the fringe of a spiritual community called Auroville where we hosted volunteer programmers working on open-source software for supporting community trade. I learned about the nature and effect of monetary systems, and new ways of creating alternatives that can be more sustaining of useful economic activity.

That the monetary system is an aspect of capitalism that needs changing was something I had accepted and mentioned in previous work,[6] but had not explored. In the *Corporate Responsibility Movement*, I outlined a concept of 'capital democracy' to explain how many activities in the CSR field are hinting at a more accountable economic system. In that theory I addressed issues of private property, limited liability, taxation and other key components of our economic systems. Yet I did not address our monetary system. Like most people working in corporate responsibility or the broader field of sustainable development, I did not fully understand how our global challenges cannot be properly addressed while private banks create about 97% of our money as debt and charge interest on it. During my time out of the corporate responsibility field, I began to understand this form of monetary system as a malignancy at the heart of our economies, meaning that our real wealth, which is found in our environment and communities, is exploited to service compound interest on perpetual debt. At first I did not see how the CSR field could relate to this insight and so after ten years I stopped writing the World Reviews and focused much more on innovation in currency and exchange systems.

In the last few years the topic of currency innovation has become more widely understood, mostly due to the growing use of the Bitcoin cyber currency. This has led to many more organisations, companies, banks and venture capitalists looking at this area, so that now I'm invited to train and advise a variety of organisations on currency innovation. There are benefits and drawbacks from the rapid scaling of new currency and exchange systems. To enable a smooth transition away from our current monetary systems to ones that enable fair and sustainable economies, the ideas, practices, alliances and organisations in the CSR field may be of some use. Therefore I have returned to CSR and responsible investment 'movements' to invite engaged scholars and progressive leaders to explore what business and financial firms can do to help.

I completed this book because I believe now is a good time for more informed dialogue and innovation on the future of our economic system and that concerned business leaders and their educators have a key role to play. When the world's business community first articulated a commitment to work on global challenges, in the early 1990s, there was a widespread disinterest in dealing with fundamental economic issues, partly because the Cold War had just ended. The 1992 Earth Summit in Rio De Janeiro, which helped consolidate the concept of 'sustainable development,' framed the challenge as one of teaming up to add more social and environmental considerations to the capitalist system pioneered by the West. Since then we have had 20 more years of this global embrace of capitalism, and are more able to identify and discuss its limitations as a system of economic and social organisation.

Our exploration of what kind of changes are needed could be enhanced by insights from a range of intellectual traditions, including sociology, political science, international development studies, history and contrarian economics, rather than the narrower management and organisation studies that currently dominate the advice and training given to business leaders. Insights from these diverse disciplines may help reveal assumptions that limit our current analysis. For instance, many participants I met at a number of summits held by the World Economic Forum appeared to assume that the world's problems require better management applied to the mainstream economic system, rather than redesigning that system. Of those who did speak of a need to redesign the system, their proposals and activities did not address the basic elements of capitalism. Those working in the CSR field might be able to help in this deeper exploration but, until now, the framing of CSR and RI, and the jobs within it, have not provided a mandate to work on or influence deeper economic governance issues. In this book Ian Doyle and I have drawn upon a variety of intellectual disciplines to support your exploration of matters of corporate irresponsibility in ways that could inspire strategies that address the scale of the public problems, rather than simply address the way those problems manifest themselves as management challenges.

In the remainder of this introduction I will look briefly at the scale and urgency of persistent social and environmental problems, and the evidence for how these are connected to the dominant economic system in the world. I will summarise some of the efforts towards systemic change that have occurred in the years within the field of corporate responsibility and responsible investment, along with their mixed results in achieving significant change. As the conversation about the future of capitalism grows, it is important to be clear about what exactly is meant by capitalism, and what in particular within it may be at fault for driving some social and environmental problems. Once this sickness is diagnosed, the possible means of healing are discussed. In particular, I focus on the potential that innovation in monetary systems holds for turning the tide of social and environmental degradation. Then I explore how professionals working and researching in the corporate responsibility field can engage in these means of healing the system. In concluding, I place this economic healing within the context of a broader healing in society and our own lives.

I hope this book, and in particular this introduction, will encourage you to explore what role businesses can play in enabling systemic changes in economic systems, in ways that could work for your own organisation. I will invite you to move out of a paradigm of curbing the excesses of the current system into a paradigm that is explicitly transformative and quietly revolutionary. I will suggest the potential for business to disrupt current unsustainable patterns of economic governance via peer-to-peer systems for sharing, exchanging and financing, as well as currency innovation. You may even be able to integrate more of these activities in your work, without having to take time out in a spiritual community in India. Though I would never argue against that . . .

Or would I? The urgency of the purpose of our work can easily be forgotten amidst the day-to-day machinations of office politics and a demanding inbox. It is important to remember that the vital signs of our world call for us to redouble our efforts, to be courageous and challenging, both within and outside our organisations. The major problems we work on are daily tragedies. In the last 24 hours, 80,000 acres of tropical rainforest have been lost.[7] In a day, over a million tonnes of toxic waste have been released into our environment.[8] In just the last 24 hours, 98,000 people on our planet died of starvation, tens of thousands of them children.[9] In just this last day, over 150 species have been driven into extinction.[10] These problems persist not because people have ignored them as many of us have been engaged for a long time, as have generations before us. There is a need for new approaches which strike at the root of the problems. In the five years chronicled in this book, there were many developments that sought to achieve a deeper and broader change in business and finance; but are they enough?

Struggling to grasp the system

To help you explore the issues chronicled in this book, we have prepared a thematic index, which is based on the set of topics identified by the ISO 26000 standard for organisational responsibility. A total of 97 book sections are categorised according to these topics, as well as by management functions and organisational sectors. A recurring theme in the analysis of my co-author Ian Doyle and I is the perception of professionals and academics of a need for more 'systemic' change in business practice (see sections numbered 31, 32, 54-58, 65, 68, 76, 84). Initiatives seeking to address root causes, or cause ripple effects to drive change beyond individual corporations appeared to grow worldwide during the five-year period we analysed. Given the global challenges we face, these steps forward were promising, but there has been a constant struggle with the limits of voluntary action and against a tide of 'financialisation' of the economy. In 2007, I was reflecting a more critical mood among some CSR professionals when suggesting that complex financial derivatives could lead to capitalism eating itself and rendering most CSR insignificant (see 'Capital cannibal', page 107).

The development of RI gave many of us working in the CSR field some hope that a more systemic approach would be possible. In the period 2001–2005 analysed in *The Corporate Responsibility Movement*, I noted that

> most work on finance and ethics had focused on questions of responsibility, not accountability, rights or democracy. Action on finance and ethics was limited to minority shareholders causing trouble for companies (shareholder activism), increasing the security of one's returns via expanded risk management assessments and corporate engagement (responsible investment), ethical venture capital (in environmental technologies, for example) or seeking moral cleanliness in one's own investments (screening out certain sectors from investment portfolios). Little had been done on the accountability of the people who invested, their demands for returns, and the people who managed their investments.

Since 2004 I had articulated the ideological limitations of the RI field as it had not explored matters of accountability of the investors themselves or the broader systemic issues.

In the five years chronicled in this book, the RI field did not evolve significantly, with the dominant trend being the industrialisation of the analysis and sale of data on environmental, social and governance (ESG) aspects of corporations. The limitations of this ESG industry to create meaningful change, and how responsible investors could be more active in driving change is a major focus in the final sections of this book (see pages 365ff.).

Beyond the CSR and RI fields, discussion about the future of capitalism has grown. Our review of CSR in 2009 was called 'Capitalism in Question' and chronicled the various books and articles that year which sought to revive capitalism through more public-mindedness from entrepreneurs and business leaders (see the introduction to 2009, pages 222ff.). Since then, others from management academia and consulting have rehearsed the same theme, most notably Joseph L. Bower, Herman Leonard and Lynn Sharp Paine,[11] Michael Porter and Mark Kramer[12] and Arun Maira.[13] These authors speak of fixing capitalism through an emphasis on the values of business leaders. They do not consider how a values-inspired approach to business could involve us seeking to reduce our own organisations' power and freedom through new regulations. No, the emphasis is once again on voluntary action, enhanced strategies and charismatic entrepreneurs. With such arguments, I cannot see how major achievements in economic ethics, such as the outlawing of slavery, would ever have been achieved. Bower *et al.* (2011) do recognise that corporate power could be channelled for changes in regulatory systems but then see no problem in an emergent world order where corporations would be deciding our fate. I am reminded of the sanity of some past politicians on this matter: 'The first truth is that the liberty of a democracy is not safe if the people tolerate the growth of private power to a point where it becomes stronger than their democratic state itself. That, in its essence, is Fascism—ownership of government by an individual, by a group, or by any other controlling private power' (Franklin D. Roosevelt, 29 April 1938).

Another side to this mainstream response to the crisis of capitalism is the emphasis on 'social enterprise', promoted by organisations like Ashoka, Acumen Fund, Schwab Foundation and LGT Venture Philanthropy. Often the argument is made that a new type of organisation is emerging that is neither governmental, for-profit or not-for-profit. Whereas there are many instances of entrepreneurs that successfully address social and environmental problems through their business activity, the current hype around them appears ideological and unhelpful. On the one hand, socially driven enterprise is as old as enterprise itself, with many of the most famous brands today being founded by people as expressions of their beliefs: for instance, the Quakers. That these companies have since been amalgamated into large, publicly listed corporations and their social mission made secondary or invisible highlights the importance of organisational ownership in maintaining a social mission (see 'CSR and ownership', page 319). Yet the current hype around social enterprise denies the importance of organisational ownership, which not only ignores this recent corporate history but also centuries of scholarship and the experience of hundreds of millions of people worldwide who work with cooperatives and mutual associations today. Not to distinguish between organisations controlled by a few who decide what to do with a surplus, and those controlled by their workers and beneficiaries and reinvest that surplus is deceitful and ignores the critical importance of inequality in driving multiple social and environmental problems (see 'Corporate responsibility for economic inequality', page 313). Those that suggest social enterprises represent a new capitalism should read up on the history of cooperatives and mutualism, as well as the current global movement now called the 'social and solidarity economy'. We might not have time to read the original texts from theorists like Pierre-Joseph Proudhon but an hour on Wikipedia would be a start, and at least instil some useful doubts and questions.[14]

My search of all papers presented at the 'Capitalism in Question' conference revealed none that explored key issues such as limited liability companies, absent shareholders, or the monetary system or even the most famous theoretical critiques of capitalism, such as that by Karl Polanyi. One panel engaged senior management academics in 'how to rethink the basic pillars of the capitalist system given its strong emphasis on ever-increasing growth' yet the discussions were not informed by the vast tradition of political theory on the subject. Faced with a daily flood of forms and emails, we may find it difficult but academics are still meant to read. An analysis of the bibliographies of papers presented at the conference revealed hardly any references to political science, sociology or development studies, nor the critical work in management studies such as that in the World Review of the *Journal of Corporate Citizenship*, or publications from United Nations agencies on these issues.[15] Given that the Academy of Management conference was hosted in Disney World, we might forgive this Mickey Mouse treatment of the organiser's theme. Yet the complete absence of depth suggests this is not an anomaly but the result of a process. Operating within an organisational culture that is wedded to contemporary discourses of success, where captains of industry are reverently studied and their courtiers in management consulting widely admired, shapes the nature of research topics. Then those topics are now explored almost exclusively by using academic journal databases, so only the most bland and mono-disciplinary texts that involve popular keywords have a chance of a glance by a researcher. This process produces a structured stupidity, reflecting the world of management academe, rather than the world around us.

To heal capitalism we won't have use for physicians who avoid underlying causes or are untrained to see them, or just want to use a sickness to display their existing prowess. So where will our physicians come from? Key may be the work arising from self-assured peripheries to the dominant paradigm: not those peripheral organisations that seek to copy the mainstream delusion of management excellence, but those that have the conviction of their own intellectual traditions. Perhaps places like my current base in the Ambleside Campus of the University of Cumbria, in the Lake District, which is home to over a century-long tradition of critical sociology, environmentalism and progressive education, could play a role.[16] Such places will need to up their game, connect with others, and begin to articulate an approach to systemic change that can influence more people—a difficult task at a time of great disruption in higher education.

I'm not steeped in political theory or the history of ideas on political economy or related philosophy. However, even a cursory reading of these fields helps one ask some more fundamental questions. To begin with, it encourages us to be clear about what we mean by capitalism, rather than assume it means 'things as they are now'. The definition provided in Wikipedia gives us a sense of the mainstream view of the concept and it indicates that capitalism is considered to involve private ownership, which is deployed to extract a profit for property owners, usually operating in a market system. Is this triumvirate of characteristics an accurate definition of capitalism? Let us first look at private property and its use for the pursuit of private profit.

Although the term 'human capital' appears in *An Inquiry into the Nature and Causes of the Wealth of Nations* by Adam Smith in 1776, in recent decades it has become normal for social scientists to regard anything as 'capital', with at least five forms of capital now discussed: natural, social, human, manufactured and financial capital. When this occurs, it is important not to ignore that something is 'capital' because of a specific power relationship: 'capital' is anything physical or virtual that someone or group can control sufficiently in order to extract an income or benefit from. A forest can be conceived of as 'capital' when it is being controlled by someone or some group to extract an income or benefit from it. The forests that are not controlled by someone to generate a yield would not be accurately described as natural capital. Yes, such a forest's impact on the environment underpins other capital and economic activity, but if not controlled by someone or group for their own revenue or benefit then 'capital' is the wrong word to describe its value or worth. Forest dwellers may be harvesting materials from the forest, and completely dependent on it for their lives, but would not consider that they 'control' the forest. Yes, the forest is valuable even though it is not 'capital', and that is partly the point I am making here: not everything valuable can be called 'capital'. Grammatically, capital-ism should simply mean a belief in capital, and a system that creates and maintains capital. Therefore, capitalism should be understood as the belief that more and more resources should be managed by specific individuals or groups to generate incomes or yields, i.e. to be managed as capital. Therefore, to believe in capitalism is to believe that it is good to control bits of existence to extract revenues or yields from them, mostly through controlling how other people interact with that bit of existence. It is a belief in creating and using property. This does not mean that one particular type of owner is necessitated in a capitalist system, as some property could be owned by non-profits, cooperatives, local or national governments. Capitalism does not have to mean that private ownership by a few is the predominant form of ownership or that capital necessarily involves use to generate a private profit, rather than a yield of some sort.

Delving back into the past, to the mid-1800s when the rapid industrialisation of Europe was inspiring a debate about the role of capitalists and capitalism, we find the Lake District's John Ruskin elaborating on the meaning of the term. In 1852 he wrote that capital 'is material by which some derivative or secondary good is produced. It is only capital proper . . . when it is thus producing something different from itself.' Ruskin was seeking to emphasise that 'capital' should be useful in supporting life.

> The best and simplest general type of capital is a well-made ploughshare. Now, if that ploughshare did nothing but beget other ploughshares, in a polypous manner, -- however the great cluster of polypous plough might glitter in the sun, it would have lost its function of capital.[17]

This qualitative assessment of what can be called 'capital' seems a world away from today's equating of capital with financial capital. Yet it reminds us that, if financial capital exists to reproduce itself rather than enable activities that generate living wealth, then it is has lost its social utility—something I return to below.

The other aspect of capitalism that is often assumed to be key is a market system. The modern era of capitalism began with the forced privatisation of resources that had previously been held in common ownership by virtue of traditional rights, and whose benefits had been more or less fairly distributed. This enclosure of the commons encouraged people to leave their land and work in cities for industrialists.[18] This process continues around the world to this day and extends into new spheres of life, where airwaves, genetics and information are increasingly commoditised and controlled for profit. The systems that develop as a result of these processes are sometimes erroneously called 'free markets', as if there are not regulations on matters such as property, contract, monopoly and legal tender that control its functioning. The growth in markets as the way we interact is clearly connected to the growth of contemporary capitalism. However, a market can exist without private property, or for-profit companies, and has done at various times and locations in history, even before the enclosure of the commons. Therefore, the equating of capitalism with free markets is false, and a criticism of capitalism does not necessarily mean a rejection of markets.

One of the more famous analysts of capitalism, Karl Marx, focused on who or what owned the means of production, how they hired labour and generated profits. Marx was important for explaining the instability of a system where all owners pay workers less than the value of the products of their work, so that over time there would not be enough money for workers to afford the produce of their efforts. It was simple maths but ignored the role of credit creation. Marx analysed how we can come to appreciate money more than real wealth, as it is transferable for so many items of wealth. He did not go much further in his analysis of money, such as the role of banking and of credit money, and neither have the well-known Marxist economists since.[19] This emphasis on control of means of production, rather than means of exchange, was a key oversight—which perhaps made it easier for international bankers to lend to communists. The nature of money, and how it is issued, is not an essential feature of any capitalist system but is the fundamental feature of the capitalism we experience today and, as such, any attempt at healing capitalism must address what I call the money problem.

The money problem

The world can seem a bit aggressive: there is always war, always a sense of threat. Some would have us believe that this is fundamental to human nature. I have come to understand such a world-view as the most insidious effect of our current monetary system and the greatest barrier to healing capitalism, society and our planet. President Eisenhower warned the world about the military-industrial complex, where industrial and banking interests would encourage military escalation for their own economic interests. A century before that, John Ruskin explained the commercial drive for constant war and xenophobia:

> It is one very awful form of the operation of wealth in Europe that it is entirely capitalists' wealth which supports unjust wars. Just wars do not need so much money to support them; for most of the men who wage such, wage them gratis; but for an unjust war, men's bodies and souls have both to be bought; and the best tools of war for them besides; which makes such war costly to the maximum; not to speak of the cost of base fear, and angry suspicion, between nations . . . And all unjust war being supportable, if not by pillage of the enemy, only by loans from capitalists, these loans are repaid by subsequent taxation of the people, who appear to have no will in the matter, the capitalists' will being the primary root of the war . . .[20]

Why would he consider capitalists, and in particular international bankers, to be so salient in war-making? Why would Britain's Chancellor of the Exchequer in 1915 comment that 'those who create and issue money and credit direct the policies of government and hold in the hollow of their hands the destiny of the people'?[21] Why would US President Andrew Jackson, tell the US senate in 1832 that 'controlling our currency, receiving our public moneys, and holding thousands of our citizens in dependence . . . would be more formidable and dangerous than a military power of the enemy'?[22] What precisely is the aspect of money and banking that they condemn?

From the crimes of rate-fixing to shock at the size of bonuses, modern banking is like salt water: good to float in if you know how but hard for us to swallow. Yet so few of us look closer at the nature of money itself, rather than the secondary questions of banker conduct. It is a fatal oversight. In most countries today, it is estimated that about 3% of our money originates from government-owned mints that make notes and coins. The rest is digital and is created by banks when they issue loans. Yes: *created*. When you or your government goes to a bank to take out a loan, the bank does not lend its own money or that of its depositors. Instead it creates that money by an electronic accounting entry in return for a contract that the borrower will pay back that amount plus interest. Nothing is being loaned; banks simply create the money on the basis of the 'borrower's' promise to pay.[23] This fact sounds unbelievable to those of us who have not thought about how modern money is issued, rather than earned. Consequently, it is often helpful to quote the central banks themselves: 'When banks make loans they create additional deposits for those that have borrowed the money,' explains the Bank of England. As Paul Tucker, the former Deputy Governor of the Bank of England, further explains: 'Banks extend credit by simply increasing the borrowing customer's current account . . . That is, banks extend credit by creating money.'[24]

Even the 'best' educational institutions are teaching their students a fictional account of how this system works today. In his best-selling *Ascent of Money*, Professor Niall Ferguson (2008) explains how students are instructed at his university:

> . . . first-year MBA students at Harvard Business School play a simplified money game. It begins with a notional central bank paying the professor $100 on behalf of the government, for which he has done some not very lucrative consulting. The professor takes the banknotes to a bank notionally operated by one of his students and deposits them there, receiving a deposit slip. Assuming, for the sake of simplicity, that this bank operates a 10 per cent reserve ratio . . . it deposits $10 with the central bank and lends the other $90 to one of its clients. While the client decides what to do with his loan, he deposits the money in another bank. This bank also has a 10 per cent reserve rule, so it deposits $9 at the central bank and lends out the remaining $81 to another of its clients . . . By the time money has been deposited at three different student banks, [the monetary base, 'M0'] . . . is equal to $100 but [the combined cash and demand deposits, 'M1'] . . . is equal to $271 ($100 + $90 + $81), neatly illustrating, albeit in a highly simplified way, how modern fractional reserve banking allows the creation of credit and hence of money.[25]

It might be neat but it is nonsense. That form of fractional reserve banking has not existed for many decades. Instead, 'changes in [a private bank's] reserves [with a Central Bank] are unrelated to changes in lending . . . the textbook treatment of money . . . can be rejected,' explained Seth B. Carpenter of the US Federal Reserve. Vitor Constâncio, Vice President of the European Central Bank, further explains that 'banks [are] taking first their credit decisions and then looking for the necessary funding and reserves of central bank money.' Simply put, this means that private banks create as much money as they determine is possible to be paid back, or that they can sell on to other institutions, given their assessment of prevailing market conditions.[26]

The key insight from a study of the history of money is that we have allowed the *credit commons* to be privatised so that it can be accessed only by appealing to some bank to grant a 'loan'.[27] By 'credit commons' we mean our ability, as free individuals and organisations, to issue credit to whomever we choose, in a form and volume that we decide, without paying interest to a bank in that process.

Today's monopoly on credit creation by private banks now drives a range of economic, social and environmental problems. If the system of capitalism is 'sick', then the current monetary system is a key cause of disease. One problem is that, as banks create the amount borrowed, but not the interest to be paid on that loan, there is more debt owed in the world than there is money to repay it.[28] Although individually we might pay off our debts, collectively the population is in debt forever and paying interest to the banks. That makes increasing inequality a mathematical certainty. Inequality is rising worldwide and 2% of the world's population controls about half the world's wealth.[29] Extreme inequality is correlated with major social problems, including crime and ill-health of all sorts, physical, mental and emotional.[30] Rich or poor, today's capitalism is literally making us sick (see 'Corporate responsibility for economic inequality', page 313).

This dynamic of bank-issued debt-based money means it exists to replicate itself, at all costs. John Ruskin's assertion that 'capital'—if of something of value—must be productive of something other than itself, makes us question whether we are deluded to consider this credit-issued money as capital at all. Therefore, might it not even be part of 'capitalism' but a mutation from it? By incessant self-replication this form of bank-money is acting like cancerous cells within the body of the economy. A metaphor of currency as blood circulating in the economy is often used, as blood helps nourish the body. With this bank-debt money, it is as if we have leukaemia, as cancerous blood cells serve themselves not the body.

A further problem arising from our money supply being bank-issued debt is that the availability of our money depends on the sentiments and intentions of bankers. If bankers lose confidence in our ability to pay, or our government's ability to pay, or simply choose to lend less in a coordinated way, then the whole economy has less money. That means less money for investment, wages and jobs. Which means we stop working for each other. That is one reason why there is mass unemployment while there remains so much that needs doing to enhance human existence. While professionals working on 'sustainability' continue to focus on initiatives and debates arising from their preoccupations with environmental protection or international development assistance, the Western financial crisis has been fundamentally restructuring the societies they exist within. Greece has suffered the greatest contraction in money supply during the recent crisis, with an annual contraction of about 20%.[31] Less money in circulation has meant cuts in wages and more unemployment. The leukaemia-like debt-money starves the socio-economic body of what it needs. The suicide rate in Greece increased by 40% in 2011.[32]

The role of banks in deciding where the newly issued money goes presents another problem as it shapes the economy and society in line with their interests, while undermining the free market, civil society and governments. Banks choose whom to issue money to in line with their aims of seeking the largest return with the lowest transaction cost and risk. So they lend to things such as consumption and property speculation, rather than to small businesses. For instance, about 80% of bank lending in the UK of late has been for property purchases. That has made house prices rise 8000% since 1950, far above the inflation in prices of other goods or assets.[33] The result of this inflation in real estate prices is that, if you are not fortunate enough to own a property, then the costs of rent, or of a mortgage, means that many people are forced to work in jobs that are destructive or demeaning and to live lives they are not happy with.[34] It is as if the leukaemia of bank-issued debt-money has metastasised, creating useless tumours around the body, which are then served by new blood vessels and drain the body of energy and resources.

The most destructive problem from this monetary system is that it requires continual economic growth to justify the necessary growth in the money supply. This stems from the fact that money is created on the basis of interest-bearing debt, so that the amount owed increases with the passage of time. Compound interest is an exponential growth function, which means that debt grows not at a constant steady pace, but at an accelerating rate. The global money system therefore requires the further continual expansion of debt in order to avoid financial collapse, as there is not enough money to service the ever-expanding debts. New loans require further economic activity which, despite a small amount of decoupling economic growth from resource consumption, means ever-greater consumption of natural resources and pollution of our biosphere.[35] Although in some countries increasing economic growth—the amount of money changing hands—may be what people desire to improve their lives, this monetary system imposes a growth imperative whatever the local context and does not allow a 'steady state' economy to emerge. Some Nobel laureates and politicians have noted the inappropriateness of growth in gross domestic product (GDP) as a goal for societies, and various initiatives are working on new metrics, such as the European Union.[36] Yet, with an interest-charging system of money creation, we have no choice but to grow the economy, otherwise there will be less new debt issued to service existing debts, so there are more defaults, foreclosures, bankruptcies, unemployment, depression and, as history shows us, crime, extremism and even war.[37]

The competition among borrowers for an insufficient supply of money also results in pressure to externalise costs onto society and environment: pollution, for instance. The interest rates charged on loans also leads to greater discounting of natural assets, as money in the bank today can be worth more than trees in a forest.[38]

The combined effects of these processes are that we experience life as difficult and requiring compromise, where we do not live the way our silenced hearts used to call us. Like the final stages of cancer where it reaches the nerves, we now experience life as pain and the ability for different parts of our social body to communicate with each other in truth begins to be lost. This requires a deeper level of healing, which I return to at the end of this introduction. Sadly, instead of addressing the needed psychological and cultural healing to keep the economic body alive, our society turns to 'fracking' for gas, nuclear power and further wars to control resources, like a form of chemotherapy when it is already too late. In summary, the current monetary system is not enabling life, but smothering it, as aptly shown by the cover of this book. The challenge is how to free ourselves and allow all forms of creativity to thrive—something we are beginning to discover.

Some have used cancer metaphors before when discussing the problems with capitalism. David Korten described the corporation as a form of cancer that will ultimately destroy the larger society upon which they actually depend for survival.[39] The entrepreneur John Mackey echoed this idea: 'the only thing in the human body that grows just for growth's sake is cancer . . . I think sometimes businesses do that because they get drunk off bigger market share or more power and bigger perks and bigger egos, and I don't think all of that scale growth is always healthy.'[40] In my exploration of how to heal capitalism, I no longer consider the corporation to be the prime issue, but the 'cancer' to be the bank-debt monetary system. The initial 'cancer' creates so many other ills, as I've described above, but they are not the prime cause.

The healing

Capitalism has become self-defeating due to over-reach into all aspects of life and is becoming unhinged from controlling frameworks and the production of real wealth: the current monetary system has driven this imbalance.

How can a process of healing begin? Having a vision of a healthy economy and society is key, to give us a sense of that for which we are aiming. Currently, the demands of the monetary system for perpetual economic growth means that politicians and economists are focused on 'healthy' numbers, rather than a healthy society. The Native American Indian Alanis Obomsawin said in 1972 that 'when the last tree is cut, the last fish is caught, and the last river is polluted; when to breathe the air is sickening, you will realize, too late, that wealth is not in bank accounts and that you can't eat money'.[41] Over a hundred years before, John Ruskin asserted a goal for economic activity. He wrote, 'the final outcome and consummation of all wealth is in the producing as many as possible full-breathed, bright-eyed, and happy-hearted human creatures'. He continued,

> There is no wealth but LIFE. Life, including all its powers of love, of joy, and of admiration. That country is the richest which nourishes the greatest number of noble and happy human beings; that man is richest who, having perfected the functions of his own life to the utmost, has also the widest helpful influence, both personal, and by means of his possessions, over the lives of others.[42]

One way to heal the rupture between finance and real wealth creation is to make capital more accountable to those affected by it. In the *Corporate Responsibility Movement* I developed a concept that connected together a variety of the approaches to increase responsibility and accountability of enterprise and finance; 'Capital democracy describes an economic system that moves towards the creation, allocation and management of capital according to the interests of everyone directly affected by that process, in order to support the self-actualisation of all.'[43] This principle implies enhanced systems to democratise ownership, trade, employment, and taxation, which I discuss in this book in the Introduction to 2009. There I describe Mahatma Gandhi's views on trusteeship, where he argued that we should not consider property owners as owners, but as trustees, who are entrusted stewardship of resources by those affected. In developing this concept of capital democracy, I reject as false the dichotomy of state ownership versus individual ownership which pervades much left-versus-right politics and economics today. Instead, more resources need to be co-produced and managed as 'commons' by active communities. Denigrated by the economics profession for years, the commons have for centuries been a successful way of managing economic life, and have experienced a renaissance in the digital sphere through open-source software and online communities.[44] Unlocking the treasury of the commons will be key to healing of capitalism and society at large.

The 'cancer' of the current monetary system must also be addressed. The restrictions on charging interest on loans within Islamic financial systems is one way to moderate the demands for growth (see 'Islamic finance', page 209). However, in most, if not all, predominantly Muslim countries, debt creation is the main origin of the money supply, with the various problems this generates explained earlier. To solve this bank-issued debt-money problem, at present there are two broad approaches. First, are the growing campaigns for monetary reform, such as the 'Positive Money' campaign in the UK. These call for government to pass legislation to end fractional or non-reserve banking and give government the role of spending and lending new money into circulation. In the last few years these campaigns have raised awareness of these issues, but have made little headway in influencing the agendas of political parties. Aside from whether it is likely that governments or politicians will soon act on this agenda, these national reform proposals do not address the need for our currency systems to be responsive to the needs of communities and businesses, and to be freely chosen by them, rather than imposed as a monopoly.

Therefore, the second approach, which has grown massively worldwide in the past few years, is to innovate one's own moneyless exchange and alternative currency systems. The best-known of the new currencies at present is Bitcoin, which is a distributed global database that maintains records of transactions between internet-enabled devices, and rewards those devices for processing the latest transactions by issuing them 'bitcoins'. Significant amounts of angel investment and venture capital are now supporting start-ups in Bitcoin-related businesses: for instance, Bitpay, which has received investment from the famous Founders' Fund. Bitcoin raises a variety of concerns about its issuance, security, governance and future economic effects, which remain to be studied and resolved. However, one thing is not in doubt: Bitcoin proves that people can create their own global currencies which do not require banks to intermediate between individuals and companies. This reminds us of the 1944 economist E.C. Riegel who wrote, 'we need not petition Congress and we need not waste time to denounce bankers, for they can neither help nor hinder our natural right to extend credit to each other, and this is the perfect basis for a money system'.[45]

Bitcoin is not yet, however, a system for extending credit to each other, and is therefore not a democratic response to the current bank-issued politically backed monetary system. The various cryptographic currencies such as Bitcoin provide a new arena for innovations in financial services. However, Bitcoin is a system where people regard the currency as wealth, and speculate on its value, rather than the currency being issued when work of useful social value is conducted. That one's computer processes some of a distributed ledger of transactions is not sufficiently useful 'work' to be an ideal means of currency issuance. Instead, the field of currency and exchange innovation can seek to reclaim the 'credit commons': that is, the ability we all have to trust and issue credit to each other, through systems that we decide and control ourselves. As Thomas Greco and I explained in our chapter on the future of money:

> It is possible to organize an entirely new structure of money, banking, and finance; one that is interest-free, decentralised, and controlled, not by banks or central governments, but by individuals and businesses that associate and organise themselves into moneyless trading networks. In brief, any group of people can organise to allocate their own collective credit amongst themselves, interest-free. This is merely an extension of the common business practice of selling on open account—'I'll ship you the goods now and you can pay me later', except it is organised, not on a bilateral basis, but within a community of many buyers and sellers. Done on a large enough scale that includes a sufficiently broad range of goods and services, such systems can avoid the dysfunctions inherent in conventional money and banking. They can open the way to more harmonious and mutually beneficial relationships that enable the emergence of true economic democracy.[46]

Known as mutual credit clearing, it is a process that is used by hundreds of thousands of businesses around the world that are members of scores of commercial 'barter' exchanges which provide the necessary accounting and other services for moneyless trading. In this process, the things you sell pay for the things you buy without using money as an intermediate exchange medium. Instead of chasing dollars, you use what you have to pay for what you need. Unlike traditional barter, which depends upon a coincidence of wants and needs between two traders who each have something the other wants, mutual credit clearing provides an accounting for trade credits, that allows traders to sell to some members and buy from others.

There are reportedly more than 400,000 companies worldwide who, in this way, trade more than $12 billion dollars' worth of goods and services annually without the use of any national currency.[47] Some systems are created with a specific focus on community development, and involve individuals rather than businesses. One of the most significant of these is the Community Exchange System (CES), which was founded in Cape Town, South Africa in 2003. Since then it has grown to around 700 systems in over 40 countries, with over 20,000 users. The core of the system is a web-based software that allows members to trade with each other using the clearing of positive and negative balances between members when they trade. The websites act as an online marketplace with all transactions being recorded. CES is one among many systems now supporting hundreds of community currencies around the world, with other notable examples being Swiss-based Community Forge and Dutch-based Qoin.[48]

The growth of mobile internet enables payment at point of sale, which means these moneyless systems can be made suitable for everyday transactions and scale rapidly. Innovation in payment technology has already scaled incredibly fast. Only five million Kenyans were banked before the creation of the Mpesa mobile payment systems just a few years ago. Now, over 17 million people in this country of 20 million adults use mobile phones for payment, accounting for over 30% of GDP. The new payment system has enabled many new start-ups, such as Mkasa and Mchanga, with services such as peer-to-peer funding of weddings or to aggregate rent payments for landlords. These systems thrive on the new payment technology, but still use national currency. The truly transformative moment arrives when they are deployed for alternative currencies, in particular mutual credit clearing. That is why my institute has worked closely with Koru Kenya, a tiny association in an informal settlement in Mombasa, to create a local mutual credit system called the Banglapesa. This project is already helping hundreds of Kenyans improve their lives, without official development assistance or government support.[49] It reminds us of E.C. Riegel's proclamation that 'you need no government aid. You need only cooperation with and from persons who, like you, have resolved to exert the money power inherent in us all. This power in each of us needs only the recognition and respect of our fellows to spring forth and exert its blessings.'[50]

Like Facebook, QQ, Twitter, LinkedIn and other networks that are purely social, I predict that some moneyless trading networks will grow exponentially and provide significant daily alternatives to bank-issued money. The vibrant field of innovation in cryptographic currencies is already enabling new experiments in self-issued credit systems, such as RipplePay, which can be used to transact personal promises of all manner of currencies without the money actually changing hands. Scaling of such innovations could be a quiet and peaceful revolution in our monetary systems, brought on not by street demonstrations or by petitioning politicians, but by working together to use the power that is already ours—to apply the resources we have to support each other's productivity and to give credit where credit is due. This approach to healing capitalism is like reprogramming cancer cells. Once a far-fetched idea, advances in gene therapy now suggest the future possibility of reprogramming the DNA of cancer cells in the body, to stop them from replicating. In the same way, different forms of money could support life rather than subjecting it to the demands of their own replication.

There will be many challenges and issues arising as this field of currency innovation grows, such as good governance, relations with national governments and tax systems, among others. There is also a likely backlash from those who misunderstand, or whose organisations consider this field of innovation to be disruptive to their core business. Our colleagues in Kenya experienced this, with the Kenyan Central Bank initially pushing for prosecution of the originators of the local Banglapesa currency, before the case was dropped. Limitations will also exist in what mutual credit systems can achieve, such as the function of large upfront financing of projects that pay returns over a long period of time. This field therefore requires more analysis, knowledge sharing and capacity building.[51]

Companies, and professionals in the CSR and RI fields, can engage usefully in these developments, as a way to contribute to this deeper healing of capitalism through transforming the bank-debt money system. All forms of business can begin to accept complementary currencies as payment, and offer to pay their employees partly in a complementary currency. They can be active in the cryptocurrency field, promoting applications that empower communities and small firms, rather than speculative activity. Mobile phone companies can help scale complementary currencies by collaborating on SMS payment systems. Retail banks can open accounts in complementary currencies. All firms can integrate complementary currencies into their philanthropy and community engagement. Firms can switch their accounts to financial institutions that practise full reserve banking, including building societies and mutual associations, such as the Cumberland Building Society, which I switched to in 2013 after moving to the Lake District, a part of the 'Move Your Money' campaign. Firms can encourage local governments to issue their own mutual credit systems, and for all governments to tax transactions in complementary currencies in those same currencies, not national money.

Firms can also back campaigns for ending fractional reserve banking, such as Positive Money in the UK. Institutional investors may have a particular rationale for supporting such campaigns. As investors in companies across the whole economy, in order to spread risk, pension funds are affected by systemic impacts on the overall value of the stock market. If one company they invest in is seeking higher returns in ways that reduce the returns of many other companies, or create instability in the system as a whole, that is not in the interests of the pension fund, and that company needs to be engaged to alter their activities (see section 98, 'An agenda for improving ESG analysis', page 360). Pension funds have an interest in a long-term thriving and diverse economy. The current fractional reserve banking system means that there is an under-funding of small and medium-sized enterprises and inflation in certain asset prices, such as housing. It also means that, due to interest payments on the very source of money, there is an ongoing extraction of wealth from the productive economy to the financial sector. This misallocation within and extraction of money from the 'real' economy of enterprises creating tangible value is not in the long-term interests of pension investors. The existing monetary system has been, and continues to be, influenced by the technical assistance and lobbying activity of banks. Therefore, institutional investors, including pension funds, could analyse the effects of fractional and non-reserve banking on long-term portfolio performance, and make relevant recommendations on the lobbying activities of the banks they invest in and the fund managers they hire.

Clearly, there is more to do to heal capitalism than change monetary systems. For instance, people active in responsible investment, either as practitioners or researchers, can no longer consider the realm of high-frequency trading and financial derivatives to be beyond their concern, as they have such a huge impact on economic systems. Reforming corporate governance, in both law and customary practice, is also important. To address a range of the most important economic governance issues, I offer the framework of 'capital democracy' (see the Introduction to 2009, pages 222ff.). Markets need unplugging from the bank-issued money system, restoring the independent countervailing power of communities and governments, and shrinking the amount of our lives that are mediated, or influenced, by for-profit firms and banks. Rather than a stronger role for the state in daily economic activity, it will involve more of our participation in co-managed commons.

Whereas there are major opportunities for entrepreneurship to forward this healing through innovative currency and moneyless exchange, this broader process is not something that can be achieved by companies working alone. It is the task of a mass social movement. Many people working within the fields of CSR and RI speak of themselves as participants in a movement, yet little insight from the history of social movements informs their strategies and tactics. Five years on from describing the emergence of the *Corporate Responsibility Movement*, it now is high time for a clearer movement mentality and activity-set to be developed, applied and researched in this field.[52] If it is not, then we would have to conclude that the best metaphor for understanding CSR and RI would be as attempts at what Herbert Marcuse called 'self-inoculation', whereby incumbent elites admit and address a little bit of evil in order to deflect attention from the greater evil.

Greater healing

Imprisoned in a concentration camp for helping shelter persecuted Jews, Corrie ten Boom once wrote that 'worry does not empty tomorrow of its sorrow, it empties today of its strength'.[53] Many of us in the corporate responsibility and sustainability fields, whether practitioners or educators, spend much time worrying. We worry that what we are doing is not enough, or is too little too late. Some of us deal with our worrying by seeking changes in things that we can control, such as reducing our own carbon footprint, or backing away from this field entirely and working instead on areas of social change where more tangible results can be obtained. A period of worry can be transformative, if we move through it into action where we accept what we think we know. To move from worry to action requires an acceptance of how bad things may be. It involves opening our minds and hearts to the deepest fears we may have about ourselves and our world. Only then can we begin a deeper healing, and move towards a greater well-being.

One of the reasons I stopped writing the World Reviews contained in this book was that I developed what's called a 'frozen shoulder'. This meant I couldn't move my right arm properly. At first, I took ibuprofen and went to the gym to work it off. In response, the condition worsened until it was painful even to move a computer mouse. I tried all manners of treatments, including cortisone injections, muscle relaxants, physiotherapy and osteopathy. I was told I would need an operation. Then one day in a café, as I was tapping on my laptop, a lady came over to my table and offered me a massage. Given the pain in my shoulder and neck, I accepted this unusual offer! After a conversation, we agreed I would come for a consultation with the lady, who was a practitioner of the Grinberg Method.[54]

Her advice, and the focus of the method, was for me to pay closer attention to my physical, mental and emotional reactions to the pain and suffering, and, by observing them, lessen any unhelpful automatic responses. It helped me realise the fear I felt with my condition—a fear of pain but also a fear of what it meant for my future capabilities. This fear led to tension in the muscles, and a negative attitude, which probably was not helping my own healing, through restricting blood flow and raising my levels of stress hormones. This process also helped me remember that, although an external intervention can help, it is in fact the body itself that performs the healing. So I focused on helping my body in general, going on a detoxification diet, working less, playing more, and taking some supplements. I began to enjoy life more, despite the painful and restricted shoulder, and at my birthday party I got drunk and punched a swinging punch bag at my friend's house—throwing punches that would, if I had not been drunk, cause me agony. I then went on holiday and did not touch a laptop for ten days. My shoulder unfroze, it stopped hurting, and I recovered normal movement.

I tell this story because it showed me how we can make our situation worse by living in denial or worrying about the pain, rather than accepting the possible implications and focusing on strengthening and enlivening the greater whole within which the specific pain is experienced. Fearing our disease, whether personal or collective, does not help the healing. Seeking to fight the disease can also be counter-productive, by creating a feeling of hate and stressful non-acceptance. Acceptance does not mean acquiescence, but a more realistic assessment of limitations and what is good that still remains. We can be more loving to ourselves, including more forgiving of the parts of us that are diseased.

In analysing the way society and medical professions describe diseases and processes of healing, Susan Sontag notes that military and capitalist concepts are often used in relation to cancer: for instance, the 'fight' against cancer.[55] In mobilising a metaphor of healing in this book, and the metaphor of cancer, I do not mean to mobilise those dominant medical metaphors of combat. Rather, more of us may stop living in denial of the limited significance of our activities, or simply worrying about capitalism and the planet, and instead we can adjust our own lives to focus on nurturing the aspects of economy and society that be healthy and remove underlying causes of disease.

'No attempt should be made to cure the body, without curing the soul,' wrote the philosopher Plato over 2,400 years ago. The 'soul' that needs healing is our separative consciousness. We need a deeper healing in our way of thinking—to help reconnect our concepts with realities. One powerful concept that needs re-embedding in the material world is our concept and measurement of 'money'.

To heal is to make whole. The Old English word *hælan* means to 'cure; save; make whole, sound and well' and is derived from the Proto-Germanic *hailjan* which means 'to make whole'.[56] As described above, capitalism involves a separating of some phenomena into an asset that is controlled for a yield. In that separation, there is potential for new interactions, new creations—new wholes. This process of separation and connection is a paradox within capitalism. Left unchecked, it has led to a damaging splitting of us from our inner selves, each other, nature, and the one consciousness that some call God. To heal these separations we could be aided by a sense of its origins. The philosopher Charles Eisenstein argues that the origins are found in the way the invention of agriculture and urban settlement required new levels of organisation that involved new levels of abstraction. That is, to organise complex interactions and specialised activities, we need to account.

The process of accounting requires categorisation of different phenomena into the same categories. Two apples are, in reality, two quite different things, that we categorise as the same thing—an apple—for the purpose of accounting. One plus one is not equal to two unless we reduce the true life of the things we categorise as the same 'one'. This process of abstraction means the uniqueness of life is overridden in calculations about how to manage society and economy. To succeed, more of us, and our organisations, seek surplus in these abstract units of account—the ultimate abstract unit being 'money'. Therefore, accumulating the abstract units can become our objective, rather than achieving something useful, and this creates the conditions whereby we can end up destroying nature and community. As Eisenstein eloquently warns:

> In the reduction of reality to number and name, in the program of owning and controlling the world, we have wrought a Tower of Babel, seeking with our finite tools to take the infinite by storm . . . The supreme irony in our Babelian quest of attaining the infinite through finite means is that we are actually enacting precisely the opposite. We are liquidating all that is infinite, sacred, and unique, converting it into the finite, the controlled, the generic, standard, and measurable . . . We are cashing in the earth, selling off our lives, reducing reality to data. Soon there will be nothing left to convert, as all social, cultural, natural, and spiritual capital is exhausted.[57]

The confusion of representation and reality is found in all aspects of life. In medicine, the approach of many specialists is to deal only with the parts of the body that have been grouped together as their specialism. A doctor specialising in dermatology will know a lot about the mechanics of the skin but far less about digestion, the nervous system, and allergies, which may be causing symptoms on the skin. Due to the economics associated with medical research, theories of knowledge and institutions of permission, specialists will also know far more about the drugs that might address the problem, than they do about other approaches to healing.[58] Therefore, medicine has become routinised, where specialists immediately look into how to put an individual through a process that uses the tools of their trade, rather than exploring ways to help the person with their own healing capacities.

When I was seven, I was suffering from a nasal allergy. Specialists in the medical domain 'Ear, Nose and Throat' had begun to accept there are such things as allergies, and so the specialist treating me proposed a series of skin pricks of different allergens to see what I was allergic to. My mother explained she did not think this was a safe idea, as my brother had eczema. 'Mother, I'm an expert,' said the specialist, before administering the pricks. Within a week the rash spread over my body and I had severe eczema for the next 12 years. Of course, a reaction to this routinised, atomised and arrogant approach to illness can go too far, by rejecting all medical approaches with the one label of 'Western', when many of the tools of such medicine are useful and life-saving. However, given the interconnectedness of living systems, I would have preferred my doctor to know a bit more outside his field of specialism than absolutely everything within that specialism. If you aren't a jack of all trades, you are a master of none.

Mainstream schooling suffers from some of the same effects of categorisation. There is utility in grouping students into year groups and ability, in turning topics into subjects with set curricula, and greater understanding into certificates for achievement. But there is also a downside, when the credentials of having 'done the time' in an official educational context seems more important for the student than one's ability to inquire and self-actualise.[59] This downside is institutionalised when the appearance of 'quality' educational processes, as represented by documents of procedures, becomes more important for university staff than challenging and inspiring students to be enthusiastic learners in their personal and professional lives. As Thomas Carlyle noted in 1829:

> . . . the mechanical genius of our time has diffused itself into quite other provinces. Not the external and physical alone is now managed by machinery, but the internal and spiritual also . . . Everything has its cunningly devised implements, its pre-established apparatus; it is not done by hand, but by machinery. Thus we have machines for Education . . . Instruction, that mysterious communing of Wisdom with Ignorance, is no longer an indefinable tentative process, requiring a study of individual aptitudes, and a perpetual variation of means and methods, to attain the same end; but a secure, universal, straightforward business, to be conducted in the gross, by proper mechanism, with such intellect as comes to hand.[60]

A focus on academic disciplines can increase this separation of 'knowledge' from the real world. In business schools, the dominance of one discipline, economics, has been particularly problematic, in promoting a false assumption of life, society and economy. It is not a new criticism. In paraphrasing John Ruskin, Mohandas K. Gandhi wrote that modern economics 'imagines that man has a body but no soul to be taken into account and frames its laws accordingly. How can such laws possibly apply to man in whom the soul is the predominant element?' He continued, 'We have seen how the ideas upon which political economy is based are misleading. Translated into action they can only make the individual and the nation unhappy. They make the poor poorer and the rich richer and none are any the happier for it.'[61] Sadly, most business schools do not explore these damaging assumptions, or the insights of wise leaders from history. Instead, most are merchants of ideology, status networks and training agencies.

Some governments are subsidising universities with millions of dollars to employ academics to publish in the highest-rated academic journals which no one reads due to their irrelevance (see 'Autistic academe', page 121). Meanwhile, many universities hire teaching-focused academics that are judged on how well they entertain and train students, rather than challenge and expand their world-views. Much harm is done by increasing confidence in the delusion that our abstractions such as 'money'; concepts such as 'the invisible hand'; and disciplines such as 'economics' are realities not stories. Within business schools there are often academics with a grounding in political science, sociology, anthropology or history, but their expertise is rarely expressed beyond the narrow confines of the business ethics class. It is time they came out of the closet and helped transform business schools into places of personal and collective transformation. To do so, leaving the corporate classroom and immersing students both in nature and in different work and living environments is essential.

Why have we been so captive to our categorisations in medicine, education, economics, organisations and beyond? Famous sociologists Michel Foucault, Max Weber, and Jacques Derrida have discussed various mechanics of social control. Yet is there something deeper at play? One explanation is that our fear of mortality means we seek to control our world, and to create a sense of permanence when transience is everywhere. Fear creates narrow-mindedness, separation and withholding one's truth, whereas love creates a broadening of perspectives, unity with others, and telling one's truth. Some of our fear comes from a belief that people are dangerous and that wealth is scarce. Many of us also assume that such ideals as ending hunger are not affordable. Yet there seems to be ample money for spending on weapons, lavish buildings or luxuries. We assume that this indicates something essential about human nature or the way we function in large groups, like nations. Many people assume that human nature is naturally competitive and selfish, and thus needs to be moderated or controlled by force for the common good. By analysing the monetary system, and seeing the energising effect of creating alternatives, we gain insight on a different perspective. We see evidence that some of the selfishness arises from a fear of scarcity that is based on the current monetary system. We see evidence that the reason why there is money for skyscrapers but not free schools is partly an outcome of how the issuing of credit is in the hands of bankers seeking high returns, low transaction costs and secure collateral. We begin to see people, in general, to be more like the people we know the best, our closest friends: that is, as people who care.

Many people working towards 'sustainability' with the corporate responsibility arena assume that it requires new checks and balances on personal behaviour, and calls for each other to be more responsible: pay more for this, don't travel on that, switch off this, don't buy that. Yet, by working on monetary issues, we begin to see that people and communities are being hampered in their ability to organise for mutual benefit. We begin to see that, through mutual credit clearing, communities can connect to their own abundance. We begin to see that people can be freed from the delusion that 'money' is wealth, and recognise, as Cumbria's John Ruskin wrote, 'there is no wealth but LIFE'. Although the past decade has seen a shift towards sustainability professionals couching their message in a positive way, about increasing personal well-being, in general the discourse is one of progress through limitation, rather than through reclaiming freedoms. Instead, by working on monetary issues, a liberatory environmentalism that seeks to unleash human nature not curb it is possible. From this a new approach to sustainability, CSR and RI can emerge where efforts are no longer directed to moderate the current system but peacefully create the new. In the words of monetary theorist E.C. Riegel:

> To desire freedom is an instinct. To secure it requires intelligence. It must be comprehended and self-asserted. To petition for it is to stultify oneself, for a petitioner is a confessed subject and lacks the spirit of a freeman. To rail and rant against tyranny is to manifest inferiority, for there is no tyranny but ignorance; to be conscious of one's powers is to lose consciousness of tyranny. Self-government is not a remote aim. It is an intimate and inescapable fact. To govern oneself is a natural imperative, and all tyranny is the miscarriage of self-government. The first requisite of freedom is to accept responsibility for the lack of it.[62]

These ideas on healing separation, delusion, fear and states of disempowerment are not new, and echo various ancient traditions. Sadly, our situation is new and unprecedented, in that we face an urgent challenge to evolve our consciousness to protect our species. In 2012, PricewaterhouseCoopers released a report that concluded it was too late to hold the future increase in global average temperatures to just 2°C. The same month the World Bank noted that, unless there is a major change in current trajectories of development, then a 4° average rise is likely by 2100. Not known as a doomsayer, the World Bank noted, 'There is . . . no certainty that adaptation to a 4°C world is possible.' Are we on course for the end of civilisation as we know it? What we know is there will be terrible disruption to the current way of life; people will suffer. How can we speak of healing when we face such a difficult future?

At an individual level, many find that suffering is a teacher, reminding us of what is important. We learn how to receive love and support, and can have a greater capacity to identify with those that are suffering. Suffering can burn away what is unnecessary and leave clarity about life, love and purpose. In his book of interviews with people who face great physical impairments, Mark Matousek describes how illness can inspire an important new consciousness. 'While hardship can certainly render us bitter, selfish, defensive, and miserable, it can also be used quite differently: as the artery of interconnection, a bridge to other people in pain . . .'[63] While not implying that we should invite or welcome suffering, we can all learn from this approach. Matousek even suggests:

> Terror can be a door to enlightenment. While traditional cultures have long understood the empowering aspects of fear and wounding, the double-edged force of passage rites to galvanize and deepen the spirit, we are too often shielded from this secret knowledge . . . Terror is fuel; wounding is power. Darkness carries the seeds of redemption. Authentic strength isn't found in our armour but at the very pit of the wounds each of us manages to survive.[64]

Could the same be true at a collective level? Could collective illness lead to a new collective consciousness? Matousek notes how 'crisis takes us to the brink of our limits and forces us to keep moving forward . . . there's vitality in facing life's extremes, including that of your own extinction'.[65] Huge suffering during the Second World War led to the creation of a welfare state in many European countries, to protect the less fortunate. Might the suffering that is likely due to climate change trigger an evolution in human consciousness? Might some of that suffering arise due to attachments to lifestyles that we could let go? Learning the lessons of the suffering created by our current extremes of capitalism may help in our psychological adaptation to climate change. Our objective must be more than healing, for wellness and well-being involves far more than being cured. New levels of freedom and vitality await us, as we free ourselves from the separations and delusions of our age and embrace whatever may emerge. From a village in Greece where we trained people in how to create and scale local currencies with open-source software, to the United Nations in Geneva where we co-organised their first conference on community currencies, the energy and joy people share in working on community currencies is palpable. The ecologist Arne Naess suggests we ask ourselves: 'In what situation do I experience the maximum satisfaction of my whole being?' To heal capitalism, we can let excitement be our compass.

Conclusion

We urgently need to heal, to make whole, our relationships to the planet and each other. To promote such healing, we must recognise that capitalism is a system that does not nor will not ever address everything or enable everything that is important. Rightly or wrongly, capitalism is understood by most to describe markets consisting of for-profit privately owned enterprise. That element of our society could be redesigned to achieve more social benefit, but also to be a smaller part of life, so that it does not encroach on all aspects of family, community, politics and the commons, in the way that it does now. Otherwise, the countervailing powers are not sufficient to moderate capitalism, and the aspects of life that are better arranged in less commercial ways are not then met.

We may need capitalism but we need less of it, and, of what remains, we must reprogramme its basic operating code, which is the monetary system, so we are no longer subject to the demands of financial capital, but rather supported by it.

Can those of us working in or on CSR and RI begin to help heal capitalism? Perhaps. The first step is to avoid wishful thinking and be more honest about the limitations of current voluntary initiatives. The second step is to learn about how massive social change has happened in the past and work together with that level of ambition. In so doing, we may not only be part of a corporate responsibility movement, but help to heal deeper malaise and so better prepare future generations for the likely difficulties presented by climate change.

Acknowledgements

The five years of reviews that we compile in this book would not have been possible without my co-authors, and in particular Ian Doyle, who believed in the approach to current affairs and business studies where we seek deeper meanings and wider lessons. Support from Professor Michael Powell and Professor Malcolm McIntosh at Griffith Business School made it possible for me to write the reviews, as well as the continued invitation from publisher John Stuart. The transition I made to a deeper yet practical critique of capitalism and an emphasis of currency innovation for social change relied on inspiration and support from Matthew Slater and Thomas Greco. The trust that Nicoletta Iacobacci at the European Broadcasting Union had in letting me 'go public' on this topic through my TEDx talk was helpful for my transition. The positive response to my new work from Peter Utting at United Nations Research Institute (UNRISD) and Hamish Jenkins at the United Nations Non-Governmental Liaison Service (UN-NGLS) helped me connect it with previous work, in the way I seek to do in the introduction to this book. Finishing the book was enabled by support from Professor Robert Hannaford at the University of Cumbria, and colleagues at the Institute for Leadership and Sustainability (IFLAS). Useful comments on a first draft were provided by John Stuart and Richard Little. Finally, I must thank you, the reader, for doing something unusual today—reading something neither for entertainment or training, nor to be able to cite something in a top academic journal. You are the kind of intellectual explorer we need to change the direction of humanity.

2006

2006: Introduction

Jem Bendell

Almost a decade ago, as the Indonesian tropical forests were burning out of control, I wrote that climate change had moved from theory to reality. But whose reality?[1] Since then we've had a decade of business-as-usual, with carbon emissions booming in tandem with economic growth across the global South and steadily climbing in most of the North.

But recently something has changed. Friends now say to me, 'so it's true, the climate is changing' and 'it's big, everyone's talking about it', and some even say 'it's because of us'. As the emphasis on climate at the 2006 Oscars illustrated, carbon is the new black. Global warming used to be a nerdy issue of scientific interest and environmental concern. Now it is a personal issue, of political interest and humanitarian concern. What made this happen? What made climate change reach a 'tipping point' to become hot gossip, even in countries like India where some might assume other matters are more pressing?

The phrase 'tipping point' refers to that dramatic moment when something unique becomes common. Popularised by Malcolm Gladwell's bestselling book of the same name, it is used to describe the point when the rate at which a process proceeds increases dramatically. Gladwell identifies three characteristics of people who have disproportionate influence over the spread of social phenomena. 'Connectors' have wide and diverse social circles, being the hubs of social networks. 'Mavens' are knowledgeable people, who are particularly aware of innovations and adopt new things and ideas. 'Salesmen' are charismatic people that help market an idea to the masses. The implication is that social change requires involvement of people with a mixture of these characteristics. But to understand how concern for climate change tipped into the mainstream, at least in the West, we need to look at the changing nature of the concept, daily experiences, and the mechanisms of communication. The growing human face of climate change, people's experience of changes to their weather, and the entertainment media's engagement in this, have all been key. The first and last of these are instructive for those of us interested in social change.

Climate tipping

First, climate change has begun to be understood as a humanitarian emergency. Studies are showing how increasing droughts, floods, forest fires, storms, erosion and sea rise, are destroying lives and livelihoods.[2] Another side to the human face of climate change is the economic impact, which has been predicted at potentially 20% of the global economy. 'Climate Change is the greatest market failure the world has ever seen', writes economist David Stern. The environment is now too important to be left to conservationists. This marks a change in what cognitive scientists might call the 'cognitive frame' of climate change, whereby the term becomes associated with human, and thus personal and moral, concepts. George Lakoff's bestselling book *Don't Think of an Elephant* popularised the theory of cognitive frames. Lakoff uses the term 'tax relief', employed by the US Bush Administration, to illustrate how words have various concepts associated with them.

> The word 'relief' has a conceptual frame associated with it . . . In order to give someone relief, there has to be an affliction and an afflicted party—somebody who's harmed by this affliction—and a reliever, somebody who gives relief to the afflicted party or takes away the harm or pain. That reliever is a hero. And if someone tries to stop the person giving relief from doing so, they're a bad guy . . . They want to keep the affliction ongoing. So when you use only one word, 'relief', all of that information is called up. That is a simple conceptual frame.[3]

Various other intellectual traditions, such as critical discourse analysis, study the power of language in shaping our sense of what exists and what is possible. 'Discourses' are a series of interlocking cognitive frames that construct our worldview. By making links back to the neuroscience of the brain, and using simple examples, cognitive scientists have been able to popularise the insight that 'language is power' more than sociologists.

Mediated truths

The second reason why climate change has tipped is the involvement of mass entertainment media. I used to think that mass media was important for communicating with, well, the masses. Not so. The mass media is important for communicating with powerful minorities. The demands on the modern professional in any line of work are such that to be successful we become highly specialised and overly busy. Our occupation becomes our preoccupation. And boy do we have to read, read, read to maintain our specialism. Consequently information doesn't penetrate very deeply if not coming from sources we assume contribute to our specialism, such as a trade magazine, business section, or top academic journal. We might scan the news but it's yet another tiring story, that doesn't reach us at a deeper level. But everyone has to relax at some point. As teachers will tell you, we all learn better when we are relaxed. So, elites can be reached in movie theatres. Another reason for the power of our cultural life is the way it provides 'social proof' for an issue: if everyone's talking about it, it must be important.[4] An equally 'Inconvenient Truth' is that Al Gore has probably done more for climate change awareness with his Oscar-winning film that he did during eight years as Vice President.

Whether working in NGOs, universities or government, it is important to learn how frames tip. Watching how the alternative fuel market boomed in 2006, and continued to do so in 2007, also suggests that frame-tipping is important for financial analysts to understand. One lesson is the importance of frames rather than facts. 'Conventional frames are pretty much fixed in the neural structures of our brains,' says Lakoff. 'In order for a fact to be comprehended, it must fit the relevant frames. If the facts contradict the frames, the frames, being fixed in the brain, will be kept and the facts ignored.' He sums this up as 'Frames trump facts.' Implication: don't just pump out your story and evidence, but change the framing, and look out for where people are doing this. Another lesson is reaching people in their leisure time, and the importance of cultural phenomena in opening people's minds to things they would otherwise consider peripheral. This relates to a third lesson, the importance of crossing worlds, and the points of interconnection between

Figure 1: **Tipping frames**

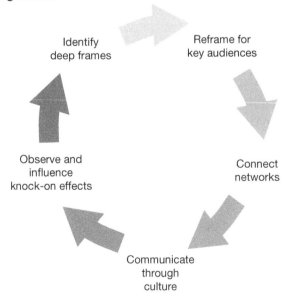

different realms of work and life. As Gladwell explains, it is through people connecting different social networks that ideas spread rapidly.

Some frames are deeper than others, in the sense that a change in them has cascading implications for a range of other assumptions and beliefs. Climate change is 'deep' in this sense, as recognising it as real and urgent means we are challenged to question our assumptions about current forms of economic development being 'progress'. Hence 'tipping frames' not only describes the process of an altered frame going mainstream, but also those frames that, once altered, lead to other frames in society reaching a tipping point. Those of us who seek to serve systemic transformations for a better world need to better understand this process of tipping frames (see Fig. 1).

A crucible for tipping frames

The range of activities relating to corporate responsibility form a site for frame-tipping, for three reasons. They bring different professions and knowledge networks together that would otherwise rarely meet. This includes the three sectors of business, government and civil society. It includes the different fields of public concern, such as environment, health, poverty and human rights, as well as those with a local and an international focus. They are also focused on framing issues, as the diverse actors seek to find a new shared language involving terms like 'partnering', 'social entrepreneurship' and 'extra-financial issues'. I previously argued that the most significant frame to tip in this field is the concept of what it is to be a professional business person. That used to mean leaving troublesome values at home but now it's coming to mean the highest expression of your values at work.[5] This relates to a broader movement towards what could be called 'work–life blending'.

Work–life blending

There is a cognitive frame around 'work' which means it is separate from 'life'. This has the dual effect of making it difficult to assimilate information from life into one's work, and making us think that to be 'professional' we should leave a lot of our 'life' experience and interests at home. A new trend is changing that. Reports suggest younger business leaders and entrepreneurs are not only wanting more work–life balance but also 'work–life blending', i.e. bringing their whole personality to work.

Various factors are driving this. Technologies are enabling home-working, which leads to the blurring of work and life. They are also allowing more entrepreneurial self-employment or side-employment, as the transaction costs of operating alone

and connecting with a global market are dramatically reduced. Demands for creativity from knowledge-based industries are inspiring more people to work outside
innovation-sapping corporate office environments. The search for more meaning
in one's work is a factor in this blending, as well as a result (see Fig. 2).

Figure 2: **Factors in work–life blending**

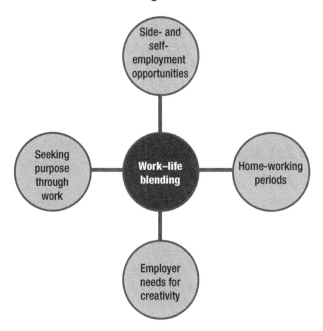

Balance is a state of equipoise; equal distribution of weight or amount. Work–life
balance suggests 'work' on one side and everything other than work on the other.
As they are separate, something can't be both 'work' and 'life' at the same time.
However, blending is to mix inseparably together. Whereas balance is the counter-
poising of separate things, blending is the integration of those things.[6] Work–life
blending is key to tipping the frame of the nature of 'work'. It has enabled me to
write in a more personal and wide-ranging style than the usual academic, UN or
corporate outlets I can use. Blogging often involves a work–life blend, including my
own (see www.jembendell.com).

This blending also relates to the third reason why corporate responsibility events
and networks are a site of frame-tipping. They bring together people who have an
interest in the state of the world, and who therefore have a strong social connection. Such people often meet in their leisure time, as illustrated by the growth of
vibrant social-professional networks of people connecting on corporate responsibility around the world. From one of the earliest social networks on this topic,
CSR Chicks, which now has thousands of members, to CSR Geneva, launched in
mid-2006 and already with over 200 members who attend breakfasts, dinners and

after-work drinks themed on different aspects of corporate responsibility, this area is extremely social. This reinforces the idea of our profession not being separate from our sense of self and allows discussions up, down and across hierarchies. It provides 'social proof' to people that they are part of a movement that sees and does business differently.

Changing frames in 2006

Changes in basic assumptions about the nature and purpose of business and work will have major knock-on effects for the behaviour of consumers, staff, investors and regulators. The 2006 review discusses various examples where cognitive frames in business, finance and accounting could be tipping: that certain assumptions about what those fields are, what they involve, and what it means to be professional within them is changing, in ways that have wide implications.

Changes in the discourse around the financial services sector are particularly important. In the section 'Reframing finance' we describe how a plethora of initiatives such as The Marathon Club, Enhanced Analytics Initiative (EAI) and UN Principles for Responsible Investment (UNPRI) are together helping reshape what finance professionals understand as being material and relevant to one's fiduciary duty.

Also important is the emergence of a positive connotation to the environmental challenge of consumption. In the section 'Consuming truths' (page 70) we describe how finding new pathways for social development that are sufficiently resource-light to be possible for a majority of the world's population over the long term, rather than the minority of a few generations of middle- to upper-class consumers, is a pro-poor vision. In the sections 'Who's leading Hu?' (page 62) and 'A different path' (page 80) we describe how new visions of sustainable development are arising in China and India. With the right leadership, development need not depend on risks such as cheap oil, inequalities such as poor pay and conditions, and the disruption of rural communities' livelihoods. As Rajesh Sehgal, Senior Law & Policy Officer at WWF-India explains, 'Indian companies can become leading exporters of and investors in sustainable goods and services, whilst emerging as key actors in promoting a proactive international sustainable development agenda'.

Whether this will lead to a tipping point in the way Asian nations generally view and pursue 'development' is currently unknown. A counter-process of reframing has been under way for sometime, with the shift to individualism and materialism most clearly illustrated in 2006 by the economic boom in Vietnam, described in the section 'Capitalism's rising star?' (page 74). The environmental and social strains of economic booms across Asia could bring things to a grinding halt, as warned by Mira Kamdar in her book *Planet India*.[7] The implications for corporate citizenship are that companies and investors need to assess how they are helping or hindering the right frameworks and incentives for innovation and delivery of the business models needed in a resource-constrained future. Rather than doing business as usual, with some social and environmental improvements, the scale, urgency and depth of the sustainability challenge requires companies to engage with other actors in society to promote governance for sustainability.

In the recent past progressive people in business, government and civil society have been uncomfortable about the ethics of 'social engineering' of public values. This is because it seems to go against the spirit of recognising people's dignity as equal people, which underlies democracy and human rights. That is a huge mistake. We are all socially conditioned. Every year billions are spent on marketing advertisements, public relations and lobbying. This is done to influence people to spend money. In doing so they feed frames such as desire, status and materialism. It is because we have left compelling mass communications to institutions that pursue narrow self-interests that we have the public attitudes we see today. The challenge is to help make people conscious of the social conditioning processes, to reduce those that are damaging, and to promote those that are beneficial to people within their communities. Consequently some organisations, such as WWF, have been calling on companies to 'talk the walk', by using their communications functions of advertising, public relations, lobbying and investor relations to articulate the type of economy and society we need, and the innovations in public policy we need to get there.

Figure 3: **Deep frames**

Figure 4: **The needed frames**

From environmentalism to societal growth

Like many established organisations in the environmental movement WWF is somewhat beset by its history. As George Lakoff explains,

> environmentalists have adopted a set of frames that doesn't reflect the vital importance of the environment to everything on Earth. The term the environment' suggests that this is an area of life separate from other areas of life like the economy and jobs, or health, or foreign policy. By not linking it to everyday issues, it sounds like a separate category, and a luxury in difficult times. Wilderness: a place for those in Birkenstocks to go hiking.

Environment implies what is around us not what we are part of. Words like protection and conservation are the opposite of positive words like freedom and change. What is needed is a positive vision for people and society: 'prosperity, security, guilt-free luxury, health, a sense of progress and meaningful hope that the future will be better than the past.'[8] The launch of One Planet Living in the UK in 2007, is one example of an attempt by a mainstream environmental group to rise to this challenge.[9]

Lakoff's analysis suggests we should examine some of the deepest frames in society. Concepts such as 'economic growth' are powerful in shaping thinking, policy and practice. 'Economic' implies efficient and important, and 'growth' implies good and natural. Much analysis suggests that a certain amount of decoupling of economic growth from resource consumption is possible, but not entirely, and so only a small amount of economic growth will probably be sustainable in the long term. The challenge is therefore to refocus on what we want from the economy, as a society. Terms like 'green growth' would not challenge but actually reinforce the dominance of the economic growth frame, as it implies green economic growth. Instead, we should articulate a new vision of 'societal growth'—the increase in well-being of all life affected by a society. Some of the deepest ideas in society are shown in Figure 3, with some of the key frame-changes that we need to work on to enable the transition to a more just and sustainable world shown in Figure 4.

Many people have a 'block' when it comes to the word 'environment', such as some developmentalists from the global South. To them, environment evokes a frame of imperialists protecting wildlife and wilderness at the expense of poor people. It is important to keep one's audiences in mind when considering what frames need to be tipped. Having said that, the deepest frame that needs tipping is our story of existence: why we are here and our relationship to everything around us. Thinkers such as Thomas Berry[10] and Ervin Lazslo[11] point to a world-view where we are not separate from 'nature' but a wonderful expression of nature's, and the universe's, ability and intention to evolve through ever greater complexity towards consciousness of itself. By bringing new insight to theology and to the natural sciences respectively, they point to a future where human purpose can be freed from the dogmas of religious institution.

Global purpose

The power of frames, and the need to work on deep frame-change, poses a challenge to those organisations we might assume are working towards the public interest, namely non-profits, charities or non-governmental organisations (NGOs). In most cases their strategies and work programmes are failing to meet the depth, scale and urgency of the challenges we face today. Due to concerns about upsetting existing donors and misplaced notions of professionalism, such as the idea an NGO should stick narrowly to the text of its mission rather than the values from which it derives and propels it, and that it should use linear models for relating action to impact to justify its budgeting rather than recognising how systemic change might require new modes of evaluation, most NGOs only work on tipping frames in minor and marginal ways. As I argued in my report for the UN on NGO accountability in 2006, international civil society organisations must not adopt old notions of business professionalism, but develop visions of excellence that are appropriate to their work, and come to a greater understanding of their common global purpose, in order to combine their efforts for deeper change.[12]

The new philanthropy from the 30-something dotcom billionaires might shake this charity mentality from mainstream NGOs, if they choose to engage. So if you are out there, Pierre, Jeff, Sergey, Larry, David or Jerry . . . we are waiting.

Watching developments in corporate responsibility during 2006 suggests that people's deepest assumptions about both business and work could be changing in cities around the world, with major implications for future competitiveness. A more subtle shift than the widely reported growth in entrepreneurialism across Asia, it is nonetheless significant. It is a shift towards moral markets. Although more research is required on the nature of this shift, it seems to be enabled by the blending of work and life, business and public purpose, news and entertainment. Although important, it is not the dominant trend in many parts of the world, such as the rapidly emerging nations. If we want to end poverty and protect the planet we have to make it the decisive trend. Although we can't legislate for personal morals, we can legislate to create market frameworks and incentives that support moral behaviour.

If there is a silver lining to the clouds of climate change, it might be in the way it wakes us up to our moral responsibilities as part of life on Earth.

1Q2006
January–March

Jem Bendell and Shilpa Shah

Food fight

Food is one of the most basic necessities of life. In 2006 an estimated 800 million people are suffering from under-nourishment and more than 5 million children will die as a result of under-nutrition. The 33rd Annual Session of the UN's Standing Committee on Nutrition convened in Geneva in March 2006 to consider the problem of malnutrition. For the first time this network of governments, UN agencies and non-governmental organisations focused on 'over-nutrition' as well as under-nutrition. Their concluding statement noted that 'Childhood obesity is becoming a recognised problem even in low income countries. More than a billion adults worldwide are overweight, of which 300 million are obese.'[1] Obesity increases the likelihood of succumbing to non-communicable diseases such as diabetes, heart disease and cancer. These contribute about 47% of the burden of disease around the world.[2] 300,000 people are reportedly eating themselves to death every year in the United States.[3] What is new is how it is a problem in lower-income countries. With one in three men overweight or obese, and one in two women, obesity levels in South Africa are now the same as in the US.[4] China already has 90 million obese people, with 200 million predicted within a decade.[5] Professor Philip James, chair of an International Obesity Task Force, says 'childhood and adolescent overweight and obesity already present massive problems . . . in many other parts of the developing world, which are already on the fast track to a massive explosion in type 2 diabetes. The economic burden from this will act as a brake on development, which depends on having a healthy and productive population.'[6]

The reasons for this explosion in obesity include physical activity and food intake. Migration into cities is resulting in less-active lifestyles, while growing consumption of processed foods is leading to higher intake of salt, sugar and fat. Today supermarkets share over 50% of global food sales, and processed food sales now account for about three-quarters of the total world food sales.[7] This market is being consolidated in the hands of fewer companies, with the largest 50 accounting for almost 30% of the global packaged food retail sales.[8] This is not a phenomenon limited to the industrialised world. In China, for example, food industry sales took off from under 100 billion yuan (€9.2 billion) in 1991 to well over 400 billion yuan (€37 billion) just ten years later.[9] Around the world, corporations increasingly comprise the food chain. From the maxim 'we are what we eat', whether we are fat or thin, healthy or sick, hungry or well nourished, hyperactive or lethargic, corporations are involved in shaping what and who we are more than ever before.

Such power commands attention. Civil society has often questioned the role of corporations in harming our nutrition. Chemical flavours and fast-food fats, mad cows and baby-milk marketing—the issues may differ around the world but a common concern has been the use and abuse of the power that corporations have today and the varying independence of public institutions from that power. In the past three years attention on the role of companies in the obesity pandemic has grown. Companies involved in the production and marketing of products containing high levels of sugar and fat have been criticised for complicity in the pandemic. Legal challenges against fast food and fizzy drink companies led *Fortune* magazine to ask, 'Is fat the next tobacco?'[10] Popular media also picked up on the issue, with highlights including the film *Super Size Me*, in which the documentary maker Morgan Spurlock wrecked his body by eating nothing but McDonald's fast food for a month; and celebrity chef Jamie Oliver's TV series on school dinners in the UK. The response from the food industry was mixed. The sugar industry's trade associations lobbied hard at the World Health Assembly to prevent any agreement between governments on adopting new regulations to reduce sugar content.[11] Many corporate representatives argued that food consumption is a question of individual choice and responsibility, and that, as multiple factors lead to obesity, specific food products should not be singled out for regulations on salt, sugar or fat content.

A focus on personal responsibility led to responses such as obesity reports on pupils by their schools.[12] However, the argument that a principle of personal choice and responsibility should determine policy responses was somewhat hollow in relation to children bombarded by advertising. Both the right and the left 'cognitive frames'—the 'strict father' and 'nurturing parent' mind-sets described by George Lakoff[13]—have a special place for intervening on the behalf of children's well-being. No surprise, then, that since 2005 a major shift in perceptions in North America and Europe seems to have occurred, with the role of the mass media and food companies in influencing children's consumption choices coming into focus. In France the government banned vending machines from schools, and the UK government announced new stringent rules on food sold in schools to be introduced during 2006. The food industry also began to respond in more positive ways. Drinks giants Cadbury Schweppes, Coca-Cola and PepsiCo agreed a deal with the William J. Clinton Foundation and the American Heart Association (AHA) so that only unsweetened juice, water and low-fat milks will be sold in elementary and middle schools across the US, with diet drinks allowed in high schools.[14] The voluntary action of these companies may be partly explained by a desire to appear as responsible adult-type organisations caring for the well-being of children, and therefore reducing the extent of social concern and regulatory intervention more broadly in terms of the marketing and sale of products to children, the content of products themselves and their consumption by the wider population of adults. However, as schools are nodes, or 'connector points' in society, so it is probable that more families will be discussing obesity and fast food and so the potential for ideas and practices to change is there.

Rather than being defensive, food companies could mobilise their market position in support of nutrition goals. There are now numerous examples of corporations becoming involved in food- and nutrition-related work, including partnerships aimed at delivering food, fortifying food, and advocating healthy eating. The 'Moving the World' partnership between TNT, an express delivery and logistics services firm, and the World Food Programme (WFP) was launched in 2002, with the aim of supporting WFP's fight against world hunger through knowledge transfer, on-the-ground logistical support and advocacy work. TNT's in-kind and financial commitments (more than US$12 million in 2005) have generated 27 projects in some 60 countries, most recently also in tsunami-affected areas of South-East Asia. Not being a food company itself, TNT has less internal issues to consider in relation to food. Some food companies have, however, also begun addressing these issues, illustrated by their participation in the new 'Healthy Eating and Active Living Global Partnership' (HEAL). This initiative aims at facilitating business action as 'part of the solution to the massive increase in chronic lifestyle-related diseases around the world linked to obesity, poor diets and a lack of physical activity'.[15] In March 2006 they co-published a report profiling companies that are beginning to take health issues more seriously and the business benefits of doing so.[16]

Yet progress is sufficient neither for public health nor for managing strategic threats and opportunities facing the food industry, according to a report published in the same month by Ethical Investment Research Services (EIRIS). 'Our research revealed little evidence of obesity-related improvement targets and key performance indicators from the multinational food and beverage firms we analysed', said report author and EIRIS research analyst Heleen Bulckens. 'Food and drink producers are waking up to the business risks associated with obesity, but significant challenges remain.'[17]

Those challenges are systemic. More voluntary action from companies in supporting changes in behaviour, and improving the nutritional content of their products, is needed and welcome. However, complex social, economic and cultural factors influence people's nutrition and physical activity. To achieve widespread public health benefits, and related benefits for economic activity, will require an open assessment and trial of a range of public policy tools to influence patterns of food production and consumption. It would be sensible for companies to start planning now for this healthier future.

Fair fight

Not only are food and drink important for what they contain but also the way they are produced. Controversy over the launch of Nestlé's first product certified as 'Fairtrade' in the UK in October 2005 continued into 2006. The association between the company awarded the 'most blatant case of corporate irresponsibility' award at the Public Eye awards in Davos in January 2005 and the green and blue Fairtrade label raised important questions about the future of the fair trade movement.[18]

The responses to the introduction of 'Nescafé Partners' Blend', a Fairtrade brand by one of the world's four largest coffee roasters, were a mixed bag. Some campaigning NGOs were sceptical of the Fairtrade certification of one product out of over 8,500 Nestlé brands, affecting the working conditions of only a small ringfenced proportion of the three million coffee farmers dependent on the Swiss food giant: the World Development Movement, based in London, argued, 'if Nestlé really believes in Fairtrade coffee it will alter its business practices, lobbying strategies and radically overhaul its business to ensure that all coffee farmers get a fair return for their efforts'.[19]

It was argued that Nestlé is using the Fairtrade label as a shield to deflect criticism about its contribution to the suppression of world coffee prices (as flagged up by Oxfam in 2002), its labour standards and its aggressive manner of marketing baby-milk substitutes in low-income countries.[20]

However, Harriet Lamb, Director of the Fair Trade Foundation, which is responsible for awarding the Fairtrade label in the UK, was enthusiastic about the development, declaring 'this is a turning point for us and for the coffee growers'.[21] *Ethical Corporation* columnist Mallen Baker argued that Nestlé had been 'unfairly roasted' by these critics and that a breakthrough of the Fairtrade label into the mainstream should be welcomed by all.[22]

The Fairtrade label is a certification awarded to products whose production and form of trade adheres to standards set by the Fairtrade Labelling Organisation International (FLO-I), an umbrella organisation which supports licensing of products for sale in 19 countries including the US, Japan and a number in Europe. Certification requires that producers integrate a range of environmental, labour rights and community development interests, and that those who purchase from such producers offer more supportive and stable contracts at prices usually above market rates.[23] Producers of coffee, tea, sugar, bananas and other products in low-income countries are given a stable, sustainable price for their products and investment into community development programmes. The Fairtrade label also acts as a signal of 'ethical' credentials to consumers on supermarket shelves; both ends of the supply chain are addressed by this movement, which has attracted the support of business and campaigning NGOs alike.

While Fairtrade products make up only a tiny percentage of their respective markets, recent years have seen a strong growth in their popularity. In Europe, the net retail value of sales of Fairtrade products in over 79,000 outlets, including 50 supermarket chains, grew to €660 million in 2005, achieving an increase of 154% on sales at the turn of the century.[24] Over 5 million producers and their families in Latin America, Asia and Africa are said to have benefited from Fairtrade relationships[25]—the number of certified producers is growing rapidly, increasing by 25% in the year 2005 alone.[26] The green and blue Fairtrade logo issued by the FLO-I is now recognised by 50% of the adult population in the UK.[27]

'Fairtrade Fortnight', an annual awareness-raising event in the UK in March was marred this year by publicity surrounding the Nestlé controversy and also by news that McDonald's, another common target of consumer boycotts, is now publicising the sales of Fairtrade coffee in 650 US east-coast stores.[28] The issue is one of trust; informed consumers and activists who have supported the growth of the fair trade movement and the Fairtrade brand feel that the movement is being co-opted by those powerful companies that it seeks to challenge. *New Internationalist* magazine argued that 'the allure of the mainstream is largely illusory. Tributaries do not change its course; they disappear into it.'[29] Whether and how to engage powerful actors in social systems, and to focus on incremental but tangible change or more transformative but often unlikely change, has been a central dilemma for social actors throughout history, and debates around the fair trade movement are one recent illustration.

The more broad your view, the more complicated and challenging this becomes. Over Valentine's Day 2006, those romantics giving their well-informed, 'ethically' minded sweethearts Fairtrade roses from Kenya may well have been rebuked for not considering the environmental damage caused by the cut-flower industry around the Lake Naivasha area. The introduction of Fairtrade certification has seen increases to workers' wages and an expansion of businesses, but local ecosystems and water supplies are being put under severe strain by the increased production and the migration of workers from northern parts of Kenya, attracted by the higher wages.[30] In addition, sweethearts may have turned their noses up at the amount of pollution caused by flying flowers in from another continent, given the growing impacts of climate change.

The growth in popularity of 'fairer trade' initiatives, such as Equitrade[31] chocolate from Madagascar and Just Change tea from India,[32] which market themselves as providing better, more stable conditions than the Fairtrade brand for only small and medium producers, reflects the growing mistrust many consumers feel towards Fairtrade.

But alternatives to Fairtrade have not all been welcomed in this way. The plethora of copycat 'fairly traded' brands and standards supported by big business—such as Kraft's 'Sustainable Development' coffee brand, produced in conjunction with the Rainforest Alliance initiative—springing up on supermarket shelves in the US and Europe have also led to concern over confusion between different 'ethical' products. These other brands may not meet the standards set by the FLO-I or uphold elements of empowerment that the Fairtrade brand seeks in relationships with producers, but are competing with Fairtrade products to produce the brightest halo to attract consumers. This echoes the banana disputes between the Rainforest

Alliance and Fairtrade movement during the 1990s, which also revolved around the dilemma of whether one step forward, a better banana, was helping or hindering a leap forward towards a sustainable and responsible one.

The question of governmental involvement in regulation of the 'ethical' market has arisen, in order to standardise the certification process and reduce conflict between the numerous emerging standards. In France, Fairtrade products are certified with the Max Havelaar label, but a number of private certification processes have also emerged over the past few years. A system of definition and qualification of Fairtrade products is expected to be introduced by the French government in 2006, aiming to standardise the meaning of 'Fairtrade' and reduce consumer confusion.[33] This move has been opposed by Max Havelaar as regulation would mean the lowering of 'fairness' standards and would also detract from the awareness-raising and lobbying aspect of Fairtrade.

Similarly, regulation of the increasingly popular market for organic food produce has raised concerns about the lowering of standards of certification. The Soil Association, one of the certification bodies of organic produce in the UK, argued that, as demand for organic produce continues to increase, 'product integrity is potentially threatened by dilution of standards world-wide'.[34] The European Commission announced new EU-wide regulations governing the certification and labelling of organic produce in December 2005, which will 'allow a certain amount of flexibility' in production methods.[35] Friends of the Earth (UK) have taken issue with the inclusion of a clause that allows products that contain a small percentage of genetically modified organisms to be labelled as organic, arguing that economic concerns are being prioritised ahead of human health and protection of the environment.[36]

That's just not fair!

In January 2006 the Just Change (India) Producer Company Ltd was launched in Tamil Nadu, India. The company is the brainchild of Stan and Mari Thekaekara, who have been working with the Adivasi ('original inhabitants' or tribal people) communities of the Nilgiri Hills in India since the 1980s. It is the latest step for Just Change, an organisation promoting alternative trading mechanisms that will benefit poor communities in both high- and low-income countries. 'We try to achieve this by directly linking poor communities and encouraging them to trade among themselves,' explained Stan Thekaekara to us.

Thekaekara found that, in spite of the successful leap from labourers to producers, the Adivasis he has worked with found they were catapulted from a local wage economy into a global market economy that is extremely vulnerable, due to the market forces determining the price of their produce. For instance, tea prices at the producer level have dropped to nearly half of what they were four years ago. 'It has become evident over the years that the strategy for poverty reduction based on the traditional approach of gaining control over assets can no longer, on its own, guarantee success,' explains Thekaekara, who is also a trustee of Oxfam GB and Visiting Fellow at Oxford University. 'We believe that lack of power and control in markets contributes significantly to poverty all over the globe.'

The launch of the company is the result of a connection made in 1994 when the Thekaekaras spent a month in the UK researching community work. In the UK, Stan and Mari found large numbers of long-term unemployed people almost completely dependent on social welfare, living in pockets of extreme deprivation. In spite of government investments into these areas, the condition of these communities did not improve significantly. The New Economics Foundation (NEF) argued that the situation in these deprived areas of Britain is somewhat similar to those of the Adivasis in India, to the extent that, despite public investments, much of the money leaks out of the local economy into large national and global economies.[37]

The Thekaekaras also noticed that poor Britons like their tea, and pay a relatively high price. As the tribal groups in India grow tea, so they thought of making a direct link to the benefit of both poor communities, by establishing a co-operative of producers and consumers. Trading began with the help of the Matson Neighbourhood Project (MNP) in Gloucester, who were working with the residents of a council estate. The Adivasis of Gudalur send their tea directly to the residents of Matson, who package and sell it both to their own community and to other local customers such as the Council.

This initiative is prototyping a new way of doing business. By sharing the ownership of the value chain, and thereby spreading the risk along that chain, the consumers and producers involved are gaining greater control of their participation in the market economy. Producers can retain ownership over their product all along the market chain and can therefore benefit from the final retail value of the product. Consumers can work directly with producers to establish a price for the product that is based on direct communication and hopefully principles of equity, rather than fluctuating and speculative markets.

It is a prototype of a new approach to both business and social change. If communities across the globe could link up to trade directly with each other, they could form a social chain which could be a powerful force for economic, social and political change. 'People need to believe in themselves and in their capacity to take control over their own economy,' states the Just Change website.[38] Their work recognises the problems and potential of disadvantaged people and communities no matter whether they live in hot or cold, rich or poor countries. As such it hints towards a new approach to international development work, as well as a different form of trade.

Three broad concepts of more responsible trade are emerging. 'Ethical trade' describes the work of large companies, such as those involved in the 'Ethical Trading Initiative', which focuses on improving workplace conditions, but does not yet address power relations and revenue distribution in value chains. 'Fairtrade' includes the same concern for better workplace conditions, but also addresses the buyer–supplier relationship, as described in the section 'Fair Fight'. As the consumer is asked to pay a premium, there is an element of charity to fair trade. The Just Change initiative does not involve a premium. In fact, the prices paid by poor consumers can be lower than the market price, as savings are made through cutting out the middleman and the payment of surplus to distant shareholders. The principle is solidarity, not charity. As such, this small initiative suggests a new form of solidarity trading could emerge as a new paradigm for people interested in working on trade for social goals. We could call it 'Just Trade'. The power of naming it thus may arise by provoking us to question what we have hitherto assumed is either 'ethical' or 'fair' in the area of trade.

Just Change is the latest example of the forms of innovation possible as information and communication technologies spread further for cheaper. Business-to-business (B2B) and peer-to-peer (P2P) applications may become sideshows to new community-to-community (C2C) collaboration in shaping 'Globalisation 2.0' by flattening power hierarchies on our planet.[39] Our global village may be creating itself a virtual village market. If successful, in the years to come the best tea in the West may be found on poor council estates, not high-class cafes.

Incredibly India

The emergence of Indian business as a confident, powerful competitor on the playing field of global commerce was confirmed by the prominence of Indian companies and culture at the 2006 World Economic Forum in Davos in January. Fareed Zakaria reported in *Newsweek* that 'no country has captured the imagination of the conference and dominated the conversation as India in 2006'.[40] The omnipresent slogan 'Incredibly India: the Biggest Democracy for Global Investors' attempted to whisk the red carpet from beneath China's feet, as the presence of the Indian business people and Bollywood music and dancers dominated the conferences and social events.

Subsequent state visits to India by US president George Bush, France's Jacques Chirac, Australia's John Howard and Saudi Arabia's King Abdullah to talk business in February and March 2006 confirmed India's 'star' status. British Foreign Secretary Jack Straw affirmed the increase of trade with India as a priority for the UK in 2006 in a key government white paper launched in March.[41] It is being courted by America, for the pivotal role it could play in negating China's likely dominance in future decades.

India's well-educated labour surplus, its booming internal markets and carrots dangled to business such as tax breaks, tariff relief and exemptions from certain labour and environmental regulations in 'special economic zones' across the country work to attract foreign investors, just as promises of exotic spices, glittering colour and noisy adventure entice tourists from all over the world. Tesco, which controls of 30% of the UK grocery market, is one of the latest big names to be looking to expand into the Indian market.[42]

Although home to over a billion people, India's 'corporate welfare' efforts to attract investment have built economic wealth on a narrow base, largely in New Delhi, Mumbai and the IT centre of Bangalore. Looking beyond the boom of foreign interest in 2006, which is underpinned by news of strong economic growth of 7.5% in 2005, the rest of India tells a different tale.

In a country as vast and diverse as this, where 17 major languages, 22,000 dialects and all the world's major religions are represented, it is the welfare and standard of living of the 75% of the population that live in rural areas that are reflected in India's low position of 127 out of 177 countries in the 2005 United Nations Human Development Index.[43] Over 300 million people in India live on less than a dollar a day. Water scarcity is considered the most pressing environmental issue followed by air pollution and loss of biodiversity. Fourteen per cent of the population still do not have sustainable access to suitable water source and 20% are undernourished.[44] Caste and gender continue to play a significant role in determining social status and lifestyle.

The infrastructure for government in India is stretched over 28 states, each with its own governance structure and each typically burdened with a history of corruption cases and a culture of inefficiency. Recent high-profile efforts by the government to address wider social problems include an anti-poverty deal, launched in February 2006, which aims to provide income for 60 million rural households[45] and a joint programme implemented with assistance from the US to increase efforts to eliminate child labour, announced in March.[46] However, the annual total the government spends on public health amounts to 200 rupees, or US$4 per capita. A bustling civil-society sector attempts to fill the gap; for example, SEWA (Self Employed Women's Association), a trade union-based national organisation originating in Gujarat, continues to roll out health, education and food security programmes assisting some of the poorest rural communities.[47]

As the prominence of Indian business has sky-rocketed, a parallel spotlight has been focused on corporate social responsibility (CSR) issues in the country. The perception of the role of corporations in social concerns is said to be undergoing a shift away from the traditional ideas of philanthropy—inspired by modern interpretations of religious philosophies promoting collective responsibility and the compassion and leadership shown by Mahatma Gandhi, Guru Nanak, Mother Teresa and others, setting up separate 'foundations' to address particular health or education needs has been a time-honoured premise of Indian business.[48]

But the prominence of activists such as author Arundhati Roy and Amit Srivastava of the campaign group India Resource Center has grown in recent years along with an awakening to the negative social and environmental impacts of the business operations courted by their government's 'corporate welfare' programmes. Even the latest mainstream Bollywood blockbuster *Rang De Basanti* delivered an inspirational message encouraging activism against powerful corporate interests and corrupt political collusion, albeit through song and choreographed dance.[49]

The future of corporate responsibility in India must involve a wide variety of participants, from the high-altitude executives in Davos to the low-caste entrepreneurs in Gudalur.

Fizzy fight

Just as *The Hindu* newspaper declared 'corporations collectively can make India a better place for every citizen' in March 2006, campaigners working to expose the harmful impacts of Coca-Cola's operations on local communities in a number of Indian states had been stepping up efforts in India and abroad.[50] Over the past four years, issues of groundwater depletion and contamination and high pesticide levels in products have bubbled to the surface, leading to the closure of a Coca-Cola plant in Plachimada, Kerala, in March 2004 and making the soft-drinks giant's name synonymous with the notion of corporate irresponsibility in households across the country.

The release of Coca-Cola's first corporate responsibility review in the UK in January 2006 and its entry into the United Nations Global Compact initiative were marred by a series of high-profile actions against the world's largest brand name in the first quarter of 2006. While Coca-Cola's report stated that the company is 'putting corporate responsibility at the heart of our business strategy',[51] *Coca-Cola: The Alternative Report*,[52] produced by London-based campaign group War on Want, focused on droughts and contaminated water supplies in Indian states including Rajasthan, Uttar Pradesh and Kerala, alleged to be caused by Coca-Cola plants there.

The company was nominated for a 'Public Eye' award at the World Economic Forum in Davos for environmental irresponsibility in January 2006, just as the University of Michigan added its name to the growing list of US colleges boycotting all Coca-Cola products.[53] The following month, court proceedings were brought against the Indian franchise of the company in relation to the suspicious death of the chairman of a village council opposing a new plant in Tamil Nadu.[54] In March, a long-standing campaign in the UK demanding that the service provider to the National Union of Students boycott all Coca-Cola products in universities came to a head as a motion for a full boycott was proposed at the annual general meeting of the union.[55]

And, perhaps more worryingly for Coca-Cola, a popular Indian television yoga guru has declared that their drinks should be used for cleaning toilets, not drinking.[56] Swami Ramdev, who has brought yoga into the homes of millions of Indians in India and abroad, referred to the high sugar content and the controversy regarding high levels of pesticides found in the soft drinks.

Coca-Cola's counter-arguments that lack of rain is the main cause of groundwater depletion have been accepted by some government and court officials, but the company's reputation with markets at home and abroad will need to be rebuilt.[57] In terms of corporate scandals in India, Coca-Cola's infamy across the world has become second only to the campaign to hold Union Carbide (now incorporated as Dow Chemicals) accountable for the chemical explosion at a Union Carbide factory in Bhopal in 1984, which killed 20,000 Bhopal residents and affected the health of a further 100,000.[58]

In comparison, the Tata group, a home-grown conglomerate of 93 companies that make everything from cars and steel to software and consulting systems, are often quoted as examples of best practice of CSR in India, due to their self-proclamation that 'an implicit sense of ethical business conduct has been the cornerstone of the Tata way in the corporate governance sphere'.[59] In 2005, its revenue grew from $17 billion to $24 billion.

But, in January 2006, 12 Adivasis in the northern state of Orissa were killed as they protested against being displaced from their land, which had been sold to Tata Steel.[60]

An ex-employee of Coca-Cola India, who worked as a CSR executive, states, 'CSR is a distant dream in India . . . CSR is more an "extra activity" that has to be squeezed in to "look good".'[61] The key opportunity for India now—as with other low-income countries—is not the numbers of companies talking about CSR and blindly replicating the current 'add-on' Western model focusing on public relations as Coca-Cola has tried to do, but the creation of a home-grown, meaningful, systemic form of CSR that addresses local issues, challenges prejudice and asserts India's position as a leading player in the global economy of the future.

At a London conference about the future of CSR across the world in March 2006, Jane Nelson, former advisor to UN Secretary-General Kofi Annan, warned, 'If India and China don't get it right then it doesn't really matter what we do in the rest of the world.'[62] While her comment should not mean we ignore the fact that so many in the West have got it wrong already, it reflects the realisation that these two very different, vast countries housing nearly half of the world's population will shape the contours of the economic and political landscape in coming decades.

Given the scale of the challenges in India, the corporate responsibility agenda there must be a systemic one. Therefore it must work to strengthen governance in the country, not sidestepping official processes citing their corrupt and over-bureaucratic nature in justification. It must address the impacts of small and medium-sized businesses instead of giving special concessions to foreign multinational interests, while giving India the confidence to stand up to global neoliberal processes that will not work for the benefit of the majority of its people—as attempted in the making of cheaper generic antiretroviral drugs for HIV and Aids sufferers, which was eventually in 2005 overruled by the intellectual property protection agreements propelled by the World Trade Organisation.[63]

India's unique social patchwork of families, communities, NGOs and small and medium-sized enterprises means that such a CSR model will have to look beyond just the urban areas, to incorporate the concerns of local communities with historical ties to land, village councils (*panchyats*) and grass-roots civil-society

organisations as well as an understanding of how caste, religion and gender inequalities have pervaded through society to replicate power differentials over the
decades.

2Q2006
April–June

Jem Bendell and Jonathan Cohen

Trials and tribulations

Sometimes complex issues are more easily understood in the negative, that is, what they are not—non-profit or non-governmental, for example. When considering the phrase 'corporate social responsibility' (CSR) or 'corporate responsibility' (CR), the inverse, or corporate irresponsibility, helps illuminate its meaning. This is particularly true in relation to what the history books may call the 9/11 of CR: Enron. In May 2006, a jury of eight women and four men in Houston, Texas, did what all of the regulators, investors, analysts, banks, boards, legal advisors and market checks and balances could not—concretely convict Enron's leaders of historic failures and human losses. Enron's emblematic emasculation embodied the turn-of-the-century corporation gone bad, and catapulted the field of CR onto the popular culture radar of North America.

The stark trajectory of Enron stood out as the iconic embodiment and public face of all that CR seeks to be the antidote to, despite competition from a veritable golden age of recent corporate scandals that have occurred primarily in the US:

- WorldCom (the biggest bankruptcy—$11 billion accounting fraud)[1]
- Global Crossing (the sixth largest bankruptcy in US history)[2]
- Adelphia ($2.3 billion in hidden debt)[3]
- Royal Ahold ($1.23 billion restatement and $1.1 billion settlement)[4]
- AIG (second restatement)[5]
- HealthSouth ($1.4 billion in false earnings)[6]
- Fannie Mae (Over $10 billion in accounting errors)[7]

Will the conviction of Ken Lay (who died in July 2006 around three months before his sentencing to a likely 30 years in jail)—former chairman and founder, on six counts including conspiracy, wire fraud and securities fraud and four counts in a separate bank-fraud trial—as well as Jeffrey Skilling—former CEO, on 18 counts of conspiracy and fraud and one (of 10) counts of insider trading—make a difference?[8] Will the convictions be a deterrent?

Ken Lay and Jeffrey Skilling were not the first corporate executives to be convicted, nor will they be the last. On the face of it, the collapse of Enron has not had much of an impact on executive compensation. However, perhaps a belated recognition by boards of their fiduciary responsibilities, and a surge in corporate governance shareholder resolution successes in the 2006 annual meeting proxy season, will start to lessen a CEO's ability to run a company into the ground.[9]

Five years after the introduction of the signature US reaction to loss of trust in the market—the Sarbanes–Oxley legislation to strengthen transparency, accountability and improved corporate governance—it remains unpopular with business in terms of its cost and the quality of auditing. Lingering implications of the reaction to Enron encompass potential mergers between stock exchanges in the US and abroad.

So, given the limits of regulatory and legal moves, does CR have a role to play in avoiding future Enrons? We should remember that Enron had staff in charge of corporate responsibility. It issued a corporate responsibility report. It lied.

Investors in particular have an interest in spotting future Enrons, and as such could be key enforcers of better corporate governance. The new mainstream of CR, typified by stakeholder dialogues and sustainability reporting, does not appear to be sufficient to empower these investors, given their reliance on self-declarations about corporate intentions and management systems, and audits from firms with a commercial interest in being regarded by their clients as both reasonable and affordable. Consequently, both responsible investors and the wider public face a credibility riddle of whom to believe when they make judgements on the social performance of companies. Three areas are important in solving this riddle: the type of information self-declared by companies, the type of auditors involved, and information gathered from other sources.

The first area where the information flow to investors could be improved is the production of more quantitative indicators of social and environmental performance rather than corporate intentions and management systems. Requirements could include guidelines for the production of basic quantitative indicators such as pollution records, average wages paid to different types of employee (including in the supply chain), non-compliance notices issued by law enforcement agencies, pending court cases, court rulings, out-of-court settlements, admonitions or investigations from intergovernmental bodies, recognised trade unions in the workplace, collective bargaining agreements, multi-enterprise codes endorsed, certifications received, political donations, memberships of trade associations, and payments to lobby groups. With such information, companies might be able to be indexed on the basis of their actual impacts on society rather than on the appearance of their management systems. The limited amount of information provided in this way raises questions not only of companies and their auditors, but of the ability of the stakeholders they engage with to move beyond issue identification for the materiality of non-financial reporting to the type of data required about those issues. Some of these performance indicators would be more difficult to compile and audit than others, with statistics on wage levels being much easier than mapping the often opaque and ad hoc nature of lobbying, or assessing its content. The usefulness of these performance indicators will still depend on the professionalism of the auditors. Initiatives such as the International Standard on Assurance Engagements (ISAE) 3000, developed by the International Auditing and Assurance Standards Board (IAASB), and the AA1000 Assurance Standard (AA1000AS), launched by AccountAbility, help ensure better practice, with the latter including attention to the auditors' capacity to deal with the stakeholder-determined issues in extra-financial reports.[10] However, self-disclosure verified by contracted auditors provides a context within which conflicts of interest can undermine effective disclosure. A comprehensive solution to credible information on company performance must include systems for gathering and processing information and opinion from society, unmediated by the companies involved

The third area for solving the credibility riddle involves generating reliable and relevant data from sources other than the companies themselves. The problem here is how to combine opinions from diverse stakeholders on different public issues into one framework, something that the Swiss investment analyst firm Covalence has been developing since 2001.[11] Its director Antoine Mach told us that 'the corporate reputation that matters, and is material to value, is not the one in the minds of management but within the web of stakeholders, with some stakeholders connected to more strands than others'. Covalence maps corporate, media and stakeholder views across 45 criteria of business contributions to human development, based on an international legal framework, to create a trackable 'ethical-quote' for each company. Another system of investment analysis that includes this broader view is Total Corporate Responsibility (TCR), developed by Frank Dixon and used by Innovest Strategic Value Advisors. It also focuses on some quantitative indicators of performance, as described above. The notable aspect of TCR is its systems approach, which considers how a company affects the societal systems it exists within, through a range of activities such as lobbying and advertising. This approach is important in three ways. First, if we assume that external performance is an indicator of internal performance, then it helps investors avoid corrupt internal practices such as those that became the norm at Enron. Second, it helps investors determine how well prepared companies are for future social and environmental change. Third, it supports companies in promoting changes in market demand and regulatory frameworks that will sustain value creation over the long term, across the whole economy. The key issue for investors is how to shift investments away from firms with a high likelihood of internal unethical behaviour. TCR seeks to drive system change by rewarding firms that are more proactive than peers in seeking to promote, rather than block, change at a systemic level. Firms working for system changes that hold all companies more responsible receive higher TCR ratings, with a hoped-for rise in stock price as a result in an effort to create a race to the top of the market.[12]

Pragmatic rights?

The weaknesses of CR governance that led to the collapse of Enron and the advent of Sarbanes–Oxley legislation in the US has implications for the challenges of CR governance at the global level. The primary global dialogue and reference point for business and human rights concerns the Special Representative of the UN Secretary-General on the Issue of Human Rights and Transnational Corporations and Other Business Enterprises (SRSG). The Interim Report issued in February 2006 by the SRSG, Harvard University Professor of International Affairs and former UN Assistant Secretary-General John Ruggie, provoked a flurry of reactions and stakeholder engagement.

The SRSG offered hope for blazing new ground in standards concerning business and human rights, and more specifically clarification of terms such as 'business spheres of activity and influence' by stating that its final report will go beyond restating what has taken place to date and contain 'normative judgments'.[13] In addition to strengthening the body of standards, a full overview of existing standards and tools and support for the most effective would move the field ahead in its application on the ground. An addition to this mix, a new Human Rights Guide for Business, was launched in June 2006 by the Business Leaders Initiative on Human Rights, the United Nations Global Compact Office and the Office of the United Nations High Commissioner for Human Rights.[14]

Amnesty International (AI) called on the SRSG to address the responsibilities of companies to protect human rights when they are in host states that are unwilling or unable to do so. Interestingly, both AI and the International Chamber of Commerce (ICC) called for clarification of the terms 'complicity' and 'sphere of influence' as used in the business and human rights context.[15]

The ICC's response to the SRSG's mandate commented that 'the state is the duty-bearer in protecting and promoting human rights' and, in its favoured monolithic monotone of the omnipotent voice of all enterprise, that 'Business does not believe there is a need for a new international framework.'[16]

The SRSG's Interim Report noted that 'it may be desirable in some circumstances for corporations to become direct bearers of international human rights obligations, especially where host governments cannot or will not enforce their obligations and where the classical international human rights regime, therefore, cannot possibly be expected to function as intended'.[17]

A letter issued by over 100 NGOs in May 2006 in response to the Interim Report called on the SRSG to take into account the UN Norms on the Responsibilities of Transnational Corporations and Other Business Enterprises with Regard to Human Rights, or simply the UN Norms for short.[18] The SRSG, however, had criticised the UN Norms in the Interim Report in unusually stark language. Criticisms levelled include 'exaggerated legal claims', by taking 'existing state-based human rights instruments and simply asserting that many of their provisions now are binding on corporations as well. But that assertion itself has little authoritative basis in international law—hard, soft, or otherwise.' Ruggie went on to say that 'All existing instruments specifically aimed at holding corporations to international human rights standards ... are of a voluntary nature. Relevant instruments that do have international legal force ... impose obligations on states, not companies.' This critique does not even encompass the most volatile elements of the UN Norms—to monitor corporations and provide for payment of reparations to victims. Further, the SRSG cites 'the flaws of the Norms' as 'a distraction from rather than a basis for moving the SRSG's mandate forward'.[19]

Approved on 13 August 2003, by the UN Sub-Commission on the Promotion and Protection of Human Rights, the UN Norms compiled a laundry list of the key human rights documents related to business under one roof, which served to focus the discussion greatly.[20] Subsequently, the UN Commission on Human Rights decided not to move ahead with the document. By virtue of this decision and the sheer lack of governmental support, the SRSG stated that the UN Norms did not possess legal standing.[21] A former high-ranking official with knowledge of the process commented that the SRSG's statement 'was the embalming oil of something that was already dead in the coffin'.

A lead in drafting the UN Norms, Professor David Weissbrodt, argues that the SRSG's critique of the Norms was 'inspired if not copied word-for-word from the advocacy of the International Chamber of Commerce (ICC) and the International Organization of Employers (IOE)' and 'relies on the tendentious and highly biased views of lawyers employed by' those organisations and 'ignores the considerable positive commentary that the Norms have generated'. He criticises the SRSG for exaggerating the potential power of the Norms, reminding us that they 'do not constitute a treaty and therefore cannot bind either states or corporations in the same way that treaties are binding if they are ratified'. Weissbrodt explains that 'the Norms principally reflect, restate, and refer to existing international standards, but apply them not only to governments but directly to businesses. The Norms are consistent with the progressive development of international law in applying standards not only to states, but also to individuals, armed opposition groups, and other non-state actors.'[22] In this sense, the Norms seek to move forward the basic concept and application of international law in line with recent developments on non-state actors, as highlighted by the establishment of the International Criminal Court. Ruggie's approach rejects that development.

Despite this, the UN Norms are still breathing, in two respects: the issues lie at the heart of the SRSG's mandate, and NGOs continue to use the UN Norms as a campaigning and learning tool, while consultants are using it in work with companies.

Human rights impact assessment standards are another area that the SRSG cited as having considerable impact on the ability of companies to meet their human rights obligations at both national and project levels, but which are in need of development. Unfortunately, the broad scope of the SRSG's mandate—an entirely unfunded mandate—means that this task will be left to others to carry out.[23]

The SRSG declares in the final paragraph of the Interim Report 'an unflinching commitment to the principle of strengthening the promotion and protection of human rights as it relates to business, coupled with a pragmatic attachment to what works best'.[24] As a school of philosophy, pragmatism suggests that beliefs qualify as valid or not, even 'true' or 'false', depending on how helpful they are in accomplishing the believer's goals. Thus it is only through their usefulness that theories and beliefs acquire meaning and validity. Even when the term is used in a more colloquial way, it often reflects this type of world-view.[25] Many human rights are widely seen, and legally recognised, as inalienable principles which are therefore absolute, not awarded by human power, not transferable to another power, and incapable of repudiation.[26]

The idea, which is held by Amnesty International, that rights should never be relative to circumstance sits uneasily with the concept of pragmatism. 'We are concerned that the approach of "principled pragmatism" to which you refer in your report may lead to underestimating the need for binding legal principles and guidelines as well as the state of applicable international law', said Amnesty's director Irene Khan in a letter to Professor Ruggie in April 2006.[27] They pointed out the limited evidence of success from voluntary initiatives and the problem of providing mechanisms of redress based on voluntary benevolence from powerful actors. It is also worth remembering that, when the Norms were originally launched, Professor Weissbrodt also claimed pragmatism in defence of criticisms from NGOs that they did not go far enough. Perhaps if there is ever to be 'principled pragmatism', it will require incorporating a set of absolute values which counterpose the relativist and opportunistic dimensions to pragmatist philosophy. Otherwise, claims to pragmatism may mask how our views have been shaped by acquiescence to those power relations that sustain our privilege. If it did, then the successful acceptance of our ideas would merely make us the intellectual totalitarians of our time.

A potential area of common thought lies in the desire by business groups such as the ICC, IOE and Business for Social Responsibility, as well as human rights groups, for more stable operating environments with better governance and rule of law.[28] The fact remains that the lack of effective global governance mechanisms, coupled with national governments that have proven woeful in preventing or holding accountable corporate involvement in human rights abuses, has resulted in a void that needs to be filled.

One step in that direction occurred when the new UN Human Rights Council convened its first meeting on 19 June 2006. The new and improved body will take up the SRSG report and serve as a key global institution for dealing with business and human rights. It will now meet throughout the year and has a mechanism to take up urgent crises. All 192 UN member states will now have their human rights record examined, resources permitting. The real test of the new UN Human Rights Council, much like the challenge more broadly for business and human rights standards, will be in its ability to hold accountable 'any Council member who commits gross and systematic violations of human rights' and 'have their rights of membership suspended by a two-thirds majority of the General Assembly'.[29]

Not banking on corruption

In what may be a hoped-for multilateral race to the top, the World Bank declared a new, comprehensive, 'long-term' anti-corruption strategy in April 2006 to leverage loans and technical assistance to developing countries and through partnerships with stakeholders.[30] The Bank has identified corruption as among the greatest obstacles to economic and social development by limiting opportunities, creating inefficiencies and impeding the delivery of services, for example; and World Bank president Paul Wolfowitz reportedly sees corruption as his signature issue.[31] Previously, individual loans were suspended in response to allegations of corruption in countries such as India, Bangladesh and Uzbekistan; however, Wolfowitz has acknowledged such a case-by-case approach 'by itself doesn't deliver effective results for the poor'.[32] To do so, 'the Bank will continue to work closely with Civil Society to provide checks and balances and promote accountability in their governments'.

The extractive industry presents the greatest challenge to the World Bank in carrying out the new long-term anti-corruption strategy. In an effort to determine existing patterns in order to inform the design of governance instruments, the UN SRSG's Interim Report surveyed 65 instances of alleged corporate human rights abuses recently reported by NGOs, which were seen as 'unlikely to be a representative sample of all situations, but of the worst'. Unsurprisingly, the extractive sector—oil, gas, and mining—constituted two-thirds of the sample of reported abuses, and 'account for most allegations of the worst abuses, including complicity in crimes against humanity; large-scale corruption; violations of labor rights; and a broad array of abuses in relation to local communities, especially indigenous people'.[33]

Moving from what had been 'an ad hoc, low visibility approach towards instances of fraud and corruption in member countries, Bank-financed projects, and among staff', the Bank now seeks to assume 'a clear leadership role among multilateral institutions'.[34] In addition to a slew of other organisations, the Bank and its private-sector financing arm, the International Finance Corporation, have supported industry-wide efforts to address the serious challenge of corruption in extractive industry practices, such as the Extractive Industries Transparency Initiative (EITI), which works toward 'improved governance in resource-rich countries through the full publication and verification of company payments and government revenues from oil, gas and mining'.[35]

The Bank's most direct impact in this area will be in its own loan portfolio. 'The proportion of new projects with accountability/anti-corruption components jumped from 0.4% in the 1995–96 fiscal years to an average of 5% in the 2004–05 fiscal years', and all Bank Country Assistance Strategies are now required to address governance issues, according to the World Bank Institute.[36] The Chad–Cameroon Oil Pipeline Project demonstrates the challenges the World Bank and its Department of Institutional Integrity face in fighting corruption in its existing projects. In what was touted as the largest private investment in Africa, the $3.7 billion dollar

Chad–Cameroon oil project, which is managed by a consortium of Exxon, Chevron and Petronas, stands as a litmus test for World Bank anti-corruption success to start at home.[37]

A 'deciding factor' in the World Bank's support for the Chad–Cameroon Oil Pipeline Project was Chad's 1999 Petroleum Revenue Management Law which required the bulk of direct revenue to be used for poverty reduction in agreed-to 'priority sectors', such as health, education and rural development, as well as a Future Generations Fund, to ensure financial savings once oil reserves are exhausted. In December 2005, the National Assembly of Chad amended the Petroleum Revenue Management Law and broadened the definition of priority sectors to include, among other areas, territorial administration and security, increased from 13.5% to 30% the share of revenue that can be allocated to non-priority sectors that are not subject to oversight and control, eliminated the Future Generations Fund and transferred its $36 million into the general budget. The World Bank, in turn, viewed the changes as a breach of contract, and on 6 January 2006 suspended new loans and grants to Chad.[38]

The Chadian government was reported to have used the first $4.5 million of the signing bonus that it received from the oil companies to purchase arms.[39] NGOs warned the World Bank against financing the project beforehand and said that its assessment of the situation in Chad, 'notorious for its corruption and human rights abuses', was based on unrealistic assumptions.[40] The World Bank's stakeholder engagement with civil society needs to take into greater account such concerns in future projects.

Subsequently, the World Bank and the Government of Chad 'signed a memorandum of understanding under which Chad committed 70 percent of its budget spending to poverty reduction programs, provided for a stabilization fund' for after the oil runs out, and made a new pledge of support for the independent oil revenue oversight authority.[41] The Bank won the round and will resume loan disbursements in education, health, community development, HIV/AIDS, agriculture, electricity, water and infrastructure.[42] Bank president Wolfowitz touted the MOU as a victory, saying 'The Chadian authorities have committed to ensuring that all oil revenues, not just the royalties, are spent on health and education and other basic needs of the poor'.[43] The corporate consortium has stayed largely out of view during the ongoing saga; however, it is unlikely that Exxon, Chevron and Petronas will successfully be able to maintain an ostrich stance through the life of the high-priced project.

Another important example of high-level collaboration to combat corruption involving corporations is the formation of a new coalition involving the World Economic Forum, the United Nations Global Compact, the International Chamber of Commerce and Transparency International,[44] the latter of which established the Business Principles for Countering Bribery.[45]

A tightening web?

If access to the internet superhighway was the first generation of the digital divide between the global North and South, and access to content via high-speed connection is the second, then impediments to the dissemination of content, whether through government censorship or corporate pay-for-play demands that result in different levels of access, is the third generation (3G) of the divide.

Structure has won a round against function, with the owners and controllers of the internet highway pipeline, whether the Chinese government on a national basis or internet network operators on a business basis, holding sway over the lords of content such as Yahoo, Google or Microsoft.

Critical Congressional hearings in Washington, DC in the first half of 2006 focused a spotlight on corporate complicity in censorship in China. Google fared worse in some parts of the media than its competitors Yahoo and Microsoft because of an apparent violation of brand identity embodied in their slogan 'Don't Be Evil'.[46]

Another aspect of the 3G digital divide, pay-for-play demands for tiers of access, speaks to a less clear-cut, but more far-reaching, potential impact. The short-term issue may be telecommunication companies charging higher prices to companies such as Google and eBay—which generate the most dissemination of data-intensive applications such as movies and video games and internet traffic—to recoup the billions of dollars needed to upgrade their networks to handle the increase in such traffic. The longer-term issue may be whether economic activity and democratic debate are available at the same level for those with access.[47]

In fact, steps in this direction were taken by AOL to charge large mass emailers for a new 'Goodmail' certified email service which bypasses spam filters and offers guaranteed delivery directly into AOL customers' inboxes.[48] A coalition with over 500 members, DearAOL.com, called the new service 'a threat to the free and open internet', and described 'pay-to-send' email as tollbooths on the currently open internet which demand 'protection money at the gates of their customers' computers' and constitute a tax on email and 'tiered services and dozens of middleman fees for every simple act of communication'. Coalition members include the AFL–CIO, Consumers Federation of America, Computer Professionals for Social Responsibility, Craig Newmark (Craig's List), Defenders of Wildlife, Democratic National Committee, Friends of the Earth, MoveOn, Oxfam America and Working Assets.[49]

The role of technology in enabling participation in democratic discourse, or 'accessible democracy', was also raised at Google's 2006 annual meeting by Amnesty International, which has issued reports citing a dramatic rise in the number of people detained or sentenced—and in cases tortured—for internet-related offences in China.[50] Adding to the glare of the spotlight, the NGO Reporters Without Borders released a report which labelled Yahoo as the 'Worst Search Censor in China'.[51] China has signed the International Covenant on Civil and Political Rights (ICCPR), which states in Article 19 that everyone shall have the right to hold opinions without interference; that everyone shall have the right to freedom of expression; and that this right shall include freedom to seek, receive and impart information and ideas of all kinds, regardless of frontiers, either orally, in writing or in print, in the form of art, or through any other media of his [or her] choice.[52]

Technology corporations have defended their practices in a strikingly similar manner, as embodied by Microsoft: 'In the case of China, we believe that despite the circumstances, the Internet has already transformed the economic, cultural and political landscape of China.'[53] This reflects the 'e-vangelical' approach of the internet generation, which believes the internet is an inherently positive force in the world. However, it does not reflect the emphasis on unbridled free markets and freely associating individuals which typified the early dot.commers. While dot.com investors remain supportive of business co-operation with, and facilitation of, government curbs on human rights, the positive promise of the internet may be broken.

3Q2006
July–September

Jem Bendell and Jonathan Cohen

Who's leading Hu?

Will endemic corruption, increasing wealth gaps, and the immense scale of environmental and health degradation from China's industrial revolution, lead to increased social unrest and an even greater media crackdown? Or will the waking economic giant leapfrog mistakes made during the West's industrial revolution? And, in answering this conundrum, will corporate citizenship play a role?

Some think so. In August 2006 a 'China CSR Map' was launched, 'to promote CSR in China through a centralized platform for the dissemination of information on organizations with CSR activities there'. Although considerable discussion and activities around CR exist in China, it is often difficult to find concrete information on which organisations are undertaking what activities. In addition to business, it involves academic institutions, service providers, media and online resource providers. To further accessibility, it is bilingual. China CSR Map is a collaboration between Deutsche Gesellschaft für Technische Zusammenarbeit (GTZ), SynTao and Transtech.[1]

Corporate citizenship appears to be relevant to Chinese companies and society for three main reasons: the influence of Western markets; the global aspirations of some Chinese companies; and the so-called development trajectory.

First, there is Western market influence. The social and environmental concerns of Western companies have been influencing construction, manufacturing and human resource practices in China, albeit to a limited and questionable extent. Even Japanese companies and those from other non-Western countries are now requesting environmental improvements from suppliers in China. Thus, to compete in certain export markets, Chinese companies will need to pay attention to how these markets adopt and practise greater responsibility. Doing so will facilitate China's navigation through the rough seas of global competition.

Recent signs indicate potential strains on future growth, partly fuelled by global trade. China has been posting an average annual gross domestic product (GDP) growth rate of 9.4% for the past 26 years, following Deng Xaioping's Four

Modernisations economic reforms.[2] But China's ranking in the World Economic Forum's Global Competitiveness Index (GCI) fell to 54 in 2006 from 48 a year ago. 'The most worrisome development is a marked drop in the quality of the institutional environment,' the report said. The culprit: the 'steep fall'—from 60 to 80—in how the Chinese institutions fared in the 2006 ranking. These institutions, spanning both public and private, had poor results in all the Index's 15 institutional indicators.[3] GCI measures the set of institutions, policies and factors that set the sustainable current and medium-term levels of economic prosperity.

As if sensing the need for change, on 25 September 2006 Chen Liangyu, a top Chinese Communist Party official in Shanghai, was booted out of the party's top leadership council, the Politburo. Mr Chen was 'the most senior official to be sacked' in a decade, or since incumbent President Hu Jintao became party secretary in 2002. The government launched an investigation that centred on the misuse of at least one-third of the 10 billion yuan ($1.2 billion) pension fund to make illegal loans and investments in real estate and other infrastructure deals.[4] Coincidentally, on the day of Mr Chen's downfall, China's auditor-in-chief disclosed that 'an unnamed company defrauded $140 million from Chinese banks and spent nearly $40 million on bribes'.[5]

To comply with international norms and to increase their competitiveness on the world stage, Worldwatch, an NGO, suggested that 'Chinese private enterprises would be wise to integrate CSR from the beginning.'[6] The global aspirations of some Chinese companies are a second reason why corporate citizenship is relevant to China. Chinese premiere Hu Jintao himself highlighted the goal of having a prominent role in global markets worthy of a great power. The Lenovo purchase of IBM and attempted takeover of Unocal by the China National Offshore Oil Company (CNOOC) is setting a trend that, according to Jack Zhai, head of global corporate finance at Deutsche Bank in Beijing, 'will continue'.[7] Besides mere ambitions, Chinese companies are expanding abroad because of market realities: constant price-cutting at home makes entry to foreign markets vital. Thin margins abroad make up for even thinner margins at home.[8]

But will going global mean going ethical? If Chinese companies seek to become global players or own global brands, they will need to pay more attention to the values and aspirations of producers and consumers in their target countries, especially those in the West. According to AccountAbility CEO Simon Zadek: 'Going global means being more responsible. We may just be on the cusp of an accountability revolution in Chinese business, or at least that part that needs to be credible in international markets, as they seek to move up the chain towards the high-value-added opportunities that come with control of global brands.'[9]

But, if Chinese companies target countries where consumer demands for responsibility are not as strong as in the West, there lies the problem. Recent Chinese foreign direct investment and foreign acquisitions have been in Asia and Africa. In both continents, the general concept of CR among local players is still largely equated to philanthropy. These countries, including its neighbouring economic power Japan, have embraced the trade opportunities with China whose robust growth and growing prosperity has enabled them to diversify their export markets and become less reliant on exports to the US. The stalling of the world trade talks has even led to a faster proliferation of bilateral and regional free-trade agreements.[10]

This has made NGO campaigners increasingly concerned about Beijing's model of 'international development', as exemplified by the country's relationship with Angola.[11] In 2004, Angola's government, battered by a long civil war, was negotiating a new loan with the International Monetary Fund (IMF) for its reconstruction. The IMF, aware of Angola's long history of corruption and poor governance since independence from Portuguese colonial rule in 1975, was keen to include measures to cut corruption and tighten the country's economic management. To the IMF official's surprise, the Angola government suddenly broke off negotiations. The Angolans had received a counter-proposal from China's export-credit agency, Exim Bank: a $2 billion loan that came with minimal rates of interest, a generous payback period, and none of the IMF's 'conditionalities'. The government in Luanda chose China's offer.

Unlike many Western companies, Chinese companies with global ambitions already serve important markets, including its own domestic market of more than a billion Chinese and where margins are squeezed to their limits. Adopting expensive above-compliance strategies on social and environmental issues have made them wary of becoming uncompetitive at home and in other markets they currently serve. Just as some factories have different labour codes for different production lines in the same factory, depending on which brand the production line is for, global Chinese companies might seek to align the CR credentials of particular products with the markets being served, rather than raise their standards globally. Oddly, this might provide new impetus for ethical labelling within those sectors that have been resistant to it until now. The impact on how companies do their business in China, however, might be limited to the size of the ethical market in the West.

The third reason why corporate responsibility may be relevant to China is because of its development trajectory. If the (questionable) assumption that the West has established a development trajectory that China is following and modelling, then just as the voluntary responsibilities of business towards society and the environment have grown in the West, then the same can be expected in China. Yet this assertion is based on many assumptions about the limited role of government to actually deliver changes in corporate practice through regulation, as well as the ability of a vibrant civil society to push for changes not demanded by government. On both counts, the situation appears quite different. The interventionist approach of the Chinese government could lead to significant rapid developments in regulations and investment for a sustainability transition; yet at the same time the same philosophy does not leave much scope for civil-society activism that could drive voluntary corporate action.

China imposed broad new restrictions on 10 September 2006 on the distribution of foreign news in the country, beefing up state regulations on the news media. Under new rules that were said to take effect immediately, the state-run New China News Agency said it would become the de facto gatekeeper for foreign news reports, photographs and graphics entering China. To censor content that endangers 'national security', the agency announced its new role and rule in its own dispatch. As chronicled by a *New York Times* article, 'President Hu Jintao has intensified a crackdown on all kinds of news media in recent months, arresting and harassing journalists, tightening regulation of Web sites and online forums, hiring tens of thousands of people to screen and block Web content deemed offensive and firing editors of state-run publications that resist official controls.'[12]

Yet it is exactly such discourse and information flow that is essential for corporate responsibility. Western-based companies such as News International and Yahoo! have been criticised for agreeing to restrictive media regulations in order to access the Chinese market. These defy the basics of corporate responsibility, like social auditing, which requires active participation and ownership of standard setting, monitoring, verification and corrective action implementation by independent representatives of the workers themselves. Without change in the social and legal context in China, it will be difficult for companies to responsibly source from China.

Still, the words of Chinese business leaders should be taken into account as a guide to indigenous driving forces for CR versus Western models. Wu Mao, Chief Economist of the Shougang Steel Group, one of the top five steel companies in China, said, 'CSR will not be promoted in China by 'lecturing' or 'teaching'. Rather, foreign companies and NGOs should share their experiences in order to promote CSR in a Chinese way.'[13]

Similarly, Chen Ying, Deputy Director of the China Enterprise Confederation (CEC), is on record as saying that corporates and foreign NGOs have demanded too much on too many issues in China. 'Rather than telling China what to do, they should let the Chinese government, companies and social organisations develop their own ideas. CEC plans to provide training to encourage more Chinese enterprises to take up CSR practices and join the Global Compact.'[14]

Death of a green salesman?

BP and Wal-mart have moved to the opposite ends of the corporate citizenship spectrum. Wal-Mart has attracted NGOs into its orbit, as exemplified by the NGO Environmental Defense relocating its project manager to Bentonville, Arkansas, home of the giant retailer's headquarters. The environmental group has set up shop in the company's 'back yard' to work on green initiatives.[15] Wal-Mart also hired former critic and Sierra Club president Adam Werbach to teach company floor employees how to consume less in their everyday lives, eat healthy food, and buy compact fluorescent light bulbs. Indeed, the so-called 'greening' of Wal-Mart has so profoundly changed the company's reputation that a prominent activist NGO decided not to campaign against Wal-Mart because they no longer make an attractive target.[16]

Meanwhile, BP, a heretofore CR leader, has drawn the scorn of public opinion over a widespread series of awful gaffes. Its record includes the following:

September 2005

The US Occupational Safety and Health Administration fined BP Products North America more than $21 million following an explosion at its Texas City plant that claimed the lives of 15 workers and injured more than 170 others.[17]

March 2006

BP's Exploration Alaska subsidiary spilled more than 200,000 gallons of crude oil near Prudhoe Bay, the largest North Slope spill ever.[18]

April 2006

US Labor Department fined BP $2.4 million for safety violations at its Ohio refinery.[19]

June 2006

The US Commodity Futures Trading Commission brings charges of price fixing.[20]

August 2006

BP shuts down the largest oil field in the United States, Prudhoe Bay, and its 400,000 barrels a day of production, due to poor maintenance.[21]

September 2006

BP executives get excoriated by elected officials and apologise during an appearance before a Congressional Committee hearing under oath, with one taking the 5th Amendment against self-incrimination.[22]

How much rope does a company with a historically acclaimed record on corporate responsibility receive when they make mistakes? Specifically, how much leeway does BP get for its atrocious recent record because of its groundbreaking role as the first oil company to publicly acknowledge the existence of global warming and the role of fossil fuels as a cause?

BP has come a long way from the days in the run-up to the 1997 Kyoto Climate Change Conference. This was the first multi-stakeholder event organised by the UN Association of USA NGO programme, together with business, the Clinton–Gore administration, and the United Nations. The US had not taken a leadership role at that point, but BP was out in front, having publicly abandoned the Global Climate Coalition, a group of influential oil companies campaigning against the validity of climate change. During the question-and-answer session that followed the presentations a radical-left NGO representative commented, 'I never thought I would say this, but BP's position is more progressive than the US government's.' How BP will regain that faith over time will make it a test case of how companies who started well, but faltered, can finish the race victoriously.

Reframing finance

At the end of August 2006 near Zurich, Switzerland, institutional investors, asset managers and listed companies gathered at the Swiss Re Centre for Global Dialogue to share thoughts on how to promote more long-term approaches to financial performance.[23] The speeches generally emphasised the challenge that short-termism in financial markets is not helpful for companies wanting to plan for long-term value creation, incorporating attention to value arising from sustainability. However, the dialogue did not progress far in identifying mechanisms for promoting long-term approaches, especially those that might be significant enough to turn the tide of short-termism that has been filled in recent years by the growth of short-selling techniques by hedge funds. The challenge was summed up well by David Russell, speaking to the *Financial Times* (*FT*): 'The investment process in the last 20 years has generally gravitated towards shorter term and relative returns. Pension funds have long-term liabilities to manage.' The senior adviser on responsible investment at the Universities Superannuation Scheme did not mince words, adding, 'We can no longer rely on short-term relative investment processes when we have liabilities stretching out for decades.'[24]

A number of initiatives seek to address this challenge. The Marathon Club is a group of investors looking at ways to encourage investment for the long term.[25] In August 2006, it released a summary of investors' responses to its discussion paper on how to promote long-term long-only investing. 'There is wide recognition that a long term approach requires a more comprehensive and in depth understanding of investment issues by trustees, prompting some respondents to suggest the need to develop appropriate governance structures and define further the scope of trustee education.'[26] Trustee awareness was identified as a key lever for change.

The importance of two other initiatives began to be recognised in 2006. Reporting on environmental, social and governance (ESG) issues grew as a result of the Enhanced Analytics Initiative (EAI), which commits its members, which include BNP Paribas, USS, Investec and Hermes, to spend 5% of their brokerage fees with firms that focus on extra-financial indicators.

In July 2006, the *FT* reported on the significance of the new UN Principles for Responsible Investment (UNPRI). These principles are backed by investors responsible for more than $4 trillion-worth of assets, or about 10% of global capital. UNPRI also commit signatories to integrate ESG, or extra-financial, issues into conventional investment analysis; to become active, responsible owners by promoting good corporate practice in these areas; and to report transparently on what actions have been taken in this area. The initiative promises to generate a global impact for the Global Compact, which is where it's now located within the UN system. Paul Clements-Hunt of the United Nations Environment Programme Finance Initiative (UNEP-FI), which conceived the UNPRI, told the *FT* that 'the signatories know they have to show that PRI will change things. It shows the investment community that these issues are mainstream.'[27]

What is noteworthy about these principles is they recognise that ESG issues have an effect on the long-term performance of companies. 'For the best part of 25 years, these factors have been a niche part of SRI [socially responsible investing],' said Marc Fox, a member of the ESG Research team at Goldman Sachs. As ESG issues enter the mainstream of investing, there has been a subtle change in terminology, reflected in the articles and press releases. No longer referred to as 'non-financial' issues, ESGs are now described as 'extra-financial', to highlight both their materiality and their additionality to the norm. Thus the conceptual frames of finance and investment might be moving towards the whole-systems theory of value and valuation.

But what of the practical implications? How does one create a truly long-term mandate? Emma Howard Boyd, Head of Socially Responsible Investment at Jupiter Asset Management, put forward a suggestion: 'You have to look at other ways of incentivising fund managers.'[28] Translating the diagnosis of systemic contradictions into proposals for specific changes in rules and norms to incentivise different practices from finance professionals is the central challenge.

NGOs aren't God, AEI reports

Not everyone was happy about the trends toward reframing finance in 2006. Certainly not a scholar at the American Enterprise Institute (AEI), Adam Lerrick, who in August wrote in the *FT* that 'vigilante non-governmental organisations have become the de facto regulators of the flow of finance to the developing world.'[29] His argument is that NGO influence on Western banks is making it more costly for entrepreneurs in emerging markets to access capital. Claims such as 'not a single dollar of multilateral funds is disbursed without NGO blessing' or that there is a 'fiat by self-anointed regulators from rich nations' make governing private finance seem so extreme and far from the truth that the argument could be ignored.

But three key issues arise. First, that financial institutions (FIs) need to demonstrate how their approach to extra-financial issues can be as much about innovating new financing for sustainable development in the Global South as it is about risk management. Hence, the work of initiatives such as New Ventures and Vantage Point are key.[30] Second, that NGOs need to be clear about how their engagement with FIs is a means of enabling economic democracy, and ensure they give voice to and are more accountable to Southern constituencies. Third, that professionals in NGOs and FIs need to develop a moral counter-frame to the one put forward by organisations such as the AEI. Phrases such as 'NGO blessing' and 'self-anointed regulators' play to the framing that George Lakoff describes as 'Strict Father God', whereby people are rewarded through success in a free market governed by electoral representative 'democracy': working hard for yourself, and doing what you are told.[31] Consequently, this framing suggests people should not develop their own ideas about rights and wrongs or seek non-governmental means to pursue them. AEI is saying to us, implicitly, that NGOs are playing God, and because they are only human are clearly getting it wrong. What might an alternative moral frame be? Perhaps that a Spirit, a God or a deeply natural quality is working through us when we take responsibility for the situations of others as well as ourselves. Imagine new ways of pursuing that. A 'Shared Spirit' frame, perhaps?

Transparency matters

August 2006 saw the conclusion of the consultation period of the European Commission's Green Paper on the European Transparency Initiative. The consultation engaged stakeholders on aspects of transparency in the European Union, such as lobbying and disclosure of data about the recipients of various EU countries.[32] Some say voluntary codes do not go far enough, particularly given their impact on legislation. While NGOs praised the development, some highlighted the fact that over €2 billion per year are channelled through them, with little attention paid to how the funds are spent. Friends of the Earth Europe, whose largest donor is the EU, claimed that the attention on NGOs is simply a distraction from the much more pressing issue of corporate accountability.[33]

If the sincerest form of flattery is imitation, then NGOs should be honoured by business front groups that trade on the NGO credibility of grass-roots organisations (which is why they have been dubbed 'Astroturf organisations', as in fake grass). One example can be found populating editorials in papers such as the *New York Daily News*, with headlines such as 'Deep-Fried Hysteria' on 29 September 2006 concerning governmental efforts to reduce obesity. There were also full-page newspaper ads, such as 'Hype', which warned readers that they have 'been force-fed a steady diet of obesity myths by the "food police," trial lawyers, and even our own government.'[34] The sponsor, the Center for Consumer Freedom, is a 'nonprofit organization dedicated to protecting consumer choices and promoting common sense'. The group was founded about 12 years ago with tobacco-company and restaurant money to fight smoking curbs in restaurants. The Center and its ads are the brainchild of a Washington lobbyist for the restaurant industry.

Given the growing use of non-profit organisations as vehicles for lobbying and advocacy by vested interests, the issue of how progressive organisations can define themselves and protect their reputations and role grows ever more important.

Consuming truths

As 2006 progressed it became clear that the challenge of climate change was once again rising in public consciousness in many parts of the world. The success of the film *An Inconvenient Truth* highlighted wide public curiosity and concern as to what is happening to our weather. The climate challenge is a consumption challenge: to promote human well-being while reducing the overall demand for carbon fuels, either directly or as embodied in the various products and services we use.

The international policy agenda on sustainable consumption (SC) continues to be touted as one of the most important out there, but real action remains lacking. The UNEP/UN DESA process, the so-called Marrakesh process, continues to have high-level meetings on SC—for example, a high-level meeting in Istanbul in August 2006 and a roundtable in Mumbai the following month. But action and enthusiasm are lacking in these meetings. Governments have not set aside budgets for this, there are no international performance targets, top-level ministers are not routinely involved, and there is no formal mechanism for reporting at the international level. In fact, the Marrakesh process was not itself mandated at the Johannesburg Summit on sustainable development, and is just an aspect of what was mandated—a vaguely conceived 'Ten Year Framework of Programmes'. At the time of writing, close to the halfway point of the ten-year framework of programmes, the international policy process has yielded not much more than a few 'task forces'—small government-funded committees, focusing on aspects of the sustainable consumption challenge, but not guaranteed to find anything new. Overall, there is hardly much enthusiasm to act proactively.

In light of this apparent impasse, a new EU-funded project SCORE (Sustainable Consumption Research Exchange), brainchild of Dutch engineer Arnold Tukker, was developed.[35] Hosted by and in collaboration with the newly minted UNEP Collaborating Centre on Sustainable Consumption and Production (CSCP) in Wuppertal, Germany, SCORE is aiming to provide a needed injection of urgency on the sustainable consumption agenda. A key task will be to help policy-makers, business and the public understand how sustainable consumption need not be a negative cost-raising fun-reducing burden, but can be a positive, opportunities-laden pathway to sustainable development.

Previously the UNEP Consumption Opportunities report sought to frame sustainable consumption in these terms.[36] It emphasised that most action on sustainable consumption has focused on impact reduction, involving pollution reduction, conservation of single stocks of resources, and preservation of ecosystems and species. Although important, the UNEP report emphasised that with the growing burden of consumption levels worldwide such impact reduction is not sufficient, and actual demand reduction is required. It pointed out this did not mean a reduction in human utility, but a reduction in the actual resource through-flow of economies. Rather than put the emphasis on the consumer, as so many are prone to do, UNEP recognised that 'systemic demand' needs reduction, which means considering industry resource wastage and the lack of service solutions to provide for human needs. Thus it argued for more efficient consumption, involving fewer resources for the same product, increasingly different consumption, involving switching to ways of meeting human need through services not products, and conscious consumption, which implies collective efforts to promote wider consideration of whether our consumption of certain resource-intensive products actually delivers significant well-being anyway.

As awareness of the environmental imperative grows, the challenge will be for businesses to find ways of succeeding within economies that must reduce their resource through-flow. More responsible products-as-usual will not be sufficient for future success. The 'dematerialisation' and optimisation of consumption patterns will be key.

Arnold Tukker of SCORE is among the leading experts who have joined the editorial board of the new Consumption Opportunities Project, which will promote the UNEP sustainable consumption framework described above.[37] The author of this original Consumption Opportunities framework, John Manoochehri, told us that

> the Marrakesh process has given us a stadium, and the governmental mandates, weak as they are, provide a partial audience. Maybe Consumption Opportunities can clarify what games are actually being played, and what the winning stakes are, and networks like SCORE can provide both coaching and even produce star players. But it remains a question of whether governments and business actually do take up the opportunities on offer, whether they really want to play.

The game may really begin if the consumption challenge can be framed in terms of creating pathways for social development that are sufficiently resource-light to be possible for a majority of the world's population over the long term, rather than the minority of a few generations of middle- to upper-class consumers.

Taming the messenger

Media's critical role in defining corporate responsibility as one that extends beyond the borders of a Western company's headquarters has long been enshrined since the exposition of sweatshop operations among Asian manufacturers contracted by major brands. Besides garments and sport shoes, the same concept has seeped through other industries, such as diamonds, mining and forest products, among others.

While sweatshop stories have become a dime a dozen, in August 2006 the big news was the story of Asia's largest electronics contract manufacturer, Taiwan-based Hong Hai Precision Industry Co., which sued mainland Chinese journalists for allegedly 'damaging its reputation'.[38] It came with a different twist: the suit took the heat off the manufacturer and its clients, which include global brands Apple, Hewlett-Packard, Dell, Sony and Nokia. Apple's famous iPod was touted as another sweatshop icon.[39]

Bringing journalists to court is a civic right of corporations, but it is also considered as part of corporate manoeuvrings to divert attention or to harass messengers of bad news. In this case, the 'messengers' involved a writer and editor of Shanghai-based newspaper, *China Business News*, which published in June 2006 a story about substandard working conditions and low pay in the factory of Foxconn, a subsidiary of Hong Hai in mainland China. To be sure, Apple sent auditors to the factory and found that, other than occasional breaching of Apple's acceptable Code of Conduct limit of 60 hours and one day off per week, especially during peak production periods, the sweatshop claims were unfounded. Hong Hai went on to slap the journalists—not the publication, as is usually the case—with a RMB30 million (approximately £2 million) libel suit that led to the freezing of the journalists' assets. The strategy backfired as progressive Chinese media made this a case of 'press freedom' versus the big bad corporation. Eventually, Hong Hai withdrew the lawsuit.[40]

Elsewhere in Asia, media organisations continue to bear the brunt when there are stories about corporate and political wrongdoings. And, since political economy continues to rule the landscape where the media organisations operate, cases of harassment abound. For example, the Philippines in South-East Asia has been touted as the 'second most dangerous country to be a journalist', next only to Iraq.[41] About 47 local journalists have been killed since 2001, most of them based in provinces where thin-skinned political and business leaders still believe retribution against unfriendly press remains under the national radar.[42] After reporting on the military's role in an election fraud, editors of *Newsbreak* magazine, an independent local publication, were sent a funeral wreath and shadowed on their way home, while their office phones were bugged.[43] Advertisers also withdrew their support for fear of political retribution to their local business operations.[44]

The foreign press, supposedly unaffected by economic and political limitations of their local counterparts, is expected to provide the big and unadulterated picture. But the experience *of Far Eastern Economic Review* (*FEER*), an affiliate of Dow Jones focusing on current events in South-East Asia and China, has been instructive. In its July/August 2006 issue, it published an interview with Chee Soon Juan, an opposition leader and vocal government critic.[45] Slighted, top-government officials reinstated a media code that requires foreign media companies to set up local office in Singapore, which could be sued whenever it publishes articles unfavourable to local leaders. For not kowtowing, *FEER* was banned in Singapore from September 2006.

The real context of the ban, according to sources of Reuters and Agence France-Press, is the timing of the *FEER* story.[46] In September, Singapore was set to host the annual meeting of the International Monetary Fund (IMF) and World Bank (WB). Singapore's officials did not want anyone 'making embarrassing noises' as the 16,000 delegates from all over the world flocked to Singapore.[47] Interestingly, the World Bank has been a staunch believer of an independent media as a factor in economic development.[48]

While Singapore's Ministry of Information stated confidently that Singapore 'will remain a good investment location . . . [since it] offers a stable, pro-business environment, and a safe, secure and vibrant place for foreigners to live, work and play', Mark Mobius, fund manager of Templeton's US$20 billion fund invested in emerging economies, affirmed that investors 'valued a free press in countries where they put their money'.[49]

If these watchdogs in Asia were limited in their ability to hold their government and, in the same breath, the corporations that operate in these countries, accountable for their actions, how can Asians appreciate the bigger goal of corporate citizenship?

This was raised by journalists who attended *Newsbreak*'s seminar on 'Covering Corporate Social Responsibility' held in September 2006 in Subic Bay, the Philippines. According to Lala Rimando, business editor of *Newsbreak*, 'It was a good opportunity to share how media should report on and criticize the companies' design and implementation of their social responsibility programs. But are the companies actually ready to walk their talk and address accountability issues on how they run their core businesses?' Exhibit one: When a tanker carrying bunker fuel owned by Petron Corporation, an oil company owned by the Philippine and Saudi Arabia governments, sank near a marine sanctuary in central Philippines, Petron initially shunned accountability for the economic costs of the oil spill although it readily provided a litany of its good works in various poor communities.[50] Judging by the September 2006 conference of Asian Forum, the biggest gathering of corporate social responsibility advocates in Asia, most Asian companies are still at the level of community philanthropy projects.[51]

These dynamics—press freedom and the practice of corporate responsibility—are crucial not only in how Asians draft their future, but also in how the West asserts its influence in Asia. After all, China, the region's biggest and most influential economy, has been growing its trading and political stake in the region in recent years.[52] So, while Western countries assert their influence in China, they might as well also consider those to whom China turns as alternative economic partners.

4Q2006
October–December

Jem Bendell and Lala Rimando

Capitalism's rising star?

The red-hot Chinese economy may remain the darling of global investors, but neighbouring Vietnam has been increasingly creeping into the spotlight. Its smaller economy and population may not rival the giant neighbour to its north, but Vietnam's rate of growth and openness to Western standards of doing business are making it an attractive destination for foreign direct investment.

This came to light when Vietnam hosted the annual Asia-Pacific Economic Cooperation (APEC) summit in November 2006. Vietnam staged the event like it was its own coming-out party. Long considered one of the less relevant economies in the South-East Asian block, the late-bloomer country welcomed dignitaries to Hanoi with freshly built or repaved roads, and even some porcelain-tiled streets, all leading to the spanking new US$250 million National Convention Center.[1]

Never mind the costs; the two-year-in-the-making facelift project achieved the desired effect as the analysts and media organisations covering the event churned out cover stories or special features hailing Vietnam as the new hot investment destination. Since then, Vietnam has been increasingly in the global news, a fact not lost in the country. Vietnam Chamber of Commerce and Industry president Dr Vu Tien Loc noted in December that Vietnam had its most number of mentions in the world media in 2006, the same year that 10% of the *Fortune* Top 500 companies arrived in Vietnam. 'Never has Vietnam been the destination of as many great groups, business communities and international investors as this year', he said.[2]

Vietnam's attraction to foreign investors is its incredible economic growth. Since 2000, gross domestic product (GDP) growth averaged 7%. Its 2005 increase of 8.4% positioned it as Asia's second-fastest-growing economy, eclipsed only by China's 10%. Thanks to the booming economy, the reported poverty rate in the past decade has shrunk from 61% to only 19%, a feat not even China can match.[3] And investors have flocked to the bourse, boosting the Ho Chi Minh Stock Index by an extraordinary 109% in 2006, making Vietnam's equity market one of the ten top performing exchanges in the world.[4] Credit Suisse vice chairman for Asia, Jose Isidro Camacho, summed it up when he told *Fortune* magazine, 'Vietnam has arrived'.[5]

Where exactly Vietnam has arrived at, and where it's going, is the focus of much of this review of 2006's final quarter. In 2006 the country came to be regarded as capitalism's newest rising star; and as such it symbolises the changes and challenges that will paint the backdrop to the future development of corporate citizenship. We explore why the country's economy has boomed, some of the positive social as well as economic implications of its opening-up to foreign influence, the dangers of unequal forms of privatisation and skyrocketing stock markets, before placing this economic and social change in the context of the country's natural environment, and the future sustainability of its development trajectory.

Understanding the boom

Foreign investors started taking a second look at Vietnam since its leaders heeded efforts of former US president Bill Clinton, who visited in 2000 to normalise relations with the former enemy. In 2000, Vietnam signed a bilateral trade agreement with the US and launched the stock market. Thereafter, it introduced new laws simplifying requirements for registering companies and creating a level playing field for both local and foreign players.[6] The timing was perfect. It emerged as the regional destination of choice for Western and Japanese investors aiming to hedge their exposure to China.

As China continues to gobble up about US$72 billion in foreign direct investments (making it the largest 'developing'-country recipient of FDI),[7] foreign investors lured by Asia's low labour costs have realised that as political winds change in China, they need to spread their business risks. Vietnam has become the first choice for Japanese firms operating in China that want to spread their investment exposure to another country. The Japanese firms doing business in Vietnam include such giants as Toyota Motor, Sony, Canon and Honda.

Vietnam's labour is cheaper than its neighbours, including China. Shortages in available factory hands in some regions of China have been driving up costs to the point that a factory worker in the mainland can earn up to five times the US$50 per month that Vietnamese workers in foreign-owned factories receive.[8] In addition, land is cheaper, with the most expensive land for factories fetching about half of what they do in China's priciest areas, and shipping from industrial capital Ho Chi Minh City is cheaper than from Thailand or Indonesia.[9]

Nevertheless, there is the potential for economic culture clash. The experience of Dutch bank ABN Amro, which has a branch in Hanoi, was revealing. In November 2006, it entered into a US$4.5 million settlement to end a dispute over a transaction with a local state-owned bank (and, not incidentally, to get four staff members out of jail). In its suit, the state-owned Incombank had blamed the four ABN Amro traders for the losses it incurred when they executed speculative foreign currency trades on behalf of an Incombank employee who was later found to be unauthorised to enter into such deals. Causing losses to a state enterprise is a serious criminal offence in Vietnam, and the arrests of the four traders has sent a chill through other foreign banks operating in the country, raising concerns about the risks of dealing with state financial institutions and other state agencies.[10] Compounding the risks is the fact that foreign exchange trading—a routine transaction elsewhere—is not yet governed by internationally consistent standards in Vietnam.

Competitive openness?

As far as low-cost and low-value labour is concerned, studies have shown that Vietnam is better at attracting socially conscious investments than China because of the latter's reported frequent violations of labour standards. This is a risk that footwear industry experts have cited in explaining why international footwear companies operating in China would look for alternative production sites.[11] Vietnam's apparently stronger labour rights regime—born of its union independence and assertiveness—positions it well in this contest.[12]

With a population 6% the size of China's, Vietnam is more dependent on the outside world, both politically and economically. Therefore, Vietnamese leaders are more likely to be sensitive to prevailing international labour rights norms than the Chinese. Workers' rights issues were one of the contentious items in Vietnam's quest for a WTO membership. But, with the issue cleared, Vietnam's accession to the trade body is expected by some to facilitate trade and capital flows, further pushing its competitiveness.

According to a US Congress-commissioned 2002 report, the strong anti-sweatshop movement, plus Vietnam's drive to clinch the good graces of the US as it was working for WTO accreditation, pushed the government and the trade unions to engage in dialogues on meeting international norms for labour.[13] In the process, Vietnam's labour standards were upgraded, an unusual example of a potential contradiction to the tendency of developing countries to participate in a 'race to the bottom' of social and environmental standards.

In fact, according to the report, the Vietnamese government and trade unions openly urged their factories to apply for SA8000, a certification of labour standards recognised by Western clients. The Chinese government, on the other hand, has always considered any reference to its labour standards as outside intervention in its internal affairs. Since criticisms of labour standards are subsumed under criticisms of human rights violations, the Chinese government has been sensitive to and adamant against any mention of this issue.[14]

For a variety of structural and historical reasons, the Vietnamese Communist Party has not taken on the authoritarian shape of its Chinese counterpart. China's leaders are more sensitive to permitting union independence since it had to deal with socially challenging and regime-threatening experiences such as the Tiananmen protest movement in 1989. Assertiveness among China's union groups has been repressed as part of the government's crackdown against the protests.[15]

However, although Vietnamese unions and labourers possess greater freedoms to advocate for workers and express grievances than their Chinese counterparts, most rights and freedoms stem not from the law, but from the discretion of the Communist Party. In other words, labour freedoms and rights in Vietnam are still vulnerable to changes in state policy.

That was not lost on the likes of US electronics giant Intel, but still it was not deterred from taking the plunge. In fact, in November 2006, as the US House of Representatives prepared to vote on granting Vietnam permanent normal trade relations, the final step in normalising relations between the two countries, Intel seemingly made a statement in support of Vietnam by announcing it would increase its investments in the building of a chip assembly and testing plant in Ho Chi Minh City from US$300 million to more than US$1 billion. The deal, which will employ some 4,000 workers, represents the biggest-ever US-led project, and was a huge and timely vote of confidence for Vietnam's long-term potential.[16] A little more than a month later, Vietnam finally clinched its WTO membership in January 2007, the culmination of a 12-year process.

Having conducted business in such Asian countries as Malaysia and the Philippines, Intel hired a Vietnamese country manager, Phu Than, to assist in dealing with the government. In an interview with *Fortune* magazine, Than shared the strategy on how Intel won over the officials by offering scholarships, training 30,000 public school teachers, and worked in close coordination with the Communist Party in testing software for its e-governance programme. 'It made coordination easier,' Than told *Fortune*.[17] While these are charged against budgets for the company's philanthropic projects, Intel is not reinventing the wheel. Microsoft made similar efforts when it was making inroads in China in the early 1990s, long before other multinationals were able to set up shop in the mainland.[18]

While it can be argued that such arrangements are mutually beneficial—the government gets the free training, software and other freebies; Intel gets the tax incentives, the permits, easy access to the bureaucrats—they highlight the fact that transnational companies, with all their resources and experiences, will also help train Vietnam's bureaucracy, which is still adjusting to the rhythm and discipline of a market-based economy. Whether the policies that emerge from this close engagement, on issues such as intellectual property protection, taxation, regulation and development priorities, are in the citizens' longer-term interests is open to debate. Weaknesses in civil society, political parties and other aspects of governance mean that this debate may not be as open and balanced as one might hope for, especially in light of environmental concerns, which we return to below.

Avoiding oligarchy

At the very least, investors in hard assets are in for a long haul. Vietnam's booming economy, however, is also attracting portfolio investors to its young stock and bond markets. Among those actively investing are foreign-managed funds, such as the Vietnam Opportunity Fund, a US$560 million closed-end fund listed on the London Stock Exchange, and the Dublin-listed US$200 million-worth Vietnam Growth Fund. We do not know of any funds considered as socially responsible investments that have descended on the Vietnamese stock exchange.

The local equity market entered the radar of most international investors when Spencer White, the chief regional strategist for Merrill Lynch, wrote a report in February 2006 that became the oft-quoted confirmation of the growth prospects of the listed local companies. White described Vietnam as 'a 10-year buy', and urged his readers to 'buy equity exposure now, for your fund, for yourself, or for your children'.[19]

There are fears that these markets are rising for an eventual fall. Investor enthusiasm has pushed total market capitalisation of the 106 listed shares to US$9.2 billion, which, considering a base of only US$510 million a year earlier, translates to a huge 1,665% increase. The number of listed companies grew from 30 to 106, of which 49 new listings were transacted in December 2006 alone.[20] There has been limited information on earnings for these new listings which used to belong wholly to the state. For years, these companies were under no obligation to publish nor ever had the discipline for financial information disclosure. No wonder buyers of their stock had few ways to gauge company performance or whether an investment was sound. Although some websites track the prices of popular stocks, reliable market data is non-existent. In other words, there is no certainty that the current prices are fair. Local investors, the majority of them neophytes, depend mostly on gossip and hope that what goes up will continue to go up.[21]

Underlying this stock market boom has been the sale of state assets, since 2000. As many as 3,600 state-owned companies have been partially privatised. Company shares were sold to employees, managers and the public who then sold them either online or directly to families and friends. Rapid privatisation in Russia led to a 'grab what you can' culture and the generation of a new class of billionaire oligarchs that moved money out of the country with damaging impacts on the nation's economy and employment. The social dislocation and injustices that followed needs to be recalled when we reflect on the current changes in Vietnam. Will the country manage its transition in a more socially just manner?

The answer may lie in the shifting values of modern Vietnam. The country is not just changing economically; it is also changing socially, with traditionally conservative attitudes gradually breaking down. As a booming economy creates a growing middle class, these people eventually demand greater freedoms. And the youth— those aged 25 and below, who account for half of the population—enjoy the spoils of economic freedom while, for the time being, not questioning the reign and rule of the Communist Party. As things are changing very fast in Vietnam, the Communist Party will have to continuously demonstrate that it can answer the questions likely to be posed by an increasingly capitalist society.

The current officials who have lived through the wars and the hardships that followed tend to adopt the 'strict father' model of George Lakoff, which refers to the tendency to discipline 'kids' or build a controlled mechanism in order to mould them to become self-reliant and obedient adults.[22] This can be gleaned from how freedoms of speech, association, religion and the media are all still sharply curtailed.[23]

But technology, especially the internet, has provided a route for those who want to escape these controls and explore freedoms that those in a 'nurturing parent' system would typically enjoy.[24] At some point, the ruling Communist Party will face a choice about whether the best way to deal with this problem is to pursue greater openness or ever-tighter control.

The underground movement of bloggers and citizen journalists known as the Free Journalists Association of Vietnam (FJAV) has started to assert its independence by gathering and disseminating news which they publish on their website. These are the stories that would be typically censored by the government, which remains a one-party state and normally does not tolerate opposing views. Every single publication in Vietnam, whether it is a newspaper or a magazine about interior design or golf, has to be registered with a Communist Party organisation. Predictably, many of the FJAV activists have been interrogated and detained.[25]

However, in a surprising effort to reach out to the techno-savvy citizens, in December 2006 former deputy prime minister Vu Khoan hosted—and engaged in—an online chat to discuss expectations as far as Vietnam's accession to the WTO is concerned. While the chat was not live, nor exactly exciting (all questions had been screened and sent beforehand, plus the discussions stayed on safe political ground), nonetheless, the fact that it happened at all shows that Vietnam's communist rulers are trying to demonstrate that they are listening to the people.[26]

How willing or prepared the leaders are to go beyond mere lip service will be further tested as foreign investors and the growing middle class hopefully continue to push for aspects of good governance, such as transparency and accountability, both in public and private arena.

A race to where?

If Vietnam is following fast in the footsteps of China, then it might be useful to take a breath (of its increasingly polluted air) and assess where exactly it is racing towards. The decrease in poverty rates is impressive, and illustrates some success of the current developments. But how lasting is that trend, and does it reveal enough about people's everyday situations? The quality of life of the 300,000 people now living in slums of Ho Chi Minh City alone, with poor access to sanitation, clean air and water, might earn wages that rank them higher than the rural areas they left, but at what cost to their health and well-being? Too often the consumption demands and investment decisions of Westerners and urban elites in Asia pressure people to abandon their communities, so the move to urban living cannot be assumed to be an expression of free will.

The World Bank reports that Vietnam's environment is under considerable stress from rapid economic growth, urbanisation and rising human pressure on relatively scarce natural resources. 'While it has gradually improved its environmental regulatory framework, Vietnam has very limited capacity for implementation. Therefore, future rapid economic growth (an expected doubling of GDP in the next 10 years) and substantial investments in infrastructure may significantly threaten the environmental sustainability of the country's development.'[27] The bank reports on signs of threats emerging, such as declining rates of catch per unit of effort in the fisheries sector, with aquaculture activities having caused a substantial decline in mangroves and wetlands, crucial for spawning fish. Drought is now becoming a concern in Vietnam,[28] and the country could be badly hit by climate change and sea-level rise.[29] For the Vietnamese environment, and consequently the Vietnamese people, there are worries that the foreign dollars pouring into the country may be more destructive, in the long run, than the chemical bombs dropped during its war with the United States.

A different path?

With global consumption levels five times what they were just 50 years ago, the natural world is buckling under the weight of demand. The impacts and costs of all this are clear: climate chaos, ecosystem stress, soil loss and degradation, groundwater depletion and toxic accumulation are just some of the headlines. The global scientific consensus on climate change proves beyond doubt that there are limits to what our atmosphere can take, and what changes to our atmosphere that our nature, agriculture, water supplies and cities can withstand.[30] The UK Government Review on the economic impacts of climate change predict a 20% reduction in Global GDP, which is equivalent to two world wars combined.[31] Already, people are losing their lives and livelihoods due to climate change.[32]

Many may applaud the social benefits of Vietnam's economic growth. But should the advancement of the economically poor in that country depend on them having to put Bangladeshis and others living in low-lying or water-stressed areas in further danger? Pollution and inefficient consumption is everyone's problem and responsibility. Over half a billion middle-class Asians are consuming significant and growing amounts of resources with negative impacts on their own rural and urban environments as well as abroad. For example, the Indian middle class now have higher-carbon-consumption lifestyles than the average citizen of the UK. As Kalpana Sharma wrote in an article in *The Hindu* newspaper in November 2006:

> The argument against putting any pressure on countries like India and China at the moment is that they were not responsible for the problem [of global climate change], so they should not be bound to slow down or change the pattern of growth. While 15 years ago this argument had some validity, today we need to re-examine it.[33]

In addition, the article reflected on the local impacts of current development paths and economic growth.

> Our current pattern of development is already making the air in our cities unfit to breathe. Our water sources are polluted, our fields are laden with chemicals that travel through the food chain into our bodies, and our forests, the lungs of this country, are disappearing faster than any effort to plant more trees. Is there any point in rapid economic growth if people have to drink, eat, and breathe poisons? In the long run we damage not just the global environment but ourselves too.

The world physically does not have enough resources, particularly energy, and sinks, particularly the atmosphere, to support or allow resource-heavy consumerist lifestyles for the majority. Consequently, the type of 'development' being pursued in Vietnam and elsewhere will neither last nor be possible for everyone. This means that resource-heavy development paths are actually elitist, and certainly not socialist. Recognising this turns the existing cognitive frame of environmental concern on its head: finding a different path to societal development that is environmentally sustainable is a pro-poor and egalitarian concern, not a mere preoccupation of the rich with post-materialist interests.

The implication is that countries in both the North and South could consider a different development path. Rather than seeing the environment as something to consider after economic growth is booming, *The Hindu* newspaper recognised the importance of setting out in the right direction from the start.

> Logic would suggest that it is better to start the process now rather than wait until it is too late. The country's economy need not suffer if there are fewer fossil fuel burning cars on the road and better public transport. The economy need not be affected if we use building techniques for our growing cities that are less energy intensive rather than following the Western pattern of glass-fronted high rises that require a huge amount of electricity to keep cool or warm as the case may be. And our energy requirements can be met if we work harder to minimise transmission losses, introduce energy saving at every level, and promote non-polluting forms of energy generation.

The challenge is to find and promote resource-light forms of development. With the right leadership, development need not depend on risks such as cheap oil, inequalities such as poor pay and conditions, and the disruption of rural communities' livelihoods. Money can be made through sustainable business. In December 2006, at the Delhi School of Economics, in the University of Delhi, launched the report 'Indian Companies in the 21st Century: An Opportunity for Innovation that can Save the Planet' was launched.[34] Rajesh Sehgal, Senior Law and Policy Officer at WWF-India, explained to us that this WWF report 'examines the scope for Indian companies to become leading exporters of, and investors in, sustainable goods and services, whilst emerging as key actors in promoting a proactive international sustainable development agenda'.

The implications for corporate citizenship are that companies and investors need to assess how they are helping or hindering the right frameworks and incentives for innovation and delivery of the business models needed in a resource-constrained future. Rather than doing business as usual, with some social and environmental improvements, the scale, urgency and depth of the sustainability challenge requires companies to engage with other actors in society to promote governance for sustainability. If this happens, then the neo-corporatist arrangements in countries such as Vietnam may, paradoxically, be beneficial in the change process. Otherwise they will merely compound the problems. If so, rather than capitalism's rising star, Vietnam could be capitalism's supernova, a commercial stellar explosion producing an extremely luminous cloud that briefly outshines its entire host galaxy before fading from view. Those countries committed to more sustainable and equitable forms of development may not twinkle so bright, yet will maintain their light.

Modern-day slavery

What Global Witness is to conflict diamonds, *Bloomberg Markets* is to modern-day slavery. Both publish investigative stories, with *Global Witness* specialising in resource-linked conflicts and corruption in trade systems, and *Bloomberg Markets* featuring people who, and issues that, move financial markets.[35] Also, they both share a record in tackling such uncomfortable issues as conflict diamonds and modern slavery.

While both topics have long been understood within non-governmental organisation (NGO) circles, they have for the most part remained outside of the public's cognisance. That ignorance will possibly be a thing of the past for conflict diamonds, which has begun to enjoy mainstream comprehension thanks to the 2006 blockbuster movie *Blood Diamond*. For most of the world's people, however, the concept of slavery is thought of as extinct, an unfortunate institution that faded into non-existence with Abraham Lincoln's Gettysburg Address.

That is not to say the media has ignored the issue. Such respected organs as *The New Yorker*[36] in the US, *The Guardian*[37] and BBC[38] in the UK, and *Frontline*[39] in India have all run special reports documenting stories of individuals forced into working conditions so substandard—and so limiting as regards the worker's ability to leave—that the description 'slavery' was appropriate. However, none of these stories generated the level of public outrage one might have expected, in part because the reports depicted incidents that had no connection with most readers' lives.

What made the cover story of *Bloomberg Markets*' December 2006 issue (a follow-up to a breaking story of affiliate *Bloomberg News* in November) notably different was that it identified the global, Western-based brands that benefit from this form of labour.[40] Authors Michael Smith and David Voreacos included comments from multinational companies—such as automakers Ford Motor Co., General Motors Corp., Nissan Motor Co. and Toyota Motor Corp., appliance maker Whirlpool Corp. and sink and bath maker Kohler Co.—after establishing through interviews and documents that raw materials for their manufacturing operations in the United States could be traced to suppliers that employed slave labour in Brazil.

By highlighting the nature of these firms' supply chains, *Bloomberg* influenced them to adopt a more rigorous approach. Most of them eventually accepted responsibility for ensuring that their business processes are not tainted by slavery of any form, at any level of their supply chains. In other words, the articles triggered a successful mobilisation of market power, which previous awareness campaigns, such as books, special reports, brochures, educational or training programmes, were unable to achieve.

The fact that a financial magazine, which is dedicated to issues that affect stakeholders in the global financial markets, took interest in dealing with the topic of slavery is a testament to how human rights issues—if effectively publicised—can impact a company's bottom line. It's also a reminder that disregarding corporate responsibility concerns will be detrimental not only to a company's reputation, but also to its financial health.

In the *Bloomberg Markets* report, the journalists joined labour inspectors as they raided some of the 1,000 charcoal-making camps in Brazil's Amazon basin to investigate reports of men, women and children being exploited to aid in the production of charcoal for companies that manufacture pig iron, a key ingredient in steel-making.

The story graphically showed workers living in squalid shacks without electricity and plumbing, drinking unsanitary water and receiving no pay. Most of the workers were recruited from poverty-stricken provinces many miles and forests away and desperate to find work. The story presented damning evidence (supported by Brazilian inspectors and customs documents) that the charcoal originating from these camps was routinely purchased by brokers for sale to steel-makers and foundries, whose semi-refined product was then purchased by some of the world's largest companies that manufacture cars, tractors, sinks and refrigerators for US consumption.

Kevin Bales, president of the Washington-based NGO Free the Slaves, argues, 'companies have an absolute obligation to understand what's in their supply chain and review it from a moral and a human standpoint'. Bales, who is also a sociology professor at London's Roehampton University, challenged corporations to step up to their responsibility of ensuring the source of products they buy and sell is not tainted by slavery. He added: 'Slavery is theft of life. It's just about the most profound loss of human dignity that you can have, short of murder.'[41]

The UN's International Labour Organisation (ILO) defines slavery or forced labour as work performed involuntarily under threat of penalty, with scarce or no compensation.[42] ILO adds that the practice occurs when 'people are subjected to psychological and/or physical coercion (the menace of penalty) in order to perform some work or service which they would otherwise not have accepted, or not have accepted at the prevailing conditions (the involuntariness)'.

It notes that human trafficking is the process by which people end up in slavery. It is defined by the United Nations Convention against Transnational Organised Crime as 'the recruitment, transportation, transfer, harbouring or receipt of persons' by such means as threat, use of force or coercion, abduction, fraud, deception, etc. 'for the purpose of exploitation'.[43]

ILO stresses that modern slavery thrives because it is lucrative. ILO estimates that global profits made from forced labourers exploited by private enterprises or agents reach US$44.3 billion every year, of which US$31.6 billion are made from trafficked victims. Everyone profits, except for the slaves, of which there are estimated to be over 12 million. These include at least 360,000 in industrialised countries, of whom at least 270,000 have been trafficked into forced labour. Approximately 43% of these are trafficked into sexual exploitation, 32% into labour exploitation and about 25% for a mix of sexual and labour reasons.[44]

Most are enslaved under a system of debt bondage, as was the case of the slaves in the Brazilian charcoal camps. Lured by recruiters and then hired by camp owners promising steady-paying jobs, they found themselves trapped in a cycle of working off their debts from exorbitantly priced basics such as tools, soap and food bought at company stores. Many go months without pay or see their wages whittled to nothing from the cost of even work-related items such as tools, boots and gloves. Lack of money, an impenetrable jungle and a long distance to travel to safety made it impossible for the slaves to leave.[45]

As soon as the *Bloomberg News* story broke at the end of 2006, those who were involved in the supply chain started to redeem themselves, obviously fearful of backlash. The car companies, in particular, almost immediately drew on their purchasing power to prod their first-tier suppliers to force all downstream vendors to avoid forced labour. The most concrete response was the move by General Motors, Ford, DaimlerChrysler and Honda to join together under the Automotive Industry Action Group to train their suppliers in how to avoid buying slave-made materials. The car association engaged Business for Social Responsibility, a San Francisco-based organisation that promotes good corporate practices, to develop the training programme which is set to commence by the second quarter of 2007. Toyota, however, decided not to join the training programme because it believes it can better resolve forced labour issues on its own. Its decision led some to question the car manufacturer's high-profile campaign for environmental innovation through its hybrid cars.[46]

One of those that voiced concern about Toyota's perceived inaction was the Interfaith Center. Representing US$700 million in investments, it campaigns for improved social and environmental standards. By publicly questioning Toyota's decision, it joined groups with financial products, such as pension and mutual funds, to assert their stake in the issue.

Ideally, the fight to rid the planet of slavery would focus global attention not only on the car showroom or the financial markets, but on the broader contexts that create the potential for slavery. The key ingredient to a slave-driven business is poverty. With over a billion people scraping by on a dollar a day, poverty breeds and feeds the supply of low-cost labourers. This is especially true in developing countries whose economies are export-dependent and have industries that are still at the mercy of Western retailers who place more value on pricing than on instituting ethics and human rights practices. Unfortunately, even in cases where governments and the private sector is responsible, corruption can undo the positives. It matters if laws are in place but enforcers turn a blind eye or are taking bribes.

That is why policy-makers, NGOs and other stakeholders in both the developing and industrialised worlds have an important role to play. They must develop strategies that address the economic, cultural and social conditions, which include illiteracy, powerlessness, inadequate governance, and the lack of economic alternatives that allow individuals to be enslaved. There are mechanisms already in place that can aid this process. For instance, the certification systems enacted for the diamond, forestry, garments, footwear and coffee industries, among others, can play a role. Some are still works in progress, but they are all striving to address the problem.

Two hundred years ago, the trading of slaves was banned by the US and UK, ending a barbaric chapter of those countries' histories. Now, as awareness is raised in our collective consciousness that slavery has persisted and evolved, no excuse can be made for not taking all necessary steps to stamp it out for good.

2007

2007: Introduction:
The global step change

Jem Bendell

In recent years a comprehensive corporate responsibility strategy has typically involved a commitment to continuous improvement, to being near the best in class and to engaging stakeholders. In 2007 that changed as the scale and urgency of social and environmental challenges became more widely understood, as well as the risks and opportunities to business. There was a wave of announcements of specific time-bound environmental targets, concerning actual performance, rather than management processes.

Awareness of climate change drove this agenda, with many companies announcing specific targets as part of their membership of initiatives such as The Climate Group, the Carbon Disclosure Project, or the WWF Climate Savers initiative (see 'Carbon: the new black', page 94; 'The green media frenzy', page 115). For instance, the household products company Reckitt Benckiser announced the target of a 20% reduction in the company's total carbon footprint by 2020, applying to all emissions associated with its products and packaging. Progress is being sought through collaboration with suppliers, measured by independent experts, and to be verified by third parties and reported annually.[1] Cisco is pioneering a system of giving each of their departments a carbon quota, with senior managers being assessed on how well they manage their carbon budget.[2]

Awareness that the carbon challenge involves reducing resource consumption and waste as a whole is encouraging the establishment of a broader set of environmental targets. In October 2007 the world's largest consumer products company Procter & Gamble announced the target of a 10% reduction in its waste and energy and water consumption by 2012, which it says would result in a 40% reduction over the decade.[3] It extended its commitment to performance goals on responsible enterprise by aiming in the next five years to sell at least $20 billion of products whose environmental impact is at least 10% less than those of previous products. We believe that this is the first time a consumer products company has set itself a financial target for developing and selling new 'greener' items as a whole, rather than for waste or energy reduction, or phasing out certain materials.

The emphasis on targets comes at a time when some key concepts in CR are being challenged. Can continuous improvement and being best in class be sufficient if there are absolute performance levels needed to avoid costs of carbon and avert a climate disaster? Should holding stakeholder dialogues be a sign of good performance when leading research institutions are finding they make little difference to aligning the interests of businesses and their stakeholders? (see 'Silence is golden', page 137). Might 2008 see the extension of this target trend to a broader range of corporate responsibility issues, such as development, labour and human rights? After all, for as long as the international community has had targets on climate change it has had targets for poverty reduction and the fulfilment of human rights, for example with the Millennium Development Goals.

This raises the question of whether companies need targets for all aspects of their social and environmental performance. Answering that depends on what we think is being achieved at present and how quickly, in relation to the goals we have. At the beginning of 2007, Lifeworth Consulting polled their 4,000 newsletter subscribers on this issue. As over 90% of the respondents are actually working in corporate responsibility, with the remaining percentage having a professional interest in it, their responses give an impression of what the profession thinks is being achieved. Lifeworth suggested two goals to measure performance by—a situation where all global economic activity is:

- 'Environmentally sustainable, by harvesting products and services within ecosystems' regenerative capacities and producing by-products that are recycled or only released safely and within a company's fair share of the Earth's capacity to absorb them'

- 'Socially responsible, by delivering benefits to all affected by their operations and supply chains, and being subject to credible systems of mandatory accountability to anyone seeking redress'

On average, corporate responsibility professionals perceived almost a doubling of the percentage of environmentally sustainable economic activity in the past decade, up from 13.2% to 22.5%. They see this increasing in the next decade, to about 47% of companies, and then increasing at a slower pace through to 2028, where they anticipate about 57% of economic activity will be environmentally sustainable. If their predicted rate of progress would continue, rather than further taper off, then overall performance would be 67.6% by 2038 and about 78% by 2050. This means that the professional corporate responsibility community, as represented by Lifeworth's subscribers, think that current rates of progress would create a sustainable economy by around 2070.

Like us, many of these respondents know how pressing the issue of climate change is. The IPCC previously stated that the world needs to see over 50% reductions in carbon emissions by 2050, and the latest science now suggests an 80% cut by that time to ensure we do not go over a critical threshold of 2° warming. That would mean at least a 20% reduction in the next 10 years, and given the growing emissions with industrialisation in the global South, possibly even double that amount in the industrialised countries to offset that. Hence WWF reminds us that 'in five years it may be too late to initiate a sustainable transition'.[4] A slower rate of change appears to be futile, and so achieving a sustainable economy by 2070 will not actually be possible.

The respondents perceived that we are working from a better starting position with social issues, but that the rate of improvement will taper off more quickly than the progress on the environment. This means these corporate responsibility professionals perceive that we are starting from a less difficult place with social issues but they will not improve as fast as with the environment, reflecting perhaps the current emphasis on the urgency of environmental challenges. We should recall that the world community made a commitment to eliminate world poverty by 2025. To do so would require economic activity to be socially responsible. Professionals estimate that on current trends only about 50% of economic activity will be socially responsible by then. It will only be about 75% by 2050.

What are the implications? A redoubling of efforts? We asked the CR professionals and they predicted a doubling of existing effort would bring achievement of a social and environmentally sustainable economy forward a decade or two. It is debatable whether that is fast enough for companies to help meet the challenge of climate change or the global commitment on poverty. What these professional perceptions indicate is that we need a global step change towards a sustainable economy, involving a step change in the way responsible business is promoted. The message is that although more of the same CR practices may continually improve performance and be welcomed by some stakeholders, best in class approaches will not deliver the sustainable global economy in time.

Understanding the nature of this global step change requires a clear vision of what that sustainable economy will look like. Such an economy will require sustainable consumption. Today global consumption levels are five times what they were just 50 years ago, and the natural world is buckling under the weight of demand. If everyone lived like Europeans, ecological footprint calculations suggest we would need three planets to support us. If everyone lived like the average Asian we would also need more than one planet. Indian middle classes have a higher per capita consumption of carbon than the average Briton. So it would be physically impossible for all the world's poor to achieve higher well-being in ways as resource-intensive as the new middle classes in Asia and elsewhere. Resource-heavy development is, by objective measures, only a possibility for a minority or for the short term. How can all of humanity live well in a way that will endure? Humanity's challenge is to find ways to improve human well-being within the limits of the Earth's resources; to stop living as if we have another planet to which we can go.

Reduction in the consumption of resources does not have to mean reducing well-being. Instead, it means a reduction in the actual resource through-flow of economies. This will require the 'dematerialisation' of systems of production-consumption (i.e. physical efficiency of those systems), and the 'optimisation' of systems of production-consumption (i.e. better management, planning and changed attitudes and behaviour in those systems). This requires a shift in economic paradigm from the linear 'take, make and waste' approach to resources to a circular 'make and remake' approach. It requires a shift towards considering what human need is being met by consumption.

Such a shift will need strong leadership from government and business. It is a common misconception that sustainable consumption is about shopping by individuals. Business is the biggest consumer of resources, and can provide alternative products and services, and government is the biggest guide of this. Individuals cannot get 10 times the amount of cars out of the same bit of steel; business can. Individuals cannot purchase public transport solutions that don't exist; business and government can provide them. Individuals cannot systematically redistribute consumption opportunities to those in need as prices for natural resources are corrected and rise; governments can. Individuals cannot get prices to rise in the market place for their produce so they have sufficient income to invest more time and resources into maintaining their lands; business and government can.

In many cases the poor may need to increase their consumption of resources to improve their quality of life. This means rich consumers must reduce their consumption rapidly towards a more fair allocation of resources, both within and between states. For any increases in poor people's quality of life to endure they must be based on more resource-efficient solutions. It makes little sense to help people today by ruining their, and our, tomorrow (see 'The rose water debate', page 104). Thus redirecting resource consumption into more sustainable infrastructures and products is key. For example, the same amount of energy might be required to build a train system as a system of airports and roads but the former will create a level of mobility with fewer ongoing energy demands.

Therefore, the 'global step change' requires a reduction, redirection and redistribution of consumption. It involves stepping:

- More **lightly**, by reducing the total level of resource consumption involved in meeting our needs and aspirations

- More **carefully**, by reducing our demands on sensitive ecosystems and exploited people

- In **the right direction**, by increasing the proportion of resources that go into creating enduring means of meeting human needs in resource-light ways

- **Together**, by increasing our support for others, particularly in developing countries, to meet their needs and aspirations through stepping forward more lightly, carefully and in the right direction

Achieving this step change will require the financial system to be more supportive of long-term value creation. Throughout 2007 awareness grew of the need to address both the societal and economic implications of our global financial system. During the year this involved greater criticism of the operations of hedge funds (see 'Capital cannibal', page 107) and private equity firms involved in leveraged buy outs (see 'Private equity, public inequity', page 109). As the year ended and the impact of the sub-prime mortgage situation led to extreme volatility in the stock markets, so this discussion was intensified, with some calling for a fundamental change in the way financial institutions are regulated and bankers are remunerated. The implications of this deeper awareness of the causes of corporate irresponsibility for the philanthropic community began to be debated, with major donors such as the Gates Foundation being criticised for not embracing mission-based investing unlike other leading foundations (see 'Donor accountability and innovation', page 125). Meanwhile the massive growth of the UN Principles for Responsible Investment, with a membership accounting for about 13 trillion dollars of assets under management, indicated that some people in the financial industry are ready and willing to take on the challenge of encouraging a sustainable world economy.

Part of the step change will require mainstreaming consciousness of the need for sustainable consumption worldwide, and encouraging behaviour change. Interestingly, in 2007 the CR spotlight swung onto some of the most iconic brands and the celebrities who endorse them. In Italy a TV programme accused top name brands such as Prada, Gucci and Dolce & Gabbana of sourcing their high-end products from factories employing workers illegally, with poor pay and conditions. A book on Italy's organised criminals even suggested that the designer suit worn by Angelina Jolie at the Oscars had been made by a tailor in the employment of the Camorra, the country's 'other Mafia' (see 'Dolce and Gomorrah', page 129). WWF sought to make sustainability desirable across the world, including in emerging markets, by pushing luxury brands to embrace social and environmental excellence as part of their brand identities. A tactic that appeared to work with their report appearing in over 50 newspapers and fashion magazines worldwide (see 'Responsible luxury', page 131). This attention coincided with leading luxury groups such as L'Oréal, which owns Giorgio Armani and Ralph Lauren, mapping out their own targets for energy, packaging and waste reductions.

We welcome this target-trend. Targets express an awareness of the scale and urgency of an issue and a willingness to engage with it. Although investing in new management processes are key, making a commitment to a performance target helps add the substance. An emphasis on purpose, performance and pace of change is what distinguishes progressive executives from the CR crowd. We think the concept of 'responsible enterprise' could describe the efforts of such executives.

We should, however, remember that targets themselves are not the mechanisms of change. It appears that many countries will miss their Kyoto targets, and the first Millennium Development Goals on primary school education have already been missed. The solution may be for wider coalitions of groups to apply themselves to the factors that shape our economy and to explore ways of collaborating to shift whole markets (see 'Change the system', page 111).

This suggests there is a research and education dimension to the global step change. 2007 saw more academic institutions begin to embrace that challenge, with many signed up to new UN Principles of Responsible Management Education (see 'The responsibility of business schools'). In the coming years we will witness, and hopefully participate in, more discussion and initiative that takes corporate responsibility to this more transformative level. The first Net Impact conference in Europe will address this agenda in June 2008. 'Sustainable Prosperity: Taking on the Global Challenge' will bring hundreds together in Geneva to share ideas on a global step change in the contribution of responsible enterprise to a sustainable world economy.[5] Our predictions for the 2008 and beyond follow:

- Many more companies will announce time-bound environmental perform-ance targets

- Some companies will announce time-bound social performance targets

- Some Asian-based multinationals will announce targets

- More Private Financial Institutions and NGOs will encourage time-bound targets from companies

- More networks and partnerships between companies and their stakeholders will focus on how to shape the market drivers that reward meeting such tar-gets, including public policy, financial systems and consumer awareness

1Q2007
January–March

Jem Bendell and Claire Veuthey

Carbon: the new black

'Do you care about the environment? We do too!' used to be the sort of advertising only marginal, 'tree-hugging' organisations would use. It is now in the marketing lexicon of UK-based easyJet, one of the most high-profile low-cost airline companies, part of a growing sector that has certainly contributed to massive increases in airline traffic in recent years. EasyJet has a prominent 'Environment' link on its website. It flaunts the company's Environment Code, its support for the UK's Stern Review, use of biodegradable chemicals, and other environment-friendly measures.[1]

EasyJet is not an exception; global warming is now on the agenda at every major business. In the first half of 2007, especially since the release of the latest Intergovernmental Panel on Climate Change (IPCC) report on climate change, its buzzword status seems even to have overtaken 'terrorism' in the media. As per our annual review of 2006, climate change has reached a tipping point, going from marginal to mainstream. To use the language of the fashion world: carbon is the new black.

Some still cling to the idea that global warming is a huge hoax. 'The Great Global Warming Swindle', a documentary transmitted on the UK's Channel 4, made strong arguments against the claim that carbon dioxide produced by industrial activity was the main reason for rising global temperatures.[2] Its key counter-argument relied on the 'solar forcing' theory, according to which the natural fluctuation in solar activity (sunspots) explains changes in global temperatures. The time period presented as evidence was between the 1940s and 1970s, when temperatures dropped in spite of rapid industrialisation and massive increases in carbon emissions. The hitch with this argument is that there could be a time-lag in the climate-changing effect of greenhouse gases (GHGs) and that sunspot activity in the past decades has been low while temperatures have risen. Even if solar forcing explained previous changes in global temperatures, it does not seem a key cause for current rises.[3]

The programme claimed two principal reasons for the existence of this supposed hoax: first, that there were institutional interests in its maintenance, e.g. that an industry of journalists, researchers and NGOs depended on a climate change myth to justify their activities. However, this conspiracy theory runs contrary to long-standing evidence of corporate funding of research questioning human-induced global warming, and lobbying against government action on carbon emissions.[4]

Secondly, the programme asserted that focusing on climate change also served other powerful interests: namely, keeping the Global South from developing, and maintaining the status quo. But the emerging world has as much, if not more, interest in maintaining global public attention on the topic of global warming. The heightened impact of climate change on the poor, particularly those vulnerable to natural disasters, illustrates climate change's global effect and that it is in the common interest to avert it. 'It is the poorest of the poor in the world, and this includes poor people even in prosperous societies, who are going to be the worst hit', said IPCC Chairman Rajendra Pachauri. 'This does become a global responsibility in my view.'[5] Christian Aid launched a campaign in February which presented global warming as the most critical matter for the world's poorest.[6] Additionally, increased attention and action taken to counter global warming—namely, the development of renewable energies—would greatly benefit the South by providing sustainable energy solutions without necessarily impeding their economic development. And the need to diversify energy supplies to reduce GHG emissions would push energy prices down, making energy accessible to the poor.[7] Finally, the strategic interests of major Western corporations—and thus of our own pensions and investments—are deeply embedded in Southern economic development. Preventing the South from reaching economic development through the artificial preservation of a global warming conspiracy would therefore be self-defeating.

Speaking in January at the World Economic Forum, Michael Cherkasky, CEO of Marsh & McLennan, warned of 'complacency' in business and government, accusing them of focusing on reacting to, rather than preventing, disaster.[8] From touring some conferences on climate change in recent months, we have found that, for those who accept the science of climate change, there is often some way to go in understanding how to act on this at work. One response has been to ignore its relevance, by taking the stance that climate change exists but overlooking how it relates to one's profession, politics or organisation. Another is to downplay it, by accepting its status as a problem but as one less important to them than issues such as HIV/Aids, poverty or terrorism, which they prefer to focus on exclusively. Others pigeonhole the topic of global warming as a 'luxury problem' only the West has the time and affluence to worry about, and so not a concern for the world's poor. Lastly, still others displace the issue by claiming that its global status requires global action, therefore implying that to change their own activities would be inadequate and thus pointless. This position is displayed both by some in industrialised countries, who argue against changing their ways unless the emerging world joins in, and developing countries, who deny responsibility for the current state of the atmosphere and refuse to incur costs for a situation they have had no historical influence on. These responses effectively render someone's acknowledgement of climate change to be inconsequential. Together they form the Ignore, Downplay,

Pigeonhole or Displace (IDPD; pronounce it 'iddy piddy') response to climate change.

Leading corporate citizens should avoid these standpoints and be clear about their inadequacy. We can't ignore or downplay climate change because it affects all of society, while energy consumption is involved in the pursuit of nearly any profession or endeavour. We can't pigeonhole it as a Western concern because it is already affecting millions of poor people worldwide. We cannot displace responsibility for action as the global nature of the challenge means that it is everyone's responsibility to act, and, if we need other people to act to be able to sustain our own actions, then this implies an additional arena of action focusing on engagement.

Green guilt offsetting?

Since the watershed moment in 2004 of HSBC announcing its intention to go 'carbon-neutral', many companies have become actively engaged in similar climate change responses. Typically, this includes a mix of energy efficiency measures, reducing consumption and waste, switching to suppliers of energy that are investing in renewables, using on-site micro-generation of power, and purchasing 'carbon offsets' for the amount of carbon still produced by their operations. In many cases the financial benefits have been clear: both DuPont and GE have taken measures that have saved them billions of dollars and substantially reduced their emissions.[9]

The Greenhouse Gas Protocol identifies three 'scopes' of emissions in order to differentiate between direct and indirect emissions. Scope 1, or direct, emissions come from sources 'directly controlled or owned by a company'; this includes emissions resulting from transportation, heating, lighting, etc. Scope 2 and 3 emissions are indirect, the former being electricity bought by the company from a third party, whereas Scope 3 covers the range of emissions resulting from the company's operations, such as the emissions caused by the use of a company's products, the transportation of purchased materials, employee travel or commuting, and waste disposal. The World Business Council for Sustainable Development (WBCSD) recommends reporting all three scopes of emission to fully understand and address the environmental impact of an organisation's activity.[10] However, in 2007, most company claims to be going carbon-neutral covered only Scope 1—direct emissions. Interesting exceptions included Unilever, which began looking at the energy consumption involved in the use of its products, and HSBC, which began calling on its suppliers to reduce carbon.[11] Meanwhile, further steps will be required from the finance sector to address the carbon profile of their investment portfolios and project financing if their claims to be addressing climate change are to be substantiated.

The lack of regulation in the voluntary market for carbon offsetting has fostered a climate of uncertainty: the complexity of choosing the kind of carbon offsets to buy, how much, and from whom, could deter individuals and organisations from doing so. For example, although popular, purchasing carbon offsets from tree planting is problematic—namely, because a standing forest can eventually release its stored carbon, and the fact that these projects don't promote structural change regarding fossil fuel dependence. Whether the carbon captured by a project would have been captured without the investment from a carbon offsetting scheme is also key for the effectiveness of this as a mechanism to combat climate change.[12]

Verifying the existence of carbon reduction projects and whether they actually add anything new is also key in a situation where unreliable sellers, or 'carbon cowboys', could operate. As with all purchases, the risk of fraud exists, with the funding of projects that turn out to be imaginary. Companies could also potentially sell the same credits several times. The Kyoto mechanism provides a tracking system to avoid this, but the lack of a central registry on the voluntary market still affords ample opportunity for abuse.[13]

In response to this, self-regulation measures have been developed by more conscientious traders. The Carbon Neutral Company, one of the biggest intermediaries, uses KPMG to audit its carbon credit accounts. Industry standards and benchmarks are being set to emulate the regulated market. Nevertheless, there remains a problem with including reforestation projects as offsets. Unless undertaken in full knowledge of the region, local plants, soil and ecosystem, replanting destroyed or damaged forests can further damage to delicate, fragile ecosystems if foreign or over-aggressive plants are mistakenly introduced. In addition, as climate change makes regions more arid, there is a risk of these new forests drying up and burning. As a result of such concerns, the Gold Standard Label has been developed to guarantee that key environmental criteria have been met. Tree planting projects are excluded from this scheme; only green energy projects (energy efficiency and renewables) are accepted, and projects must also contribute to broader sustainable development goals and be verified by an independent third party.[14] The absence of a credible system of endorsement for 'carbon sequestration' projects, such as reforestation or underground carbon capture, is one area where business could partner with expert and authoritative groups to find verifiable solutions.

The carbon offsetting agenda is being driven by the need to communicate to consumers that 'something is being done' by the business community. But, when all is said and done on offsetting, too much is said and too little done to make a real impact on reducing emissions. A closer look at the leaders of 'climate neutrality' by the World Development Movement (WDM) is revealing.[15] HSBC states that 'we achieved carbon neutrality in September 2005 through our carbon neutral pilot project'. However, WDM in analysis of HSBC's website found that its CO_2 emissions actually rose from 585,000 tonnes in 2004 to 663,000 tonnes of CO_2 in 2005. Barclays launched a scheme with Climate Care to promote offsetting to Barclays' customers travelling abroad. Meanwhile, Barclays claimed: 'Carbon neutral flights really need not cost the earth. Offsetting a flight to New York costs around £12. It's so easy and cheap for everyone to get involved, that it could really take off.' While encouraging its customers to offset CO_2 emissions, the latest figures for Barclays' CO_2 emissions show a rise from 200,145 tonnes in 2004 to 207,650 in 2005. It appears that the advertising in this area is either inaccurate or disingenuous, with further misrepresentations identified by WDM in January 2007 including:

- BSkyB claims in its 2005 Corporate Social Responsibility report that carbon emissions are '0% . . . after carbon offsetting'

- Lastminute.com advertises offsetting alongside selling its flights and holidays. It says: 'Offsetting lets you repair the damage done by your emissions by funding projects that reduce CO_2'

- Climate Care states: 'Offsetting means paying someone to reduce CO_2 in the atmosphere by the same amount that your activities add. In this way you can 'neutralise' or 'balance' the CO_2 added by your activities'

For it to be a means of climate change reduction rather than just 'green guilt offsetting' for consumers and staff, carbon offsetting will need to be a minor part of a comprehensive package of initiatives to reduce all three areas of an organisation's emissions. And corporate communications will need to exercise a little more rigour on this topic than is apparently being applied at the moment.

The buzz on biofuel

In March 2007, US President George Bush met with the three largest automotive manufacturers in the US to discuss reducing US gasoline consumption by 20%. The discussions centred around ethanol, with GM, Ford and Chrysler agreeing to develop cars able to run on biofuel, or at least a mix of 85% biofuel and 15% gasoline. Derived from renewable sources, domestically produced, with minimal direct GHG emissions, biofuels appear to be a promising alternative. Biofuels range from energy crops raised solely for ethanol production (soybeans, corn) to biowaste made from agricultural and animal waste, and, except for GHGs emitted during transportation and production, biofuel combustion itself does not release carbon dioxide. It can also be mixed with gasoline to up to 20%, lessening reliance on fossil fuels and decreasing carbon dioxide emissions.

But it has become apparent recently that the production and sale of biofuels doesn't provide as neat an answer as had been hoped for. Problems with crop growth and its regulation, limited environmental benefits, serious potential damage and effects on the global economy present major limitations to its viability in the struggle against global warming. The GHG emissions and environmental damage generated during production vary greatly depending on the type of biofuel. 'Biowaste', or waste-derived biofuel, is produced by 'digestion' of agricultural byproducts and biodegradable waste, and does not generate significant carbon dioxide. However, production of biofuel derived from energy crops grown specifically for energy generation (including sugar-, soy- or corn-based ethanol, methanol and biogas) sometimes use fossil fuels, arguably countering the initial benefits.[16] Growing soybeans and corn also requires nitrogen-rich fertilisers, which, when run off by rains into nearby rivers, could cause significant environmental damage.[17] In March 2007, European leaders agreed to make biofuel 10% of all European transport fuel by 2020. This has encouraged countries such as Indonesia to increase palm oil production, which has traditionally been developed at the expense of the rainforest and has led to large-scale forest fires, which are a major contributor of GHGs. In spite of this, 'no mandatory certification exists at present that will guarantee that tropical rainforests [. . .] are not destroyed for the production of palm oil', said Andris Piebalgs, the European Energy Commissioner. Such inadequate regulation, in spite of the laudable intention, might actually worsen global warming by accelerating the destruction of tropical forests.[18]

The first signs of the social implications of using food for fuel also became apparent in early 2007. 'The growth of the biofuel industry has triggered increases not only in the prices of corn, oilseeds, and other grains but also in the prices of seemingly unrelated crops and products. [. . .] Rising feed prices are also hitting the livestock and poultry industries', noted experts Ford Runge and Benjamin Senauer.[19] Rising food prices in the US or other rich nations could perhaps be considered worthwhile for the production of environment-friendly fuel. But in poor countries, such as Mexico, the sudden 50% increase in the price of corn-based tortillas in January pushed people to the streets in protest, after which the President was pressured to agree to cap corn flour prices. Increasingly, warns Noam Chomsky in the *Independent News*, as starchy food staples—corn and sugar cane in the Americas, cassava in sub-Saharan Africa—are snatched up for ethanol production, the poor will have fewer and fewer options to feed themselves.[20]

It appears there are no simple technical fixes. Carbon offsetting and waste-derived biofuels could play a role if properly regulated. There is a role for leading businesses to help find the right regulatory frameworks, both statutory and professional, and at national and international levels, to allow business to apply its entrepreneurial flair to the climate challenge. In addition, as the limits of the current solutions are all too apparent, business could support government frameworks for the development of other renewable energy resources and new forms of consumer–producer collaboration so that people can gain the utility they require for less resources and energy.

Drowning in oil?

In early 2007 the ramifications of the Russian government's December 21st deal with Shell over the Sakhalin II oil project were becoming clear. Shell had lost half of its 55% share of the $20 billion project, as a result of a suspension of the project due to environmental breaches. The government-owned oil company Gazprom had taken a majority stake.

In the Western media these actions were portrayed as part of a move against private ownership of Russia's oil and gas industry which had started with the destruction of Yukos and continued with the state regaining control of Gazprom, which then acquired Sibneft. The state-owned share of total oil production has increased from 16% in 2000 to almost 40%. The suggestion was that the Russian Ministry of Natural Resources' concerns about ecological impacts of Sakhalin II project did not reflect a new environmental concern, but were a tactical use of such concerns to achieve the state's political and economic goals—a move back to resource nationalism.[21]

Clearly, there are legitimate concerns about the environmental impacts of the project, particularly concerning the whale population. The project has been the focus of a campaign by NGOs such as WWF, the International Fund for Animal Welfare (IFAW), Friends of the Earth (FOE) and regional and Russian groups, which has delayed the agreement of loans by the European Bank for Reconstruction and Development (EBRD) and the UK's Export Credit Guarantee Department (ECDG). It was this delay that meant Shell did not have the level of involvement of the UK government (through the ECDG) and other Western governments (via the EBRD) that might have put more pressure on the Kremlin to maintain its existing agreements with Shell. Consequently, 'the world has watched', according to US Deputy Secretary of Energy Clayton Sell, in March 2007, 'as the Russian government has taken greater and greater control over Russia's energy resources, while private entities have been marginalized'.[22]

'The outcome of the "Sakhalin Episode" marks a clear change in the "rules of the game" in terms of the role of foreign investors in the Russian oil and gas industry', concludes analyst Dr Michael Bradshaw of Leicester University.[23] A wider look around the world at resource nationalism in other countries such as Venezuela suggests that, despite record profits, the future of 'Big Oil' multinationals will not be easy.

In the last ten years, the confrontation between Shell and Greenpeace over the disposal of the Brent Spar oil platform in the north Atlantic has come to be regarded as a turning point in corporate citizenship, when business leaders woke up to the power of civil society and public calls for them to be more responsible. In time, the confrontation with NGOs over Sakhalin should come to be regarded as an even more seminal moment in the history of the corporation and its relations with society. By delaying loans and guarantees from government-backed agencies and giving the Russian government a reason to suspend the project, environmental campaigning has cost the company thousands of times more money in assets and lost future earnings than Brent Spar, and poses a greater challenge to the very core of Shell's business. This challenge is twofold.

First, it involves the asymmetrical pressures from civil society. Currently, international oil companies (IOCs) face far higher pressure from a critical media, an active civil society and informed communities in their home countries than many of the nationally owned or promoted oil companies in Russia, China, Malaysia and Brazil, among others. Consequently, they are pushed to adopt higher standards, and are more quickly criticised when failing to meet them, with real financial implications. This poses a strategic challenge for IOCs, which could mean operating community and government relations in entirely new ways in host countries. For example, IOCs may find it beneficial to support the development of an effective civil society and critical media in countries with oil reserves, and work towards improved international regulations on social and environmental issues, including international mechanisms for enforcement. As a matter of long-term survival, IOCs might also sensibly support an international convention on corporate accountability.

The second part of the challenge involves examining the future opportunities for energy generation. In light of resource nationalism, Shell and some other IOCs have begun to focus on the niche of projects that require the most sophisticated technology, to secure oil from difficult regions such as the Arctic or unconventional sources such as Canadian oil sands and liquefied coal. The problems with this are obvious. Getting oil from sand or coal consumes huge amounts of energy, and thus greatly increases pollution, while despoiling pristine environments such as the Arctic, which will generate huge outcry, not just from NGOs but from the public at large.

In the short term Shell and others may be able to pursue this strategy because of high oil prices and security concerns in the US and Canada about energy independence. But, in the long term, oil price fluctuations, the growing cost of carbon and growing awareness that the changing climate is itself a security threat will likely derail it.

In a BBC debate, Solar Century director Jeremy Leggett asked Shell's CEO Jeroen van der Veer whether it is possible for the company to go into the Arctic and Canadian oil sands and for the world's atmosphere to stay below the 450 parts per million of carbon identified as a crucial threshold to avoid a catastrophic acceleration in global warming by the IPCC. When pushed, van der Veer replied that 'we are not responsible for deciding the energy mix of the world'.[24] This is reminiscent of the stance Shell took in the mid 1990s on involvement in public matters, before the Brent Spar and Ken Saro-Wiwa episodes led them to accept their influence and express an intention to use it responsibly. Clearly, everyone is responsible for deciding the energy mix of the world, with some more influential than others. Companies such as Shell have major influence in political processes and the economics that frame political discourse. CEOs in such companies with sufficient awareness and courage must face these difficult conundrums to find a long-term viable strategy.

James Leaton, a key figure in the coalition of NGOs working on Sakhalin Island, thinks there is a way forward. He told us that 'Oil companies are about project management, technology and marketing, to supply liquid hydrocarbons for transport fuels. Unless they start putting these skills and resources to more sustainable options, companies like Shell, who are investing in more carbon-intensive fuels, will be stranded in a carbon-constrained world.'

For Shell and other oil companies to explore new directions more vigorously is a tough challenge, requiring significant refocusing, retraining and restructuring. It would necessarily involve levels of risk taking, innovation and flexibility that might not be generally associated with the mind-set of large bureaucratic organisations. In addition, for such a reorientation to work, IOCs would require an appropriate regulatory environment and the right signals and cooperation from consumers, investors, staff and suppliers. Whether they take up this challenge will determine whether the IOCs help us drown in oil or begin to genuinely build an ark of alternatives.

The Sakhalin episode was not an outright victory for campaigners. The environmental record of Gazprom is hardly excellent, and in January 2007 the EBRD announced it was no longer considering the current financing package for Sakhalin II. 'With the departure of the EBRD, the NGOs have lost an opportunity to leverage compliance on environmental and social issues', noted Dr Bradshaw. Organisations concerned with the operations of the oil industry, and the extractives industry as a whole, will need to develop new ways of applying pressure on companies from emerging economies, many of which are nationally owned. Consequently, in the search for new levers, their attention may shift further to the private project finance markets and to intergovernmental agreements. It would make sense for the IOCs to work with NGOs on such efforts to mainstream attention on social and environmental issues by private project financiers, and to promote more enforceable international standards. In the BBC debate, Leggett suggested Shell's shareholders wouldn't let van der Veer respond to the real implications of climate change. Many of those shareholders are institutions that invest in other companies. Engaging shareholders to facilitate understanding of their longer-term interests and the implications for needed social change and regulatory innovations, in all financial centres, is a key task for contemporary corporate citizenship.

Work–life blending

With the global search for talent, employers have paid increasing attention to their 'work–life balance' policies to attract potential employees. Some have rejected this as an inappropriate label for what they call 'work–life *blending*': 'balance' implies a distinct separation between 'work' and 'life', whereas 'blending' describes the inseparable mix of the two. As The Future Laboratory's January 2007 report explained, the evolution and spread of technology, as well as changing expectations regarding one's job, made work–life blending one of the main trends impacting the world of work.[25] Today, according to their report, nearly half of all workers (46.8%) have jobs that involve them working away from the office. From this, 41% of the men who spend time out of the office say that it constitutes more than ten hours (or more than a day) each week.

Work–life blending is a growing phenomenon, to which several factors have contributed: mounting expectations of constant connectedness both at work and home blurs the boundaries between previously compartmentalised 'work' and 'life'. Technologies enable easier access to telecommuting, as well as self- and side-employment, or other DIY escape routes from traditional corporate settings. As a result, a new generation of workers happily email friends from work, and polish the next day's presentation from home.[26] They also increasingly seek meaning in their work. This application of a 'consumer's judgement' to their career means that they are more likely to look for a profession that is fulfilling—in ways other than financial—if their current job doesn't fit their values.[27]

The rejection of the implication of a 'work–life balance'—that work is so awful it shouldn't be considered as part of life—is one of the main thrusts for 'blending's new popularity. As blogger Ryan Healy wrote, we would never consider looking for a family–life balance or a friend–life balance; why would a work–life balance make any more sense, especially if, as Healy thinks, this balance is doomed to fail?[28]

Someone personally invested in work will probably: care more about their work and its results; work harder to reach objectives; and do a better job. Having a profession that reflects this sense of self means they will probably try to tease out issues with friends, in the same way they would a strictly 'personal' issue, which could be conducive to more creative problem-solving.[29] Some argue that too many hours in the office makes one's marginal productivity plummet, and therefore being able to alternate the time allotted to various activities during the day could also help to avoid being overwhelmed or burnt out. Finally, Healy claims that making one's schedule fit one's needs is not novel but, if sought, requires flexibility—i.e. the willingness to do a little work at home if necessary. Work–life blending involves not worrying about which tasks go in the 'work' box and which go in the 'life' box.

Critics would point out that this blending is only something geographically flexible twentysomethings with white-collar jobs and no family obligations would seek. Once Wednesday afternoon piano lessons kick in, taking extra time to put the finishing touches on Thursday's presentation might become difficult, even unacceptable. Not all jobs can be done from home; those that can usually require a significant investment in the appropriate technology. So work–life blending is really practical only in a region with widespread, reliable and accessible technological infrastructure, where having a cell phone, personal computer, printer, scanner, BlackBerry and/or fax machine are part of the way of life, and for individuals of a certain professional standing.[30]

Beyond the caveats, however, the focus on work–life blending is increasing. Whether this is a positive development is yet to be determined. A survey released by Digital Life America in February 2007 showed that owners of BlackBerry-like devices in the USA were split about whether these gadgets further bind one to one's work or not: one-third agreed, one-third was indifferent and one-third disagreed.[31] The same survey showed that users of such technology tended to work more, felt that they didn't have enough personal time, but also that they earned more. 'Contrary to shiny happy ads suggesting we do more in less time, in fact, there is evidence to suggest that we simply do more, more of the time. [. . .] While being "always on" is natural for young people, many of those in the 25–54 age group with families and corporate jobs are struggling with work– life blending. There is a need for the mainstream workplace culture to offer ways to counterbalance', said Digital Life America analysts.[32] Dartmouth's Tuck School of Business panellists agreed that technologies such as the BlackBerry have a tendency to make work become very present in one's personal life, making the determination of family time a challenge.[33] Donna Hall, Director of Marketing Strategies at Digital Life America, explained the feeling of being too tightly bound to work by business technologies as resentment for this intrusion: 'Many have been given a BlackBerry by their employers. The expectation on the part of the employer is that once they have it they will be accessible at all times. There are no more boundaries or times when they are unreachable, even on vacation.'[34] Finally, not only is better technology pushing us to work more overall, it has raised expectations—and stress levels—for documents previously written in weeks to be produced in hours.

One could therefore wonder whether work–life blending is as healthy as it appears: if one is very invested in one's work and stress levels are high at the office, how and when does one relax, or reflect about work? 'Going home' might just mean moving one's body between two locations; one called 'work' and one called 'home'. For some, being able to make a clear distinction, be it geographical or chronological, can be important to one's capacity to let go and enjoy the present. Plus, sharing both personal and professional life with the same people can be problematic— excusing sloppy work or behaviour in a friend is easier than in a co-worker with whom there may be little emotional bond.

Time will reveal whether more work-life blending will mean the extension of corporate consumption of people's time, or an empowering of people so they can 'consume' a wider choice of working options. Individuals, which include workers, demand more affordable custom-made solutions for everything: grocery shopping, friendship and, yes, work. As Ryan Healy laments, there are those who are still 'thinking of work and life as a constant tug of war. If you are doing something you love then why can't they be one and the same? The goal of a blended life is not living to work and it's not working to live. The goal is to have a life.'[35]

The rose water debate

'So, this Valentine's Day, you can be a romantic, reduce your environmental impact and help make poverty history. This is about social justice and making it easier, not harder, for African people to make a decent living.' So argued the British International Development Secretary Hilary Benn in February 2007, calling on British consumers to buy flowers from Kenya.[36] Much of this production comes from the shores of Lake Naivasha, 120 km north-west of Nairobi in the scenic Rift Valley. The Kenya Flower Council (KFC) says flower farming is an important economic activity for the country. 'This is the fastest growing sector of the economy, only second to tea', said Loice Mwangi. In 2005, Kenya exported 81,000 tons of cut flowers and earned US$350 million (KES24 billion). The sector today employs between 50,000 and 70,000 people, with another one million depending on the farms through auxiliary services, according to Jane Ngige, the KFC head.

Benn's comments came as some were questioning the suitability of these burgeoning imports of flowers from Kenya into Europe. Kenyan journalist Ochieng' Ogodo also wrote in February how 'Beneath the graceful expression of love the roses convey and the lucrative business flower production is, there is the hidden cost little known to many: environmental degradation, socio-economic imbalance, blatant human rights violation, and adverse health consequences for workers.' Ogodo warned 'it [Lake Naivasha] could soon become little more than a turbid, smelly pond, threatening the livelihoods of over 300,000 people living around its shores'.[37]

It is estimated that the flower farms are extracting around 20,000 m^3 of water daily from the lake. Many think this is an underestimate, as there are now more than 2,000 hectares of land covered by the steel and plastic greenhouses where the flowers are grown. Each hectare of flowers grown with even the most efficient watering mechanism uses about 40 m^3 of water a day, but flowers grown in the open use three times this amount. Some experts have estimated that at this rate of consumption the lake will be lost within 10 or 15 years. According to Earthwatch-supported ecologist Dr David Harper of the University of Leicester, 'The companies will not be able to grow flowers then because the water will become too alkaline. The companies are shooting themselves in the foot.'[38]

Dr Julius Kipng'etich, head of the Kenya Wildlife Service (KWS), is one senior Kenyan official brave enough to openly question the industry, in the face of its vested interests. 'For a water-stressed country like Kenya, we have to ask ourselves: Is it a sustainable industry? It is a challenge for us.' Another is Peter Kenneth, Assistant Minister of Finance and himself a flower farmer near Nairobi, who said, 'There is a danger that Rift Valley lakes will dry up. You can see that conflict will break out. Kenya needs to understand what the real cost of a poor environment is.'[39]

WWF calculated that the UK importation of flowers from Kenya consumes 2,216,120 m^3 of water each year from Kenya. This includes the 'virtual' water—the total water used in the production of a crop or the processes of a given product. The adjective 'virtual' refers to the fact that most of the water used in production is not visible in the end product. It is sometimes described as 'embedded' water. 'When consumers buy a Kenyan rose, do they consider the 2.7 litres of blue water that was evaporated for its production or that this polluted 1.3 litres of water resources in Kenya?' asked Stuart Orr.[40]

The flower debate in the media has mainly been about climate change, and whether it was sensible to promote the flying of products such as flowers thousands of miles to an end market. The fact that countries with scarce water resources are exporting those resources around the world through horticultural and agricultural produce poses an equally important concern that must be grappled with by business. Deciding how to respond is difficult when mixed messages are coming from civil society and government, both at home and in the exporting countries.

The case of flowers from Kenya highlights a problem that will not easily be resolved. Traditional promoters of development, such as the UK's Department for International Development (DFID) and various UN agencies, are not conceptually and organisationally well prepared for supporting social progress in the emerging world, within the context of scarce natural resources and growing concerns over climate change. As these agencies struggle with retooling themselves, leading companies will need to work out how best to address the intersecting concerns of poverty, climate and natural resources.

Good corporate citizens should be listening to people in the global South who want to improve their lives in harmony with nature and who question the growing reliance on those export industries that harm their livelihoods through heavy resource consumption and pollution. In this regard, it is worth noting the declaration of African civil-society organisations at the World Social Forum 2007 in Nairobi, Kenya, in January:

> We reject these new foreign systems that will encourage Africa's land and water to be privatised for growing inappropriate export crops, biofuels and carbon sinks, instead of food for our own people. We pledge to intensify our work for food sovereignty by conserving our own seed and enhancing our traditional organic systems of agriculture, in order to meet the uncertainties and challenges that will be faced by present and future generations. Agricultural innovation must be farmer-led, responding to local needs and sustainability. We celebrate Africa's wealth and heritage of seed, knowledge and innovation. We will resist these misguided, top-down but heavily-funded initiatives from the North, which show little or no understanding or respect for our complex systems. We ask that we be allowed to define our own path forward.

2Q2007
April–June

Jem Bendell and Jonathan Cohen

Cannibal capital

In June 2007 the world's biggest unions launched a multi-fronted campaign to impact sections of the financial industry, with a series of protests and policy proposals at the G8 meeting of industrial nations in Germany. Members of the International Trade Union Confederation, the world's largest union federation representing more than 168 million workers around the world, pressed various ministers about the problems associated with hedge funds and private equity.[1] These two forms of financial operator have both boomed in recent years, and each poses different challenges to corporate citizenship, which were becoming clearer during the first half of 2007.

Hedge funds have boomed since the turn of the millennium while many stock markets were not doing so well. This is because they focused on betting that stocks would go down. They did this by short-selling, which is the practice of borrowing shares with a promise to give them back at a later time. The trader sells them when the share price is high and then buys them back—to fulfil the promise—after that price falls, thus making a profit from a fall in share price. This works well when the interest on the borrowed shares is low, and the time elapsed before buying back the shares is also short, so that overall interest charges do not eat into the difference in share price obtained. Some hedge funds therefore even do these trades in a matter of minutes.

Over 8,000 hedge funds exist, mostly in the US and UK. As their influence has grown, hedge funds have come under attack from regulators, pension funds, and even some business executives complaining about 'short-termism', a lack of transparency, and increased volatility in share prices. The average stock ownership period has fallen during recent years, from an average of two years in 1998, to 14.6 months in 2000 and just 9.4 months by 2007. Some major companies have seen their share prices fall by 30% in a single week after hedge funds have targeted them.[2] The problem for corporate citizenship is that this short-term pressure does not encourage companies to plan for the long term and thus invest in research, in staff development, community relations and so forth. Business groups, such as The Conference Board and Business Roundtable, published reports last year that revealed that a focus on short-term earnings undermines companies' ability to create long-term value.

Another reason for notoriety and criticism is the eye-popping amount of money hedge funds make. Hedge fund managers can take 20% of the profits generated in trades, with the top hedge fund manager, Steve Cohen, earning around a billion dollars a year.[3] Leaving aside concerns about the ethics of a financial system that can create such earnings amidst such inequality, cumulatively these earnings draw on the collective wealth of the asset owners and employees, an issue we return to below.

This points to the key question about hedge funds: are they good for the economy? If hedge funds make a significant proportion of their money from betting against poor-performing stocks, then do they have an interest in the overall market declining? Man Group CEO Stanley Fink said on the BBC in 2006 that if you think that there will be no union action, no political changes or new regulations, then invest in equities, but if you think there could be, then invest in hedge funds.[4] Does that imply Man Group has a strategic interest in volatility, or even in general economic decline? Most hedge funds have an edge because of their short-selling, and so they may have a strategic interest in economic downturn in general, but then that would involve a situation where there would be less money to be made in future, which would reduce the pot from which they can draw: they would have got a bigger piece of a smaller pie.

How have hedge funds responded? Some have parroted the old Milton Friedman rationale that they have created huge wealth for the financial centres that have supported them, like London, and have increased liquidity of money, which they suggest is helpful for the market as a whole. Looking at the corporate social responsibility report of Man Group, the largest hedge fund in the world, the question of the societal benefit or impact of hedging is ignored. It recognises responsibilities to all those with which they have a 'direct relationship' or have an interest in or concern about Man Group, but there is no evidence of the company addressing how its core business impacts on the wider population. Their ethical policy states they will not 'take any stance in respect of politics and religion which is not a neutral one', which seems difficult to square with the important role of financial regulations in providing a framework for instruments such as short-selling, and is not up with the latest thinking on progressive corporate political engagement, described in these pages.[5]

More hedge funds floated on stock markets, and attracted large sums from around the world. Man Group financial performance was reported as strong because of Japanese interest in buying shares and giving their money over to manage.[6] With all that money coming in, the share price of hedge funds has the potential to do well. But what of the underlying conditions? Hedge funds did well as the market fell but, as the market is on the up, the key innovation of hedge fund—short-selling—is no longer such a great bet. If the new capital injection is herd behaviour, perhaps a hedge fund bubble could be forming.[7] The irony would be if a hedge fund manager spotted this and created a fund to short-sell publicly listed hedge funds that focus on short-selling stocks. Now that hedge funds can be retailed, such a 'hedge-cutter' fund might attract interest from disgruntled CEOs.

Private equity, public inequity

Another segment of the financial industry that received some heat in 2007 was private equity. In June, while more than a hundred bankers and investors attended a dealmaker conference at the New York Stock Exchange, two union groups protested the growing and, in their view, 'unchecked power of these well-heeled and secretive investment firms'. Andrew McDonald, director of the private equity campaign for the Service Employees International Union (SEIU), which represents 1.8 million workers, told Reuters that 'America is waking up to the fact that private equity is everywhere and it has a huge impact not only on the economy but workers and communities'. In April, the SEIU had unveiled a report highlighting its concerns about buy-outs, which can lead to job cuts, the elimination of pension plans and cuts in health coverage.[8]

Buy-out firms have been active for more than 20 years, but in early 2007 scrutiny of them grew. The floating of the Blackstone Group, the takeover of iconic companies such as Chrysler, Hertz and Tommy Hilfiger, and the billions of dollars made by the dealmakers, have helped raise their public profile. Key to their recent growth has been an era of cheap debt. This has enabled many private equity firms to punch way above the weight of their own bank balance. Worldwide, the private equity industry is thought to have about $300 billion in cash, which might amount to $1 trillion in spending power when firms borrow against their capital, according to Ernst & Young.

Ben Schiller summarises the main criticism of private equity firms as being that 'after buying out companies, they load them with debt, take out the cash, and then sell the emaciated carcass a few years later. In Germany, private equity firms have famously been described as locusts for their asset-stripping activities.'[9] Key here is the widespread use of leveraged buy-outs (LBOs), which involves borrowing other people's money to buy other people's companies in return for giving them your debts and demanding large dividends. For instance, the private equity partners who took over the British retailer Debenhams increased the company's debt from £100 million to £1.9 billion, paid themselves dividends of £1.3 billion, tripling their investment in just over two years.[10] To the non-financier this sounds somewhat like getting a mortgage from a bank to buy a house and giving the existing tenants the debt and upping their rent. Nice 'work' if you can get it.

Unions are particularly concerned with job cuts. They cite the example of the Automobile Association (AA), where new owners Permira and CVC cut 3,400 jobs within months of taking it over.[11] However, in April 2007 a study by the *Financial Times* suggested that the 30 largest private equity deals made between 2003 and 2004 in the UK have created 36,000 new jobs, many in the country. In response, Paul Kenny, general secretary of the union GMB, said, 'The FT finding that some companies owned by private equity grew jobs and turnover does not invalidate the GMB experience of job losses at the hands of private equity in the mature sectors of the economy like AA and Birds Eye, and the related tax breaks, asset-stripping, saddling of thriving companies with massive debts and culture of secrecy.'[12]

In addition, recent evidence suggests that short-term pressures on executives from these LBOs and hedge fund activity are limiting investment in various areas, not only employment. In a 2006 survey of 400 senior US executives by the *Journal of Accounting and Economics*, four-fifths of respondents said they would cut spending on research and development, advertising, maintenance and hiring to meet their quarterly targets.[13]

Some commentators on corporate social responsibility argue that 'there is nothing inherent to the private equity model that should mean that privately owned businesses must be inherently less sustainable or less responsible than [publicly listed companies]', and see the issue merely as one of increasing the knowledge of private equity managers and their stakeholders about best practice.[14] That is a convenient position to take if selling advisory services and seeing a major new market from the backlash against private equity firms. However, there can be no denying the 'tax breaks, asset-stripping, saddling thriving companies with massive debts and the culture of secrecy' that Kenny describes poses problems for how companies create value for society. 'When you have something in private equity you don't have the public visibility about corporate social responsibility activities in the same way as with public companies,' says Arthur Probert from Tomorrow's Company.[15]

Private equity managers themselves have differing perspectives on corporate social responsibility. On the one hand, there is evidence of progressive behaviour. Private equity firms made their $32 billion takeover of energy company TXU dependent on the firm cancelling 8 out of 11 coal-fired power stations on environmental grounds. David Russell, head of responsible investment at the Universities Superannuation Scheme, a pension fund with £29 billion assets under management, explained that all of the fund's current private equity assets are invested in wind farms.[16]

However, some of the large PE investors take a dim view of how societal concerns relate to them. At a Treasury select committee in the UK, CVC Capital managing partner Donald Mackenzie said, 'A lot of public companies we speak to spent too much time on regulatory issues, social responsibility and corporate governance . . . And they forget their prime purpose—which is to grow the company as rapidly as possible.'[17] One sector already causing concern is retailing. In May 2007, Somerfield Stores, UK grocer, pulled out of the Ethical Trading Initiative after being bought out by private equity group Apax Partners. Mallen Baker of Business in the Community sees PE managers demanding a new rigour in corporate social responsibility thinking. 'They are skeptical, because flawed arguments based on wishful thinking are the sorts of things they pride themselves on being able to see through.'[18] However, the idea that there can be a business case for voluntary corporate action on all social and environmental issues has already been shown up as wishful thinking and the agenda has moved on to focus on creating the right frameworks and drivers for business to be more responsible, accountable and sustainable. That requires a systemic view, appreciating the importance of value creation across the whole economy in the long term, and a sense of moral purpose to act beyond, but not in contest with, what is financially sensible for one's own company today. If the financial system empowers those who take no such long-term or broader view and seek to maximise short-term returns based on debt to equity calculations, then we have a problem that can not be resolved by Blackstone or Primera, for instance, hiring a corporate social responsibility manager and joining a few relevant membership organisations.

However, apart from some in the trade union movement, by mid-2007 the connections were not being clearly made between these new financial powerhouses and the interests of wider society. In Melbourne, Australia, the top business conference of the year was packed with seminars about social and environmental challenges. During a panel on Private Equity during this 'Future Summit' the audience sat hushed listening almost in awe to the millionaire dealmakers on stage and did not ask any questions about how PE is helping or hindering a sustainable Australian economy.[19] In May, PE even made it into *Vanity Fair*'s annual 'Green Issue'. Nearly all articles addressed crucial issues such as climate change. The one on private equity marvelled at the billions that PE firms are making by 'doing the math', mentioned some protests, but concluded 'just deal me in'.[20]

Change the system

The connections between the basic models of corporate financing and their potential for creating societal as well as private wealth needs exploring. Currently the focus of initiatives about the regulation of PE and hedge funds focuses on the two Ts: transparency and tax.

Peter Linthwaite, director of the British Private Equity and Venture Capital Association, which represents hundreds of private equity firms, acknowledges that there is 'a wider base of people with a legitimate interest' in the industry and 'there will be more people than just the investors and employees who will want to know about how these companies are run'.[21] Faced with potential regulation, his association has convened a group to develop a voluntary code to promote transparency in the industry. Chaired by Sir David Walker, former chairman of Morgan Stanley, the group's ten members include industry leaders such as David Blitzer, senior managing director of Blackstone, and Lord Hollick, a partner at Kohlberg Kravis Roberts (KKR).

Transparent behaviour can still be problem behaviour. Bill Stein, writing in the *New York Times*, focused on the question of taxation. 'Long ago, I had a European history teacher named Mrs Enright. She explained to me that one of the causes of the French Revolution was the sad truth that the aristocracy was not taxed at all, while the workers and burghers were taxed highly. Is this our future?'[22] Stein argued that the US must 'make the tax on private equity and hedge funds approximate [to] the treatment of other highly paid people—or it can continue down the road to the Bastille'. In the UK, some PE managers told the Treasury they would support tax rises on carried interest, the share of profits that account for most of dealmakers' pay.

Some commentators, particularly in the US, vociferously disagree. 'What we don't need is government intervention to restrain a model that genuinely creates wealth in a world that needs wealth creation. What we will, and should, see is a greater requirement for transparency and accountability in how the sector goes about its business,' argued Mallen Baker in May. However, given that the pressures from financial markets are often pointed to by corporate leaders as barriers to more effective corporate contributions to sustainable development, it seems too early to argue against government intervention, especially when it is government that has shaped the rules and trading environment that have given birth to these innovative financial practices in the first place. The techniques of highly leveraged buy-outs and short-selling are so problematic for long-term corporate planning that by using such instruments hedge funds and private equity could be cannibalising capitalism, eating it up from within.

Currently it is the institutional investors who pay the price, as they have to invest across the whole market to reduce their risks, and so they buy the heavily indebted stocks when they are sold back onto the stock market by PE firms. Yet about half of the $1.1 trillion under management by PE comes from such institutions, including esteemed US pension groups such as CalPERS and even university endowment funds and central banks. Even within existing regulations on fiduciary duty this practice could be challenged. Because, if the value of the whole portfolio of investments is taken into account, not just the performance of individual equities and instruments, then by pumping up a system that costs their portfolio as a whole, through funding PE, trustees could be in contravention of their fiduciary duty. Yet they face a prisoner's dilemma: if they stay out of PE and hedge funds, their wider portfolios will still suffer while they miss out on the short-term earnings from these financial players. So although the ITUC are examining the possibility of blocking member pension funds from investing in buy-outs firms that engage in activities detrimental to workers' rights,[23] a broader international response will be required. Interestingly, some institutional investors in the UN Principles for Responsible Investment (UNPRI) initiative have established a working group on private equity.

This situation suggests that institutional investors should take greater leadership in considering the kind of financial system that is supportive of their members' interests and work towards that. Therefore, not only do such institutions need to establish what forms of hedging and PE might be compatible with long-term value creation and the broader interests of their members, but develop an understanding of the kind of global financial system that will deliver that goal. The implication might be a new public policy agenda from investors seeking to promote more patient and accountable capital. With this understanding the pressures from the European Commission on the Swedish government to remove 'preferential treatment' of investors with long-standing share ownership could be seen as against their interests.

As we reflect on the responsibilities of financial institutions it would be useful to consider how an understanding of the responsibilities of non-financial corporations has developed since 1990s, in the West. There has been a shift away from an agenda where business managers sought to satisfy themselves that they were being smarter about managing their social and environmental impacts for financial returns, or in agreement with their own ethical preferences, towards an understanding that as managers of powerful organisations they needed to be more accountable to those they affected. This is a matter of principle, underpinned by notions of equality, dignity and fair play: stakeholders should be respected. This same shift in thinking has not occurred in the realm of responsible finance. Instead, six broad types of approach can now be seen. One approach is to buy into a narrow range of stocks that are preferred for a mixture of financial and ethical reasons, such as clean technology funds. Another approach has been to invest across the board, but screen out those companies in sectors you don't like, such as tobacco or armaments. A third approach has been to buy into those stocks that are the best performing of their class on ethical issues that concern you. A fourth approach has been to engage with companies you have stocks in to seek improvement in their performance on ethical issues, within the framework of what's financially material, such as some of the members of the UNPRI. A new approach is emerging, whereby investors seek to engage companies on the basis of a broader understanding of what is material to the performance of the portfolio as a whole, what James Gifford of the UNPRI calls 'portfolio wide materiality'. Lastly, some institutional investors recognise that their members have concerns beyond the financial, and so they want to uphold certain traditions and values. The question of the accountability of the owners, and finding a new accord between financial property rights and duties, defined as capital accountability by one of these authors in a UN publication in 2004, has not been discussed in responsible investment circles.[24] Indeed, most regulatory innovations in recent years have helped make capital less patient and accountable.

The lack of engagement on either regulatory issues or matters of their own accountability by financial institutions could be a result of the lack of informed pressure coming from civil society. NGOs have focused much of their effort—for example, through BankTrack, a network that tracks the impact of the private financial sector on sustainability[25]—on either project finance, which is only about 1% of global finance, or on ranking the high-street banks' incorporation of social and environmental issues into their wider lending practices. The problematic practices of the financial services in areas such as currency speculation, offshore trusts, short-selling and leveraged buy-outs have not been engaged by most mainstream

NGOs. There could be two reasons for this. First is the brain drain from NGOs into the worlds of socially responsible investment and corporate social responsibility management or consulting. Many of the leading people in responsible finance, such as Nick Robins, Rob Lake, Raj Thamotheram and Steve Waygood, left NGOs. Second is the institutionalisation of NGOs, so they become less innovative and more risk-averse over time. It is more of a challenge to make the case to your membership for why, for instance, currency speculation should be curbed to promote sustainable development than why a fence should be put around a forest to protect a bird. Given climate change, driven by dynamics of global finance, the latter may be increasingly futile, but it's still an easier communications option, which makes it an easier fundraising message. The rapid changes in finance mean there is an urgent need for a reversal of that brain drain, and for people from the business side to join with NGOs, unions and others who are interested in addressing the root causes of corporate social irresponsibility.

Food is going to the dogs

A staple of NGO fundraising appeals for years has been to highlight the amount of money Americans spend on pet food compared to the notably smaller amount one is asked to contribute to the cause in question. Americans love their pets. They spend money on their pets as if they were kids. Pet food alone is a $14-billion-a-year industry.[26] In fact, it has been said that, for baby-boomers, pets have now become the kids, because people are treating them that way. So we should not be surprised by the stink caused in April 2007 by a story of pet food from China that killed furry loved ones in homes across America.

Add a sense of helplessness and fear[27] about the supply chain when human food was also thought to be toxic,[28] when the tainted pet food was linked to chickens from Indiana and hogs from California,[29] multiple varieties of farm-raised seafood were detained at the border,[30] mix in a touch of greed to the scandal when a pet food company officer sold stock before the recall,[31] and the makings for a major story are in place—the kind of story that most readers can relate to.

The steady drum beat of stories about food containing illegal substances, such as forbidden carcinogenic chemicals and drugs such as antibiotics, continued in relation to an ever-widening array of food products. Stories included substances prohibited by Chinese authorities, and the removal of more than 10,000 tubes of Chinese-made toothpaste from stores in the Dominican Republic. The European Union had the foresight to develop a rapid electronic alert system in response to such risks, specifically from China.[32]

The global sourcing of ingredients in processed foods and a doubling of food imports to $80 billion, according to the US International Trade Commission, as a result of the lowering of trade barriers some ten years ago, pointed to a further exponential spread of concern, which led to the *New York Times* calling America's food import rules 'relatively permissible' and its inspection regime 'weak'.[33]

China's sheer lack of quality control and widespread corruption quickly became the main story. The world's most populous country responded by exhibiting a close variation of the five stages of grief,[34] starting with denial.[35] Anger was directed internally—by sentencing to death the top drug regulator for taking bribes,[36] as well as externally toward the US for blocking suspect imports. Bargaining resulted in the Chinese rejection of water, seafood and fruit imports from other countries such as Australia and the US.[37] Depression and, finally, a modicum of acceptance ensued with the announcement of new and stricter food safety standards,[38] as well as the closure of 180 food factories.[39]

Consider the huge trade surplus involved—China had an approximately $150 billion surplus[40] with the US and replaced it as the largest exporter in the world in 2006,[41] with expectations for an unprecedented $100 billion surplus in the first half of 2007 alone. The sheer volume of products from China that enter the United States, and the rest of the world, promised that what started as a pet food scandal would be a story . . . with legs.

The green media frenzy

Mainstream media thrives on catastrophe, shock and misery, so perhaps the notable increase in coverage of green issues and green business issues shouldn't be surprising. The United States has often been seen as behind the rest of the industrialised world in its awareness of environmental issues. In 2007, it became apparent that the trend of featuring environmental issues in the mass media via news, television shows and popular culture was spiralling as never before.

The Global Warming Survival Guide stared out from the cover of *Time* magazine's April 9 issue, and included '51 Things You Can Do', which stated 'You—along with scientists, businesses and governments—can create paths to cut carbon emissions'.[42] *Time*'s June 18 issue urged readers to 'Take Your Planet to Work (Going Green at the Office)', and noted that 'One office worker can use a quarter ton of materials in a year'.[43]

As mentioned above, *Vanity Fair* unveiled its 'Green Issue' in May 2007, which featured articles on lawsuits against Chevron for destructive oil drilling in the Ecuadoran Amazon, 'The Rise of Big Water', as an industry, a sleek new electric car, and also skewered energy industry executives in the article 'Texas Chainsaw Management'. (Yes, and that one on private equity.)[44]

The Discovery Channel launched the first 24-hour television network dedicated to green lifestyle programming, Planet Green, in April 2007. The initiative includes a $50 million investment in new original content and a multi-platform offering with interactive tools and comprehensive 'how to' resources. Planet Green will begin airing in 2008 and is expected to debut in over 50 million US homes.[45] Meanwhile, the cable network's Health Channel covered 'Green Yard' programming, and its Travel Channel featured an 'Eco Lodges' episode.

The Sundance Channel launched a weekly bloc of environmental programming in the month called The Green. The Green kicked off each bloc with an original documentary series that took a look at 'the leading edge of a new green world'. The first few segments focused on alternative fuel, green building and eco-fashion.[46] Both the Discovery and Sundance channels created advisory committees with a selection of notable names and organisations to support programme development, partnership outreach and corporate innovation activities.

A key actor in the climate change debate took notice of the increased media attention and responded by buying 'Let's Talk about Climate Change' full-page ads in the major publications such as the *Washington Post*. That key actor was none other than Exxon. When the biggest climate change denier nonchalantly changes tack to engage the issue on its own terms rather than insisting it doesn't exist, it has conceded the fight. The vice president for public affairs of the world's largest publicly traded oil company, Kenneth P. Cohen, said that the company never denied the existence of climate change.[47] No, they have only heavily funded those that do.

The main classic rock 'n' roll radio station in the Washington DC area, 94.7 FM, has banked that green is good, to paraphrase Gordon Gekko in the movie *Wall Street*, with a new name—The Globe—and mission: 'We want to be a part of the solution.' Its website lists its top 12 priorities, which include 'The Globe' at number one, and 'Think Globally, Act Locally' at number three, with regular on-air tips on how to go green with energy, electronics, landscaping, cars and shopping, and ads featuring global positioning gadgets with the pitch that they can find the nearest place to recycle garbage.[48] Green Weddings graced the cover of the *Washington Post* 'Home' section in its 21 June edition, and declared that the '$73 billion wedding industry is paying more attention to the environmental implications of their choices'.[49]

Even *Wine Spectator* magazine's June 30 issue declared 'Wine Goes Green'. Articles examined how producers make wine while reducing pollution and conserving energy with solar panels to subterranean cellars, and new organic wine-making methods.[50]

Being consumed

Against this backdrop of environmental concern, the topic of sustainable consumption has been aired more often at corporate social responsibility conferences. A twist on the familiar subject occurred in June 2007 at Canada's largest oil conference. A representative of the US National Petroleum Council told several hundred oilmen that in order to address worldwide energy needs an abundant new source was needed, and announced the launch of Vivoleum—a fuel made by 'transforming the billions of people who die into oil': all a hoax devised by the Yes Men.[51]

Andy Bichelbaum of the Yes Men, a political prankster group, posed as the representative, and was thrown out along with a companion after handing out Vivoleum memorial candles purportedly made from the remains of an ExxonMobil worker who had died following the clean-up of a toxic waste spill. The janitor, in a video tribute, announced that he wished to be transformed into candles after his death. The candles were actually said to be made of paraffin, beeswax and human hair.[52]

Vivoleum.com, the spoof website, quickly got yanked off the internet the next day, along with the Yes Men's email service, in reaction to a complaint whose source their internet service provider declined to provide. The provider also made the Yes Men remove all mention of Exxon, who was ostensibly the manufacturer of Vivoleum, from TheYesMen.org, before email service was restored.[53]

The hoax about the sustainable consumption *of* consumers conjured up shades of the cult 1973 science fiction movie *Soylent Green*, which revealed in the dénouement that the main ingredient of the essential food source in society was, in fact, people.[54]

The Yes Men were making a number of points. One is how we are ourselves consumed by the economy we have created. In his 2007 book *Consumed*, Benjamin Barber develops the theme. He suggests our global economy is designed to overproduce goods and necessitates the corporate targeting of children to make them demand more products and services.[55] Barber asserts that in place of the Protestant ethic once associated with capitalism—encouraging self-restraint, preparation for the future, protection of children and community, which he sees as characteristics of adulthood—we are constantly being seduced into an 'infantilist' ethic of consumption. The system we have created, he says, has as its primary goal not the manufacture of goods we need, but the needs themselves. For the sustainable consumption agenda to be embraced by business people and the larger public, there is a need to understand how product and service design, marketing and advertising can be done in ways that communicate to people about consumption opportunities without their being consumed by debt from overspending, environmental destruction from overdevelopment, and personal dissatisfaction from perpetual want.

3Q2007
July–September

Jem Bendell

The responsibility of business schools

In July 2007, the UN Principles for Responsible Management Education (UN PRME) were launched in Geneva. They call for the incorporation of universal values in curricula and research, and are offered as a guiding framework for academic institutions to advance the broader cause of corporate social responsibility (see Box 1). The Principles have been developed by an international task force of 60 deans, university presidents and official representatives of leading business schools. The initiative has been co-convened by the United Nations Global Compact, the Association to Advance Collegiate Schools of Business (AACSB International), the European Foundation for Management Development (EFMD), the Aspen Institute's Business and Society Program, the Globally Responsible Leadership Initiative (GRLI) and Net Impact.

Box 1: **The principles for responsible management education**

Source: www.unglobalcompact.com/HowToParticipate/academic_network/index.html#bus_ed

As institutions of higher learning involved in the education of current and future managers we are voluntarily committed to engaging in a continuous process of improvement of the following Principles, reporting on progress to all our stakeholders and exchanging effective practices with other academic institutions:

- Principle 1: Purpose. We will develop the capabilities of students to be future generators of sustainable value for business and society at large and to work for an inclusive and sustainable global economy.
- Principle 2: Values. We will incorporate into our academic activities and curricula the values of global social responsibility as portrayed in international initiatives such as the United Nations Global Compact.

- Principle 3: Method. We will create educational frameworks, materials, processes and environments that enable effective learning experiences for responsible leadership.
- Principle 4: Research. We will engage in conceptual and empirical research that advances our understanding about the role, dynamics and impact of corporations in the creation of sustainable social, environmental and economic value.
- Principle 5: Partnership. We will interact with managers of business corporations to extend our knowledge of their challenges in meeting social and environmental responsibilities and to explore jointly effective approaches to meeting these challenges.
- Principle 6: Dialogue. We will facilitate and support dialogue and debate among educators, business, government, consumers, media, civil society organizations and other interested groups and stakeholders on critical issues related to global social responsibility and sustainability.

The launch of the Principles is the latest illustration of a trend in management education that appears to be responding to criticism of business schools from business, students and wider society during the first years of the 21st century. *The Economist* recalled,

> five years ago, business schools, particularly in America, came under attack from all sides. Fairly or not, they took some of the blame for the corporate scandals that erupted at firms such as Enron and WorldCom. Jeffrey Skilling, the former boss of Enron, was a star of the Harvard Business School class of 1979. Other corporate villains and their lackeys have boasted MBAs. Many agreed with one commentator that the only way to solve the ethical problems of corporate America was to fire everyone under 35 with an MBA.[1]

Even esteemed professors of management were critical. In an article published in 2005, the late Sumantra Ghoshal of London Business School argued that, by assuming executives are the self-interested agents of shareholders, driven by maximisation of their self-interest, business-school teachers had freed their students from 'any sense of moral responsibility'.[2] Applications for MBA courses began to dip and graduating MBAs began to experience great difficulty in finding work, according to *The Economist*.

Since 1999, the World Resources Institute (WRI) and the Aspen Institute's Business and Society Program have been publishing reviews of the social and environmental content of MBA programmes. The 2007 report ranked universities on their incorporation of such issues into the business curriculum, as well as their research. The top ten of the schools studied in 2007 are listed in Table 8. The global rankings are dominated by North American business schools which might reflect the methodology of the rankings, including the way different issues are weighted. Nevertheless, the publication of this ranking has increased the pressure and incentive for business schools to consider corporate responsibility in their teaching and research.

Table 8: **The top ten business schools for corporate responsibility, according to the US-based Aspen Institute**

Source: www.beyondgreypinstripes.org/rankings/index.cfm

More information from www.beyondgreypinstripes.org

Rank	University	Country	Student opportunity	Student exposure	Course content	Faculty research
1	Stanford	USA	1	11	2	3
2	Michigan (Ross)	USA	10	27	4	1
3	York (Schulich)	CAN	2	6	17	5
4	UC Berkeley (Haas)	USA	4	32	1	5
5	Notre Dame (Mendoza)	USA	5	15	17	9
6	Columbia	USA	13	13	7	16
7	Cornell (Johnson)	USA	6	24	11	20
8	Duquesne (Donahue)	USA	21	1	27	29
9	Yale	USA	3	18	5	69
10	IE Business School	ESP	8	5	7	52

Some of the more recent innovations in teaching challenge the normal approach of management education entirely. *The Economist* described the new approach taken by Yale School of Management during 2007.

> Instead of the well-worn method of teaching functional subjects, such as marketing, strategy, accounting and so forth, students who are now completing their first year at Yale are taught with eight courses that each address different themes, such as the customer, the employee, the investor, competitors, business and society, and innovation.

To rewrite the curriculum, weekly meetings of multidisciplinary teams discussed what each subject could bring to a course. This encourages the faculty out of their academic silos and enables them to see the bigger picture, something returned to below.

Globally, one of the most active projects to transform management education to promote corporate responsibility in business has been the Globally Responsible Leadership Initiative (GRLI), which was launched in 2004 by senior representatives from 21 companies, business schools and centres for leadership learning. The partnership's Co-founder and General Secretary, Anders Aspling, who is also Dean of Vlerick Leuven Gent Business School in Belgium, explains that 'business schools and centres for leadership learning can play a pivotal role, alongside business, in developing the present and future leaders required to ensure that business is a force for good'. Michael Powell, Pro Vice Chancellor of Griffith Business School, the first Australian business school to be involved in the GRLI, says that 'it is important to connect with those professors and deans around the world who are seeking to provide a new form of management education, so we can support each other in our efforts'.

Autistic academe

There is much to collaborate on, because if management education is to be transformed it will require a changing of the incentives for the current unhelpful patterns of behaviour by faculty. This is an issue for all social science, not just management education. *The Economist*'s analysis of the challenge facing business schools alludes to one of these broader challenges: the incentives shaping research. 'Business-school faculty members often seem to place greater weight on winning the approval of peers in their academic discipline than on gaining the approval of their business-school colleagues'. The way to win that approval is by publishing in the A-rated academic journals. This is because, in the name of accountability, around the world, academics' performance has increasingly become rated on the basis of their publications in journals that are held in high regard in a particular discipline. Aside from the fact that this discourages multidisciplinarity, the highest-rated academic journals usually uphold a particular concept of valid research, which expects research questions to arise from theory rather than practice, and incorporates many hallmarks of a positivist paradigm of science. Consequently, these assessment systems have promoted three main hallmarks of an academic approach around the world. First, a focus on particular details at the expense of context to a degree where one's analysis is irrelevant, often coupled with an elaborate verbosity on minor details. Second, a dislike or inability to explore the values and emotions of others as significant phenomena in society and a dislike or inability to reflect on one's own values and emotions as key in shaping one's research. Third, an inclination for repeating procedures, as in particular research methods, rather than changing one's approach depending on circumstances in order to achieve useful outcomes.

Is it mere coincidence that each of these hallmarks of the esteemed 'academic' approach are the same as the main symptoms of autistic spectrum disorders (ASD)? Also called autism spectrum conditions (ASC), these are a range of psychological conditions characterised by widespread abnormalities of social interactions and communication, as well as severely restricted interests and highly repetitive behaviour.[3] Autistic traits have been recognised as beneficial for disciplines such as science, mathematics, engineering and computer programming, with some people with ASD displaying extraordinary powers of calculation.[4] As a letter-writer in

New Scientist once noted, 'many people with this condition go undiagnosed right through life and are often academically very successful'.[5] That people with autism can play a useful role in society should be welcomed but, if societies' institutions of knowledge production demand it of people in order that they have a successful career, we may produce more mentally impaired societies as a whole.

In management academia the problem has been compounded by the dominance of economics, widely understood as the most autistic of social sciences for its extreme and scientifically questionable assumption of so-called 'rational' human beings who act according to narrow self-interests.[6] *The Corporation* film and book made a name for itself for suggesting that, as defined in law, the corporation was psychopathic in terms of not having regard for the well-being of others, and previous studies have reported on psychological studies of psychopathic traits in successful business executives.[7] Encouragement from an autistic academe for the disregard of values and emotions can only support psychopathic behaviour in business.

As the business environment evolves with growing social complexity, so these traditionally dominant ideological assumptions in business schools are making them less relevant to modern business practice. A survey by Egon Zehnder, a recruitment firm, found that just one in five of the international corporate executives it polled thought that an MBA prepares people for real-life management.[8] As business schools are, *The Economist* notes, 'where academic theory and the practical world engage with each other', the current situation is a huge missed opportunity for research and practice to infuse each other in ways that benefit society as a whole.

How effective might the various initiatives be in promoting change? The UN Principles are a useful start, but perhaps they do not yet fully address the factors that are creating the current situation. *The Economist* notes that 'One problem is the shortage of talent available to provide the blend of academic excellence and practical insight that everyone wants'. The reason for this is the current incentive system for academics. Therefore collaboration on changes in professional standards and incentives, such as teaching and research assessments at national and international levels, will be required to support the right kind of faculty development. This means the role of regulators, funders and employers needs examining. In addition, the Principles do not address the internal mechanics of a change process in a university, such as the adoption of a policy and communication of this across the university, allocating resources, setting benchmarks, creating staff incentives, and reporting on performance. This will also need to come. Finally, the Principles could be seen as culturally Western and perhaps too specific on the question of what constitutes 'responsible' management education. The Principles mention environment and stakeholder relations, for example, and there were debates in the drafting process about mentioning ethics and diversity, among other issues. Perhaps the Principles could be more fluid and adaptable, allowing different organisations to have their own understanding of responsible management education that is culturally specific and sensitive to their understanding of the market needs, while connecting with the universal values at the heart of the UN Charter and declaration of human rights. This broader approach, while also paying attention to the internal change processes and accountability, is the one taken by a sister initiative, the UN Principles on Responsible Investment (UNPRI).

Many business schools saw their founding mission as the professionalisation of the management of business, in much the same way as medical schools have institutionalised medicine. Professions usually have at least four elements: an accepted body of knowledge; a system for certifying proficiency of that knowledge before it can be practised; a commitment to the public good; and an enforceable code of ethics. Perhaps we could benefit from a managers' equivalent of the Hippocratic oath in medicine.

Those who teach can do

The old saying goes that 'those who can, do; those who can't, teach'. With corporate responsibility it is important that this negative view of teachers and scholars does not gain further support. The authenticity of academic institutions professing responsible business, manifested by how they themselves operate responsibly, is important. Although not yet an explicit principle, the UN PRME explains how signatories 'understand that our own organizational practices should serve as example of the values and attitudes we convey to our students'.[9] Fortunately during 2007 there were signs of significant progress in one area of this: the environment.

In June, the leaders of 284 American colleges and universities from 45 states which represent about 15% of the country's higher-education institutions announced the American College and University Presidents Climate Commitment, a pact that urges educational institutions to eliminate greenhouse gas emissions. Their pact calls for development of a plan to achieve climate neutrality as soon as possible, as well as publicly reporting the action plan, inventory of carbon emissions, and periodic progress. Signatories are required to choose at least two actions from a list including building all new constructions to at least the US Green Building Council's LEED Silver standard, supporting shareholder resolutions addressing climate change and sustainability issues in companies in which the school invests, and purchasing energy from renewable resources.[10]

Earlier in 2007, *BusinessWeek* magazine announced 'The Greening of America's Campuses', while the Association for the Advancement of Sustainability in Higher Education (AASHE) revealed 'an explosion of activity around sustainability on campuses across the US and Canada'.[11] More than 600 environmental projects were reported on North American campuses during the previous year. The combined green power purchases of the top ten higher-education purchasers in the US tripled in 2006. AASHE's own growth during 2006 mirrored the trends highlighted in the report, with membership having more than quintupled since the beginning of the year.[12]

New Europe, new drivers

A UN Development Programme (UNDP) study on CR in Central and Eastern Europe revealed that civil society is a missing element in holding corporations accountable for their impacts on society and environment in the region. In contrast to Western Europe, where CR is influenced by the active pressure from various civil society organisations (CSOs), the CR agenda in Central and Eastern Europe is driven mainly by companies themselves, especially large corporations and international organisations present in the region.[13] The impact of civil and consumer groups is still limited owing to underdevelopment of the non-governmental sector. Indre Kleinaite of the Lithuanian sustainable enterprise network Gyva.net said that 'the Soviet system formed a passive society who then developed an obsession with the market economy as a panacea for all their inherited problems, and paying most attention aspiring to Western ideals of consumerism'.

The UNDP report was the first comprehensive regional study on the level of CR implementation in eight Eastern and Central European countries. The conference to launch the report was opened by Ms Kori Udovicki, UN Assistant Secretary-General, who stressed that 'Eastern Europe has learned that markets are indispensable for fast growth, but we also need institutions that can remedy the less positive consequences of the drive for profits. CR is one such tool to help ensure that everyone benefits from growth'. Mr Richard Howitt, MEP, Rapporteur on CR, called for more support from the European Parliament (EP) and European Commission (EC) for involving CSOs and small and medium-sized enterprises (SMEs) in the region. Ms Lyra Jakuleviciene, Head of UNDP Lithuania and leader of the regional CR project, concluded, 'while there are some success stories to be proud of, there is also plenty of work to be done'.

In recent years there have been signs of growing civil society activism in Lithuania, albeit leading to a backlash from some in business and government. Since 1991, when Lithuania regained its independence from the Soviet Union, privatisation was undertaken to move towards a market economy. One case has now inflamed civil society protests. The private owners of a popular cinema named 'Lietuva' (Lithuania) in Vilnius decided to demolish it and build apartments instead. Over the period 2005–2007 a number of protests merged into a civil society movement for public spaces and public interest, which has delayed the property development process.

In July 2007, a lawsuit was launched by the developers against four activists for inquiring into the real-estate project. Gediminas Urbonas, artist and one of those activists, says that this constitutes an unprecedented attack on public expression.

He adds, 'it is a very concrete illustration of how capital squashes public discourse by paralyzing active individuals'. The activists called for financial support from people to be able to hire lawyers to defend the case in the court.[14] The case sparked an active media debate from free-market advocates labelling the case a 'falsification of public interest', arguing that a few independent film lovers are pretending to represent the public by calling the movement a symbolic fight for Lithuania.[15] However, as a free and active civil society is a necessary driver of corporate responsibility, a corporate backlash against social activism will not be helpful.

Meanwhile, identifying other drivers for CR in the region is important. One such driver could be the need to address the widespread emigration of skilled people from Central and Eastern Europe. Unemployment is no longer an issue in countries such as Lithuania where thousands of people have left to pursue better-paid jobs elsewhere in Europe, especially the UK and Ireland. This means local businesses are now lacking workers and experiencing skills shortages. Could businesses have been more attentive to this social trend and taken measures to improve the pay and conditions of workers so more might have chosen to stay in countries such as Lithuania? Might CR in the workplace be one way to tempt them back?

In the absence of a tradition of NGO advocacy funded by donations from individual citizens, it is likely that new social enterprises will be a key way for social and environmental concerns to be articulated in post-Soviet states. The success of Latvian high-end cosmetics company Mádara is illustrative of how young Eastern Europeans motivated by social consciousness can express themselves. The company makes completely natural flower and herb cosmetics for body and facial care. These products are made only from plant extracts, natural oils, butters and waxes, without petroleum ingredients, chemical preservatives, parabens, artificial colourants and other potentially harmful substances. For all print and packaging, Mádara uses paper from forests certified under the Forest Stewardship Council (FSC), a system of sustainable wood supply that WWF helped to create in the early 1990s. The paper is manufactured in accordance with a strict environmental policy that calls for minimal carbon emissions and the recycling of water. According to co-founder Zane Rugina, the brand 'tells a story about a healthy and natural lifestyle, about dignity and respect towards secrets of natural beauty'.[16]

The debate about CR in Eastern Europe is part of a broader debate about the type of economic system countries in the region want to shape. Canadian activist Naomi Klein once wrote that 'the alternative to capitalism isn't communism, it's decentralized power'.[17] Indre Kleinaite explains that 'in the post-Soviet Union some are now arguing the alternative to communism is not just capitalism, but a balanced system that allows both private and public interests to go hand in hand like two forces in a union where none of them is dominating the other'.

Donor accountability and innovation

In July 2007, One World Trust published a report on the accountability of new institutions created to donate large sums for the long-term funding of post-conflict reconstruction and peace-building.[18] These 'Multi-Donor Trust Funds' aim is to ensure coherent funding rather than piecemeal, ad hoc cherry-picking of projects by donors, smoothing out lumpy income streams and providing consistency. However, the report argues that as they are multi-million-dollar funds for the reconstruction of a country or region it is also essential that there are adequate accountability mechanisms in place, and provides recommendations for improvement. This was the latest report in an emerging trend to consider 'donor accountability'.

Earlier in 2007 the former director of a large charitable foundation, Joel Fleishman, published a book that called foundations a 'great American secret' and raised the concern that 'foundations are not, in effect, accountable to anyone'. They are required to file annual tax returns and to give away a mandated percentage of their assets each year, but there is no 'authority' that monitors what they fund, nor do they publish information on their failures. Only a tiny fraction even print an annual report.[19]

In a book edited by the Ford Foundation's Lisa Jordan and launched at the UN earlier in the year, an agenda for donor accountability was mapped out. This expanded the call made by the UN Non-governmental Liaison Service report on NGO accountability late last year for greater focus on donor accountability.[20] Four principles were outlined for more accountable donors. First, donors should seek to make their generation of funds both transparent and more democratically accountable to those affected by the activities involved. This would mean that the assets of charitable foundations should be managed in the most responsible manner, ensuring companies invested in are accountable to their stakeholders. Second, donors should seek to make the administration of their activities both transparent and more democratically accountable. This involves issues such as the governance of the fund, the salaries of the officers and so on. The third principle suggests that donors should enhance the transparency and democratic accountability of their grant-making decisions and of the activities they fund. Therefore applicants and recipients could be given new ways for feeding back to grant-makers. Finally, donors should take steps to influence the regulatory environment in order to ensure support for democratic accountability, and thereby address the broader processes that give rise to the need for giving in the first place.[21]

As Fleishman's book illustrates, most donors are nowhere near this fourfold approach to their accountability, with many not recognising accountability issues of concern at all, and most not understanding how the way their funds are generated could have as much an impact on the mission they serve as the donations they then make with those funds. One foundation that has come under the spotlight is the Gates Foundation. According to the *LA Times*:

The Gates Foundation has poured $218 million into polio and measles immunization and research worldwide, including in the Niger Delta. At the same time the foundation is funding inoculations to protect health, it has invested $423 million in Eni, Royal Dutch Shell, Exxon Mobil Corp., Chevron Corp. and Total of France—the companies responsible for most of the flares blanketing the delta with pollution—beyond anything permitted in the United States or Europe.[22]

In response, the foundation first announced a systematic review of all of its investments to determine whether it should consider divestment from some companies.[23] Later, it revoked this pledge and said it would continue its current practices.[24] In May, the *LA Times* kept the Gates Foundation-gate story alive by focusing on Darfur and PetroChina, an oil company in which Gates trustee Warren Buffett owns a large stake via his Berkshire Hathaway company. PetroChina is heavily invested in oil extraction in the Sudan.[25]

The decision not to change investing practice was explained by the Gates Foundation as follows:

> Many of the companies mentioned in the *Los Angeles Times* articles, such as Ford, Kraft, Fannie Mae, Nestlé, and General Electric, do a lot of work that some people like, as well as work that some people do not like. Some activities might even be viewed positively by some people and negatively by others . . . Shareholder activism is one factor that can influence corporate behavior. The foundation is a passive investor because we want to stay focused on our core issues.[26]

In other words, every year the Gates Foundation will put 5% of its money to good causes while 95% of its money continues to be asked to do whatever will deliver the returns. Or, simpler still, doing something good with more than 5% of its power is just too 'complex'. Speaking of the problems described in the *LA Times* as caused by corporate activities invested in by the Bill and Melinda Gates Foundation, its CEO Patty Stonesifer explained that 'it is naive to suggest that an individual stockholder can stop that suffering. Changes in our investment practices would have little or no impact on these issues'.[27] Would it be naive for us to think that the CEO of the largest foundation in the world has not heard of the world's leading institutional investors in the UNPRI, accounting for $10 trillion of assets under management, engaging on precisely that agenda and to deliver long-term returns? Or would they be naive in doing this? One foundation that has joined the UNPRI is the Nathan Cummings Foundation. Yet most of the tens of thousands of foundations in the world, and mainstream human rights, development and environment charities, have their funds managed without any attention to responsible investing.[28] It would make sense for them all to join the UNPRI as asset owners. If they are not managing their assets responsibly, why should private investors listen to what they have to say on the subject? In September 2007, the UK Social Investment Forum (UKSIF) and Ethical Investment Research Service (EIRIS) teamed up to launch an online resource to help promote charities manage their assets more responsibly, assisting those that are beginning to address the issue.[29]

If large foundations such as Gates joined initiatives such as the UNPRI, they might learn more about modern finance and explore innovative approaches to creating change. As Fleishman notes, there is a whole field of mission-based investing in development, with venture philanthropy, funding social enterprise, corporate engagement, and using your assets to leverage other private finance into funding the right kinds of business. One project seeking to do this met in Geneva in September 2007. A partnership between WWF and the UNEP Finance Initiative, it looks at how NGOs, donors and private financial institutions can work together to reduce the risk of investing in sustainable SMEs in emerging markets.[30] One mechanism they are exploring is whether foundations could use their assets to write letters of guarantee to cover initial losses of private funds invested in social or sustainable enterprise, and thus reduce the risk profile sufficiently to drive more private finance into those businesses.

Once foundations become more engaged in mission-based investing, and using their assets in new ways, perhaps they might even stumble across a way of making leveraged buyouts or short-selling a progressive activity. Perhaps one day, when the necessary procedures and insurances are worked out, large philanthropic foundations could lend stock to activist not-for-profit hedge funds, charging no interest but requiring a percentage of profits, so the hedge fund could short-sell companies that don't help the achievement of the foundation's mission? Lessons could be learned from Karmabanque, which is currently running an ethical activist hedge fund.[31]

4Q2007
October–December

Jem Bendell

Dolce and Gomorrah

Publicly challenging corporations is considered a dangerous business in many parts of the global South, as recognised by *Ethical Corporation* magazine in their selection of the Best Ethical Leaders of 2007, which included the anti-corruption journalist Lala Rimando, from the Philippines, the second most dangerous place to be a reporter after Iraq.[1] But that a leading journalist on corporate irresponsibility and crime in Europe required police protection during 2007, after a 'highly credible death threat', was a stark reminder of the continued problems with organised crime, corruption and related commercial interests in the 'developed' world. Roberto Saviano had written a book on the Camorra, the lesser-known yet more powerful branch of the Italian mafia, based around Naples.

In November 2007 the English translation of *Gomorrah: Italy's Other Mafia* was published, and made the book review sections of leading newspapers, though not the business news or lifestyle sections. Perhaps journalists, or their editors, did not want to detonate the full explosiveness of this book, given the significant income they receive from high-end brand advertising. The book reports that a white suit worn by one of the world's most famous women, Angelina Jolie, on the red carpet at the Oscars, was made by someone employed by organised criminals accused of multiple murders. No wonder, then, that the publishers decided not to mention that the suit worn by Ms Jolie was from Dolce & Gabbana. Bloggers such as BabelMed made the connection, as could anyone searching Google for images of Ms Jolie at previous Oscar awards.[2]

Although this is a brand bomb waiting to explode, Saviona's analysis is wider than an attack on one company. He describes a widespread system of commercial dependence between Italy's fashion industry and organised crime around Naples, so extensive that it suggests many famous brands will be contaminated by association. He describes an auction process where multiple suppliers compete to try to meet an order, with the fashion brand paying only one of the suppliers: the one that meets the quality, quantity and deadline first. As they are not paid until after delivery, Saviano says most bidders are financed by the Camorra. He also suggests that the well-made products that are made for the fashion labels but are surplus to requirements subsequently find their way into the counterfeit market, through the Camorra. He argues this system keeps prices paid to suppliers by the fashion brands as low as possible, so they do not challenge the counterfeiting directly.

In December 2007 an Italian TV documentary on Rai 3, entitled 'Slaves of Luxury', dug deeper into the supply chains of leading Italian fashion labels.[3] The programme detailed cases of illegal Chinese immigrant labour in Italy making accessories for D&G, as well as Prada and other leading brands. The programme had an audience of four million and the forums on Rai's website were swamped with concerned viewers.[4]

'We asked to meet with Dolce & Gabbana also, considering that we found their trademark [in the factories with illegal labour], but their response was "no comment",' explained Rai 3's Milena Gabanelli. Given that Ms Jolie was still being photographed wearing D&G-branded products during 2007, the risk to her own reputation as a conscious global citizen remained. One option for her might be the Star Charter for responsible brand endorsement, launched in a report by WWF-UK in November 2007, which offers six principles to guide celebrities.[5]

Some brands did respond to the TV journalists. One was Prada, whose group communication and external relations director Tomaso Galli explained that the company has 'two different kinds of inspectors, those who check quality and those who control the working conditions of the suppliers. But we're not the police and our inspectors do not have an unlimited access to all areas and documents. Regrettably, situations like the one described in the show, which we agree are unacceptable, may occasionally occur notwithstanding our controls, but they are odd and the show did not bother to mention what the overwhelming reality is.'[6] This does not refute TV presenter Sabrina Giannini's point that companies such as Prada inspect labour conditions only after the contracts are signed, and take quality, price and punctuality far more seriously. 'The compliance with the rules could be verified from the start, thus five months earlier, and it was sufficient to ask the proprietor for the pay envelopes and registration numbers of the employees,' she explained. Furthermore, the programme shows that Prada's 'piattine' nylon bags retailing in Milan for €440 are bought from suppliers for just €28. 'Is the proprietor [of the factory] the one exploiting his workers, or is it Prada that pays too little and, right from the start, must realise that at these prices it is possible to produce only under certain conditions?' she asked.[7]

Three judgements have been issued by the Public Prosecutor's office in Florence, against the owners of Chinese firms in Italy that exploited illegal labour to produce shoe soles for Christian Dior and Gucci, and handbags for Gianfranco Ferré. Despite these few cases, it is a situation 'that as a whole is tolerated, perhaps to prevent these companies from going directly to China,' argued Milena Gabanelli.

The programme discussed the damage these practices may have on the 'Made in Italy' label and brand. 'What the world envies us for is precisely the prestige of our fabrics and the skill of our artisans. If this is not preserved, there is a risk of ruining a unique heritage. But instead, there are those who prefer investing a great deal in advertising, perhaps overlooking the substance,' said Sabrina Giannini. CEO of luxury brand Tod's, Diego Della Valle, agreed on the programme: 'I tell other important brands like our own that we must be very careful not to water down the great consideration that the world has of articles made in Italy . . . When people have money, especially in these emerging countries, they want to buy the major Italian brands, and also articles made in Italy, but this serves especially to preserve the great Italian handicrafts sector. Well, for 10 or 15 years now I have been saying that, if we don't watch out, we will lose the "Made in Italy" little by little.'

Responsible luxury

How Mr Della Valle's sentiments have translated into effective action is debatable, given that his company, Tod's, came bottom of the first worldwide ranking on the social and environmental performance of the world's largest luxury brands, which was published by WWF-UK in November 2007. *Deeper Luxury: Quality and Style when the World Matters*[8] was covered by over 50 newspapers and magazines worldwide, and numerous blogs, with the *Financial Times* headline 'Luxury brands fail to make ethical grade'.[9] UN corporate reporting expert Dr Anthony Miller commented that the luxury goods industry looked like it was 'having its own Nike moment', referring to the mid-90s criticism of labour practices in Nike's supply chain which made the company invest heavily in its corporate responsibility programme.[10] FashionUK commented the report 'could herald a huge change in the way global luxury brands operate'.[11]

Leading industry executives speaking at the *International Herald Tribune* (*IHT*) conference on luxury, in Moscow, on the day of the report's launch, portrayed a growing awareness of the importance of ethical performance. Laurence Graff, chairman of Graff Diamonds, and Yves Carcelle, chairman and chief executive of Louis Vuitton, spoke positively of their companies' responsibilities. Tom Ford, the former Gucci top designer, said that 'we need to replace hollow with deep'.[12] However, in Condé Nast Portfolio.com, Lauren Goldstein Crowe contrasted 'The Words v. the Reality', citing the WWF-UK report as an opportunity for needed leadership on this agenda.[13]

The industry response to the report was mixed. Within days, Just-Style.com reported that 'PPR Group commits to improving sustainability' as a result of the publication.[14] Pierre Simoncelli, Managing Director of Sustainable Development at L'Oréal, which owns luxury brands such as Ralph Lauren and Giorgio Armani, said the report 'demonstrates that a quality product must involve a quality value chain, where everyone in that chain benefits and their environment is sustained. Bendell and Kleanthous' analysis should be welcomed as an important contribution to the strategic planning of all high-end brands and their suppliers.' However, the director of the Council for Responsible Jewellery Practices was not pleased, slamming the report for what he saw as its negative tone.[15] WWF-UK's co-author of the report Anthony Kleanthous explained in the *Guardian* that, although 'press coverage has focused on the ranking, and on what these companies are failing to do right for the environment . . . the main thrust of the report looks to a future in which the very definition of luxury deepens to include not only technical and aesthetic quality, but also environmental and social responsibility'.[16]

The longest chapter focuses on commercial reasons for that new approach to luxury. It examines key challenges facing the industry and suggests that greater depth and authenticity is a strategic response. These challenges include modern technology, which means that what's on the catwalk today can be copied and in high-street retailers within weeks, and growing levels of counterfeiting—both of which, the report suggests, require brands to offer something deeper than purely appearance. Sales growth in societies with high social inequality means that luxury brands face a crisis of legitimacy and a regulatory backlash, the report says, so their products will increasingly need to benefit the local economy with good jobs. The more youthful profile of luxury consumers worldwide means luxury brands need to find ways to build in value to casual fashion items, without making them non-casual, with sustainability and ethics an obvious approach, the authors contend. The report also argues that the increasing availability of luxury items means that brands must find new ways of maintaining their cachet, rather than relying on the memory they were once scarce and exclusive, and that superior social and environmental performance is a way to restore that cachet. The report therefore offers a business case for responsible enterprise that does not depend solely on levels of consumer awareness. The consulting firm hired by WWF to research and co-write the report, Lifeworth, subsequently launched the Authentic Luxury Network to bring together executives, designers, analysts and entrepreneurs who want to lead the creation of more sustainable and ethical luxury.[17]

The scale of the environmental challenge is so great and pressing, and the reach of NGOs into Asian societies currently so limited, that, if the brands that affluent Asians esteem can excel in sustainability, then awareness of sustainable living may grow in emerging economies fast enough to curb global consumption and pollution within environmental limits. Other efforts to promote that awareness are growing. For instance, the Malaysian government embraced the concept of eco-fashion and luxury, through the launch of the ecoStyle awards, with entertainment company IMG. The award was established to honour several leading international designers, acknowledging their efforts to present stylish sustainable initiatives and opportunities to the world. Nominees included Anna Cohen, Q Collection furniture, Stella McCartney and Terra Plana footwear. In December the winner, Dr Ken Yeang, a leading green architect, was announced at the ecoStyle Gala event in Kuala Lumpur.[18]

Outsourcing intellects

Perhaps sensing this growing attention to luxury ethics, in November 2007 the *Harvard Business Review* provided an in-depth case study on the commercial pros and cons of outsourcing the production of a fictional British luxury brand, which in many respects mirrored the situation with Burberry.[19] That British luxury apparel company had previously raised some concerns in the industry and with unions when it closed its Welsh factory in Treochy earlier in 2007 as it moved more of its production to Asia.[20]

Case studies have long been recognised as useful teaching aids for the way they can encourage debate and reflection. After the fictional case *HBR* included the feedback from four different fashion industry experts. However, what was surprising was that all commentators agreed about the commercial imperative of outsourcing production to places with cheaper labour. Research by marketing agencies, cited in the *Deeper Luxury* report, suggests that there are strong commercial reasons for luxury brands to maintain high labour standards throughout their supply chain wherever they source from, as well as maintaining a significant proportion of their workforce in the country associated with their brand. Affluent Asian consumers do not expect an expensive British brand to be made in factories on the outskirts of their own cities. 'Brand-savvy consumers in India and China are not happy to pay for a premium label assembled in their own backyard,' reported the fashion chronicler *Monocle*.[21] This is one reason why the Chinese owners of MG Cars are investing in British production. The debate over 'Made in Italy' sparked by Rai 3 also illustrates awareness of the importance of providence, but also the importance of maintaining what values and practices a region is meant to embody. Luxury brands involve building in value to the product more than taking out cost. If luxury industry executives are blinkered by mainstream management models into simple cost-cutting strategies, then they may be liquidating the cultural capital of the brand: its heritage and its current contribution to society.

Although the importance of providence and country of origin is being recognised as important in the high-end marketplace, economic globalisation is doing more than shift the geographies of production beneath the brand. They are also shifting the geographies of ownership. This is not new. For instance, Gucci has not been owned by Italians since the early 1990s, but by Arabs, and then the French group PPR, while the British luxury brand Mulberry, known for its attention to heritage and British values, is owned by Singaporean billionaire Christina Ong. In addition to MG Cars being owned by a Chinese firm, Lotus Cars has been owned by the Malaysian firm Proton for many years. Despite this, towards the end of 2007 some high-end brand managers expressed concern over takeovers by firms from the global South. There were debates about the effect on brand value, management and employment practice of Tata taking over Jaguar Cars. Then the management of Orient-Express gave a snooty response to interest from Tata's hotel business.[22] Tata Hotels then protested to the Securities and Exchange Commission for what they called Orient-Express's 'fossilised thinking'.[23] As this globalisation of owner-ship continues, so high-end brands will be less able to rely on consumers' assumptions that the national identity of a brand defines its quality and style. The values beneath those national identities will need uncovering and upholding.

Sustaining conversation

Also in November 2007, *The A to Z of Corporate Social Responsibility* was published, including over 300 entries spanning 544 pages.[24] A useful resource, it also high-lights the growth in terminology concerning companies' relations with society. Some of the most frequent terms used in the West in the last two decades feature: such as environmental management, sustainability, stakeholders, corporate social responsibility, corporate accountability and corporate citizenship. As our 2006 annual review identified, the meeting of people and organisations in discussion about CSR is a phenomenon that could tip cognitive frames about the role of business in society, so definitions are important. The concept of 'luxury' was identi-fied at the top of a pyramid of cognitive frames about progress and quality that influence the business environment and need to change as part of a cultural shift towards sustainability.

One term that began being used quite extensively during 2007—sustainable enterprise—does not appear in the *A to Z*. In 2007, conferences in California and Cornwall employed the theme.[25] The University of North Carolina has established a Center for Sustainable Enterprise, as has the Stuart Graduate School of Business,[26] while Cornell University now has a Center for Sustainable *Global* Enterprise.[27] Coventry University, UK, is launching an MA in Sustainable Enterprise, and at the British House of Lords, 'The Roundtable in Sustainable Enterprise' met throughout 2007 to discuss policy innovations.[28] The buzz continued in 2008 with the Impact Conference *Leadership for Sustainable Enterprise* in June.[29]

The growing popularity of the term reflects a number of trends. First, that cor-porate responsibility is still often regarded as, and practised as, corporate phi-lanthropy, whether by its advocates or critics. Commentators from McKinsey, Foundation Strategy Group Advisors and the Eden Project, among others, often describe a 'straw man' of CR as a form of guilty philanthropy that can distract us from the commercial opportunities in addressing societal needs.

Second, that corporate citizenship has become an unclear term more of intel-lectual discussion than practical use. It was promoted in the late 1990s as a way of emphasising corporate leadership in addressing societal problems, helping move the focus away from internal operational responsibilities to a broader focus on part-nerships.[30] The notion of it actually describing corporations behaving as citizens, and thus as members of political communities that govern their rights and free-doms, has not taken off in the business world, although it remains in civil society, academia and policy fields as 'corporate accountability'.[31] The term has now been further elaborated and reworked to suggest that, as people are dependent on corporations for the realisation of their rights as citizens, we are somehow in an era of corporate citizenship.[32] The debate about problems with corporates having rights in US courts of law and in some international trade agreements complicates this further, and thus the term is not as widely used in the business world.

A third reason is the upsurge in interest in entrepreneurship coming from California. That interest is backed by billionaires in their thirties, who founded companies such as eBay, Google, MySpace, etc. They have poured funds into projects and people that use entrepreneurial approaches to solve social problems. The term being used by groups such as the Skoll Foundation and Schwab Foundation to describe this approach is 'social enterprise'. Some use the term purely to describe for-profit enterprises and entrepreneurs that solve social problems. Others make no distinction between whether the enterprises are for-profit, not-for-profit or charitable. This leads to a situation where people who would previously have identified themselves as activist, or community worker, now win prizes as social entrepreneurs. The pen is mightier than the sword, when signing cheques. Muddying the distinction between those who use market approaches but do not seek to make profits for shareholders, and those who do, will only be useful to the latter—and their investors. The focus on and excitement with enterprise is, however, relevant, as it reminds us of the transformative role of disruptive innovations that move markets to new patterns of social provision and power relation.

Fourth, the resurgence of interest in the environment and how the commercial implications of this are now clear, with vast amounts of money flowing into environmental technologies. Consequently, 'sustainable enterprise' appears to capture the new mood. A definition might be: sustainable enterprise describes innovative commercial activity that generates sustainable development. Expect to see it in the second edition of the *A to Z*. Also expect to see debates, papers and perhaps even conferences about the difference between 'social enterprise' and 'sustainable enterprise'. Then expect to see CSR champions who want some of that enterprise buzz rebranding themselves as working in 'responsible enterprise'. While we are at it, let us offer a definition: 'responsible enterprise' describes innovative commercial activity that actively considers its social and environmental effects; it may help resolve social problems or promote sustainable development but the foremost purpose is commercial.

That is not to be facetious, but to recall the use, power and limitations of language. Terms that become popular—as 'social enterprise' is, and 'sustainable enterprise' is becoming—are useful as they help convene people to share ideas. Hundreds of people conferencing in rural Cornwall in October 2007 are a reminder of that. The emphasis on enterprise is useful, as it is hopeful and encourages a practical and action-oriented focus. Yet the power of language is also to exclude. Thus, growing attention on social and sustainable enterprise may draw attention away from how to deal with unsustainable and anti-social enterprise, and how to address challenges that cannot be solved through the marketplace, let alone the system of wealth accumulation and financing known as capitalism. Issues of governance and power may be marginalised by the concept, yet working for policy frameworks that guide innovation and profit seeking towards more socially and environmentally appropriate activities is important.

Just as a map is not the terrain, language is not the reality it describes but a reality of its own. Words are our choices about how we wish to conceive of the world. French painter Georges Braque once said, 'to define a thing is to substitute the definition for the thing itself'.[33] That is not inevitable but a risk. Intellectual debate and teaching can be constrained by not seeing beyond the words used. Critical discourse analysis, the deconstruction of the meanings in terms and the power relations they embody and exert, can help us to see through words; but this analysis needs to be connected to and integrated with practical experiences of the matters at hand if not to be lost in itself.

When looking at the issues discussed in the name of sustainable enterprise, what is new? At the Eden Project in October 2007, Professor Malcolm McIntosh, from the Applied Research Centre in Human Security at Coventry University, explained, 'this conference is about hope and excitement'. Stories from successful entrepreneurs such as Cate Le Grice Mack, founder of Norwood Rare Breeds Organic Farm, enthused the participants. Representatives from larger corporations, such as Phil Smith of CISCO systems, explained how a commitment to sustainability helped energise their staff. The existence of a niche for eco-products and of a motivation-based business case for large corporations is not new. Neither is the disbelief from informed delegates when they hear speakers such as James Smith, chairman of Shell UK, saying 'sustainability can't be bolted on. It has to be part of the core business strategy' during his opening address. Shell's core strategy is investing in high-technology approaches to access unconventional or difficult-to-reach fossil fuels. Discussions revealed a split of opinion between those calling for fundamental change to match the size of the problem and others who backed incremental steps to achieve the same goals. It's a debate that has raged throughout human history, and been a fault line between those working towards more mandatory corporate and capital accountability and those who propose more active responsibility.

The event closed with Tim Smit, co-founder of the Eden Project, boldly stating that 'within 30 years almost every major company will be a social enterprise'. Whatever the changes in business culture and regulation in the coming decades, it is likely we will witness a new buzz term before then. New terminology may sustain a conversation, but not necessarily a change. Whatever people label people in future, let's hope it empowers us all to act.

Silence is golden

Also in October 2007, a conference was held at INSEAD outside Paris to discuss the findings of a major EU-funded study on corporate responsibility that had been coordinated by the European Academy of Business in Society (EABIS). It focused on the extent of alignment between stakeholders' views and demands for corporate responsibility and companies' own views on that and whether more alignment correlated with business performance.[34] The summary report concluded, 'those that have established processes for managing dialogue with their stakeholders are no more likely to have achieved high levels of alignment than those that take a more ad hoc approach to monitoring and responding to external concerns. Stakeholder engagement is an established touchstone of CSR best practice—but could it really be that it is a waste of everybody's time?' The overarching finding was that positive stakeholder relations are important to business performance and that these cannot be achieved by processes such as structured stakeholder dialogues but perhaps by aligning core business with the interests of the most stakeholders. If companies are naturally aware of societal challenges, then stakeholders will not complain, and costly add-on initiatives to engage them beyond the normal course of business will not be required. In a free society, stakeholder silence is golden. The findings were not entirely new, but the fact of an EU-backed project involving esteemed management institutions and a large data set to back up the conclusions will be useful to champions of real change in corporations to create business models that benefit a broader set of stakeholders.

The report and conference discussed implications of these findings. One insight was that fewer resources should be paid to formal stakeholder dialogues and more attention to creating organisational cultures and systems that reconnect staff with their communities and personal values, so that they can organically innovate new business models that are inherently more aligned with societal needs. One limitation in both the report and conference appeared during the discussion of how non-business stakeholders could change in light of the research.

The study is limited in its understanding of the stakeholder universe and this impairs its conclusions. A key limitation is in understanding the strategies of non-governmental organisations. For instance, the report recommends that, as 'companies with high alignment are more often found in countries, industries and competitive niches characterised by rapid change than by those where business models and social norms are more stable', so NGOs should focus their engagement with these companies. That might make sense for market researchers but NGOs often choose to focus on the companies that are most resistant to change, and seek to create contexts that will shift them, deciding who to focus on for broader concerns about what will drive social change. The WWF work on the luxury sector discussed earlier is a case in point. Another example of a mistaken assumption about NGOs is that they will decide to invest their resources in better engaging in internal change dynamics of companies. The report says NGOs 'need to substantially upgrade their understanding of corporate processes and their skills in coordinating and cooperating to drive and support internal change'. However, NGOs will need to assess whether CR will deliver a sufficient scale and pace of social change compared to other activities they could be involved in, such as lobbying for regulation, before deciding to invest in such skill development. Some would argue that if business wants these changes then they can pay consultants. NGOs' management would also assess whether investing in such skills relates to their own business model in terms of maintaining a distinctive role in society that will attract sufficient media attention to generate public and donor support. Calling on pensioners to donate $10 a week to finance you being skilled at understanding accounting or marketing is not an easy sell.

A second key limitation of the Response study's understanding of stakeholders is that it does not account for differing states of civil society across Europe. In Eastern Europe the history of civil society is very different from the West; so not finding dissonance in expectations of stakeholders and companies there is a function of a relative lack of a tradition of independent informed critical civil society and media.

These mistakes are inevitable given that stakeholders were treated as sources of data not objects of study, nor played any role in guiding the objectives of the inquiry. It is ironic that a research project about stakeholder engagement had no real stakeholder engagement in its design, governance or assessment. It is also ironic that one of the conclusions of the report is the importance of managers developing social consciousness (through various relaxation techniques), and thus an ability to appreciate interconnections and different points of view. What is the social consciousness of EABIS and the research partners? Asking for data from stakeholders and then chatting together about it in the safety of an elite management institution, pontificating on what the implications might be for stakeholders? That would appear to manifest a hierarchical and protective mind-set, rather than an open and boundary-crossing consciousness, which would involve recognising the equal dignity and autonomy of others, not just their relevance to you and your employers.

To include stakeholders will require not only humility but a preparedness for discomfort in grappling with insights from interdisciplinary areas such as development and civil society studies, which more effectively integrate sociology and political science with the traditional theoretical bases of management studies. EABIS could make a start by commissioning a stakeholder assessment of the implications and limitations of the study, with sociology, political science and development studies specialists in support, and then base a research project on the findings. They might also assess what stakeholders could get from EABIS and what they could bring, and consider changes to organisation membership and governance as a result.

The Response project has been important in suggesting CR should not be a practice, a profession, a department, but that companies can evolve so all staff in all departments consider both financial and societal value. We need top-to-bottom sustainable enterprises. Oops, it's that term again.

2008

2008: Introduction

Jem Bendell and Chew Ng

Talking turns

An important shift in power in past years, now hastened by the economic crisis that began in 2008, has been away from the Western world, towards the rest of the world, including the East. That shift compounds a turning towards the East that is evident in how business impacts on society, and vice versa. 'Responsible enterprise' is commercial activity that voluntarily considers its social and environmental effects.[1] The relationship between business and society is ubiquitous in relevance around the world, and so we may surmise that the 'Eastern Turn' in world power will be reflected in responsible enterprise issues, initiatives, and analysis.

Investigating this 'Eastern Turn' in responsible enterprise, we feel like the poet W.B. Yeats, who described the essence of Asia as its 'vague immensities'. We are, after all, speaking of a region with the majority of our world's people. However we think it an important shift to chronicle, and to encourage debate about, as we believe it has implications for how we achieve a fair and sustainable world through more conscious approaches to enterprise and finance. We aim to describe some aspects of this Eastern Turn, and some implications that are beginning to appear for business, civil society and government from different directions of the compass. In doing so, we intend to stimulate debate about the future of sustainable and responsible enterprise in a multi-polar world.

By speaking of 'East' we are describing the Middle East, Asia and the Asia-Pacific region (not yet including Australia and New Zealand, due to the dominance of 'Western culture' in their recent history). In this introduction we briefly describe the global power shift to Asia and the importance of the region for global sustainable development and, therefore, global responsible enterprise. We note a historical Western dominance in Corporate Responsibility (CR), before discussing the rise of responsible enterprise challenges within Asia, due to domestic changes, and in the world that involve Asian firms and investors. In doing so we refer to events during 2008 that highlight these challenges. Then we focus in more detail on the rise of responsible enterprise practices and initiatives within Asia. We describe how Asia has become the leader in environmental management systems and sustainability reporting. Next, we examine the extent to which business studies has analysed related issues, and find that there has been a rise in academic attention to Asia in journals dealing with aspects of responsible enterprise and finance. We then reflect on the nature of corporate responsibility issues and initiatives in different parts of Asia, and the extent to which an Asian agenda is emerging, could emerge, and what the implications could be for how that process occurs.

Our main conclusion is that diverse Asian approaches to responsible enterprise will increasingly affect business practices around the globe. We argue that not only can this development be welcomed, but it is essential to achieve a fair and sustainable world, and now is an important moment for people interested in business–society relations to engage in elaborating greater understanding about Asian approaches to responsible enterprise and finance. We call for further democratising of the way the Asian responsible enterprise community of practitioners, policy-makers and experts are developing their own agendas, and warn of some of the cultural challenges for professionals in both the East and West. We conclude by returning to the fundamental reflections about economic systems that the financial crisis is provoking, and suggest that key Eastern liberation leaders could offer us some insight into forms of political-economic system fit for a fair and sustainable world, as well as the way to bring them into being.

The power shift

The years of growth of technology and industry across many parts of Asia has created a new level of economic power. Being so populous, half of the largest 10 private employers of the world are from Asia.[2] Asia's foreign currency reserves are around US$4 trillion, well over half the world's total.[3] The Gross Domestic Product (GDP) of Asia is about US$14 trillion, overtaking that of the US, with Asia's share in world merchandise exports standing at 27.9%, up from 19.1% in 1983. In 2008, the majority of Asia's trade was, for the first time in modern economic history, within Asia.[4] Also that year was the first time that the number of middle class people in Asia exceeded that in the West.[5]

The power shift was symbolised in March 2008 when Indian conglomerate Tata completed its purchase of British car brands Jaguar and Land Rover.[6] That stimulated debate about the loss of British iconic brands to the East. That acquisition was simply the latest in a trend over many years that has seen luxury car company Lotus bought by a Malaysian firm, and the luxury fashion firm Mulberry bought by a Singaporean firm, to name just two famed British brands. In sport, the purchase of Manchester City football club by a Thai businessman and former prime minister, then sale in 2008 to a member of the Royal Family from Abu Dhabi, further highlighted the changing global economy.[7] This shift also extends to technology innovations, as highlighted by the data on internet traffic. In 1999, 91% of data from Asia passed through the United States at some point on its journey. By 2008 that number had fallen to 54%.[8]

The financial crisis beginning in 2008 gave this power shift a further push, because at root it is a Western financial crisis, and although the ripples spread around the world, it was the West's financial institutions and governments who were most affected through a loss of capital and confidence (see 'The end of financial triumphalism', page 197). As the BBC economics editor described it, 'the credit crunch is creating a new world order in banking and finance . . . It's a world in which the Chinese state, if it coordinated the investments of its cash-rich institutions, could end up owning more-or-less the entire financial system of the US and the UK.'[9] The implications of the financial crisis was something we paid much attention to in our analysis during 2008, in sections titled 'The end of financial triumphalism' (page 197), 'Beyond the Western financial crisis' (page 202), 'Islamic finance' (page 209) and 'Sovereign wealth fund responsibility' (page 212). The political philosopher John Gray, summed up some implications of the crisis in *The Observer* in September 2008:

> Here is a historic geopolitical shift, in which the balance of power in the world is being altered irrevocably . . . The era of American global leadership, reaching back to the Second World War, is over . . . The American free-market creed has self-destructed while countries that retained overall control of markets have been vindicated . . . In a change as far-reaching in its implications as the fall of the Soviet Union, an entire model of government and the economy has collapsed . . . .How symbolic that Chinese astronauts take a spacewalk while the US Treasury Secretary is on his knees.[10]

The following month Professor Gray might also have mentioned India launching their first lunar mission, to further illustrate that the shift is beyond the economic.[11] Mark Leonard, with the European Council for Foreign Relations, said in June 2008 that 'it's not just economic and military power that's shifting from West to East. China is emerging as an intellectual power. It's coming up with its own ideas, which are very influential, which other people are copying.' He explained to policy makers in the West that 'the debate we're having about managing China's rise has got a mirror image in China, where they're having an argument about how to manage the West's decline.'[12] Writing in his book before the financial crisis broke, in early 2008, Kishore Mahbubani notes that 'for centuries, the Asians (Chinese, Indians, Muslims, and others) have been bystanders in world history. Now they are ready to become co-drivers.'[13] The need to convene a Group of 20 of the world's largest nations, rather than a G7 or G8, as in previous years, further highlights the historic shift.

These economic changes will also impact on development cooperation because of the changing budgets of governments, and of civil society in general, due to the shifting incomes of middle classes worldwide.[14] Given the role of development cooperation and of civil society campaigning in shaping corporate responsibility agendas, this is likely to be significant for the future of responsible enterprise, something we return to below.

Another dimension to the shift is cultural. The Malaysian politician Anwar Ibrahim has often spoken of an 'Asian renaissance' that is emerging in line with new economic power and cultural confidence. 'By Asian renaissance we mean the revival of the arts and science under the influence of classical models based on strong moral and religious foundations; a cultural resurgence dominated by a reflowering of art and literature, architecture and music and advancements in science and technology,' he explains.[15] One indicator was that throughout 2008 art critics were reporting contemporary Chinese art as the hottest market in the art world.[16] Cultural confidence pervades people's identities and will therefore shape their assumptions and beliefs about the way enterprise should be conducted, amongst their other attitudes to life and work.

Ibrahim has noted how the shift in power has 'given rise to the self-induced fear on the part of the West that its civilisation is on the verge of being overwhelmed by a horde of marauding Asians'.[17] The concept of an inevitable 'clash of civilisations' between the West and East has been developed by some contemporary Western philosophers.[18] We believe that is a perspective arising from an ignorance of the diversity of Asian cultures and the interpolation between East and West through the ages. We also think it unhelpful in enabling the world to come together to face common global challenges such as climate change. But nor do we think the rise of Asia is something for Asians to feel pride about. Power is not in itself a source of pride; the manner of its generation and application can be. There is no pride to be had in power derived from exploitation or unsustainable processes, or if used in irresponsible ways. With new found power comes new found responsibilities, which extend beyond traditional concerns for family, ethnicity, nation or region. 'Asians must not repeat the mistakes and excesses of the past inflicted upon them by multinational corporations,' asserts Anwar Ibrahim.[19] In this 2008 review we will explore how responsibilities are evolving in the business community in Asia.

The importance of Asia

Asia is the most important region of our world for achieving global well-being. One reason is simply the region we call Asia is where most of us live. That has implications for both consumption and creativity.

The Asia-Pacific region requires about 40% of the world's bio-productive capacity. China is the second greatest consumer in the world, using up 15% of the world's total biocapacity (although per capita basis it is 69th position in the world). China currently needs an equivalent land area of two Chinas to meet its needs and absorb its waste. If it were to follow the United States' example, where the per capita requirement is equivalent to 10 hectares, it would require the world's entire biocapacity.[20] Decisions made today about infrastructure and other aspects of economic development will determine the environmental demands and impacts of societies in Asia for decades to come.

In being so populous, Asia is also home to diverse societies, each with their own creativity and technological prowess. The challenges of resource scarcity, ecological degradation, climate change, as well as social challenges of non-communicable and infectious disease, mean that we need to draw upon the ingenuity of all the world's peoples. Commercially, Asia is no longer simply a region where resources and human labour can be sourced more cheaply than elsewhere. Instead, it is a place where engineers, scientists, programmers, and entrepreneurs are pushing the boundaries of their professions.

Another reason for the importance of Asia to global well-being arises from its reach around the world. Companies from China, India, Indonesia and Malaysia, are investing in business across the world, in Asia, Africa and Latin America, as well as the West. For example, bilateral trade between China and Africa exceeded US$100 billion in 2008 (see 'Beyond the Western financial crisis', page 202). This trade and investment presents many opportunities for everyone concerned, but also problems in terms of negative impacts on certain stakeholders and the environment, as we discuss next.

The Rise of Asian responsible enterprise challenges

Responsible enterprise challenges are emerging in Asia and in the rest of the world due to the activities of Asian firms. Such challenges arise because of the impacts of economic activity, but also because of changes in society that affect the way people view companies and their ability to engage with them.

Within Asia, economic development has brought many gains as well as new problems. The environment has become a major concern across many parts of Asia in recent years. A report from the UN in 2008 mapped the scale of the pollution problem and its implications for human health. The brownish haze, sometimes more than a mile thick and visible from aeroplanes, stretches from the Arabian Peninsula to the Yellow Sea. The UN report identified 13 cities as brown-cloud hot spots, among them Bangkok, Cairo, New Delhi, Tehran and Seoul. It also demonstrated how 'atmospheric brown clouds' are dramatically reducing sunlight in many Chinese cities and leading to decreased crop yields in rural India. The impact on public health is significant. '340,000 people in China and India die each year from cardiovascular and respiratory diseases that can be traced to the emissions from coal-burning factories, diesel trucks and wood-burning stoves,' reported the *New York Times*.[21]

Research done by marketing agencies during 2008 tell us that this pollution is leading to high levels of local environmental concern. Agencies of the marketing services company WPP Group found that Chinese consumers see the environment as a higher priority than do their US and UK counterparts. 31% of Chinese consumers told them that the environment was a higher priority than the economy, compared to 28% in the UK. The French market research agency Institut Français d'Opinion Publique et d'études de marché (IFOP) found similar results, with a higher percentage of Chinese, Indian and Japanese respondents saying they were very concerned about environmental problems than people from the US or Western Europe (Fig. 5). Sixty-nine per cent of Chinese respondents to WPP's research said that they expected to spend more on environmentally friendly products in the next year. Sixty per cent said they think about the environment when they shop. IFOP found more Chinese consumers thought the environment is important or essential to consider when they shop than US, Italian or French respondents (Fig. 6). The way different respondents understand the concept of 'the environment', for instance whether it relates to personal health or public good, would have an impact on responses, as well as cultural influences when being surveyed, and so more analysis is required.[22] However, these research findings indicate that environmental awareness exists in Asia, and connections can be made to consumer behaviour, thus constituting a local business case to address sustainability issues within Asia.

Figure 5: **IFOP Research on comparative environmental concern**

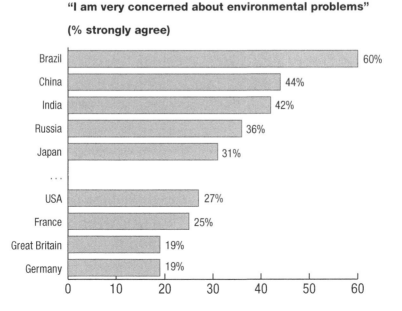

"I am very concerned about environmental problems"

(% strongly agree)

Figure 6: **IFOP Research on comparative consumer environmental concern**

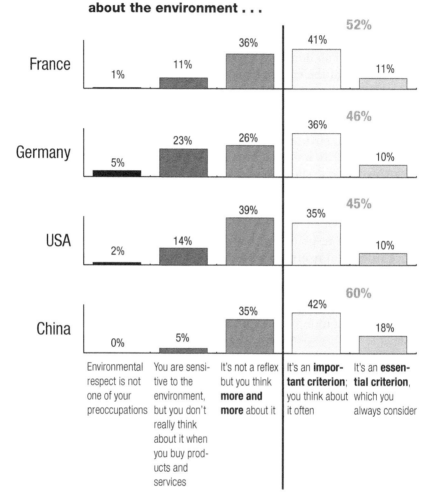

When you buy a product or a service, would you say, about the environment . . .

	Environmental respect is not one of your preoccupations	You are sensitive to the environment, but you don't really think about it when you buy products and services	It's not a reflex but you think **more and more** about it	It's an **important criterion**; you think about it often	It's an **essential criterion**, which you always consider
France	1%	11%	36%	41%	11% (52%)
Germany	5%	23%	26%	36%	10% (46%)
USA	2%	14%	39%	35%	10% (45%)
China	0%	5%	35%	42%	18% (60%)

The speed of economic development, as well as changes in traditional political systems and cultural norms, has contributed to a growth in corruption across Asia—a key responsible enterprise challenge (see 'Olympian graft', page 170). The exporting of corruption across Asia, as businessmen bribe politicians in other Asian countries, reached extreme and blatant levels during 2008, with the exposure of arrangements that were being made between Chinese businessmen and the husband of the Philippine President Gloria Arroyo (see 'Foreign direct corruption', page 172).

Economic development has also brought changes in social life, generating problems typical in higher-income societies such as obesity. In Kuwait, almost three-quarters of the population above 15 years old are overweight or obese, the eighth worst rate in the world. Not far behind are the United Arab Emirates, Saudi Arabia, Bahrain and Qatar, according to the World Health Organisation. The causes are increased wealth, so people have access to household help, motorised transport and a carbohydrate-rich diet. The impacts of this affluence are costly. Only the Pacific island of Nauru has a higher diabetes rate than the United Arab Emirates. Already food companies are being asked to provide healthier options. For instance, food engineers at Al Islami Foods, a halal foods company based in Dubai, were reported in the middle of 2008 to have been working on reducing carbohydrates and fat in their chicken burgers, sausages and sandwiches.[23]

As mentioned earlier, estimates in the *Economist* suggest that sometime in 2008 the number of middle-class people in Asia exceeded that in the West.[24] The economic definition of *middle class* concerns the percentage of one's expenditure that is entirely discretionary. A middle class can therefore be more discerning consumers, creating a direct driver of responsible enterprise. In addition, middle-class people have more disposable income to donate to common causes, thereby supporting a professional civil society, and can consume more media services, thereby stimulating civil discourse. Recognising the growth in giving, RBS Coutts launched a philanthropy advisory service for Asian donors in 2008.[25] The terrible Sichuan earthquake on May 12 led to many Chinese people giving to relief charities for the first time. In time the increased levels of philanthropy might lead to a more vocal civil society, in which case they may express opinions on matters of responsible enterprise that relate to their organisational mandates.

A range of Asian responsible enterprise challenges are arising due to the operations of Asian firms in other parts of Asia and around the world.[26] For instance, although Chinese investment in Africa is helping finance new infrastructure, it raises concerns about corrupt payments, and the knock-on effects on effective and accountable governance (see 'Beyond the Western financial crisis', page 202).

Western corporate responsibility professionals have been waking up to the global implications of a new era of Asian commercial power. They realise that unless Asian firms embrace their corporate responsibilities then in a global market the efforts to promote responsible enterprise in the West will be futile. At the first European conference of the corporate responsibility association, Net Impact, Simon Zadek told the audience that the important corporations on the world stage now include those from Brazil, Russia, India and China, and that engaging them is a central challenge for people interested in making an impact on corporate responsibility (see 'Movement East', page 189).

During 2008, Lifeworth Consulting conducted a survey of the 4,000 subscribers to their bulletin, asking about their view of the future of research needs on responsible business. Respondents considered that the most important regions for future research are in Asia. Other regions with emerging nations were also ranked highly, as shown by Figure 8, in the section 'Movement East' (page 190).

The Rise of responsible enterprise initiatives within Asia

The contemporary era of research, practice, and education on matters of corporate responsibility has been dominated by the West. Transnational Corporations (TNCs), non-governmental organisations (NGOs), consulting firms and academic institutions from Europe and North America have led the agenda, amidst strong domestic drivers for voluntary corporate responses to societal issues, including consumer awareness, independent media, active civil society and an ambivalence towards government intervention. Changes are afoot. In the past years not only have Asian responsible enterprise challenges grown, but also Asian responsible enterprise initiatives, according to a report for the UN Conference on Trade and Development in November 2008, by the ethical investment research organisation EIRIS.[27]

In 2008, there were dozens of conferences on corporate responsibility across the region, indicating at least an enthusiasm for discussing the topic. The IBM study of CEOs found that Asian respondents placed higher importance on their social responsibilities than those from other regions (see 'Movement East', page 189). Corporate responsibility reporting is another indicator. At the CSR Asia Summit in Bangkok, Leontien Plugge, of the Global Reporting Initiative (GRI), highlighted that Asia is now the second largest reporting region, with an exceptionally high rate of sustainability reporting in Japan. Our analysis of Asian companies reporting in accordance with GRI guidelines since 1999, is shown in Table 9. It shows that of the 20 Asian countries with companies reporting to GRI standards, 12 began reporting in the last four years (Cambodia, Indonesia, Israel, Jordan, Pakistan, Palestine, Philippines, Saudi Arabia, Singapore, Thailand, Turkey and UAE). Reporting levels in Asia in 2008 were up 133% on the previous year. As some Asian governments and stock exchanges announced in 2007 that they will introduce requirements to report on corporate sustainability and responsibility, reporting rates are set to increase further (see 'From CSR in Asia to Asian CSR', page 217).

Table 9: **Asian company GRI Reports since 1999**

Country	1999	2000	2001	2002	2003	2004	2005	2006	2007	2008
Bangladesh	0	0	0	0	1	0	0	1	0	0
Cambodia	0	0	0	0	0	0	0	1	0	0
China	0	0	1	4	1	3	4	5	4	14
India	0	0	1	4	1	5	3	6	5	16
Indonesia	0	0	0	0	0	0	0	2	3	7
Israel	0	0	0	0	0	0	2	0	3	4
Japan	1	7	23	17	14	20	20	17	15	47
Jordan	0	0	0	0	0	0	0	0	1	1
Malaysia	0	0	0	1	1	1	0	1	1	4
Pakistan	0	0	0	0	0	0	0	0	1	1
Palestine	0	0	0	0	0	0	0	0	1	0
Philippines	0	0	0	0	0	0	1	1	1	5
Republic of Korea	0	0	0	0	2	4	7	14	26	35
Saudi Arabia	0	0	0	0	0	0	0	0	0	1
Singapore	0	0	0	0	0	0	0	0	0	2
Sri Lanka	0	0	1	0	0	0	0	1	0	0
Taiwan	0	0	0	1	0	0	0	1	0	6
Thailand	0	0	0	0	0	0	0	0	0	2
Turkey	0	0	0	0	0	0	1	0	0	0
United Arab Emirates	0	0	0	0	0	0	0	0	2	2
Total	**1**	**7**	**26**	**27**	**20**	**33**	**38**	**50**	**63**	**147**

Governments have been key to this increase in reporting. In general, the Eastern Turn in responsible enterprise is being encouraged by government policies. In 2008, Asian governments regularly announced new policies and regulations to promote change, from a new environmental tax in China,[28] to a new child-labour-free product label in India.[29]

The relative distribution of environmental management system certifications around the world is another indicator of the pursuit of responsible enterprise in different countries. By the end of 2007 there were 71,458 ISO 14001 certifications in the Far East (Table 10). That was 46% of certifications worldwide, up from 42% in 2005 and making it the leading region for total certifications. The number of certifications in the Far East was up from 46,844 in 2005, which is an increase of 52%, compared to an average increase worldwide of 39% on 2005 figures. This indicates the comparatively rapid uptake of ISO 14001 in Asia in recent years. The country with the most certifications in 2007 was China with 30,489, up by 240% on 2005, indicating a massive uptake of environmental management systems in China during the last few years. Japan and South Korea are also in the top 10 countries for ISO 14001 certifications (Fig. 7).[30]

Table 10: **Total ISO 14001 certifications in the Far East from December 2005 to December 2007**

Source: ISO, *The ISO Survey: 2007* (Geneva: ISO, 2008): 27.

Far East	Dec 2005		Dec 2006	Dec 2007
	Total	of which 14001:2004		
Bhutan	–	–	–	3
Brunei Darrusalam	4		4	4
Cambodia	1	–	2	2
China	12,683	1,385	18,842	30,489
Hong Kong, China	385	385	509	522
Macau, China	15	15	17	18
Taipei, Chinese	1,556	1,556	1,633	1,674
Fiji	1	–	–	–
Indonesia	430	252	369	625
Japan	23,466	10,576	22,593	27,955
Korea, Democratic People's Republic of	97	53	91	474
Korea, Republic of	4,955	3,692	5,893	6,392
Lao, People's Democratic Republic	–	–	–	1
Malaysia	694	246	593	667
Myanmar	3	3	–	1
Nepal	2	–	4	9
Papua New Guinea	4	4	3	4
Philippines	408	197	458	637
Samoa	1	–	1	1
Singapore	887	289	716	602
Thailand	1,120	51	1,369	1,020
Vanuatu	5	–	–	–
Vietnam	127	55	189	358

Figure 7: **Top countries for ISO 14001 certifications in December 2007**

Source: ISO, *The ISO Survey: 2007* (Geneva: ISO, 2008): 10.

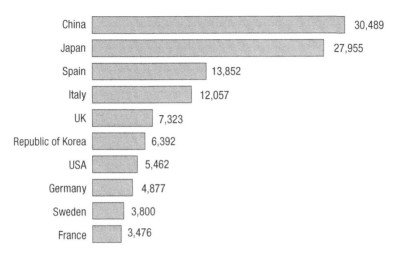

China	30,489
Japan	27,955
Spain	13,852
Italy	12,057
UK	7,323
Republic of Korea	6,392
USA	5,462
Germany	4,877
Sweden	3,800
France	3,476

A plethora of responsible enterprise institutes have emerged across Asia. Qatar CSR and CSR ASEAN were born in 2008, following the previous year when CSR Centre Bangladesh, CSR Kuwait and CSR Bahrain were established. CSR ASEAN is important given its international reach and connection with government. Established by the ASEAN Foundation, it brings together ten ASEAN countries.[31] A sample of Asia-based CSR initiatives and advisory services are listed in Table 11, showing the majority have been created in the last few years.

Table 11: **A selection of Asia-based CSR institutes**

Country	Institute	Founded	Website
Bahrain	CSR Bahrain	2007	www.bahraincsr.com
Bangladesh	CSR Centre	2007	www.csrcentre-bd.org
Hong Kong	Community Business	2003	www.communitybusiness.org.hk
India	Partners in Change	1995	www.picindia.org
India	Centre for Social Markets	2000	www.csmworld.org
Indonesia	CSR Indonesia	2006	www.csrindonesia.com
Kuwait	CSR Kuwait	2007	www.csrkuwait.com
Malaysia	Malaysian Institute of Corporate Governance	1998	www.micg.org.my/home.htm
PR China	Institute of Contemporary Observation	2001	www.ico-china.org

→

Country	Institute	Founded	Website
Philippines	League of Corporate Foundations	1991	www.lcf.org.ph
Qatar	Qatar CSR	2008	www.qatarcsr.net
Singapore	Singapore Compact	2004	www.csrsingapore.org
South Korea	Korea Labour Institute	1988	www.kli.re.kr
Thailand	NGO-Biz Network	2004	www.ngobiz.org
Various	CSR Asia	2004	www.csr-asia.com
Various	Robin Hood Asia	2003	www.robinhoodasia.com
Various	CSR ASEAN	2008	www.aseanfoundation.org/csr/index.php

There was also progress in responsible investment during 2008. Symbolically important, but also practically useful given the economic shifts discussed here, The UN Principles for Responsible Investment (UNPRI) held its 2008 annual meeting in South Korea. The UNPRI is the largest responsible investment initiative in the world, and the number of its Asian signatories has been growing rapidly in the past year.[32] Given the growth of interest in responsible investment in that country, UK-based EIRIS has partnered with KO-CSR of Korea to research Korean companies.

The emergence of a variety of responsible enterprise institutes and initiatives across the region could lead to a new wave of ideas and practices with the potential to influence international agendas. One example of innovation from the region is the new management and reporting tool 'imPACT'. This approach brings together dynamic stakeholder engagement with a new approach to communication. Developed jointly by Edelman and CSR Asia, the imPACT philosophy is based on the understanding that many companies face critical societal challenges which they can play a role in addressing through outcome-oriented partnerships. Thus, CSR actions can be mobilised around issues such as climate change, water, human rights, poverty alleviation or health, so that companies become partners in addressing public need, rather than making minor improvements on a diverse set of issues aimed to benefit corporate reputation. Emphasis is placed on shared responsibility and joint accountability with the other organisations and sectors with which a company engages (see 'From CSR in Asia to Asian CSR', page 217).

ImPACT arises due to a recognition of the nature of responsible enterprise challenges in Asia. The diverse cultural traditions of the region are also likely to give rise to more novel approaches. Today more Chinese leaders are speaking either overtly or implicitly about traditional Confucian and Taoist values. Some socially responsible entrepreneurs are even described as Confucian entrepreneurs (see 'Foreign direct corruption', page 172). The potential for philosophical traditions of Asia to encourage innovations in responsible enterprise and finance is something we return to in concluding our introduction.

Focusing on policies, partnerships, management systems and reports, as well as activities using the label 'corporate social responsibility', as indicators of positive contributions from business in society, can be misleading. Instead, the actual business activity is more revealing of the contribution to society. It is in this way that some Asian companies are in the vanguard of a fair and sustainable economy, through technological and business-process innovation.

Social enterprise—innovative commercial activity that seeks to solve social problems—has been growing in Asia. The level of activity was reflected in 2008, with the first Asia Social Entrepreneurs Summit (ASES) held in South Korea[33] and Singapore's Social Innovation Park organising their first Global Social Innovation Forum.[34] One of the longest-running initiatives to promote social enterprise is the Ashoka Foundation. Each year they select and fund Ashoka Fellows, as social entrepreneurs who 'have innovative solutions to social problems and the potential to change patterns across society'.[35] Asia is the region that has produced the most Ashoka Fellows (Table 12).

Table 12: **Regional Distribution of Ashoka Fellows**

Source: The Ashoka Fellows Database; www.ashoka.org/search/fellows, accessed April 2009

Region	Number of Ashoka Fellows
Africa	278
Asia (not including Middle East)	608
Europe	225
Middle East and North Africa	42
North America	279
South America	519

The potential for Asia to bring social enterprise to the world is illustrated by Nobel peace prize winner Muhammad Yunus and the Grameen Bank. Created 30 years ago to provide micro loans to groups of women in Bangladesh to help them achieve economic self reliance, the bank now has 7.34 million active borrowers, 97% of whom are women. Since its inception, the bank has distributed about US$6.55 billion in loans with a 98% recovery rate.[36] One unusual feature of the Grameen Bank is that it is owned by the poor borrowers of the bank, most of whom are women. Of the total equity of the bank, the borrowers own 94%, and the remaining 6% is owned by the Government of Bangladesh.[37] In 2008 the bank began making micro-finance loans in the United States, and has already lent about US$1.5 million to more than 600 people in Queens, New York. Yunus explains 'we're not a "third world" bank but a good bank coming to America.'[38]

One area requiring sustainable innovation is personal transportation. In 2008, *Newsweek* reported that the largest electric car company in the world is Reva

Electric Car Company from Bangalore, India, which produces the G-Wiz.[39] It now faces competition from BYD Auto, a Chinese automobile manufacturer based in Shenzhen, China.[40] It is part of the BYD Company Limited, which makes 65% of the world's nickel-cadmium batteries and 30% of the world's lithium-ion mobile phone batteries. With this experience and capacity, BYD Auto has been making strides in the provision of electric and dual-fuel automobiles. On 15 December 2008, BYD launched their new mid size F6 sedan, which uses iron-phosphate based battery, and can be recharged to 70% of capacity in 10 minutes at special stations, and in a number of hours through normal electric plugs. The cost effective manufacturing capacities in Shenzhen mean that unlike other car companies BYD can produce most of the components in its cars itself, such as the air-conditioning, lights, seat-belts and electronics.[41] Consequently, it can offer its electric cars for US$22,000— far less than the electric cars being made in the West. The company seeks to become the top car company in the world, and attracted interest from Warren Buffett, who in 2008 bought a 10% share of the company for US$230 million. Far on the other side of Asia, an Israeli company is innovating solutions to the infrastructure problem which holds back the uptake of electric vehicles. Better Place is building a huge network of charging points and battery swapping systems in a number of countries, including Israel and Australia, to enable existing car companies to offer electric models that are compatible with the system. They are innovating a new business model where consumers will pay for the mileage they drive, and thus car producers will earn revenues from the amount of charging their customers use. This parallels the business models of manufacturers of mobile phones and computer printers.[42] As car companies in the US struggle and require government support, the dawn of a new era of transportation is appearing in the East.

Nevertheless, sustainable innovation within Asia often involves Western enterprise and finance. Both Better Place and BYD have drawn upon western capital and technologies. In 2008, the power company NorthWind added five new turbines to the Bangui village wind farm in Ilocos Norte province, northern Philippines, raising its capacity to 33 MW, enabling the company to provide half the province's power needs. NorthWind is the result of Danish engineering, with support from the Danish International Development Agency (Danida), the Philippines' almost infinite coastline, and the World Bank's Prototype Carbon Fund (PCF), which enables NorthWind to sell 'carbon emission reduction credits' under the Clean Development Mechanism (CDM) of the Kyoto Protocol.[43] Sustainable innovations in Asia will continue to benefit from East–West exchange. That is important, as the evidence from just these two areas of mobility and banking-the-poor highlight how the world can benefit from the rise of Asian responsible enterprise.

The Eastern Turn in academe

As in most areas of academia, the English language predominates in the field of research on responsible enterprise and finance. Many of the journals in related fields, such as corporate governance, business ethics and environmental management, originate from Western institutions and convene editorial and review boards of Western academics. As a result we might expect such journals to provide relatively more coverage of Western concepts and practices than those from other parts of the world.

The practitioners surveyed by Lifeworth Consulting called for more research on responsible enterprise and finance in Asia (see 'Movement East', page 189). We therefore examined the level of research attention being paid to responsible enterprise issues in Asia since the turn of the century, from within a group of eight English-language, Western-originating, academic journals that deal with different aspects of business in society. The results of this analysis are shown in Table 13. It shows that in 2008 the number of journal articles concerning Asia was double that of the average number for the previous seven years.[44] The journals *Corporate Governance: An International Review* and *Corporate Social Responsibility and Environmental Management* have increased their coverage of Asia significantly in recent years. In April 2008, the *Journal of Business Ethics* published a special issue on the importance of cross-fertilisation of Eastern and Western ethical traditions in the study and practice of business ethics.[45] Taken together, the evidence from these journals is that more of the management academe has begun to turn Eastwards in its analysis of responsible enterprise. The full list of countries searched, the databases used and the titles of the articles found, are provided in Appendix 2. Furthermore, in 2009 EIRIS found similar trends in the growth of Asian CSR activity as highlighted by our analysis.[46]

Table 13: **Academic analysis of responsible enterprise issues related to Asia**

Journal	2000	2001	2002	2003	2004	2005	2006	2007	2008
Business and Society	0	1	0	0	0	4	0	1	0
Business and Society Review	1	0	2	3	3	2	2	3	2
Business Ethics: A European Review	2	7	2	4	0	0	0	1	3
Business Strategy and the Environment	0	0	4	2	1	3	1	3	3
Corporate Governance: An International Review	3	1	1	0	4	21	8	21	8
Corporate Social Responsibility and Environmental Management	2	0	0	0	1	6	4	5	4
Journal of Business Ethics	10	16	18	23	17	19	10	21	62
Journal of Corporate Citizenship	n/a	1	3	3	12	5	6	4	4
Total	**18**	**26**	**30**	**35**	**38**	**60**	**31**	**59**	**86**

Characteristics and implications of Asian responsible enterprise

The growth of Asian companies and initiatives using the terminology of corporate social responsibility (CSR) to describe the social and environmental performance and effectiveness of their business, has encouraged discussion of what 'CSR' in Asia is like, most often in contrast to the West. Conversations often focus on assessing the level of corporate responsibility across an economy,[47] and what similarities there are in CR activities in Asia which contrast with that practised in the West.[48] Typically, some express the view that CR is less developed than in the West, whereas others argue there is an implicit form of CR among many Asian enterprises that needs to be codified and communicated. The assumption at work in many of these conversations is that Asia is following the West: either by 'catching up' with Western CR practices, or in codifying and communicating its own indigenous approaches to socially and environmentally effective enterprise in ways that can be reported to Western companies, NGOs, investors and consumers.[49] This is a natural response to how Western firms have increasingly been requesting compliance from their suppliers, subsidiaries and business partners in Asia to non-statutory codes on social or environmental performance: CR performance is regarded as a means of remaining competitive in international markets. However, such a view ignores that beneath the acronym, CR is the matter of how business and society relate, which is as local as it is international. It also overlooks the rapid changes within Asia, such as the growth in the middle class, environmental awareness, and new media, and the depletion of natural resources which are creating new risks and opportunities for businesses. As you have read this far, let alone the rest of this review of 2008, we hope you can set aside the assumption of East following West. In which case, what might be the reasons for reflecting on the similarities in Asian forms of responsible enterprise that are distinctive to the West?

- To inspire. Inspiration for people in Asia and across the world can arise through revealing the diverse approaches to social advancement from across Asia.

- To interrogate. Critical assessment of whether certain Asian approaches to responsible enterprise are a by-product of social imbalances, or arise from positive social values.

- To inform. Critical reflection on whether certain approaches promoted as globally responsible are actually appropriate is important in a global economy with a growing network of standards and codes.

- To influence. Assessment of where the power exists in business and society in Asia, and what factors shape the social and environmental effectiveness of enterprise is important to understand how to influence performance in the future.

In future consideration of the characteristics of Asian responsible enterprise, each possible characteristic should be interrogated, to then inspire and inform globally, but ultimately, to seek to influence. At the same time, 'being the cradle of great civilisations Asia is anything but monolithic', and so all generalisations should be held lightly.[50] With this in mind our tentative hypothesis is in comparison to the West, contemporary Asian responsible enterprise is: familial, governmental, practical, informal, religious, and non-global. We briefly discuss each characteristic.

Familial

Comparatively more companies in Asia are owned privately by families.[51] Not beholden to shareholders, they bring their own values and interests to their companies, including priorities on social and environmental performance. On the one hand this can raise ethical issues concerning nepotism and class stratification, while on the other it presents a great diversity of possible ethical approaches and the ability for unusual innovations on particular social or environmental issues.[52] One example of the extensive influence of family in business is the importance of family-related notions of social capital in Chinese culture, called *Guānxi*. It has been the subject of an ongoing debate about its ethical implications in the *Journal of Business Ethics* for the past decade.[53]

On the matter of influencing practice, recognising the familial nature of business means that traditional social networks are key. Although the majority of family businesses are small or medium-sized, the role of families in controlling some large transnational corporations, suggests that professionals or activists who seek high leverage points of influence to promote responsible enterprise should seek to engage through social networks as much as professional channels.

Governmental

The role of government is important in shaping responsible enterprise in Asia.[54] Unlike the West, in many Asian countries the government is traditionally expected to lead on matters of national development. The importance of government in shaping responsible enterprise practice is highlighted by the difference in environmental management performance between Japan, Hong Kong and Singapore. Of the Japanese companies they assessed in Japan, 80% were considered by EIRIS as having either an advanced or good management response to environmental issues, better than for Europe, North America and Australasia. That compared to well below 10% in Hong Kong and Singapore. The head of research at EIRIS, Stephen Hine, explained that 'the Japanese government has long encouraged as well as regulated companies to adopt environmental management systems such as ISO 14000 whereas in HK and Singapore this has not traditionally been the case'.[55]

After the economic crisis of 2008, state-owned enterprises and sovereign wealth funds have grown in significance both within Asia and abroad. The efficiency and accountability of state-owned enterprises when compared to private companies has sometimes been challenged.[56] Yet the potential is there, for governments to exert novel forms of influence on business practices if they wish to use that influence. In 2008 the Chinese government announced that corporate responsibility reports would be mandatory for all state-owned enterprises—half of all such reports issued in China that year were from state-owned enterprises.[57]

The growing role of government as an industry owner and investor poses a challenge for how they can be an active and responsible owner and investor without creating political controversies due to being seen as pursuing national interests through their international firms and investments (see 'Sovereign wealth fund responsibility', page 212).

A more significant implication of this role for government is the intellectual scope it may provide for more systemic interventions in markets, including the basics of business incorporation and money-creation (see 'From bail-outs to better capitalism', page 194; 'The end of financial triumphalism', page 197). In Jem Bendell's previous book, *The Corporate Responsibility Movement*, it is argued that an interlocking framework of ideas for how to redesign economic actors and systems is emerging: 'Capital democracy describes an economic system that moves towards the creation, allocation and management of capital according to the interests of everyone directly affected by that process, in order to support the self-actualisation of all.'[58] It is an agenda that requires government action to realise; perhaps this is more likely for some governments within Asia, given wider acceptance of their role in intervening in markets when compared to the West.

Practical

The challenges of development are inescapable across most of Asia. Concerns with the effective rule of law, given levels of corruption in the public sector, and with basic material needs, given levels of poverty and an absence of comprehensive state welfare provision, and with consumer health, given toxicity sometimes found in food, beverages and water supplies due to weak regulation, and with basic equality, given racial tensions and the subjugation of women, mean responsible enterprise initiative is focused on these practical challenges.[59] Therefore much activity is, paradoxically, either philanthropic (and thus not addressing how business processes avoid adding to public problems) or innovative, seeking enterprise solutions to particularly public challenges. The common element to both corporate philanthropy and social enterprise is that they seek immediate and tangible returns on investment of time and resources. However, one problem is that an expectation of 'tangible' returns may reduce attention to more systemic actions that are harder to demonstrate impact. In addition, this approach may hamper the potential comprehensiveness in how Asian enterprises approach their social and environmental effectiveness, something we turn to now.

Informal

The business sector in Asia is very diverse and in some countries less regulated than in the West, by either government or private standards, and likewise many of the social and environmental activities of business are informal. Informality also derives from high level of family ownership, described above. This characteristic can lead to an unsystematic approach to assessment of social and environmental aspects of business. This is highlighted by a high variability in what social and environmental issues companies address. Evidence from a 2008 EIRIS report suggest that the range of performance on social and environmental issues is more variable in Asia than the West. As evoked above, over 80% of Japanese companies were assessed as having either an advance or good management response to environmental issues, better than for Europe, North America and Australasia. However, amongst companies with a very high or high risk exposure on climate change only 17% of Japanese companies have developed a good response, according to EIRIS. 'This seeming "lag" on climate change may be due to the fact that it is only relatively recently that companies have been exhorted to deal directly with climate change and we would expect a dramatic increase in these figures in coming years,' explained Mr Hine from EIRIS.[60]

In one study of the corporate responsibility reports in China in 2009, Guo Weiyuan found their approaches varied widely, and their quality 'leaves much to be desired'. There are a variety of ways that companies can identify issues and stakeholders and prioritise them, some focusing most on near-term financial implications, others looking at the importance of a business's activities to society in making their judgement about what to prioritise.

Jia Feng, deputy director of the Publicity and Education Center of the Ministry of Environmental Protection, in China, explained when looking at the study, that the way to develop a strategy 'is not whether a cause is worthy but whether it presents an opportunity to create mutual value. That is, a meaningful benefit for society that is also valuable to the business.' Without systematic approaches to the identification and prioritisation of issues, companies may not be as strategic or effective in either delivering societal or financial value through their efforts at responsible enterprise. For instance, an analysis of the most urgent issues addressing the region, where the chance for effective action diminishes with time and the issue affects the most number of people, would likely identify deforestation in Borneo as a top issue for many companies with supply chains using wood, minerals or palm oil. The impacts on biodiversity, climate, air quality and water supplies are massive.[61]

The informal sector is a major part of economic activity in Asia. This poses particular challenges for social protection, as domestic workers, for instance, are vulnerable to employment abuse (see 'Glassed: women and CSR', page 179). One implication is that encouraging public awareness and respect for informal sector workers through social marketing may be necessary to improve practice in this sector. Another is the importance of working with migrant labourer organisations to improve their ability to educate, engage and represent migrant workers.

Religious

Anwar Ibrahim suggests that a key difference between East and West is the general level of religiosity in the former.[62] This may be an over generalisation, given the level of religiosity in the US, and the major changes in Asian urban cultures today. Within 'religiosity' are the quite distinct phenomena of an emphasis on tradition, spiritual consciousness, and group identity. The world's major religions are well represented in Asia. In the West responsible enterprise is often framed in terms of secular or humanist universal values rather than specific religious beliefs, even if individuals hold such beliefs. In Asia, religion is becoming more overt within business, particularly in post-Communist societies.[63]

Kasit Piromya, the Director of International Affairs of the Democrat Party of Thailand, and the Thailand representative of the Caux Round Table, spoke at the CSR Asia Summit about a parallel between Buddhist philosophy and responsible business, owing to the emphasis on stakeholder interdependence:

> Buddhist monks live according to the principle of interconnectivity with the community and the environment; they are one with their stakeholders. Similarly, every individual belongs to an organization, and ultimately to society. So every individual, while working to earn a living and enjoy the rewards, is inter-dependent on the business community and society as a whole. Along with its stakeholders business is a part of a whole and thus the need for social responsibility and good governance. In particular, large multinational corporations have a global responsibility, and not only to their financial stakeholders [see 'From CSR in Asia to Asian CSR', page 217].

There are parallels in this thinking within Islam. Centuries ago, Muslim thinkers conceived and expounded the concept of *al-wahda fi 'l-kathra*, which presupposes the essential oneness and transcendent connectedness of the apparent diversity on the surface. The emphasis on non-duality between heaven and earth, consciousness and matter, self and other, pervades most Eastern religions, even the Abrahamic faiths.

On the one hand we could conclude that this emphasis on connectedness will encourage responsible enterprise. However, the changes in Asia due to economic development are important. Today some regard Asians as increasingly pursuing Western objectives with Asian intentions, with problematic and unsustainable outcomes, both personally and socially. Some regard a typical Asian intention to be social harmony, yet others consider this to be a desire for conformity and thus less noble. The belief in harmony or conformity, is a manifestation in form of a level of consciousness which equates one's personhood with a collective. If that outer form is disconnected for the consciousness that gives it meaning and context, then people can be exploited and made to doubt their natural tendencies to compassion and fairness.

The religiosity will mean that the idea of conducting business in harmony with each other and our planet may find deep rhetorical resonance in many Asian communities in the coming years. However, this religiosity poses difficult questions about whether responsible enterprise might be attempted in paternalist rather than rights-based ways, and for the benefit of particular groups not others. Whether this happens will depend on the relative importance of cultural forms or spiritual consciousness in shaping the actions of business leaders.

One area where the religiousness of Asian responsible enterprise could give rise to interesting challenges is Islamic finance. This field of finance is fast approaching a trillion dollars of assets under management and was much less affected by the economic crisis due to its restrictions on investing in debt. The core principles of Islamic finance provide insight into a way of financing that can be more stable and sustainable (see 'Islamic finance', page 209). However, currently the Islamic investors, and the Western investees, are not comfortable about Islamic values guiding practices of companies in the West. As a result, the code agreed for Sovereign Wealth Funds during 2008 is likely to discourage active value-based ownership, apart from a loophole agreed by the Norwegians whose responsible investment activities are less contentious in the West (see 'Sovereign wealth fund responsibility', page 212).

One implication for influence is that religious institutions throughout Asia will be important to the future of responsible enterprise.

Non-global

Most Asian firms we have experience of are not explicit with a vision for the way their company will do business around the world, let alone a vision for how any business should be conducted anywhere in the world, or to work for that global objective. Often nationalism is a key motivator for greater contributions to society from leading companies in Asia, such as JN Tata.[64]

The colonial legacy of the West, its modern era of leadership within inter-governmental institutions, and its levels of education and wealth, have led many Westerners to have an opinion about the state of the world and its people (for better or worse). Anwar Ibrahim summarises this West's sense of itself as 'having something unique and benevolent to disseminate to others'.[65] To risk a vast generalisation, many Asians do not have that sense of global responsibility or global purpose. You will be hard pressed to find an Asian who is concerned about the rights of workers in factories in Scotland, for instance, in the way some Scottish people are concerned about the rights of workers in Asia. We have been met by laughter whenever asking such questions in Asia. Yet patterns of ownership and investment described here show how Asians are acquiring a global role, influencing billions of workers, consumers and community members. Cultivating a sense of global responsibility is key.

There were sparks of this new global responsibility from within the responsible enterprise community during 2008. The global vision of Muhammad Yunus, taking microfinance to the low income communities in the United States, is one example, as is the creation of a Global Social Innovators Forum (GSIF) by Singapore MP Penny Low (see 'From CSR in Asia to Asian CSR', page 217).

One implication for those in the West who are active in making the world a fairer and sustainable place is to find, engage and support similarly committed people with an internationalist view in the East. An implication for responsible enterprise professionals in the East is to seek to evolve indigenously derived principles and agendas that resonate with existing international principles, and seek to apply them globally, not just domestically or in the Asian region.

Democratising responsible enterprise in Asia and the world

Many of these characteristics are not unique to Asia, but are found in Latin America and Africa. They are characteristics of a 'Southern' form responsible enterprise. Discussing differences between East and West has always been popular and current shifts in power make it more so. However, we should never lose sight of how these are simply imagined communities with imaginary boundaries. Some fall into a trap of describing the East or West as entirely separate and internally coherent entities that act as conscious beings, so that 'the West' can be said to 'worry' about 'the East', for instance.[66] The problem is that by trying to distinguish one from the other we may deny aspects of both that are universal, and restrict their identity to past forms, rather than an unfolding of possibilities.

The division between 'East' and 'West' is a product of European history and literature over hundreds of years, which made a distinction between European Christendom and the cultures it was coming to know to its east. The Western world and Western culture are imagined today often as typified by rationalism, science, freedom of thought, individualism, human rights, democratic values, and either Christianity or secularism. In describing an Eastern Turn we are not describing a turn away from these cultural traditions. First, because we do not recognise them as owned by a place called 'West'. The foundations of contemporary rational thought and mathematics are found in ancient conceptual developments in the Middle East.[67] Not only did Christianity arise from the Middle East but it arrived and thrived in India even before it took hold in Rome.[68]

The second reason we do not imply a turning away from certain values is that we do not accept the implication that there are not equally important traditions that emphasise personal liberty and democratic values from within Asia. Anwar Ibrahim has reflected on these various traditions and reminds us that the struggles against colonialism in Asia and subsequent 'national independence would not have been possible without the prior cultivation of the spirit of liberty and nurturing of the aspiration for a just social order'.[69] One of the most eloquent summaries of the interface between rationalism, freedom, spirituality and progress was made by Filipino José Rizal in 1883, when he lectured a Spanish audience that 'humanity will not be redeemed while reason is not free, while faith would want to impose itself against the facts, while whims are laws and where there are nations that subjugate others'. We may recall that democracy was thriving in many countries in the East before it arrived in Spain, to further highlight the fallacy of assuming West and East to be a distinction based on a historical embrace of different values.[70] Therefore we agree with Ibrahim's assertion that

> it is altogether shameful, if ingenious, to cite Asian values as an excuse for autocratic practices and denial of basic rights and civil liberties. To say that freedom is western or unasian is to offer our own traditions, as well as our forefathers who gave their lives in the struggle against tyranny and injustice.[71]

Even the religion most often cited as justifying forms of hierarchy, Confucianism, does not provide a rebuttal of the need for personal freedom. Confucius advocated the primacy of the self, the individual and the community as *sine qua non* for human flourishing.[72]

Instead, in describing an Eastern Turn we point to an opening up of possibilities of beliefs and approaches to all aspects of society, and thus a questioning of some assumptions that underlie existing debates and activities on corporate responsibility. The Eastern Turn is not a turning-away from the West but away from an assumption of a singular source of imagination. It is not a turning-away from the values people often ascribe to Western culture, but an opening up to a broader dialogue of values.[73] With this in mind, before we conclude this introduction we wish to sound two warnings, one for Eastern professionals, the other for Western.

As discussed earlier, Asian companies' voluntary engagement with the social and environmental performance of their business has been much influenced by the West. This approach may risk downplaying or even ignoring local stakeholder interests in the role and performance of business. In discussions with CR professionals in Singapore, Hong Kong and Malaysia we heard the view that most local stakeholder interests in business performance can be articulated through government, and, where that is not the case, that those stakeholder interests are not particularly urgent. That view may be a result of the dominant role of the state in many Asian countries and the variable, still often weak, levels of civil society organising, media independence and political debate.[74] We consider this state of affairs may hamper the emergence of domestic responsible enterprise agendas in some countries in Asia.

Such an emergence may also be hampered by the imbalance in domestic voices involved in shaping the future of responsible enterprise in Asia. The evidence from five CSR conferences in Asia during 2008, is that the corporate responsibility debate in Asia is shaped by business leaders, government officials and high-society elites, rather people who are directly impacted within the region.

There is some evidence for this elitist approach to CR from analyses of the lack of performance by large Asian firms on issues that are awkward for elites: corruption and labour rights. Only about 5% of Japanese companies with a high risk exposure to corruption were found by EIRIS to have a good response and none had an advanced one, which is less than that of assessed companies in Europe, North America and Australasia. Japan also performed less well than those regions on labour rights, with no assessed company with a high risk exposure to supply chain labour issues having better than a limited management response and nearly 80% having no evidence at all of a response.[75]

If Western imposition and local elitism dominates responsible enterprise agendas in Asia, rather than a more organic emergence of ideas and innovations from dialogues and contestations of people from across the region, the loss will be both Asia's and the world's. One implication, therefore, is the need for greater awareness of the levels and nature of endogenous desire across Asia for socially progressive enterprise, and the relative roles of government, business and wider civil society in shaping and responding to that desire (see 'From CSR in Asia to Asian CSR', page 217).

Researchers and consultants from the West can relate to this eastern turn in power in progressive or regressive ways. One lesson from this economic crisis is the danger of intellectuals seeking favour with the powerful and therefore ignoring fundamental problems (see 'Rent-a-geek', page 206). At this time of new levels of global exchange, we would do well to watch our own interests and emotions.

A growing trend is for Western CR professionals to look East. This is due to an awareness of where key challenges lie, but also because of the changing market for professional services, accentuated by the recession in Europe and US. As consultants with much to learn about the cultures where they are offering services, clearly they may be humble and polite in offering their views. However, in the same breath as speaking of the need to learn from cultures of the world, some CR consultants and advocates have been expressing doubts about values such as human rights, in particular labour and political rights. We must be careful not to repeat the mistakes of environmental consultants in the 1990s who extended their offerings to social advisory, and often fundamentally misunderstood notions of labour rights, in ways that initially made them more attractive to those corporate clients not wanting to address thorny issues of trade union rights and gender equality. The current global shifts provide wonderful possibilities for personal and professional development, no more so than helping Westerners escape, on the one hand, the asphyxiating arrogance of assuming one's culture to be the most advanced, and on the other, a confusion about meaning and purpose in one's life.

Conclusion: a global Satyagraha

The night has ended,
Put out the light of the lamp of thine own narrow corner smudged with smoke,
The great morning which is for all appears in the east,
Let its light reveal us to each other who walk on the same path of pilgrimage.[76]

Rabindranath Tagore wrote his poetry at a time of heightened creativity due to new exchanges between East and West, which was also a time of struggle and emergence, with the retreat of the British Empire and the birth of India. Our current period resonates with such momentous times, as economic systems are shaken and people think again about the order of things.

We have described the Eastern Turn in responsible enterprise as a shift in the location of responsible enterprise challenges and the origin of responsible enterprise ideas and initiatives, arising because of the growing power and development of the Middle East and Asia. We have argued that it is not a turning-away from the West but an opening-up to insights from all directions. The rise of Asia reminds us of the diversity of our world, and therefore the diversity of ideas about social, economy and politics. In this sense, 2008 witnessed *The Return of History.*[77] Yet, rather than seeing our future history as a repeat of ancient conflicts, 'the challenge at hand is to conceive a common vision of the future which goes beyond our current concerns and preoccupations, advancing towards the creation of a global community, dominated neither by the East or the West, but dedicated to the ideals of both'.[78]

Progressive professionals in both the West and East have much to gain from reconnecting with, and debating, the wisdoms across Asia. For instance, one of the greatest leaders from recent Asian history is Mohandas K. Gandhi. His views are relevant to the future of the global economy and our work on responsible enterprise and finance in at least five ways: economic purpose, economic equality, appropriate technology, self-reliance, and trusteeship.

To begin with, he saw economic activity as significant and meaningful, not merely in terms of what was produced, but how and by whom, and with what implications for the community. Challenging both the caste system and negativity between religions, he promoted the equality of all peoples, which meant non-discrimination in employment and economic affairs. He also believed that technology could be good if it did necessary work, but bad if it put people out of work. This philosophy led him to spend many hours working on the spinning wheel, a technology that was appropriate to the economic level of villagers across India at the time. Another important aspect of the spinning wheel was how it generated self-reliance. Gandhi spoke of *swadeshi* or economic self-sufficiency, as the only way that India would achieve self-determination. He called on his country-people not to pay into the system of empire by buying foreign clothes. In our current context the implication here is not simply that we produce for ourselves, but that we seek to become independent of systems of exploitation for our own livelihoods and lifestyles.

These aspects of Gandhian economics are well documented and discussed. Like many business folk the world over, some Indian executives do not see the relevance of these approaches to modern business, viewing them as anachronistic. Yet, in a resource-constrained and climate-threatened world, where hyper-inequality fuels violence, the need for principles and practices of equality, appropriateness and self-reliance to pervade business is clear.

Gandhi's views on 'trusteeship' resonate with the latest thinking within the corporate responsibility movement. More of us have come to understand that we need to redesign the systems of corporate governance and finance in order to create more sustainable and responsible economies, and that business executives can and should engage in public policy debates to promote that re-design:

> In a democratic society, property rights should only exist because people collectively decide to uphold them; they are not inalienable but are upheld by society as a matter of choice. Therefore, if society confers us the right of property, then we have obligations to that society. Today property rights have become so divorced from this democratic control that they are undermining other human rights. A reawakening to a basic principle is required: there can be no property right without property duties, or obligations. From such a principle, it should not be left up to the powerful to decide if they are responsible or not, or if they are carrying out their obligations or not. Instead, the focus shifts to the governance of capital by those who are affected by it.[79]

The Mahatma's view of trusteeship is the same, but elegant in its simplicity. It arises from an understanding that everything is owned by everyone, and wealth is owned by those who generate it. Thus the one who controls an asset is not an owner but a trustee, being given control of that asset by society. Gandhi wrote 'I am inviting those people who consider themselves as owners today to act as trustees, i.e., owners, not in their own right, but owners in the right of those whom they have exploited.'[80] In the *Harijan* paper, his views on trusteeship of property were later documented to clarify: 'it does not recognize any right of private ownership of property except so far as it may be permitted by society for its own welfare' and 'under State-regulated trusteeship, an individual will not be free to hold or use his wealth for selfish satisfaction or in disregard of the interests of society'.[81] He also wrote that 'for the present owners of wealth . . . they will be allowed to retain the stewardship of their possessions and to use their talent, to increase the wealth, not for their own sakes, but for the sake of the nation and, therefore, without exploitation'.[82] All those years ago the Mahatma was proposing an economic system that many people are only beginning to conceive of today.

Some Indian industrialists supported Gandhi and applied some of his ideas to their own business, such as G.D. Birla. The concepts of equality and trusteeship inform some Indian companies' voluntary corporate responsibility efforts today.[83] However, the concept of trusteeship has much untapped potential as an economic system, if codified into public policy and regulation. The current crisis demonstrates the need to globalise trusteeship, or capital democracy, as an approach that can be debated and interpreted into new principles and policies for economics, finance and enterprise. In addition, it is clear that concepts of appropriate technology and self-reliance have much more to offer both to corporate strategy and public policy than currently the case. It is to be seen whether contemporary Indian business leaders can mobilise these concepts and play a role in bringing them to the world.

The life of Gandhi is important not only for his views on economic systems but also on how to bring them into being. In *The Corporate Responsibility Movement*, Jem Bendell argues that the global challenges we face mean those of us who work to make business better must start thinking and planning like a movement:

> The corporate responsibility movement is a loosely organised but sustained effort by individuals both inside and outside the private sector, who seek to use or change specific corporate practices, whole corporations, or entire systems of corporate activity, in accordance with their personal commitment to public goals and the expectations of wider society.[84]

As a movement leader, we could learn from Gandhi's mastery of symbolic communication combined with personal authenticity, his embrace of both dialogue and direct action, his respect for people no matter the differences, and his demonstration that we must ourselves disengage with systems that do not align with our values. More of us can mobilise our networks and knowledge for transformative ends. And if it means changing our lives to be less economically dependent on the status quo, then that's what we must do.

The poet Tagore particularly identified with Gandhi's philosophy of liberation which he called Satyagraha. *Satya* means 'truth', *Graha* means both 'involved in' and 'total' (or perhaps 'global'). Gandhi used *satyagraha* to describe a non-violent way of life, that does not participate in oppression wherever it occurs, and challenges it in non-violent ways. It became synonymous with India's liberation movement. Gandhi believed that *satyagraha* required fearless yet convivial dialogue about the truth of society and efforts to live by that truth. As stakeholder dialogue has been a central methodology for responsible enterprise practitioners around the globe, we could embrace a new degree of fearless yet convivial dialogue to seek out truths for the future of business and society—a new global *satyagraha*. Such an international and cross-cultural dialogue could encourage a multitude of Asian approaches to responsible enterprise to positively affect business practices around the globe.

1Q2008
January–March

Jem Bendell, Lala Rimando and Claire Veuthey

Sexpenses

Those seeking more leadership from government and judiciary on promoting corporate accountability often praised the work of Eliot Spitzer, then New York State Attorney General. He pursued matters of corporate crime and malpractice, on issues such as price fixing in the technology sector and stock price manipulation in the financial sector, costing companies billions of dollars in fines.[1] This is not a man the financial services industry would wish to have around amidst the credit crisis with its requests for unusual support from the government and federal reserve. On 10 March 2008, the *New York Times* reported that Spitzer was a client of a prostitution ring. Two days later, he announced his resignation as governor of New York, citing 'private failings'.[2] Journalist Greg Palast suggested the timing of the news was too convenient:

> While New York Governor Eliot Spitzer was paying an 'escort' $4,300 in a hotel room in Washington, just down the road, George Bush's new Federal Reserve Board Chairman, Ben Bernanke, was secretly handing over $200 billion in a tryst with mortgage bank industry speculators. Both acts were wanton, wicked and lewd. But there's a BIG difference. The Governor was using his own checkbook. Bush's man Bernanke was using ours.[3]

Sex scandals have long been the downfall of politicians. They are less often the downfall of leaders in business and civil society, unless involving children. However, both the growing prominence of such leaders in society, and the widespread use of sex workers in business circles, means that such scandals are likely to arise in future. In February, the role of sex in one of the biggest corruption scandals in Germany came to light.[4] In illegal transfers that cost the company €2.5 million, VW worker representatives accepted 'special bonuses', such as opulent trips and extravagant nights out involving prostitutes in places such as Brazil and Korea in exchange for favourable policy votes.[5] A former German MP, Hans-Jürgen Uhl, and the ex-CEO Ferdinand Piech may also be involved, the newspapers reported. Labour relations have been a source of national German pride, with VW in particular historically being a bastion of worker rights. But the current scandal has exposed the potential risk of close relations between executives and labour leaders. This has led to some to call for a broadening of the concept of corporate responsibility and accountability that has shaped German corporate governance for decades, with the bilateral engagement between management and unions now seen as an insufficient mechanism for socially accountable corporate governance.

This case is not unique. An oil executive was sentenced in February for awarding his favourite American prostitute a contract to pay for her services with company funds—on top of raiding company coffers for trips to massage parlours and strip clubs.[6] The payment of sexual services were also part of the bribes paid by Chinese businessmen to government officials in the Philippines, which we discuss below. Our discussions with business people from Geneva to Singapore suggest that corporate hospitality for clients often involves arranging sexual services, and can be facilitated by major hotel companies, through opaque or false billing records.

The question we consider here is not prostitution per se. Its legal status differs from country to country; a particular problem for Elliot Spitzer was that it is illegal in New York State. The moral and pragmatic arguments on how and whether to control the industry also vary. The key issues for corporate responsibility, however, concern corruption, governance, health and gender, as well as the reputational risks involved.

It is widely accepted, and defined in law, that a corporation should not be plying clients or partners with personal gifts, beyond hospitality. This stands whether the bribe consists of an object, straight cash, or a service. All resources a company disburses should be purchases linked to its core business and administrative needs or somehow connected to serving the interests of the organisation's owners via legal means. Bribery skews the competitive market and sets an unfortunate precedent for business relations; agreements are signed and sales made for the wrong reasons. Bribery within the context of stakeholder relations, particularly when these relations constitute processes of corporate governance, give rise to particular concerns, as revealed in the VW case.

The purchase of sexual services, however, adds insult to injury with a new dimension to institutional responsibility and corporate norms of individual behaviour. Especially where sex tourism is rampant and responsible for the exploitation, trafficking and exposure to disease of millions of children and women, and generally a reflection of a dearth of economic opportunities, and poor education and welfare systems, businesses should take a particularly strong stand against their employees' use of prostitutes' services on the company dime. Accepting cultural arguments to excuse using sex workers for business ends is cowardly and opportunistic. Considering bars with sex workers as one might restaurants, in terms of business locales providing a service that can make potential clients feel at ease and see the company favourably, obfuscates the participation in a vicious system of exploitation and social marginalisation; and therefore cannot be equated to a lavish meal out. That line should be clearly drawn. Let's not forget the risk of contracting and spreading disease, even if using protection: for the 'beneficiary', his or her partner at home, and the person providing the service. In addition, business environments that treat such sexual services as a normal way of doing business effectively discriminate against women in their own organisations, who are excluded from the bonds made and deals done in such settings. Moreover, responsible investors may be horrified to learn that what has been charged as 'food' at a hotel by a corporate executive was actually sex. Given the reputational risk associated with such practices if they hit the newspapers, there is also a material financial reason for investors to be concerned.

Targeted solutions to such practices are, however, hard to establish. A group of organisations including the UN World Tourism Organisation, Accor Hotels, and NGOs advocating the end of child prostitution, set up the Code of Conduct for the Protection of Children from Sexual Commercial Exploitation in Travel and Tourism in 1997, committing to take steps to help prevent the facilitation of child sexual exploitation. A vital first step is an explicit repudiation of this mode of deal-making by companies themselves, as well as a credible threat of serious sanction for individuals that do not abide by the employer's code of conduct. The extension of such measures to address the sexist nature of much corporate hospitality is also necessary. Given the large number of women involved in corporate responsibility, it is surprising that sex on expenses, and sexist hospitality more generally, has not yet become more of an issue. Many senior female business travellers have had first-hand experience of returning to a hotel room while the men continue their night in a club. Might some greater solidarity with the women in those bars emerge?

Olympian graft

As well as being the year that China first hosted the Olympics, 2008 marked the 30th anniversary of the beginning of that country's programme of economic reform. The major social and economic changes that have occurred in those 30 years mean that corruption has become a major problem in Chinese society, as temptations have grown and social traditions declined. Thus, corruption has been a concern surrounding the Olympics. In January, state media reported that 38 people were arrested in Beijing during 2007 in a crackdown on corruption connected to the Olympics. Beijing's communist party chief Liu Qi, who also heads the Beijing Olympic organising committee, said the Games must be run in an 'open and transparent' manner, and previously ordered the stepping-up of audits and inspections on Olympic-related activities. The highest-profile Olympic graft case so far has yet to come to court. Liu Zhihua, a former vice mayor of Beijing, was fired in June 2006 after allegations of massive bribes concerning Olympic venues that cost more than a billion dollars to build.[7]

China has been increasing its anti-corruption drive in the past years, especially in major cities, where a number of scandals and shady deals involving top officials have been exposed. Wrongdoers have been fined, given jail terms or even death sentences. Such cases included the arrest of Shanghai's party boss, who had been a member of the Communist Party's Politburo, the power core in China, and the execution of the former head of the national food and drug regulation body. China ratified the United Nations Anti-Corruption Convention in 2005 to curb the flight of corruption officials who abscond with public funds abroad. It even participated in the anti-corruption initiatives of the Asia-Pacific Economic Cooperation and the Organisation for Economic Cooperation and Development (OECD), although it has not yet signed the OECD Convention on Combating Bribery.

Despite this stream of high-profile efforts to align national with international anti-corruption initiatives, Minxin Pei, director of the China programme at Carnegie Endowment, a Washington-based policy study group, revealed in his report that, in reality, only a 'small proportion' of officials tainted by corruption are punished. He told journalists that 'The odds of an average corrupt official going to jail are at most three out of 100, making corruption a high-return, low-risk activity.'[8]

Pei's report, entitled *Corruption Threatens China's Future, showed that, despite the Chinese government's* more than 1,200 laws, rules and directives against corruption, implementation has been inconsistent and ineffective.[9] Analysts explain that China, as an economy, has been undergoing profound structural change. The general lack of obedience to the law is attributed to increasing market competition and the growing domestic economic gap. After the collapse of the promised cradle-to-grave life-long protection, many citizens doubted that their hard and honest effort under the new open-market economy would be enough to provide a decent income. According to the *Asia Times*, business people assume that, if they have bought political backing, they can get investigations into their affairs called off and stories in the state media killed.[10]

In the 2007 Transparency International Corruption Perceptions Index, China ranked 73rd out of 156 countries. It was, however, a few notches higher than China's 78th place the year before. The index tracks how business people perceive corruption in a country. China is not the worst in Asia, but it's in the company of many much poorer countries, such as Laos.

Pei is not convinced that corruption is just a stage in China's development. He believes rather that it is actually a failure of political reform:

> The Chinese government has consistently resisted steps to further reduce the role of the state in the economy, increase judicial independence and mobilise the power of the media and civil society, even though international experience shows that only such full-fledged efforts can root out systemic corruption.[11]

But, because of China's one-party system, these channels don't exist. Local Chinese party secretaries have sweeping control over the local media, legislatures and courts, breeding corruption and abuse of power.

Pei said that the direct costs of corruption, which could be as much as $86 billion each year, posed a 'lethal threat' to the country's economic development. He acknowledged that corruption has not yet derailed China's economic rise, sparked a social revolution, or deterred Western investors. 'But it would be foolish to conclude that the Chinese system has an infinite capacity to absorb the mounting costs of corruption. Eventually, growth will falter.'[12]

At a meeting of the Central Commission for Discipline Inspection (CCDI) in January, Chinese premiere Hu Jintao echoed much of this critique, warning that increasing levels of corruption could eventually destroy the Chinese Communist Party. He reviewed various regime changes across the world since the 1960s. Other than those due to foreign interference, he said the two main factors for change were the ruling party's corruption, and social problems associated with economic recession.[13] At the meeting special efforts were outlined in the fields of environmental protection, food and medicine safety, work safety, and land appropriation: areas where corruption has particularly direct impacts on the general population. In addition, supervision will be intensified on the management of social security funds and the special fund for poverty and disaster relief, an issue that came into light later in the year after a catastrophic earthquake.[14]

That many ordinary Chinese are concerned about corruption was highlighted just a few weeks before Hu's speech, when the new website of China's National Bureau of Corruption Prevention (NBCP) crashed soon after it was launched, 'as Chinese people logged on in their droves to complain about corruption among the official ranks'.[15] An NBCP official, who declined to be named, confirmed the breakdown had occurred because 'the number of visitors was very large and beyond our expectations'.[16] The scale of the problem indicates that firms in China will need to leapfrog the development of corporate responsibility in the West from compliance and philanthropy to become involved in promoting good governance (as 'corporate citizenship' means to some people).

Foreign direct corruption

As corruption at home is tackled, attention has turned to the role of Chinese businesses in corruption scandals around the world. In February, the Philippines media and legislators were desperately trying to find one relatively unknown forestry official named Rodolfo Lozada. He was supposed to give a tell-all testimony in a senate investigation about a botched telecommunications deal between a Chinese supplier and the Philippines government, but evaded his summons by going abroad and was then whisked away by authorities when he returned. He appeared two days later, at 2:30 am, on live television, to recount who abducted him, how he was persuaded and bribed by government officials to keep silent about his involvement in the controversial deal, and how his conscience made him come clean.[17]

Certainly, Lozada could not claim to be an angel. During his senate testimonies, he admitted profiting from kickbacks on government deals through his friendship with the economic planning secretary who approved the telecommunications project. He said this project would have been pushed through with little or no attention if the kickback had been limited to the agreed $65 million. But various individuals—apparently emboldened by the alleged willingness of the Chinese suppliers to pay extra—wanted to bloat the project's worth to $330 million so they could pocket up to $200 million. He said the economic planning secretary asked him to 'moderate their greed'.[18]

The project involved a nationwide broadband network that would link government offices and allow the education ministry to beam instructional materials to far-flung public schools isolated by mountain ranges or located in islands. Whistleblowers, including Lozada, named an election official and the husband of Philippines president Gloria Arroyo as project 'facilitators' (political backers). President Arroyo signed it days before the May 2007 national election when her allies, who would ensure she would not be impeached, won majority seats in congress.

The failed project's main beneficiary would have been Zhong Xing Telecommunication Equipment Company Limited (ZTE), one of China's biggest telecommunication makers. ZTE, a partly state-owned company, is growing its emerging-markets portfolio and the supply contract with the Philippines government would have been a coup. But vocal Filipino critics from civil society, academia and the media have criticised the ZTE contract with their government, arguing that it violates several Philippines laws, including rules that call for competitive bidding for government procurement contracts. Whistleblowers recounted during the senate investigations how the ZTE officials wined, dined, provided women entertainers to, gave free trips to, and paid an advanced 'facilitation' payment of about $41 million to their Filipino political backers who helped them clinch the deal. Eventually, President Arroyo not only nullified the deal but also suspended other Chinese-funded projects in the country worth some $2 billion.

Had the Philippines' active and free press and dynamic civil society not exposed ZTE officials' actions to clinch the broadband project, bribery and corruption may just have been hidden away as a business-as-usual inevitability. So, is this an indication of how Chinese state-owned companies are bringing their economic ambitions to the developing world?

It is not often that cheap, long-term loans from China encounter public wariness in a beneficiary country. China has also been generous in dispensing loans, some interest-free or as outright grants, to poor debtor African states that embraced no-strings-attached financing for electrification, highways, railways, hospitals and schools. Such financing is in stark contrast to the austerity demands and long list of social, environmental, human rights, fiscal policy, publicly declared political affiliation, and ethical requirements of multilateral agencies, such as IMF and the World Bank. China announced that, through its Export and Import Bank, it will ramp up infrastructure and trade financing to Africa to $20 billion over the next three years and that it would also write off unpaid debts. In return, not only did China outflank the United States, Japan and the European countries in clinching supply deals on oil and other minerals from these natural-resource-rich but development-poor nations, it also means serious business for some 800 Chinese state-owned enterprises (SOEs) now active in the continent.[19]

ZTE is considered as one of China's 'National Champions', backed by China's fat foreign exchange reserves that are funnelled through state-owned lending channels, which then lend *de facto* subsidised, low-cost funds to ZTE's customers.[20]

In China's telecommunications industry, two giant equipment companies have emerged: Huawei and ZTE. They seem to be a study in contrast on Chinese companies' outbound investments.

Both have been feverishly expanding overseas and edging out their Western counterparts not only by being price cutters but because they understand that some developing markets have a 'just give me the phone' attitude, a far cry from, say, Nokia, whose customers are locked into the Finnish company's standardised products and systems. But as *CFO Asia* described, there are key differences between the two. For example, Huawei is privately owned, while ZTE has a share structure that is an amalgam of public and state ownership (about half of the shares belong to state-owned agencies and senior management; the balance are listed in Shanghai and Hong Kong bourses). They also differ in style, and perhaps even in general approach. While both are headquartered in Shenzhen, *CFO Asia* described Huawei's as a palatial Silicon Valley-like campus, while ZTE's has the official feel of a government office. ZTE's showcase lobby reportedly has LCD screens flashing pictures of government ministers and political leaders from Sudan, Eritrea, Niger, Algeria, Libya and Zambia where ZTE has already clinched equipment deals.

But perhaps the most telling difference is the overseas markets they have secured. Huawei has made inroads in the more lucrative developed markets of North America and Europe. It has won contracts with operators in France, Germany, Spain, the UK and Australia.[21] On the other hand, ZTE's sales executives have become wizards at selling products in the developing markets of Africa, Latin America and Asia.[22]

No wonder, then, that Huawei seems more attuned to the global standards of sustainability. In 2004, Huawei joined the UN Global Compact.[23] On the other hand, ZTE reported on its website limited corporate social responsibility (CSR) goals, which focused more on product, supplier and philanthropic concerns.[24] There was no mention of any ethical or legal standards that it vowed to uphold in its overseas transactions. In fact, consultancy firm CSR-Asia censured ZTE for vying to invest in a proposed cyber-city in Burma, which has a notorious human rights record.[25]

However, the mere fact that ZTE has begun to document its CSR goals is a step in the right direction. This could have been a response either to its need to project a caring image to outsiders, or conformity to government-led initiatives, such as those from the State Council's State-owned Assets Supervision and Administration Commission (SASAC), which oversees and regulates SOEs, such as ZTE. In January 2008, SASAC issued an instructing document that aims to guide SOEs in fulfilling and reporting about their social responsibilities, and in turn improving their competitiveness and sustainability. This guideline was based on CSR issues revealed from SASAC's in-depth study, which was initiated as a result of the ongoing and increasing debate on CSR in both the international and national arenas. It listed eight major CSR content points that SOEs should follow. While labour issues, product safety and environmental concerns are prominent in the document, at the top of the list is this: 'Comply with laws and regulations, moral standards, business ethics, and industrial regulations and conduct their business honestly. They should . . . *eliminate corrupted behaviours in all business activities*' [emphasis added].[26]

The failed ZTE contract in the Philippines, however, is a glaring contradiction between what is preached and what is happening in practice. How these CSR reports will contrast with actual progress and achievements on CSR issues such as corruption remains to be seen.

If corruption in China is exported elsewhere through loans and contract agreements, a twin threat occurs. If the return from a project is insufficient to pay off the loans, this could lead to bad debt, which in time might create a new debt crisis in emerging nations, with similar negative developmental impacts to the previous debt crisis fuelled by Western lenders. The costs of such a situation would also mount for China. It is in China's best interest, therefore, that it safeguards the long-term viability of its overseas investments' beneficiaries and promotes enlightened self-interest among the outbound Chinese investors. If it does not, then there are also risks to be faced, as future governments in foreign countries seek to penalise companies that bribed previous administrations.

Back in China, the head of the CCDI, He Guoqiang, said in January that 'the key to winning our war against official corruption is to put punishment and prevention on equal footing'. He said, 'We will place equal efforts in punishing crooked officials for their misconduct, as well as in establishing an anti-corruption system to get rid of corruption at its root.'[27] Some consider one of those roots to be the shifting cultural norms in China, as Maoist Communism has been fundamentally transformed. Consequently, more Chinese leaders are speaking either overtly or implicitly about traditional Confucian and Taoist values. Some socially responsible entrepreneurs are even described as Confucian entrepreneurs.[28] Confucianism, like all spiritual and religious traditions, has a mixed history in how it shaped, or was used to justify, forms of governance and trade. Its role in the future of China is unclear, and even more unclear is whether it will influence the way China does business with the rest of the world. The concept of *Ren* in Confucianism emphasises interconnectedness. A more conscious approach to the broader relations it has with all the peoples of the nations it is investing in may prove a wiser approach, in the long term.

Targeting change

In previous years a comprehensive corporate responsibility strategy has typically involved a commitment to continuous improvement, to being near the best in class, and engaging stakeholders. Our review for the 2007 year argues this consensus was shifting, as the scale and urgency of social and environmental challenges became more widely understood, along with the risks and opportunities to business. The review chronicled a wave of announcements of specific time-bound environmental targets from companies, concerning actual performance, rather than management processes.

In just the first month of 2008 dozens more targets were set by companies. For instance, Heinz pledged to provide free micronutrient assistance to 10 million children at risk of iron-deficiency anaemia by 2010; Coca-Cola Hellenic Bottling Company announced plans to reduce CO_2 emissions from production by more than 20% by the end of 2009; HP announced a target to reduce PC energy usage by 25% by 2010; and the law firm Freshfields Bruckhaus Deringer planned to increase its *pro bono* activities by 30% by 2009. Perhaps winning the prize for the most ear-catching target, Renault-Nissan announced plans to sell entirely electric cars in Israel by 2011.

This shift to performance targets reflects 'the urgency of the global challenges we now face, such as on water, food, poverty', argued Professor David Grayson of the Doughty Centre at Cranfield University. That urgency 'makes the search for better models of sustainable development ever more critical'.[29] Our 2007 review predicted that this focus on the pace of innovation and entrepreneurial activity to addressing societal challenges would lead to a shift in language about 'corporate social responsibility', with terms such as 'sustainable', 'social enterprise' and 'responsible enterprise' becoming more common.

We should, however, remember that targets themselves are not the mechanisms of change. It appears that many countries will miss their Kyoto targets, and the first Millennium Development Goals on primary school education have already been missed. In addition, studies have long shown that focusing on meeting targets can have unintended consequences and undermine true progress. The solution may be for wider coalitions of groups to apply themselves to the factors that shape our economy: to explore ways of collaborating to shift whole markets.

Drinking problem

In February 2008, London Mayor Ken Livingstone launched London On Tap, a campaign encouraging consumers to ask for tap water in restaurants and pubs for environmental reasons. Jenny Jones, Green Party member for the London Assembly, called the bottled water market 'one of the biggest con jobs of the last two decades', adding that 'Selling water in bottles and burning massive quantities of fossil fuels for its transportation does not make economic or environmental sense.'[30]

San Francisco Mayor Gavin Newsom passed an outright ban on the purchase of bottled water by city departments in July 2007; New York City officials heavily promoted tap water over bottled that same summer; and officials in Minneapolis, Salt Lake City, Chicago, Rome, Florence and Paris have taken similar actions. On top of being 500 times more expensive, bottled water comes with a heavy carbon footprint: from the oil used to make the plastic bottles most water comes in, to the carbon emitted during transportation and refrigeration, to the millions of bottles that end up in landfills.[31] And the market is booming: the world spends $100 billion on bottled water every year; in the United States its sales are second only to carbon-ated soft drinks.[32] The Worldwatch Institute has previously calculated that this is a similar amount to that required to ensure the whole world has potable tap water.

More than 25% of bottled water is treated tap water, including Pepsi's Aquafina and Coca-Cola's Dasani. In many parts of the developed world there is no particular health value in drinking bottled water rather than water from the tap. In fact, laws governing the testing of bottled water are much less stringent than those cover-ing tap water: New York City tap water was analysed some 346,000 times in 2006.[33] Given this fact, much of the advertising that claims bottled water is beneficial to health could be challenged.

Principally, though, the corporate responsibility problem lies with the bottles. According to the Earth Policy Institute, more than 17 million barrels of oil are needed every year to produce the 29 billion plastic water bottles used in the United States alone. Less than a quarter of these are recycled; the bottles that end up in landfills take four centuries to biodegrade.[34] Add to this the emissions generated through pumping, processing, refrigeration and transportation, since 25% of bottled water is imported relative to where it is consumed, and its environmental impact per litre is estimated to be up to 300 times that of tap water.[35]

Kim Jeffery, president and CEO of Nestlé Waters North America, does not like the comparison with tap water. He argues that consumers don't choose between bot-tled and tap water but between bottled water and other bottled drinks, which are sugar-loaded or otherwise unhealthy. In addition, he highlights that water is one of hundreds of beverages to come in plastic bottles. According to Jeffery, water bottles constitute less than 1% of municipal solid waste in landfills.

All of this raises the question: is it legitimate to target bottled water producers? Is similar attention being paid to really big water users, such as agriculture, or old and inefficient infrastructure? Part of the bottled water focus is due to the fact that large corporations are easy, cohesive advocacy targets. But of all drinks sold in plastic bottles, water is the easiest to replace instantly—in most industrial countries—it is quasi-ubiquitous, safe and cheap, and in this regard makes for an excellent advo-cacy target, since the public can act instantaneously.

Those pushing for extended producer responsibility would demand that compa-nies take responsibility for their containers' life-cycle. But producers have shunned deposit programmes and emphasised community recycling, for which they are not responsible and incur no costs. There are, however, signs of change: in September 2007, Coca-Cola announced its intent to build the world's largest recycling plant in order to recycle and re-use the entirety of its plastic packaging in the United States.[36] Unfortunately, there was no specified time-frame. Nestlé and Coca-Cola are reducing the plastic in certain bottle sizes by 20–30% to diminish plastic waste and the energy spent in making the bottles. Nestlé produces its own bottles on-site, so they don't have to be shipped to the plants, which would add to emissions. An option that seems greatly ignored could be a shift towards materials that are more easily biodegradable, such as hemp- and natural fibre-based pseudo-plastics, which are made without resins and break down much more quickly than petro-chemical-based plastics. Finally, producers could offer a re-usable bottle, or join in on the trend of directly encouraging re-use by selling water at a discount to those who bring their own container. Regarding emissions, the problem applies more widely than this industry; legislation and political pressure could encourage the use of modes of transport with lighter footprints.

Legislators could offer consumers a real incentive for bottle return, e.g. a deposit law charging a small sum for each bottle on purchase, which is refunded on return. In the US, states that have deposit laws and community recycling have much better rates of return than the national rate, but they are in a stark minority. Again, there are signs of change: Massachusetts Congressman Ed Markey has called for what amounts to a nationwide deposit law on single-use beverage containers, though his programme is still to be fleshed out, as it currently lacks crucial specifics such as management and sources of funding. A final way to target bottled water consumption is to look at it practically: people also buy bottled water because having a portable form of hydration is practical, since it's not given that there will be a clean source of water wherever one is. In Bath, where council bottled water costs were running into the thousands of pounds annually and a ban on bottled water in all council offices was recently passed, activists have additionally called for the rehabilitation of public water fountains.

As with most environmental dilemmas, the problem is structural: it has to do with how we live and consume in daily and seemingly inconsequential ways. Campaigns such as London On Tap, which seek to raise awareness about our societal disconnect with the environmental and commercial systems we function in, are only a first step to jolt consumers towards simpler, cheaper and more environmentally friendly modes of consumption.

This is not to say that this is not a matter of corporate responsibility. Nestlé articulates its new approach to corporate strategy is one of creating 'shared value' for its shareholders and society. Its 2007 annual corporate responsibility report highlights a range of commercial initiatives that are generating revenues while addressing social problems.[37] Such initiatives are laudable, but any reader of its report could justifiably ask whether this 'shared value' approach is really central to the Nestlé core business. It is difficult to see which social or environmental problem is being addressed, which social value being created, by the sale of bottled water in industrialised countries, rather than adding to existing problems of pollution and waste. The arguments offered by their CEO do not resonate with a 'shared value' approach. Given that many of the examples offered by companies of how they can address social challenges through business are in practice making less of a rate of return than that expected from the business as a whole, are not scalable, and are dependent on government or NGO subsidy through partnership, we may question whether they really embody a new strategy. Perhaps they could be more appropriately understood as an advanced form of an established strategy: effective public relations through corporate philanthropy.

2Q2008

April–June

Jem Bendell and Sandy Lin

Glassed: women and CSR

In June, the 18th Global Summit of Women was held in Vietnam. Known informally as the 'Davos for Women', the Summit attracted over 900 participants from 72 countries and regions.[1] The list of sponsors for the Global Summit of Women included corporate powerhouses such as Microsoft, IBM, Pfizer and FedEx. Despite the scale of the event, the Summit did not garner international press coverage. An internet search revealed that press materials were limited to major dailies in Vietnam, Malaysia and China. The Summit aims to be a celebration of women's achievement. In the Opening Address, Irene Navidad focused on how women have the ability to run businesses successfully. '41% of Rwanda's businesses are owned by women,' she explained. 'The march of female entrepreneurship from agribusiness to tourism came out of the sad opportunity emerging from the genocide, which left agricultural lands, for example, in the hands of women whose husbands, sons and fathers were slaughtered. To survive, women—many of whom had no training or exposure to managing property or farms—had to take control simply in order for their families to survive. With the help of international agencies which provided training and loans to the women, Rwanda came back to life.'[2] This advancement of women out of adversity echoes progress made in women's rights in Europe after World War II, as women had been depended on in factories and farms during the fighting.

There was disquiet being expressed in some media that progress made in the West over the last decades on women's rights, as economies had boomed, are falling back, and look likely to slip further due to an economic downturn. 'So you thought the gender equality cause had come a long way in the last 30 years? Well think again. Not only is gender discrimination in the workplace alive and kicking, it's actually getting worse,' argued the British newspaper *The Independent* in May. It reported on a survey of more than 100 British recruitment agencies, which revealed that 70% had been asked by clients to avoid hiring pregnant women or women of childbearing age.[3] The *New York Times* then reported that women were being laid off faster in the economic downturn.[4]

How is the corporate social responsibility (CSR) profession addressing gender issues? New research published by the International Centre for Corporate Social Responsibility (ICCSR) found that the potential role of business as a vehicle to advance women's issues is often overlooked in corporate responsibility work.[5] In describing the state of CSR and gender equality in the EU, Dr Irmgard Schultz, co-founder of the Institute for Social-Ecological Research (ISOE), states: 'the potential of CSR to promote EU policy goals for gender equality is hardly recognised by the public'.[6] This was evident in a survey conducted by responsible enterprise consulting firm Lifeworth on 'Women and CSR', which invited current members of the mailing list 'CSR Chicks' to share their views. Sixty-four per cent of respondents, who were all female CSR practitioners, stated that their membership of the (gender-specific) network had not led them to think about the role of CSR in women's advancement before the survey was conducted. Fifty-eight per cent reported that gender issues are 'not a top priority' in their organisation's corporate responsibility efforts, 36% that it is one of the top ten priorities, and 6% that it is one of the top three priorities.

With intergovernmental organisations launching several key gender initiatives in 2008, more corporate responsibility practitioners may awaken to a gender perspective. One such initiative was the Danish government's launch of the MDG3 Global Call for Action Campaign, which urged for gender equality and women's empowerment to be put higher up in the international agenda.[7] In a symbolic gesture representing the ignition of a global resolve, they planned for more than 100 MDG3 torches to travel around the world as they are passed to representatives of governments, the private sector, civil society, individuals from North and South and international organisations.[8] Responding to the call to 'do something extra', intergovernmental organisations have taken on a leading role to facilitate and strengthen advocacy on gender equality. On International Women's Day 2008, the Organisation for Economic Cooperation and Development (OECD)'s Development Centre launched Wikigender, an internet portal that aims to foster a bottom-up dialogue on the importance of gender equality. Along with the introduction of the Gender, Institutions and Development Database to determine and analyse obstacles to women's economic development, the OECD aims to fill in the knowledge gap about gender discrimination that is often rooted in social institutions such as norms, traditions and family law.[9]

Following the OECD's lead, in June the International Labour Organisation (ILO) embarked on an awareness-raising campaign. Speaking about the year-long ILO Global Campaign for Gender Equality that will lead up to the ILO conference scheduled in 2009 on 'Gender Equality at the Heart of Decent Work', ILO Director-General Juan Somavia stated, 'although progress is being made, gender equality is still lagging behind in the rapidly changing world of work'. Indeed, despite substantial progress in the closing of the gender pay gap, women are finding out that money and power do not go hand in hand. In the Mastercard Master Index of

Women's Advancement released in March, women in the Asia-Pacific region continue to feel that they are under-represented in managerial positions.[10] The survey measured women's socioeconomic progress according to four indicators. The first two objective indicators are the ratio of female to male participation in labour force and in tertiary education based on source data from national bureau statistics. The remaining two subjective indicators measure female and male perceptions of whether they hold managerial positions and earn above-average income. Their findings that women do not have the same opportunities as men in the workplace corresponded with the ILO report on Global Employment Trends for Women 2008 released in Geneva in the same month. It revealed that, even though more women are working than ever before, they are still clustered in 'low-productivity, low-paid and vulnerable jobs, with no social protection, basic rights nor voice at work'.[11] In Hong Kong in June, Devi Novianti from Christian Action noted there is a particular challenge for domestic helpers, with sexual harassment being a concern. Equal Opportunities Officer Cynthia Lam emphasised that awareness-raising activities, such as training, are key.[12]

It is problematic that the gender impacts of business operations still register low on the radar of CSR programmes and priorities, given that women are disproportionately affected by social and environmental issues. A report released in April by the UN Food and Agriculture Organisation (FAO) on the gender implications of biofuels production asserts that, in light of the increase in food prices, women 'tend to be particularly exposed to chronic and transitory food insecurity, due also to their limited access to income generating activities'.[13] Co-author of the paper Yianna Lambrou said: 'Unless policies are adopted in developing countries to strengthen the participation of small farmers, especially women in biofuel production by increasing their access to land, capital and technology—gender inequalities are likely to become more marked and women's vulnerability to hunger and poverty further exacerbated.'

In high-income nations, key gender issues for business centre on women on boards and the related issue of career mentoring and grooming for leadership roles, equal opportunity and diversity management in employment, segregation in the context of male/female professions and the reconciliation of a work–life balance.[14] Although women in the developed world may face different socioeconomic challenges as a result of their gender identity, common among women of the North and South is a lack of decision-making power, as well as an absence of control and access to resources such as financial credit, technology and property.

The lack of attention paid to gender issues in the corporate world was highlighted by the main CSR-relevant news-making study of the quarter: the IBM report *Global CEO Study: The Enterprise of the Future*.[15] Its survey of over 1,000 CEOs worldwide found that perceiving consumer interests in the social dimension of business has become a key strategic issue. Perhaps women leaders might be involved in this strategic shift? We asked the authors, but found that they had not included a gender variable in their study. On our request they kindly 'drove it' into their data, to find that 5% of their surveyed CEOs are women. 'We did not do any additional analysis using this variable, but it will for the future certainly be interesting,' explained Dr Phaedra Kortekaas of IBM. The 5% figure and the oversight of the relevance of the variable suggest that gender mainstreaming, let alone equality, has some way to go in the corporate world.

Given the scale of the challenge, why is there a lack of gender consciousness in CSR, even though many women are personally involved as CSR practitioners? Interviews with executives led Kate Grosser and Jeremy Moon to conclude 'a lack of civil society engagement with business about gender equality in the workplace'.[16] As civil society pressure plays an important role in shaping corporate responsibility agendas, unless the efforts of the ILO, OECD and others to raise the profile of gender issues changes civil society engagement, leadership will need to come from companies. However, Judi Marshall, a leading writer on women in management, suggests that gender issues may not be raised by women business people in the context of corporate responsibility 'because the challenges CSR might address are [seen as] more important than creating trivial gender skirmishes'.[17] Indeed, gender equality often 'disappears' behind broader CSR preoccupations with labour rights, human rights or the environment. As a result, a gender perspective has not emerged as a key issue, or framing of issues, within CSR. ISOE's study on the banking sector found that there is 'an urgent need to clarify and define gender equality as an indispensable dimension of CSR'.[18]

Professor Marshall attributes the lack of shaping power by women in CSR to the fact that women remain at the margins of CSR leadership. She cites Vandana Shiva and the late Anita Roddick as examples of well-known women who have used raw messages to challenge gender power dynamics. Marshall asserts that their 'discordant and confronting' style of leadership contributes to their marginalisation as activists, *vis-à-vis* more 'tempered radicals' such as Al Gore and environmental scientist James Lovelock, who have found mainstream credibility. It is perhaps time for the CSR narrative to be shaped by a more diverse group of voices. Gender differences in leadership style leads Marshall to wonder if the white male dominance of CSR leadership is 'simply a mirroring of dominant notions of management, business and organizational scholarship'.[19] Additional reasons for this lack of a gendered engagement in CSR may be the absence of gender solidarity due to competitive attitudes both professionally and personally, and a deliberate downplaying of gender issues by female captains in industry, for personal reasons.

This is illustrated by the attitude of the most powerful female CEO in American history, Carly Fiorina, who was fired from her tenure at Hewlett-Packard after five and a half years on the job. In her memoir entitled *Tough Choices*, Fiorina describes that she did not want to talk about her gender or the glass ceiling as she felt these topics were distractions from the mission at hand and might cause alienation among the vast majority of her employees. Fiorina further states that she made a deliberate choice to downplay issues of gender in interviews with the media, as she did not want to draw attention to herself. This lack of clear leadership on women's issues was reflected by results from the Lifeworth survey of the CSR Chicks mailing list. Only 34% of the respondents, all female CSR practitioners, answered yes to the question 'Has the most senior woman in your organisation that you have some direct experience of, mentioned their activities to improve the organisation's impact on women?' Respondents considered 'Personal Leadership from Women CSR Professionals' to be the most important activity within CSR to advance women over the next five years, with 46.0% considering it 'very important'.

Servane Mouazan, managing director of Ogunte, which works on women's leadership development, told *JCC* that more women business executives need to connect with women who are serving their local communities more broadly. She said the Global Summit of Women is an example of how successful women can develop an elite view, by praising themselves for their own success and their support for women and girls in poverty. Thus a critical perspective of how their own societies, institutions and personal behaviours affect women is overlooked. This lack of critical perspective, and the kind of reticence expressed by Ms Fiorina, does not promote awareness of the nature of gender discrimination. Consequently, misunderstandings of attempts to promote diversity at work are widespread. For instance, in a paper to be presented at the Engendering Leadership conference held at the University of Western Australia, Rhonda Pyper suggested that white males can see affirmative action as about providing special privilege rather than levelling power imbalances. While Pyper was describing these change initiatives in the context of equity legislation in Canada, one wonders if the same may be said about reactions to the Equality Bill that was passed in the UK in June.[20]

The pressing need for CSR practitioners to win the 'hearts and minds' of middle-level management to promote gender equality is acknowledged by the ISOE banking case study, where it was found that instruments that are sensitising for gender equality (against gender stereotypes) contributed to the success of CSR initiatives adopted by one of the two banks surveyed in the study. It is only through this process of winning the 'people's case' for gender equality that a change in attitudes will translate to a corresponding change in organisational behaviour. While gender issues may be less easily discussed than climate change, relying on the business case alone to carry broader normative perspectives is unwise, as the societal change desired requires a change in the emotional basis of gendered relations.

The emotional baggage surrounding gendered power relations is reflected in the varied definitions that have been used to bring meaning to the word 'gender', ranging from the use of gender as a concept, an ideology, a perspective, a role, a paradigm, a mechanism and a value. The confusion surrounding the use of the term brings up the question of 'the political reasons for the disappearance of other problematics, concepts, and words ("women," "feminism," and "patriarchy" probably being the most significant) for which progressively but rapidly gender has been efficiently substituted'.[21] While the use of gender as a catch-all term does not eradicate the 'fight' against patriarchy, male domination, power relations between the sexes and the equality/inequality between men and women, one wonders if the term 'gender' now holds any meaning at all, especially when the richness of detail and the sharing of meaning and experience of other concepts it embraces are now subsumed in a single word. Perhaps 'gender' is now a term that is used unknowingly and carelessly to 'enable analyses that disregard patriarchal relations of domination', with the unintended consequence that 'gender' is now a word to legitimise 'the absence of any relation of domination, any system of domination, any thought of domination, of all domination'.[22]

If business is to take on a more active role in women's advancement, existing CSR instruments to promote women's equality must be strengthened. In examining the gender practices of UK companies claiming best practice, the International Centre for Corporate Social Responsibility found that, although there has been 'some improved reporting of performance information' relating to gender equality, the level of reporting was still limited. Authors Kate Grosser and Jeremy Moon attribute this to 'the fact that companies committed to gender equality perceive little advantage to reporting quality information, where market, social and governmental actors appear neither to demand nor reward it, and where media attention risks misuse and misinterpretation of data'.[23] Perhaps an improvement in gendered data collection and impact assessment will occur if the investors in companies begin to make this a priority. Despite conclusive evidence about the business case for gender equality being presented by Catalyst in reports published in 2004 and in 2008, there is limited pressure from the responsible investment community on these issues.[24] Providing 'Evidence of Business Case for Gender Equality' was the second most important activity for CSR to advance women over the next five years, according to respondents to the Lifeworth survey. The launch of the 'Women's Principles' by investment firm Calvert, in partnership with the United Nations Development Fund for Women (UNIFEM) in 2004, has not yet led to a widespread focus on corporate responsibilities for empowering and investing in women worldwide.[25] As the asset management industry has generally been dominated by men, as are corporate boards, the discussion of women at investor relations meetings probably leaves a lot to be desired.

The conclusion must be that real change will occur if women decide to lead the agenda themselves. 'What Rwandan women demonstrated is that in order to create change in their lives, they looked to themselves first,' explained Irene Navidad in Hanoi. 'That is why I say over and over to women everywhere—it is not enough to envision change, you must see yourself as the agent of change. This next century is ours, and we women are poised to demonstrate to the world that the economies of each of our countries can only flourish, as it did in Rwanda, if we are given the chance to lead. But like the Rwandan women, do not wait for leadership to come calling, remember that it's not enough to envision change, you must see yourself as the agent of change.'[26]

Inspi(RED) marketing or (RED)wash?

In June the largest student and alumni network on corporate responsibility, Net Impact, organised its first European conference; or, to be more precise, volunteers from the University of Geneva and INSEAD organised it ably for them. The efforts of students in bringing together hundreds of delegates for a packed programme indicates the importance of Net Impact as a key connector in an emerging movement of young professionals that are 'socialising' business, as much as socialising with business. Or so we may hope. More on that later.

One of the highlights for an audience yearning for the possibility of both a corporate career and a clear conscience was a plenary on Product(RED) and its contribution to the Global Fund to Fight AIDS, Tuberculosis and Malaria. Launched in 2006 by U2 singer and activist Paul Hewson (known popularly as Bono), Product(RED) is 'a brand designed to engage business and consumer power in the fight against AIDS in Africa'. It works with the 'world's best brands' to make unique (RED)-branded products and direct up to 50% of their gross profits to the Global Fund to Fight AIDS, TB and Malaria, to fund African HIV/AIDS programmes with a focus on the health of women and children. (RED) explains it 'is not a charity or campaign' but 'an economic initiative that aims to deliver a sustainable flow of private sector money to the Global Fund'.[27] Greta Thomas told a few hundred delegates at the conference in Geneva that Product(RED) is 'the most successful cause marketing initiative in history', having raised over 100 million dollars for the Global Fund, through about 350 co-branded products in 60 countries. Product partners include Converse, Gap, Motorola, Emporio Armani, Apple, Hallmark, Dell, Microsoft and American Express. (RED) reports there are currently more than 45,000 people on antiretroviral medication in Ghana, Swaziland and Rwanda owing to support from these funds.

Great stuff. So who could be complaining? Around the time of its launch, some NGOs grumbled. '(RED) is unlikely to raise significant amounts of money to close the funding gap of US$3 billion over 2006–7 and risks giving business a good cover story without pressing them for a more substantial contribution,' wrote Aditi Sharma, International HIV/AIDS Campaign Coordinator with ActionAid International. But (RED) couldn't be held responsible for the woeful response of the wider private sector at the time of the call for donations. A more worrying attack for (RED) came a year later when *Advertising Age*, a key magazine for that profession, published an article that argued the brands involved in (RED) had spent far more on advertising than had been raised for the global fund at that point in time. They had got their figures slightly wrong, so boss and co-owner of the company behind (RED), Bobby Shriver, slammed the article. His riposte did, however, contain evidence that the companies had spent almost twice as much on advertising than had been raised by (RED) for AIDS work at that time. The criticism must have hurt, as 15 months later Ms Thomas mentioned it from the podium, and explained that, as people are going to continue being materialistic, and businesses are going to continue to advertise, it's worth looking to get some good out of that process. The president of (RED), Tamsin Smith, told the *New York Times*, 'We're not encouraging people to buy more, but if they're going to buy a pair of Armani sunglasses, we're trying to get a cut of that for a good cause,' she said.[28]

With people doing such ingenious, well-meaning and useful work, it can seem rather mean to pick holes. But someone has to do the unpleasant jobs. 'Not encouraging people to buy more'? Was that really part of their pitch to Dell when asking the computer company to pay a big licence fee upfront, as Dell planned a prime-time 2008 SuperBowl advertising slot in the United States for its (RED) laptop. All cause marketing, all advertising, all sponsorship, all PR is ultimately directed at encouraging people to buy from a particular company. Let us accept that and consider whether or not it is a good thing for the cause concerned that people buy more from a particular company.

From the floor of the conference the prolific writer on responsible business Wayne Visser asked the question that was in the minds of many who work on corporate responsibility issues: how does (RED) deal with the social responsibility of its product partners? Although Dr Visser chose not to give examples of (RED)'s product partners engaging in commerce that is ultimately detrimental to the cause, he would be aware that a UN study has found that corporations may be undermining the global fight against AIDS due to the impacts of their value chains on the conditions for HIV transmission and progression, and by not seeking to address these.[29] For example, cobalt is a necessary component of all mobile phones. Cobalt is predominantly found in the Congo. A vigorous mining industry has sprung up to service this need. And mining has been key to the spread of AIDS in Africa. So we are entitled to ask about the *negative* impact on the fight against HIV of purchasing, for example, Motorola(RED) phones. It can be put quite bluntly: an initiative that promotes more business-as-usual in these high-risk sectors by encouraging sales is in fact exacerbating the spread of HIV/AIDS.[30]

In response to concerns about its product partners, (RED) espoused a set of principles, among which are: '(RED) respects its employees and asks its partners to do the same with their employees and the people who help make their products or deliver their services' and '(RED) promotes HIV/AIDS workplace policies and practices'. To this end, it is working with the Global Business Coalition against HIV. In 2008 Motorola was not yet a member of this coalition; and the company's 2007 CSR report does not mention working on HIV/AIDS workplace policies and programmes with its suppliers. In that report the auditor Verité calls for Motorola to do more on promoting awareness among its suppliers of the company's code on various aspects of labour relations.[31] So there is no evidence that Motorola has improved the impacts of its value chain to a degree that could give one confidence in a statement that one of its products is 'Designed to Eliminate AIDS in Africa', as its advertising claims.

Ms Thomas responded to Dr Visser by suggesting that when a company 'signs up for Product(RED) it is arguably putting a great big target on its forehead for spotlighting its broader CSR activities'. This spotlight effect is yet to be seen in Motorola's policies and programmes on HIV/AIDS. So, perhaps by writing this article we are in some way helping (RED) achieve this spotlight effect. We are happy to help, but might a more hands-on approach from (RED) more usefully consider the product partners as well as the intended beneficiaries in Africa?

The head of Private Sector Resource Mobilisation at the Global Fund, David Evans, declared from the podium that '(RED) involvement can be the start of a conversation with a company and in creating a deeper engagement with your cause'. He explained the Fund's discussions with Nike—which is a (RED) partner through its ownership of Converse—about what could be done on gender issues, given the 'feminisation' of the AIDS epidemic. 'Financial contributions . . . can't be the end of a conversation; it has to be the start,' he said.

Ms Thomas explained that (RED) encourages companies where possible to source or manufacture in Africa, in order to create employment in export industries. Some of the partners have sought to create positive relationships with African entrepreneurs as part of their (RED) commitment. Designer Giorgio Armani said, 'as I set about designing my first collection of Emporio Armani(RED) products I wanted to create a tangible and personal connection with Africa. What better way than to incorporate the striking art of Owusu-Ankomah . . . ?' Armani is now sourcing materials for its T-shirts from Mozambique, although no information is provided on its website or that of (RED) about the working conditions. More enterprise in low-income countries, whatever the enterprise and whatever the employment conditions, is not in itself progressive: the problems in the mining and manufacturing sectors provide a simple illustration of that. Creating decent work in sustainable enterprises must be the goal.[32] The US company GAP was more forthcoming about its aims for its (RED) products to make a positive contribution beyond the fundraising. The company has worked to ensure decent labour conditions in the factories there. Of particular relevance is its work on HIV/AIDS in the garment sector in Lesotho. It has funded the Apparel Lesotho Alliance to Fight AIDS (ALAFA), to provide HIV testing and treatment options to thousands of garment workers. GAP has also lent its expertise on dyes and yarns, thus building local capacity to enter the Western market.[33]

Aside from questions of how much is being raised compared to the marketing spend, and whether the participating companies are doing much on the HIV/AIDS impacts of their value chains, others have raised a broader critique about consumerism. The critics say it sends a message to the public that the current economic system and its large corporations are part of the solution to social challenges such as HIV/AIDS rather than an obstacle to their abatement. A political economic analysis of the reasons why governments, communities and individuals have been unable to protect and then look after themselves adequately can raise questions about the current system of corporate globalisation. One group called Product(RE) argues that 'simply buying an item or advertising support for a cause will not solve an epidemic . . . it takes thinking more critically and consciously about how we consume'. It launched a counter-campaign that raises funds for HIV/AIDS in Africa through the reclaiming and recycling of consumer products, branded with a (RE)D logo, which involves (RE)cycling. They argue that (RED) 'implies that corporations, branding and consumption are a necessary and healthy part of involvement in a cause . . . [but such] marketing is not only manipulative, but damaging. It claims to erase any guilt from shopping by offering products that aim to be not only ethically neutral but activist in nature . . . "This is for the greater good", supplants doubts about the questionable origins or future life of an object.'[34] Could Product(RED) be a form of (RED)wash, a corporate pretence towards social benefit, perhaps more insidious than 'greenwash', the pretence of environmental friendliness by business?

The company that owns the (RED) brand, Persuaders LLC, was not impressed, and its lawyers took steps against the (RE)D initiative. With that, the company is asserting that its critics should be legally accountable for any breach of copyright. However, others may question to whom the Persuaders LLC, or its owners Paul Hewson and Bobby Shriver, should be accountable to in respect of their product partners' direct and indirect impacts on public health. Because, when pressed on the criticisms we have outlined here, (RED) spokespersons remind us, 'we are a business, not a charity'.[35] As a business with a growing role in the fight against AIDS, Persuaders LLC now requires more attention to its own social responsibility. The first step is transparency. Persuaders LLC does not have a website. Its co-owners are two of the richest men in the world, one of whom wrote the disinguous statement '(RED) "shareholders" are the poorest of the world's poor'.[36] That sounds like a great idea. However, while it is owned by people who don't need the money, and encourages people to buy into their brand to give money to charity, it is important to know how much income (RED) receives from the process. It does not divulge the licence fees it is paid to set up the product partnerships, what percentage of its own turnover (if any) it is taking as profit, or what levels of accountability it aspires to in operational issues such as its own overheads and salaries.

The contract between the Fund and Persuaders LLC is not public and neither are those between Persuaders and the participating companies. One person working on the project told us that the participating companies can pull out of the scheme if Bono is not involved in future. If the Fund's projections are correct, then this would mean in future almost 10% of the Fund's work would depend on the interest and health of one rock star. People and institutions change over time, for better or worse, and so systems should be 'future-proof'. A lack of transparency means concerned people cannot check these issues.

Another concern has been raised by some NGOs about the influence of (RED), and its corporate partners, on the Global Fund. That fund is governed by rules that ensure human need, not donor interest, determines the activities it funds. However, (RED) wished to promote itself to consumers by highlighting who was benefiting, and so a compromise was reached whereby (RED) could identify itself with projects in Africa, but not further, and the connecting of a participating company to a specific project was done following careful procedures. In subsequent years further specificity has been allowed, including specific countries and types of intended beneficiary. As a result other corporate donors can now brand their philanthropy in the same way. If corporate giving increases, this could cause problems for the system of needs-driven grant-making. The influence of business interests on the strategy of (RED) is illustrated by Persuaders currently considering whether to expand their giving to Asia, so that Asian companies may be more inclined to join (RED).

There seems to be a pattern emerging in the way (RED) responds to criticism. When criticised that it is not doing enough for the social cause, it reminds people it is a business not a charity. When criticised for not being a good business, it reminds everyone of its charitable contributions. Given (RED)'s offices in London are within the PR company Freud, one might be inclined to think this double-speak is carefully conceived. However, it is more likely that it reflects unreconstructed notions of business and charity. Cause marketing maintains that dichotomy: business makes money, charity takes it, and the political economic order stays the same. That order is being eroded by corporate responsibility and social enterprise, which seek to create social benefit through core business operations. (RED) is not part of that movement. It could be. It could be a catalyst for mainstream corporate responsibility, starting by ensuring that the value chains of its product partners have the best possible workplace policies and programmes on HIV/AIDS.

The Global Fund is leading the way in tackling HIV/AIDS, tuberculosis and malaria. It has unrivalled levels of transparency on matters other than corporate engagement. The private sector, (RED) included, must respect that transparency and needs-driven governance process. The key is to keep the goal in sight. Although for (RED) 'in the end it's about the dollars', the Fund's purpose is not about raising cash, but about reducing disease; is not about spending money on grantees, but ultimately about reducing the need for people to need such charity in the first place. Unless the Fund and its private sector partners keep that in view and seek to tackle the root causes of the problems, including the way economic processes and companies are involved, then they will fail their historic mandate.

Movement East?

At the same Net Impact conference, Simon Zadek of AccountAbility encouraged younger delegates to think about why they were interested in the conference. Perhaps in the future being a CSR manager in a company such as Motorola could be an important role to play; or perhaps not, he mused. He challenged delegates to consider what the challenges of tomorrow's world will be, rather than focusing on what has emerged over the last decade. The emerging corporations on the world stage are from Brazil, India, China and Russia, he explained, and engaging them is key. This view is shared by other Western practitioners, such as Jane Nelson, with Harvard University, who has emphasised that India and China need to embrace corporate responsibility or other efforts are futile.[37] Policy Advisor Eddie Rich,[38] of the Extractive Industries Transparency Initiative, agrees that the influence of companies from these countries is key to the effort against corruption worldwide. It was promising, therefore, that the IBM study of CEOs found that Asian respondents were placing higher importance on their social responsibilities than those from other regions.

As a contribution to the UN Principles for Responsible Management Education working group on Research Priorities, in April Lifeworth conducted a survey of the 4,000 subscribers to its bulletin on CSR about their view of the future of research needs on responsible business. Respondents considered that the most important regions for future CSR research are in Asia. Other regions with emerging nations were also ranked highly, as shown in Figure 8.[39]

Figure 8: **Where should we focus in future?**

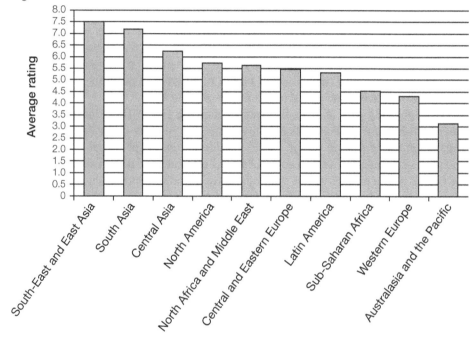

Dr Zadek wondered out loud whether it would be the Chinese oil firm Sinopec, rather than Shell, that would have more influence on sustainable development in years to come, for good or ill, and whether Net Impact delegates would seek jobs in the more challenging companies and environments in order to maximise their influence. 'What's your appetite?' That question encourages us to reflect on whether corporate responsibility is emerging as a profession or social movement, or both. If processes of professionalisation dominate, with codes and qualifications determining what is considered appropriate, will that help or hinder the transformative potential of people working in this space? Many of those people speak of being part of a movement: a search for 'corporate social responsibility movement' delivers 13,700 hits on Google.[40] If it *is* a social movement, what are the implications for priorities of work, and of research?

The field of social movement studies is large, and draws on experiences as diverse as the civil rights movement, the feminist movement and the environmental movement. The basic insights of these historical experiences and analyses are that people in a movement benefit from developing an understanding of common values and goals. They benefit from a sense of shared identity, from knowledge of the repertoires of action that movement participants use, and the elites that they engage with. They consider methods of entryism into those elites and the dangers of co-optation, because they recognise the role of power in both shaping the problems they seek to overcome and the opportunities for change. Consequently, they discuss strategies for influencing the political opportunities they can seize, and choose terminology on the basis of its potential to mobilise people and create deeper change. People participating in movements often recognise particular convening processes, networks and organisations as key to the movement's success and evolution. In light of this context of the history of social movements, the corporate responsibility movement, if there is such a thing, still has some way to progress. The limited evidence of gender consciousness and solidarity among women working in corporate responsibility, discussed above, may be a symptom of a movement that does not yet know itself. Whether the outcome of networks such as Net Impact will be the socialising of business, rather than merely the business of socialising, is yet to be seen. The potential for a movement to emerge and have a historic impact on society is explored in more detail by Jem Bendell in *The Corporate Responsibility Movement*.[41]

3Q2008
July–September

Jem Bendell, Niaz Alam and Barbara Wettstein

Hungry bubbles

Money, money, money. By mid-2008 money was certainly making the world go round, first in a spin, then a downward spiral. The financial system really unravelled in the third quarter of 2008. Yet, before the credit crunch became a credit calamity, at the top of the world's agenda was the huge inflation in the price of food, with some pointing an accusing finger at that soon-to-be-endangered species—the investment banker.

As the world saw a doubling in wheat prices and tripling in rice prices in a year, leading to food riots in over a dozen countries, Olivier De Schutter, the United Nations special rapporteur on the right to food, said that, although climate change played a part, 'speculation in commodity markets, driven in part by investors seeking havens from slumping stocks has . . . contributed heavily to hunger by pushing food prices out of reach for tens of millions'.[1] In the last few years, regulations and advice have been changed to enable large institutional investors to buy into commodities-tracking funds, thus allowing huge sums to pour into this sector and its derivatives, such as options and futures. 'This has been a serious factor aggravating the crisis,' Mr De Schutter said, with some retailers and global agribusiness firms benefiting disproportionately from the price hikes.

One implication of this situation for investor responsibility is that investors need to assess more carefully the societal and longer-term economic implications of any regulatory changes they seek. Investors have been incorporating the political affairs of the corporations they invest in as part of their environmental, social and governance (ESG) assessment, but what of the political involvement of the private financial institutions themselves? Might we expect their own political influence to be consistent with the longer-term interests of the people whose money they manage? It is an issue we return to below when considering the influence of financial institutions and their former staff on the regulators.

Although clearly a topic of increasing concern and research, the food crisis had not produced a concerted response by socially responsible investment (SRI) organisations. This disparity is reflected in the varied views collated in June in an *Investment Week* survey of UK ethical investment analysts by Sarah Griffiths.[2] Gonzalo Baranda of JPMorgan Asset Management said the food crisis was in part driven by long-term trends of 'an increasing world population and a change in consumption patterns in rapidly growing emerging markets with, for instance, an increase in the consumption of meat', but that 'growth in demand for heavily subsidised biofuels' were an exacerbating factor.

Speaking to Jeffrey MacDonald of the *Christian Science Monitor* in August,[3] Lloyd Kurtz, principal at Nelson Capital Management, a private money-management firm in Palo Alto, California, said, 'It's hard to figure out who to blame for the food crisis. Social investment has been most influential when there was an actor that could be identified—e.g., the tobacco companies, the South African apartheid regime, etc. But the causes of the global food crisis are multifaceted . . . That's probably why you haven't seen a coherent response from the social-investment community.'

One response came in June when the Interfaith Center on Corporate Responsibility launched an initiative to tackle food-related issues and propose investing guidelines for its 275 institutional investor members with projects aiming to encourage sustainable agriculture worldwide. Joachim von Braun, director-general of the International Food Policy Research Institute, a food-security think-tank in Washington, DC, also looked at what investors might do to positively help the situation. He advised that 'The mobilization of capital for agricultural growth, especially in the small-farm economy, definitely cannot come only from the public sector. So the private sector has a very important role to play in order to mitigate and overcome the current food crisis.' He urged social investors to shun commodity futures trading and instead provide 'what small-farm agriculture really needs, [which] is long-term investment'. Von Braun added that 'Ethically motivated investors should stay away from grain- and oilseed-based biofuels because these biofuels by now are the cause of about one-third of the overall increase in food prices.' In select cases, he told the *Christian Science Monitor*, development of certain biofuels can be justified, but 'the large-scale investment in Europe and North America has been extremely damaging to world food security'.

The price of many foodstuffs fell back somewhat in the third quarter of 2008, but the price inflation forewarned of likely future scenarios, as climate impacts increase, groundwater and soils are depleted, industrial agriculture becomes more expensive due to peaking oil production, and global finance herds from one asset class to another. Socially responsible investors need to consider these root causes. A key factor has been that investment seeks the greatest returns without pricing in externalities such as carbon, or the risk to future generations from a food supply dependent on oil. This gives rise to situations such as in the Philippines, which went from a net exporter to the largest importer of rice in a matter of decades, as investment poured into its business process outsourcing industry, and government and industry turned their backs on domestic agriculture. Supporting the resilience of communities and economies should be a key dimension to responsible investment, with encouragement given to the government facilitation of investment to build such resilience.

Another issue highlighted by food inflation is the bubbling nature of our financial system. Most countries use a debt-money system, where money is created by private banks in the form of loans. Consequently, as Chris Martenson explained on Sea Change Radio, there is not enough money in the world to pay back all the debt. It leads to a situation where the economy must continually grow because of compound interest. This, he argues, leads to inevitable economic bubbles.[4] Any form of bubble can cause a problem for asset owners, who lose out far more when the bubble bursts, compared to the financial services professionals, who can make a personal fortune on commissions as the bubble inflates. A bubble affecting the price of goods that are needed by disadvantaged people (think rice rather than shares in 'buy.com') presents a double whammy, as many people are hurt as the bubble inflates. If a bubble becomes too large, due to an inability to create units of value out of thin air (think derivatives of mortgage-backed securities) bought by people with access to sufficient credit (think 'sufficient' to keep the process going until they get their bonus), then you have the mother of all bubbles, which leads to a financial crisis. As institutional investors such as pension funds invest in the whole economy, they are particularly vulnerable to boom-and-bust cycles, and yet we might expect them to be particularly able and willing to influence the economy, as part of their duty to their policy holders. Yet, as we will see, this has not happened, and people who have saved for their whole lives are as a consequence hurt by a lack of systemic fiduciary duty shown by those meant to safeguard their future.

From bail-outs to better capitalism

People began to realise just how bad the situation with the financial industry was when governments began bailing out major banks and insurers. They started in the US, in March, with investment bank Bear Stearns. Then, in the space of ten days in September, the two mortgage giants Fannie Mae and Freddie Mac were taken over by the federal government as was one of the world's biggest insurers, American International Group (AIG). During the same period the four remaining large independent banks disappeared. Lehman Brothers was allowed to fail, Bank of America acquired Merrill Lynch at a discounted price while Goldman Sachs and Morgan Stanley turned themselves into regulated banks.

The Federal Reserve System (Fed)'s lax monetary policy, leading to abundant liquidity in the system, and loosening lending practices combined to cause a crisis in sub-prime mortgages in the US. What transformed this into a global financial crisis was the complex and opaque securitisation process and the shadow banking system made of off-balance-sheet vehicles, special-purpose vehicles and the like.

Yet, as the crisis developed, it became clear that the whole system of highly lever-aged banking had become unstable and unsustainable.

In a first plan to rescue the financial system, the US Treasury Secretary Hank Paulson and the Chairman of the Board of Governors of the Fed, Ben Bernanke, had Congress pass a vast bail-out of US financial institutions whereby the Treasury Department can buy up to $700 billion in toxic mortgage-backed securities or recapitalise the banks.[5] This dramatic turn of events raised many questions and was widely commented upon. Were these bail-outs necessary? Should taxpayers' money be used to bail out private companies that failed because of their excessive risk taking? What should regulators and government demand in return? In other words, who should pay the price for yesterday's recklessness?

That bankers were going to be bailed out, while homeowners still struggled, was galling to many. Robert Borosage, president of the Institute for America's Future, said, 'many homeowners were misled by predatory lenders to taking mortgages that they didn't understand and couldn't afford. It would be simply obscene to help the predators and not those that they preyed on.'[6] Some also questioned the revolving door between bankers and regulators, and whether people such as Paulson, who became super-rich from working in one of the firms whose practices had helped create the crisis, should be deciding how to hand out billions to the same sector.[7] They could point to investment firms scrambling for the oversight of all the assets that the Treasury planned to buy, so they could receive hundreds of millions of dol-lars in fees.[8] News that the bankruptcy courts had released $2.5 billion to secure Lehman Brothers bonus payments, at a time when savers were still losing out, was just one example of a situation that seemed to many like a systemic abuse of power by a professional elite of regulators, judiciary and bankers.[9]

The bail-outs were defended by the fact that these financial institutions were 'too big' or 'too interconnected' to fail and that failure would have caused a systemic risk. If governments and regulators have let financial institutions become so big that they cannot be allowed to collapse, shouldn't they be encouraging more com-petition and more diversity? This is at least the view of trade unions. UNI Finance Global Union, the global trade union for finance workers, has repeatedly called for a diverse finance market that includes not only private banks and insurance com-panies but also public banks, savings banks and insurances, cooperative banks, mutual insurance companies and foundations.[10] However, this does not seem to be the view of governments and regulators who were pushing failing institutions into the arms of healthier ones (for example, the acquisition of Merrill Lynch by Bank of America in the United States or the takeover of HBOS by Lloyds TSB in the United Kingdom). As Lina Saigol, a *Financial Times* columnist, argued, this 'new genera-tion of gargantuan institutions [will have] the power to dictate the next financial boom and bust'.[11] With the new injection of funds from governments, many banks turned their attention to attempts at buying each other out, and thus compound-ing the problems associated with market domination by too few players, rather than getting back to the business of lending money to people in the business of making things for others.

Another issue raised by the bail-outs was that of moral hazard. Many commentators, including *Financial Times* columnist John Gapper, argued that the rescue of AIG 'encourages the idea that institutions can run amok in markets and will be bailed out. Indeed, the bigger they are and the worse they have behaved, the more likely it is to happen.'[12] Other critics called these events 'a perfect demonstration of Wall Street socialism'[13] and the 'socialisation of finance'.[14] It is true that the financial industry seems to have understood better than any other how to privatise gains but socialise losses. After all, in 2007, Daniel Mudd, the CEO of Fannie Mae, reaped a 7% pay increase to $13.4 million while his company was losing $2.1 billion and its shares fell 33%.[15]

In many cases the bail-outs became part-nationalisations of the banks involved. This gave governments some additional influence over their practices, yet most politicians were cautious about what influence they would exert, and merely spoke about future executive pay. This timidity is an issue we return to in the following section, when discussing the broader implications of the financial crisis.

The irony of increasing government ownership of the banks is that taxpayers may face a double whammy of their own. Not only have they bought up bad debts, but they have bought into potentially massive legal liabilities. In a comment in *The Guardian*, Nick Leeson, the trader who brought down Barings Bank in 1995, said, 'For my role in the collapse of Barings I was pursued around the world, and ended up being sentenced to six and half years in a Singaporean jail. Who is going to go after the reckless individuals responsible for the financial catastrophe? Apparently no one.'[16] However, as time passed there appeared to be growing pressure to hold companies as well as individuals responsible for the global financial crisis. On 24 September, regulators announced the broadening of the investigations into the collapse of the sub-prime mortgage market to include Fannie Mae, Freddie Mac, Lehman Brothers and AIG.[17] In addition, many observers expected a sharp rise in shareholder lawsuits against investment banks and other financial institutions following the millions of dollars of losses they made by gambling money in asset-backed securities and the like.[18] Lawsuits were emerging from Hong Kong to Paris to Reykjavik.

These actions slam the legal door after the capital horse has bolted. Rather than punishing the individuals who profited from using other people's money to buy derivatives they did not fully understand, but knew could turn a profit in time for their next bonus, this legal action will cost the companies' new owners, including the taxpayer. First the bankers, then the lawyers, will have bled the collective purse. As this situation becomes visible to the general public, calls for the people who made millions from speculating with their money to replenish their depleted pension funds may grow. There could be investigation into whether there was abuse of fiduciary duty by those who received large bonuses through creating, investing, rating or trading in mortgage-backed securities or credit-default swaps since the deregulation of those markets in 1999. Given the mobility of capital, such processes would require international cooperation, to freeze assets of those being investigated. If this happened, it would remind us of the words of Interface CEO Ray

Anderson, who said that people like him would in future be regarded as criminals for doing things that at the time they considered normal business. Letting bankers live as millionaires, some as billionaires, from creating a crisis that has emptied the pensions funds and now the coffers of government, would sadly stand as a testament to systemic injustices of contemporary societies. However, it is unlikely that governments will want to see such a wave of litigation. As such, there may be growing calls for some form of 'financial truth and reconciliation' commission, to explore how this crisis developed, where fault lies, and how to repatriate some savings.

The end of financial triumphalism

Time will tell what the lessons of the financial crisis really are. One way of exploring the lessons is to look at how people were apportioning the blame at the time. From lenders to investors to regulators, it seemed everyone had blood on their hands. As Bill Gross, chief investment officer at Pimco, the world's biggest bond fund, put it, 'we are all to blame. For the most part, you can throw in central bankers, Wall Street, investment bankers and you can throw investors into the pot as well as mortgage bankers and regulators who looked the other way.'[19]

Joseph Stiglitz, winner of the 2001 Nobel Prize for Economics, summarised the main debate around the financial industry and its social responsibility: 'In both the UK and the US, about 40 per cent of corporate profits go to the finance industry. What is the social function of the industry that justifies that generous money? The industry exists for managing risk and allocating capital. Well, it clearly didn't do either very well [. . .] The idea that banks should self-regulate, relying on their own risk management systems and rating agencies, is absurd. We lost sight of why regulation is needed. The trouble is that regulators are too close to the people they are regulating. There was a party going on and nobody wanted to be a party pooper.'[20]

It is true that clues of the crisis to come were abundantly available to regulators. As early as 1993, the Interfaith Center on Corporate Responsibility (ICCR), a faith-based investors' association, warned of the risks to households, communities and investors associated with sub-prime lending.[21] In 2000, a House of Representatives hearing addressed many of the issues that were blamed for the sub-prime market woes, in particular abuses by mortgage lenders.[22] In December 2006, a report by the Center for Responsible Lending, a not-for-profit organisation based in North Carolina (USA), published a report showing that, despite low interest rates and a favourable economic environment, foreclosure rates in the sub-prime market were very high (almost 20%). The report held predatory lending practices such as adjustable rate mortgages, no- or low-doc loans and pre-payment penalties as culpable.[23]

There is also evidence that regulators knew about the loosening of lending standards. The Fed's survey on bank lending practices revealed a deep fall in standards beginning in 2004 until the end of the housing boom in 2006.[24] In addition, global institutions, such as the Bank of International Settlements, issued warnings of the risks associated to parts of the US housing market in 2004.[25]

If the evidence was so clear, how could the regulators let the party go on? According to former International Monetary Fund (IMF) Chief Economist Kenneth Rogoff, governments and central bankers fell prey to 'financial triumphalism',[26] the idea that light regulation and a self-correcting financial market are not only enough to maintain discipline but can help economies to grow faster. That the IMF did little to curb this process, and a lot to increase it through influencing financial liberalisation, raises a serious question mark over its legitimacy and proficiency in helping solve the problems now. It was the International Labour Organisation of the UN that has been warning in recent years of the excessive financialisation of the economy.[27]

Financial derivatives had became so complex that people trading in them did not really know how they worked, just that they were offered from reputable institutions and were receiving good credit ratings. The more complicated a product, the more ingenious, and the more profitable, or so it seemed. Some call this approach the greater fool theory, or pyramid selling: so long as someone else is willing to buy, then the prices can keep going up. Some talk about a collapse of trust, but that is misrepresenting what was involved in the market and emptying the term 'trust' of any meaning. Trust involves people. Most trades are done through a computer, often automatically. Finance professionals did not so much as trust, but they assumed—that complexity, ingenuity, a famous institution, and large market power, were all signifiers of financial value. With the onset of the credit crunch they now assume almost the opposite—hence inter-bank lending grinding to a halt.

Credit ratings agencies took some heat for an apparent lack of rigour in their valuation of complex derivatives. Developments in accounting, with the introduction of mark-to-market or 'fair value' approaches, facilitated a global-market groupthink of 'it is valuable because many of us think that many other people think it is valuable'. The credit ratings agencies are involved in a process that sociologists call 'social construction', i.e. where assumptions, beliefs and norms are constructed by people and organisations in society. The larger and more famous the ratings agencies, the more authoritative their ratings are and the greater impact on perceptions and thus of the market price of what they value. Thus within the current system there is an implicit value in play—that might is right. The socially constructed nature of financial markets was discussed at length by financier George Soros. Yet he did not articulate a value basis from which such processes could be more accurate and beneficial. Sociologists and stakeholder dialogue experts have different views on how a socially constructed concept of something's nature or worth can be made legitimate and effective, with some advocating forms of 'communicative action' in the process as a way to achieve a participatory and intelligent view of phenomena. There is no such 'communicative action' in the valuing of assets in the financial markets.

Perhaps the underlying reason for this situation is a lack of sociological and political-historical understanding within the financial services sector and its regulators. Finance services professionals, like most people, are naturally competent in objectivist or positivist approaches to understanding reality, and so, when they work in fields that are relativist in their nature, they are not at ease with exploring how we might wish to shape the ways in which we decide what the value of something is, and so just fall back on mob rule—where something is valued according to the sum of the views of the most powerful. If we are explicit about values, then we might seek a credit ratings system that allows new entrants, balances views, moderates the influence of strategic commercial self-interest and seeks to arrive at socially beneficial forms of valuation, such as using a five-capitals model of valuation.[28] In this way the financial system might be able to learn something from the corporate responsibility community. A lack of political-historical understanding also contributed to the problem, according to Harvard historian Niall Ferguson. He said that most people in the industry and its regulators do not have memories stretching back before the 1980s, so they do not understand how financial systems have evolved over time and how they can collapse.[29]

This philosophical turn may seem to some readers to be miles away from matters of corporate citizenship. What are the implications of this financial crisis for corporate responsibility and responsible finance? A few immediately appear. First is the issue some dub 'the political bottom line'.[30] Intense lobbying by the financial industry helps explain how the financial crisis took shape. According to the non-profit advocacy organisation Common Cause, the mortgage lending industry spent nearly US$210 million between 1999 and 2006 in lobbying activities as well as political campaigns contributions to both Democratic and Republican politicians that helped persuade the US Congress to refrain from passing regulation that would restrict predatory lending practices.[31] In addition, economist Robert Kuttner blamed the repealing of key protections put in place by the New Deal for contributing to the crisis.[32] An example of this is the Gramm–Leach–Bliley Act (1999), which eliminated restrictions on affiliations between commercial banks and investment banks. Senator Phil Gramm, who led the charge to pass this bill, has close ties with the financial industry: he is a vice chairman at UBS Investment Bank and was paid by the Swiss bank to lobby Congress on mortgage-related legislation.[33] The political affairs of corporations are a key element of social responsibility, implying transparency and consultation on the societal impact of the forms of regulatory change sought by investors.

A second implication for corporate responsibility, and responsible finance, is that much of the work being done in our area is fiddling around the edges, and not addressing fundamental economic issues. The Enron collapse led *Business Ethics* editor Marjorie Kelly to question whether work on corporate responsibility risked being beside the point, and called for more focus on the fundamentals of corporate law and financing.[34] In the book *The Corporate Responsibility Movement*, it is argued that corporate responsibility is evolving in a way that can address these deeper challenges.[35] 'The corporate responsibility movement is a loosely organised but sustained effort by individuals both inside and outside the private sector, who seek to use or change specific corporate practices, whole corporations, or entire systems of corporate activity, in accordance with their personal commitment to public goals and the expectations of wider society.' The analysis suggests an interlocking framework is slowly emerging, which seeks to integrate economic and social principles, dubbed 'capital democracy' by the author, Jem Bendell. 'Capital democracy describes an economic system that moves towards the creation, allocation and management of capital according to the interests of everyone directly affected by that process, in order to support the self-actualisation of all'.

Might the financial crisis spur professionals in the corporate responsibility and responsible finance fields to take up this deeper agenda? One process holding back an embrace of that agenda is the way that work in this field has been defined as a particular set of professional practices rather than an evolving field of societal expectation on business and finance. This delineation of a field of practice meant that, in August, the United Nations Principles on Responsible Investment (UNPRI) could put out a press release reporting 'Rapid growth in Responsible Investment despite credit crisis'.[36] They were referring to new signatories, yet many of those same signatories were being lambasted at the same time for irresponsibly investing in ill-understood derivative markets. Until now the field of investor responsibility has been defined by the investors themselves. Therefore the focus has been on the social, environmental and governance (ESG) performance of the firms they invest in. But, with the financial crisis, they are beginning to have to look in the ESG mirror, as the public and civil society increasingly question the financial institutions themselves.

Perhaps the lasting impact on the corporate responsibility field will be that the more critical perspectives, such as those often reported in these pages, will receive greater attention from the shapers of the mainstream agenda on corporate responsibility. They will be able to quote people in high places. In Europe, for instance, some political leaders have called for an end to laissez-faire capitalism. In a political rally in the French city of Toulon, French President Nicolas Sarkozy said that 'the idea of the all-powerful market that must not be constrained by any rules, by any political intervention, was mad. The idea that markets were always right was mad.'[37]

Trade unions have also reiterated their calls for more regulation. The Trade Union Advisory Committee (TUAC) to the Organisation for Economic Cooperation and Development (OECD) issued a statement in September spelling out what governments should demand in return for taxpayers' money. According to TUAC, 'international cooperation should go far beyond what is currently under consideration—i.e. reviewing prudential rules for banks and "encouraging" more transparency on the market place. It is the national and global regulatory architecture that needs to be restored so that financial markets return to their primary function: to ensure stable and cost-effective financing of the real economy.'[38]

UNI Finance Global Union also called for a fundamental overhaul of the financial industry based on tougher regulation, more transparency, long-term investment and sustainable growth.[39] In June, it released a statement with 13 key demands on the regulation of finance markets. These asked regulators to act on issues such as pay systems for executives, consumer protection, sales targets, and tax breaks for private equity.[40]

Given the caution with which governments were saying they would seek to influence banks and change the banking system, the unions have some work ahead. This is not surprising given how in recent decades monetary policy has been turned into a technical not political issue—symbolised by the establishment of independence for national banks. Yet the recent financial crisis has made publics around the world more aware of the political nature of their monetary systems. Most governments oversee a system whereby private banks print money, and loan it out as debt, thereby benefiting from the system of money creation in a way no one else in the economy does. In return for that privilege, we could expect that governments might influence the way they then loan out that money. But they don't. Why is this monetary process beyond the political process? Why can't the contracts governing how the private banks issue money incorporate restrictions on the way that money is used, to promote the objectives set through government? For instance, guidance could be given on the employment or carbon created by the activities funded by the loans. Perhaps corporate responsibility could be embedded in the money system?[41] Rising awareness due to the financial crisis might lead to more discussion of policy innovations in monetary systems, yet governments do not seem ready to lead that process in 2008.

At a time of crisis it is natural to look for a quick fix. Yet, once the gold dust settles, it is clear that deeper questions must be asked, and discussed by a broader range of people than international financial institutions and the finance ministers of powerful nations. Any economic historian will tell you that 'moral sentiments' precede 'the wealth of nations'. We should be considering what values we want to further through the design of financial systems. Being clearer about the values embedded within and furthered by the current financial system, and whether that's suitable for this century, would be a good start. Steve Waddell, of the Global Finance Initiative (GFI), said, 'although stability is clearly the major concern, there are also significant concerns about the social and environmental impacts of finance. Indeed, increasingly there are suggestions that stability cannot be realized without more categorically considering these broader impacts. There is no formal, open and inclusive public space to develop a global strategy to address these concerns.'[42] Along with the Network for Sustainable Financial Markets, the GFI is one of a number of initiatives of progressive professionals thinking big on the future of finance.[43]

Beyond the Western financial crisis

'The credit crunch is creating a new world order in banking and finance . . . It's a world in which the Chinese state, if it co-ordinated the investments of its cash-rich institutions, could end up owning more-or-less the entire financial system of the US and the UK.' That was the view of BBC business editor Robert Peston.[44] Although the financial crisis seemed global, the origins began in the highly leveraged West, and posed a greater long-term threat to the economic systems of post-industrial economies than to rapidly industrialising ones. Looking forward on how this period of history—what we now refer to as 'the credit crunch'—will be appraised, the term 'Western Financial Crisis' might be a strong candidate. If a New Financial Order is emerging, it is clear that China will play a significant role in how it is formed.

Mark Leonard of the European Council for Foreign Relations said, 'it's not just economic and military power that's shifting from West to East. China is emerging as an intellectual power. It's coming up with its own ideas, which are very influential, which other people are copying.' He explained that 'the debate we're having about managing China's rise has got a mirror image in China, where they're having an argument about how to manage the West's decline. In the US, they're talking about what mix to have of containment and engagement, to try to get the China that they want. But what's interesting is that the Chinese are thinking about how they can shape an America that is organised in a way that benefits their interests.'[45]

Some worry about the growing role of China on the world stage; others welcome it. As expected, the focus of the world's attention on the Summer Olympic Games in Beijing led to widespread coverage of China's poor human rights record and its occupation of Tibet, and PetroChina's oil investments in Sudan, which human rights campaigners have long argued is complicit with genocide occurring in the Darfur region.[46]

With calls for Olympic boycotts made by some campaigners falling on deaf ears, the London *Times* (which is owned by News International, a company with significant investments in China) collected together a series of articles on its website examining some weaknesses in anti-China arguments. One *Times* commentator noted that 'The lowlife double standards that informed Western views of the vicious Easterner 60 years ago are being rehabilitated in the modern era by human rights activists, who are calling on Western democracies to put pressure on China over its occupation of Tibet and its human rights abuses.' The logic of this argument about racially motivated fears was somewhat confused when the author added 'the West has no moral authority to lecture anyone, including China, about rights and democracy. Here in Britain, free speech has been curbed through the creation of new thought crimes (see the Racial and Religious Hatred Act).'[47]

A more compelling pro-China argument rests on indications that some African nations are increasingly welcoming and voluntarily preferring Chinese state-led investment projects over Western private investment. South African-based commentator Janine Erasmus reported in September that 'China has become Africa's third-largest trade partner, after the US and former colonial power France. According to a report by China's General Administration of Customs, bilateral trade between China and Africa will exceed R803 billion ($100 billion) in 2008, two years earlier than predicted.[48]

'The trend is attributed to escalating shipments of natural resources to China, especially crude oil, mainly from Sudan, Chad, Nigeria, the Republic of Congo and Angola, metals from Ghana, Gabon, the Democratic Republic of Congo, Zambia, and South Africa, as well as cobalt and other minerals. At the same time, goods manufactured in China are increasingly sought after by African consumers. During the first half of 2008, exports to China from Africa rose 92 percent to R240 billion ($30 billion), while the continent imported goods to the value of R184 billion ($23 billion), an increase of 40 percent according to the Chinese customs authority.'

One key advantage for China in what is often viewed as a 'new scramble for Africa' has been the ability of its state-controlled banks to finance infrastructure investment as part of its trading arrangements. In the Democratic Republic of Congo, China 'is estimated to have pumped in $9 billion for developing the mines and building roads and hospitals. In exchange it will be allowed to mine in the mineral rich Congo for 22 years. Despite heavy criticism from opposition parties the government has continued to defend the deal. It has described it as the "Marshall plan" it needed, to rebuild the country and ensure it reaches double digit growth levels.'[49]

When the mines reach full production capacity, China will be extracting 4,000 tons of copper from six mines. Deputy Minister of Mines Victor Kasongo told South African television that 'It was important for Congo to have infrastructure to sustain. It is not by Congo's fault [that] others couldn't give us the money or access the market. So we had to take our own responsibility to bring growth forward. The China deal came to replace the promise we had with western countries.'[50]

According to the contract, China is expected to build close to 4,000 km of road connecting the country's major economic hubs, 26 hospitals and improve 250 km of road in Kinshasa alone. Opposition members have criticised the deal, arguing that it favours Chinese firms who receive much of the building work. With China, Brazil and India tying up infrastructure or loan deals in several African countries, often in return for oil, metals and other commodity resources, concerns have been raised among traditional lenders such as the International Monetary Fund (IMF) and World Bank.

In response to these concerns African members of the IMF meeting in August in Mauritania issued a declaration pledging 'greater transparency in their dealings with China and other so-called non-traditional sources of finance'.[51] IMF Managing Director Dominique Strauss-Kahn told Reuters in August that 'It is good news that there are new sources of financing, but we have to be very careful in order that this new financial help does not destroy the original policies of the Bretton Woods institutions'.[52] A report released in July 2008 by the World Bank[53] states that China, together with India and several Gulf nations, is financing a number of large infrastructure projects, such as hydropower schemes and transport schemes, across sub-Saharan Africa which may have positive impacts in the drive to reduce poverty. World Bank vice president for Africa Obiageli Katryn Ezekwesili has remarked, 'China's growing infrastructure commitments in Africa are helping to address the huge infrastructure deficit of the continent.'[54]

In an era of globalisation, it is natural that Western firms will face increasing competition around the world. What was perhaps unforeseen by Western policy-makers was the scale of the impact of state support for Chinese investment. Rosalind McLymont writing in the New Jersey-based *Shipping Digest* reports that 'China's two-way trade with Africa surged past $70 billion in 2007, compared with less than $1 billion in 1980, while US trade with Africa grew to about $85 billion from about $23 billion in the same period . . . Between 1998 and 2006, Africa's exports to China increased 2,126 percent against 402 percent in exports to the United States. To facilitate those exports, Beijing set up most-preferential-treatment agreements with 20 African countries, including tariff-free treatment on 454 products imported from the least developed nations.' She also noted that 'With $1.7 trillion in cash reserves, compared to the United States' $62 billion, Beijing has much more leverage for deals in Africa than Washington does.'[55]

The scale of growing South–South cooperation and investment led by China represents a new challenge to traditional Western-led North–South investment. While some Western companies have responded to the corporate responsibility agenda by building infrastructure and increasing the transparency of their dealings with developing-country governments (for instance, BP in Angola), the willingness of private international capital to take long-term risks is more constrained than recent state-facilitated Chinese arrangements in Africa. One consequence is that, while Western hydrocarbon companies may have led the oil boom in African nations, as the centre of global economic power shifts 'eastwards and southwards' contracts for infrastructure and future development are increasingly going to Southern-based companies, with China, Brazil and India posing a growing challenge to Western dominance in world trade. Along with that will be a reduction in Western influence on the corporate responsibility agenda, as new challenges, views and initiatives emerge among a more diverse field of business activity.

Rainbows in the storm

As money was such a dominant issue in the third quarter of the year, let us round up some of the news in the socially responsible investing (SRI) field that caught our eye. Because, even though the financial crisis has overshadowed all other stories for all types of investors, there was no let-up in campaigns and news stories targeted at influencing socially responsible investors, particularly in relation to investments in countries with poor human rights records.

Action in Zimbabwe was one such rainbow amid the financial storms. In June, international concern about rigged elections and political violence led to renewed calls for companies to review their investments in the hyper-inflation-ravaged country. Standard Chartered, the UK-listed international bank, came under the spotlight following reports that the Foreign Office was investigating one case of a possible breach of EU sanctions.

The influential newsletter *Africa Confidential* alleged that Standard Chartered, together with Barclays and the insurance firm Old Mutual, was one of three British-based groups thought to have provided an estimated $1 billion (£500 million) in direct and indirect funding to Robert Mugabe's administration. *The Independent on Sunday* quoted internal Foreign Office emails expressing concern about the bank's activities, with one message stating 'I'd say Standard Chartered is my prime concern. I've not asked them whether they've made any of these loan payments, but there's a good chance that they may have been forced to do so by the Reserve Bank of Zimbabwe. Officials said that, if a sanctions-busting case is proven, 'we will take appropriate action. We are determined to see that EU sanctions are properly enforced.'[56]

In July, *The Observer* reported that Shell was considering pulling out of Zimbabwe 'amid claims that President Robert Mugabe was reserving the distribution of fuel at petrol pumps for party supporters'.[57] A study by London-based Ethical Investment Research Services quoted by the paper showed that Britain is the largest foreign investor in Zimbabwe with holdings in more than a quarter of the 82 companies that have their parents listed on overseas stock exchanges.

In response to public concerns, UK Prime Minister Gordon Brown asked companies doing business in Zimbabwe to 'reconsider' their position. The Foreign Office said this meant that they should look at board members and shareholders of their subsidiaries to see if regime members were directly benefiting.

While—in common with other long-standing investors in the country such as Unilever, British American Tobacco and the mining corporations Anglo American and Rio Tinto—Standard Chartered Bank pledged to stay in Zimbabwe, some non-resource companies with smaller commitments did respond, with Tesco announcing that it would 'stop sourcing products from Zimbabwe as long as the political crisis persisted'; and the Mayor of London promised that London Transport's 'Oyster Card' supplier EDS would not renew its contract with the Munich-based company Giesecke & Devrient, because the latter provided banknotes to Zimbabwe's central bank. The communications company WPP meanwhile sold its 25% stake in Imago Young & Rubicam which had been advising the regime 'for just $1 to the majority shareholder, Sharon Mugabe, who is also chief executive'.[58]

July also saw renewed focus on Western investments in Burma (Myanmar) with the publication of a new report by Burma Campaign UK, 'Insuring Repression', accusing foreign insurance companies of working closely with the regime's insurance company to ensure that foreign businesses can operate in Burma.[59] Sixteen companies were highlighted as their members or subsidiaries sell insurance to companies in Burma, including Lloyds of London, Hannover Re, Catlin, Atrium,

XL, Tokio Marine, Sompo Japan and Mitsui Sumitomo. Johnny Chatterton, author of the report and Campaigns Officer at Burma Campaign UK, said, 'By selling insurance to companies operating in Burma these companies are propping up a regime that rules through fear—raping, torturing and killing Burma's civilians. These companies are putting profit before ethics, they are helping to finance a regime that less than a year ago was shooting peaceful protesters on the streets of Rangoon.' The Campaign criticised the EU for failing to follow the US in imposing targeted financial sanctions that would prevent insurance companies from selling insurance to companies in Burma and praised a number of companies that have taken the decision not to provide insurance to companies there, including AIG, Allianz, AON, AVIVA, AXA, ING, Munich Re, SCOR, Swiss Re and Willis.

In July, there was interesting news for those following the increasing public interest in and scrutiny of SRI funds when Pax World Management Corp. agreed to pay a $500,000 fine to the US Securities and Exchange Commission (SEC) because it had failed to follow its own socially responsible investing criteria over a five-year period, when two of its mutual funds invested in off-limits industries such as gambling and liquor, and oil and gas exploration. David Bergers, head of the SEC's Boston office, said it apparently was the first case the agency has brought due to violations by a mutual fund firm that purports to use social as well as financial screening criteria in making investments.[60] After the failures at Pax, the socially responsible investment industry estimated by the US Social Investment Forum to hold more than $2.7 trillion in investor assets last year could come under closer scrutiny.

Rent-a-geek

'We see things as we are, not as they are' it says in the Talmud. If we are someone who wants to benefit from society's resources and respect, and who therefore associates with the people, organisations and ideas 'in power', how will we see 'things'? Will we see them in a way that accepts, even praises, the status quo, and scoff at ideas that seem to challenge power? As you are reading this review, and have got to this stage of what is a rather long review, you are likely someone who takes pride in 'knowing' about things. But what are you actually coming to know, if you do not look inside yourself? In the face of a financial meltdown, the head-scratching of people who like to think they know things, and know some things better than others, should serve as a lesson.

During the third quarter, in classrooms and canteens of business schools around the world, business school professors were muttering about 'necessary oversight' and 'greater transparency'. Many could not bring themselves to use the 'R' word: regulation. It does not take an expensive education to know that markets require regulation, so the stupidity of thinking that deregulation of financial markets would be beneficial had to arise from a process of social conditioning, willingly partici-pated in by careerist academics.

'Since the early days of recorded history there have always existed a class of peo-ple who will sell their intellectual prowess to those in power. The exceptions seem so rare that they are talked about for centuries afterwards. The most famous being Socrates. More typical are those who come up with reasons that the status quo is the appropriate organization of society and that those in power are the perfect persons to be running things,' explains Robert Feinman.[61] Until the 18th century religious leaders played a key role in providing justifications for power, such as the 'divine right of kings'. Their influence waned with the Age of Enlightenment and modern science. 'What is needed is a "scientific" rationale for the organization of society. This role has now been taken over by economists. Through the use of statistics and mathematical theories they have been able to produce whatever justification was desired by those employing them. Proof of their intellectual dishonesty is easily found. For every economist who can "prove" the effectiveness of, say, trickle down economics there is another who can demonstrate that such policies are a complete failure,' says Feinman. In business studies this approach is sometimes taken to the extreme, when an academic's concept finds its validity through being adopted by a famous CEO. Therefore, professors in more traditional disciplines have sometimes regarded business academics as intellectual rentboys of corporate elites.

The alternative should not be a retreat to the libraries, but to be clear about the type of business and business person a business school seeks to inform. The differ-ence between a management guru and a management geek is not only the style of communication and the reach of their ideas, but also how they see a wider context and serve a higher purpose.

The World Economic Forum (WEF) likes to think it is the leading intellectual forum on the world of business. As the financial system unravelled, their minor *mea culpas* mixed with 'told you so' was particularly revealing. In interviews with Bloomberg, leading staff at the WEF said 'chief executive officers who gathered in Davos, Switzerland, over the last five years didn't listen to warnings from their peers. Davos organizers also say they failed to play tough with the financial-indus-try bosses, opting to accept their funding and let them turn Davos into a rave-up for Wall Street excesses.'[62]

Leaders of the Forum have been putting their failure down to excess, rather than principle. 'We let it get out of control, and attention was taken away from the speed and complexity of how the world's challenges built up,' said its founder Klaus Schwab. If not as much money had been taken from Wall Street speakers at Davos, would the WEF really have been much smarter? Hardly. The lesson is that an institution that pays its bills by convening the world's largest companies to enter-tain them at high-powered meetings will be beset by systemic sycophancy. Some WEF staff complained that delegates did not listen seriously to helpful sessions on emerging bubbles. But what do they expect when you are in the Alps and Angelina Jolie might be at the bar? The hubris of the Forum is that they see themselves as an emerging power in global governance as significant as the UN. Yet it would be a truly crazy planet if the world's largest corporations would be able to set the agenda for policies across the world.

A Davos delegate for seven years, the World Bank Director of Governance and Anti-corruption, Daniel Kaufmann, warned finance bosses 'about global risk and the abusive nature of their actions, but they had no incentive to change ... why should they have listened to us? I see it with my 10-year-old daughter, who scolds me because I don't put the garbage in the correct bin. Let's not delude ourselves. It's impossible to teach old dogs and investment bankers new tricks unless you change the incentive structure.'[63] This implies that if one is truly committed to improving the state of the world then one must reach out beyond the old dogs and fat cats. More than that, you must seek to be accountable to others. Perhaps if the WEF had listened to the protesters outside their luxury hotels, rather than their hand-picked corporate-sponsored NGO leaders, they might have developed a better sense of the state of the world. The WEF staff mistakenly thought such protests were about specific social and environmental concerns, which they could then effectively incorporate into the agenda. Other staff realised that the criticisms were of an economic kind, particularly as the alternative World Social Forum developed. They thought it was a disagreement about which economic theory was best to encourage social development. But the protesters do not challenge what the WEF delegates believe in, but rather their legitimacy to decide for others.

That message has not sunk in. For 2009, Schwab says his goal is to transform Davos into the 'Bretton Woods of the new millennium', a meeting targeted at establishing a fresh set of global rules for commercial and financial relations, much as the original Bretton Woods conference in New Hampshire did in the summer of 1944.[64] Doing that in their current form, with their current membership, is bound to cause deep concern across civil society. The World Economic Forum might soon find that not only were they the greatest fans of the Emperor's new clothes: they *were* those clothes. For the WEF to avoid being an intellectually insubstantial adornment to power, it will need to reconsider its membership structure and its approach to dialogue. This will become even more important if its Global Agenda Councils, which met for the first time in 2008, are to play a useful role in informing how we tackle global challenges.

4Q2008
October–December

Jem Bendell, Chew Ng and Niaz Alam

Looking East

As 2008 drew to a close, some of the long-term implications of the financial crisis were beginning to be seen. The shift of economic power from the West to 'the rest', which had been chronicled or predicted for some time, appeared now to be inevitable, as Western governments took on huge debts to bail out their struggling banks and companies, and stimulate their economies with public spending. This has implications for the future terrain of corporate social responsibility (CSR) issues, concepts and practice. In this review of the final quarter of 2008, we examine some of dimensions to the underlying shifts in economic power and their implications for corporate citizenship. These shifts include the growing importance of Islamic finance and of state-owned funds as investors and owners of companies worldwide, and the increasing initiatives on corporate responsibility across Asia.

Islamic finance

In November 2008, the US Treasury Department announced that it would convene an 'Islamic Finance 101' Forum to teach Islamic Finance to US banking regulatory agencies, Congress and other parts of the executive branch in Washington, DC.[1] Collaborating with the Harvard University's Islamic Finance Project, the purpose of this Forum is 'to help inform the policy community about Islamic financial services which are an increasingly important part of the global financial industry'.[2]

Islamic finance is a banking system that is characterised by five principles of Shari'ah or Islamic Law. These include: prohibition of interest (*riba*), prohibition of uncertainty and excessive speculation (*gharar*), prohibition of certain economic activities (including the consumption of alcohol and tobacco, gambling and pornography), share of profits or losses (*musharakah*), and use of asset-based financing (*murabaha*).[3] Islamic finance is concentrated in the Middle East and

South-East Asia (predominately Indonesia and Malaysia) but is spreading into North Africa and Europe. It is regulated by the Islamic Financial Services Board (IFSB), an international standard-setting body which 'promotes and enhances the soundness and stability of the Islamic financial services industry by issuing global prudential standards and guiding principles for the industry'.[4] In 2008 the spread of Islamic finance in Western economies was highlighted when Dublin-based maritime communications group Blue Ocean Wireless secured access to debt funding of $25 million (€17 million) from Bank of London and The Middle East plc (BLME), a Shari'ah-compliant wholesale bank based in the City of London representing what 'is thought to be the first time that an Irish company has availed of Islamic finance'[5]

Islamic finance accounts for approximately US$700 billion of assets and is growing at 10–30% annually, according to Moody's Investors Service. Wall Street now offers an Islamic mutual fund and an Islamic index. The importance of the Islamic finance principles has been accepted by the UK Financial Services Authority,[6] the World Bank and the International Monetary Fund. In December 2008, the Associated Press reported that France became the latest country to woo Islamic banks.[7] Finance minister Ms Christine Lagarde, who believes that Western financial institutions could learn a thing or two from Islamic finance, promised to make necessary adjustments to the French regulatory framework so that Paris could become a major marketplace in Islamic finance.

The turmoil in global financial markets since mid-2008 has raised serious questions about prudential lending and borrowing practices, risk management and corporate governance.[8] Added to these are two behavioural problems: greed and fear.[9] The Secretary General of the Franco-Arab Chamber of Commerce, Dr Saleh Al Tayar, claimed that the €4.9 billion loss suffered by Société Générale SA as a result of Jerome Kerviel's unauthorised trading could not have happened in an Islamic financial institution.[10] And Mohammed Awan maintains that the global financial crisis 'would not have occurred if Islamic principles were applied in international financial markets'.[11] This is because, under Shari'ah principles, one cannot 'sell debt against debt'. In turn, greed leads to sale of dubiously rated collateralised debts. A further reason advanced is that Islamic finance principles require deals to be based on tangible assets that require tight controls over debt levels.

In relation to *sukuk* (bond) issues, Shari'ah rules require bondholders to be undivided partners in the underlying asset(s) that are being financed. Accordingly, the effect on Islamic financial institutions has been muted as *sukuk* instruments are generally held to maturity.[12] Thus, narrow yield spreads provide less occasion for speculation in secondary markets. Some proponents argue there is minimal probability of default with *sukuks* since issuers are able to meet payment obligations.[13]

Moody's in its November 2008 report shows that Islamic financial institutions have been quite resilient in the current global financial crisis. As an interesting aside, no Islamic bank has acknowledged investing in Bernard Madoff's US$50 billion fraudulent Ponzi scheme.[14] The resilience of Islamic finance is summarised by Zarina Anwar[15] as follows:

> The development of Islamic finance in general is also important from the perspective of financial stability . . . The Shariah-based approach contains in-built checks and balances through risk- and profit-sharing structures. More critically, it demands a high level of disclosure and transparency in the financial system which is consistent with the principles of sound securities regulation as well as in compliance with Shariah requirements. This is not to say that Islamic asset markets have not been affected by the current turmoil. Indeed it has, and the value of Shariah compliant equities has declined in tandem with that of global equities. But it has been shown that Islamic finance in various segments of the market has been able to weather the storm relatively better than its conventional counterpart.

Nevertheless, the impact of an economic downturn and evaporating asset values was having an effect on Islamic financial institutions, and led to a number of events at the end of 2008 to discuss measures to mitigate those impacts. For example, on 25 October 2008, the Islamic Development Bank convened an urgent meeting to discuss the impact of the global financial crisis on the Islamic banking industry and agreed on policy initiatives to tackle the challenges and opportunities for the industry. In November in Kuala Lumpur, the IFSB and the Institute of International Finance (IIF) jointly organised a conference, entitled *Enhancing the Resilience and Stability of the Islamic Financial System*, to examine whether the Islamic financial system is strong enough to weather the crisis. The connectedness of global finance and the global economy means that, although principles may protect Islamic financial institutions from the extreme impacts of the financial crisis, they cannot be insulated entirely. This raises a question that has hitherto been avoided by the Islamic finance community: should they engage more assertively in international policy processes to promote their principles to non-Islamic governments and financial institutions, for mutual benefit? An affirmative would imply a reversal of a dominant assumption of recent centuries: that the 'West' has a version of economics that is suitable for the rest of the world, while non-Western approaches are seen as exotic, at best filling a niche, at worst being mere artefacts from pre-modern societies. That is an assumption that some non-Western communities have been complicit in maintaining, by assuming their own ways of organising are specific to their society, rather than relevant for all societies.

The rest of the world could benefit from the Islamic financial community assuming a greater role in international initiatives to achieve financial stability. That is not only because of the problems described above, but because Islamic finance recognises the deep problems associated with interest. As money enters economies as debt, being lent by banks with interest, organisations and people have to pay back more than they originally borrow. This creates a growth imperative, as the economy must keep expanding in order that the interest is paid. That poses a problem for a world of finite resources. Interest also promotes a competitive approach to society, as people need to acquire more money than they began with, because of the interest payments. In his description of money systems, one of the originators of the euro, Bernard Lietaer, explains how interest-money therefore necessitates increasing economic inequality.[16] Although many financial institutions would be wary of Islamic finance principles being seen as a blueprint for a new global financial system, as it would curtail many of their lucrative but risky activities, leaders of the 'real economy' could support such a view, as they would benefit from a more stable financial system. That is not to say that Islamic finance does not present areas for substantial refinement. First, the emphasis on debtors having tangible assets could restrict loans to the economically disadvantaged, such as those currently being helped through microfinance. In addition, the processes for discriminating against certain economic activities or systems of financing on the grounds of their being considered morally inappropriate would need to be refined. For instance, the *sukuk* market declined at one point in 2008 as a 'Bahrain-based group of Islamic scholars decreed . . . that most bonds ran afoul of religious rules . . . Only one that complies with the edict has been issued, pushing up borrowing costs on projects including $200 billion of real-estate developments in the United Arab Emirates capital'.[17] The growth of Islamic finance therefore raises challenging questions about the accountability of those who have greater power in interpreting religious texts and their contemporary spiritual implications. This highlights how an 'Eastern turn' in economic power is likely to present a range of novel questions for corporate responsibility.

Sovereign wealth fund responsibility

As the banking crisis deepened, media attention increased on the role and size of sovereign wealth funds (SWFs), which played a major role in the multi-billion-dollar bailouts of Western banks such as Citigroup and UBS. Rising energy prices and trade surpluses by exporting nations enabled SWFs to grow to control assets worth an estimated $3 trillion, a figure that the Organisation for Economic Cooperation and Development (OECD) estimated could increase to around $10–12 trillion by 2012. The rise of these government-owned foreign investment funds is, the BBC notes, 'one sign of the shift in the balance of power in the world economy from Western industrialised countries to new emerging market giants like China and the oil-rich Middle East'.[18]

How does the emergence of SWFs relate to corporate responsibility? In at least two ways. First, as investors and owners of companies, they become relevant for assessment by firms with policies on those with whom they do business. Second, as asset owners they have responsibilities to their ultimate beneficiaries, which are their national governments, and to others they affect through their investment decisions: sovereign wealth fund CSR.

The first area was highlighted when The Co-operative Bank in the UK publicly stated a policy on SWFs, based on its policies excluding business with companies connected to countries with poor human rights records. One league table of the world's 12 largest SWFs, shows that only four are from countries with democratically elected governments, although neither Russia nor Singapore was rated as fully free by Freedom House. Barry Clavin, The Co-operative Bank's ethical policies manager, explained, 'our policy precludes us from investing in an oppressive regime or in businesses and investments owned by an oppressive regime. Any business more than 20 per cent-owned by a blacklisted sovereign wealth fund will be turned down for business.'[19] Given the growth of SWF investing in Western companies, that stance may become difficult to maintain, as well as raising questions about its efficacy in either promoting social change or more effectively managing financially relevant human rights risks.

The second area of relevance for corporate citizenship is that of the SWFs' own responsibilities as private institutions—both to their beneficiaries and wider stakeholders. As the SWF assets are state-owned, we might expect them to be managed as those states see fit. The investments of SWFs have therefore raised concerns in the West that (Western) strategic assets such as banks and energy firms may end up in the hands of (unstable or unfriendly) foreign governments.[20] Concerns of stakeholders in countries receiving inward investment from SWFs therefore became more widely discussed during 2008. A McKinsey report on the topic even cited Venezuela's President Hugo Chavez as an example 'of a political leader who mixed investments with politics'[21] as an illustration of the growing calls for new rules for SWF investments.

Traditionally, however, despite periodic press coverage about human rights abuses by some SWF regimes, both investor and investee country governments have taken a laissez-faire approach to the role of SWFs, with investee nations tending to welcome investments and SWFs tending to shy away from controversy and any appearance of interference in other states' affairs. For instance, China, Singapore and Saudi Arabia have historically downplayed the extent of their governments' potential influence on investments in the West.[22] On the other side of the SWF coin, as Western economies tend to be the major recipients of their investment funds, the OECD has argued the world economy benefits from the growth of sovereign wealth funds, 'which recycle the trade surpluses earned by oil producers and manufacturing exporters like China back into the world economy' and point out that OECD countries should be as open to investment as they have called on other countries to be.[23] The occasional high-profile protectionist stances by US lawmakers to foreign investment (for example, objecting to Dubai Ports' takeover of UK company P&O because of its US port interests on 'security grounds') have been atypical or driven by short-term political concerns. More frequently, the default position has been for governments to avoid public interference as far as possible.

This debate led to some increased transparency: for instance, by the Government of Singapore Investment Corp. (GIC), which publicly released its annual report for the first time in 2008 'to help allay Western fears that their investments are politically motivated',[24] following GIC's $18 billion investments in the struggling UBS and Citigroup.

Table 7: **OECD estimates and Freedom House human rights ratings, June 2008**

Sources: SWF Institute, IFSL estimates and Freedom House rankings; originally published in *The Times*, 21 May 2008

Fund	US$ (billions)	State and Freedom House rating
Abu Dhabi Investment Council	875	UAE not free
Government Pension Fund of Norway	380	Norway free
Government of Singapore Investment Corp.	330	Singapore partly free
Saudi Arabia—various	300	Saudi Arabia not free
Kuwait Investment Authority	250	Kuwait partly free
China Investment Corp	200	China not free
Hong Kong Monetary Authority	163	Hong Kong partly free; China not free
Temasek Holdings	159	Singapore partly free
Stabilisation Fund	157	Russia not free
Australian Future Fund	61	Australia free
Qatar Investment Authority	50	Qatar not free
Libya Arab Foreign Investment Co.	50	Libya not free

Note. This table is used to illustrate The Co-operative Bank's SWF stance; it is based on estimates that may underplay the influence of some countries via Bank investments and currency reserves (such as Japan and China) as well as excluding Western public pension funds that are regulated and potentially influenced by their governments.

Given the continuing concerns from recipient countries, and the potential backlash against SWF investments, an IMF-hosted working group involving 23 investing and recipient countries agreed a voluntary code to increase transparency by SWFs in order to 'promote a clearer understanding of the institutional framework, governance, and investment operations of SWF, thereby fostering trust and confidence in the international financial system'.[25] It was a challenging task, given the SWFs all have different sources of capital, different legal statuses, different mandates and different investment policies. In October the working group released the Santiago Principles—also known as the Generally Accepted Principles and Practices (GAPP). The principles cover areas such as SWFs' meeting of local recipient regulatory requirements, making public disclosures in a variety of areas, and investing on the basis of economic and risk-and-return considerations. The principles were founded on the notion of keeping politics out of the way of SWF investment, whether the politics of the recipient or investor country.

Although some questioned whether the code would really restrict political involvement in the management of the funds and thus the companies they invest in, what matters more for corporate responsibility and responsible investment is the way the code reasserts the primacy of financial value over other values, and limits fiduciary duty to solely financial considerations. Thus, SWF managers may become more accountable through procedures associated with the measurement of the financial performance of their funds, yet less accountable to the people whose savings created the funds in the first place, because their interests are assumed to be purely financial. If, as a result, managers of large companies worldwide can access funds that are purely interested in financial returns, this may not help achieve greater corporate accountability, and could undermine the move towards more active and responsible ownership typified by the development of the UN Principles for Responsible Investment (UNPRI).

In 2008 one SWF was a member of the UNPRI. The Norwegian Government Pension Fund–Global, with an estimated US$390 billion-worth of assets, is the world's second largest SWF after the Abu Dhabi Investment Authority. It highlighted its uniquely active ethical policy by selling its US$500 million stake in Rio Tinto, a leading UK-based mining company for potentially subjecting it to 'grossly unethical conduct'. Norway's finance minister, Kristin Halvorsen, said its concerns related to Rio Tinto's joint venture with US-based Freeport McMoRan, a company excluded by the fund in 2006, for a mining operation in the Indonesian province of West Papua. In a statement on the ministry's website, she said,

> Exclusion of a company from the fund reflects our unwillingness to run an unacceptable risk of contributing to grossly unethical conduct. The council on ethics has concluded that Rio Tinto is directly involved, through its participation in the Grasberg mine in Indonesia, in the severe environmental damage caused by that mining operation.[26]

The Grasberg complex is the biggest gold mine and third largest copper mine in the world. Environmental groups and local people are concerned with the environmental damage caused by dumping millions of tonnes of ore waste into the local river. In 2007, a study published by the campaigning charity War on Want claimed that local people had suffered serious human rights and environmental abuses. Rio Tinto spokesman Nick Cobban expressed surprise to the *Guardian* at the Norwegian move, saying, 'Our immediate response is one of surprise and disappointment. We have an exemplary record in environmental matters—world leading, in fact—and they are given the very highest priority in everything we do.'[27] The *Guardian* also quoted Ruth Tanner, campaigns and policy director at War on Want, welcoming the decision to exclude Rio Tinto and challenging other funds to follow its lead: 'The Norwegian government has again put its money where its mouth is to ensure a real ethical investment policy. Now other pension funds should follow Norway's example.'[28]

The unprecedented level of investment transparency practised by Norway's SWF potentially makes it easy for other investors to follow suit and to leverage its global influence. Norway's SWF invests profits from oil and gas in a portfolio of around 7,000 companies around the world. The fund's ethical policy is based on applying to its investments the spirit of international agreements and ethical norms (such as ILO [International Labour Organisation] conventions) signed by the Norwegian government.

The bulk of the fund's ethical activity is in common with a growing number of public pension funds, largely based on engagement with companies in which it is invested. What sets it apart is the combination of the sheer size of its holdings and the ability and willingness of its Ethics Council (governed separately by the Ministry of Finance) to recommend shares for disinvestment. Of the 27 companies disinvested by Norway's investment programme on ethical grounds since 2005, the majority relate to governmental objections to certain types of military and nuclear weapons hardware. Boeing, Raytheon, Northrop Grumman and Lockheed are among the leading US arms companies excluded along with Britain's leading arms manufacturer BAE Systems, Thales of France and UK support services group Serco, which was removed in 2007 because of its involvement in the UK Atomic Weapons Establishment at Aldermaston.[29] The Norwegian Ethics Council has also disinvested from major companies for 'serious, systematic or gross violations of ethical norms', notably Wal-Mart for alleged complicity in breaches of international labour standards (including child labour, gender discrimination and the blocking of unionisation attempts). As the fund itself acknowledges, while disinvestment may continue to be applied in some high-profile cases, its preferred strategy remains engagement on a broad range of ethical issues.

As you may have noticed, this actively responsible approach from Norway's SWF is a form of politics: it derives from the interests of the Norwegian government in certain social and environmental principles. Therefore, its engagement in the development of the SWF code led to an interesting compromise, illustrated by the paradoxical Principle 19. It reads that 'The SWF's investment decisions should aim to maximize risk-adjusted financial returns in a manner consistent with its invest-ment policy, and based on economic and financial grounds', but then continues in a subprinciple that 'If investment decisions are subject to other than economic and financial considerations, these should be clearly set out in the investment policy and be publicly disclosed', further qualifying that 'The management of an SWF's assets should be consistent with what is generally accepted as sound asset man-agement principles.' Principle 21 goes further in describing the nature of the share-holder activism and engagement that will be acceptable, saying, 'if an SWF chooses to exercise its ownership rights, it should do so in a manner that is consistent with its investment policy and protects the financial value of its investments'. These principles limit the exercise of social responsibility from SWFs, including Norway, to approaches that have demonstrable financial benefits. An 'enhanced risk man-agement' approach to responsible investment is only one approach, with some recognising how individual savers, as human beings, have interests that extend beyond the financial, whatever time-frame is applied.

The code is what one would expect from a group convened by the IMF, given its ideological bias towards traditional financial disciplines, and the fact that this code was developed to defend SWFs from Western scepticism. A much-needed dialogue would focus on what active responsible ownership can look like when being pursued by SWFs from the Gulf or Asia, rather than Scandinavia. Just because the latter have been historically more active on their concerns for people in other countries, and come from a cultural and political tradition less complicated for the West than those from the Middle or Far East, does not mean that only their form of shareholder activism should be welcomed. Without such dialogue on what are universally acceptable ways of governments, or any organisation, pursuing their full range of interests through their commercial activities, this code will soon lose legitimacy among SWF nations, and, as world power shifts, may be increasingly ignored.

For now, the code means the SWFs are tethered to the shareholder-value paradigm and thus environmental, social and governance (ESG) concerns can be forwarded only in terms of enhanced risk management. Therefore, the opportunity lies in corporate responsibility advocates seizing on Principle 22's statement that 'The SWF should have a framework that identifies, assesses, and manages the risks of its operations' and promoting a fuller understanding of ESG-related risk management.

From CSR in Asia to Asian CSR

The shift in power from the West to the 'rest' indicates a growing role for Asian enterprise, not only within Asia itself but also in the rest of the world. Consequently, the evolution of corporate responsibility concepts, policies, practices and initiatives across the region is important worldwide. In the last quarter of 2008 a flurry of conferences confirmed the growth of corporate responsibility as a topic of business interest in the region. Despite the economic downturn, Singapore hosted a number of these events, beginning in October with the Asia Pacific Academy of Business in Society (APABIS) gathering academics and business people to develop this emerging network.[30] The following month delegates amassed at the Asian Forum on CSR,[31] which focused on giving executives a platform to promote their corporate responsibility programmes, and then at the Global Social Innovators Forum,[32] which celebrated individuals who are innovating new approaches in both business and charity, to address public challenges.

The most content-driven event of the conferencing season was the CSR Asia Summit in Bangkok, which brought together innovative practitioners from different sectors, chosen by the leading specialist consultants on corporate responsibility in the region, CSR Asia.[33] The very growth of this organisation, now with dozens of staff in five offices, is an indicator of the development of the responsible business agenda. At the summit, Leontien Plugge of the Global Reporting Initiative high-lighted that Asia is now the second largest reporting region, although this is mainly due to the high rate of sustainability reporting in Japan. As some Asian governments and stock exchanges had announced during 2008 that they will introduce requirements to report on CSR and sustainability, other countries' reporting rates are set to increase.[34] To gauge the general level of CSR disclosure at present, the 'CSR Asia Business Barometer 2008' was launched at the event. This report compares the CSR disclosure of the 20 largest listed companies in Hong Kong, Malaysia, Singapore and Thailand. Commenting on the results, CSR Asia's Executive Director Erin Lyon said that 'companies listed in Hong Kong demonstrate a superior quality of CSR disclosure' although 'the majority of companies listed in each of the countries have significant room for improved disclosure'. CLP (China Light & Power) came top of their ranking. A potential concern for the United Nations' efforts in this field emerged from the study, as Ms Lyon noted that Global Compact membership had no measurable impact whatsoever on the level of disclosure of companies in the region.[35]

The discussions at these conferences give some insight into the emerging dimensions of Asian CSR, as a global phenomenon, rather than just CSR in Asia. First, the philosophical bases for corporate responsibility are being discussed. Kasit Piro-mya, the Director of International Affairs of the Democrat Party of Thailand, and the Thailand representative of the Caux Round Table, spoke at the CSR Asia Summit about a parallel between Buddhist philosophy and CSR, owing to the emphasis on stakeholder interdependence:

> Buddhist monks live according to the principle of interconnectivity with the community and the environment; they are one with their stakeholders. Similarly, every individual belongs to an organization, and ultimately to society. So every individual, while working to earn a living and enjoy the rewards, is inter-dependent on the business community and society as a whole. Along with its stakeholders business is a part of a whole and thus the need for social responsibility and good governance. In particular, large multinational corporations have a global responsibility, and not only to their financial stakeholders.[36]

As Buddhism is one of the many spiritual traditions in the region, there is much to be drawn on in elaborating on concepts and motives for Asian CSR.

The second dimension to the evolution of an Asian CSR is the innovation that is occurring in CSR from within the region that may have a global impact. The conference in Bangkok hosted a workshop exploring a new initiative in reporting—imPACT. This approach brings together dynamic stakeholder engagement with a new approach to communication. Developed jointly by Edelman and CSR Asia, the imPACT philosophy is based on the understanding that many companies face critical societal challenges that they can play a role in addressing through outcome-oriented partnerships. Thus, CSR actions can be mobilised around issues such as climate change, water, human rights, poverty alleviation or health, so that companies become partners in addressing public need, rather than making minor improvements on a diverse set of issues aimed to benefit corporate reputation. Emphasis is placed on shared responsibility and joint accountability with the other organisations and sectors with which a company engages.[37]

A third dimension to the evolution of Asian CSR is the growing recognition within individual Asian countries of having the potential to play a global role. This was highlighted by the awards given out at the Global Social Innovators Forum (GSIF). The event was hosted by the Singapore-based Social Innovation Park (SIP), and focused on celebrating global leaders in social enterprise. Founder and President of SIP Penny Low said that

> SIP Fellow Awards recognize outstanding and high achieving individuals who are creating systemic change in the community that they live and work in. Role models in their own fields, these individuals are action leaders, who are shaping the future in their own way and by doing what they do best. They are the future world leaders of the globe.[38]

The Distinguished Fellow Award went to Jet Li, the Chinese actor, for his fundraising activities during 2008. One of the Fellow Awards went to Amit Wanchoo, Managing Director of Eaton Laboratories, for his work with the poor in Kashmir. In his acceptance speech Dr Wanchoo explained that 'in economically challenging times like these, social innovation remains more pertinent and relevant than ever'. He explained that 'social entrepreneurship brings together everyone's strengths to create the greatest social impact possible. I believe that collaborative innovations can help in sowing the seeds of positive change in this world for the well being of the whole of humanity. We collaborate not as different sectors but as one people with one dream of a better world.'[39] In discussions with Jem Bendell, Penny Low recognised the significance of this growing international outlook: 'The SIP Fellow Award and the SIP Distinguished Fellow Award are the first Singapore-originated awards given to international recipients who excel in the field of social innovation.'

Although there is great potential for diverse approaches to emerge and impact on the global experience of corporate responsibility, the development of CSR in Asia also poses a number of unique challenges. Currently, many Asian companies' voluntary engagement with the social and environmental performance of their business has been very influenced by the West. Therefore, at the conferences chronicled above, senior managers and government officials expressed the view that the main motivation for improved corporate responsibility is to achieve better relations with CSR-sensitive export markets. This approach can downplay or even ignore local stakeholder interests in the role and performance of business. The assumption is made that local stakeholder interests in business performance can be articulated through government, and, where that is not the case, that those stakeholder interests are not particularly valid. This view is a result of the dominant role of the state in many Asian countries and the variable, often weak, levels of civil society organising, media independence and political debate. This state of affairs may hamper the emergence of domestic CSR agendas in Asia.

Such an emergence may also be hampered by the imbalance in domestic voices involved in shaping the future of CSR. The evidence from these conferences is that the corporate responsibility debate in Asia is being influenced not by those who are directly impacted within the region, but by business leaders, government officials and high-society elites. This may be why, even now, CSR is most often construed by Asian business leaders as corporate philanthropy. This is highlighted by the fact that all of the 2008 Asian CSR awards went to philanthropic projects, bar the workplace award for Microsoft Philippines (a company that was not facing difficult workplace issues, does not have a trade union nor a systematic approach to checking what international labour standards apply to its operations). Further illustrating an emphasis on philanthropy rather than economic justice, at the GSIF most of the examples of 'social enterprise' were actually charitable activities involving some trading, such as the sale of charity-branded goods. The discussion of actions transforming core business practices on issues that have involved significant conflicts with affected stakeholders were conspicuous by their absence.

Although there are signs that at both conceptual and practical levels we are seeing the emergence of Asian CSR rather than simply more CSR in Asia, currently the majority of activities carrying the CSR tag are a mix of Western imposition and preening by local elites. If this subjugated dimension to CSR in Asia dominates practice, rather than a more organic emergence of ideas and innovations from dialogues and contestations of peoples from across the region, the loss will be both Asia's and the world's. One implication, therefore, is the need for greater awareness of the levels and nature of endogenous desire across Asia for socially progressive enterprise, and the relative roles of government, business and wider civil society in shaping and responding to that desire.

2009

2009: Introduction: Capitalism in question

Jem Bendell

Not many people want to look back on 2009. Not if they are thinking about the state of the world. Indeed, the decade as a whole does not look too distinguished, given steepling carbon emissions, new frictions and restrictions due to security concerns, and the mortgaging of future generations' welfare to prop up banking-as-usual in some countries. On a scale of human progress, to some the decade counted for nought—hence the aptness of our new label for the decade: The Noughties.

But bear with me. There is reason to look back at 2009 one more time. Looking at a year, indeed a decade, gives us a framework to look for patterns, for wider realities than our immediate day-to-day concerns. To do that can help us awaken to truths we may fear to see. Truths that could shape our future action in the corporate responsibility field and beyond. It's time to take the bitter pill and wake up to the underlying causes of our common problems.

The first key insight from the 2009 year is a reminder that government matters, and that government can act. Although a hands-on role for the state has been the norm in some countries, the past two decades witnessed a rolling-back of government involvement even in (former) communist countries such as China, Vietnam and Cambodia. In 2009, as new government regulations were announced, further nationalisations of financial institutions became necessary, and economic stimulus packages were agreed around the world, government once again took on a position to shape economic activity. Asian countries committed $1.153 trillion in stimulus money, with the spending plans ranging from 1% of GDP up to 4.4% with the Philippines and 12% with China. According to the European Commission, the executive arm of the 27-nation bloc, EU stimulus amounted to between 3.3% and 4% of GDP. The US committed $787 billion, or about 5.5% of GDP (see 'The return of government', page 240).

Much of the corporate social responsibility (CSR) field has been predicated on a belief that government is constrained by global finance and can, or should, intervene in markets only to a limited extent. The giving of huge amounts of money to private banks may suggest that global finance is still dominant, but it also shows that sometimes, when called on to act, most governments will intervene in markets in dramatic ways. The inclusion of social and environmental considerations into the various stimulus packages undertaken in 2009 indicates that these aspects of business have become a mainstream idea in policy circles (see 'The sustainability of stimulus', page 241). Indeed, the relative percentage of stimulus spent on 'green' industries was relatively higher in China and South Korea than elsewhere, highlighting the rise of environmental business awareness in East Asia.[1] However, what these stimulus packages also reveal is the dependence of governments around the world on maintaining economic growth rates—a situation that is not without environmental cost and social disruption (see 'If the problem is the prescription . . .', page 246). The implications for CSR of the problems with compelling economies to grow in a resource-constrained world was discussed in our review of 2007 above.[2]

The impasse reached in Copenhagen, at the 15th conference of parties to the UN Framework Convention on Climate Change, also highlighted how governments are constrained by a policy paradigm of promoting relatively short-term economic growth in their own countries. Although some companies pushed in good faith for intergovernmental action, the impasse also highlighted the perverse effects on policy of commercial interests, which had led to over a decade of talks on carbon capping and trading, rather than simpler more efficient approaches to carbon reduction such as carbon charging. Something that, rather ironically, had been in place in Copenhagen since the early 1990s (see 'The impasse on climate', page 280).

Bankers in question

The Copenhagen stalemate was one reason why many people who are concerned at the state of our world sounded downhearted at the close of 2009. The news that bankers were pulling in huge bonuses, while recession continued, led to incredulity, even disgust. Earlier in the year, an opinion poll in the US had revealed for one of the first times greater trust for politicians than for business leaders.[3] Bankers have been increasingly attacked from even conservative commentators as 'robber barons', 'economic vandals', 'vulture capitalists'. Bankers therefore began their public relations fight-back, the content and tone of which opened up the debate even further. Lloyd Blankfein, Goldman Sachs's Chairman and Chief Executive, declared his and his colleagues' huge bonuses a reward for doing 'God's work'. His explanation was that 'We help companies to grow by helping them to raise capital. Companies that grow create wealth. This, in turn, allows people to have jobs that create more growth and more wealth. It's a virtuous cycle.' He summarises that 'We have a social purpose.'[4]

It's a view not shared by critics who see Goldman and other investment banks as profiting from inflating one bubble to the next. In concluding a stunning analysis in *Rolling Stone*, which shows just how popular the debate about capitalism is becoming, Goldman Sachs was described as 'a great vampire squid wrapped around the face of humanity, relentlessly jamming its blood funnel into anything that smells like money'.[5] *The Sunday Times* explained the ability of large investment banks to predict market movements because they help move those markets through advising various clients. Like 'a huge casino in which the house knows every hand at the table and uses that information to enrich itself at the expense of everyone else'.[6] Hollywood reflects the new interest in debating capitalism. In his latest documentary, *Capitalism: A Love Story*, Michael Moore drives up to the New York office of Goldman Sachs in an armoured money van, jumps out carrying a sack with a giant dollar sign on it, looks up at the building and shouts: 'We're here to get the money back for the American people!'[7]

As well as some anger at bankers, the financial crisis has led many in the West to ask deeper questions about finance in general and, therefore, about capitalism. At the start of the crisis, European leaders were heard blaming the Anglo-Saxon model of capitalism. The arguments of such leaders including President Sarkozy of France, helped remind people of the different models of capitalism. 'Purely financial capitalism has perverted the logic of capitalism', he said. 'Financial capitalism is a system of irresponsibility and . . . is amoral. It is a system where the logic of the market excuses everything . . . Either we re-found capitalism or we destroy it.'[8]

Different forms of capitalism have different implications for voluntary corporate responsibility, and during 2009 some began looking at the experience of Francophone business to gain a broader perspective (see 'Francophone CSR', page 259; 'Francophone African CSR', page 264). Although certain European nations, including France, did not do as badly during the financial crisis as some Western nations, they still suffered and questions were asked of their forms of capitalism as well. The Prime Minister of Russia, Vladimir Putin, suggested, 'The entire economic growth system, where one regional centre prints money without respite and consumes material wealth, while another regional centre manufactures inexpensive goods and saves money printed by other governments, has suffered a major setback.' He continued, 'the economy of the future must become an economy of real values. How to achieve this is not so clear-cut. Let us think about it together.'[9]

Top business leaders also began expressing doubts about capitalism. 'The global financial crisis and recession has Kazuo Inamori rethinking capitalism', reported *USA TODAY*. He is the founder of Kyocera, a Japanese manufacturer of products ranging from ceramics to cellphones, with annual revenue around $13 billion. 'Capitalism was able to bring previously unknown levels of prosperity to humankind. We have now fallen into an unprecedented recession brought about by capitalism', he explained. 'Overcoming the current difficulties will require us to refine the free-market economic model . . . We must use the wisdom of humankind to modify the current form of capitalism into a more moderate version . . . We need to seek profits supported by sound ethics and a strong sense of morality.' He considered the environmental conundrum of economic expansion key to this needed rethink. Said the 77-year-old elder-statesman of Japanese business:

> There is a limit to the amount of food and energy on the planet. It should be clear to anyone that an endlessly more affluent and comfortable life-style is impossible to maintain in light of the finite nature of the Earth's resources. It is impossible for humankind to prosper on this planet indefinitely under the current form of capitalism. The time has come to fundamentally rethink how nature and living beings can coexist and live symbiotically within the limited space of our planet.[10]

With the passing of the Cold War, people assumed that capitalism was as natural as day, rather than a political economic construct that has been in struggle with other economic forms. Not any more. 2009 was the year that capitalism became political again.

Capitalism writing on the wall

Publishers realised that capitalism is now in question. A number of books came out that sought to provide historical context for the financial crisis, including *A Cultural History of Finance*,[11] *Debating Varieties of Capitalism*[12] and *Contested Capitalism: The Political Origins of Financial Institutions*.[13] Looking at the less academic books in English, targeted more at the mass market, gives us insight into the contours of the emerging debate, at least in the West. Some books provided lively reads that put the crisis down to 'too much'—whether too much greed, too much leverage, too much power to move markets. *Hoodwinked: An Economic Hit Man Reveals Why the World Financial Markets Imploded—and What We Need to Do to Remake Them* gave an insider's view that was so raw it will inspire many to seek deep changes in the economic system, but such changes were not the focus of the book.[14] In *Debt Spiral: How Credit Failed Capitalism*, Martin Lowy focused on the need to control leverage and derivatives better, and stop financial players influencing the rules of the game.[15] Robert J. Barbera argued that some instability is *The Cost of Capitalism*, with the upside being the innovation and growth that it creates.[16] In *The Trouble with Markets: Saving Capitalism from Itself* R.P. Bootle looked a little deeper at the values and emotions that contributed to the crisis, but did not conclude a need to change the basic factors that reward certain values and behaviours, such as the interest-based money system.[17] Indeed, when looked at together, these critiques suggest that some new regulations can fix the problems of capitalism. That is an analysis that even some bankers would concur with, including the Goldman Sachs CEO: 'If we didn't understand the limits of unfettered capitalism before, we sure do now. Anything that makes the system better, safer, is good for us.'[18]

Other analysts painted a far more damning picture. In *Cornered: The New Monopoly Capitalism and the Economics of Destruction*[19] the regular *Harpers* and *Financial Times* contributor Barry Lynn asks us to look beneath the current crisis to recognise the consolidation of power in all sectors of the US economy, a process mirrored around the world. The financial crisis is therefore argued to be just the most recent result of government regulatory functions being captured by monopoly forces. Lynn proposes major government intervention to break up monopolies, but does not address other failings of capitalism. Another new book described some processes by which such monopoly control is developed. From research across Eastern Europe to the US, anthropologist Janine R. Wedel described how a *Shadow Elite* of individuals move seamlessly between government, private sector, academe and NGOs to manipulate the agendas of society. However, as a descriptive piece, solutions were not offered for how to transform that undemocratic influence.[20]

Another set of recent books seek to do something that previously seemed neither necessary or interesting—to defend capitalism. Steve Forbes and Elizabeth Ames explained *How Capitalism Will Save Us: Why Free People and Free Markets Are the Best Answer in Today's Economy.*[21] Others spoke of *The Capitalist Spirit: How Each and Every One of Us Can Make A Giant Difference in Our Fast-Changing World.*[22] Authors Brian S. Wesbury and Amity Shlaes reassured readers that *It's Not as Bad as You Think: Why Capitalism Trumps Fear and the Economy Will Thrive.* 'When planes crash, no one questions the science of fluid dynamics. Capitalism is also a natural force. It is an organic method . . .', they proclaimed.[23] Developing the idea that capitalism is a natural force, Howard Bloom described *The Genius of the Beast*, and his 'radical re-vision of capitalism'.[24] That vision involves us recognising that capitalism is not about financial tricks, but a system that arises from, and helps us to tap, 'our imagination, our desire to feel useful, our desire to help others, and our desire to be recognized for contributing to the welfare of humanity'. He suggests that capitalism does not have its roots only in the Protestant work ethic, but from our human natures and, even the creative process of the cosmos. These claims led spiritual commentator Andrew Cohen of EnlightenNext to endorse the book thus: 'By tracing the capitalist impulse to innovate all the way back to its humble origins in bacteria and ants, Bloom conveys a powerful moral and evolutionary imperative for us to reinvent ourselves and reinvigorate this system for the sake of our collective future'. Bloom certainly provides a colourful dimension to the capitalism question.

Some people have sought to brand the new capitalism. 'Creative capitalism' is the favoured term of Bill Gates, Warren Buffett and other business leaders, and was the title of a new book on their ideas published at the end of 2009.[25] John Mackey, the CEO of Whole Foods, the $8 billion retail giant, prefers the term 'conscious capitalism'. He uses the term to describe approaches to business that focus on social purpose as much as profit, and balance the interests of different stakeholders. In his new book Mackey says that 'conscious capitalism . . . will become the dominant paradigm of business in the 21st century'.[26] He enthuses that 'voluntary cooperation and spontaneous order . . . when channeled through free markets, lead to the continuous evolution and progress of humanity'. He told *Fast Company* magazine that 'self-interest and altruism can not only coexist, they can both thrive simultaneously without a lot of government meddling'.[27] Mackey is certainly up for a debate about capitalism. 'If we are truly interested in spreading capitalism throughout the world (I certainly am)', he wrote in *Reason Magazine*, 'we need to do a better job marketing it.' He plans 'Catalyzing Conscious Capitalism' summits in the US, Europe and India, and the creation of a 'Conscious Capitalism Alliance'. Perhaps to demonstrate his belief in turning any phenomena into capital, he has trademarked the phase 'Conscious Capitalist'. Some may see Mackey as an advocate of corporate social responsibility and social enterprise. Others may see him as a right-wing ideologue, especially given his public questioning of climate science and challenging of President Obama's proposed public option for health insurance. What his efforts certainly tell us is that capitalism is now open for debate.

My own book, the *Corporate Responsibility Movement*, came out in early 2009 and also sought to join this debate about capitalism. The perspective I provided came from an analysis of recent years of campaigns for, and initiatives on, greater corporate responsibility. I concluded that many practitioners in the corporate responsibility field understood themselves as part of a social movement working, in their own ways, towards the transformation of business and finance. As journalist Bill Baue suggested in his look back at 2009:

> Perhaps the biggest CSR development of the year was not readily visible, as it was an idea: that CSR represents not just a trend or professional discipline, but a social movement. In other words, CSR is not a random collection of ad hoc, discrete actions to revise corporate behaviour, but rather a coherent aggregation of sustained, widespread efforts to reform (or even revolutionize) the role of corporations, shifting from negative to positive impacts on society, environment, and economy.[28]

I argued in my new book that social movements not only share identities, types of resources, and contexts for action, but they also share goals—a sense of what they are collectively working towards. Therefore I looked at what CSR practitioners are doing and what their motivations are, and concluded that they shared an interest in more democratic economic systems. I developed that interest into a theory of more democratic capitalism and offered it to the corporate responsibility movement as one potential coherent vision, that could allow us to work more in concert—more effectively as a movement.

Calling it for what it is

Many practitioners, researchers and promoters of voluntary action by business on their social responsibilities recognise the constraints put on companies by the nature of markets, and specifically the pressures from financial institutions.

However, until now most of their focus has remained on corporations, and not on those financial institutions. Their work on finance was largely limited to voluntary guidelines on project finance and the retailing of 'ethical' funds to concerned savers. The more recent mushrooming of investor engagement with companies on their social and environmental performance, stimulated by the UN Principles for Responsible Investment (UNPRI), is limited to asset management and what is considered in the investors' financial interest. These are useful beginnings and signs of the growing interest in transforming business by transforming finance. However, what is needed now is a better understanding of the underlying principles and mechanisms of finance, and greater clarity on the principles that would underpin a more fair and sustainable economic system. In the remainder of this introduction, I map out a potential organising concept for the corporate responsibility movement.

First, it is important to cut through the rhetoric and public relations, and recognise the system for what it currently is. In direct contradiction to the statements by the CEO of Goldman Sachs that their social function is funding companies, according to figures from the federal reserve in the US, in 2005, about 1 dollar in every 100 trading on Wall Street was reaching companies, with the other 99 all speculatively invested.[29] Marjorie Kelly even found that the financial institutions had sucked more money out of companies than they had put in:

> New equity sales were a negative source of funding in 15 out of the 20 years from 1981 to 2000 . . . The net outflow since 1981 for new equity issues was negative 540 dollars billion. Rather than capitalizing companies, the stock market has been de-capitalizing them . . . It's inaccurate even to speak of stockholders as investors for more truthfully they are extractors. When we buy stock, we are not contributing capital: we are buying the right to extract wealth.[30]

Back in the 1990s economist David Korten had provided a powerful summary of the situation:

> The problem is this: a predatory global financial system, driven by the single imperative of making ever more money for who already have lots of it, is rapidly depleting the real capital—the human, social, natural and even physical capital—upon which our wellbeing depends. Pathology enters the economic system when money, once convenient as a means of facilitating commerce, comes to define the life purpose of individuals and society. The truly troubling part is that so many of us have become willing accomplices to what is best described as a war of money against life. It starts, in part, from our failure to recognize that money is not wealth. In our confusion, we concentrate on the money to the neglect of those things that actually sustain a good life.[31]

So what do we want from an economic system? I believe we want a system that is run by the people who collectively make up that system: a democratic economic system. Democracy arises from a belief in self-determining one's life-world. A number of other human rights stem from this, once we recognise the material foundations of self-determination and self-actualisation: namely, the right to basic necessities of life, which includes a safe environment. David Korten states that 'there are few rights more fundamental than the right of people to create caring, sustainable communities and to control their own resources, economies and means of livelihood'.[32]

From this approach to human rights and democratic governance, organisations or persons that affect you and your community, especially when they affect the material foundations to your self-determination, must be able to be influenced by you and your community. In other words, they must be accountable. Therefore over twenty years ago organisation theorist Henry Mintzberg was asking us 'how can we call our society democratic when many of its most powerful institutions are closed to governance from the outside and are run as oligarchies from within?'[33] If we believe in human rights and the spirit of democracy, then we should use that framework for understanding corporate responsibility and the type of corporate and financial system we desire.

The editor of *Business Ethics* magazine Marjorie Kelly explained that democracy is in the economic arena:

> about shaping the system forces that act on all corporations. It's about consciously crafting new democratic system structures, structures of voice, structures of decision making, structures of conflict resolution, structures of accountability. Eventually this will mean changes in law. But legal changes must be of a different sort than we've attempted thus far. Laws controlling corporations now amount to a patchwork of regulations about working conditions, pollution, or consumer well-being, focusing on outcomes rather than underlying mechanisms. Thus we've been like home-owners chopping down nuisance trees which continually spring back, because we have failed to eradicate the roots.[34]

There are direct implications of this for capitalism. But first, in any dialogue about capitalism it is important to understand it in the plural, as capitalisms. Richard Whitley, Professor of Organizational Sociology at the Manchester Business School, has documented clearly that corporate law, labour markets and so on differ across the world, so there are very different forms of capitalism.[35] One lesson from that is we should choose the form we want. In doing that we must clarify what is the basic essence of these different capitalisms. Wikipedia can be a good source for common wisdom. Here is the 'crowd-sourced' definition:

> Capitalism is the economic system in which the means of production are owned by private persons, and operated for profit, and where investments, distribution, income, production and pricing of goods and services are predominantly determined through the operation of a free market.[36]

It has recently become popular in social science to regard anything as 'capital', with at least five forms of capital now discussed: natural, social, human, manufactured and financial capital.[37] When this occurs, it is important not to ignore that something is 'capital' because of a specific power relationship: 'Capital' is anything physical or virtual that some person or group can control sufficiently in order to extract an income or benefit from it. A forest can be conceived of as 'capital' when it is being controlled by someone or some group to extract an income or benefit from it. The forests that are not controlled by someone to generate a yield would not be accurately described as natural capital. Yes, such a forest's impact on the environment underpins other capital and economic activity, but if not controlled by some person or group for their own revenue or benefit then capital is the wrong word to describe its value or worth. Forest dwellers may be harvesting materials from the forest and completely dependent on it for their lives, but neither they nor their adversaries in oil exploration, for instance, would consider that they 'control' the forest. Yes, the forest is valuable even though it is not 'capital', and that is partly the point I am making here: not everything valuable can be called capital.

With the financial crisis the 'ism' seemed to be falling off capital. Grammatically, capitalism should simply mean a belief in capital, and a system that creates and maintains capital. Therefore, capitalism should be understood as the belief that more and more resources should be managed by specific individuals or groups to generate incomes or yields, i.e. to be managed as capital. Therefore, to believe in capitalism is to believe that it is good to control bits of existence to extract revenues or yields from them, mostly through controlling how other people interact with that bit of existence. It is a belief in creating and using property. This simple definition is often lost in the debates about capitalism, with many of the writers mentioned earlier using the term to describe entrepreneurship, markets, or patterns of government non-intervention.

The definition provided on Wikipedia indicates the 'ism' involves the private ownership of capital, and the management of it to extract a profit for those owners, rather than just a revenue or benefit. This aspect of capitalism is not definitive, as economies in different countries have different forms of ownership and profit-taking. Even in so-called free-market economies, the state owns large portions of capital and includes regulations on who can own capital, particularly if they are a large firm giving rise to competition issues.[38]

Towards capital democracy

If we believe in democracy, then this process of how material or virtual phenomena are turned into capital, by whom, and how this directly affects people, should be examined more closely. This means looking at the process of private property creation and use. Financial capital is one expression of property rights. In a democratic society, property rights should only exist because people collectively decide to uphold them; they are not inalienable but are upheld by society as a matter of choice. Therefore, if society confers us the right of property, then we have obligations to that society. Today, property rights have become so divorced from this democratic control that they are undermining other human rights. A reawakening to a basic principle is required: there can be no property right without property duties, or obligations. From such a principle, it should not be left up to the powerful to decide if they are responsible or not, or if they are carrying out their obligations or not. Instead, the focus shifts to the governance of capital by those who are affected by it: a concept that I previously dubbed 'capital accountability' in a report for the United Nations.[39]

As mentioned above, most work on finance and ethics has focused on questions of responsibility, not accountability, rights or democracy. Action on finance and ethics is limited to minority shareholders causing trouble for companies (shareholder activism), increasing the security of one's returns via expanded risk management assessments and corporate engagement (responsible investment), ethical venture capital (in environmental technologies, for example), or seeking moral cleanliness in one's own investments (screening out certain sectors from investment portfolios). Little has been done on the accountability of the people who invested, their demands for returns, and the people who managed their investments.

The fact that most current work on responsible or sustainable finance is based on a voluntarist view of responsibility is problematic from a democratic perspective. When funding an activity, people should not only have a responsibility to know what happens with their property but should also be accountable to those who are affected by it. An obligation should therefore exist for owners of capital to only invest in activities that are accountable to those affected by them. If owners do not carry out their obligations, they should lose the right to the specific property involved. In essence this principle would mean investors ensuring that those who manage their money require that the activities they fund/own are accountable to those affected. Thus when banks lend or when fund managers buy stocks—that is, when an activity is financed—the companies involved must be accountable to the people affected by that activity. Mechanisms would then be needed to ensure that banks, fund managers and, in turn, individual absent owners of capital carried out their obligations to ensure companies followed these accountability guidelines. Clearly this would pose a challenge to the current financial markets, where the derivatives markets have multiple links in a chain before affecting people—the consequences of which in 2008–2009 illustrated the importance of restoring some accountability to the real economy. Another dimension to capital democracy would be ensuring that processes of the capitalisation of aspects of life are more open to public discussion and review; for instance, intellectual property claims over genetic code need to be matters of public debate and consultation.

Combining democratic and economic philosophy in this particular way is not entirely new. Indian independence leader Mohandas K. Gandhi, articulated a concept of 'trusteeship' in some of his writings. This arose from his view that everything is owned by everyone, and wealth is owned by those who generate it. Thus the one who controls an asset is not an owner but a *trustee*, being given control of that asset by society. Gandhi wrote, 'I am inviting those people who consider themselves as owners today to act as trustees, i.e., owners, not in their own right, but owners in the right of those whom they have exploited.'[40] In the *Harijan* paper his views on trusteeship of property were later documented to clarify: 'It does not recognize any right of private ownership of property except so far as it may be permitted by society for its own welfare' and 'under State-regulated trusteeship, an individual will not be free to hold or use his wealth for selfish satisfaction or in disregard of the interests of society'. He also wrote that 'for the present owners of wealth . . . they will be allowed to retain the stewardship of their possessions and to use their talent, to increase the wealth, not for their own sakes, but for the sake of the nation and, therefore, without exploitation'.[41] Gandhi did not develop these ideas further, as he had other preoccupations, such as generating economic self-sufficiency, inter-communal understanding, and the non-violent expulsion of the British Empire. The concept there remains to be developed and applied further.

Promoting capital accountability today implies creating more 'present' ownership. Owners of property are often more accountable if they are present with that property. For example, an owner of a factory experiences a face-to-face form of accountability by seeing those affected by the activities of his or her property. Closing the distance between those who own property and those who are affected by it can also be promoted by increasing employee, customer, supplier and community ownership of that property. Jeff Gates therefore argued for more 'up-close ownership' so as 'to link a nation's people to their workplace, their community, their economy, their environment—and to each other'.[42] Sharing the risks associated with an economic activity is another way of increasing the involvement of owners.

Creating more present ownership is also part of a process democratising capital ownership in general, and efforts from within both governments and large corporations to encourage a greater diversity of capital ownership across an economy should be supported. This takes us beyond capital accountability to a broader economic democratisation agenda. I offer the term 'Capital Democracy' to describe an economic system that moves towards the creation, allocation and management of capital according to the interests of everyone directly affected by that process, in order to support the self-actualisation of all. This principle would mean not only more effort to hold capital accountable and democratise ownership, as described above, but also democratising money, democratising trade, democratising employment, and democratising taxation, as I will now outline.

A key area for democratisation is the money system. There are two main aspects to that challenge: currency speculation and the creation of money. Currency speculators on international financial markets have no accountability to the people affected by the volatility in the cost of borrowing, devaluations and so forth that they help accentuate. At a minimum, owning the 'property' of money should confer duties to the society or societies that underpin that currency. The concept of capital democracy might suggest that all financial transactions be taxed, due to the transactor's obligation to the social infrastructure that provides the opportunity for their transaction. Such a measure could end short-term currency speculation. It would also create resources that could permit the reduction or abolishing of other taxes, such as some income taxes.

The other aspect of democratising the money system concerns not the way money is traded but the way it is created. Money enters the economy as debt, as it is provided to private banks who then lend it out, with interest attached. Consequently, we have a system where the total amount of money in the world is not sufficient to pay the total debts of the world—and never will. We are a perpetually indebted planet. The system helps explain the findings of Marjorie Kelly and others that the financial institutions are a net drain in wealth of real businesses, and further condemns the veracity of Goldman's claims of social purpose. Such indebtedness is a form of social control, as the amount of economic activity must continue to grow, which necessitates resource consumption and commodification beyond the levels we might otherwise choose. Not only is it logically impossible and ecologically mad to create a system that demands perpetual growth, it is not democratic for this decision about growth to be out of the hands of people. Today people are asked to spend, spend, spend, and borrow, borrow, borrow, in order to keep the economic system from collapsing. Democracy requires choice, and that necessity for growth is no choice. In addition, this process of money creation means that the private banks are given opportunities to grow their profits in ways that are not available to others. You or I cannot go to a central bank and receive permission to create money out of nothing. The private banks do this and loan it out at interest, which creates a systematic driver of inequality in society. An interest-based money system, where currencies are issued not by governments but by central banks, often with private shareholders, indebts governments and thus requires higher taxation. Yet such a money system is not a necessary part of capitalism. And for the reasons just outlined, it would not be a feature of truly democratic capitalism.

What might more democratic alternatives involve? One source of ideas is the system of Islamic banking. Many Islamic institutions consider usury, and thus interest, to be wrong, due to some principles in Shari'ah law. First, money should only be a medium of exchange, a way of defining the value of a thing; it has no value in itself, and therefore should not be allowed to give rise to more money. The human effort, initiative and risk involved in a productive venture are more important than the money used to finance it. Second, a lender must share the risk with the borrower: that is, the potential profits or losses that arise out of the enterprise for which the money was lent. Third, transactions should be entered into honestly with the minimum of uncertainty, risk and speculation. Fourth, investments should not support practices or products that are incompatible with the core beliefs of Islam. As a result, the charging of interest, trading in futures, speculation on currencies and investment in products such as alcohol, were not permissible for many Islamic financial firms. In practice, Islamic banks usually work by taking an equity stake in the enterprises they help finance. It is a matter we explored in some detail in our review of the 2008 year. The crash of 2008–2009 has stimulated more worldwide interest in Islamic banking, as it becomes apparent that a more accurate description of the economic system in most of the West is not capitalism but moneyism—a belief in helping money to make more money no matter what the connection to real, non-financial capital in the economy.

The democratisation of markets and trade is also an important part of the capital democracy agenda. The way market access is regulated not just by governments but by large corporations which can drive down prices paid to producers is something that needs addressing. It underlies the lack of resources available to suppliers which translates into poor labour practices and environmental protections. The democratisation of employment is also a central aspect of capital democracy, including who has access to employment, how their wages and conditions are set, and whether there is freedom from discrimination in those processes.

Democratising taxation is another key aspect of capital democracy. The underpinning of democracy is that we have a government, and the underpinning of a government's ability to govern is tax revenue. The democratic view is that we should all contribute to collective costs for collective needs, and the wealthier we are the more we should give. The current situation does not live up to that ideal, due to extensive corporate welfare and regressive taxation where the poor and middle class often pay proportionally and sometimes even absolutely more than some companies and wealthy individuals. Therefore, taxation has become as much a regressive and illegitimate process as it is progressive and legitimate. The concept of capital democracy would suggest restoring progressive and fair taxation, which in the context of a global economy necessitates greater international cooperation on, and harmonisation of, tax codes. In this annual review, we explore this issue and the currently limited attempts of the G20 to collaborate on corporate taxation more effectively (see 'Responsible tax management', page 252).

In 2009 there were more discussions about how to transform our economies to a more sustainable and fair situation. Some frame this as a transformation to a 'sustainable enterprise economy' (SEE). In November 2009 this idea was discussed at the Asia Pacific Academy of Business in Society (APABIS) at Griffith University's Asia Pacific Centre for Sustainable Enterprise (see 'The pulse of CSR in Asia', page 296). Characteristics of such an economy include companies applying their capacities for innovation to the sustainability challenge (see 'Sustaining innovation', page 301). I believe that the transition to a sustainable enterprise economy will not be achieved without addressing the deeper causes of our malaise, which are found in the legal forms we have created called corporations and banks, and the separation of principles of democracy from economy in the design of those forms.

We don't just need to reform capitalism; we need to reformat it. I have chosen the term 'Capital Democracy' for this vision of economy, as it is about a form of capitalism and an application of democracy.[43] It calls for returning decisions about capital to the people affected by it. What might happen when those who are affected by capital can govern it more effectively? They might choose to support profit-taking and the existing ownership patterns, if they determined these to form a useful system—or they might not. The important thing is that it would be their choice and not imposed by outsiders autocratically supporting or abolishing property rights. Thus the true revolution in economic democracy is not about abolishing capitalism or extending capitalism, but about creating choices for people to transform, reform or remove corporations and capital in certain contexts. This democratisation of capitalism could be the ultimate goal of the corporate responsibility movement: the seeds of these ideas are already to be found in the existing analysis and practices of many people working on corporate responsibility today.

Will the emerging movement begin to articulate a common vision? There is more chance than ever before, given our levels of connectivity. Bill Baue explains that CSR professionals were

> initially slow on the uptake of social media and other interactive technologies to connect with their stakeholders, but [are] increasingly building online networks to advance a more community-based approach to corporate accountability and sustainability—most notably, Timberland's Voices of Challenge stakeholder engagement website. Corporate adoption of Web 2.0 tools shows promise of fuelling the CSR movement into the new year and decade.[44]

Implications for management and research

This discussion of economic systems can seem distant from the day-to-day preoccupations of most executives and the academics who seek to research about, or educate, them. Yet making such connections will be important if the corporate responsibility movement is to have a substantial and lasting effect on commerce and society. In addition, as we enter a period of potential reconfiguration of economic governance, leaders of organisations will need to better understand the issues, actors and dynamics to be successful. There are four implications from this need that I employ in my management education: moral consciousness, transfunctional competence, systems thinking, and responsible political engagement. These four areas can also inform a range of topics for academic research.

Moral consciousness is not often a goal of management education. Business ethics courses can help students understand different ethical frameworks that they or others use or could use to explain their actions. However, actually encouraging a deeper sense of moral consciousness and how that then applies to one's work, is not that usual in business schools. In my teaching the awareness and values of the individual are important to explore and develop, and to be kept in mind during all aspects of management practice. Unless we are conscious moral actors we will not be able to engage usefully in processes concerning the common good. In 2009, the founder of Kyocera, Kazuo Inamori, reflected on the need for more moral leadership within business. 'Top executives should manage their companies by earning reasonable profits through modesty, not arrogance, and taking care of employees, customers, business partners and all other stakeholders with a caring heart. I think it's time for corporate CEOs of the capitalist society to be seriously questioned on whether they have these necessary qualities of leadership.'[45]

'Trans-functional competence' is a term to describe the ability of people to transcend organisational silos and the single lenses that come from specialisms in marketing, finance, human resources, strategic planning, operations and so on. The new popularity of design thinking, like systems thinking, reflects how organisations are trying various ways to overcome silos (see 'Sustaining innovation', page 301). Having teams of experts from different specialisms is one way in which organisations try to overcome these silos, but they are rarely more than the sum of their parts. Instead, if managers develop a competence for trans-disciplinarity or trans-functionality, they can draw on the expertise in different specialisms, while rejecting certain knowledge claims from those disciplines that they can spot as the result of unhelpful assumptions or preoccupations. Key to this is understanding a knowledge claim in its full context: to distinguish between what it reveals and what is simply a projection of its method, theory, and assumptions. Two of the best underlying factors in developing trans-functional competence are critical discourse analysis, and the philosophy of science, as they enable people to deconstruct the truth claims they hear. Without such trans-functional competence, executives will not be effective agents in mobilising their moral consciousness.

'Systems thinking' is a well-established field within management studies. It encourages us to see our world as relationships between things rather than separate things. Therefore, it helps people understand contexts and dynamic processes that they participate in every day. It also encourages a focus on how to create new self-sustaining relationships which could grow to influence and eventually transform wider systems. Greater 'systems thinking' can also encourage a de-centring of the firm in the mind of managers, so they look at issues from a broader perspective, and see opportunities for mutual benefit, as well as impediments to lasting progress. Teaching systems thinking requires a diverse pedagogy, which includes exercises, role play and games, as much as it does standard lecturing.

'Responsible political engagement' is a key implication of an awareness of the need to transform our economic systems. The nature of a company's direct and indirect political influence is now understood as a key dimension of its CSR.[46] How to be responsible in one's lobbying is a more difficult question, as the corporate lobbying of climate policy has shown. Although, on first look, corporate lobbying for government action on carbon emissions may look responsible, much of it has been for ineffective, inefficient and unfair systems of carbon cap-and-trade, which led the intergovernmental process into stalemate in Copenhagen (see 'The impasse on climate', page 280). In the future, well-established principles of stakeholder engagement, transparency and accountability which apply to other aspects of CSR should be applied to corporate lobbying. I explore these issues with my students, and in so doing draw on various insights from political science and sociology. This reflects how management studies could benefit from more input from a wider range of social sciences.

Helping management students develop competencies in these areas will help them navigate the complex social and political challenges that large organisations will continue to face. Teaching management students about capitalism or democracy, or indeed about capital democracy, would not be as empowering or as meaningful as giving them the ability to critique and synthesise for themselves, from their own passionate standpoint.

How should executives respond to the deeper critiques and debates that I outline in this review? It is difficult to say, as I have not yet had many conversations with senior executives on this agenda. My strategy advisory has hitherto focused on sector-specific changes and challenges. However, some initial ideas about implications for management include:

- Become proactive in influencing the research and teaching agendas of business schools to address this agenda, including the competencies outlined above

- Develop a policy and programme to promote responsible political engagement by the company and the associations of which it is part

- Shift strategic thinking from firm-centric stakeholder management to a more democratic stakeholder engagement that seeks mutual benefit in addressing social challenges together

- Examine the firm's governance and model of ownership, including whether both the purpose of the company can be legally defined to serve a social purpose, and whether greater levels of employee and customer ownership can be promoted

- Become involved in initiatives that are seeking to transform economic systems, such as The Finance Lab, Corporation 20/20 and the Transforming Capitalism project of MIT[47]

- Explore how your company could begin participating in non-interest-bearing complementary currencies, such as by offering to pay suppliers and staff an option to receive a percentage of payments in a local currency, and accepting such currencies for some payment

- Working towards a shift in the Responsible Investment field from investor-determined interests in environmental, social and governance issues, to Accountable Investment, where investors would have an obligation to respond to stakeholder-defined interests

- Engage those NGOs, unions and other organisations that are working on a more transformative agenda

Broader transformations

Although I believe a sustainable economy is impossible without a reformatting of capitalism, it is unknown whether a system of capital democracy would create an environmentally sustainable society. As capital democracy involves making more economic decisions accountable to those affected by them, then this process would promote environmental sustainability to the extent of people's awareness and commitment to that aim. Perhaps the democratic spirit of people would be cultivated through an experience of democratic institutions and practices and the resultant increased sharing of resources equitably, and so concern for collective challenges such as environmental ones would be addressed better than they are now. However, there are some limitations in the framework: the concept of inter-generational equity does not fit within a framework of democratic principles and rights. However, given current life-spans, the rights of children should require us to consider the potential impact of today's decisions on the situation in eighty years' time. Whether capital is managed with a longer time horizon would depend on the views in society.

A democracy and human rights framework does not protect either the welfare of non-human life or its freedom from extinction. However, human concern for these matters would translate into their view of what aspects of the natural world should be capitalised and how that capital should be owned and managed. Therefore, the extent of concern for animal welfare and biodiversity would depend, once again, on levels of human awareness. There is no guarantee, either, that a more demo-cratic economic system would calm consumerism sufficiently for the economy to exist within the biocapacity of the Earth.

Capital democracy will not be a panacea, and to attain global well-being and restore the biosphere will require a democratisation of other aspects of life—in-volving an awakening of all to our connectedness, to each other, and the planet we live on. My previous involvement in world summit protests, NGOs, business, the United Nations and academia helped me realise that we would miss the point if we blame a particular economic or political system for everything, or propose another system as the total solution. Some systems are better than others; they feed certain aspects of human character not others. But ultimately the outcome of any social or organisational system will depend on us. Over the five years I witnessed common characteristics in people and groups working in all the arenas I engaged. Every-where there was compassion, humility and inquisitiveness. Yet everywhere there was also pride, fear, manipulation and ego. Everywhere including in myself.

I concluded, with David Murphy, in my first book, which looked at cross-sectoral partnerships for corporate responsibility, with the following hope:

> Perhaps we are on the verge of something bigger. People are beginning to recognise their small part in the wider world. People are beginning to think of the implications of their actions and people are beginning to lis-ten to each other. Indeed, people are beginning to consider the needs of a

'we society' and not just a 'me society'. If these changes help to breakdown some of the alienation and competition we feel in work, in the street, in academia, even in our personal lives, then we may just stumble across a new way forward and reinvent the future.[48]

Over ten years on, I do see something bigger. The barriers are being shaken between everything—including business and society, research and action, science and spirituality, progress and traditional wisdom. People are turning away from the idea that they should be consumers of politics, culture and society, and instead act as citizens in all areas of life. In this light the corporate responsibility movement, and the emerging common agenda for capital democracy, can be seen as one dimension of a growing global democracy movement.

My hope today is that a spirit of democracy and global citizenship is carried into the spheres of belief, religion and spirituality to lead to a transformation of consciousness that will make any new political-economic systems we create function for the well-being of all life on Earth.

1Q2009
January–March

Jem Bendell and Jonathan Cohen

The return of government

A major implication of the global financial crisis is the return of government to a leading role in national economies. A hands-on role for the state has been the norm in some countries, but the past two decades witnessed a rolling-back of government involvement even in communist or former communist countries such as China, Vietnam and Cambodia. In 2009, as new government regulations were announced, as further nationalisations of financial institutions became necessary, and as economic stimulus packages were agreed around the world, government once again took on a position to shape economic activity. How it would use that role, and the implications for social and environmental performance of business, will only be understood in the years to come, but there were some early signs in the first quarter of 2009. In this review we note the scale of the stimulus packages, the sustainable business dimensions of these spending announcements, and the implications for achieving a sustainable economy, before recalling what the private sector is meant to be good for—innovation—and looking at how a return of greater government shaping of our economies might relate to the need for sustainable innovation. We also consider what the post-crisis situation spells for the future of the community of professionals working in corporate social responsibility (CSR).

Reviewing the world of government responses to the global economic downturn revealed an unprecedented international effort to prop up economic growth and employment. In March 2009, the International Monetary Fund called for stimulus of approximately 2% of gross domestic product (GDP) each year for 2009–2010, depending on national circumstances.[1] Asian countries committed $1.153 trillion in stimulus money,[2] with the spending plans ranging from 1–12% of GDP, with the Philippines at 4.4% and China at 12%.[3] According to the European Commission, the executive arm of the 27-nation bloc, EU stimulus amounted to between 3.3% and 4% of GDP.[4] The US committed $787 billion, or about 5.5% of GDP.

In Latin America, larger economies—Argentina, Brazil, Chile, Mexico and Peru, with lower debt-to-GDP ratios, announced stimulus plans. Smaller economies with debt that was already over 50% of GDP in cases before the collapse in exports didn't have the public finances for stimulus plans.[5]

Combined with the nationalisation of troubled industries, the growth of government spending under the stimulus packages highlights how governments around the globe now have a central economic leadership role that could drive the next phase of CSR—not merely through regulation of private industry, but by being the client, investor, lender, insurer and marketeer.

We discuss how government is using this power in the following section. However, one CSR challenge that is set to grow on account of this greater role of government is that of corruption, cronyism and inappropriate lobbying. Industries that rely on government as their main consumer have a track record of being politically involved; such industries include arms, construction and pharmaceuticals. Now that government is becoming an even bigger client of a diverse range of industrial sectors, so the scope for unprofessional practice, corruption and uncompetitive lobbying to occur is increasing. If untrammelled markets and central decision-making aren't the answer—and shared governance is—then transparency is essential in rebuilding lost trust. The return of government with $2.8 trillion in stimulus opens the door to unprecedented scrutiny of spending which will be inextricably linked to the private sector, blurring and extending lines of accountability.

The sheer scale of deficit-financed stimulus spending, with public money passing into and propping up private for-profit institutions—which threatens in some cases to bankrupt governments and essential services—has tightened the screws of corporate governance because of a macro-economic system dependent on corporate welfare.

In consideration of this, China announced the deployment of inspection teams to monitor all aspects of stimulus funding, including planning, procurement, construction and quality. Inspectors will 'check whether the money is used to build office buildings or guesthouses of party and government departments'.[6] China wasn't the only country placing an emphasis on transparency. A new US Recovery Act Accountability and Transparency Board was created to conduct oversight of recovery spending.[7] Further, US Treasury Secretary Tim Geithner told the House Financial Services Committee, 'We need much stronger standards for openness, transparency, and plain common sense language throughout the financial system.'[8]

The sustainability of stimulus

In March 2009, the chief executive of Business for Social Responsibility, Aron Cramer, posited that this period marks the end of an era that started in the late 1970s with the rise of Ronald Reagan and Margaret Thatcher, privatisation, shrinking government, and the Washington Consensus.[9] It has been an era in which some of the world's biggest celebrities have been CEOs. However, with the sudden collapse in trust in business and markets, the pendulum has begun swinging back towards greater reliance on the public sector for the safeguarding of public security and prosperity.[10] This has implications for the future of corporate citizenship.

Even before the crisis fully revealed itself, a blueprint emerged for subsequent stimulus plans—'A Green New Deal' (GND).[11] A report from British civil society organisations called for a 'structural transformation of the regulation of financial systems, and major changes to taxation systems', and 'New Deal size investment in renewable energy and green jobs to create the basis for a low carbon economy'.

Elements of 'A Green New Deal' could be found in various national stimulus packages, with more than $430 billion addressing GND elements, according to a report from HSBC in February 2009. Report co-author Nick Robins wrote, 'We believe that these commitments are but the first instalment of further efforts by governments to use low-carbon growth as a key lever for economic recovery.'[12]

Stimulus plans can be evaluated based on how quickly they get economies back up and running, but the added value in their 'Green New Deal' elements lies in how much they leverage the investment and also build the future infrastructure for a low-carbon economy that will pay dividends for generations to follow. Government stimulus plans focused investment in the following categories: renewable energy electricity grids, mass transit, low-carbon vehicles, building efficiency and environmental conservation, as well as education and healthcare. In addition, government restructuring of tax codes and financial incentives was a common option for codifying and spurring sustainable economic development.

A report issued by the UN Environment Programme in February 2009, 'A Global Green New Deal', stated that energy efficiency improvements and green tax credits in stimulus plans are particularly effective because they 'continue well beyond the initial investment period and offer higher employment compared to jobs created by conventional tax cuts and road infrastructure investments that end once the money is spent'. Additionally, they offer greater return on investment to households through lower energy bills. Investments that provide alternatives to car use reduce pollution and emissions as well as creating employment.[13]

Further, the Peterson Institute for International Economics and World Resources Institute report from February 2009, *Green Economic Stimulus Creates Jobs, Saves Taxpayers Money*, wrote, 'On average, green recovery programs create 30,000 jobs for every $1 billion in government spending.'[14] The Center for American Progress released a report, *Green Recovery: A Program to Create Good Jobs and Start Building a Low-Carbon Economy*, which estimated that US Green stimulus spending would engender a '20 percent increase in job creation over more traditional infrastructure spending'.[15]

Crunch the green numbers of stimulus plans from a given country and, aside from the absolute amounts, their percentage of overall spending demonstrated commitment to 'Green New Deal' elements.

China led the way with $221 billion in spending on GND elements or some 38% of stimulus, while the US allocated $94 billion or about 12%. South Korea meanwhile devoted about $31 billion on GND initiatives or just over 80%—by far the highest proportion of any country. EU social safety nets resulted in a smaller stimulus, although the climate change dimension was seen as greater than in the US, due to a focus on low-carbon investment in France, Germany, and at the EU level, according to the UNEP report.[16]

Opportunities for large capital-intensive infrastructure improvements will not come along again any time soon as economies gradually recover to newly emerging levels. Government procurement stands as the single greatest vehicle to scale up corporate social responsibility practices moving ahead, particularly through the adoption of standards to codify change.

Were China to follow up its impressive green stimulus spending with a similar commitment to government procurement in a top-down regime, it could quickly demonstrate the possibilities of unprecedented CSR scale. This would not exactly be new policy either, as China announced a new 'green procurement' policy in late 2006 based on a list of recommended products carrying 'China's only national eco-label, which an official explained could make the government "the real driving force for industry to develop green technology"'.[17]

In fact, scale is the heretofore unrealised holy grail of CSR: the International Council on Local Environmental Initiatives (ICLEI) has documented green procurement by numerous countries and localities,[18] with Denmark and Japan cited as particular successes.[19] 'Following the introduction of the 2001 national law on green purchasing in Japan,[20] the price of environmentally friendly product alternatives, such as recycled paper, has dropped to equal the nongreen alternatives', according to *Moving the Market*, a report from the EcoProcura conference on sustainable procurement.[21] Other municipalities and governments have taken similar initial steps, such as the Queensland government announcement in August 2007 of a new 'green' IT procurement plan, covering all government agency purchases of PCs, laptops and servers.[22] Mexico decreed in 2008 that it would green its procurement of paper and wood products and buy chlorine-free paper made of at least 50% recycled material.[23]

One example of the importance of monitoring follow-up to stated commitments and adherence to related standards, however, can be found in the UN Office for Project Services (UNOPS). It announced with great fanfare in June 2000 that it would be the first UN Entity to sign on to the SA8000 labour standard to improve the social accountability of its procurement process with suppliers and vendors, as well as its own facilities; but later quietly dropped that commitment.[24] While the agency's procurement policy claims observance of relevant International Labour Organization agreements, the third-party certification and monitoring inherent in the application of SA8000, which provides credibility, is nowhere to be found.[25]

External third-party verification and assurance stand as the most trustworthy governance bulwark against corruption, incompetence and squandering of a generation's Green New Deal legacy. The potential exists for a wave of new demand for CSR auditors and the education and training necessary to prepare them to close the loop on the gap between stimulus spending and accountability. Without transparently communicated accountability measures, subsequent instalments of governmental low-carbon investment may not materialise, as anticipated by Robins and HSBC.

In addition to procurement, a harbinger of a greater governmental role in socially responsible investing can be found in the response to the global financial crisis by the board of the UN Principles for Responsible Investment (UNPRI), an investor initiative that includes some of the world's largest pension funds. UNPRI released a public statement from the board in March 2009 that 'urged fellow institutional investors to accept their share of responsibility for the current crisis, to work together to improve risk management practices, and create a culture of "active ownership" in response to the crisis'.[26] The board includes representatives from governments such as Brazil, New Zealand, South Africa, Thailand, the US and the UK.

Implications for companies and countries from the surge in government spending can be found in the following key areas:

- China committed more to renewable electricity grid infrastructure than any other country—$70 billion[27]—while the US devoted $11 billion as well as $6 billion in renewable energy loan guarantees for power generation and transmission,[28] and France spent over $4 billion[29]

- Mass transit necessarily entails a long-term view, which China's green stimulus package took by spending $85 billion on rail transport.[30] The US included $17.7 billion for energy-efficient transportation,[31] and South Korea spent $7 billion on railroads and mass transit.[32] Brazil in turn said it would rely completely on private-sector investment to build a high-speed train between Rio de Janeiro and São Paulo, which limited government debt, but placed the project in doubt due to a difficult credit climate[33]

- Spending on low-carbon vehicles was included in stimulus by the US, South Korea, France, Denmark and Spain. The US gave $2 billion to US manufacturers of advanced vehicle batteries and battery systems, and spent $600 million to replace older vehicles owned by the federal, state and local governments with alternative-fuel and plug-in automobiles—and this does not include measures taken to bail out the automotive industry

- South Korea spent almost $1.5 billion on fuel-efficient vehicles and clean fuels,[34] whereas France included over $500 million in incentives to do away with older vehicles and spur purchase of new, environmentally friendlier models.[35] Denmark instituted a new green vehicle tax that will make it cheaper to buy energy-efficient vehicles but more expensive to use cars, and Spain's stimulus called for plans to install an electric car infrastructure in Seville, Madrid and Barcelona with cars to be purchased with state subsidies of up to 30%[36]

- Retrofitting buildings for energy efficiency was included in stimulus packages by countries such as Japan, Germany, the US, South Korea and Australia.

Japan spent the most in this category, $12.5 billion, Germany second at a shade over $10 billion,[37] while the US Spent $5 billion for low-income weatherisation programmes, and $4.5 billion for federal building energy efficiency renovations and repairs.[38] South Korea included approximately $6 billion for environmentally friendly buildings and schools, and Australia spent $2.5 billion[39]

- South Korea stood out as the single most prominent country to focus on environmental conservation as a vehicle for economic stimulus with a commitment of over $10 billion for river restoration, more than any other single part of its stimulus plan, with another $1.7 billion on forest restoration as well[40]

- Latin American countries—Argentina, Chile, whose stimulus constituted the largest percentage of GDP in the region, Mexico and Peru, all allocated money for social programmes in areas such as education and healthcare,[41] as did Eastern Europe countries, such as Bulgaria, to a lesser extent[42]

- Government restructuring of tax codes and financial incentives were a favourite measure of many countries, including Denmark, the US, France and the Czech Republic. Denmark took one of the strongest tax reform measures of any country and instituted binding incremental emission caps on industry, with the resultant revenue to be used in green tax reform that decreases taxes on labour and increases taxes on pollution.[43] The US committed approximately $20 billion in clean energy tax incentives.[44] France instituted a tax system for CO_2 emissions from cars,[45] and the Czech government provided tax incentives for new car purchases[46]

Meanwhile, the UK's green fiscal stimulus was described by Parliament's Environmental Audit Committee as 'welcome, but too small—especially given that most funding was already committed, and will be offset by reduced spending in 2010–11'. Instead, it called for 'improving the energy efficiency of existing buildings as the number one priority. Such programmes are labour-intensive and do not require development of new technology.' The EAC further stated, 'It is disappointing that the wider stimulus package contains hundreds of millions of pounds for road building and widening',[47] which embodies the paradox of competition between carbon- versus sustainable-based spending.

Keeping talk of a Global Green New Deal in perspective, Manish Bapna, executive vice president of the World Resources Institute, said, 'Even the most aggressive short-term stimulus spending will have only a modest impact on emissions. Recovery efforts should be designed to set the stage for comprehensive energy and climate policies.'[48]

While green stimulus spending of $430 billion is significant, it needs to be seen as only the start of ongoing green government spending so the other $2.3 trillion or so in stimulus does not work at cross-purposes.

If the problem is the prescription . . .

So has this financial crisis been used as an opportunity to create a new and more sustainable model of capitalism? Inherently built into the litany of government stimulus plans is the paradox of restarting a carbon-based economic engine while at the same time trying to build a new, green road. In the face of withering criticism of business practices amid the fallout caused by the global financial crisis, the very assumption of the macro-economic basis for stimulus policy prescriptions—i.e. growth—has once again been called into question. The UK Sustainable Development Commission, an independent advisory body to the government established in April 2006, released a report on 30 March 2009, *Prosperity without Growth? The Transition to a Sustainable Economy*. The report argued that 'the market was not undone by rogue individuals or the turning of a blind eye by incompetent regulators. It was undone by growth itself.'[49]

Viewing the problem as the prescription, the report stated, 'the broad assumption behind all these recovery packages is that they will be successful in stimulating consumption growth again. Credit will flow, consumers will spend, business productivity will return and the wheels of the machine will start turning. The outcome (assuming it works) will be thoroughly predictable', consumption will be driven forwards, with 'no means of anyone getting off the treadmill'.[50]

Starting with the view that the impacts of unfettered economic expansion and resource use associated with it 'are already unsustainable', the report equated the doubling of the global economy over the last 25 years with the degradation of 'an estimated 60% of the world's ecosystems' and an increase in global carbon emissions by 40% since 1990. These critics view the economy as a subset of the macro ecosystem of the planet, rather than the opposite.[51]

In an idealised zero-waste economy, a steady state of activity would occur where renewable resources would not be used any more quickly than the ecosystem can replace them. Non-renewable resources would not be used any more quickly than renewable substitutes could be developed. Waste and pollution would not be emitted any more quickly than it could be absorbed sustainably.[52] In short, as Professor Tim Jackson, the UK Sustainable Development Commissioner for Economics said, the ideal economy provides the ability for people to flourish 'within the limits of the natural environment'.[53]

The steady state economic critique challenges the current model: 'The truth is that there is as yet no credible, socially just, ecologically sustainable scenario of continually growing incomes for a world of nine billion people. Simplistic assumptions that capitalism's propensity for efficiency will allow us to stabilise the climate and protect against resource scarcity are nothing short of delusional.'[54]

Taking its philosophical views to the extreme, the report views the choice as either an increase in consumption for all up to the level of the most prosperous, which is unsustainable, or a levelling-off 'in which incomes are distributed equally across nations' and 'growth in the richer nations is curtailed or some kind of completely unforeseen technological breakthrough happens'.[55]

The question of social equity is an important one to raise in the context of sustainability. It is clear that highly unequal incomes in and between societies leads to the degradation or waste of resources,[56] as well as negative impacts on personal health and well-being.[57] The UK Sustainable Development Commission has thus highlighted an important issue that cannot be ignored—a redistribution of resource consumption opportunities. This issue was identified in our 2007 year reflection: the need to reduce, redirect and redistribute resource consumption to achieve a sustainable globe. One implication for business is that of gaining greater insight into how to operate in ways that do not create high inequality, and even provide opportunities for social advancement of disadvantaged groups. However, it also raises the question of what form of 'equitable' resource consumption can be aspired to. There are, to our knowledge, no internationally agreed principles about an equitable consumption of the world's resources. Suggestions that 'incomes are distributed equally across nations'[58] appear illogical as well as impractical, given the diversity of lifestyles and livelihoods, from artisanal fisher in the Pacific island of Palawan to a taxi driver in Manhattan. Yet it encourages us to engage in a debate about how consumption levels can justifiably be related to individual wants and societal contributions.

While characterising economic growth as the path to over-consumption, advocates of steady state economics argue for growth of a different kind, 'moral growth'.[59] Herman Daly has said changes in both institutions and values are necessary, but changing the latter is more important.[60] Demonstrating the range of views questioning basic assumptions of unrestrained growth, German President and former head of the International Monetary Fund Horst Köhler asked in a 24 March 2009 speech, 'How much is enough?' He answered by saying, 'We should know that we can no longer rely mainly on economic growth as the solution to our problems and the peacemaker in our societies.'[61]

Peace, however, was in short supply as nationwide strikes broke out in France with well over a million people in the streets angry that companies cut jobs while executives received bonuses. Employees at French 3M and Sony France held executives hostage over disputes about terms for laid-off staff.[62] In response to popular pressure, the government banned 'bonuses and stock options for executives' whose companies received bailout money.[63] The riots at the G20 summit in London also highlighted the level of unrest at the existing economic and political system that lies under the surface of 'normal' society. As such, it is an important period for citizens interested in contributing to a positive relationship between business and society to participate in this systemic debate, and relevant initiatives aiding informed policy-making.

To be effective in this new policy context CSR professionals will need to look up from their specific activities, and consider the kind of economy and society they are seeking to bring into being. In this reflection of goals and change strategies, they could learn much from how social movements past and present have arisen and impacted on society. It is that insight that led Jem Bendell to explore social movements theories and their implications for the contemporary CSR field.[64]

One area of human activity that appears to need wholesale transformation in light of climate change is transportation. In the first two months of 2009, sales of cars were higher in China than the US for the first time in history. For people concerned with spiralling carbon dioxide pollution, this appears a disturbing statistic. It comes after news that Indian firm Tata intends to produce its Nano model to enable millions more Indians to own a car.[65] However, this growing cloud of carbon could have a silver lining—in the technological and business process innovation that is occurring in the growing Chinese car industry.

A Chinese automobile manufacturer based in Shenzhen, China, BYD Auto is part of the BYD Company Limited, which makes 65% of the world's nickel–cadmium batteries and 30% of the world's lithium-ion mobile phone batteries. With this experience and capacity, BYD Auto has been making strides in the provision of electric and dual-fuel automobiles. This includes a mid-size sedan, which uses an iron-phosphate-based battery, and can be recharged to 70% of capacity in ten minutes at special stations, and in a number of hours through normal electric plugs. The cost-effective manufacturing capacities in Shenzhen mean that, unlike other car companies, BYD can produce most of the components in its cars itself, such as the air-conditioning, lights, seatbelts and electronics.[66] Consequently, it can offer its electric cars for less than the electric cars being made in the West. 'We are committed to a green future for our planet', said Wang Chuanfu, chairman of BYD, at the Detroit Auto Show in January 2009. 'We have the ability, the capability and the desire to be a significant part of the solution.'[67] His company has attracted interest from Warren Buffett, who bought a 10% share of the company for US$230 million. Buffett thinks BYD 'has a shot at becoming the world's largest automaker, primarily by selling electric cars, as well as a leader in the fast-growing solar power industry'.[68] The new model it unveiled in March 2009 showed that it was not an innovator in aesthetics, as it closely resembled Toyota's Lexus.[69] However, the real design innovation for BYD is in the engine—a form of innovation more important for sustainability.

More dual-engine, hybrid cars and electric cars will not, however, create sustainable mobility systems, consuming more resources than mass public transport systems, especially if trains and buses are designed and operated with carbon emissions in mind. Yet individual car use is likely to remain key for many people. An insight into how individual car usage could be redesigned has emerged from an Israeli company called Better Place. It is innovating solutions to the infrastructure problem which holds back the uptake of electric vehicles. Better Place is building a huge network of charging points and battery-swapping systems in a number of countries, including Israel and Australia, to enable existing car companies to offer electric models that are compatible with the system. It is innovating a new business model where consumers will pay for the mileage they drive, and thus car producers will earn revenue from the amount of charging their customers do. This parallels the business models of manufacturers of mobile phones and computer printers.[70]

The way consumers use their new electric transportation will also be key to its sustainability. Thus transportation sharing initiatives are an important dimension to sustainable mobility. Zipcar, the world's largest car sharing service, is now in 50 US cities, as well as in Vancouver, Toronto and London. The company has increasingly rolled out its innovative business model beyond individual consumers to universities, and now governments, with an agreement reached on 5 February 2009 with the city of Seattle, WA, for use by over 10,000 employees,[71] and a partnership with the city of San Francisco, 19 February 2009, to increase the number of electric plug-in hybrid vehicles in their fleet as well as the advent of new charging stations at city hall.[72]

Whether personal mobility services can be transformed in time to offset the growth in emissions due to a growing global demand for mobility will be key to how humanity reduces its carbon emissions. This could be helped if the stimulus packages targeted those firms ready with solutions, and that bailouts were conditional on link-ups with those firms with appropriate technologies and business models for low-carbon societies. Concerns about the leakage of government stimulus or bailout funds outside a country may be missing the point: the best use of public funds is in investing in the businesses of the future, no matter their nationality. If the US government had invested its billions in BYD and Better Place, as an owner, rather than putting its money into failing US automakers, the US citizen might now own a stronger asset, and be better supporting the climate fight. The political difficulty of governments taking such an internationalist perspective to their own spending further highlights the difficulty they face in playing a positive role in guiding sustainable innovation. Arguing the case for internationalist approaches to encouraging and scaling up sustainable innovations is therefore a central responsibility for leading business executives at this time of dual economic and climate crises.

The challenge of transitioning to sustainable mobility highlights the need for government to be a partner in stimulating the necessary innovations for fair and sustainable societies. 'It may be understandable, but disproportionate effort continues to be lavished on shoring up the dinosaurs of the old order, rather than investing in the new pioneers, who are working hard—and often against the odds—to incubate and scale market solutions essential for a sustainable future', claimed a report released by Volans in early 2009. The authors, John Elkington, Alejandro Litovsky and Charmian Love, describe a 'Phoenix Economy' that is 'focused on providing social and environmental solutions, where markets and governments have failed'.[73]

One policy innovation in the first months of 2009 was 'cash for clunkers', which gained traction under the German stimulus where 'vehicles over nine years old traded in for new, environmentally friendlier models received rebates of $3,172'. Subsequently, Germany experienced the highest February car sales level in a decade. China slashed taxes on small, fuel-efficient vehicles, which increased their monthly sales 19%. Similar programmes hit the road in France, Italy and Spain.[74] Given the complexity of creating new systems of electric recharging and car sharing that are financially viable, there is still much for government to do in shaping sustainable mobility.

From right to relevance

The global financial crisis might better be termed 'The Great Breakdown'. For what has occurred is a breakdown in governance and accountability that lies at the root of the financial events, and the breakdown in public trust and legitimacy of the current system due to the spending of unprecedented sums of public money to fix private losses due to high-risk profit-seeking. How may the CSR field be relevant to this new context?

The chief executive of AccountAbility, Simon Zadek, summed up the landscape clearly:

> After 2008, no one in their right minds will ever again question the negative impact of irresponsible business practices, the source of the world's first global recession along with its consequences of millions upon millions of jobs lost, houses repossessed, families broken, and economies shattered. Never again will anyone be able to look smug in demanding advocates of corporate responsibility to 'prove it'. The financial community, at enormous cost to us all, has done what no one else has quite managed, to make our point, loudly, globally, and irrevocably.[75]

Despite the centrality of corporate irresponsibility in causing 'The Great Breakdown', some predicted CSR's demise in the face of bottom-line cuts and crises, with the *Financial Times* anticipating CSR professionals 'will be told to take a gap year indefinitely', for example.[76] CSR risked being seen as merely an add-on in recovery efforts, since in Western nations all else took a back seat to securing the banking system and ensuring employment did not collapse.

Nevertheless, the existence of Green New Deal elements in stimulus packages around the world highlights how some of the issues that the CSR community advances have made their way into the mainstream of government planning. Further government leadership is necessary, especially to scale the sustainable and social enterprises described in *The Phoenix Economy*. If such enterprises 'are to succeed, they will still need substantial assistance from governments, foundations, investors and businesses', notes Volans. They identify opportunities for facilitation, collaboration and support, in a Phoenix Economy Manifesto for governments.[77]

As government returns to a central role in shaping economic activity, so the potential to support a new sustainable enterprise economy, or prop up the old, has grown significantly. SustainAbility's founder John Elkington predicted in January 2009 that executives 'will be expected to help design the new order, not simply to massage the old'.[78] The leaders and institutions in the CSR field will be tested by their ability to effectively advocate and lobby governments to ensure the unprecedented sums of stimulus money are transparently governed, and spent and implemented effectively. They will need to push government farther and faster than it planned on going now that it is a client, investor, lender, insurer and marketeer. They will need to think and act as a movement.

2Q2009
April–June

Ian Doyle and Jem Bendell

Responsible tax management

The fallout from the Western financial crisis continued to bring government back into the picture in respect to how business–society relations should unfold. In April 2009, leaders of the world's 20 largest economies met in an attempt to revise the rules of global finance and reform the world's financial institutions. One of the key agenda items at the G20 concerned one basic corporate contribution to society: the payment of taxes. Leaders sought agreement on controlling tax havens and exchanging tax information—no doubt one attempt to recoup the large borrowings necessary for bailing out the banks. The outcome was an official communiqué with a commitment by the G20 'to take action against non-cooperative jurisdictions, including tax havens' and to deploy sanctions to protect public finances and financial systems.[1] While the G20 leaders can be congratulated for publicly taking a stance against jurisdictions that lack transparency in respect to the exchange of tax information, and demonstrating a willingness to act at a political level, it raises the question of what is the ethical responsibility of the corporation when it comes to using tax havens. As deputy director of the Centre of European Reform Ms Katinka Barysch questions, in commenting on the G20 agenda prior to the meeting, is addressing tax havens the real issue, or should it be improving global economic governance?[2]

For instance, the day before the summit, the French justice department announced a preliminary investigation into the possible fraudulent activity of the French oil giant Total. According to *Reuters*, Elf Trading SA which is a subsidiary of Total, was suspected of laundering money via tax haven accounts in Liechtenstein.[3] Total has since refuted the claims by acknowledging that the French government is aware of the tax havens in which they operate, none of which is in Liechtenstein.[4]

Irrespective of the outcome of the investigation, this particular example highlights the fact that, for some corporations, using tax havens is a normal part of everyday business, permitted by the government, and supported by a legal framework that enables their use.[5] So should corporations be taking advantage of such jurisdictions just because they can? Corporate social responsibility (CSR) has long been framed by the notions of social justice and environmental responsibility, but what about the ethical dimensions of a business's financial obligations to society through government taxes? If corporate governance is management's balance between economic and social goals, what is the scope of each of these concepts? Can economic responsibility be simply defined as a corporation's duty to produce goods and services while providing appropriately paid employment and still earning a profit for its stakeholders? Is it democratic for an organisation to privately define what its economic responsibilities are, and to use whatever tax management vehicles to accomplish them? As taxation is the major source of revenue for governments in maintaining social cohesion, do companies have the right to exempt themselves from paying tax for the benefit of private interests?

Questions relating to tax justice and CSR are not new. In the book *The Corporate Responsibility Movement*, Mr John Christensen, coordinator of the Tax Justice Network, argued that

> . . . curiously the CSR debate, which has touched on virtually every other area of corporate engagement with broader society, has only recently begun to question companies in the area where their corporate citizenship is most tangible and most important—the payment of tax.[6]

In a 2007 KPMG discussion paper entitled *Tax and Corporate Social Responsibility*, Mr David Williams of KPMG's Tax Business School stated that

> The application of CSR to tax issues, however, is an area that has not as yet received a great deal of attention . . . [partly because] . . . the payment of tax liabilities is, to a great extent, a non-discretionary matter . . . [as companies] . . . can deal only with public authorities, and only on the terms laid down by them.[7]

With governments now making a stoic attempt to clamp down on tax havens in light of the G20, there is a renewed impetus for corporations to reflect on the ethical dimensions of their tax strategies, and this to be assessed in terms of CSR. The difficulties facing governments in achieving international cooperation on taxation makes it important for business leaders to voluntarily explore what a responsible approach to tax management could involve, and encourage ways for governments to generate tax revenues from companies in ways that do not undermine the relative competitiveness of certain firms.

The importance of progressive business people engaging in this debate became clear as the first governmental initiatives regarding the new focus on taxation were already appearing flawed in 2009.

Triumphant claims by the G20 that 'the era of banking secrecy [was] over' were somewhat premature due to the political and administrative barriers in enforcing transparency under the current arrangements. For example, the G20 agreed to name and shame those countries and jurisdictions that are yet to comply with the international standard for exchange of tax information, according to the Organisation for Economic Cooperation and Development (OECD). The definition of a secrecy jurisdiction or tax haven is important to note. The central feature of a haven is that its laws and other measures can be used to evade (the illegal and deliberate failure to pay tax), or avoid (the minimisation of tax liability by lawful methods), the tax laws or regulations of other jurisdictions. According to the OECD, tax havens have four characteristics that facilitate both tax evasion and tax avoidance:

- Low or zero tax rates, as an indicator to determine situations in which analysis of the other criteria is necessary

- Lack of tax information exchange with other countries

- A high degree of bank secrecy

- And lack of real economic activity associated with the income generated[8]

However, in a Tax Justice Network (TJN) report to identify tax havens and offshore finance centres (OFCs), they conclude that there is no precise definition of either concept and suggest that OFCs are a purer form of tax haven.[9] This is because the regulatory criteria such as that of the OECD above, may not be consistent with other organisations and they are based on different methods and indicators to identify such jurisdictions. The City of London in the United Kingdom is a case in point as it has a preferential tax regime that exempts foreign source income from resident-country tax. This means that, by residing in Britain, wealthy internationals can find tax solace to avoid taxation on their foreign earnings.[10] According to OECD criteria it is not a tax haven but, according to the International Monetary Fund (IMF)'s criteria, it is.[11] Judging by the number of wealthy individuals having flocked to London, in practice the IMF's definition appears closer to the mark.[12]

The ironic corollary, of course, is that the 'name and shame' game being played by the G20 powers is not being applied in a universal sense, so it is not surprising that, with the large influx of wealth coming into Britain, the City of London is considered the world's largest OFC. The City of London is not a borough of London per se, but a defined geographical area within London that is home to Britain's largest 'offshore' financial district. It is managed by the City of London Corporation which is also the political representative body. According to TJN, it is the most powerful lobby in Britain and possibly the world and, as a result

> . . . exerts enormous political influence to resist regulation and extract tax exemption. It has fostered criminality by ensuring that the City ranks amongst the least accountable of financial centres on the face of the Earth.[13]

This kind of power is not surprising because the City of London Corporation is in effect the provider of services that would normally be fulfilled by the local authority and is thus an example of a private company operating under the auspices of a public service.[14] Promoting sustainability is a part of the corporation's 'offer' and this is outlined in a partial sustainability policy.[15] That policy makes no mention of tax justice, nor is there mention of human rights, labour or anti-corruption issues as per the Global Compact. For such a powerful institution that attracts so much international money, could it set the standard by implementing these principles themselves? The anti-corruption measure alone would mean that they would be engaged to work *against* corruption providing a potential barrier to the investment of corrupt money. Being a financial district, it could promote the UN Principles for Responsible Investment. While the City has put in place the London Principles in conjunction with Forum for the Future, the principles are only a guide to the conditions to enhance the financing of sustainable development; the integrity of their own operations is not in question.[16] This may be the explanation as to why the corporation limits their reporting to community activities through the London Benchmarking Group, with no social and environmental report ever being published by them.[17]

The City of London was not the only jurisdiction that escaped the OECD list. Hong Kong and Macau did not make it either, distorting the progress that needs to be made by China, nor was there mention of the US states Delaware, Wyoming or Nevada. With the French pushing hard to combat tax havens, it was also a little ironic that they let one of their own *paradis fiscal* (tax haven), namely French Polynesia, slip away unannounced.[18]

While Hong Kong and Macau have committed to the internationally agreed tax standard, but have not yet substantially implemented it, the omission gives the impression that China is well on its way to implementing the standard; yet, in actual fact, two of its biggest financial centres are far from being ready. By calling these jurisdictions 'Special Administrative Regions', those that write the rules are manipulating language and in turn deflecting the attention towards tax havens other than their own.[19]

But what constitutes progress, or substantial implementation of the international standard is in itself questionable. The subjectivity of the OECD's method is demonstrated in a letter from the OECD Secretary-General Angel Gurría to the Luxembourg Justice Minister prior to the summit.[20] Mr Gurría stated, 'the OECD noted that a good indicator of progress was whether or not a jurisdiction [had] twelve or more agreements that [met] the OECD standards' which the OECD subsequently confirmed in their June 2009 progress report on countering offshore tax evasion.[21] What form an agreement takes is important to note because there are two types: Double Taxation Agreements (DTAs) and Tax Information Exchange Agreements (TIEAs). A DTA is a treaty between states to avoid the double taxation of income and thus indicating that taxation is a structural part of each nation's economic stability. But, for jurisdictions with no or low taxes, this type of agreement is not considered appropriate and the preferred type of treaty is a TIEA. TJN estimates that there are anywhere between 50 and 72 secrecy jurisdictions in the world, yet there are well over 100 countries with which they could negotiate information exchange agreements. With only 55 TIEAs having been signed between OECD countries and secrecy jurisdictions prior to the G20, the so-called indicator of progress is clearly not applicable in any universal sense.[22]

So, having satisfied the OECD requirements, do these agreements enforce a greater transparency? In a *Financial Times* (*FT*) article in April 2009, Raymond Baker of Global Financial Integrity explained that without serious reforms to undermine the vehicles used to ensure secrecy, these agreements will be ineffective.[23] Firstly, countries such as Switzerland have laws that prevent such exchanges so, without changes to these laws, an extremely time-consuming process, the agreements will have little effect. Secondly, in the event that there is tax evasion, according to OECD guidelines there must be proof of the fraud to authorise any exchange of information. Such a course of action is an impediment because a detailed case must be made, with the criteria set out in a lengthy legal document.[24] Furthermore, in light of the many jurisdictions that require absolutely no traceability to set up accounts, how will it be possible to establish fraudulent activity?[25] In May, a political scientist at Australia's Griffith University, Dr Jason Sharman, demonstrated just how rife the problem is by circumventing prohibitions on banking secrecy and forming seventeen anonymous shell companies and five secret bank accounts with only AUS$20,000 and the internet.[26] Thirteen of these shell companies were in OECD countries and, of the secret accounts, four were in the United States and Great Britain.

In an article from Tax Analysts they say,

> Before deterrence of evasion can begin, a haven must negotiate bilateral tax information exchange agreements, enact legislation, and—usually after a multiyear transition period—set up and maintain the bureaucratic machinery to enforce the agreements[27]

Again the poor lose, leaving a question mark over the political feasibility of the G20's confidence to eliminate tax havens.

Ultimately, for the agreements to work, the blockages to effective exchange need to be removed. Raymond Baker puts it succinctly in his *FT* article:

> What needs to happen now is for the G20 to broaden its dialogue on information exchange agreements, international co-operation and international financial protocols. Most effective in curtailing the massive illicit outflows from developing countries would be a requirement for automatic cross-border exchange of tax information on personal and business accounts and country-by-country reporting of sales, profits and taxes paid by multinationals.[28]

The emphasis on automatic cross-border exchange is imperative if the G20 are serious about tax exchange and ensures a level playing field in respect to transparency. Exchange upon request is simply too burdensome on an administrative and cost level. In an Internal Revenue Service (IRS) study on compliance, the IRS observed that the compliance rate is 96% when there is comprehensive information reporting requirements as in the case of US dividends and interest, which is analogous to automatic information exchange. When there is little or no information reporting required, the compliance rate drops to 46%, suggesting that the 'upon request' approach is not sufficiently coercive in assuring the exchange of tax information.[29]

If the G20 had the political will, there are a variety of ways to economically coerce tax havens into exchanging tax information, including restrictions on providing financial services such as wire transfers, or the refusal of deductions related to transactions with listed tax havens, to name two. Sanctioning tax havens is not the only solution either. The revenue lost by governments is significantly more than the fee and service income that tax havens earn so there is also scope for incentives to ensure that tax-haven economies do not crash.[30] Regulatory measures such as the adoption of a General Anti-Avoidance Principle (GAAP) as tabled in the British parliament by Mr Michael Meacher MP in May 2009, could also provide recourse in tax avoidance issues.[31] Such legislation would give courts the power to decide on whether certain tax practices are being used to avoid paying tax and thereby also assisting directors in understanding their duties on the payment of tax.[32]

More poignantly, however, the tragedy of the G20 was not the superficial statements that did not recognise the systemic complexity underlying the tax haven and secrecy jurisdiction problems. The tragedy was that the G20 leaders missed their opportunity to create a new financial system: one that incorporates responsible governance, the environment and the social well-being of every citizen; a financial system no longer focused on short-term gain but rather long-term sustainability; one that seeks a cooperative role between corporations and governments for the benefit of society instead of the accumulation of private wealth; and one where worth in monetary terms is secondary to the values that encapsulate the greater good. Moreover, it was an inevitable outcome when the very committee advising the G20 comprised some of the biggest names in banking orthodoxy, in turn limiting any possibility of an alternative dialogue.[33]

The implications for the CSR movement are many. In an April 2009 report, the French magazine *Alternatives Economiques* (*Economic Alternatives*) reported that apart from four companies in the CAC 40 (the French equivalent to the Dow Jones or FTSE), for which information was not available, all companies had subsidiaries in a tax haven or secrecy jurisdiction of some sort, many in the City of London. The admission by Total that the French government was aware of their activities in such jurisdictions reduces this number to three. While illegal activity cannot be implied by this observation, it nonetheless shows the ubiquitous use of such jurisdictions by large companies—the locational smoke to the tax avoidance fire. Topping the list was BNP Paribas with 189 subsidiaries, with another three French banks making the top ten. While BNP asserts that it uses such jurisdictions for the purposes of its international branches, and states it in its 2007 and 2008 CSR reports, it does not mention why there is such a large concentration (40% in the City of London) nor their purpose.[34]

There are also repercussions for responsible investment (RI) managers and indeed banks offering socially responsible or ethical investment products. In the case of BNP Paribas, which has a number of funds dedicated to ethical and responsible investment, should there be more detailed disclosure in respect to tax havens, not only for the funds themselves, but for the very institution promoting them?[35] Such disclosure could include the purpose of the tax havens, and their contribution to the profitability of the group, which would be a measure of the legitimacy of such subsidiaries. Similarly, the ratings agencies that analyse environmental, social and governance (ESG) performance could verify how the tax havens are used to ensure the ethical integrity of the funds and the institution. According to Mr Robin Edme, President of FrenchSIF, and Vice-President of EuroSIF, current rating agency practices do not address this issue explicitly, but it is an area that is now a strong point of discussion for investors, and hence examining the financial industry sector is already a major concern.[36]

But questioning the effectiveness of a tax agreement or justifying the purpose of a tax haven are side issues to the essential question underlying all the systemic complexity of tax transparency: are corporations actually paying the tax they should be paying and what are the appropriate levels of tax management? What about the ethical dimension of tax avoidance? Is not tax avoidance totally incompatible with the claims of good corporate citizenship? A 2005 survey entitled *Tax, Risk and Corporate Governance* conducted by Henderson Global Investors showed that most companies did not address the questions related to tax strategy and CSR, while some perceived that there was a tension between the two.[37] How this in turn can be measured will be another dilemma for the rating agencies as it represents an overlap between ethics and the claimed objective notions of accounting, a subject already raised in Issue 6 of the *Journal of Corporate Citizenship* following the Enron scandal.[38]

As an example, PricewaterhouseCoopers has developed an initiative 'Total Tax Contribution', a tool for companies to demonstrate their effective tax contribution to society and improve transparency in recognition of this nexus.[39] But, as Mr Richard Murphy of Tax Research LLP cautions, transparency is far from improved as the PwC framework is simply the addition of various different taxes such as VAT, national insurance and employee payroll tax, and thus not a reflection of whether a reasonable amount of tax is being paid. The individual components in the computation have no value either because the reporting framework has no requirement to state the underlying base data: that is to say, for example, the profit or employee payroll on which the tax calculation was based; nor does it take into consideration the location of *where* the profits were made.[40] John Christensen calls it a 'crock of nonsense' and has recommended that corporations looking for a more prudent approach to tax justice should consider the 'SEE What You Are Buying Into' labelling scheme, which incorporates tax justice issues as part of their matrix of social, environmental and ethical issues.[41]

The SEE scheme's approach incorporates the base data necessary to determine whether an appropriate amount of tax is being paid, where the

> 'Appropriate levels of tax' are the rates stipulated by the relevant tax authority within the country where the company's tax liability falls minus 3%. [The 3% is recognition that accounting and taxable profits are not always identical.]

To become SEE-listed, companies are required to respond to 35 closed questions on a range of social, environmental and ethical (SEE) issues. SEE What You Are Buying Into Ltd initiates a dialogue with companies in the event that there is a question mark over their responses or they are unclear. To answer the tax question, co-authored with TJN, companies must declare the date of publication of their financial statements for the last two financial years, the applicable tax bracket for their business, and the percentage of tax that they paid. If they are not paying the defined appropriate rate, they must additionally explain and justify why not. All details are housed on the SEE What You Are Buying Into website where they are available for public scrutiny, comment and rating. Thus businesses participating in the scheme offer a transparent picture of their performance on tax, among many other material corporate responsibility matters.

SEE Company's approach could indicate a change in the wind for an area of CSR that remains undeveloped, but the issue of tax havens and secrecy jurisdictions has a long way to go because what it demonstrates is that the law, in the interim, is not sufficient. When the legal undercurrent supports the corporate machine for the purposes of gain, it is very easy for corporations to hide behind the law without actually breaking it. As a result, questions of legitimacy, social responsibility and managerial discretion are difficult to challenge. But, if the law is not equal for everyone, then values are the ultimate guide in determining how a business person understands their role in society, and whether they should adopt a more political role. What the tax haven agenda questions, from a CSR perspective, is: are companies willing to be transparent so that they are whole participants in society? It also raises the issue of whether both ethical and practical considerations could lead more business people to push for more effective intergovernmental action on tax matters, so their own companies can make a fair contribution, without being unfairly disadvantaged by those who avoid taxes more actively. These issues have been in the background of CSR for some time and, after the economic crisis, they are set to become even more important.

Francophone CSR

Interest in French approaches to capitalism and economic management has grown in some circles as a result of the Western financial crisis. Pointing to the deregulation of the financial services sector, many commentators regard the crisis as emanating from an Anglo-Saxon model of capitalism, where the government is meant to enable market forces, rather than curb them. Experience of business– society relations in France may become increasingly relevant to discussions of the role of government and business across the West. Therefore the French experience of voluntary corporate responsibility, and its connection to government, is worth reflecting on.

In May 2009, HEC Paris hosted their sixth annual Social Business Conference in conjunction with Net Impact, bringing together mostly MBA students and some professionals. The session on Sustainable Finance proved to be an interesting indicator on how mind-sets, with respect to responsible investing, are changing in France. Jean-Philippe Desmartin, the SRI Research Manager from Oddo Securities (France's largest independent investment broker), stated that the socially responsible investment (SRI) market was in an exciting transition phase. In respect to their own client base, the number of institutional investors that required investment services that incorporated ESG criteria had increased from approximately 150 in 2005 to 350 in 2008. More importantly, he added that there had been a shift in paradigm because, out of their responsible investment client base, 80% selected a predefined product with ESG criteria as part of their portfolio in 2005 but, by 2008, 50% were using their own ESG criteria to select their whole portfolio.

Supporting this trend, in June 2009, Novethic, the French government-sponsored research centre for CSR and SRI, released their annual review on responsible investment in France.[42] They stated that, for the first time since their inaugural 2002 review, there was more money invested according to ESG criteria, directly tailored by institutional investors' ethical needs, than in predefined products. This subtle change represented an ethical reflection within the investment selection process *on the buy side* that went beyond mere portfolio diversification in the interests of spreading risk, to incorporating values other than profit-making. In a country where the public has traditionally looked to the government as their guiding force, it was also a sign that the French are mobilising in respect to issues related to the broader dimensions of sustainable development.

France is also an interesting case as it is one of the world's largest economic powers and has a presence right around the globe.[43] Apart from their European neighbours, the French also have departments (administrative divisions of the state) that neighbour Australia, Brazil, Venezuela and Canada, and so their economic influence is a genuinely global phenomenon.[44] France is also characterised by a public sector that supports a centralised political system which in turn influences relationships between business and society. So, in a country where the roles of business and government are defined differently, the discourse around CSR will naturally be impacted.

The concept of 'corporate social responsibility' (CSR) is a source of confusion for linguistic reasons because in the French language there is no distinction between the word 'responsibility' and the legal concept of 'liability'. In French, 'responsibility' can also be likened to 'accountability'.[45] In the same vein, the word 'social' in English integrates society as part of its meaning which therefore includes external stakeholders. In French, however, 'society' is translated to *société* but it has two adjectives, *sociale* and *sociétale*. The adjective *sociale* is traditionally linked more directly to labour-related issues. Conversely, the word *sociétale* focuses on broader matters relating to society at large and hence external stakeholders.[46] Using one and not the other, however, risks excluding certain aspects of CSR that would normally be implicit in the English definition. An added confusion is that the French translation of CSR, *responsabilité sociale de l'entreprise* (RSE) is the same acronym for *responsabilité sociale et environnementale*, which makes no explicit reference to a corporation, raising the question of whether such concepts should be simplified to accommodate international dialogue. The terms 'corporate responsibility' and 'responsible enterprise' would be better alternatives for this reason.

It is worth noting, however, that not all francophone territories reflect these distinctions. The French Canadian province of Québec shares the Anglo-Saxon definition of CSR, probably due to the influence of the surrounding Anglophone provinces embedded within a federation, and the United States.[47]

Québec is nonetheless active on CSR issues with a social network called Cataléthique, previously the Montreal chapter of Net Impact, and a research centre dedicated to CSR and sustainable development at the University of Québec in Montréal. Québec also boasts a political party, Québec Solidaire (Solidarity Québec), which seeks to address systemic issues relating to the financial crisis.[48] In their May 2009 manifesto, *Pour Sortir de la Crise: Dépasser le capitalisme?* ('Resolving the Crisis: Going Beyond Capitalism?'), they propose an economic platform that is a vehicle for promoting social and environmental values and they openly challenge the *laissez-faire* approach to markets, specifying that, without systemic change, the moralisation of the financial sector will simply be a short-term solution, in turn raising the same questions of the financial triumphalism of self-regulating markets.[49]

Beyond the linguistic challenges of a French CSR, there are also particularities related to history and culture. The French recognise the essential role of government, which is expected to exercise its influence, and so it is of no surprise that there is a considerable body of legislation relating to CSR. Two examples are mandatory corporate social reporting, introduced in 1977, and the 2001 legislation requiring listed companies to include some 40 social and environmental indicators in their annual reports to shareholders which impacts some 700 companies.[50] This legislation is nonetheless not without its flaws because there are neither sanctions nor external audit requirements. In a 2004 report submitted to the French government, most small to medium listed companies were found to provide inadequate information, perhaps explained by the lack of sanctions.[51] This document also highlighted that publishing the reports had little effect because the public discourse linked to social and environmental reporting was undeveloped. This may be linked to the historical context of the initial social reporting guidelines created in 1977 which were submitted to a government agency rather than being open to public scrutiny. So, while the legislation is not necessarily well applied due to the above factors, and also because of the traditional understanding of 'social', at least the government has underlined the legitimacy for the concepts of CSR.[52] It also means that French corporations will be looking toward the government for continued guidance in the future.

A more recent example is France's Grenelle de l'environnement which is the French equivalent of a commission for the environment. The initial phase, 'Grenelle I', provided the general objectives and the second phase will outline in more detail its application. While the redrafting of the initial phase was still being debated in the

National Assembly as of June 2009, one of the agenda items for the second phase is governance with respect to carbon emissions.[53] According to the French Energy and Environmental Management Agency (ADEME in French) in their May 2009 *Grenelle II* report, the legislation will oblige all companies with high emission levels and more than 500 employees to report on their carbon footprints by 2011.[54] The same legislation will also require that all non-SMEs (small to medium enterprises) will be subject to the same environmental and social reporting requirements as that of listed companies, levelling the playing field in respect to the original 2001 law.

The legislation will also address the low number of companies with environmental certification. ADEME estimates that there are around 6,000 French companies that have been certified to ISO 14001, and that such programmes remain inaccessible for smaller organisations. As a result, the legislation will provide fiscal incentives for SMEs to improve environmental reporting. It is worth noting that there is a proportional increase in the number of French companies being ISO 14001-certified with an approximate doubling between 2006 and 2008 based on ADEME estimates.[55] The long-awaited guide to social responsibility, ISO 26000, may prove to be more accessible as it provides guidance rather than a certifiable standard. Seeing that French municipalities have already developed an application guide for its implementation based on the drafts, this may serve as an example for French companies, irrespective of their size.[56] Furthermore, there promises to be a ripple effect as ISO 26000 will affect the procurement and tendering processes when dealing with the state departments.

The low number of environmental certifications is also reflected in the number of directors that are wholly responsible for CSR issues. In a March 2009 study, Cadre Emploi (the French job search engine for managers) estimated that there were around 100 directors in total dedicated to CSR within French corporations.[57] However, these positions are not necessarily answerable to top management, indicating that CSR for some of these companies is not a strategic issue but merely an exercise in communications.

But, while the French look to the government for guidance, a number of initiatives indicate that the French public is alert to the CSR agenda. The Sustainable Luxury Fair in May 2009 offered a novel perspective on how luxury goods can contribute to a more sustainable world and how contemporary art can be a catalyst in raising awareness with respect to sustainability issues.[58] The fair featured a number of eco-inventions and eco-luxury goods as well as an exhibition called 'Consumer', an artistic interpretation challenging participants to look at the systemic cycle of consumption. The fair was also an indicator that various sectors and communities in France are now taking it upon themselves to promote sustainability rather than relying on government intervention.

The academic community has not been silent either. In contrast to the aesthetic aspects of the Sustainable Luxury Fair, a more sober approach to CSR was evident at the Symposium for CSR Indicators in Lyon held the following month.[59] Organised by the Socioeconomic Institute of Firms and Organisations (ISEOR in French), the symposium led an academic reflection on the harmonisation of the plethora of norms and standards available to organisations in order to provide better measurements for CSR. What was interesting to note, however, was that, while being organised by a French institute, the symposium was conducted in French, Spanish and English, reflecting not only its international character, but also indicating a possible convergence in respect to CSR concepts.

In a rather innocuous article in the *Financial Times* in June 2009, there was further suggestion of this convergence with Groupe ESC Rouen, announcing a name change to Rouen Business School in an attempt to diversify internationally.[60] While Rouen Business School is not necessarily renowned for CSR, this rebranding reflected a continuing trend towards opening up French schools to international perspectives and students to the French experience.[61] As Antal and Sobczak have observed in their study on CSR in France, historically the orientation of French management researchers has been limited to a national focus, with some exposure to other francophone territories such as Belgium, Canada and Switzerland through conferences and publications.[62] So, while French business schools were providing international training, they had little influence on global research and theories because of the language barrier. While not directly linked to CSR per se, the promise of more articles in English from French management schools with an international focus will continue to reduce the gap between different concepts of CSR, including the role of government.

These changes also represent a cultural shift for the French. For historical reasons that date back to the Revolution, some claim that the French have a relatively higher distrust of private actors to provide the general good, and hence their faith in the government.[63] Albeit a small percentage, with the French public becoming more and more active with respect to sustainability issues, these examples illustrate that not all the French are willing to wait for the government to always take the lead. More importantly, though, the government has been willing to explore different ways of using its influence. Encouraging voluntary initiatives, such as ISO 26000, are a testament to the fact that the French government sees room for mandatory approaches and voluntary initiatives. It also indicates that there is a new openness in accepting CSR definitions that are traditionally not a part of French culture.

This is also reflected at policy level. A January 2007 release by the Ministry of Sustainable Development as part of the government's National Sustainable Development Strategy stated that,

> Although sustainable development is a growing concern, the ways in which companies act are very diverse. In order to facilitate their efforts towards sustainable development, a consensus was reached on the necessary balance between voluntary efforts and legal and regulatory measures.[64]

In her analysis of EU, UK and French CSR Policy, Dr Jenny Fairbrass of the University of Bradford observed that this is an adjustment to the French government's contribution to the 2001 Green Paper defining the EU's CSR policy.[65] At the time of writing, the French government saw voluntary initiatives as useful in assisting corporations in going beyond the law, but the principles of CSR should be embedded in the law as opposed to being mainstreamed in line with market forces. It stated,

> The Green Paper . . . affirms that voluntary instruments [. . .] are neither a substitute nor an alternative for regulation. The legal and regulated framework is, in effect, indispensable for guaranteeing equality of treatment of all workers.[66] [Fairbrass' translation]

As there are strong parallels between UK and EU policies in respect to voluntary initiatives, Fairbrass concludes that this is a sign of convergence in approaches to CSR at a national level. Seeing that the French government has taken the lead on harmonising their sustainable development strategy with that of the EU, continued Europeanisation of French traditions will no doubt lead to a progressive merging of CSR concepts in the future.[67]

The question is whether actors from other countries can draw on French concepts of CSR. What the French CSR experience has demonstrated is a willingness to let the government play a role in guiding business and its relationship to society. So, while the government intervention is far from being perfect, it has legitimised the concept of CSR and mainstreamed it through a regulatory framework, as opposed to market-led initiatives. This interaction with public authorities may prove a useful model for stakeholders in other countries in attempting to further the dialogue around CSR.

In the same vein, French CSR has been driven by the internal dimensions of business as it relates to labour issues. This has been, and remains, a traditional focus within France. The regulations around labour could also be a source of debate but, more importantly, how non-francophone actors could learn from the traditional processes that embed such regulation.[68] The ISEOR conference in Lyon is an example of how thinking is going beyond borders and also how researchers are trying to tap into the French experience. As France begins to develop its own field of corporate responsibility, it stands ready to exert greater influence on the international field of corporate responsibility.

Francophone African CSR

May 2009 also marked the seventh meeting of the ISO 26000 working group in Québec City. In conjunction with the meeting, a public conference was organised with the objective of helping stakeholders to understand the implementation and the organisational impacts of ISO 26000.[69]

One of the sessions was dedicated to *How Africa Puts Sustainable Development in Action in its Industry*, which analysed an Ivory Coast corporation, Sifca. Sifca is a private agro-industrial company of over 11,000 employees with a presence in the Ivory Coast, Liberia, Nigeria, Ghana and Benin, and has several strategic partnerships including Michelin.[70] Its principal areas of industry are sugar, palm oil and rubber.

Sifca's focus is an interesting one as it highlights the community-oriented nature of its CSR, also confirming a GTZ impact study in 2007 which concluded that African CSR projects were primarily aimed at local communities and poverty reduction.[71] Sifca's focal point is to meet workers' immediate needs through health and safety. To do this, each site has a working group dedicated to sustainable development, suggesting that suppliers and workers are conscious of social responsibility and that they are being integrated at the beginning of the supply chain. Furthermore, it also demonstrates that CSR is understood as a participative process whereby the structure allows workers to initiate continuous improvements to respond to social needs. An example is Sifca's response in adapting to the rural nature of the supply chain: redeployed workers are provided lodging and, according to Mr Franck Eba, Sifca's head of sustainable development, the company pays for the electricity and water costs as well.[72]

At a governance level, the company has also undergone a pre-audit based on SA8000, ISO 14001 and OHSAS 18001, which was conducted by the Belgian CSR consulting specialists Cap Conseil, and they plan to issue their first sustainability report in July 2009.[73]

However, Sifca is the exception in francophone Africa. While Sifca is actively embedding CSR as part of its strategy, it has assumed large levels of responsibility that the state would normally provide. Its active conviction to meet the needs of workers to make up for weak state welfare is commendable, but it stresses an urgent need for institutional development at a government level.[74] Quoting Mr Eba, 'We just can't do it all.'

African concepts of CSR also reflect this as the philanthropic side is prioritised, due to its immediacy in providing economic welfare, over the more governance-related ethical dimensions of CSR and the environment.[75] As Wayne Visser, CEO of CSR International, has observed

> . . . economic responsibilities still get the most emphasis. However, philanthropy is given second highest priority, followed by legal and then ethical responsibilities.[76]

Dr Ulf Richter, Assistant Professor for Political Economy at the International University of Grand Bassam in the Ivory Coast also confirms, '. . . most see it [African CSR] as quality management and the fight against poverty'.[77] ISO statistics would lend support to these statements. In a 2007 report, francophone countries including non sub-Saharan nations had proportionately higher numbers of ISO 9001 quality assurance certifications to ensure trade with developed countries, with only a handful of ISO 14001 certifications, potentially ignoring environmental considerations.[78]

There are also other complicating factors at play. While the same GTZ study concluded that the role and interest of governments in respect to CSR is lacking in sub-Saharan countries, conditions for funding require that governments focus on poverty reduction, and so CSR is understandably not a primary focus. It would also be easy to look at the number of Global Reporting Initiative (GRI) reports from 2006 to 2008 and conclude that francophone Africa was completely inactive with respect to CSR, as there were none.[79] But the landscape of French-African economic activity in general is not geared to respond to an initiative such as the GRI because most businesses are SMEs and there are few TNCs of French-African origin.[80] The Global Compact may actually be a better measure due to its accessibility and less onerous reporting requirements. According to the Global Compact 2008 annual review, of the French sub-Saharan countries, Senegal and the Ivory Coast had a Global Compact network with another emerging network in Cameroon.[81]

The case of Sifca shows there is an opportunity for TNCs to learn from a French-African company and its activities within local communities. An analysis of its local working groups dedicated to sustainable development could provide insights into traditional ways of embedding social responsibility at the bottom of the supply chain and, more importantly, potentially open doors to a better understanding and respect of the French-African CSR experience.

3Q2009
July–September

Jem Bendell, Ian Doyle and Emma Irwin

Mindful mining

The plethora of initiatives that support more responsible business practices is the source of continuing debate. Not only is the number of initiatives a point of confusion, but also their respective scope and relevance to a corporation's needs, as well as their governance and accountability to affected stakeholders. This complexity led the new Ethical Corporation Institute to publish *The Guide to Industry Initiatives in CSR*.[1]

Due to its international nature and the variety of social and environmental issues and interest involved, the mining sector has its own array of corporate responsibility initiatives. This is because other sectors that depend on mining, such as jewellery, are under increasingly close scrutiny over the origin of their precious metals and gemstones. On the social side, issues include: working conditions and labour standards; the human rights of local people; fair trade and conflict-free raw materials; artisanal and small-scale mining; community development and investment; communication, engagement and equitable participation with all stakeholders; and respect for local cultures, traditions and indigenous peoples. There are just as many issues to consider on the environmental side, such as minimising the adverse impacts throughout all stages of a project, including: implementation of environmental management systems; responsible resource extraction and use with respect to ecosystems and biodiversity; responsible use of hazardous and toxic materials; climate change; responsible waste management; and mine closure. Underpinning all of these concerns, particularly in lower-income countries, are apprehensions over the potential involvement of mining operations in bribery, corruption and the possible exploitation of weaker institutions and economic structures. The tax management practices of some mining companies have also been challenged.[2]

As a result of these ethical considerations, companies as diverse as Wal-Mart, Tiffany and Cartier have established their own initiatives to responsibly source their jewellery products. Wal-Mart, for example, has developed a system to track each piece of jewellery sold as part of its 'Love, Earth' collection.[3] Many companies have sought to work together on the difficult issues involved. The most well known of the collaborative initiatives is the Kimberley Process which addresses the problem of diamonds sourced in conflict zones. However, there are now more than half a dozen international multi-enterprise and sometimes multi-stakeholder initiatives that address the broader range of social and environmental aspects of mining.

Some of these initiatives, such as the Responsible Jewellery Council (RJC), have sought to provide a comprehensive solution. The RJC's difficulties in the third quarter of 2009 remind us of the ongoing contest over the legitimacy of corporate responsibility initiatives. In August 2009, a coalition group of civil society representatives withdrew from the RJC's public consultation of their second draft Mining Supplement for their assurance standard, and rejected the RJC's offer to participate in its Consultative Panel.[4] The coalition declined to contribute, citing the RJC's refusal to adopt a sufficiently participatory multi-stakeholder process during its standards development as the cause. They argued that it inadequately engaged with civil society representatives such as NGOs; local communities in mining regions; and artisanal and small-scale miner representatives as equal stakeholders.

This should not come as a surprise when considering that the RJC was founded in 2005 by a group of jewellery companies. Its objective is to reinforce consumer confidence in the jewellery sector by promoting responsible practices throughout jewellery company supply chains—from mine to market. The RJC's past attacks on NGO analyses of related industries may not have created the impression that it is open to differences of opinion or priority.[5]

The RJC's proposed certification system includes a set of voluntary standards on business ethics, human rights, social and environmental issues and mechanisms for verifying responsible business practices through 'third-party auditing'.[6] However, its system has been the subject of debate from the outset with concerns that it only serves to benefit its members and avoids key issues such as traceability of materials in the supply chain. The nature of its third-party verification system is also open to questions of independence given that the entire initiative is industry-led and -governed.[7]

The credibility of RJC's certification system is not just linked to the process of certification, but also to the effectiveness of the standards. When questioned how the standards would prevent the unsafe use of mercury by children extracting gold, which invariably finds its way into the EU and US markets, Mr Michael Rae, CEO of the RJC, honestly acknowledged

> Well, frankly, we won't, because it's not something that we are saying we are doing.[8]

In light of the NGO pull-out from the public consultation, and with the admission by the RJC's CEO that its certification system will not guarantee traceability, it would seem that these concerns are justified.

Furthermore, the August 2009 version of the draft Mining Supplement ignored many of the coalition's recommendations with respect to social and environmental criteria as per its October 2008 letter.[9] These included a number of fundamental social and environmental requirements such as free, prior and informed consent (FPIC) for indigenous peoples, and the importance of obtaining community consent for resettlement.

The RJC responded with two public letters in September 2009, clarifying its position in respect to the NGOs' concerns. It requested that the NGOs reconsider their decision not to contribute to the consultation process, extending the time-frame of the consultation to allow for further input, and addressing the issue of independent, third-party verification. However, the failure to give equal voice to stakeholders weakens the legitimacy of the standard.[10] Moreover, the omission of representation of local and small-scale mining communities as a key stakeholder group risks giving preference to the larger conglomerates within the mining sector.

Transparence SA has been a member of RJC since mid-2007 and has taken an ethical stance with respect to its supply chain so that customers can have a guarantee of the material's origin. While offering a retail platform for its responsibly sourced jewellery, it has also taken a leadership role by connecting sources of ethical stones and metals to other luxury jewellery designers. The brands it works with include: Cred, FiFi Bijoux, Oria Jewels, Noën and the luxury brand Garavelli. Transparence SA's founder, Veerle van Wauwe, explained to the *Journal of Corporate Citizenship* that

> RJC won't build supply, it will just certify existing sources. New actors need to emerge, who develop solutions to the environmental and social challenges of mining, otherwise those who need most support will be left behind.[11]

As a result of concerns over the direction of the RJC, the NGO coalition opted in favour of the Initiative for Responsible Mining Assurance (IRMA) as a more constructive process of engagement for certification purposes.[12] While IRMA has a broader scope with respect to the mining sector in general, it does incorporate jewellery-related supply chains, thus covering many of the same issues as the RJC system. In cooperation with civil society representatives, it is creating a set of standards that encapsulate best practice for the industry through a constructive multi-stakeholder dialogue process that gives equal voice to all participants.

The Communities and Small-Scale Mining Initiative (CASM) is another example of a multi-stakeholder and participatory dialogue process. It is a global multi-disciplinary networking and coordinating forum chaired by the UK Department for International Development and the World Bank which aims to reduce poverty by improving the environmental, social and economic performance of artisanal and small-scale mining in developing countries.[13] In September 2009, CASM's annual conference in Mozambique focused on the role that artisanal and small-scale mining can play in rural development and poverty alleviation.[14] In a World Bank press release in the same month, Mrs Esperanca Laurinda Nhiuane Bias, Mozambique's Minister of Mineral Resources, expressed the government's support for the initiative due to

> ... the important contributions of artisanal and small-scale mining in reducing rural poverty, creating employment, providing diverse services, developing small industries and reducing the migration of our youth from the rural areas to cities by ensuring sustainable economic growth in these rural areas.[15]

Artisanal and small-scale mining (ASM) is practised by people who live in the poorest and most remote rural areas around the world, people who normally have few livelihood alternatives. Due to its marginalised status, ASM often falls outside the scope of legal and regulatory frameworks, and, furthermore, is illegal in some countries. It is not uncommon for entire families to work at an ASM site with men, women and children each having their own designated roles and responsibilities within the ASM site structure.

Typically, ASM exposes workers to extremely poor and hazardous working conditions, with little or no awareness of health and safety standards and a high rate of major incidents, including fatalities.[16] The handling of toxic materials such as mercury (for artisanal gold mining) without protective equipment or clothing is the norm. There is also a high prevalence of poor health issues and disease among ASM communities, including vulnerability to malaria, tuberculosis, cholera, HIV and Aids.

Given that ASM lacks institutional support in the majority of countries in which it occurs, exact numbers regarding how many people are involved are not known. However, CASM estimates that approximately 20 million men, women and children in over 50 developing countries are directly employed in the sector, with 100 million more dependent on it for their livelihoods.[17] Women are estimated to constitute approximately 30% of the ASM sector, and the International Labour Organisation (ILO) estimates that approximately 1–1.5 million children are currently employed in ASM, and the numbers are rapidly increasing.[18] CASM also estimates that there are many more people engaged globally in ASM than are employed by large mining companies. As the global demand for mineral commodities grows and prices rise, the number of people engaged in ASM worldwide is expected to increase correspondingly.

Many ASM communities are located on the fringes and perimeters of large-scale mining (LSM) operations, and frequently in among them. The presence of multinational companies with LSM operations in traditional ASM areas also creates potential conflicts around issues of land ownership rights and the right to mine generally. Many companies often face the daily reality of 'illegal' or 'artisanal' mining, including child labour in, on and around their operations. As such, the relationship between LSM operations and artisanal miners has generally tended to be one fraught with mistrust and resentment. However, some companies appear to be learning that building constructive relationships is a far more effective risk management strategy than attempting to eliminate the artisanal miners through increased security measures, or by hoping that the problem will simply go away. As Mr Anthony Kwesi Aubynn, corporate affairs director for GoldFields Ltd's Ghanaian operations, asserts,

It is widely recognized that maintaining harmonious relationship between large-scale multinational mining companies and local operators is crucial if both parties are to maximize their contributions to the economy and livelihoods of the operational areas.[19]

Gold and gemstones attract the majority of artisanal and small-scale miners. CASM estimates that 75% of all gemstones and 15–20% of the total global mineral supply are from ASM sources: a strong indicator of the importance of ASM to the global minerals market.[20] The corollary is that with such a large proportion of the world supply coming from ASM, most jewellery brands will have some contact to this type of sourcing, potentially exposing themselves to brand and reputation risks. However, the potential for companies to contribute to the long-term social and economic development beyond mining is equally as important if they are willing to engage with these communities.[21] If integrated legitimately into responsible international mineral and metal supply chains and 'formalised' by national governments, ASM represents a huge opportunity for sustainable development for millions of people worldwide. It is also significant that the challenges facing the ASM sector fully reflect those of the United Nations Millennium Development Goals (MDGs), including: health, environment, gender, education, child labour and poverty eradication.[22]

The key challenge for a responsible mining sector is how to effectively manage ASM and its associated risks without compromising companies' CSR/sustainability commitments. Several mining companies have already begun engaging with ASM in and around their concessions, realising that constructive engagement and steps towards 'coexistence' promise far greater benefits, and less risk, than the alternatives, including making a real contribution to poverty alleviation and upholding human rights. LSM companies are also in a position to make a significant contribution by facilitating dialogue, awareness and understanding of ASM at the government level. If this can be achieved in countries of operation, it may then be possible to use leverage to obtain formal recognition of ASM at national policy levels. ASM engagement initiatives at site or project level are increasingly integrated into broader community relations strategies, and include, for example: procurement or purchasing schemes, education and training programmes that could potentially lead to employment opportunities, capacity-building or alternative livelihood programmes and other community development initiatives.[23]

Indeed, CASM has an ongoing working group dedicated to the relationship between LSM and ASM—one of the agenda items at CASM's conference in Mozambique.[24] Collaboration between LSM companies and ASM communities, as well as other stakeholders including retailers and jewellery companies, is increasingly becoming a way to ensure inclusion of those in marginalised mining communities. This also addresses the issue of traceability, whereby stones and metals can be traced back to their origin or source.

However, these initiatives will be of limited impact if the corporate precious metal buyers do not begin to support them. Veerle van Wauwe of Transparence wonders,

Will large companies just sit and watch to see what happens? If they are serious about it, they need to start investing now in solutions in artisanal mining. They could commit to start buying from these sources that are under development, to help them achieve commercial viability.[25]

Executives in the jewellery business have expressed to us their worries about the complexity of working on artisanal mining, the potential reputational hazards, and the limited volumes that can be produced from ethical artisanal production. This position demonstrates an approach to corporate responsibility that is reactive and defensive, seeking to avoid perception of malpractice, rather than a strategic approach that seeks to make as much of a positive difference as possible through integrated responsible business practice.

It was therefore significant when, in July 2009, Cartier announced that it had formed a partnership with the Goldlake Group, owners of Eurocantera. Eurocantera is a 'responsible' gold mine in Honduras that works in partnership with artisanal miners, utilising an innovative process requiring only water to extract alluvial gold, rather than cyanide or other harmful chemicals.[26] The initial three-year agreement assures the entire purchase of Eurocantera's gold production for the 2009–2010 fiscal year, and at least the same amount for the two following years.[27] While the supply of gold from Eurocantera will represent only a small part of Cartier's supply needs, the significance of the agreement is nonetheless an important one for the luxury brand. Ms Pamela Caillens, Cartier's Director of Corporate Responsibility, affirms

> Eurocantera gold is only a portion of our supply at this stage, but it's an important step. We want our purchasing decisions [to] make a difference in the way gold is extracted, by helping leaders and pioneers like Goldlake to develop, and by inspiring others.[28]

Mine's fair

The first company to devote itself entirely to the 'ethical' production of gold was the Green Gold Corporation ('Oro Verde'): a pioneering community cooperative initiative based in the Choco region of Colombia. It has developed its own Certified Green Gold Program and is currently the only 'fairtrade' gold available on the international market.[29] In 2004, it participated in the establishment of the Alliance for Responsible Mining (ARM), a multi-stakeholder, miner's-based initiative to promote responsible mining which is developing a 'fairmined' (fairtrade) mark and certification system for responsibly ASM-sourced minerals.[30]

ARM was one of the first multi-stakeholder initiatives to specifically address ASM, closing the final public consultation to finalise its 'Standard Zero' for fairtrade artisanal gold and associated silver and platinum in September 2009.[31] Standard

Zero was first created in 2007 in collaboration with the Fairtrade Labelling Organisation (FLO) and comprises a system that has adapted FLO's standards for small producers to an ASM context. Standard Zero certification aims to assure a path from mine to market to provide consumers with a guarantee of the mineral's origins and ensure that workers at every level of the supply chain are subject to appropriate working conditions and fair pay. Nine pilot projects have been under way to test the system's traceability claims before undertaking the final phase to integrate the consultation input.[32] ARM's 'fairmined' mark was expected to be available by mid-2010.

For mining companies, and those in the jewellery sector in particular, these programmes represent a change in the wind with respect to corporate responsibility. Simply being part of an initiative will no longer hold credence if it is not part of a larger multi-stakeholder dialogue process that provides equal voice around social and environmental issues. Initiatives such as IRMA, CASM and ARM have identified the importance of engaging with community groups in the mining sector for the purposes of transparency. More significantly, however, the latter initiatives have gone a step further by partnering with local communities, a step towards achieving the MDGs.

Civil society withdrawal from the RJC public consultation indicates more than a disagreement with respect to process and values. It signifies that, unless initiatives take an approach that is inclusive and accountable, there will continue to be new initiatives, adding complexity to responsible enterprise efforts. Some may argue that this competition in standards is healthy and the market will decide. However, there are pragmatic implications for representative organisations that have limited time to invest in building, promoting and monitoring standards. Calls for unifying them into one coherent system can no longer be ignored, raising questions about the most unified way to better industry practices.[33] All initiatives will do well by not only improving stakeholder dialogue, but by making a concerted effort to consolidate standards to simplify the process for all involved.

The case of competing standards in the responsible mining field is an example of the complexity associated with the growth of 'global private regulation' that has emerged in the past decades around the social and environmental dimensions of trade.[34] As traditional forms of legitimacy through government involvement and control do not apply in private forms of regulation, so new questions arise about the accountability of standards and their application.[35] The International Social and Environmental Accreditation and Labelling Alliance (ISEAL Alliance) is an organisation that was established to help professionalise this field of standard-setting and certification. As a membership organisation of standard-setters, it needs to balance its own priorities and its need for income. How it manages that balance will be key to whether 'private' standards truly serve the public good. Ultimately, the growth of private standards today provide an opportunity for the United Nations to offer guidelines in this field, something that was once envisaged for the Global Compact.[36] At this time, practitioners and researchers involved in this field should consider the extent to which any standard is governed by stakeholders, whether a standards body is compromised by requiring successful certifications for its income, what forms of complaints procedures are in place, and whether its processes for assessment and monitoring actually empower those affected by the business activities concerned.

For companies in the mining and jewellery sectors, examples such as ARM and Eurocantera provide a vision for better mining by meeting community priorities. These developments address issues that can guide companies towards innovation that benefits humanity and serve ends that go beyond profit. Veerle van Wauwe's hope is that

> it is time to create a more equitable value chain, empowering mining communities and delivering tangible results for human and sustainable economic development in these communities. Slowly but surely, I have to believe that we will succeed and make a real difference.

Beyond beauty

The beauty industry is a source of both blemish and rejuvenation when it comes to their social responsibility. The recent proliferation in the number of natural and organic cosmetic manufacturers in the beauty industry represents a return to the sourcing of natural, rather than synthetic, ingredients and the recognition of better environmental and social practices.[37] Despite this encouraging trend, it is not indicative of greater corporate responsibility within the larger luxury conglomerates, as it has been led, primarily, by small to medium-sized businesses.[38]

Two major beauty industry events held in September 2009 illustrated this. Beyond Beauty Paris is Europe's largest expo for the beauty and wellness sector, grouping beauty product brands and their suppliers, as well as services, such as spas and beauty institutes. Apart from providing an opportunity for brands to market their products, the event addresses business issues linked to the beauty industry, including sustainability. In previous years, issues such as fairtrade, ethics and toxicity have been conference topics. In 2009, issues relating to sustainable packaging were on the agenda. While the expo has a selective approach to such issues, it is nonetheless an indicator that the beauty industry is somewhat alert to environmental and social performance. More importantly, however, the themes up for discussion were peripheral in comparison to the actions of companies that have sustainability at the very heart of their operations. Concerns over the toxicity of beauty products, ethical sourcing, bio-piracy, animal testing and societal development have been drivers for many small to medium enterprises in creating niche products that are not only respectful of nature, but ecologically restorative as well. These companies are letting their products do the talking and, despite the small market share, their efforts are now becoming recognised by their peers.

Demonstrating this trend were the eventual winners of the various industry prizes up for grabs that aim to recognise the most promising new brands on the cosmetics market. In recognition of the growth in the natural and organics market niche, the 'Beauty Organic Award' was added to the three existing awards.[39] Despite the one prize category dedicated to organics, all four awards were won by companies producing natural and organic products. This is all the more impressive when considering that none of the judging criteria included performance with respect to sustainability—perhaps sending a message to the better-known luxury brands that synthetic chemicals do not need to be a part of cosmetic ingredients.[40]

The winner of the Beauty Organic Award was Aïny, which Beyond Beauty described as a

> ... brand which brings indigenous people's sacred, shamanic sciences together with modern innovations of cosmetology to invite us to take a new look at cosmetics.

The 'new look' that Beyond Beauty is talking about is an approach to cosmetics that incorporates an environmental ethic that goes beyond organic ingredients and an aesthetisation of beauty. Not all of Aïny's products are certified organic, but they practise fairtrade and work with local communities to protect their cultural assets and traditional knowledge about plants. To do this, they have a bio-piracy policy so that no patent can be registered and partner with the local indigenous organisations, helping them to protect their rights. They are 'One Voice' certified as part of their stance against animal testing.[41] As such, beauty is situated within a larger ecological system, recognising connections between self and community, ethics and aesthetics, humans and nature.[42] Consequently, beauty is captured in what the product represents, not just the benefits for personal appearance.[43] Moreover, these products reconnect the notion of health to beauty through community values and relationship.

Cosmetic responsibility

The LVMH Research symposium was the second of the September 2009 events and proved to be a somewhat different affair. The day-long symposium served as an intellectual platform to study how cosmetics contribute to the emotional well-being of women. An impressive array of studies were presented by speakers from various academic disciplines such as psychiatry, philosophy, psycho-physiology and psycho-sensoriality, as well as industry professionals, providing a theoretically rich analysis of self-esteem and a playing field for new ideas.[44] Absent from the seminars were any discussions about sustainability or corporate responsibility.

The first study provided the context and sought to position the beauty industry in terms of its legitimacy as a source of wellness services. The analysis illustrated that physical appearance was one of the five categories that women value in terms of their well-being.[45] Other categories included health, relationships and work satisfaction, with health topping the priority list. The study revealed that women in general were dissatisfied with their physical appearance, manifesting a continuing trend further to the 2004 report by the Campaign for Real Beauty, where 69% of women expressed the same dissatisfaction in this area.[46] The LVMH study showed that women felt better after applying cosmetic products, and in addition to the physical benefits, the cosmetics facilitated a psychological and psycho-socio function (that is to say, integration in society) in improving women's self-esteem. Consequently, the authors argued that the beauty industry was at the service of all women, helping them to boost their self-confidence through cosmetics.[47]

While the conclusion served to support the industry's *raison d'être*, perhaps a greater opportunity was overlooked to explore the deeper issues as to *why* women feel dissatisfied with their appearance in the first place. This was highlighted by an amusing anecdote when a participant in the audience asked, 'Why don't men wear make-up, then?' Barbara Polla, a symposium participant and author of *Les hommes, ce qui les rend beaux* (*Men: What Makes Them Beautiful*), responded that in her 200 research interviews for her book, every man interviewed thought he was beautiful.[48] The humorous anecdote served to illustrate that women's beauty has been aestheticised in such a way that their intrinsic qualities are undermined by a psycho-toxic version of beauty, whereby beauty has become synonymous with physical appearance.

Furthermore, Ms Polla's comments lent support to the *2004 Campaign for Real Beauty Study* which showed that 60% of women believe that 'society expects women to enhance their physical attractiveness'. It isn't any wonder that many women in these studies saw the functional purpose of cosmetics as a camouflage.

Contrary to the LVMH study, *The Real Truth about Beauty* report demonstrated that cosmetics are potentially more destructive in facilitating psycho-social function because beauty defined aesthetically creates social divisions. As such, the report revealed that 45% of women believe that 'women who are more beautiful have greater opportunities in life'. This is not surprising given that 47% of women also believe that 'only the most physically attractive women are portrayed in popular culture'.[49] In Asian countries, it isn't just the most physically attractive women that are portrayed in popular culture, but women with lighter complexions that fit a Western ideal: beauty brand advertising promotes skin whitening products that lighten the skin. Such an approach is not only a reductionist view of beauty that ignores beauty in all its diversity, but it is unattainable for any woman that has a darker complexion, resulting in social hierarchies.[50] Thus, creation of dissatisfaction is the goal of beauty product advertising, to the detriment of psycho-social function.[51]

Similarly, in what has become known as the globalisation of eating disorders, a Harvard Medical School study, conducted by the anthropologist Anne Becker, demonstrated the power television has over the public. Within three years of introducing television to Fiji in 1995, 11% of women reported vomiting to control weight and 62% had dieted in some way. Prior to television being introduced, there had been no reported cases of eating disorders and most women, no matter what their size, were comfortable with their bodies.[52] While this second example is not directly linked to the beauty industry per se, it does demonstrate the power of the media and the ability it has to influence the public—something that beauty brands need to be conscious of in their marketing.

Moreover, the purported psycho-social benefits of cosmetic use are a poor filter by which to analyse self-esteem. *The Real Truth about Beauty* report revealed that women who are satisfied with their beauty are *significantly more likely* than those that are less satisfied to define beauty by non-physical factors. The corollary is that women that are less satisfied are more likely to think that cosmetics make a woman beautiful.[53]

Given the self-esteem problems that this is causing for women, perhaps the beauty industry will better understand the effect of cosmetics as a whole by looking more closely at their psycho-toxic marketing strategies that project an unattainable beauty. Cosmetics themselves might not be blamed for the undermining of women's sense of physical self-esteem, but through their marketing they could add to the problem by promoting unattainable forms of beauty (and at times artificial forms, through digitally airbrushed images).[54] This in turn creates a want that cannot be satisfied.[55]

This issue became evident during the symposium's opening address on self-esteem and identity by Dr Christophe André, a practising psychiatrist. During the question time following his presentation, when asked about the potential effect of photo-touching on the psyche, he craftily avoided the question by suggesting that the issue was not photo-touching per se, but the individual's ability to recognise that the images may not necessarily be real, rendering void any ethical responsibility on the part of the company. He also added that such a practice could 'also serve as motivation for women' [translated from French].[56]

Given the evidence to the contrary of the power of marketing, this so-called motivation hasn't proved to be so positive for the psyche in Fiji. What the motivation represents is also a question. Would the motivation be to attain such beauty or to facilitate better social positioning? Because cosmetics are often considered luxury goods, and luxury goods confer status and an air of success on the person, perhaps this is the reason why it is no surprise that women feel better upon application.[57] Therefore, the conclusions of the studies presented at the LVMH symposium were hardly insightful about the specific role of the ability to alter one's appearance. Instead, if a social role for cosmetics is sought, then it requires attention to the full relations of production, marketing and consumption of cosmetics—how they are produced and how they are marketed.

The concept of the metrosexual is an example of how marketing has influenced the male body image. Mark Simpson invented the label further to his book *Male Impersonators*, 'which analyzed the effect an increasingly aestheticized and inauthentic world was having on masculinity', to describe

> a new, narcissistic, media-saturated, self-conscious kind of masculinity
> . . . produced by Hollywood, advertising and glossy magazines to replace
> traditional, repressed, unreflexive, unmoisturized masculinity . . .[58]

Part of this trend is male body depilation. In a January 2008 article entitled 'Men seeking Beckham effect go wild for Boyzilians', the *The Guardian* investigated the new trend for men to remove pubic hair further to Giorgio Armani advertisements featuring 'a trimmed around the edges' David Beckham modelling their latest underwear. In the same article, the increasing trend was confirmed by Mr Phil Swinford of the British Association of Beauty Therapy and Cosmetology stating that

> Overall, just 5% of beauty treatments are carried out on men, but as the whole market is increasing, so too are the number of men wanting treatments. Four years ago hardly any women were getting Brazilians or other intimate waxing, let alone men, but now more and more salons are offering it.[59]

But, if the depilation of women's body hair is to be indicative, this emerging trend is sure to continue if the marketers have their way. In her thesis on the history of American women and hair removal, Kirsten Hansen analysed how marketing was a key influence in creating the need for American women to shave their armpits. From the first hair removal advertisement in *Harper's Bazaar* magazine in 1915 when the practice of armpit depilation was relatively unknown, women were assaulted with marketing until, in the 1930s, it had become common practice among average consumers.[60] What the example of male body depilation highlights, however, is that the beauty industry, like many others, is in the business of creating want that is in direct contrast to sustainability. Not only do its messages have an impact on people, but also an impact on the planet by encouraging consumption.

The final two presentations of the symposium emphasised that such strategies were not accidental, either. The presentation on psycho-sensoriality described 'Affective Design', whereby product materials and packaging provide the emotional stimuli to improve self-esteem, suggesting a more manipulative approach to cosmetic manufacture. Ms Edwige Blanc, Director of Della Vita, a consultancy that specialises in brand marketing, offered some insight into how to successfully market luxury products. Three categories of luxury were defined: 'Top-of-the-line' or 'Up-market', 'Premium Luxury' and 'Ultimate Luxury'; absent from the categories was 'Sustainable Luxury'. On consideration of the characteristics for marketing Ultimate Luxury, this was not surprising. Ms Blanc outlined that, for the effective marketing of Ultimate Luxury, there needs to be a sense of transgression and dilapidation, the latter being likened to over-abundance and waste. Apart from the fact that this seemed strangely out of place at a time when the world is looking for sustainable solutions to improve the living conditions of all people and the planet, such sentiments are contrary to the etymology of the word *cosmetic* which is derived from *kosmos*. *Kosmos* means to order, to arrange, or to adorn; yet the very dilapidation called for in marketing 'Ultimate Luxury' suggests chaos rather than order.

Redefining beauty

These contrasting approaches within the beauty industry demonstrate the gulf that exists in how beauty is defined and the support mechanisms used to defend these views. In light of *The Real Truth about Beauty* report which revealed that happiness, kindness, confidence, dignity and humour are powerful components of female beauty, as well as the physical attributes, it would seem that women's self-esteem would be better served through products such as Aïny's, which re-appropriate a fuller sense of the meaning of beauty. Furthermore, their community approach facilitates a breaking-down of traditional social, cultural and ecological hierarchies that perpetuate certain structures to the exclusion of others.[61]

In the same vein, natural and organic products recognise the environmental sensibilities of the consumer and thus incorporate meaning into the product beyond improving one's personal appearance and image of success. Due to the continuing and increasing demand for these types of beauty products, it would seem logical that the larger conglomerates, such as LVMH, position themselves in a way that goes beyond just stimulating the emotions, but connects with real issues that are important to women and their self-esteem. An approach could be to include an environmental aesthetic when marketing, rather than the wasteful implications of 'Ultimate Luxury', which would influence how consumers think about resources and consumption. While this risks being a touch-up of the greenwashing kind, an engaged corporation would also need to demonstrate greater responsibility right throughout the organisation. This aesthetic would then not be marked by image politics, but a sense of beauty that reflects a greater ecological integrity, embracing a natural beauty and its intrinsic value. Perhaps then cosmetics could celebrate the harmony of women's self-esteem, with nature and with production: a new realignment with the *kosmos*.

4Q2009
October–December

Jem Bendell,* Ian Doyle and Nicky Black

The impasse on climate

In December 2009, the attention of the world's media turned to Copenhagen and the Summit to negotiate an agreement on international action on climate change. Given widespread international concern about carbon emissions leading to abrupt climate changes, the expectations of some were high. However, by the end of two weeks, the conference's 'noting' of an accord that specified no firm target for limiting the global temperature rise, no commitment to creating a legal treaty, no target year for peaking carbon emissions, and no clear mechanism for creating an internationally equivalent price for carbon emissions, meant that the summit appeared to many as a disappointment. Some delegations were calling it a disaster for their nations. Yet others welcomed the collapse of the summit, for reasons we will explain below. The way the summit unfolded led some commentators to suggest it marked a new era in international relations. This new era is discussed to some extent in our 2008 year reflection, as the growing economic power of nations previously grouped together as the 'third' or 'developing' world presents major implications for the terrain of corporate responsibility worldwide. The full implications for responsible management research and practice need to be explored: the goal of our reflection for the 2009 year.

At the end of the Copenhagen Summit everyone was being blamed. Many leaders from the G77 block of countries pointed the finger at the high-income nations of the EU and at the USA, and in particular at their plans to obtain an agreement that the Danish hosts had drafted which many said favoured the richer nations. Others pointed the finger at the Chinese, who did little to help the talks progress; and then, during the last days, convened meetings of large non-Western economies to set out what they wanted in an agreement and what they did not, and who said they would not accept any international targets in the agreement, not even for

---

* Sole author of pages 280-96.

the 'developed' nations. Despite this approach from China, the leaders of the G77 delegation blamed only the West for the limited commitments. The fact that the lead negotiator for the G77 was from an oil-exporting nation, whose controversial government is dependent on Chinese investment, was not reflected by most media or indeed the non-governmental organisations (NGOs). The previous lead negotiator for the G77, a renowned ethical and tough negotiator, was removed just before the conference by the President of the Philippines, a lady whose husband has been embroiled in corruption scandals involving multi-million-dollar payments from Chinese businesses. Then the campaign group Avaaz blamed the corporate lobbyists from the US (where over 2,000 lobbyists now work on climate change policy), who, they said, made it impossible for the US president to have much credibility in signing any agreement, given the attitudes of the US Congress. As a result, Avaaz launched a campaign against the US Chamber of Commerce. Others in civil society began blaming themselves for having been wrong-footed and not realising where the real power lay, and for wasting too much time advocating what the EU and US should do, rather than working on encouraging climate mitigation ambitions in other powerful nations.

So there was much going on beneath the surface that may never be fully understood. What is clear, however, is that most countries came to the talks with narrow and short-term economic self-interests framing their agendas, whether personal or national, and in such a situation the dominant economic force of the 21st century, China, held sway. Prior to the negotiations I was in meetings that made it clear that negotiators on one Asian nation's delegation to the Summit were told not to agree anything that would cost the country money. We presume their political bosses had not read the Stern report on what the costs really are of not doing anything to reduce global carbon emissions. At that meeting I attended, the environment minister sat next to the CEO of one of the largest oil companies in the country. The minister explained to me he favoured a voluntary approach. We return to the issue of responsible lobbying below.

The Copenhagen Summit helped the world see how climate negotiations are not about preventing climate change. Even if the world had implemented the Kyoto Protocol to the full, it would only have delayed global warming by six years, yet CO_2 emissions are now 40% above 1990's level: the amount Kyoto was meant to return them to. The ambitions were always too low, but the Copenhagen Summit illustrates clearly that we have reached an impasse in how global challenges can be addressed through the interactions of nation-states. The global ideology of economic growth overhangs all deliberations, as nations seek to protect their growth rates, rather than their populations (and failing to see the difference, thus demonstrating their ideology). Additionally, the assumption that regulations add costs and reduce growth, rather than stimulating innovation, remains widespread. Yet, as Paul Toni of WWF Australia explained when interviewed at the Asia Pacific Academy of Business in Society (APABIS), environmental regulations cost far less than predictions from those against them and drive innovation.

Forward thinkers must now question how to overcome the inter-governmental impasse and organise ourselves better this century. John Sauven, executive director of Greenpeace UK, said: 'It is now evident that beating global warming will require a radically different model of politics than the one on display here in Copenhagen.' Much has been said of the growing power of civil society and, more recently, of well-intentioned business leaders in helping encourage governments to act. While some NGOs, such as Avaaz, have argued that Copenhagen shows the mobilisation of a people's movement around the world, and that it must continue, and others praised the role of the media, it nevertheless appeared that civil society was, as stated above, somewhat wrong-footed. The limited scope and role of civil society in countries such as China means that NGOs play a very cautious role and seek favour with leaders. This can be seen in WWF China's comments before the Summit, among others, that China would not be able to cut its emissions in order to meet a 2° warming target, and therefore other countries would need to cut their emissions further. It can also be seen in AccountAbility's report released in November 2009, which stated in the third person that its national environmental initiatives give

> China a convincing voice in efforts to achieve a global agreement on how to manage the economic, social and environmental threats of climate change. China is now recognised as a part of the select group of countries that are doing most to investigate and devise policies to build low carbon competitiveness.

They may be sensible to build bridges and understanding, but it suggests that a vibrant grassroots civil society engaging in robust dialogue with leaders is not a feature of politics in some countries. Therefore, civil society groups will need to do some soul-searching and consider how best to influence non-Western governments. The lead author has been applying his own ideas about this for three years now, but that's another story.

The paradox of business lobbying on climate

Business communities have been vocal on climate policy nationally and internationally for almost two decades. In the late 1980s it was left to scientists to debate their various predictions about rates and consequences of climate change. In the history of climate change policies the role of business has been inauspicious, given how large corporations mobilised throughout the 1990s to create uncertainty about the science of anthropogenic global warming. For instance, 'in the 1990s the Global Climate Coalition (GCC)—a front group for 50 major oil, coal, auto and chemical corporations and trade associations—played a key role in delaying and weakening international climate agreements, mainly by pressuring US politicians', says Oscar Reyes of the Corner House. In his December 2009 article he continues:

the GCC successfully lobbied Washington to ensure that no binding targets were included in the UN Framework Convention on Climate Change, agreed at the 1992 Rio Earth Summit. It also promoted a 1997 Senate resolution where US legislators expressed unanimous opposition to legally binding greenhouse gas reductions unless developing countries (responsible for a fraction of the current and historical emissions) adopted the same rules. Al Gore, the US chief negotiator at the time, took this message to the UN climate negotiations and 'demanded a series of loopholes [in the Kyoto Protocol] big enough to drive a Hummer through,' as British journalist George Monbiot put it.

Today, however, the situation is much more complex. Many companies and their associations, such as the US Chamber of Commerce, still deny that curbing carbon emissions is a priority for public policy and lobby against, or focus on obtaining exemptions or special treatment for their own sectors in order to reduce costs. For instance, in the US, Washington DC 'can now boast more than four climate lobbyists for every member of Congress'. A negative approach to carbon regulation is not welcomed by many executives today, a recent example being Apple, who withdrew from the Chamber in protest in October 2009. In a letter to the president of the US Chamber of Commerce, Apple's Catherine Novelli wrote: 'we strongly object to the Chamber's recent comments opposing the EPA's effort to limit greenhouse gases', further explaining: 'Apple supports regulating greenhouse gas emissions, and it is frustrating to find the chamber at odds with us in this effort.'

Groups such as the Climate Disclosure Project, the Institutional Investors Group on Climate Change, and the Business Leaders Initiative on Climate Change, now bring together large swathes of the private sector that lobby privately and advocate publicly on the need for an intergovernmental agreement on climate change. On the one hand, this is very promising, representing a wiser approach to business, one that recognises systemic threats to value creation, and the role of government in providing frameworks for innovation. The impact can be seen to be positive, such as the work of HSBC in analysing the environmental components of government stimulus packages, as Jonathan Cohen and I discussed earlier in our review of 2009.

On the other hand, we will argue below that further legitimisation of corporate involvement in public policy development presents a threat not only to effective action on curbing climate change, but to accountable and efficient governance in general. This new paradox of private sector policy advocacy is highlighted by the very agenda of the Copenhagen talks—the development of carbon cap-and-trade markets. The paradox is not that we see business lobbying both for and against international agreements; they are doing so due to their understanding of the commercial costs and opportunities of climate change. The paradox is that to move intergovernmental processes forward, we will need business influence, yet corporate lobbying is plagued by narrow short-term commercial interests that have, to date, damaged the intergovernmental process, by, on the one hand, holding it back and, on the other, shaping its agenda in misguided ways. To understand this paradox, we must understand the history, limitations and injustices of cap-and-trade systems.

The carbon scam

The focus of discussions of the UN Framework Convention on Climate Change (UNFCCC) has been about capping carbon emissions and mechanisms to trade permits to pollute the atmosphere with carbon. The Kyoto Protocol established the concept of carbon offsets, where an enterprise can be financed to adopt technologies or practices to reduce its current or predicted carbon emissions and the reduction in emissions can be deducted from the company or government paying for the necessary changes. The UN Clean Development Mechanism (CDM) resulted from this approach, as did the development of carbon emissions trading schemes (ETS). The reason that this was adopted as the best policy option in 1997, when the Protocol was adopted, was that the United States, and then Vice President Al Gore, proposed it as the only option it would sign. This was after intensive lobbying by Enron, the corrupt company that had profited significantly from trading in energy derivatives and the cap-and-trade sulphur markets in the United States. After the Protocol was agreed, Enron's senior director for environmental policy, John Palmisano, celebrated it as an agreement that was full of 'immediate business opportunities'. The other countries followed, yet ultimately Kyoto was never ratified by the United States. (Perhaps the memory of how a US president can sign up, but yet the Congress can vote no, meant that China wasn't interested in high-level bilateral meetings with Obama on climate.)

The reason for the focus on cap and trade, and the reason for it being adopted since by other governments, is simple: it posed the least threat to the polluting industries of all the policy tools available, and offered the creation of a whole new market for the financial service providers. Other options, such as outlawing certain practices or introducing carbon taxes, were therefore sidelined at that time in intergovernmental negotiations. For instance, a carbon tax was proposed at the EU level during the 1990s but failed due to industrial lobbying.

A focus on cap and trade at the UNFCCC negotiations these past decades has been a monumental waste of time and resources. It has been a waste because carbon cap-and-trade systems are ineffective, inefficient, unfair, unworkable, extremely difficult to agree at an intergovernmental level and can alienate people from decisive action on carbon emissions. I will explain each limitation in turn.

Cap and trade is **ineffective** in delivering real cuts in carbon emissions, according to the top climate scientists and economists who have invented it. One example of its ineffectiveness comes from the post-Soviet states. The Soviet Union was given a huge allocation of carbon emissions permits in the early 1990s.

But the following year, it collapsed, and its industrial base went into freefall—along with its carbon emissions. It was never going to release those gases after all. Johann Hari, in *The Independent*, explained:

> But Russia and the Eastern European countries have held on to them in all negotiations as 'theirs'. Now, they are selling them to rich countries who want to purchase 'cuts'. Under the current system, the US can buy them from Romania and say they have cut emissions—even though they are nothing but a legal fiction.

Those permits account for 10 gigatonnes of CO_2, which dwarf the 6 gigatonne savings that would come from the entire developed world cutting its emissions by 40% by 2020. Another aspect of ineffectiveness is how cuts through carbon trading are recorded twice. Hari explains:

> If Britain pays China to abandon a coal power station and construct a hydro-electric dam instead, Britain pockets the reduction in carbon emissions . . . [so it can] keep a coal power station open at home. But at the same time, China also counts this change as part of its overall cuts. So one tonne of carbon cuts is counted twice. This means the whole system is riddled with exaggeration—and the figure for overall global cuts is a con.

Research from Stanford University on 3,000 projects applying for carbon offset funding found that they did not need the funds. They concluded that between one-third and two-thirds of all the total carbon development mechanism offsets do not represent actual emission cuts and that this trend would get worse. One of the world's leading climate scientists, James Hansen, who blew the warming whistle in the 1980s, explained that the belief that the European emissions trading scheme has had an effect on emissions is completely misguided: 'what happened was the products that had been made in their countries began to be made in other countries, which were burning the cheapest form of fossil fuel, so the total emissions actually increased'. Given these problems, it should be no surprise then that one *Wall Street Journal* poll found that 54% of economists, a constituency not normally keen on taxation, preferred a carbon tax to any other option for effectiveness in reducing emissions.

Cap-and-trade systems are **inefficient and unfair**. Permits for polluting are allocated to current large polluters, who then make a disproportionate profit from carbon trading. Patrick O'Connor and Alex Safari explain:

> In the lead-up to the handout of carbon credits in Europe, the major polluters lobbied their national governments and ratcheted up reported emissions in order to claim many more credits than they actually required. Once the market came into effect in January 2005 they then returned to business as usual. Without reducing any emissions, businesses were able to sell their surplus credits for significant sums. British oil companies BP and Shell, for example, made £17.9 million and £20.7 million ($40 million and $46 million) respectively through the sale of their carbon credits.

A recent example comes from Tata. In Redcar, North Yorkshire, UK, 1,700 workers lost their jobs when the owner of the Corus steelworks decided to close its plant. By stopping production at Redcar and increasing production in locations outside ETS areas, Corus/Tata is able to sell its carbon allowances from the EU, but with no impact on carbon emissions. 'By ceasing to emit a potential six million tonnes of CO_2 a year, Corus will benefit from carbon allowances which could soon, according to European Commission projections, be worth up to £600 million over the three years before current allocations expire,' wrote Christopher Booker in *The Telegraph*.

The carbon trades are conducted by financial institutions, who charge fees that accrue to shareholders, not those needing to adapt to climate changes or rising prices. These financial institutions also create derivatives, which lead to speculative activity that benefits only the institutions themselves, and poses an unnecessary cost on economic systems and consumers. Today the carbon trading market is worth over $100 billion and 'at today's European carbon price, yearly carbon emissions have a market value of more than €500bn, a figure which could increase significantly' as a global ceiling took effect. It would increase a lot more, as banks developed secondary derivatives markets. Indeed, Bloomberg notes that carbon trading will become centred around derivatives. Lisa Kassenaar wrote that

> the banks are preparing to do with carbon what they've done before: 'design and market derivatives contracts that will help client companies hedge their price risk over the long term. They're also ready to sell carbon-related financial products to outside investors.' The secondary carbon market in derivatives will be many multiples larger than the primary market.

No surprise, then, that, in 2009, Goldman Sachs bought Constellation Energy's carbon trading operation along with a number of other carbon-trading-related investments. That also helped me to understand one hedge fund manager I met who had quit his job, and in a year blew millions in charitable donations to create climate action NGOs to be seen as experts in carbon markets, and build a brand that could net greater fortunes, with the added bonus of a veneer of cool. There's nothing like talking about saving the planet over a glass of champagne on the top floor of the Ritz Carlton.

The problem with this behaviour is its effect on society and on attempts to curb carbon emissions in socially acceptable ways. Hedge fund manager Michael Masters, founder of Masters Capital Management LLC, says, 'speculators will end up controlling U.S. carbon prices, and their participation could trigger the same type of boom-and-bust cycles that have buffeted other commodities'. In a report on the matter by Friends of the Earth (FoE) US, carbon trading was identified as a derivatives market which may eventually be bigger than the credit derivatives market, which collapsed so spectacularly. Interestingly, one of the key architects of the 'credit default swaps', which played a key role in that collapse, is now heading environmental businesses at a major bank, focusing on carbon markets. Michelle Chan, a senior policy analyst in San Francisco for Friends of the Earth, says that given their recent history, the banks' ability to turn climate change into a new commodities market should be curbed. Her report earlier in 2009 pointed out that regulation of secondary carbon markets were effectively non-existent. She said the carbon markets already have all the ingredients for a sub-prime carbon market, in particular futures contracts to deliver carbon that carry a relatively high risk of not being fulfilled. Others have been more assertive in damning banks such as Goldman Sachs. Chronicling the bank's involvement in carbon trading in the EU and its push for such a system in the US, Matt Taibbi says that, with Goldman's push for cap and trade, they are seeking to create more bubbles to manipulate markets, 'creating what may be the biggest and most audacious bubble yet'. Revealingly, earlier in 2009, Goldman Sachs representatives said in court that their software could help manipulate markets in unfair ways.

Another aspect of the inefficiency and unfairness that arise from cap-and-trade systems stem from how governments must allocate permits, which leads to huge levels of lobbying and agreements, which favour special interests. In some countries this situation would create a new arena for corruption. An example of the special-interest shakedown that arises from this situation is the sectoral focus being advanced by the World Business Council for Sustainable Development. On the one hand, it is great that some companies are clubbing together in sectors to voluntarily reduce emissions, such as the postal and cement sectors. On the other hand, it is inappropriate for sectors to seek their own special allocation of carbon permits so they can avoid paying the same cost of carbon as other enterprises. That would not only be unfair but the jostling for position makes it a highly inefficient policy, unless you are a lobbyist. As Chad Holliday, chairman of DuPont, noted, "companies do not fall into easy categories any more and it would be very difficult to put companies and their emissions into nice, neat boxes".

These new inefficiencies in the effective organising of economy and society come at a time when nations need to re-tool to low-carbon societies. In addition, the system is fundamentally unfair, which has implications for the public support for climate action, which we return to below.

Cap-and-trade systems are also currently **unworkable**, with huge levels of fraud. Fox News reported that 'the top cops in Europe say carbon-trading has fallen prey to an organized crime scheme that has robbed the continent of $7.4 billion'. The problem of fraud and insider trading in the carbon markets was also highlighted in the FoE US report. The situation was highlighted by the German artist Dirk Fleischmann, who visited a reforestation site in the Philippines that he had donated to as part of a voluntary carbon offset scheme run by Carbonme.org. He found out that the forest project managers had never heard of Carbon Me and received funds from another source. Carbon Me replied that their small print detailed how the projects promoted on their website were for illustration only and that they would not necessarily be the ones that received funds. Their terms read: 'Carbon Me with its tree-planting partners will use its/their best endeavours to ensure the trees are planted in the chosen areas. There may be instances when it is not possible to plant a tree in the area requested. In these cases Carbon Me and/or its tree-planting partner reserve the right to plant the trees in the next best or most similar location.' It is difficult to see what best endeavours they used to plant trees in a forest that was already being planted by another funder. The real funder sued Carbon Me for copyright infringement. It is a story Fleischmann chronicles on his blog.

In arguing for a focus on cap and trade, most people argue it is the only practical option. 'In the actual world, a global scheme of tradeable emissions quotas is the best solution', said an editorial in the *FT* just before Copenhagen. In their book *The Hot Topic*, Gabrielle Walker and Sir David King assert that cap and trade is politically more achievable than other measures such as carbon taxes. Yet this statement is undermined by their identification of the political prerequisites for such a deal, including agreement on a global emissions cap and the distribution of emissions rights. The co-editor of *The Economics and Politics of Climate Change*, Cameron Hepburn, points out that seeking agreement on caps and allocations puts difficult issues of distribution and compensation at the heart of the international negotiations, which has clearly contributed to the impasse. The past 18 years of climate negotiations have shown how difficult it is for governments to agree on caps and allocations. Some argue for a convergence of carbon intensity of gross domestic product (GDP), others for a convergence of per capita GDP before caps can be considered. Some argue that convergence of allocations is only fair, yet it is nonsensical to argue that a fishing community in the Philippines, for instance, would need or want to emit the same amount of carbon as a citizen of Singapore. To assume so is to assume one concept of human progress. Globally applied cap-and-trade systems are also **internationally improbable,** as national allocations of carbon caps are extremely difficult to agree at an intergovernmental level. The difficulties in reaching agreement has led to crucial time being lost.

The fifth main way that a cap-and-trade focus is hindering global action on climate change is that it is **alienating** some of the public from action on carbon emissions. Much of the media that is critical of any action on climate change focuses on the scam that is carbon cap and trade. Rather than arguing for effective, efficient and fair action on climate change, the majority of the anti-cap-and-trade analysis rejects action on climate change altogether. In addition, it analyses the personal motivations of leading figures in the climate change field, such as Al Gore and the IPCC chair and highlights how much they have to gain personally from cap-and-trade systems—thereby giving the impression that the darlings of mainstream environmentalism are actually charlatans. For instance, looking at the leading role Al Gore has played in shaping cap and trade, and his business interests in the carbon market, *The Telegraph* predicts that 'Al Gore could become the world's first carbon billionaire', a theme picked up in the *New York Times*. *The Telegraph* also pointed out that the chair of the Intergovernmental Panel on Climate Change is an industrialist, with a long career in oil and heavy industries. Rajendra Pachauri

was, for instance, a director until 2003 of India Oil, the country's largest commercial enterprise, and until this year remained as a director of the National Thermal Power Generating Corporation, its largest electricity producer. In 2005, he set up GloriOil, a Texas firm specialising in technology which allows the last remaining reserves to be extracted from oilfields otherwise at the end of their useful life.

Given all these limitations, it should be no surprise that some government leaders were so critical of the approach of the West. The President of Bolivia exclaimed, 'Capitalism wants to address climate change with carbon markets. We denounce those markets and the countries which [promote them]. It's time to stop making money from the disgrace that they have perpetrated.'

For there to begin to be total reductions in carbon emissions through behaviour change and technological innovations, 'you have to put an honest price on carbon, which is going to have to gradually rise over time', explains climate scientist James Hansen. As prices will rise, the mechanism for doing that will need to be broadly perceived as socially legitimate. There is a great history of struggles against unfair taxes, such as the British salt taxes in India to the poll taxes imposed in the 1980s in the UK. If the polluters and bankers are receiving the cash from price rises and there is no immediate and corresponding reduction in carbon emissions, there will be a justified and overwhelming backlash. The social legitimacy of any system for increasing the price of carbon is therefore key, and should be the focus of intergovernmental deliberations.

The global carbon charge

We need to encourage behaviour change, guide innovations, and invest in helping people maintain or develop their quality of life while limiting their carbon emissions and adapting to the increasing impacts of climate change. A globally agreed, nationally implemented carbon tax, applied upstream at the point of energy production for commercial distribution, would have been far simpler to agree and implement that the cap-and-trade approach pursued since 1997.

Arguments against such a global carbon charge include that it would fund unaccountable governance, or would be socially regressive, or couldn't specify limits for carbon emissions. Each argument is woefully mistaken.

For instance, a framework for how governments introduce a national or regional carbon charge could be agreed through international treaty. The revenues could be collected and distributed nationally, according to internationally agreed criteria and therefore be accountable to both citizens of that state and the international community. The importance of an international framework for such national carbon charges has many elements. First, it is important for all nations that carbon charges are introduced in a synchronised way, in order not to unfairly distort trade or to allow carbon leakage when businesses seek the lowest carbon taxes. For instance, we do not want to see aircraft flying further distances to get refuelled in countries with lower carbon charges. Second, it is important that countries agree on whether there should be initially differential rates of carbon charge depending on the levels of economic development, and what the yearly escalator of the level of the charge should be in order for it to change behaviour and stimulate innovation without causing the kind of traumatic abrupt changes in post-Soviet states in the early 1990s. Third, countries need to encourage each other to make commitments that would ensure that there would not be a public backlash and the revenues would be used in a sensible way. Therefore an international commitment on distribution of the charge revenues is needed, so that governments agree to invest them in helping vulnerable people to adapt to climate impacts and to the initial effect of the charge in increasing costs of fulfilling their basic needs such as food and energy. Part of this commitment could be to pay a percentage of collected revenues to an international fund, focused on both mitigation, such as forest protection and reforestation, and adaptation, helping finance the costs of climate-related humanitarian emergencies. Fourth, countries would need to agree on mechanisms for imposing legitimate tariffs on products and services from countries that are independently adjudicated to be not applying the carbon tax appropriately (or who are not signatories to the agreement). Given the need for an agreement to have such real teeth, and the trade importance of such an agreement, the World Trade Organisation could be one option to host the negotiation and policing of such a 'General Agreement on Carbon Charging and Related Measures'.

The argument that a carbon tax could be socially regressive ignores the realities of what needs to occur for behaviours to change: the cost of carbon must go up and therefore prices will rise. As the *Financial Times* editorial before the summit explained, 'politicians must tell their electorates the truth: power, transportation, and carbon-intensive products must become markedly more expensive'. Therefore, for any policy initiative to be effective it must address the social consequences of such a price rise. Cap-and-trade systems lead to the revenues from increased prices going to the polluters and banks, and therefore not to those who need support to change. A carbon charge administered by the government could be invested in the necessary social support. In addition, to ensure that price changes are not so abrupt as to disrupt people's lives in the way shock therapy in post-Soviet states did, then increases in carbon prices must be controlled, which is not possible if the financial speculators inflate a carbon bubble. If a carbon tax is socially regressive, then a cap-and-trade system is socially degenerate.

The other argument made against carbon charges by Tim Flannery, Chief Commissioner of the Australian Climate Commission, among others, is that with a charge one can not lock in a specific limit for carbon emissions. That assumes a specific limit is actually feasible through cap-and-trade systems; the discussion above has shown it is not. A charge is a mechanism that can be increased to the degree that it generates the behaviour changes and technological changes required. Other policy instruments may also be needed to deliver quick cuts, such as prohibitions on certain industries, such as tar sands exploitation, unsustainable logging, and on certain behaviours such as leaving neon signs on at night and air-conditioning units set extremely low. The focus must be on what works, not empty promises on paper.

The existence of carbon charging in a number of countries shows that it is possible. Finland, Denmark, Netherlands, Sweden and Norway established carbon taxes in the early 1990s. In the last two years interest in carbon taxes grew, with US state of California introducing a carbon tax in 2008, and in 2009 France detailed a new carbon tax set at €17 (US$25) per tonne of CO_2, as did the Republic of Ireland, set at €15 per tonne. A number of East Asian nations are examining how to introduce their own carbon taxes, including China. For corporations that operate in markets around the world, the existence of carbon charges is already of commercial importance even if their own country of origin does not yet impose one. The international trade challenges that such carbon charges pose was highlighted at the close of the year; President Sarkozy of France said that a carbon tariff on European Union borders was necessary to balance international trade for French enterprises. 'I will fight for a carbon tax levied on EU borders', for products from countries that did not impose their own carbon charges, he said—something that made immediate news in China. Meanwhile, Minnesota passed a measure to stop carbon at its border with North Dakota. To encourage the switch to clean renewable energy, Minnesota plans to add a carbon charge of between $4 and $34 per ton of carbon dioxide emissions to the cost of coal-fired electricity, to begin in 2012. It is inevitable that trade disputes will emerge on such issues, and therefore now is the time to work towards an effective and fair global framework for carbon charging.

Some analysts of the impasse at Copenhagen are looking at other governance mechanisms to deliver the needed changes. For instance, Simon Zadek, formerly with AccountAbility, is interested in the extent to which voluntary multi-stakeholder processes might deliver changes. However, approaches that are neither governmental nor global will not bring global emissions down. It is not sufficient for some to reduce their emissions—there has to be global action.

Positive lobbying?

Although the lobbying by climate change sceptics received the most media criticism, as well as the campaign attention of Avaaz, most of the visible corporate lobbying of the 15th meeting of Conference of Parties to the UNFCCC was in favour of an agreement. WWF made this situation clear by adding up the market capitalisation of firms that had signed on to various initiatives: US$11 trillion. For instance, the Corporate Leaders Group on Climate Change launched the Copenhagen Communiqué, and received the support of 1,000 business CEOs from across all G20 countries. It called for 'an ambitious, robust and equitable global deal on climate change that responds credibly to the scale and urgency of the crises facing the world today', including 'a reduction of 50–85% by 2050' of greenhouse gases. Their focus was on agreement that could support carbon markets, and there was no mention of carbon charges. Signing a communiqué is one thing, but other businesses have invested heavily in influencing policy agendas on climate to obtain the kind of cap-and-trade systems they desire. The Center for Responsive Politics (CPR) reported that Goldman Sachs personnel donated nearly four-and-a-half million dollars to the Democratic Party in the US, with almost a million of that going to Barack Obama. Goldman staff were Obama's largest private contributor and together were 'the biggest business donor to Democrats in 2008', according to a (CPR) report.

The continuing dominance of the cap-and-trade policy paradigm is illustrated by the mitigation report of the Intergovernmental Panel on Climate Change, chaired by Indian energy industrialist Dr Pachauri. In a large report on policy measures to reduce carbon emissions, there was only one line on carbon charges, summarising research that proposes 'all countries agree to a common, international GHG emission tax; several of the proposals suggest beginning with a carbon tax limited to emissions from fossil fuel combustion'.

As the Copenhagen Summit showed, an impasse was being reached with the current climate policy paradigm, and more people began to wonder whether we had been working on the wrong agenda. Even Al Gore, a man particularly responsibly for the past 18-year focus on cap and trade, said in a speech at Copenhagen that he personally favoured a carbon tax, although he still did not argue for it and recommended remaining focused on cap and trade. Earlier in 2009, the chief executives of Caterpillar Inc. and FedEx said they prefer a tax on carbon dioxide emissions and criticised the cap-and-trade measure being debated in Congress. ExxonMobil's CEO Rex Tillerson has also said a carbon charge made more sense than carbon trading, as it is 'a more direct and transparent approach'. This attitude is shared by some business leaders even in places where one might not expect it. In answer to a question I put to a seminar on climate change at the CSR Asia Summit in Kuala Lumpur in October 2009, an executive from China Light and Power (CLP) explained that she would favour a carbon charge as it would allow them to know what the price of carbon would be over time and thus start planning their major infrastructure investments accordingly. With the current uncertainty, she said, it was impossible to factor in carbon costs to strategic and project planning in a way that would be decisive.

Today, many business leaders see the seriousness of the climate challenge. Yet they are working on an agenda that was set in 1997, when there was not the same will to take decisive and swift action on carbon emissions. In addition, such concerned business leaders currently face two problems. The first is that the cap-and-trade train has left the station, and there is now a community of business, banks, NGOs and others who have a vested interest in cap-and-trade systems being expanded and would see a global carbon charge as undermining their financial self-interests. Second, it appears that there is no multi-enterprise or multi-stakeholder initiative that is explicitly against cap and trade and for a global carbon charging framework.

Part of the reason for that is the failure of international civil society to articulate a principled position on climate justice. On the one hand, it appears there is a coming-together of environment and social concerns with development charities such as Oxfam and Christian Aid advocating tough action on climate change, and African human rights activist Kumi Naidoo taking the helm of Greenpeace International. However, the development groups are often very careful before campaigning on issues of justice or against corporate power, and usually do so with the safety-in-numbers of coalitions; and climate is a new issue for them. On the other hand, environmental groups have been suffering a loss of expertise in the past decades as talented staff joined the private sector, and my own experience with them suggests they have lost a lot of confidence and ambition in the past 10 years, as they focus on sounding reasonable and attracting large grants from major donors as their traditional base of individual members shrinks in the West. As a result, there are few voices for economic justice in the international sphere today.

Without coalitions pushing for effective action, commitments to carbon charges may remain off-hand comments in speeches, seminars and newspaper interviews, rather than a concerted campaign for change. My latest book argues the need for explicitly normative associations of businesses that advance changes in society that are collective, not private, in benefit, as such associations are crucial to the manifestation of the corporate responsibility movement. Existing initiatives on climate could come to play such a role, but to do so they would need to more clearly understand what constitutes responsible lobbying.

Earlier in 2009 consultants Kyle Peterson and Mark Pfitzer tackled the relationship between lobbying and corporate social responsibility (CSR) in the Stanford Social Innovation Review. In the article, the authors advocate ending the traditional divide between a company's corporate social responsibility (CSR) and lobbying activities. They list a variety of areas where companies have advocated policy changes which the authors believe have benefited both the businesses and society. They write that companies can 'create tremendous social value and business benefit, ... leverage their true expertise and natural advantages, and ... build more active, two-way relationships with policymakers and nonprofits'. It may appear a win–win, but that depends on the nature of the lobbying, and the follow-on impacts of improved relations with regulators and policy influencers. That is another dimension of the paradox. Governmental processes need encouragement, and that can come from responsible businesses. However, it is clear that corporate lobbying can influence agendas that are damaging to effective, efficient and fair policy outcomes. How should responsible business leaders navigate that paradox? This is discussed in my 2005 paper for *Business Strategy and the Environment*, called 'The Political Bottom Line'. In it Professor Kate Kearins and I argued that what constitutes 'good' corporate lobbying is not simply what companies themselves consider to be good for society. Instead, some broad principles that are widely accepted in responsible business management should be applied to the development of lobbying positions. This would imply the transparency of one's lobbying, seeking accountability to weaker stakeholders' interests in the development and implementation of one's lobbying, and support for international agreements and principles that are already agreed by intergovernmental processes or accords between independent civil society organisations. As corporate lobbying involves the use of power to affect us all, it is not responsible for companies to simply satisfy themselves of the rightness of their policy positions, or seek consultations only with business-funded organisations to inform their positions. True accountability must be at the heart of responsible lobbying.

It is by the application of this philosophy that responsible business leaders might manage the paradox identified at the beginning of this section. That is the paradox where intergovernmental processes are bogged down as countries are too influenced by commercial interests, whereas, conversely, there is a need for globally responsible business leadership to move things forward, with the reality of such business influence currently having perverse effects on policy agendas. Ultimately, the way a person manages that paradox will come down to their consciousness and courage: something we return to in concluding.

Businesses and governments need to learn the lessons of the current impasse—fast. There is a potential that a backlash against the cap-and-trade carbon systems will overflow into alienation with a corporatised political process. If it appears that the use of political access and public goodwill accorded to corporations for engaging in an issue of major concern has actually helped them to seek profits in ways that threaten civilisation, then there will be major implications for our political systems, and rightly so. First, it will challenge the foundation of the modern corporate responsibility field, which is founded on the idea that everyone can benefit if a business becomes active in considering and managing its social impacts. Instead, CR would be viewed in its full context as either deliberately political public relations (PR) or consequentially political PR, creating that deadly side effect of poisoning political processes. Second, it will lead more people to see existing forms of governance as not only unfair, but dangerous to society, and thus encourage more radical action.

It is important for responsible business leaders to act now, as the lessons of Copenhagen will be learned fast by the whizz-kids at Goldman Sachs and others in the cap-and-trade business. They will recognise that persuading China to come on board will be key to any global expansion of carbon markets. Perhaps Chinese officials are biding their time until the country pollutes enough, and can record it enough, to benefit from future international allocations of emissions permits. On the other hand, as revealed by the November 2009 report from AccountAbility, there is strong evidence to suggest that many Chinese leaders are aware of the problem of climate change and are investing heavily in low-carbon development paths. In that case they may prefer a carbon charging arrangement, where their own levels of carbon charging would be considered internationally acceptable so they won't experience tariffs at the borders of countries that have or will have such charges in future. However, other more sinister options remain, if responsible leaders do not act now. For instance, one scenario is where the elites in emerging economies consider that their ever-increasing stakes in international banks mean that a global cap-and-trade system could allow them to extract rents indefinitely from populations around the world.

Old truths, new urgency

Corporate involvement in intergovernmental policy deliberations will be either good or bad depending on the context of that involvement and the intentions of those involved. Blanket support or criticism for corporate influence misses the point: we have complex societies where people in many walks of life can exert a positive or negative influence as far as public matters are concerned. The implication is that we need people in business who find themselves engaged in policy deliberations to reflect on their work as a vocation as much as a profession: to understand themselves as part of a global social movement seeking to transform economies—to be citizens of the world not just subjects of their employer.

We need business professionals to be active members of a real social movement to transform economies. I myself have protested in the past, at G8 Summits. However, what I know of the machines of business, government and intergovernmental bodies, it is clear to me that no amount of marches, vigils, songs, videos or emails from general publics will in themselves shift things. Instead, they must be complemented by people taking risks in their professional lives. Outsider activism can raise an issue on an agenda, but such activism does not shape the policy response, and it is at that moment of developing policy that the effectiveness, efficiency and fairness of an intervention is determined. It is for this reason that I believe thinking and acting as a 'corporate responsibility movement' is crucial, and explore it in some depth in the introduction to my book *The Corporate Responsibility Movement*.

To serve the common good, all of us can do well to remember that just because we work on a matter of public concern does not mean we work for the public benefit. Just because we always thought we were doing good, does not mean that we do so today. Just because we proved our commitment in our activist or NGO days does not mean we are moral agents today in our new roles. We must no longer simply hope that we are having some effect or hope that something useful might come of our work in business, finance or public policy. Instead, we must make our judgement now, and live with the consequences.

In exploring the impasse and paradoxes surrounding global climate politics and the way business leaders have engaged with that, one core theme emerges, which is not at all new; indeed, it is an age-old truth. Whether something we do is good or bad depends not only on the act itself, but on our intention and the context of our act. It is not what we do, but what love we bring to doing it that matters. If we act with loving compassion for humanity and nature, and therefore subsume our self-interest to that wider scene, then the right course of action in any professional situation will become clear.

Although these are age-old issues, the current context is unprecedented. We are on the edge of a crash in current civilisation due to abrupt climatic changes. We risk the fear of this trauma allowing selfish individuals to seek their own ends, and subjugate people to unfair systems where the poor have to pay premiums to polluters and banks, just for the right to eat and heat their homes. At Copenhagen, Matthew

Stilwell of the Institute for Governance and Sustainable Development said of cap-and-trade systems: 'This is a colonial moment... You've carved up the last remaining unowned resource and allocated it to the wealthy.' At this critical time we need global solidarity, not new attempts to exploit the weak.

During the most famous PowerPoint presentation ever, 'An Inconvenient Truth', Al Gore said of climate change: 'I consider it to be a moral issue.' As such, we can reflect on the morality we and others exhibit in our work. Is it people's greed that seeks to exploit our fears, and our fears that let us stand aside or offer excuses, and some people's pride that tempts them to bask in the praise and funds of the greedy? Are these characteristics a contemporary manifestation of evil, hidden by a mask of technical language and convivial appearances? If so, then the gravestone to our species, standing among countless others we took with us, would aptly read: 'We had enough atmosphere for everyone's need, but not everyone's greed.'

But we need not be despondent. Whether an event is positive or negative is in part due to how we respond to it. The good news is that the failures at Copenhagen brought world attention to these issues, so that people can learn and a new agenda could emerge. 'Copenhagen has soured into a con—but from the wreckage, there could arise a stronger demand for a true solution' wrote Johann Hari. Climate scientists James Hansen concurs: 'I'm actually quite pleased with what happened at Copenhagen,' he said on radio, 'because now we have basically a blank slate.' Copenhagen could be a new beginning, a call to action for globally responsible leaders.

The pulse of CSR in Asia

The final quarter of 2009 confirmed the continuing interest in the nexus between sustainability and business in the Asia region with conferences focusing on the topic.

Singapore is a major hub for international conferences as well as education. It is already home to the Social Innovation Park,[69] which organises the Global Social Innovators Forum (GSIF) annually, and Syinc, a network which connects people to seek innovative solutions for social change.[70] In October 2009, the Singapore Management University debuted on the business-and-society conferencing scene with its 'Social iCon' to explore what it calls 'social innovation'.[71] The concept of social innovation is popular in Singapore, perhaps because it allows people to discuss social progress in a space outside the governmental sector, yet without overtly challenging the government, since phrases such as 'social change' can raise an eyebrow in some countries. The use of the term 'innovation' also resonates with the enthusiasm for all things 'new' across East Asia at the moment, due to the close embrace of modernity, and the rapid economic changes happening there.

The conference itself, of about 300 delegates, was populated mostly by non-profit-sector professionals and business people who volunteer. It appears common in Singapore for civil society leaders to also have full-time day jobs in business or government, perhaps due to the limited civil society funding, and the current low status of being in the voluntary sector. This also reflects how volunteering has a form of cultural cachet if it is something one does in one's leisure time as an extra-professional activity. A key impact of events such as Social iCon could be to help promote the idea that working on social progress outside of the governmental sector is a worthwhile profession.

The speakers were a diverse mix of charity leaders doing traditional charity projects such as housing development; entrepreneurs running small businesses that deliver some social benefit in creative ways; and a few large corporations who sought to promote the positive social impact of their companies. One such company at the conference was Second Life, the world's largest user-created online 'virtual community', whose chief executive argued that they create social value through the amount of charitable donations that have been made through the platform. He was not challenged on whether these were donations that would have been made in other ways, and if that small aspect of Second Life qualifies it to be seen as a social enterprise. It appeared that the spirit of the conference was to celebrate action, not to inquire into the form and impact of that action, and its contribution to social progress.

Given this emphasis on celebration, the level of discussion was limited. The lack of debate did little to develop a shared concept of what social innovation may entail—a particular shame given that the concept, and its articulation in the Asian context, is weakly understood. Without an easy frame of reference within which to relate different contributions, the sheer diversity of presentations, and the selection of moderators for their perceived status rather than their ability to synthesise lessons from specific cases, meant that opportunities for deeper synthesis were sorely lacking. Although the focus on innovation at Social iCon and the GSIF can create a positive outlook, it can also impede the discussion from discussing longer-term struggles. With a focus on celebrating innovation, the spirit of the audience is to applaud people for doing easily recognisable and non-contentious 'good' things in (apparently) new ways. In such a setting, a woman working for 30 years training migrant workers while struggling against a sceptical government might not be an obvious choice for the speakers' roster. In comparison, a more likely candidate would be the wife of a millionaire who set up an orphanage for children after the tsunami, especially if there is a transfer of skills to make items that can be sold, thereby generating revenues for the orphanage. As a result, there is a danger of narcissism and political conservativism in the 'social innovation' field in Asia, which could undermine learning about progress in business–society relations.

Despite the general tone of the event, there were some inspiring people who are applying the concepts of sustainability in innovative yet practical ways. The best example of this was Tri Mumpuni, Executive Director of IBEKA, in Indonesia. 'We are tackling the challenges of rural electrification and economic development by creating community-owned micro-hydropower systems throughout Indonesia,' she explained in a very small breakout session. 'We use micro-hydro, so our electrification can be managed by communities. By giving communities equity in the operations and training them to manage the micro-hydropower systems technically and financially, we are creating jobs and revenues, as well as an environmentally sustainable source of electricity.' The integration of ecological, economic and community needs in this small-scale work is an inspiration for those hoping for non-carbon-intensive development.

Notable by their absence from Social iCon were CSR managers of large corporates in Singapore or the region. The profile of the delegates contrasted with those at CSR Asia's event a few days later in neighbouring Kuala Lumpur.[72] The CSR Asia conference marked a watershed. It also had 300 delegates, compared to 100 the previous year, who were mostly CSR or PR managers from the private sector. The majority were from East Asia, and were not from the base of the supply chain. There was a distinct lack of voices from wider society such as consultants, unions, religious institutions, strongly critical NGOs and academics, none of whom were on the speakers' list. Only the voice of a rogue journalist seemed to challenge the status quo. So the homogenous character of the conference raised not only questions about racial diversity but also diversity of classes and sectors. This illustrates that CSR in Asia is now as much about large firms adopting their own CSR approaches as it is being driven by the need to conform to social and environmental audits from overseas. This was further emphasised at the close of the conference when CSR Asia co-founder Steven Frost commented that Asia now has its own CSR constituency and is developing its own CSR agendas.

Despite promoting the conference as being about sustainability, there was only one presentation that looked closely at new business models that place an integrated notion of sustainability at its heart. This was from Shokay founder Marie So, also a graduate of Harvard University. She explained how the company 'aims to impact the lives of Tibetan herders in China oppressed by poverty. By introducing luxury yak down to the global market, we hope to create a market for yak fibre, thus increasing the value of the raw fibre to provide herders with long-term employment and a greater sustainable income.' She explained that, as the business is doing well, with a new partnership agreed with luxury brand Shanghai Tang for 2010, Shokay's development impact is fourfold: direct income generation, preserving the local culture, promoting sustainable use of the environment, and community development. 'We currently work with 2,600 people, providing a sustainable source of employment and income to these herders. By setting up fibre cooperatives in each sub-village, it is our goal to help grow each ecosystem to provide a safe and transparent vehicle for addressing local development.'[73]

In light of Marie So's involvement in international networks such as that convened by CSR Asia, there is a strong chance that there are other innovators who are embodying forms of business that can be part of a fair and sustainable economy. If a conference organiser could go about finding these innovators, profiling them, provide funding to attend, helping them to learn how to present in ways of mutual benefit, and organising workshops where people can learn from their experiences but also work on their challenges, then that would be a powerful event.

Could such an event be an academic conference? Probably not, unless conferences come to be understood as potential mechanisms for research rather than just research dissemination and discussion. In November 2009, the Asia Pacific Academy of Business in Society (APABIS) conducted its third international conference entitled *Finding Solutions to Global Problems*. Drawing together practitioners and researchers from across business, civil society, government and academia, the conference aimed to explore the role of stakeholder engagement, new social partnerships and strategic alliances in the transition to what it termed a 'sustainable enterprise economy' (SEE).

Hosted by the Asia Pacific Centre for Sustainable Enterprise (APCSE), at Griffith University, the conference was set against a background of three interlinked global imperatives: responding to climate change, the global financial crisis, and a moral crisis within economic practice—themes that echoed through many of the presentations. It also aimed to showcase the challenges and opportunities, strategic partnerships, innovation and education/skills-training necessary for a transition to a SEE.

While the usual case studies proved fruitful in providing examples of programmes and initiatives that organisations are implementing to contribute to sustainability, probably the most challenging session highlighted a re-conceptualisation of what 'economy' means. Illustrating the multi-disciplinary approach of the conference, this plenary brought together an unlikely mix of speakers: namely, the CEO of a large employment company, the head of an Indian corporate foundation, a sustainable fund manager, and an engineering and research projects consultant, to talk about change and action for the new economy.

Nick Fleming, Chief Sustainability Officer at Sinclair Knight Merz and participant of the plenary panel, described a sustainable economy as one that not only works towards sustainable development but also demythologises traditional models of scarcity, and counters the power structures that support and maintain such paradigms. He proposed we think of a sustainable economy with 'the notion of abundance replaced by limits. Economic value replaced by real societal value—with erosion recognised. Regulated commerce that promotes societal benefit.'

Matthew Tukaki, CEO of Drake International, and Ashoke Joshi of the TVS Srinivasan Services Trust (TVS-SST), recounted the practical challenges of developing and promoting the skills necessary for sustainability in both developing and developed economies. In relation to climate change, Tukaki explained, 'We're going to see a lot of debate about what green jobs are or what a green collar worker will be. Our focus is on developing the skills, jobs and industry to respond to climate change. Most of the arguments against trading schemes, for example, focus on the jobs that will go. Lost in the debate are the jobs created. We're working to make that happen; to create the skills for the transition.'

Describing the skills training and health services provided to 80,000 rural Indian families through the TVS Motor Company's social trust, Ashoke Joshi evoked both the vast spectrum of material and social justice issues in working toward a SEE, but also the profound economic, social and political upheavals involved. Sharing a case study from a company factory, Joshi described an initiative run by the trust and funded by the government, which trained local women to cook chapattis, with an understanding that the factory would buy them at a set rate if they were of a high-enough standard. Today the women make 25,000 chapattis, of which the factory buys a fifth, and markets the rest to other factories up to 50 km away. However, 'As the women started making money the menfolk became jealous; they felt the women were getting powerful, and worried they would lose their authority. So they came up with an ingenious argument. They said, "You've been cooking chapattis in the community hall, which is meant for meetings only, so you can't do it here anymore." So that almost ended the programme. But by then the women were strong enough, had the confidence, had some money and went to the bank. They bought land, built a factory and now have a balance of 6 million rupees. So then you had domestic violence. But that is getting better now.'

The approach of the conference was well received by most participants. As one plenary speaker noted, 'I've been on many sustainability panels, but to have people approaching the topic from such different places—that's very rare. It made for an interesting conversation.'

For the Asia-Pacific region this might be one of the most significant contributions of the conference, given the current pattern of development of CSR in the region. As discussed in our review of the 2008 year, if CSR in the Asia-Pacific develops as a mix of the interests of Westerners and, increasingly, local elites, it will not respond to those that are directly impacted by business activities within the Asia-Pacific.

The APABIS conference hoped to offer something different to the elite focus of CSR for Asia through its cross-sector and multi-disciplinary approaches that embraced differences, and to spark the creative thinking necessary to envision a SEE. By incorporating stakeholders other than business managers and government officials, there was a deepening of the systemic reflection necessary to envision new economic concepts. As a result, there was a new focus on economic justice rather than the more philanthropic concepts of CSR that are dominant in Asia, indicating a potential shift in how the Asia-Pacific region is starting to think about CSR. However, while more than 20 nationalities were present at the conference and case studies presented in breakout sessions were drawn from throughout the region (including Australia, New Zealand, Vietnam, Indonesia, Japan, India, Myanmar [Burma] and Fiji), the conference participants were overwhelmingly from Australasia, although there also was strong representation from Japan and Vietnam. If APABIS is to become an important forum for cross-cultural and cross-sectoral dialogue on matters of business in society, there is much work to be done.

Both the conference's approach and its focus were nevertheless not without their critics, illustrating in turn the challenges of systemic change. As argued by Professor Jean Palutikof, Director of the Australian National Climate Change Adaptation Research Facility, 'the sustainable enterprise economy means very little to me—I think it is used to disguise the fact that no one is doing much about carbon emissions'.

While the conference highlighted and bemoaned the 'silo mentality' found in government, business and industry, and academia, at times the format and participants struggled to break out of the well-worn stand-and-present routine. Disciplinary and institutional divides are well recognised as limits to exchange and innovation in thinking and processes to adapt to the sustainability imperative. While striving to bridge these divides, this conference demonstrated both the need and the difficulty in engaging in what could be called 'trans-disciplinary' conversations; the importance of moderators skilled in conversations on systemic issues; and the promotion and further development of these more innovative conference formats.

Sustaining innovation

The Singapore conference on social innovation also reflects the popularity of the term 'innovation' in management conferences and initiatives on business–society relations. Two design conferences in the fourth quarter of 2009 also suggest that the nexus between sustainable enterprise and design is an emerging trend. The International Design Conference on Sustainability and Design in Mumbai in November explored the theme of Sustainability, Design and Enterprise.[74] A month earlier, the Design Management Institute (DMI) held its annual conference entitled 'Design, Complexity and Change' to present case studies that draw out lessons on how design can help reframe, rethink and reinvent futures.[75] They illustrate how design is a concept that goes beyond the creation of products and is concerned with exploring the role of design in sustaining, developing and integrating human ideas into broader ecological and cultural environments.

So what does innovation mean? According to BusinessDictionary.com, innovation is the 'process by which an idea or invention is translated into a good or service for which people will pay. To be called an innovation, an idea must be replicable at an economical cost and must satisfy a specific need. Innovation involves deliberate application of information, imagination, and initiative in deriving greater or different value from resources, and encompasses all processes by which new ideas are generated and converted into useful products.'[76] It is in essence a systematic and systemic approach that directs acts of invention towards a shared purpose, this purpose being of public benefit in the case of social, sustainable or responsible innovation.[77]

Recognising the systemic change necessary for such complex innovation, Paul Toni presented WWF's *Climate Solutions 2* report as part of the APABIS conference in November 2009. The report modelled the ability to grow low-carbon industries within a market economy and highlighted some of the challenges to such innovation. On the practical side, such industries have constraints to growth caused by limits to resource, technology, capital and workforce size and skills but, as Toni explained, 'these limits are measurable and make it possible to calculate the time required to transform the energy and non-energy sectors to avoid a 2° warming'. According to Toni, 'there are 24 low-carbon resources, industries and practices available today that are sufficiently large to provide 9 billion people with significant economic development'. However, the maximum possible rate of growth for these industries is lower than 30% a year. Therefore, unless public policy creates the right frameworks for massive investment in such industries to achieve the 30% annual growth rate needed from 2014 onwards, it will not be possible to achieve the necessary reductions in carbon emissions to keep world temperature rises below the 2° threshold.[78] So, systemically, there are innovation constraints as well.

As such, Paul Toni argued that there are three main reasons why innovations are held back, or at least not promoted by government. First, 'incumbent firms argue to maintain the status quo—how can they do otherwise without breaching their duty to the shareholders?' he explained. Second, 'industry associations are particularly vocal opponents of change because they represent the whole spectrum of opinions in the industry—including those of the least efficient companies and least prepared'. Third, 'Departments of Industry are usually supportive of incumbents for similar reasons and are seldom promoters of change.' As a consequence, regulations that would compel innovations are fought against, usually with the argument that they are too costly and would cost jobs. However, Toni presented evidence showing that industry calculations of the cost of regulations in the fields of asbestos, benzene, coke ovens and vinyl chloride were exaggerated by between 50% and 1,500% before regulations were introduced. Part of the reason was that, once regulations came into effect, industry began to innovate and find cost savings in so doing. Therefore, he called on governments to influence markets and promote the rapid scaling of needed technologies.[79]

Other deep-seated impediments to sustainable innovation from within businesses themselves were explored in a Boston Consulting Group (BCG) publication in October 2009 entitled *The Business of Sustainability*. The report detailed the results of a global survey of over 1,500 corporate executives and managers which sought to better understand the business implications of sustainability.[80] One of the conclusions of the report was that, although 92% of businesses were trying to address sustainability issues, most companies struggled on execution demonstrating a lack of coherence between the desire to act and the ability to implement bold action. The report detailed that one of the major obstacles was the difficulty in modelling a business case for sustainability due to three major factors:

- Forecasting and planning beyond the one- to five-year time horizon typical of most investment frameworks

- Gauging the system-wide effects of sustainability investments

- Planning amid high uncertainty

While these three points illustrate the ambiguity that businesses face, they also demonstrate the typical decision-making mechanisms that businesses use in determining future direction. Expanding on the third point in particular, the report stipulated that 'Strategic planning, as traditionally practiced, is deductive—companies draw on a series of standard gauges to predict where the market is heading and then design and execute strategies on the basis of those calculations. But sustainability drivers are anything but predictable, potentially requiring companies to adopt entirely new concepts and frameworks.'[81]

In criticising deductive logic, where theories arrived at through past experience are used to predict what will happen in future, BCG were giving voice to other forms of knowledge in a domain traditionally dominated by economics, as illustrated by a range of strategy management journals. Economics is a discipline that is highly reductionist and determinist, meaning that, to provide insight into society, it reduces complex interactions into a few key variables (reductionism), and then seeks correlations between the variables as a means of identifying cause and effect (determinism). As such, economics has its limits in revealing insight into complex realities. Beyond economics, many of the tools used to describe major trends in society that inform the fields in which companies focus their innovation depend on quantitative data, including analysis of the subjective opinions and experiences of individuals through surveys. The reliance on what can be inscribed and aggregated not only enables some useful macroscopic views of trends, but also means there is a temporal and physical distance between the analyst and the realities studied. The data shows how things used to be, not how they could be, and does not provide insight into the complexity of people's lived experiences. It is as if, by looking for the 'helicopter view' of a situation, one has to travel away from the phenomenon to look back at it through a telescope. What is lost from this approach is not only an understanding of complex consumer needs and wants, but also the potential for a conversation with consumers about what they might want, and how their expressed behaviours might not actually be how they would wish to behave if they had other choices. For instance, the reason that people spend two hours in traffic everyday might be an observed preference, as it is their behaviour, but it is not necessarily their desired preference.

A key lesson here is that, in order to become better at strategy, businesses need to get closer to consumers. But the main focus of BCG was on the restrictive effects of business executives requiring 'proof' of a business plan, where what constitutes proof is narrowly defined, before making a decision to invest in innovation. This was also the focus in *Fast Company* magazine in November 2009. Being interviewed on innovation in business, Roger Martin, Dean of the Rotman School of Management at the University of Toronto, explains that 'Most companies try to be innovative, but the enemy of innovation is the mandate to "prove it." You cannot prove a new idea in advance . . .'.[82]

The alternative, he suggests, requires 'design thinking'. A simple definition of design thinking is any process that applies the methods of industrial designers to problems beyond the scope of how a product should look. 'Design thinking' is a user-based approach that observes people in order to create practical solutions in product design and for social problems. It focuses on the nature of the problem itself. Put this way, such a methodology means that products are created in sync with consumer needs rather than creating a product and pushing it into the marketplace. Mr Martin suggests that design thinking is a conduit between the intuition of new ideas and the more structured approaches of analysis which 'enables the organization to balance exploration and exploitation, invention of business and administration of business, originality and mastery'.[83]

This suggests that, by thinking like a designer, organisations may be freed from the burden of proof so that the *best solution* can be explored rather than the illusion of what can be proven.

A November 2009 special report in *Bloomberg BusinessWeek* highlighted how design thinking is impacting business.[84] The article illustrated how companies such as Procter & Gamble (P&G), GE Healthcare and Philips Lighting use design thinking to solve their problems. At P&G, the number of design facilitators has grown from 100 to 175 since 2008 in an attempt to embed such methodologies throughout the organisation; and, judging by their enormous growth between 2000 and 2008 when revenue doubled from $40 billion to $83 billion, it isn't surprising that their performance is being heralded as a triumph of design thinking.[85] GE Healthcare has also adopted design thinking and, according to a 2003 report by the Danish Design Center, increased design activity such as design-related employee training boosted the company's revenue on average by 40% more than other companies over a five-year period.[86]

These earnings may convince companies that 'design thinking' is central to the future of innovation, but what might it imply for the social and environmental performance of business, including the challenge of scaling innovation as rapidly as described above? There are two areas of potential benefit. First, as design thinking challenges dominant views of what constitutes proven knowledge in strategic planning, and allows for more complexity and uncertainty in decision-making, so investments in innovation may gain more attention. This is because, as BCG noted, 'Decisions regarding sustainability have to be made against a backdrop of high uncertainty. Myriad factors muddy the waters because their timing and magnitude of impact are unknown. Such factors include government legislation, demands by customers and employees, and geopolitical events.'[87]

Second, design thinking could encourage businesses to respond to the needs of consumers, rather than seeking ways of marketing existing things to them. This is closely connected to developing a functional perspective on what consumers do, and why they do it. With this view, a car is no longer just a car, but a means of fulfilling a range of functions to the consumer, such as mobility, status and fun. With that perspective and recognition of growing resource constraints, changing values and technologies, designers could explore how to serve those needs in different ways. Thus needs for mobility, status and fun could be provided separately, or more sustainable transport solutions infused with characteristics that meet the non-mobility functions of existing cars. Making bicycles cool, for instance, or providing more ticket classes and benefits in public transport. The importance of taking a consumer need perspective, or 'functional approach', and seeking to meet that within resource constraints, was identified by the UN Environment Programme as a key sustainability policy paradigm for governments in 2001.[88]

The shift in mind-set in design thinking is one that moves from regarding a product as simply a physical thing to regarding it as part of a set of relationships that fulfil various purposes for different people; and so those relationships are as important as the thing in itself. In marketing, this view is often discussed in terms of focusing more on the experience of the consumer. There are also strong resonances here with systems thinking, which emphasises that everything is a set of relationships.

The use of design thinking in business innovation has the potential for encouraging more sustainable design, but it depends on what criteria the observation of users is based, the choice of their needs to be explored, and the intention of the company. In the case of P&G designing cosmetic products, for instance, do their designers question their users about the wider consequences of the products, or the reasons why consumers have particular 'needs' and tastes? In light of the Environmental Working Group's cosmetic safety database which details hundreds of P&G products containing potentially harmful toxic chemicals, perhaps user observation needs to be coupled with user education in order not to avoid certain environmental and social issues.[89] Design may be used to support innovation and the bottom line, but there is also the risk that the broader ecological boundaries are deliberately circumvented to the detriment of others. So, despite the enormous potential of design thinking as highlighted by the examples of P&G and GE, until environmental and social issues become part of the purpose of the organisation, new products may not necessarily be more sustainable.

That said, P&G is starting to apply sustainability criteria to some of its products. Called 'Sustainable Innovation Products' or SIPs, P&G has a goal to deliver $50 billion in cumulative sales of products with improved environmental impact by 2012. SIPs must have an overall use reduction of 10% in the areas of transport, energy, water or materials, or have replaced non-renewable materials with renewable ones.[90]

Design thinking is not a magic bullet for social and environmental effectiveness of corporations, and should not be understood as a new function within business, but just one way of practising a more connected and holistic way of doing business. A *Harvard Business Publishing* article in October 2009 suggested that the success of design thinking is as much about embracing different points of view as it is design methodologies.[91] Although Peter Merholz, the author of the article, founded a company that is dedicated to experience design, he suggests that the effectiveness of design thinking is that it embraces many different experiences and disciplines. He affirms that 'What we must understand is that in this savagely complex world, we need to bring as broad a diversity of viewpoints and perspectives to bear on whatever challenges we have in front of us. While it's wise to question the supremacy of "business thinking," shifting the focus only to "design thinking" will mean you're missing out on countless possibilities.'

His comments supported an article in *Fast Company* earlier in 2009 that com-mented on the role of Claudia Kotchka, P&G's first-ever VP for design strategy.[92] The author, Dev Patnaik, CEO and founder of Jump Associates, a firm that helps companies create new businesses and reinvent existing ones, was quick to point out that Ms Kotchka was an accountant by training and spent most of her pro-fessional life in marketing and thus had no design experience when she started the role. He insists that what design thinking ultimately embodies is the 'conscious blending of different fields of thought to discover and develop opportunities that were previously unseen by the status quo'.

So, while Ms Kotchka immersed herself in design thinking, combining it with her other experiences was what made her such a powerful example of design. As Mr Patnaik concluded, 'To walk away concluding that design thinking is what makes P&G great would be like going to the movies and concluding that Indiana Jones is a great hero because he always wears a hat.'

It should be of no surprise that corporations using design thinking are now employing people from the social sciences such as sociologists, anthropologists, ethnologists and the like because they can open up thinking through entirely dif-ferent points of view. The key here is the need to transcend organisational silos and the single lenses that come from specialisation in marketing, finance, human resources, strategic planning, operations and so on. The new popularity of design thinking, like systems thinking, reflects how organisations are trying various ways to overcome silos. Having teams of experts from different specialisations is one way that organisations try to overcome these silos, but they are rarely more than the sum of their parts. Instead, if managers develop a competence for trans-discipli-narity or trans-functionality, they can draw on the expertise in different speciali-sations, while rejecting certain knowledge claims from those disciplines that they can spot as the result of unhelpful assumptions or preoccupations. Key to this is understanding a knowledge claim in its full context: to distinguish between what it reveals and what is simply a projection of its method, theory and assumptions. Two of the best underlying factors in developing trans-functional competence are critical discourse analysis and the philosophy of science, as they enable people to deconstruct the truth claims they hear.

Furthermore, the organisational silos are there for a reason: they have helped incumbent organisations to control their activities, and regulate any potentially disruptive changes. As a means to shore up success, corporations have created organisational structures to maintain their financial commitments. As many large organisations are either financed by debt or equity, there are requirements to ensure that debt is paid back on a predetermined schedule or that shareholders are paid a return; and so it is understandable that companies have ordered their organisations to meet these demands.[93] According to Roger Martin, the conse-quences of such arrangements for organisational functions are many, and of note for CR professionals. (1) Organisations will take the risks associated with exploring new ideas only when there is a clear potential for a significantly enhanced finan-cial return; investments in new approaches that would deliver similar returns to existing practices are not favoured. (2) Owing to the outflow of money, there are limited resources that can be dedicated to innovation—thus, ironically, working against their own long-term interest. (3) As a result, meeting the budget is the first measure of operational success as opposed to, for example, better environmental performance. And (4) because the nature of the work environment demands reliability for financial purposes, work itself is secondary to the business of making and selling, often demoting people to machine-like tasks and blocking creative potential.[94] A corollary to the last point is that work then becomes a measure of time. The consequence is that performance is measured according to quantity and time rather than quality and objectives, potentially leaving the problem to be addressed unsolved in the interest of rapid turnaround.[95]

It is not just a top-down process that enforces silos in organisations. Rather, to be effective in addressing challenges in ways that integrate insights from various organisational functions, one must be highly intelligent and enthusiastic about the organisation's purpose. If one is tired at work, or not deeply interested in the goal of the organisation, then learning the ropes of a particular discipline, and being satisfied one is a trained practitioner in that discipline, is a natural option. The same is true of management schools, where academics have the added pressure of the expert expectation, so that choosing to put boundaries around one's expertise is an easier way of life.

While corporate responsibility (CR) professionals are presenting sustainability as a source of business opportunity, little is said about those dominant structural aspects of business that are implicitly opposed to innovation. In the case of business, the requirement to 'guarantee' profitability means that businesses depend on mechanisms and processes that have demonstrated reliability in working toward this goal.[96] But, in the face of climate change, financial crises and continual uncertainty, this raises the question of whether the organisational mechanisms that support profit-making are as much hampering as stimulating innovation on challenges such as climate change. For professionals working in CR, examining deep-seated impediments to sustainable innovation is important.

Stakeholder dialogue is an area of corporate responsibility where design thinking could have a direct application. Concerns over the effectiveness of stakeholder dialogues in aligning the interests of business and their stakeholders raise the question of why there is little innovation when there is a veritable abundance of differing viewpoints at the table.[97] This would suggest that there are tools necessary from a process point of view to create a shared sense of problem, to explore the *best solutions* and then channel these ideas through to the implementation phase. In light of the diversity parallel with design thinking, perhaps the missing element in innovation through stakeholder dialogue is design facilitation, an admittedly ambitious project. For, while the design facilitator may be able to unite the stakeholders present to solve a problem, the trickle-down effect might be a little less effective if the organisational structures behind them are naturally resistant to innovation. Consequently, the greatest challenge facing the CR movement may not be providing creative ideas for businesses but helping organisations to break free of paradigms that they've established in attempts to shore up profits and returns for shareholders. If business is to unleash its sustainability creativity, the CR movement will need to not only promote more design thinking, but also transform existing organisational structures that have been designed to resist change. This is where public policy could play a role with a few interventions at the root of the problem, such as obliging corporations to retain a certain percentage of profits to be used for innovation to address a public need.

Indeed, if there is one message from 2009 for the corporate responsibility arena, it is that government can still intervene in markets in game-changing ways—the real question is: for whom? The growing debates about the forms of capitalism that a fair a sustainable society requires will cast new light on such government action.

2010

2010: Introduction

Jem Bendell

By 2010, the global impact of the financial crisis made more people aware of the importance of economic governance to all manner of social and environmental concerns. As analysts of the field of corporate responsibility, our attention therefore turned increasingly to basic economic questions, and how voluntary activity would address some of the systemic flaws in capitalism. Our review of 2009 had been called 'Capitalism in Question', and in 2010 we looked to see the extent to which the CSR field was providing useful answers to these difficult questions.

Despite the fierce winds of financial malpractice, it appeared that the corporate social responsibility and responsible investment fields had become increasingly sheltered and self-referential, considering a growth in uptake of CSR as indicative of success. For instance, the UN Global Compact's 10th anniversary was celebrated in New York, without much serious questioning of whether it had been significant in the broad trajectory of economic trends in the previous decade (see 'From Global Compact to global impact', page 329).

Therefore our reviews were often about analysing limitations and absences in this field, rather than chronicling major new initiatives. It was time to take stock of the corporate responsibility movement at an application level: although the 2010 year was a watershed moment with the launch of ISO 26000, the International Organisation for Standardisation's guide to organisational responsibility, did such institutionalisation represent an accurate understanding of the role of business in shaping economic systems?

Our 2010 analysis highlighted that business leadership is falling short in two ways. First, business leaders are having trouble extrapolating what social responsibility could mean beyond their immediate financial interests. For instance, a theme that was common in many societies worldwide throughout 2010 was growing economic inequality. With so many companies claiming to have fully embedded corporate responsibility, we wondered whether companies would be proactive on this agenda, rather than wait for campaigner or regulatory pressure. We conducted our own analysis of firms' corporate responsibility policies to see if they addressed inequality in particular, such as through pay-rations. The study was conclusive in that nearly all corporate responsibility reports analysed had not addressed the economic inequality issue (see 'Corporate responsibility for economic inequality', page 313). This suggests business leaders still have far to go in being proactive on social and economic concerns.

We then asked the question of what economic inequality might mean at governance and operational levels, and discovered that there was a lack of attention to the relationship of ownership and economic inequality within businesses themselves (see 'CSR and ownership', page 319). What we observed, therefore, was a danger that corporate responsibility was following formulaic tendencies rather than being a values-based system that inspires people and organisations to more holistic approaches to business that benefit society as a whole.

Another area for potential leadership is climate change, where in 2010 the discussions about adaptation to, rather than simply mitigation of, climate change, grew in earnest. We explored how corporations might seek to build resilience through their business continuity policies in ways that could support suppliers and communities in developing countries that will be most affected by climate change. Could business continuity efforts be vehicles of solidarity in times of need (see 'CSR and disaster risk reduction', page 378)? The online Oxford Dictionary defines solidarity as: 'unity or agreement of feeling or action, especially among individuals with a common interest; mutual support within a group'. Our reflection showed that opportunities for business exist to create mutual support in preventative ways during times of hardship. However, to do so would require companies to redefine the boundaries of those they include as part of their common interest.

Societal leadership, to promote systemic change to benefit most stakeholders, also appeared a difficult challenge for professionals working within sustainable finance fields. We conducted an analysis of the impact and limitations of the field of environmental, social and governance (ESG) analysis field. We found that the sector is having little impact in driving behaviour change in corporations; and the various actors in the chain, from institutional investors to fund managers to ESG analysts to corporations, all seemed to point the finger of blame for a lack of change to another link in the chain (see 'ESG analysis in deep water', page 343; 'The source of the matter', page 345; 'Inside the analysts', page 346; Mixing materialities', page 350; 'Drilling the depths of ESG', page 354; 'Impediments and drivers of change in ESG analysis', page 357; 'The politics of finance', page 363; 'An agenda for improving ESG analysis', page 360).

Which brings us to the second point: very few businesses have begun to explore how to adapt their business models to be actively engaged for the good of society. While a managerial approach to corporate responsibility is a necessary part of an organisation, such discipline risks becoming an exercise in methodological competence if it does not help one reflect on the social utility of a business.

For this reason we looked at the business response to sustainable development and the evolving business models that try to address development issues. Some such as the 'Bottom of the Pyramid' model, were clearly off the mark and have done little to break the poverty cycle for those that most need it. Others, such as the concept of 'Inclusive Business' were encouraging, but with a caveat: to create scalable transformative change, the role of government needs to be an essential part of the process (see 'The buzz on business in development', page 334; 'The business of inclusion', page 337).

As we questioned the mainstream CSR field, we also began to look more closely at the importance of personal values in creating change, and the role of business schools in developing leaders of the future. While business leaders acknowledge the importance of addressing sustainability issues, not only at a societal level, but also from a business point of view, most companies struggled on execution, demonstrating a lack of coherence between the desire to act and the ability to implement bold action. So we proposed some building blocks for responsible holistic business education as a way of better equipping future managers for the challenges that sustainability presents. As such, in developing globally responsible leaders, business schools would not only need to set exemplary standards in terms of their own corporate responsibility and the teaching of same (see 'Practising what we preach', page 365), but schools would need to facilitate the journey of students so that they give voice to their values.

Ultimately, our sense that the CSR field was not providing sufficient space for critical questioning and radical action meant that at the end of 2010 we withdrew from writing quarterly reviews, to take stock, synthesise our analysis, and redirect our own efforts. One of the results of this reflection is the more radical critique provided in the extended introduction of this title (pages 1ff.). Our view is that the economic governance questions will not diminish, and so the CSR movement will begin to address them and, in time, we hope that the analysis we provided in 2010, contained in the following pages, will be of relevance and use.

1Q2010
January–March

Jem Bendell, Hanniah Tariq, Ian Doyle and Janna Greve

Corporate responsibility for economic inequality

In February 2010, the World Business Council for Sustainable Development (WBCSD) launched its *Vision 2050* report at the World CEO Forum in India.[1] The report was compiled by 29 leading global companies seeking to lay out a sustainable pathway to ensure the well-being of a global population of 9 billion people so that, by the year 2050, all will enjoy health, food, shelter, energy, mobility, education and other basics of life. The focus on how to shape the world for the benefit of all and how to bring it into reality marks a shift in the field of corporate responsibility. Rather than being reactive to pressures from various stakeholders and managing an organisation's internal or value chain relations in more responsible ways, this represents a broadening of the role of business in contributing to issues of public interest. This embrace of societal leadership was chronicled in *The Corporate Responsibility Movement*, published in 2009.[2] Such a shift poses a range of novel challenges for globally responsible leadership. In particular, how equipped is the private sector to support its leaders to appreciate the wide scope of human interests, and whether the visions and action plans will be limited through commercial interests? If that is the case, then stakeholder dialogue, and certain universal principles, will become a more important factor to bear in mind when it comes to the practice and discourse relating to corporate responsibility.

At the launch of the report, the WBCSD's president Mr Björn Stigson announced optimistically that

> The world already [had] the knowledge, science, technologies, skills and financial resources needed to achieve *Vision 2050*. However, concerted global action in the next decade will be required to bring these capabilities and resources together, putting the world on the path to sustainability.[3]

The solution was defined as one of technical capacity and the barrier to its effectiveness seen as a lack of collective action to mobilise such capacities for sustainability. Other organisations have identified quite different challenges for the achievement of a good society. For instance, many development agencies, including the UN Development Programme, previously identified power differentials as central to the ills of the world, and thus a lack of accountability of key decision-makers and institutions to those that are affected by their actions.[4] An unavoidable question faced by anyone looking at the future of humanity is whether everyone can thrive within ecological limits, if the current levels of economic inequality between nations and within them are to continue. Clearly, as recognised by the UN Environment Programme, a certain amount of redistribution of resource consumption will be required to achieve globally sustainable levels of consumption.[5]

The environmental challenge therefore means a new focus on wealth redistribution is required, although this was not explored in the WBCSD *Vision 2050* report.[6] Highlighting the challenge was a February 2010 article from the NGO Share the World's Resources. As the author, Mr Justin Frewen explains,

> It is simply not possible to effectively tackle poverty by relying solely on improving economic performance. The problem of socio-economic inequality has to be openly recognised and tackled. Failure to adopt such an approach will result in the gains from economic development flowing into the coffers of the wealthier sections of the population, leaving the poor as badly off as ever.[7]

The *Oxford Handbook of Economic Inequality* defines economic inequality as the disparity in the distribution of income and assets and its effect on constraining or creating the opportunities for people to live the lives they want to live.[8] The term describes inequality not only among individuals and groups within society but also geographical regions and nations.

Statistics indicate that it is on the increase worldwide. According to Richard Wilkinson, a social researcher on inequalities, and Professor Kate Pickett of the University of York and co-authors of the book *The Spirit Level*, UK and US income inequality has increased nearly 40% for the period 1979–2006 and 1975–2005 respectively.[9] In regards to wealth, the US non-governmental organisation (NGO) Inequality.org cited research from the Economic Policy Institute that the wealth of the richest 1% of US households was 125 times greater than the typical household in 1962 but, by 2004, it was 190 times. Furthermore, the same 1% owned 34.3% of the nation's private wealth.[10] So, despite the equalising effect that the economic crisis has had on an international level, inequalities are increasing within countries.

Supporting this trend was the *Wall Street Journal*'s 'Wealth Report', which indicated that, in 2009, the number of US households with a net worth of more than a $1 million (not including their primary residence) jumped by 16%, and ultra-high-net-worth households with assets greater than $5 million increased by 17%. Considering the implications of future cuts in public spending and rises in taxation due to the high unemployment and a government needing to service a huge budget deficit, the economically poor are unlikely to be participants in this trend—as Robert Frank states in the report 'Capital has recovered. Labor hasn't.'[11] In addition, in February 2010 in the UK, another country hit hard by the financial crisis, a National Equity Panel report showed that economic inequalities appear intractable, persisting from generation to generation.[12]

Recognising the challenge of the increasing concentration of wealth, Chinese Premier Mr Wen Jiabao announced at the start of China's annual parliamentary session in March that it will be a priority to develop new policy that reduces the gap between rich and poor in light of China's forecasted growth. He said,

> We will not only make the 'pie' of social wealth bigger by developing the economy, but also distribute it well . . . [We will] resolutely reverse the widening income gap.[13]

Economic inequality is therefore set to become a more important issue for businesses. Although the *Vision 2050* report from the WBCSD acknowledged social issues in its vision of a sustainable world, by not examining inequality it left a key issue sidelined.[14] How might business executives and others in the corporate responsibility field respond to growing levels of economic inequality, and rising public concern with it? Some see this is as public relations issue. In January 2010, Lifeworth Consulting launched its 2009 review of corporate responsibility entitled *Capitalism in Question*, which examined a range of new books written by business leaders that seek to defend capitalism as the best economic system for collective well-being.[15] One of the main defences against criticisms of economic inequality is that it is a necessary dimension to a capitalist system, as it is the outcome of incentives for work and innovation. However, such an argument will find it difficult to justify when considering the intergenerational persistence of inequality, which suggests economic reward is not based on merit, and is thus not a motivating factor for work and innovation. In addition, it raises questions of fairness that are unlikely to be won or provide the grounds for useful initiative. Rather, the first step to any decent engagement with this issue is to understand the problem better—the impact of economic inequality on society as a whole, and the potential impacts on business success.

One aspect of the problem of economic inequality is that it is both a result and driver of other forms of inequality in society.[16] Current discourse on inequality is usually linked to the treatment of individuals as it relates to gender, race, religion, ethnicity, age, or sexual orientation, which can translate into less economic opportunity and security, thus maintaining a cycle of economic inequality. Therefore, if one is concerned with such inequalities, it follows that economic inequalities need to be addressed. However, economic inequality is an issue in and of itself, aside from how it relates to other social divisions. One mistaken assumption is that the only problem with economic inequality per se is the existence of poverty. The extension of this assumption is that working on poverty reduction will resolve economic inequality—a mistaken supposition because the impact of any activity on economic inequality depends on the relative distribution of revenues from that activity. If staff and shareholders gain relatively more than those in poverty, then economic inequality is not reduced. Poverty is a persistent concern and companies are important to poverty reduction, with more becoming active in this area in a conscious way, rather than contributing simply as a by-product of their success.[17] Such a focus is not only important for the reduction of poverty, but for social and environmental reasons, as economic inequality is also a driver for the various dimensions of social inequality and also environmental destruction.

Research shows that the more unequal a society, the less peaceful, happy and healthy it is. Societies are less peaceful because crime rates rise amid inequality. They are less happy because there is more dissatisfaction among the economically poor, and more fear and alienation among the rich. This may feed through to quality of life, and thus the more unequal the society, the more ill health there is.[18] These dimensions were highlighted in the 2005 UN report *The Inequality Predicament*, which explained that general social cohesion and citizen well-being are negatively impacted by high rates of inequality.[19] A January 2010 *Newsweek* article entitled *The Recession Generation* confirmed this finding. Senior editor for international business and economics coverage, Rana Foroohar, while commenting on the consequences of the growing divide between the fortunes of big American firms and the average American worker, reported that the

> . . . division between capital and labor and the permanently high unemployment that it seems to encourage not only depresses wages, it depresses people; a large body of research shows they tend to withdraw from their communities and societies after being laid off . . . Parental unemployment has huge negative consequences for children, making them more likely to fall behind in school, repeat grades, and exhibit anxiety disorders.[20]

Research also shows that the environment suffers in more unequal societies. That is because, on the one hand, economically desperate people are not able to think of the future, and may have to degrade their environment in order to survive, and thus be forced to over-exploit their lands or seas. On the other hand, extremely wealthy people can be profligate in their use of resources, either as a matter of habit or taste or because of a concern for protecting themselves and their wealth from others.[21] Given these connections, even people with a narrow understanding of sustainability as an environmental challenge would still need to address inequality for such reasons. The inequality–environment nexus is increased with attempts to cut carbon emissions, as this inevitably raises the costs of products and services that require energy from carbon fuels. Unless climate-related policies address economic inequalities at the same time, they are unlikely to be socially just or politically sustainable.[22]

Once a deeper understanding of inequality is attained, it is important to understand how business relates to economic inequality through the way it is owned and governed. The relationship between dominant models of business ownership and the distribution of wealth in a given system is poorly understood. One study calls it 'a major challenge for future research.'[23] The logic of profit, as the extraction and distribution of a surplus from an economic activity to specific beneficiaries, such as shareholders, suggests that certain private forms of ownership are net central-isers of wealth. Research chronicled in 'Capitalism in Question' even found that stock markets have been extracting wealth from companies more than they have been capitalising them over the past decade.[24] Therefore, although corporations may be involved in raising the incomes of the poor, if not owned by the poor them-selves, as in the case of the Grameen Bank, they are adding to economic inequality through their activities. Poverty may be reduced in the short term, but the prob-lems of growing inequality remain. Economic inequality is clearly a difficult issue for most executives in privately held or publicly traded corporations to engage in: so how do they?

A 2010 study in the *Journal of Corporate Citizenship* by Lifeworth Consulting analysed the world's best corporate responsibility reports: 271 reports classified as A+ by the Global Reporting Initiative in 2009, of which 267 were able to be searched from online sources, were analysed for any mention of the term 'inequality', in the appropriate languages.[25] The reports that mentioned inequality were reviewed to determine how the organisation understood the issue, and how they addressed it. Dozens of reports mentioned poverty, but only 15 mentioned inequality: namely those of Abeinsa, Befesa, Banco Bradesco, Caja de Burgos, Caja Navarres, Compan-hia Paulista de Força e Luz Energia (CPFL Energia), Environmental Management Corporation (EMC), Garrigues, Larsen & Toubro, NovoNordisk, Obrascon-Huarte-Lain (OHL), Otto Group, Telefónica S.A., The Co-operative Group and United Microelectronics Corporation (UMC). Seven of these companies mention inequal-ity only in terms of gender, or age, or ethnicity, or other non-economic groupings or identities. Eight of the companies do mention the problem of inequality in general socio-economic terms, and their initiatives for addressing it. These companies are Abeinsa, Banco Bradesco, Caja de Burgos, Caja Navarres, Larsen & Toubro, Otto Group, Telefónica S.A., and The Co-operative Group. According to Lifeworth's find-ings, only 3% of the world's best corporate responsibility reports that were able to be searched online, mentioned the problem of economic inequality as an issue to address, with none explaining the specific problems of economic inequality, in terms of its impacts on well-being, security and the environment.

How do these few companies address economic inequality? In most cases through philanthropic activity, rather than core business. Banco Bradesco pro-motes staff volunteering to help targeted groups.[26] The Otto Group mentions its initiative to promote trade with economically disadvantaged cotton producers.[27] Caja de Burgos and Larsen & Toubro promote skills development and education among target groups.[28] The latter of these is the only company to make it clear that economic equality is a problem in society, although it does not explain why. The Larsen & Toubro report reads:

> India is a constellation of cities, towns and villages categorised by isolated and uneven growth. This growing divide between the rich and poor econ-omies has serious social implications for the country. It is imperative that

India aims for inclusive growth. On our part, we are leveraging our coun-trywide presence and capabilities to reduce disparities through specific interventions in education and healthcare. Our regular and close interac-tions with the local community members have enabled us to identify their pressing needs and we have strategically aligned our interests with those of the community. We view skill building and training as the most potent means of empowerment. Our 'Construction Skills Training Institutes' provide the unemployed rural workforce access to certified training and thereby helps them increase their employability and secure a livelihood.[29]

Only one company states the importance of economic equality as a central prin-ciple. Not surprisingly, that company is The Co-operative Group, which reminds us that 'member economic participation' is one of the principles of the co-operative movement. Its report notes that

social inclusion is about promoting greater equality between the most disadvantaged groups and the rest of society, to ensure that every person and community can play a full role in society. Financial inclusion is con-sidered a key component of social inclusion, and, since 1998, has occu-pied a firm foothold on the UK Government's political agenda.[30]

However, its report does not detail how it applies that principle of economic equal-ity in its relations with other stakeholders.

Only one company, Telefonica S.A., in its international divisions, specifically identified negative impacts of economic inequality to the business itself. It states that economic inequality restricts the market for mobile telephony so that there is a business case for acting to reduce such inequality. However, it does not specify why inequality, rather than poverty, is a specific concern, and does not present substan-tial initiatives on it.[31] This analysis of CR reports does not mean that companies, or specific individuals in companies, are not acting on a broader understanding of the problems of economic inequality in important ways but that, if they are, it is not yet reflected in their main CR communications.

This lack of attention to economic inequality is not surprising as the ISO 26000 draft and the Global Reporting Initiative (GRI) guidelines do not discuss the issue. However, the potential for more to be done through the GRI exists, as its guide-lines already suggest that companies disclose the distribution of revenues to stake-holders including staff, government and capital providers. In an analysis of two environmental, social and governance (ESG) methodologies to which Lifeworth Consulting had access, the investment analysis process also lacked a specific focus on economic inequality.

Could business executives working on voluntary corporate responsibility do more on this agenda? Or is active engagement with economic inequality impossi-ble both practically and ideologically for privately owned companies, whose prof-its accrue to shareholders, not those people involved in the economic activities? So suggests Dr Mick Blowfield, a Senior Research Fellow with the Smith School of Enterprise and the Environment at Oxford University. He states that 'CSR is not a revolutionary construct so will not result in fundamental shifts in imbalances of power and equality.' He adds that most work on economic inequality has focused on the question of raising and equalising wages within companies, particularly in supply chains, and improving supply chain transactions so suppliers receive a better financial deal in return for, and in support of, social and environmental improvements. Board remuneration has also been a hot topic, particularly for investors. Could this agenda be extended? Or is the transformative potential of voluntary responsibility essentially limited?

Answers will unfold through the actions of individual managers. At the very least one might expect a concern for economic inequality to encourage more action of the types we described above, and on promoting working arrangements that enable the less economically advantaged to participate more gainfully in a firm. For instance, companies can implement new working arrangements to allow people such as women with children to do their work and prevent job loss due to a family situation. They could also encourage such approaches from those they do business with. Such initiatives would not, however, address a systemic cause of growing inequality—the very ownership of so many for-profit corporations. Perhaps even the most fundamental attribute of business is not beyond the corporate responsibility lens, as some developments with employee share-ownership illustrated during the first months of 2010.

CSR and ownership

In March 2010 one British retailer announced it was sharing a GBP151 million bonus with its entire staff. The John Lewis Partnership (JLP) is 100% owned by its 70,000 staff. Its founder, John Spedan Lewis, created a governance system that would be both commercially viable while being democratic, giving every partner a voice in the business they co-own.[32] All employees received an equal percentage of profits for the last three years.[33] The respective figures were 20%, 13% and 15% for the 2008, 2009 and 2010 years—the bonuses equating to around two months' salary. The fact that profit is distributed equally reflects the efforts of every member of staff rather than concentrating bonus and power distribution only at a directorship level. As Mr Andy Street, JLP's managing director, explained in response to whether he deserved such a bonus, 'The partners must judge whether I've earned my bonus this year.'[34] The JLP model challenges the mythology that, to be important to both the governance and profitability of a company, one must be at 'the top'.[35]

The John Lewis Partnership reminds us that one way of addressing economic inequality successfully is through the very ownership of the business. As public liability companies (PLCs) generally focus on wealth generation or profit making through shareholder capitalism, they are influenced by short-term pressures. Yet, despite being the most common form of ownership model, alternatives such as cooperatives, or the hybrid, the employee-owned, or the completely mission-guided corporation do exist.[36] These ownership structures allow for new perspectives on the normative distribution of the generated capital to the various stakeholder groups, thus promoting 'the ownership solution' to the crises of capitalism, to quote Jeff Gates in his best-selling book some years ago.[37]

More specifically, these forms of ownership represent more democratic ways to manage organisations as they equalise power relations and decision-making processes. Additionally, these forms of ownership may decrease the distance between the stakeholder communities and allow for better stakeholder dialogue at ground level. Thus, it minimises risks in regard to stakeholder management and makes the fulfilment of corporate responsibility measures in support of various stakeholder communities more plausible and probable.[38] More significantly, as these models focus on the needs of the people, on job security and community welfare and not merely on profits, they can make a valuable contribution also in defeating economic inequality. Thus, as Mark Goyder, founding director of Tomorrow's Company asserts, shareholders' 'priorities and behaviours are aligned with the long-term interests of the company, and with the health of the soil in which it's being nourished'.[39]

Organic Valley has a mission is to save the family farm. It is one of the US's most well-known organic brands with over US$500 million in revenue, owned by the farmers that produce its products and operated in the form of a cooperative.[40] Another example of employee ownership is the Carris Companies. Its focus is on investing in employee quality of life through economic, educational and social accessibility provided by the company, and this in spite of the many workers who are unskilled at the time of employment. To do this, the company is 100% employee-owned and -governed, thus creating equality and sustaining the greater context of its employees beyond the workplace. What is significant about the Carris Companies is that the company transformed its initial structure to enable 100% employee ownership.[41] This indicates that it may be possible for privately owned companies to explore how to pluralise their ownership and make more employees co-owners.

One novel form of cooperative was profiled in NovEthic in the first months of 2010. Founded in Paris in 2004, Coopaname employs nearly 400 people. Seemingly unaffected by the economic crisis, the cooperative's turnover grew 20–30% in 2009. Its members create their own activity within the existing business. 'Rather than engaging in business creation or opt for the status of self-employed entrepreneur, they join in a company and they share and gain a salary from that,' explains Stéphane Veyer, CEO of Coopaname. The cooperative is open to anyone wishing to experience this form of employee entrepreneurship. 'Today is a very risky bet' for starting a business, says Veyer, and many people want autonomy from large corporations, but not necessarily to build a large business themselves. 'The primary interest of the cooperative is that there is no risk taking. Individuals do not need to borrow money, or to pledge their personal assets. At worst, they will not earn much money, but they do not lose much in case of a failure,' says the CEO. Risk is shared across the cooperative, covering potential losses and providing the option to cease trading more flexibly than in the case of a conventional closure of a business. In addition, it means less paperwork for launching a business, and keeping one's normal status within employment law. Another advantage of this particular cooperative model is project support, coaching and monitoring. Members do not have to do accounting and administrative management, as these services are also shared. A third of Coopaname activities are related to crafts and fashion, a third to services for individuals and a third to knowledge services. Ten per cent of each employee's sales allows Coopaname to cover the costs of running the company, supporting a team of eight people responsible for central administration. Stéphane Veyer also emphasises the human relations in this type of participatory work. Regular meetings are organised to allow the sharing of experiences and information and generate new business ideas. He asserts, 'It is a very contemporary theme, unlike the cheesy image of cooperatives too often widespread . . . Very often, the economic and social innovation comes from these groups.'[42]

In March 2010, Sappi, the global pulp and paper group, announced a black economic empowerment deal in South Africa which would represent an empowerment transfer of approximately 30% of the company's South African business to employees, black managers, a community foundation and strategic partner companies. Commenting on the deal, Sappi Limited CEO Ralph Boëttger asserted 'broad-based black economic empowerment is a key requirement for sustainable growth and social development in South Africa, . . . [and that] . . . the transaction recognises the crucial role that our staff play in making the company a success.'[43]

A similar deal was initiated in February by Rezidor, the multinational hotel group who expanded its partnership with Mvelaphanda Holdings, a black-empowered company based in South Africa. The deal would ensure that all existing and future Rezidor hotels in South Africa, Lesotho and Swaziland would be managed by Mvelaphanda Holdings.[44]

The South African government has been trying to address inequality through its Broad Based Black Economic Empowerment Act of 2003 (BBBEE). The BBBEE is designed to broaden the economic base of the country after apartheid.[45] A January 2010 article from *BusinessWeek* in South Africa cited a 'Who Owns Whom?' empowerment survey which suggested that the policy has been an effective strategy with 69 transactions worth R82.7 billion completed between January 2007 and August 2009.[46] But, while this is an indicator of how black empowerment policy is starting to be integrated into the gross domestic product of the South African economy, it is not necessarily a true reflection of overall equality. An Organisation for Economic Cooperation and Development (OECD) report released in January 2010 concluded that the gap between the rich and poor in South Africa had not only widened between race groups but also within race groups, suggesting that the government needs other policies besides black empowerment to redistribute wealth.[47]

Companies could also help promote more economic inequality within their spheres of influence by seeking to work with more employee-owned enterprises, either as suppliers or business partners. This philosophy can also apply to the informal sector, where many people work for themselves in family units. For cooperatives such as the John Lewis Partnership, The Cooperative Group, or Coopaname, this would appear a natural application of their philosophy.

Yet, despite these emerging models, it is early days for an economic inequality agenda within corporate responsibility, with some even thinking that it is not possible. There are certainly some important issues to address, beyond the challenge of how a privately owned company might seek to pluralise its ownership. For example, how should social enterprises respond to this analysis? Many such entrepreneurs talk about seeking private investment and one day going public. Yet, back in 2006, Anita Roddick said that 'going public' was the worst thing she'd done in the history of The Body Shop. Until that point, the link between her ideas and the company's practices had been direct. Once the business was publicly listed, she had to present her ideas to the board which more often than not said, 'you can't do that: you'd be stealing from the shareholders'. From that point on, she recounted, there was less sustainability-oriented innovation in the company.[48]

What are the implications for the initiatives developing metrics for social impact? None of initiatives that we are aware of examines how the ownership of the organisations involved in a particular social project then affect inequality. Indeed, the discourse on social enterprise, promoted by Schwab Foundation, Acumen Fund, among others, tends to make no distinction between organisations on the grounds of their ownership. Given an awareness of the downsides of economic inequality, rather than poverty alone, this approach will not be tenable.

What are the implications for responsible investment? On the one hand, an awareness of the societal and long-term financial harm of high economic inequality could necessitate a new reflection on what to seek from companies and what that means for their own ownership stakes and rights. On the other hand, economic inequality might not be such a bad thing for investors. That is because, drawing on Marxist analysis, a pool of poorly paid people who are concerned about keeping their jobs while surrounded by poorer unemployed people, can be seen as functional to capitalists because it depresses workers' demands for improved pay and conditions. Sociological research indicates that in some countries the levels of intransigent inequality are not being perceived by the poor in society, who believe conversely that they are living in a less class-based society and have more opportunities for upwards economic mobility.[49] In this sense, some people are living in what we can term 'glass corridors', with barriers to their opportunities invisible to them but, nevertheless, shaping the course of their lives.[50] Is it a step too far for responsible investors to explore the financial implications of different levels of economic inequality? If they cannot, or the evidence of a business case for reducing economic inequality is unclear, what are the implications for proponents of responsible investment and the regulators of investors?

It seems that economic inequality will become a challenging area in the future of corporate responsibility, social enterprise and responsible investment, as well as an added reason for innovations in forms of enterprise ownership.

Unveiling corporate responsibility in the Muslim world

The high rate of economic growth in the Middle East has created a veritable Mecca of economic and infrastructural development. In the main, this also brought a single-minded attitude of making money without due consideration for the resources and people necessary to maintain such growth. Highlighting this concern was the 2010 Human Rights Watch (HRW) *World Report* released in January 2010 which summarised human rights conditions in more than 90 countries and territories worldwide.[51] Reflecting this exploitation, the report strongly condemned the Gulf States for their role in human rights abuses of migrant labourers.[52] The starkest reminder of this trend was the announcement in March 2010 by the NGO Migrant Rights that every two days a migrant worker attempts or commits suicide in Kuwait.[53] This followed another Migrant Rights article in January 2010 which asserted that one of the top five migrants' rights stories in the Middle East for 2009 was the widespread abuse of workers' rights by the private sector.[54] This is not a recent trend, as Human Rights Watch also documented in a May 2009 report that labour and human rights abuses were 'commonplace' among migrant workers in the United Arab Emirates (UAE).[55] The report also detailed that workers regularly endured extremely low wages, restrictions on freedom to associate, unfair recruitment policies, self-coverage of medical and administrative expenses and illegal control of passports and visas. Furthermore, despite attempts by the government to reduce such abuses, they had not improved since they were last documented by the organisation in 2006.[56]

These findings directly touch on a problem of limited responsible business practices among companies in Muslim regions. In a February 2010 article entitled *Islam and CSR* in the *Journal of Business Ethics*, authors Geoffrey Williams, CEO of OWW Consulting, which specialises in CSR, and John Zinkin, Associate Professor at Nottingham University Business School stated that

> empirical papers in this area appear to show that Muslims may not be as concerned about ethical business behaviour as members of other religions [and that] Muslims score elements that are assumed to matter in determining socially responsible business behaviour less highly than people of other religions.[57]

In a survey of Middle East executives in January 2010, the Sustainability Advisory Group reported that most of the 106 businesses questioned were not addressing environmental issues. In response to the survey, Dr Mohammed Raouf, the manager of the environment programme at the Gulf Research Centre, confirmed that 'The results represent the Middle East; the awareness of stakeholders here is not as high as in the West.'[58]

A possible reason, according to an exploratory study on CR conducted in the UAE in 2007, is that most CSR activity in the UAE is performed by multinational corporations such as Intel, DHL or Shell, and not by local businesses.[59] The same study confirmed a general lack of defined policies of the kind found in the West, supporting an Arab Planning Institute's 2009 conference finding that current CSR was at a nascent stage in the region (Middle East and North Africa [MENA]).[60]

This finding is supported by a 2008 report by the Dubai-based Hawkamah Corporate Governance Institute. It found that no publicly listed company in the MENA region followed best practice when it came to corporate governance, primarily due to the fact that it was not required.[61]

The report also highlighted a number of traditional factors that contribute to the state of CSR in the region such as:

> the region's historic isolation from the global economy, large regional banks that were on hand to provide cash for companies, strong economic growth, and undeveloped capital markets. The Gulf's family-owned businesses, which account for some 90% of commerce in the region, often shy away from disclosing details of their business affairs; and in many cases, government-related enterprises are murky, too.

The Gulf States are not the only region with limited voluntary CSR initiatives. A February 2010 release by the French NGO the Fédération Internationale des Ligues des Droit de l'Homme, which defends human rights, reported that multinationals abuse workers' rights with impunity in Algeria.[62] In light of CSR WeltWeit (the German information portal on CSR)'s comments that it is still the exception for Algerian companies to take on responsibilities in the social arena, it would seem that Algeria is still developing in this area.[63]

An absence of companies and governments from Muslim regions within various international dialogues on voluntary regulation will not help in addressing current limits in their responsible business practice. One recommendation of HRW's 2006 report was that companies should consider joining the UN Global Compact and implementing its human-rights- and labour-law-based principles.[64] In another 2006 study on CSR in the MENA region, Melsa Ararat, the Director of the Corporate Governance Forum of Turkey, observed that 'International campaigns, programs, projects such as Global Compact, WB-IFC and UNDP programs were only prevalent in Turkey, Lebanon, Egypt.'[65]

Yet, by 2009, only an estimated 10% of the signatories to the United Nations Global Compact (UNGC) and just seven members of the United Nations Principles on Responsible Investment (UNPRI) belong to the world's top 10 Muslim countries by population.[66] None of the governments or companies party to the Voluntary Principles on Human Rights and Security is from a Muslim region, which is a significant absence given that a large proportion of the world's oil supply is from largely Muslim regions.[67]

There is an apparent paradox between these observations on limited engagement in corporate responsibility in predominantly Muslim countries, and the view that there is inherent harmony between Islamic principles and the general discourse of responsible business practice. In the same study on Islam and CSR, Zinkin and Williams also found that not only are Islamic principles completely compatible with those suggested by the UN Global Compact but that 'Islam exceeds the requirements of the Global Compact in a number of important ways.'[68]

It has also been observed by Johan Graafland and colleagues that there is a convergence between Islamic business ethics and socially responsible business conduct.[69]

In light of this alignment between Muslim values and responsible business, perhaps the global discourse on CR could benefit from its contribution to responsible business practice. Interestingly enough, in a January 2010 release from the Sustainability Advisory Group, Mrs Gayatri Raghwa, an environmental education specialist at the Environmental Agency Abu Dhabi (EAD), affirmed that 'Islam puts big emphasis on conserving natural resources. We should use the power of religion.'[70]

So, despite the common perceptions that CR in the Muslim world is less of a priority, a vibrant discussion is beginning that could shape business society relations and potentially international dialogue around CR. It is a discussion made more urgent by the growing international influence of business and finance from Muslim countries, as part of an 'Eastern Turn' in global economic power, presaged in Lifeworth's 2008 annual review of responsible enterprise.[71]

Muslim CR in transition

Philanthropy is often the most visible aspect of corporate responsibility in Muslim regions with Gulf Cooperation Council (GCC) countries donating approximately $15–20 billion in 2009.[72] This impulse can be seen to be a result of the community responsibility and charitable giving discourse found in the religion. However, this focus on philanthropy should not be taken to mean an ad hoc approach to CSR, as, given the poor performance of governments on social provision in a many Muslim regions, business has had no choice but to be involved in reducing the social and environmental problems and create a safer environment to conduct business. It is also important to note that the perception of philanthropy in the region as unstructured giving does not take into account the responsiveness implicit in the nature of such social transactions. In Saudi Arabia, for instance, it was observed that the 'business community is very much tuned to the development challenges facing the kingdom'.[73] Companies in the UAE are also displaying 'strong, yet perhaps indirect awareness of CSR and some proactive practices' despite the lack of public policy as found in the West.[74]

Yet governments in the Muslim world are also increasingly defining the agenda for CSR. In response to the widespread abuse of workers' rights, Ziad Baroud, Lebanon's Minister of Interior, informed relevant stakeholders in December 2009 that the 'government will be taking steps towards the protection of migrant domestic workers in Lebanon.'[75] In Turkey, Morocco, Palestine and Jordan the public sector is helping characterise the role of business with the introduction of corporate governance codes, disclosure and reporting requirements and labour laws.[76] The Indonesian government previously enacted a law that expects companies to take on CSR-related activities.[77] Meanwhile, the government in the UAE is carefully reinforcing the concept of a positive business role in society with a conference held on *Corporate Social Responsibility as a National Duty* in Dubai in 2009; and in Egypt the first national conference on CSR was promoted by the Ministry of Investment in 2008.[78]

Some countries with large Muslim populations such as Indonesia are also displaying increasing interest in corporate responsibility and its intersection with personal religious values. While interviewing employees at a steel plant in Indonesia, Daromir Rudnyckyj, assistant professor at the University of Victoria, found that there is 'increasing focus on relating Islamic practice to daily work at official company functions'.[79] Consultancies such as the Emotional and Spiritual Quotient (ESQ) Leadership Center are also emerging in Indonesia which carry out 'spiritual training', or ESQ training, which is 'business management, life-coaching, and self-help principles with Islamic history and examples from the life of the Prophet Muhammad'.[80] ESQ is being implemented in human resource development by state-owned and private enterprises as well as government offices in Indonesia.[81]

Thus, despite the perception that corporate responsibility in the Muslim world is in its infancy, there are strong indicators that is gaining momentum. The negative view could be a result of the fact that measures that attempt to 'implement predetermined and so-called universal recipes often demand a style of cooperation that does not exist locally'.[82] In Saudi Arabia, for example, Emtairah *et al.* found that 'contrary to expectations drawn from external reviews, CSR in Saudi Arabia can be characterised as responsive within the existing normative and institutional pressures in the local context'.[83]

Local support and facilitation for CSR is observed to be growing in Muslim regions. For example, a key trend in the Middle East according to the Sustainability Advisory Group is a 'strengthening of the agenda' since the first CSR conferences were held in the UAE and Kuwait in 2004.[84] They also found that across the Middle East there is an emerging trend of recognition through awards such as the *CSR Arabia Award* launched in 2008 by the Emirates Environmental Group and the GCC's *CSR Award Scheme*.[85]

Standards are also being developed simultaneously to guide companies in assessing their role and impact. In 2009 the Accounting and Auditing Organisation for Islamic Financial Institutions (AAOIFI)[86] developed the AAOIFI Standard 7 on CSR in order to ascertain standards on the definition of corporate social responsibility for these institutions.[87] According to the institution, the principles are applicable across the board for Islamic institutions regardless of the legal form, country of incorporation or size.[88] However, in order to maintain flexibility that respects diverse operating environments, the standards are divided into mandatory and recommended sections allowing adaptability to local circumstances.

Training support for practitioners is increasing in the region with a CSR Practitioner Workshop held in Dubai, UAE, in January 2010 by the Centre for Sustainability and Excellence (CSE).[89] This increase in professional support can be observed to be a response to new indices, guidelines and principles emerging in the Muslim world. For example, the Saudi Arabian Responsible Competitiveness Index (SARCI) was developed by the Saudi Arabian General Investment Authority, the King Khalid Foundation and AccountAbility in 2008, intended to help companies evaluate and control their social, environmental and economic impact.[90]

CSR and the Muslim paradox

Despite the absence of companies and governments from Muslim countries in many international CSR initiatives, dialogue on CSR in the Muslim world is not limited to within national boundaries. Saudi Arabia hosted a CSR conference in late 2008 in conjunction with the World Bank Institute, the United Nations and Harvard University.[91] Kosta Petrov, conference manager for the 5th annual CSR summit held in Dubai of the same year confirmed that, 'despite the image sometimes portrayed of regional companies, more and more are demonstrating their leadership by advancing responsible corporate citizenship'.[92]

The international exposure that has been generated by such events raises the question of engaging in more effective forms of mutual exchange and learning for CSR to be able to build on the rich cultural values that inherently exist in societies—in this case Muslim societies. Throughout the development of the concept and practice of CSR, lessons learned characterise it as a contextual business response to external and internal drivers rather than an absolute model that can be followed and replicated in developing countries. Consequently, views and approaches towards corporate responsibility have been observed to differ according to region and circumstance even within relatively similar countries.[93]

One of the major problems with the concept of CSR according to Dr Michael Hopkins, course director of the advanced CSR certificate at the University of Geneva, is that there are multitudes of definitions but no overall agreement about the nature of it.[94] This problem acutely manifests itself in the Muslim world as, despite individual efforts within different sectors, there is a lack of a consolidated view and engagement on the business role in society. This was the observation in a November 2009 survey carried out by the Sustainability Advisory Group on Middle Eastern Leaders' opinions. Across the UAE, in Saudi Arabia, Lebanon, Oman, Palestine, Jordan and Qatar, approximately 30% of the respondents felt that the largest impediment to implementing CSR was the challenge of defining what CSR means to their businesses.[95] In a similar survey carried out in Turkey it was found that 'there is confusion over the definition of Corporate Social Responsibility (CSR) and this confusion reflects [sic] itself on the practices of CSR.'[96]

What this demonstrates is a cultural divide which needs to be addressed so that Muslim businesses can engage more productively in the global dialogue around CSR. In order to facilitate engagement, the current discourse on CSR will have to be rendered applicable to the specific context of businesses. Research on corporate governance in the Middle East conducted by Schieffer, Lessem and Al-Jayyousi shows that the 'human–social dimensions and the relevance of originally western topics (e.g. CSR) only became evident through a re-rooting of such concepts in local soil'.[97]

Hence discovering the distinctive impulses of the Muslim world could offer new perspectives on the global debate around corporate responsibility.[98] One area where the Muslim faith could have a real impact is in the world of finance. As Shari'ah or Islamic law shapes the Islamic banking system, and the religion prohibits excessive speculation, bans certain economic activities and also the charging interest while encouraging profit sharing, Islamic principles could be used to shape more responsible approaches to finance.[99]

While there is inadequate work done on labour and human rights, and the Muslim presence in the global dialogue around CSR is only starting to emerge, some innovators and leaders in the Muslim world are actively trying to define and promote the appropriate role of business in society. Williams and Zinkin claim that this 'paradox is due to the failure of western businesses to communicate credibly the relevance and importance of the CSR model to the Muslim world'.[100] But the reverse is also true—so that there is a deeper, more holistic concept of CSR for the Muslim world, there will also need to be a space to effectively convey its own agenda within the context of a globalised economy.

As the authors of *The Eastern Turn in Responsible Enterprise* conclude: 'The rise of Asia reminds us of the diversity of our world, and therefore the diversity of ideas about social, economy and politics . . .' They quote Anwar Ibrahim, former deputy prime minister of Malaysia, in explaining how 'the challenge at hand is to conceive a common vision of the future which goes beyond our current concerns and preoccupations, advancing towards the creation of a global community, dominated neither by the East or the West, but dedicated to the ideals of both'.[101]

2Q2010
April–June

Jem Bendell, Ian Doyle and Tapan Sarker

From Global Compact to global impact

In June 2010, the largest corporate responsibility (CR) initiative in the world, the United Nations Global Compact (UNGC), celebrated ten years since its launch, with a Leaders Summit in New York. Celebration was justified, as the UNGC has done more than any initiative to globalise the idea that voluntarily enhancing the social, environmental and ethical performance of business can be both good for business, and important for the world. But introspection was also required, for two main reasons. First, the relationship between business and society has not improved markedly in the last ten years, with problems including spiralling inequality, rising carbon emissions, commodity inflation and speculation, and financial crises, all suggesting ineffective economic governance. As a result, corporate responsibility (CR) practitioners need to grapple more clearly with these systemic problems if they are to provide significant solutions for sustainable development. Second, as CR is now an established agenda and there are hundreds of CR initiatives worldwide, so the role for the UN in the CR space will need to evolve. Therefore the UNGC may need to clarify its role, specifically what the UN brings to CR and what CR brings to the UN. Given that the UN is the premier global political forum, and the UNGC is about business, so global economic governance would appear a natural and needed niche for the UNGC to embrace. Therefore, to coincide with the anniversary, the *Journal of Corporate Citizenship* published an analysis of the currently limited role of the UNGC in addressing economic governance.[1] It argued the need for business support for an enhanced role for the UN in helping member states regulate markets for the common good.

   The tenth anniversary prompted others to discuss the role of the UNGC, both past and future.[2] The Leaders Summit reflected some of that thinking, with emphasis placed on the need to reach a 'tipping point' in corporate responsibility and sustainability. Yet, if it is to be effective over the next ten years in encouraging that tipping point, the UNGC may need to evolve its approach. Previously the international reach and pulling power of the UN flag was enough to make the UNGC a remarkable contribution, but in future it may need to add a third strength: interfacing CR with economic governance challenges. In doing that, its secretariat and participants could enhance their understanding of four interconnected areas: social change processes, the ethics and accountability of new governance mechanisms, ways and means of reforming economic governance towards sustainable development, and the evolving role of the UN in world affairs, including economic affairs.

Some limitations of the UNGC's current approach were illustrated by (not within) the report on CEO opinions on CR and sustainability, by an international consulting firm, which set the tone for the Leaders Summit. On the one hand, it had some useful analysis of cross-cutting changes that are needed in mainstream CR, such as changes to the investment practices and regulations to internalise more externalities.[3] It is promising to see such ideas expressed by CEOs, as hitherto they had only been discussed by more critical analysts.[4] On the other hand, the report and the research behind it appeared designed to make the participating businesses feel comfortable, avoiding challenging questions. So much so that, of the 766 CEOs who responded, 81% agreed that CR issues are 'fully embedded into the strategy and operations of my company'.

The identity of those CEOs was not revealed, so some participants speculated on whether BP's Tony Hayward had participated in the survey. *The Economist* even reflected that, as BP had been considered a leader in CR and a member of the UNGC, the deep-water disaster was casting an 'oily cloud' over the celebrations in New York. They wrote, 'Among the many victims of BP's catastrophic oil spill in the Gulf of Mexico is the campaign to promote socially responsible behaviour among big companies.'[5] Writing before the Summit in the *FT*, Professor David Scheffer, of the Northwestern University School of Law in Chicago, wrote that the BP disaster illustrates how 'corporate self-regulation and public oversight have failed. We need to rethink how companies operate in a fragile world and how governments monitor them.'[6] Over 5,000 CEO members of the UNGC did not even respond to the opinion survey requested of them by the UN. Some delegates thought the questions were rather bland, with delegate Dr Ven Pillay of the University of Pretoria wondering why CEOs were not asked direct questions such as whether they would have their bonuses linked to independent measures of their firm's social and environmental performance: surely not a worry for them if CR is embedded in strategy and operations already?

The report was what one would expect from a consultancy that seeks to tickle not ruffle the feathers of c-suite executives. That 81% figure may do wonders in drumming up new business from CEOs feeling they are behind the game. Over the past decade the UNGC has utilised the pro bono support of management consultants to establish its work programmes, and been keen to appear a trusted and careful partner of business. Yet might the UNGC have reached a stage after ten years where it need not concern itself with appearing corporate-friendly and focus more on setting an ambitious change agenda, generating and disseminating methodologically sound, incisive and informative data on the realities of corporate responses to sustainable development? If so, are the academics up to it? There is less institutional self-interest in a university spending resources on a CEO opinion survey—they can not leverage the relations and profile in the same way after such a study.

This illustrates one area where the UNGC could evolve its practices to meet new needs. In light of the pro bono input from established consulting firms to build UNGC programmes, the consulting firms received high-profile access and acclaim in return. This approach helped the UN to speak the language of business, and be understood. However, the established consulting firms rarely challenge large corporations as they seek to serve them, and they rarely propose innovative ideas with impact because their business model does not allow time for a depth of reflection and research. Going forward, the UNGC needs to reach out beyond the conservative consulting firms in order to better encourage learning on how to reach a tipping point.

The hope of having a wider systemic impact was expressed by the UNGC secretariat, in part by their increasing use of the terminology of sustainable development as an integrated goal for economy and society, which corporate responsibility initiatives should work towards. This new emphasis was captured well by Professor Malcolm McIntosh of Griffith Business School, during the leaders' commentaries posted on the summit website.[7] A goal of reaching 20,000 members in ten years was presented by the UNGC as a vision in keeping with its new emphasis on systemic change, which raises questions about people's understanding of 'systemic'. Member recruitment has been a key focus for the UNGC during its first ten years. That has meant it has sought to appear a safe and trusted partner to most corporations. However, that approach has meant that some more challenging issues have been sidestepped or sidelined. To achieve greater change, these difficult issues need to be addressed, which will mean some companies become nervous or critical. Might the time be right for the UNGC to show leadership in pressing ahead in concert with true global leaders, rather than seeking to satisfy a greater number of business members?

The Deputy Director of the UN Global Compact, Gavin Power, expressed a more ambitious call that 'companies and investors must now work together to identify and overcome the barriers that prevent sustainability from being permanently embedded into the majority of global business activity'.[8] In releasing *The Blueprint for Corporate Sustainability Leadership* the UNGC sought to define what it wants to see from participants, though they made it clear this document did not constitute a new requirement. The blueprint includes some useful emphasis on 'taking action in support of broader UN goals and issues' including 'advocacy and public policy engagement'.[9] It is a start in outlining the importance of contributing to a movement for a transformation in economy, but it provides thin advice on what is a highly complex area. The phrase 'tipping point' was used throughout the Leaders Summit, which was appropriate given we were in the city that is home to journalist Malcolm Gladwell who popularised the term. However, as any social scientist who has read his book understands, there is no clear theory of what a 'tipping point' is or how it is reached. If our topic here is how to create systemic change, where sufficient numbers of individuals or organisations change in order to re-pattern the way most of us behave, then there are many fields of social science that we can draw upon. Draw on them we must, if we are to be serious and not rhetorical about seeking systemic change.

Insights on social change processes (in society and in meetings) can come from organisational change management, marketing, innovation and entrepreneurship, behavioural economics, social movements studies, network sciences, systems theories and cybernetics, institutional theory, social psychology, sociologies of power, design thinking, theories of art practice, and more. As sustainability and CR professionals begin to talk more explicitly about catalysing change in society, they need to find ways to draw upon such fields, integrate their insights and make them practical for practitioners and policy-makers.

Two examples of the application of schools of thought on social change to the CR field are social movements theory[10] and network sciences.[11] However, the fields receiving the most attention are those that are most known to management consultants—such as marketing (the basis of most of the evidence in the book *Tipping Point*) and organisational change management (for instance, the current popularity of the U-process to structure the design and facilitation of change-oriented meetings). It is not certain that the leading management consultants recognise the wealth of knowledge on social change. For instance, in April 2010, McKinsey published a matrix on social change, suggesting it was a new contribution,[12] when it was an unintentional recycling of philosopher Ken Wilber's four-quadrant model of the locations of change.[13]

If the Leaders Summit marks the beginning of a wider acknowledgement among CR and sustainable business professions of the need to serve systemic transformations, then it needs to be followed rapidly by a new awareness about where to learn about such change. The famous management consultancies may not be the places to look for the relevant expertise, as there is a level of conceptual development required that costs time and money that most consulting firms cannot afford.

As becoming smarter about social change processes is a key imperative for the UNGC and its members, then being smarter about the ethics of shaping such change is also key. The UNGC is said by some, such as the official summit blogger Professor Dirk Matten, to be a part of an emerging global governance architecture.[14] If initiatives such as the UNGC and other private regulatory initiatives do achieve such power so that governance is a useful term to describe their role, then this raises issues of accountability and fairness. In whose name do they govern?[15] A prerequisite for addressing this issue and developing appropriate processes is for it to be recognised as warranting attention. Too often when people raise these issues, including at the Leaders Summit, senior business people cite how their business-like approach means they do not have time for such philosophical debates.

To become smarter about the new mechanisms of governance, we could look towards the political economists who have been looking at business–state relations in depth for decades. The UN's own research institute on development issues published a book in 2010 looking at precisely this issue.[16] Through conceptual and historical analysis, as well as case studies from Brazil, Chile, India, Mexico, Peru,

Russia and South Africa, this book examined the means by which corporations influence social, labour market and development policy, the reasons for their positions and the scope of their influence. It demonstrated how, under appropriate conditions, and with the right guidance, the inevitable political influence of large firms can be prevented from undermining inclusive development. Such in-depth examinations of the issues have not found a place within the debates and initiatives of the UNGC these past years. One reason for this is the interests of the political economists themselves, where the focus is on academic publishing rather than engaging policy-makers, civil society and companies to see how their insights are relevant to practice. Another reason appears to be the limited interest from UNGC participants and conveners in engaging with intellectually challenging analyses, where synergies with voluntary corporate action are not immediately obvious. If these silos persist for the next ten years then we will not progress far in enhancing the accountability and ethics of the emerging forms of private governance.

A third area to become smarter about is economic governance. The question at the heart of CR in general and the UNGC in particular is the impact of business and finance on society. The most important changes in that relationship have gone unaddressed by the UNGC. In recent years the financial crisis has highlighted the social impact of changes in market governance. Key issues include monetary reform and commodity market regulation, as recognised by the G20 French presidency. Large corporations and their associations have an impact on those policy deliberations, so their positions on these issues should be under examination and discussion within the UNGC.[17] The UNGC has stayed clear of issues of trade and investment policy in the last ten years. This approach has allowed it to move the CR agenda forward without protracted and highly politicised debates about trade agreements. However, the time has now come for core economic governance issues to be addressed, as well as the influence of business over related policy-making, if a tipping point in CR is to be reached. UNGC has increased its work on the public policy dimensions of CR, for instance with the Bertelsmann Foundation[18] and through a *Guide on Responsible Business in Conflict-Affected and High-Risk Areas*, which was particularly welcomed by Asian business delegates during speeches from the podium.[19] This work will be important to scale up; indeed, it could be the start of a more comprehensive engagement with economic governance issues at national and international levels.

A fourth and related area for smarter action in future is the role of the UN in global economic governance. Since its creation post World War II, the UN has been marginalised on economic issues by the traditional economic powers. Countries in the OECD and G8 have worked for the World Bank, International Monetary Fund (IMF), World Trade Organisation (WTO) and Bank of International Settlements (BIS) to be the key agents of global economic governance, because that is where they dominate the agenda and/or decisions. The UN is the closest we get to a democratic process representing interests of governments of the world, and so its initiatives on economic governance issues have the backing of the majority of the world's governments, unlike the institutions mentioned above, or latterly the G20 club of powerful nations. Various parts of the UN system have sought a voice on the recent financial crisis, and been roundly ignored by the world's largest economies. Indeed, recommendations from its agencies such as UNCTAD would, if heeded, have averted the current levels of economic inequality and instability that arose from a market fundamentalism imposed on nations by the IMF and World Bank. Some officials within the UNGC may have their own views on economic governance, trade and development, but the UN has in its mandate a role on economic governance. Moreover, as economic power continues to shift from the West to the rest, it is likely that as we emerge from this financial crisis, the majority of UN member states will no longer acquiesce to the dominance of global economic governance by institutions that are not representative of their interests. Therefore, thinking ahead about the future of the UN, it would make sense for the UNGC to consider whether the interests of the majority of its business participants will best be served by a revamped role for the UN in global economic governance. That agenda may not be interesting to some company members based in the OECD or G8 countries, which have been the traditional leaders of CR and active in UNGC. However, the majority of UNGC members are from the rest of the world, and together could become the new leaders in a new phase of CR focused on systemic change in economic governance, that revitalises role of the UN in a more multi-polar world.

Simply through its existence, the UNGC has provided us new opportunities to imagine pathways towards sustainable futures for the planet. That is due to the incredible efforts of Georg Kell and his dedicated band of professionals and volunteers, who have been inspired by the idea that this could be a historic and game-changing initiative. Ten years in, now could be a time for the same level of bold creativity that gave rise to the Compact in the first place: to move from a global compact to a global impact. Some bureaucrats close to Ban Ki-moon regard him more as an administrator than a visionary leader.[20] If that means we won't see the UNGC secretariat leading the way in addressing economic governance issues, then it will be necessary for the progressive participants to join together and form smaller groups that can learn together about social change, governance accountability, pressing economic challenges, and a revitalised role for the UN in global economic governance. If the UNGC does not address these areas in tangible ways in the coming years, then those people who say the UNGC was designed to avoid core economic justice issues will be the ones writing its history.

The buzz on business in development

Several events in the second quarter of 2010 highlighted the increasing attention to the role of business in development. In April, the World Business Council for Sustainable Development (WBCSD) launched the *Inclusive Business Challenge* to encourage more leadership from business in meeting the Millennium Development

Goals (MDGs).[21] Also that month an international summit in New Delhi focused on corporate social responsibility (CSR) as a strategy for inclusive development.[22] In New York, the Business Civic Leadership Center (BCLC) and United Nations Office for Partnerships hosted a conference on the theme of *Investing in the Millennium Development Goals*.[23] In May, the 2010 World Business and Development Awards were launched. Present was Mr Jean Rozwadowski, Secretary-General of the International Chamber of Commerce (ICC), who said that 'increasingly the private sector is a critical component for increasing aid effectiveness and achieving the Millennium Development Goals'.[24] The positive contributions of business to development were also highlighted in a report launched in June 2010 in Amsterdam by the National Committee for International Cooperation and Sustainable Development (NCDO),[25] and with two reports at the Leaders Summit in New York. *A Global Compact for Development* presented a range of initiatives and support for business to contribute to development, and *Innovating for a Brighter Future: The Role of Business in Achieving the MDGs* discussed progress made since 2000 on this agenda with the UNGC.[26]

Given this growing attention to the role of business in development, it is important for a moment to step back from the language and the institutions involved, and note that business did development before development did development. This is to say that business is the process of making and trading things with and for each other and is therefore a process through which people, families and societies advance—the very meaning of 'development'. It has only been since the late 1940s that the modern concept of international development as a project that would be pursued by national aid agencies, international bodies and non-governmental organisations began to take shape.[27] In the past few years this 'international development community' has begun to engage business in new ways, rather than simply through seeking its regulation by government for more social development gain. In addition, with the rise in voluntary acceptance of corporate responsibility for impacts on society, and new creative thinking about how social and environmental challenges can become drivers of innovation, so companies have been looking again at the preoccupations of the international development community. In 2005 authors Jem Bendell and Wayne Visser called for the two academic communities connected to each area, namely business studies and international development studies, to find more means of sharing their insights and learning from each other.[28] Events and discussions in the second quarter of 2010 highlighted the need for still further engagement across disciplines, and between businesses and experts in international development.

The passing of the influential management academic C.K. Prahalad in April 2010 led to a new wave of discussion of one concept about business and development that some corporations have been pursuing for the past five years: namely, business directed at the Bottom, or Base, of the Pyramid (BoP).[29] BoP discussions and initiatives centre on the development of products for the poor in ways that are commercially viable. The type of initiatives praised and the problems with these from a deeper development understanding, highlight how there is still much to be learned.

As Anand Kumar, assistant professor of marketing at IIMA, has pointed out, many existing initiatives fail to target those who are truly needy. Instead, many corporations engaged in BoP focus on providing non-essential products to those with disposable income.[30] Some BoP initiatives also see large multinational corporations displacing local competition and local labour by importing goods, materials and labour.[31] Too often there is a net benefit for the multinational corporation but no enduring benefit to the disadvantaged communities in the form of employment or infrastructure.[32] As Aneel Karnani, associate professor of strategy at the University of Michigan, suggests, the eradication of deprivation will require firms to buy from the poor,[33] instead of simply selling to them.[34] Furthermore, Suparna Chatterjee, adjunct to the department of Economics at Xavier University, suggests that 'there is very little evidence that selling to the poor is a profitable venture which benefits large companies as well as the poor . . . [and] one must not just talk about fortune at the bottom of the pyramid but also fortune for the bottom of the pyramid.'[35] The main fallacy of BoP approaches has been to assume that reducing prices through techniques such as smaller servings constitutes a form of social development, when, if these are simply consumer goods, then it does nothing about the problem of people being cash-poor.

But, in light of the calls for greater dialogue between academic disciplines and the above challenges, little progress has been made at a conceptual level with BoP. Numerous examples show how enterprise can be undertaken to deliver specific development impacts, yet these rarely involve international companies in ways that meet their normal expected return on investment. That situation casts doubt on the rhetoric that 'shared value' is a non-philanthropic strategy guiding the whole of a large corporation such as Nestlé.[36] Instead, the successful examples of enterprise solutions to social development problems are usefully described by the term 'social enterprise'. The concept of social enterprise appears more useful than BoP, as the examples discussed usually have a clear social purpose at their heart, rather than seeing the poor as simply a new market for making a fortune. Seeking enterprise solutions to social challenges of all kinds is an important approach, as it promises scale without reliance on continued charity. The community of people engaging around the idea of social enterprise is one of the most dynamic in the field of business–society relations, as was demonstrated by the energy at both the Skoll Foundation and Schwab Foundation forums on social entrepreneurship in April 2010.[37]

One of the most famed examples of entrepreneurship being the vehicle for advancement of millions of poor people is that of the Grameen group of businesses, whose founder Muhammad Yunus received a Nobel Peace Prize in 2006.[38] In addition to the well-known work on micro-finance, providing small loans to groups of women to start businesses, Grameen is engaged in sustainable energy and telecommunications. The severe energy shortage in his home country Bangladesh contributes to its environmental degradation, poverty and inequality.[39] The Grameen Bank has sought to combat this by providing solar technology to individual households at the same cost as kerosene.[40] Since the project began in 1996, the

Grameen Bank reports it has installed more than 285,000 solar hot water systems, constructed 7,000 Biogas stoves, produced 40,000 improved cooking stoves, created 20,000 green jobs, and trained 3,000 women as Renewable Energy Technicians.[41]

Providing telecommunications was soon recognised as an important means for enhancing the economic and social development of rural areas of Bangladesh, where isolation and poor infrastructure is the norm.[42] With this in mind, the Grameen Bank established GrameenPhone as a joint venture with Norway's Telenor.[43] GrameenPhone makes telephone services available to rural villages in Bangladesh, by one member of a community taking a loan to acquire the handset, which is financed by charging the rest of the community for access. After almost ten years of operation, there are now 50 million telephone users in the country, 80% of these being mobile phones, making GrameenPhone the leading telecommunications provider in Bangladesh.[44]

A question that has interested some consulting firms, including Volans, as well as many business schools with research centres on development, is how large corporations and investors can relate to these social enterprises and to the cause of international development more broadly. The Grameen case demonstrates there are opportunities for partnership, as they have done with Telenor, Danone and others. The finance, resources, technologies, staff skills and access to markets that large corporations can bring are important to social enterprises. Yet what can companies do beyond partnership with social enterprises or seeking to develop new products for BoP markets? Discussions and initiatives in response to this question have given rise to the popularity of 'inclusive business' as a framework for understanding business contributions to development.

The business of inclusion

The term 'Inclusive Business' describes the belief that business can have a greater positive impact on development by adapting their core business to encourage development outcomes, rather than through new niche BoP initiatives, corporate philanthropy or support for social enterprises.[45] 'Inclusive business' is defined by the United Nations Development Programme (UNDP) as 'business models that create value by providing products and services to or sourcing from the poor, including the earned income strategies of non-governmental organisations'.[46] The focus is less on small enterprises seeking to address social needs profitably, but large firms being able to adjust their core businesses to benefit more people as either consumer, employee or supplier.

An April 2010 report by the International Finance Corporation (IFC) entitled *Scaling Up Inclusive Business* marked a watershed in the discussion of business contributions to development, as it uncovered some myths and mapped out a new agenda.[47] First, they found that most companies that engage in more inclusive business practices do not do it for reputation, risk management or innovation promotion. Those traditional drivers of voluntary responsibility are not sufficient to make a real difference to investment strategy. Instead, there has to be an obvious model for sales growth for companies to invest significantly in including more people in the sphere of their positive impact.

Second, they did not find any success from specialist base-of-the-pyramid approaches, but a 'whole-pyramid approach'. Beth Jenkins and her co-authors explained that

> most of the commercially viable, scalable examples . . . take more of a 'whole pyramid' approach in which the poor are segments within a much broader overall market, supplier base, or distribution network . . . Cemar, for example, was required by law to electrify the entire state of Maranhão in Brazil's low-income northeast region. The company was permitted to charge higher-income, higher-usage customers higher tariffs—enabling it to cross-subsidize those with low requirements and abilities to pay, with the government providing additional subsidies. In the telecommunications cases, the companies started in markets at the top of the pyramid to develop steady revenue streams and recoup their infrastructure investments, which eventually put them in a position to develop products and distribution channels for lower-income clients, with lower average revenues per user.

They continue that their findings

> may signal that new or more nuanced thinking is warranted on some of the assumptions that have become generally accepted knowledge in the inclusive business space—for instance, that doing business with the world's [poor] will require radical innovations in technology and business models.[48]

Instead, it points to the needed role of government.

This leads to their third key finding, which is the essential role of governments in creating enabling conditions and even imperatives for inclusive business. One of the most successful examples in the report was from the Philippines, and the often highly charged issue of private provision of water services. The report highlighted how the Manila Water Company is effectively providing water for impoverished communities due to the company and the government planning to ensure the successful meeting of public need and private expectations. Through a series of partnerships between the company, municipal governments and local communities, low-income neighbourhoods not only have access to water but are themselves central to the efficiency and cost-savings components of Manila Water's inclusive business model. Metering systems were developed to ensure ease of monitoring and transparency and where such systems were not practical, usually in very poor communities, bulk metering and cost-sharing programmes were introduced which permitted self-monitoring through collective responsibility. The community is engaged to administer collections and maintain the system which directly supports local employment, generating a local interest in the entire system, including on-time payment, discouraging water theft. The resulting benefit to the community is superior service and water quality while actively participating in keeping the costs of water low.[49] In many countries the private provision of water by large corporations has created criticism and even protest. Perhaps one of the most important means of ensuring that the costs have been kept down and thus maintained Manila Water's licence to operate is that the government required the company to cross-subsidise, so that they charge wealthier consumers more in order to fund the infrastructure for poorer consumers. This suggests a key government role to encourage some forms of inclusive business, including through regulations that require inclusive practices in return for licences.[50]

A fourth finding was the general lack of good examples of inclusive business by large firms. 'Large-scale success stories—reaching large numbers of poor people directly or via replication—are still the exception, not the rule,' wrote Beth Jenkins and her co-authors.[51] Given the companies in their investment portfolio are receiving funds from a development-oriented institution, one might assume some examples of inclusive business, yet only about 100 were found to have a potential inclusive business dimension, in addition to about 100 micro-finance initiatives. That is roughly 13% of the IFC investment portfolio.[52]

The fifth finding, and main purpose of the report, is the need for greater collaboration on enabling conditions for inclusive business, if they are to be mainstreamed beyond the current low level. For this purpose, more collective action is called for on issues such the dual evaluation of business activities, the development of in-depth market information on the needs, aspirations, capabilities and limitations of low-income consumers and producers, as well as on awareness-raising, education and training for low-income consumers, suppliers, distributors and retailers. In a seminar on this topic co-hosted by IFC and Harvard University, participants described a need for 'greater transparency [from potential donors to inclusive business projects] about what is possible and on what terms; faster decision-making and execution; and more judicious, strategic communication with external parties and the public at large'.[53] Therefore donors will need to become clearer about what kinds of projects are worthy of support and what management systems need to be in place to promote success. Some donors have measurement systems, such as the IFC's own *Development Outcome Tracking System*; however, such systems do not yet include the social and environmental standards that are already agreed by the wider international community as important aspects of sustainable development. Other goals, such as the MDGs, and standards, such as the ILO conventions, were not designed for business directly, while the UNGC only provides generic principles that are not comprehensive (not including health, for instance). Attempts to make broad goals such as the MDGs relevant to companies by using them as the basis for measurement tools, as with the MDG Scan, are useful for bringing attention to core business contributions to development, but they do not assess the full impact of business. For instance, the data on employment creation does not distinguish between a decent job and forced labour. Standards such as the ISO 26000 social responsibility standard, which was agreed in 2010, may prove useful, but, as it focuses mostly on reducing negative impacts of business practice, it will not be sufficient for guiding inclusive business and social enterprise, where the intention is to generate positive impacts in specific ways.

Therefore, during a keynote at the launch of the report on Dutch companies use of the MDG Scan, Dr Jem Bendell, called for a more holistic and integrated approach to business contributions to development and their measurement—a form of sustainable inclusive business. He said the field had grown enough now for a new management system for sustainable inclusive business, which could form the basis of new trainings and education. To begin with, it is necessary to define the personal qualities of managers (see Box 2) and the characteristics of business projects (see Box 3) that enable beneficial engagements by large enterprises in low-income communities.[54] These qualities and characteristics could be sought in those recipients of funds for sustainable inclusive business projects.

Box 2: **Personal qualities of managers of sustainable inclusive business**

There are key personal qualities that are important for business executives in large corporations to move their organisation towards helping poverty reduction in a sustainable way.

1. Active: aspiring to be a conscious agent of sustainable development in ways that involve core business

2. Coherent: addressing both the positive and negative impacts on low-income communities of current and planned business activities, leaving no issue ignored for long

3. Self-aware: focusing on your new USP—your 'Unique Serving Points'—by identifying the special capabilities you bring to a particular situation

4. Transformative: seeking enterprise opportunities that disrupt obstacles to social progress

5. Creative: using methods and indicators that promote creative team-working to innovate new solutions

6. Inquiring: learning together with unusual colleagues, sharing your own approaches while appreciating low-income communities and their organisations as co-innovators, while increasing your understanding of the complexity of development issues (including by applying the project characteristics)

Box 3: **Project characteristics of sustainable inclusive business initiatives**

A particular business project should have the following characteristics in order make a positive contribution to sustainable development:

1. Provides products, services or decent work to lower-income communities in ways that stimulate more sustainable production and consumption patterns as a whole

2. If out-competing goods and services produced by locally owned operations, then offers superior eco-social qualities to existing options, and provides local employment

3. Supports a mixed-ownership economy

4. Provides new sources of capital to community members

5. Provides community members with new access to markets, on stable and transparent terms

6. Transfers appropriate technology and skills to community members

7. Generates a return on investment that is acceptable to the company to be part of a scalable business, without future reliance on cash or in-kind subsidy from government or voluntary sector partners

8. Supports good governance and enabling conditions in the local community and nationally, in accordance with relevant UN principles on human rights and development

9. Involves mechanisms for participatory monitoring, evaluation and learning that address each of the preceding characteristics, to inform future strategy and operations

Projects that do not exhibit these characteristics may create some benefit, but risk causing new problems in the communities they affect, and therefore having unintended negative consequences for both sustainable development and the performance and reputation of the organisations involved.

The MDGs have played a useful role by focusing minds with time-bound goals. They helped keep poverty and development on the international agenda during a time of competing priorities and policy agendas, such as anti-terrorism. They do not, however, provide or inform a strategy for social development and therefore are weak guides to corporate strategy. With only five years to go to 2015, it is clear we are not on track to meet the MDGs. In the coming years this will make more people realise the futility and unhelpfulness of separating out interconnected symptoms of underlying systemic inequalities and injustices in politics and economy. In 2010 the limitations of a goal-focus began to be discussed by different parts of the development community. Amnesty International published a call for 'all governments to ensure all MDG initiatives are consistent with human rights', as they had witnessed how a focus on the goals had led to matters of accountability and rights being sidelined at times.[55] In May 2010, the UN Non-governmental Liaison Service

(UN-NGLS) published a report on the role of employment generation in meeting development objectives.[56] A key point made was that, on a large scale, the poor are not helped by targeting them in particular. Instead, poverty is reduced by helping enterprises generate decent work that create not only the products and services but also the wages for people to buy them. Therefore the creation of decent work opportunities with fair wages is key to all poverty reduction and social development, no matter how the poverty is then manifested. As these realisations spread, it is likely that matters of inequality and human rights will once again become key to the business and development agenda. As a result business leaders may need to learn the fuller lexicon of development, 'where the keywords are not simply market access, linkages with [international companies], philanthropy or infrastructure development through privatisation, but [also] rights-based development, equity, regulation, sustainability and local development'.[57]

If business leaders can then ally with the cause of fairer and more sustainable societies, then this engagement will be worthwhile. It is six years since aforementioned authors Jem Bendell and Wayne Visser called for engagement between the professions and academes of business and development. That the silos have persisted raises questions about the courage and commitment of the professionals involved to move outside their comfort zones for the sake of others. The integrating of insights across these fields remains the courageous cause of true leaders.

3Q2010
July–September

Jem Bendell

ESG analysis in deep water

One of the most important corporate irresponsibility stories of 2010 was the explosion and spill from the BP Deepwater Horizon oil rig in the Gulf of Mexico, destroying fisheries and tourism, as well as creating lasting ecological damage and health concerns. The leak was finally plugged in September 2010, ending five months of oil leaking into the Gulf. The spill raised critical issues about regulatory capture, dependence on oil; and whether international oil companies are either commercially or morally sensible to focus their efforts on extracting hydrocarbon fuels from the most technically challenging parts of the planet, rather than addressing issues of resource nationalism and their long-term strategy for profitability in a carbon-constrained world. For the community of practitioners and researchers in the field of corporate social responsibility (CSR), also known as 'corporate citizenship', the BP disaster raised deeper questions about the usefulness of voluntary CSR policies and reports, as well as the credibility and usefulness of the new profession of analysts and raters of corporate Environmental, Social and Governance (ESG) performance and the espoused commitments of institutional investors to Responsible Investment (RI). In September 2010 the Secretary General of the UN Conference on Trade and Development (UNCTAD), Supachai Panitchpakdi, reflected this concern, in the opening of its report on the state of global CSR and RI communications:

> In the wake of the BP oil disaster in the Gulf of Mexico, questions have been raised about the meaningfulness of voluntary corporate responsibility communications and the analysis of these by responsible investors. This report makes clear that both CSR communications and ESG analyses must now improve, to better indicate the contributions and impacts of business, rather than simply offer an engagement with the issues.[1]

In the preceding month there had been a flurry of emails about the implications of the BP disaster on the mailing list of academics run by the UN-backed Principles for Responsible Investment (UNPRI). Dr Neil Eccles, head of the Responsible Investment Unit, and the University of South Africa, had kicked it off by noting that

BP had just been delisted from the Dow Jones Sustainability Index. 'What the hell are oil companies doing on a sustainability index at all?' he asked, before noting that the FTSE4Good Environmental Leaders Europe 40 Index still listed BP as their top-ranked company.[2] Dozens of academics and reflective practitioners chimed in with different views, reflecting a general debate within the CSR, ESG and RI professions about the implications of BP for their trade, and for their aspirations for what they might achieve. The leading National Public Radio (NPR) radio show Marketplace also debated what the BP situation meant for RI.[3]

Also in August 2010, the French arm of Friends of the Earth (Les Amis de la Terre) slammed the majority of France's Socially Responsible Investment (SRI) funds as being 'illegitimate'. The organisation said in its report, analysing 89 SRI funds, that 71 of them invested in companies it considered as 'controversial' for 'disastrous' social and environmental practices. They mentioned BP, but also Total, France Télécom, BNP Paribas and AXA.[4] Amidst this growing debate about the role of ESG analysts, indices, SRI funds and RI in general, the consulting firm SustainAbility released a study on ESG raters. They had inventoried over 100 sustainability ratings and their attributes and surveyed over 1,000 sustainability professionals on their perceptions of ratings;[5] 'We sense a greater degree of interest and angst this Fall amongst companies and others who follow and use ratings,' said Michael Sadowski from SustainAbility:

> This may be driven in part by the proliferation of ratings and the continued opacity of the raters' methodologies and selection processes. Yet we believe there is something more profound and promising happening: ratings are being taken more seriously. Companies are starting to link executive compensation to their standing in ratings. Mainstream asset managers are switching on to the ESG agenda. And citizens and consumers are starting to pay attention to sustainability issues. While this is good news, it is more important than ever that we get ratings right.[6]

The key message here is that as the scale of RI grows and ESG analysts and indices proliferate, so participants in this field will be challenged to demonstrate effectiveness and accountability. That was also the main message from the UNCTAD report, which said that CSR reporting and RI commitments are now so widespread worldwide that they could influence trade and investment flows and there is a need to ensure they do that effectively for sustainable development outcomes rather than having perverse or inefficient effects.[7]

Data on signatories to the UNPRI released in September 2010 indicated that US$22 trillion—over 10% of the estimated total value of global capital markets—are now being managed by institutions committed to social and environmental responsibility in investing.[8] Meanwhile, Eurosif's 2010 European SRI Study revealed the expansion of the European SRI market; now totalling approximately €5 trillion assets under management (AuM).[9] Taken together, this growth in RI and SRI means a growth in demand for the research services of ESG analysts and the indices they inform or produce. No wonder, then, that of the 108 ESG ratings examined by SustainAbility, only 21 existed in 2000.[10]

This growth has led to growing interest from major players in the financial analysis. During 2010 acquisitions continued as MSCI, one of the world's largest investment research houses, completed its acquisition of the risk and corporate governance advisory firm Riskmetrics.[11] That followed a number of takeovers in 2009: namely the KLD and Innovest acquisitions by Riskmetrics; the ASSET4 and Point Carbon buy-out by the news and information giant Thomson Reuters; the mergers of Centre Info and INrate and Jantzi Research and Sustainalytics; and the takeover of the environmental data provider New Energy Finance by Bloomberg.[12] 'We believe this will be a long-term growth area for us. We've really only just begun,'[13] said Peter Grauer, Chairman of Bloomberg, at an ESG conference.

The implications of this growth and investment in ESG analysts and raters are summarised well by the founder of the Global Reporting Initiative, Allen White:

> The confluence of multiple forces is escalating the demand and supply of ESG information. Whether ESG will achieve its full potential as a sustainability driver depends on the standards of transparency, integrity and rigor that govern these rapidly expanding markets.

The BP disaster therefore brought into sharp relief an issue that has been growing for some time. It is time to shine some light on the hitherto deep-water horizons of how ESG analysts and raters conduct their business and how asset managers use such information.

The source of the matter

Both the SustainAbility and UNCTAD studies identified a number of weaknesses in the current practices of some ESG analysts and raters. From those studies, discussions on the UNPRI academic mailing list, and specific questions put to ESG analysts themselves and the users of such information, nine key weaknesses to address as the ESG market grows can be identified.[14]

The first key weakness is that many ESG analysts and raters rely predominantly on information published or provided directly by the companies being assessed, or by media that republish corporate communications. That is problematic because companies with challenging ESG issues are more likely to communicate on these issues and, when they do, it is with their particular opinion and choice of issues and data. 'More than 60% of the ratings in the inventory depend wholly or in part on information submitted directly to ratings organisations, thereby rewarding companies with the greatest capacity to respond to ratings requests rather than those with the best performance,' reported SustainAbility.[15]

For instance, Company A may report that it has an environmental policy, whereas company B does not—where Company A is a gold-mining company facing a range of challenges, concerning biodiversity destruction, pollution and influencing the spread of infectious disease, whereas Company B is a solar power company, facing many fewer ESG issues and providing a particular societal value. In addition, even if verified by an auditing firm, corporate ESG communications provide the corporate view of what are material issues and how they are being addressed, yet ESG issues are highly contestable, and more so than the verification of financial accounts.

Noting how BP was often 'best in class', Karen Reiner, a senior analyst at RepRisk, argued in *Responsible Investor*, 'for investment decision-making purposes investment managers cannot only rely on the information provided by the company itself, but rather should primarily use independent assessments of the company's associated ESG risks.'[16] Her employer, like Covalence and some other reputation trackers, focus on collecting information from a variety of sources to build an assessment of a company's reputation on ESG issues.

A second key weakness is the focus on analysing management policies and processes rather than the actual ESG impacts and outcomes of the companies being assessed. This is problematic because companies with challenging ESG issues are likely to have more developed policies and programmes, but that does not mean they have the least negative or most positive impacts. CSR communications provide an indication of the awareness of a company on some ESG issues, their efforts on those issues, and their intention to share information and begin to be assessed on such issues. In other words, their communications demonstrate engagement with their wider responsibilities, rather than social or environmental performance being achieved. Although there are some protocols for reporting on actual performance (e.g. the GRI G3 guidelines), they are not widely used and need further development. There are some exceptions, such as Trucost, which provides quantitative data on resource consumption and pollution, but the majority of ESG analysts still focus on process not performance. These first two weaknesses result in some companies with the most significant impacts being rated very highly by ESG analysts.

Given these limitations, why do fund managers buy such data? One reason is to simply tick the box that ESG issues have been considered. Another reason is because of the theory that the existence of CSR management systems, rather than performance and impacts on ESG issues, provides an insight into how intelligent and open the management is, which indicates how well the company will perform financially.

Inside the analysts

The third weakness in current ESG analysis is that most assess companies within a downside risk framework, focusing on the management of negative externalities that can lead to damage to reputation or litigation. That is problematic because it does not consider which companies are likely to succeed by creating more social or environmental value for society, particularly where doing business in certain countries may imply a higher potential for both positive or negative impacts. The CEO of Timberland, Jeff Swartz, asserts that,

> although many CSR funds have updated their 'screens' in recent years to ensure that they're considering a company based on both positive and negative merit, the punishment is still more powerful—and prevalent—than the reward.[17]

The negative risk management focus means that the enterprises innovating the technologies and approaches that are solutions to major social and environmental problems can be under-valued by some ESG analysts. In addition, the UNCTAD report noted that as RI grows and ESG analysis begins to effect trade and investment decisions, so an overemphasis on downside risk could have a protectionist effect on trade and investment. This is because some countries are considered by ESG analysts to present higher risks of social or environmental problems and therefore companies sourcing or operating in them are expected to have enhanced CSR policies otherwise they are marked down. Besides the fact that this categorisation of countries can be contested, as there are cultural issues shaping an analyst's perception of the location of social and environmental risks, this ignores that there could be more benefit gained from investment in such countries, through the creation of decent work and technology transfer.

As a result some ESG analysts, such as Maplecroft, are offering information services focusing on innovations in lower-income countries. One organisation trying to rate companies according to their current or future positive impacts is the Global Impact Investing Network (GIIN), a not-for-profit organisation dedicated to increasing the effectiveness of 'impact investing'. Impact investments aim to solve social or environmental challenges while generating profit. Rather than focus on the traditional ESG methodologies that analyse the actions of organisations to minimise socially negative behaviour, Ms Sarah Gelfand, director of GIIN's Impact Reporting and Investment Standards (IRIS), explains that 'The difference here is that we're trying to look at the proactive, mission-driven organisations that maximise positive impact.' Ms Gelfand adds:

> This absolutely is meant to build a market for the for-profit investing world to participate, and to use standards, auditing practices, and rating agencies that would make [impact investing] more accessible to the broader investment community.[18]

Another benefit of GIIN's system is that it generates data that allows investors to better compare the social benefit of their investments. This approach seeks to inform investors so that they can assess 'whether 20 seasonal jobs on a Kenyan coffee farm produce the same social good as 20 full-time positions at a textile factory in Guatemala—and help investors use that information alongside financial returns data'.[19] The mainstream ESG analysts could learn from these developments in impact investing.

A fourth weakness of much ESG analysis is that they use limited frameworks for understanding the complex and evolving field of corporate responsibility, with reductionist methods to assess companies, due to commercial constraints on the time, skills and advice available to them. This also means combining issues that perhaps should not be treated equally, and a masking of the cultural bias of the analyst organisation and the individual analysts by presenting interpretations as numbers.

As most ESG analysts keep their methodologies private, it is not so easy for researchers or clients to examine the completeness of the coverage of ESG issues relating to a particular business. However, from the three different ESG methodologies I have seen, it is clear that they vary in how up to date their understanding of CSR is. In addition, when ESG analysts publish reports on industry sectors one can gain an insight into what issues do not appear to be addressed. For instance, at the launch of a report on the palm oil industry in Singapore in September, I was surprised to find out that one very large palm oil company was ranked highly by the ESG analyst, while their spokesperson was arguing against any form of government action on the problem of the industries involved in incentivising forest clearance by burning. When pressed, the ESG rater explained that a company's public policy stance and lobbying activity was not considered within the assessments. That was despite the issue of a firm's political activity being recognised as an important aspect of its CSR since five years ago, when accounting bodies, NGOs, consulting firms, UN reports and leading peer-reviewed academic journals explained its importance to understanding CSR both from financial and moral standpoints.[20]

The ESG analyst in question uses a framework for assessing CSR practices that was developed by leading experts in the field, so the limitation in its comprehensiveness is not a result of a relative lack of expertise. In addition, they decided to upgrade their framework to include political activities after this issue was raised, showing that limitations were not the result of a disinterest in continual improvement. Rather, the lesson here is that as CSR is an evolving field of issues and practices, and will become more complex as different countries and cultures develop their own understandings and priorities, so a proprietary methodology will not evolve well given that developing complexity.

The second aspect of this weakness is in the actual analysis of those topics that are included. ESG analysts turn assessments of performance into numerical ratings, such as on a scale of 1 to 5 for whether a practice is considered sufficient or not. That gives an impression of unbiased 'data' when in fact it is all interpretation. In addition, very different issues as varied as policies on carbon management and child labour, are combined to produce overall scores. The process of weighting the different categories, including a 1 to 1 weighting for each, is again a matter of interpretation. For instance, if an analyst has twice as many environmental criteria to assess than social, and weights them all as equal, then the result is that environmental issues are being weighted as more important. As such, the numerical scores produced are a result of the cultural assumptions and priorities of the ESG analysts and their clients. Given that the data is socially constructed in this way it is important to understand how those judgements are made, yet this is impossible with most ESG analysts who keep such processes private.

Numbers will remain useful in ESG metrics, and in particular for producing comparable data on actual social or environmental performance. For instance, in a 2004 *World Review* in the *Journal of Corporate Citizenship*, a need was highlighted for CSR reports to include more numbers on issues such as the percentage differentials of pay depending on race and gender, or the number of court cases concluded or pending or out-of-court settlements reached in a given period. Such figures need to be produced according to agreed and transparent guidelines. In addition to numbers, however, there is a need for more nuanced descriptive data on the ESG approach, activities and performance of individual companies. This was noted by the European Federation of Financial Analysts Societies (EFFAS), and the Germany's Society of Investment Professionals (DVFA), in their combined report on Key Performance Indicators for ESG assessment. They suggested the need for 'KPN'—Key Performance Narratives, whereby KPNs consist of responses to one to two questions, given that some aspects of ESG cannot be expressed as numbers alone, thus requiring descriptions to put such numbers into context.[21]

There are commercial reasons for this weakness in ESG methodologies. The founder of Innovest (which is now part of MSCI), Matthew J. Kiernan, explained that one of the 'dirty little secrets' of the industry is asset managers' reluctance to pay for quality ESG research relative to the prices at which traditional financial research and analysis are purchased: 'Institutional investors are much keener on getting the research in principle than on paying a living wage for it,' he said.[22] That is because many users of ESG research just used it to tick a box that they have included ESG considerations. Therefore the commercial incentive is to produce research that can be used to cheaply tick a box, rather than more comprehensive analysis which is more costly and might not be purchased.

A fifth weakness in ESG analysis is the concerns over the independence of the analysis and rankings, due to conflicts of interest. There are at least four key areas for conflict of interest, which arise when ESG analysts and rating agencies:

- Sell services to the companies (including listed financial firms) that they analyse and rate, or are co-owned by consultants who sell such services. Therefore the rater could be tempted to favour a client in the ranking

- Are owned or invested in by the companies they rate (including their pension funds). Therefore the rater could be tempted to favour their owners or investors

- Produce ratings that are solicited or funded by clients, or their publication, launch and dissemination is sponsored by one of the rated companies. Therefore the rater could be tempted to favour that company or its interests in the ranking, in that or future rankings

- Are active in investment management. Therefore the rater may want to artificially improve a company's grade to keep it in the portfolio for financial considerations

As the use of ESG analysis in investment management grows, so these conflicts of interest will become more concerning. Clearly, credibility is important for the ESG analysts and this provides a commercial rationale for managing these conflicts of interest. However, is that enough? It is important to recognise the difficulties presented by existing conflicts of interest in the financial services community, as highlighted in extreme fashion by the Enron collapse and the sub-prime mortgage debacle. For Enron's off-balance-sheet losses to be hidden in separate investment vehicles (which lent exclusively to Enron and were governed by Enron executives) the banks needed to agree to fund these new vehicles. In doing so they would win commissions on the deals. In addition, the financial analysts nearly always gave positive buy recommendations for Enron stock, and were rewarded for that by their banks receiving business from Enron.[23] That experience suggests conflicts of interest require professional codes and government regulations to ensure their effective management. Part of that will be new levels of transparency. Antoine Mach, the head of Covalence, believes that these potential conflicts of interest mean that 'there is a need for more disclosure regarding who are the ESG agencies' clients, be they companies or investors'.

The experience with Enron also suggests that, until there are scandals that threaten the whole sector, most enterprises and professions have sought to be given the freedom to adopt their own codes of practice for managing such issues. We are likely to see this pattern play out with ESG analysts, whereby they will seek to define their own codes for managing conflict of interest, either soon, or after some future scandal. However, it would appear to be in the interests of both ESG clients and the companies being rated to promote good practice and thus ensure appropriate codes and regulations, something returned to below.

Mixing materialities

A sixth weakness in ESG analysis is that the materiality of ESG issues for financial performance of investments and the materiality of those issues to the affected stakeholders and wider society are often conflated. Some assess the importance of an ESG issue on their estimation of whether it could affect financial performance, while others involve more moral judgements about what to assess, score and weight. For both approaches, the credibility and accountability of those judgements are in doubt.

Some ESG professionals regard this field as one of enhanced financial analysis, or smarter investing. One such investment professional, Nicholas A.J. Taylor, explained on the UNPRI mailing list that 'I see ESG/Sustainability as about risk management, not morality. Thus what "ought to be" is not considered relevant.' That view became popular in distinguishing the new emphasis on RI promoted by UNPRI, which presented ESG issues as materially relevant to all assets, rather than being something that financial institutions could consider if developing a specific investment option for ethically concerned clients, which had been the norm for SRI prior to 2005. The former has been termed enhanced 'value-based investing' and the latter 'values-based investing'. Others professionals in this field disagree with such a distinction: they argue that ethical concerns do or should influence ESG assessments and investment decisions. Some of those seek to square this circle by arguing that an opening ethical focus can then lead to superior financial performance. That view was well expressed by a leader in the field on the UNPRI mailing list, Dr Craig Mackenzie of the University of Edinburgh, and former head of the ESG team at F&C:

> One of the central insights of the ESG agenda is that 'What ought to be' is frequently highly 'relevant'. Failure to manage ESG issues is such a big risk for companies because key stakeholders have strong moral opinions, and will rise up in moral indignation, boycotting companies that breach moral expectations and asking their elected representatives to punish them severely and extract swingeing restitution. BP's recent experience with the US populus is a case in point. People don't simply want BP to clean up the oil, they want to punish BP; many want to see it go out of business. These are moral responses. So in a world where people have strong views on what companies 'ought' to do, managing risk is not just technical issue. It is one that requires an understanding, debating and engaging with social expectations about responsible behaviour.

However, on the same list, the head of the Responsible Investment Unit at the University of South Africa, Dr Neil Eccles, pointed out that if financial interests are used to justify ESG analysis in any way, even if not directly, then this can challenge the assumption that ESG analysis is necessarily going to improve social, environmental or governance outcomes. He wrote:

> If ESG/responsible/sustainability investment is all about investment risk management, then we can simply combine ESG analysis and derivative instruments to manage investment risk. So if we happened to have hindsight grade ESG analysis which told us that one of BP's wells was going to blow its top somewhere off the US coast, we could 'manage this risk' by short selling BP stocks—and while we are at it we might even engage with BP management to cut costs on safety just to make sure of our investment strategy!? This manages risk. Of course it doesn't in any way address the moral issues of BP's (or any other oil company for that matter) wells blowing their top and messing up people's lives. Which I actually suspect most of us in the RI space actually want to see. Some will invoke universal ownership and long-termism to dress up this moral objective so that is appears to satisfy investment rationality and the 'amoral high ground'. But others will argue that these theories are not yet mature enough to be convincing and so we get nowhere.

This online debate exposed some of the conceptual ambiguities at the heart of both the CSR and ESG fields, which are often papered over in reports, analysis and ratings. The data in CSR reports and ESG analysis rarely distinguishes between the materiality of an issue to an organisation and its materiality (or relevance) to society. These are not always the same. For instance, due to questions of reputation, a company or investor may focus on eradicating child labour within their supply chain, yet an affected community may seek more labour rights in order to press for better pay and conditions, which would then allow them to put their children in school, by their own choice. The assumption that what is bad for society is bad for investors and therefore there will always be an alignment of interests is naïve. The case of carbon trading highlights this. For an investor a company's leadership in promoting carbon markets can be seen as addressing an ESG issue in commercially useful ways. Indeed it presents more potential for revenues than if the company was active in pushing for a carbon tax and working to reduce its carbon intensity. Yet many climate policy analysts would argue that advocating for a carbon tax is the more responsible approach.[24] If the ESG analyst is looking at what improves return on investment, then it would be unfounded to assume their assessment would correlate with the public interest.

For those with an interest in the financial significance of ESG issues, the way ESG analysts make estimations on whether an issue, country, industry or initiative presents a higher or lower risk is important, yet this conceptual ambiguity and a lack of transparency on how analysts apply their own conceptual framework means that ESG analysis is currently a weak financial tool.

On the other hand, for those with a broader interest in the ethical dimensions of investing, this ambiguity also presents problems. As described above, some believe ESG analysis and RI have a moral role to play in society. Craig Mackenzie asserted 'that the ESG investment community has a very powerful role to play in pursuing ethical goals . . . and will only come into its full maturity if it develops a richer understanding of its relationship to ethics. There is an R in PRI.' What would a mature approach imply? To begin with, answering the question of whose values, whose ethics, and whose morality matters. Answering that question casts light on whether the ethical approach to ESG is actually very ethical at all. That is understood by the Head of Covalence, Antoine Mach, who explained that 'In addition to issues of independence and methodological robustness, we have to deal with the problem of defining ethics. So I believe controversies about ESG ratings are here to last.'

In practice the morals that matter in ESG analysis and RI are the ones held by the asset owners. Craig Mackenzie noted that 'for most shareholders there are limits to pursuing a public-interest agenda imposed by fiduciary duty (e.g. advocating actions that will destroy material shareholder value).' The President & Group CEO, Fifth Capital Ltd, Miroslaw Izienicki, explained in the same online discussion that 'one of the fundamental concepts of investment regulation is that the intermediary must "know their client" and demonstrate a mandate.' Might, therefore, the application of a more explicitly values-based agenda in ESG analysis and RI lead to privileging the values of the wealthy and powerful? For instance, it would be interesting to see how the Western business communities might respond to explicitly morality-based engagement by Sovereign Wealth Funds from Arab nations. In such a case we might hear people complaining that the morality of might is not right, and that there are universal codes of human rights.

What is really happening in the ESG field at this time is neither an application of enhanced financial materiality or of a clearly understood ethical system. Instead the cultural assumptions and norms of the professional community of ESG specialists and their clients are being applied in ESG analysis, often rushed and without critical self-awareness. This situation is made possible by how the 'R' in PRI is left undefined. It is highlighted well by Neil Eccles's rhetorical question to members of the UNPRI mailing list: 'If the Niger Delta were the Mississippi Delta, I wonder whether Shell would still be on the Dow Jones Sustainability Index? Although the pollution in the Niger Delta is chronic rather than acute, I think that it runs to about the same level of catastrophe.' Whether your interest is 'financial' or 'moral', the conceptual ambiguities and incoherence in the ESG field confer a fundamental weakness in current ESG analysis and ratings. To aid in clarifying the different concepts I have heard over the years, I offer a typology of different philosophies of responsible finance in Box 4. I include two approaches, which I rarely hear, but which are based on concepts of universal human rights, and I first outlined in 2004.[25]

Box 4: **Philosophies of responsible finance**

1. Smarter Finance—considering environmental, social and governance (ESG) issues for an enhanced assessment of financial materiality in the near term and for single assets, projects or loans

2. Holistic Finance—considering ESG issues due to materiality for longer-term returns, and also due to interactions between assets in a whole portfolio (where the actions of one asset can help or damage another), or where some projects or loans reduce the performance of other financial products in the same portfolio. Some call this the Universal Owner concept

3. Moral Finance—considering certain ESG issues either as a bank manager or asset manager as the owner of the assets asks them to consider certain ESG issues because of their particular values or morals (i.e. where owners have interests other than the financial and where these override the financial concern), or because the bank/asset manager holds certain values or morals (this latter form raises questions about whether fiduciary duty is being upheld; the former form raises questions about how fiduciary duty is often assumed in practice or by law to only concern the financial interests of owners rather than their other interests)

4. Accountable Investing—considering ESG issues out of a general principle that it is important, on moral grounds, for economic activity to be accountable to those affected by it, and that private financial institutions need to be accountable for their impacts on society for all their activities

→

that impact on stakeholders. This concept was first introduced in a UN paper in 2004 as 'capital accountability'

5. Accountable Finance—considering all activities and instruments of Private Financial Institutions (PFIs), not only asset management, for their accountability to those who are affected by them

Most ESG professionals appear to apply a mixture of the first three approaches. At the time of writing I do not know anyone applying approach 4 or 5, although a few ESG professionals have recognised these as the approach to work towards.

Drilling the depths of ESG

The weaknesses and challenges I have described above are enough to raise serious questions about the usefulness of current ESG analysis. There are three additional weaknesses that serve to make the CSR, ESG and RI areas somewhat murkier for everyone involved.

As SustainAbility's report noted, not only do ESG analysts often produce ratings but the ratings they produce are then incorporated into composite ratings. The seventh weakness of ESG analysts is that the indices they produce, or supply data to, incorporate all forms of enterprise, including ones that would never be considered sustainable or socially progressive, and by doing that they confuse the issue of what is responsible investing for fund managers and private investors, as well as regulators and the wider public.

An example of this was mentioned at the start, when people criticised Dow Jones and FTSE for listing BP in their sustainability and responsibility indices. That BP was replaced in the list by controversial oil company and military contractor Halliburton, sparked even more ridicule for such indices.[26] Halliburton was included as it was assessed to be in the top 10% among companies in the oil field services sector. Companies from most economic sectors can be in such indices if they are assessed as engaging ESG issues and actively managing associated risks. The existence of such indices could lead to public antagonism towards ESG and RI in general, as well as confusing ethically minded investors, and therefore undermining the potential for funds to flow to socially and environmentally beneficial companies. My colleague at Lifeworth Consulting, and former financial advisor, Ian Doyle, also believes that it reinforces an assumption of the primacy of financial interests over all else:

> by not focussing on investing in companies that are doing good and in turn creating a vision of the world beyond finance, such analysis reinforces the system within which it is situated, namely an economic one that demands a return, without shedding any light onto the social effectiveness of such

investments. This is exemplified by the all too common statements like, 'there is no sacrifice in returns by investing in SRI' and 'long-term profitability needs to incorporate ESG'.

This situation frustrates many leaders in social and sustainable enterprise. The CEO of Timberland, Jeff Swartz, explains that 'Too much "social investing" seems to me "screen and criticize" rather than invest behind CEOs and Boards that make real commitments to commerce and justice.' He continued that 'we've earned a decent reputation as sustainable business and responsible brand . . . and yet SRIs only hold about one percent of our shares.' He recommended that

> CSR funds need to take a more thoughtful approach to company screenings, in recognition that as the world of CSR has evolved, so too their criteria for judging a company's performance should be more sophisticated . . . CSR money managers should stop just Index investing—weighting their entire portfolio as per the market—and start making some principled, concentrated investments in companies whose social mission they believe in.[27]

The eighth weakness I identified in current practice is that most ESG analysts and raters do not integrate their ESG products and ratings with the mainstream financial analysis products and ratings that their own firms, owners or business partners offer clients, partly because of a commercial interest in maintaining different products. That is problematic as it restricts the potential to integrate ESG considerations in normal financial investment analysis. As CSR consultant Ian Doyle explains, 'we need a new system through which to interpret data, not new filters on an old system where short-term narrow financial returns remain prime. To do this ESG research cannot be a stand-alone consideration but must be as integrated as the financial considerations of the investment itself.' With the wave of acquisitions in the ESG analyst market over the last two years, there are now ESG reports and indices being produced by teams of people in the same building where sub-prime litigation risk reports and indices, political risk reports and indices, and mainstream financial reports and indices are being produced. Such lack of integration is untenable, as ESG analysts can take up some of their own responsibility and leadership, rather than blaming the client, and trial new forms of integrated assessments.

The ninth weakness is that most ESG analysts are not transparent about their methods of research, analysis and ranking, or about their general operations, for stakeholders and regulators to assess their credibility in light of the various issues outlined above. The SustainAbility study found that 88% of professionals think disclosure of methodology is important for the credibility of an analyst or rater. The professionals have a practical interest in improved ESG analysis. On the finance side, it means they could conduct their fiduciary duty better, or enact their own or their clients' moral interests more effectively, depending on the approach they take. On the corporate side, it means they could be recognised appropriately by investors when leading their companies towards superior performance on ESG issues. But there is a broader constituency that has an interest in improved ESG analysis, and that is all of us. Because, as RI grows, so ESG analysis and ratings will take on a quasi-governance role over enterprise, trade and investment. How effective, efficient, fair and accountable it will be as a system of 'global private regulation' will be a matter of growing public interest.

At a time when information is becoming more widely available, and online collaboration the norm, it is difficult to see what social justification there is for proprietary ESG methodologies. Instead, it appears a way of hiding from criticism, even ridicule, given the major flaws in many ESG analyst practices that I and others have chronicled. With a light cast on their inner workings, the newly acquired ESG empires may have few clothes to display. It seems only a matter of time before such a light is shone, and ESG analysts will need to improve their processes and evolve their business models accordingly—something I explore below.

The various weaknesses identified above are summarised in Box 5. The implication is that we urgently need more clarity in distinguishing between actual ESG impacts, the perceptions of stakeholders, the strategic competence of management, and the readiness of the organisation for responsible and sustainable innovations.

Box 5: **The nine limitations of ESG analysis**

Many ESG analysts and raters:

1. Rely predominantly on information published or provided directly by the companies being assessed, or by media that republish corporate communications. That is problematic because companies with challenging ESG issues are more likely to communicate on these issues, and when they do it is with their particular opinion and choice of issues and data

2. Focus their analysis on management policies and processes not on the actual ESG impacts and outcomes of the companies assessed. That is problematic because companies with challenging ESG issues are likely to have more developed policies and programmes, but that does not mean they have the least negative or most positive impacts

3. Assess companies within a downside risk framework, focusing on the management of negative externalities that can lead to damage to reputation or litigation. That is problematic because it does not consider which companies are creating more social or environmental value for society—particularly where doing business in certain countries may be imply greater potential for both positive or negative impacts

4. Use limited frameworks for understanding the complex and evolving field of corporate responsibility, and reductionist methods to assess companies, due to their commercial interests limiting the time, skills and advice available to them. This also means combining issues that perhaps should not be treated equally, and a numerical masking of cultural bias of the analyst organisation and the individual analysts

5. Are not completely independent from the companies that they are rating, with a variety of conflicts of interest that need to be managed

→

6. Conflate the materiality of ESG issues for financial performance of investments and the materiality of those issues to affected stakeholders and wider society. Some make assessments based on financial materiality and others involve more moral judgements. In both cases the credibility and accountability of those judgements are in doubt

7. Run indices or supply data to indices that include all forms of enterprise including ones that can never be sustainable, and thus blur the issue of what is responsible investing for fund managers and private investors, as well as regulators and the wider public

8. Do not integrate their ESG analysis products and ratings with the mainstream financial analysis products and ratings that their own firms or owners offer clients, partly because of a commercial interest in maintaining different products. That is problematic as it restricts the potential to integrate ESG considerations in normal financial investment analysis

9. Are not transparent about their methods of research, analysis and ranking, or about their general operations, for stakeholders and regulators to assess their credibility in light of the weaknesses described above

Impediments and drivers of change in ESG analysis

It would appear that many stakeholders in ESG analysis have an interest in the improvement of current practice. The clients of ESG analysts and raters have an interest in receiving good insights into either the financial or moral implications of firms' strategies and performance on many ESG issues. The assessed companies have an interest in coherent and accurate forms of assessment and ranking, so that they can be recognised for the CSR efforts. Various CEOs have said that investors need to support companies for investing in sustainability, yet effective ESG analysis and advice is critical for such support from investors.[28] The ESG raters themselves have an interest in building the credibility of their own operations and the concept of ESG analysis in general. Some are taking their own steps, such as Covalence, which lists its clients on its website and in connection with its reports, and detailing the methodology it uses. However, if other raters do not take such steps, then the sector as a whole could be damaged, and so there could be a collective interest in collective action, as we see in many professions, leading to professional standards being developed and monitored over time. The wider CSR profession has an interest in the financial system supporting CSR and sustainability leadership, and ESG analysis is key in making that connection. Other stakeholders in companies, from professional campaign groups, to trade unions to communities living near commercial operations, all have an interest in the more responsive and responsible companies being recognised by investors, and the more irresponsible ones finding it more difficult to obtain financing. Therefore they also have a stake in ESG analysis working effectively.

Since 2005 we have seen more government regulations requiring CSR reporting from listed companies, and the disclosure of approaches to ESG issues by financial institutions. Noting this trend, Dr Anthony Miller from UNCTAD explained that 'Regulators can work to strengthen the mechanisms through which institutional shareholders are able to influence the ESG practices of the companies in which they invest, while also encouraging investors to formally articulate their stance on ESG issues in public reports.' Such measures are based on an assumption that these are useful practices, helping nudge corporate and investor behaviour towards public goals. Therefore they have an interest in ESG analysis being accurate enough to actually achieve that nudging effect: they have an interest therefore in not any form of reporting and engagement, but quality reporting and effective engagement. Otherwise, as discussed above, the growth of ESG and RI could have perverse impacts on trade and investment for sustainable development.

Despite all these interests in quality ESG analysis, the types of criticisms outlined have been heard in some form or another for many years, while the industry of ESG analysts has grown without much significant change.[29] That begs the question: why? Could it be that the ESG analysts were too focused on business development than doing a socially progressive job? That they assumed they were doing a socially progressive job? Could it be that stakeholders and regulators simply did not understand enough about this field in order to become involved and shape practices? Could it be that companies feared criticising ESG analysts in case this backfired in the assessments they received? Some of the causes of inertia in dealing with core problems in what is an innovative field of practice may need further examination if things do not move forward now. Various participants in this field, however, point the finger at investment managers, for not being sufficiently interested in ESG issues to demand quality analysis, and, crucially, then pay for it.

Given that so many asset owners and managers are signed up to responsible investment via the UNPRI, one might wonder how this can be the case. It is important to note that currently the UNPRI focuses on encouraging its signatories to become more engaged responsible owners, not on what the substance of that actually means. Therefore some argue that, despite its emphasis on reporting, the UNPRI leaves us no wiser as to what actually occurs in investment decisions on ESG issues. One academic from Oxford University even suggested that 'the UNPRI, after early successes in legitimizing the responsible investment ideology, appears to be acting as a shroud of legitimacy for traditional "non-responsible" investment practices.'[30]

Other initiatives in the responsible investment field could be challenged for not addressing the lack of transparency. The Responsible Investment Association of Australasia (RIAA) is professionalising SRI, in a country with one of the highest proportions of pension funds signed up to the UNPRI, at 43%.[31] The RIAA offers

responsible investment certifications for fund managers, pension funds and financial advisers. Its certification programme currently does not specify standards for
the practice of responsible investment, but how RI activities should be disclosed.
Bringing assessment to claims made by fund managers, RIAA may help to address
confusion about what are or are not ethical funds. However, its audits are conducted by a commercial firm using its own confidential and proprietary methodology for assessment. As such, it misses an opportunity to cast some light on opaque
practices. As the field of RI is professionalised, we should remember lessons from
the lack of transparency in normal fund management. For instance, some investment research houses knew about the sub-prime meltdown before it happened
and, rather than warning all their clients or the public, they incorporated it into
their data for their own benefit.[32]

There are a few examples that cast doubt on the meaningfulness of investor
expressions of responsibility. One test case was the blacklisting of Rio Tinto by the
Norwegian Government Pension Fund in September 2008. At the time their Fund's
'Ethical Committee' announced they had sold USD$1 billion in Rio Tinto stock for
grossly unethical conduct at the jointly operated Grasberg mine in West Papua (also
known as Irian Jaya, Indonesia). More than three months of engagement took place
prior to Rio Tinto stock being offloaded. In addition, Rio Tinto would have been
aware that the co-owner of the mine, Freeport-McMoRan, had been pressed by the
Norwegian Fund over the Grasberg mine for some five months in 2005 before being
blacklisted. Some proponents of RI said that this illustrated the limits of adopting a
negative screen, or avoiding bad companies. Innovest, which is now part of MSCI,
issued a statement which claimed that the Norwegian Pension Fund had

> taken a traditional approach to SRI by screening out a company that does
> not meet its value-based mandate. In contrast, Innovest rates Rio Tinto
> highly because the company is a sustainable-mining leader relative to
> sector peers. And while Rio Tinto's involvement in Grasberg is of concern,
> Innovest feels the company is managing its overall ESG risks well, which
> should add to increased shareholder value over the long term.

Such a conclusion ignores the Norwegian fund's engagement with Rio Tinto in
the months running up to their decision to divest, and the lack of progress they
achieved from that engagement.

BP also received much engagement from investors on its social and environmental performance. Despite the peculiar ESG rankings that used BP's CSR reports to
place them at the top, investment managers who knew more about actual performance were already concerned and pushing BP to change.

> Between May 2008 and April 2010 BP consistently ranked among the most
> environmentally and socially controversial firms [on a reputation index
> tracking news media, NGO reports, court cases, among other sources],
> suggesting that its true risk exposure was always high, a fact that was not
> often taken into account by other types of analysis. This warning sign
> offered an indication of its serious risk exposure in terms of environmental

and social concerns, particularly with respect to health and safety issues in the US, even prior to the Deepwater Horizon oil-rig explosion.[33]

Having been criticised for ditching Rio Tinto, the Norwegian Government Pension Fund stayed with BP despite this negative information. In August 2010 they reported having lost €1.1 billion with their investment in BP.[34] It appears that even large investors can't change company practices unless they work in concert with other investors. But it appears they can stop being complicit in ecological destruction and human rights abuse, and reduce their associated risks, by divesting in companies that pose such risks.

There are some developments in the past year that mean the time could be right for the interests identified above to outweigh the forces of inertia. The scale of commitment to RI is now so high, and the ESG market so large, that this is attracting more scrutiny. The acquisition of ESG raters by mainstream financial analyst firms means that more integration of ESG mainstream financial analysis is possible. An internationalising RI and CSR means that more difficult cross-cultural issues will emerge and need resolving. The growth of social media and open-source software means that new forms of collaboration are possible. Growing awareness of how the financial system is not working in the public interest will also lead to more criticism and innovative thinking about how to evolve better systems. The true underlying materiality of how our environment is coping with our ever growing demands for resources, the weirdness of our weather, and high-profile disasters such as BP's, will also continue to raise questions about what is being achieved in the name of responsible investment. We could, therefore, be on the cusp of a new agenda for improving ESG analysis, and in turn the meaning and practice of responsible investment.

An agenda for improving ESG analysis

To improve ESG analysis will require new training, codes of conduct for ESG analysts, more open-source approaches to analysis, higher revenues for code-abiding analysts and new regulations and government funding to guide practice. I discuss each in turn.

The Australian government donated 2.5 million Australian dollars to the RIAA to develop the Responsible Investment Academy, which will develop training programmes. It is a move that could significantly increase the quality of practice in this emerging profession. The implication for professional practice from the critiques of current ESG and RI practice I have outlined is that such trainings need to encourage critical evaluation of current practices and an awareness of how professional interests may sometimes militate against the public interest. Therefore, although the outlining of current best practices is important in any course on RI, as this is an emerging profession, training also needs to explore the limitations of current CSR reporting, ESG analysis and RI reporting, and the personal ethics and systemic risks of profiting from an opaque marketplace. If conceptual development and associated trainings are led within the two fields of finance and accounting, rather than drawing on sociological, political and organisational sciences, then there may be major limitations in effectiveness for either social change or enhanced investment.

A code of conduct for ESG analysts and raters is needed. Such a code does not need to include all the requirements placed on financial analysis, as some of that is inappropriate. However, in many areas it should go beyond what is required of normal financial analysts, as ESG raters are doing things that are more complex, contested and subjective. In addition, as they often claim to have a positive social impact through promoting CSR, this suggests more scrutiny of how they achieve what is required. Such a code would need to provide answers to all the nine weaknesses outlined above. Therefore it would need to encourage the use of multiple sources of information, assessments of actual performance, disclosed and thorough methodologies that provide clarity on the different theories of materiality, continual learning and dialogue about CSR topics and cross-cultural issues, management of conflicts of interest, and products that integrate ESG into mainstream financial analysis.

Some ESG analysts may not wish to develop or adopt such a substantive code, yet only a substantive and demanding code that will require changes in ESG analyst practice will deliver for the interests of various stakeholders. Therefore it is important for all the stakeholders in ESG analysis to participate in a process to develop such a code. Upon its conclusion, ESG analysts could be invited to adopt the code and be audited. The benefit of doing so would ideally be the securing of more business from clients—something I return to below.

In addition to improving general ESG practice through a code, it is also important for new forms of open source ESG analysis to be developed. *Responsible Investor* magazine reported on a new initiative entitled the Global Initiative for Sustainable Ratings (GISR), designed to create a transparent sustainability ratings framework as a response to the proliferation of ratings products that have created confusion in the marketplace.[35] The initiative has a goal to provide sustainability ratings products that are publicly available at no or nominal cost through an independent, non-commercial, multi-stakeholder process. Mark Tulay, former Head of ESG Solutions at RiskMetrics, explained:

> We believe it is time for an independent, non-commercial initiative to produce a white paper on the rating agencies and, more broadly, to chart a longer term strategy for building a world-class, normative ratings framework to guide capital, procurement and business–NGO partnerships toward companies that are true sustainability leaders.[36]

If initiatives like GISR develop, then other ESG analysts may need to evolve their business models to add value to clients in new ways. They will need to develop competencies that distinguish them from competitors. Geography, technology, interpretation and display of information, and being seen as providing an authoritative analysis from a particular standpoint, will all form part of those evolving business models.

There have been efforts to enhance the practices of financial analysts in the past: in particular the now defunct Enhanced Analytics Initiative (EAI). The problem with EAI was that investment managers did not want to pay for more and better ESG analysis. That is in a situation where investment managers spend millions on investment research, but the ESG research industry, including the sell side, only receive a fraction of that. That provides a real indication of what most investors think is valuable to informing their investment decisions: most ESG issues are currently not considered financially material by investment managers. Therefore if ESG analysts are going to up their game and adopt the type of code suggested above, there will need to be a shift in how investment managers view ESG issues. Indeed, they would need to incentivise code uptake by committing to buy more from code-certified ESG analysts and raters. The difficulty here is that investors do not seem likely to take such steps voluntarily—the failure of EAI suggesting as much. Therefore we come to the role of regulation.

Given the amount of resources now being put into ESG communications, and the growing range of institutions claiming to practise RI, governments could consider influencing the effectiveness of these activities in promoting fair and sustainable markets. That could mean more than providing funds, and actually providing direction on what is in the public's interest. To address the conundrum where everyone seems to welcome RI as a good thing but little is being done by investment managers to resource quality ESG assessments, so governments could revise what is considered fiduciary duty. There are strong arguments for fiduciary duty being revised to include comprehensive assessment of ESG factors, and therefore that asset managers should seek independent, specialist, comprehensive and contemporary assessment of ESG risks and opportunities relating to whatever asset they are holding, buying or selling.

On the surface, the donation from the Australian government may be a measure of its commitment to incorporating ESG into investment analysis, but the RIAA is part of an industry serving its client and seeking profit, and so the positive public impact cannot simply be assumed. As the sociological study of professions has shown, professions need some visible hand of public interest, from the state, guiding their work. Given the international and complex nature of these issues, it lends itself to deliberation at the intergovernmental level. Organisations such as the United Nation Conference of Trade and Development (UNCTAD) could host processes to clarify goals, weaknesses, and the various approaches to improving performance. They could even host the process to develop a code of conduct for ESG analysts: concerns over the power of standard setters and assessors in world trade means that an independent body such as UNCTAD needs to balance the interests at play.

The politics of finance

If the practices of ESG analysts are improved we will see some progress in advancing the CSR and sustainability agenda. However, as I have alluded to above, to achieve that requires a larger shift in the way financial institutions work. It is important to note that considered and patient asset management is only a part of the financial sector and thus only part of their wider impact on economies and societies. There is a key difference between trading-based investment strategies and ownership-based investment strategies, with the former becoming more profitable given the ease of short-selling and leveraging positions, and rising volatility in asset prices. If you take a trading-based approach, then ESG issues will never be material to your decisions. Therefore, if the shifts described above are to be significant, then a broader reshaping of financial practices is needed, and the only way for that to come will be through governments changing the rules.

In addition to trading-based strategies, there are a variety of other financial practices that are unhelpful either to financial market functioning, non-financial economic activity, and broader economic development, as well as in turn various social and environmental issues. Those forms of investment practice include high-frequency arbitrage, leveraged short-selling, highly leveraged buy-outs, short-term currency speculation, dark pool market trades, and unregulated commodity derivatives, among other things. As a larger share of a financial institution's profits come from such activities, how interested will they be in investing in quality ESG analysis?

If such financial practices do not serve any public purpose, but cause public problems, should there be a proper discussion about whether to outlaw them or tax them heavily? Where is that debate today? Is it too complicated for unions and NGOs? Too tangential for companies? Too personally risky for politicians? Previously Western governments benefited from such financial imagination, but with the bailouts, crisis-caused recessions and sovereign debt crises, even they are not benefiting from these financial practices any more. In the past there has been a presumed innocence of financial products and services and this is likely to shift towards a presumed guilt, as the impacts of the financial crises are felt in universities, hospitals and homes. There is likely to be a new wave of political activism around these issues, and intergovernmental coordination of the debates and dialogues. For CSR, ESG and RI communities of research and practice to be more than a sideshow to history will require them to engage in these issues. Indeed, by engaging in them it may become clearer the goals of an emerging corporate responsibility movement.[37] It is difficult to know what may result, but the most responsible financial institutions are likely to be the ones that prosper in this more observed and critiqued marketplace.

Clearly there were other important events and developments in the third quarter of 2010. Nonetheless, given the growing and decisive role of finance in shaping corporate practice, and the major debates about ESG and RI that the BP disaster then sparked, in retrospect it will be seen as a key issue of the quarter, and the 2010 year as a whole. As the financial turmoil of recent years has shown, even if you are not interested in finance, it is interested in you (and your employer and your government).

4Q2010
October–December

Ian Doyle, Wayne Visser and Jem Bendell

Practising what we preach

When the concept of business education—or management science—first developed, it was largely with progressive and egalitarian intentions. By outlining the skills that could be learned and mastered by anyone with the right talent and application, the concept challenged the assumption that future bosses would always be the sons of former bosses. There was a meritocratic thrust that businesses are rational enterprises that can be run by anyone with the relevant skills, regardless of social background.[1] That original intention is not often acknowledged today, as more business schools worldwide aspire to be considered elite institutions embedded in elite social, economic and political circles. When considering their social role, the issue of how elite performance and elite access can be applied to social progress has not been adequately explored by the world's top business schools. Efforts at social responsibility are largely focused on the content of teaching and research, or adopting some environmental measures for internal operations, rather than a full embrace of social purpose relevant for today's challenges and its application to all organisational functions. This lack of a comprehensive embrace of social purpose is highlighted by how some of the top business schools have stumbled in their response to the issue of economic and social inequality.

2010 saw increasing concern over growing economic inequality within nations. During the year the implications of this growing inequality began to be perceived for business, investors and business schools, rather than society at large. In November 2010, the United Nations' latest *Human Development Report* was published, featuring for the first time a metric to take account of growing inequality within countries, so that the income of elites does not mask the situation.[2] The new Inequality-adjusted Human Development Index (IHDI) is a measure of the level of human development of people in a society that accounts for inequality. Across 139 countries, the average loss in the Human Development Index (HDI) due to inequality was found to be about 22%.[3] Some of the commercial and moral implications for business and finance of these levels of economic inequality were explored above in the section *Corporate Responsibility for Social Inequality*, in which we reported on research by Lifeworth Consulting that found neither leading companies nor corporate responsibility organisations have been addressing economic inequality.[4]

In November 2010 the commercial implications became more widely recognised, as the International Monetary Fund (IMF) published a working paper that argued high economic inequality can trigger economic crises, which led to lively discussions on *The Economist* website and elsewhere.[5] The IMF authors Michael Kumhof and Romain Ranciere wrote that

> Both [the Depression and current recession] were preceded by a sharp increase in income and wealth inequality, and by a similarly sharp increase in debt-to-income ratios among lower- and middle-income households. When those debt-to-income ratios started to be perceived as unsustainable, it became a trigger for the crisis.

With various models and data, they explained how 'the key mechanism' for this connection between inequality and crisis is

> reflected in a rapid growth in the size of the financial sector, is the recycling of part of the additional income gained by high income households back to the rest of the population by way of loans, thereby allowing the latter to sustain consumption levels, at least for a while. But without the prospect of a recovery in the incomes of poor and middle income households over a reasonable time horizon, the inevitable result is that loans keep growing, and therefore so does leverage and the probability of a major crisis that, in the real world, typically also has severe implications for the real economy.[6]

Research released in October 2010 continued to show how, in some countries, the public are not aware of the levels of inequality and still believe that their societies are becoming more, not less, socially mobile.[7] However, in some countries there is more awareness of persistent inequality and a lack of social mobility, even if those countries are not the most unequal or socially immobile. In France, for example, debates about inequality and social mobility raged during 2010. This debate led to a challenge earlier in the year from French politicians and top business that the elite educational institutions, including the famous French business schools, respond to the need for more opportunity for the economically disadvantaged. That challenge, the initial reaction and then response from elite business schools in France, highlights the issue of the social responsibility and role of business schools, and educational institutions more generally. As such, it gave significant impetus to efforts to clarify those responsibilities, and broaden the focus from simply more socially responsive course content.

An article in *La Presse* highlighted how French business schools were resisting French government efforts to increase social diversity within their classes. In a country whose motto includes the word 'equality', the government proposed that the schools give 30% of places to students receiving financial aid due to modest family incomes. In response to the government proposal, the *Conférences des*

Grandes Ecoles (CGE) which manages the elite educational institutions stated that such quotas 'would inevitably cause a drop in the average'.[8] Not surprisingly, the comments were met with protest in France. The French Commissioner for Diversity and Equality, Mr Yazid Sabeg, slammed the CGE's criticism. He said, the suggestion that

> . . . because more marginalised people have access to our grandes écoles, there is a weakening of the level and quality of teaching received and the average in general, it is an adulteration and an absolutely scandalous claim.[9]

The French Minister for Education, Mr Luc Chatel, replied in similar fashion, exclaiming his shock and affirmed his determination to change the current system because it 'produces only social inequality'.[10]

Research by François Dubet, professor of sociology at Bordeaux University, confirmed this view.[11] Of the children of professionals that entered high school in France in 1995, 80% were still studying ten years later and only 10% had not obtained their higher school certificates, while only 30% of working-class children continued onto tertiary education with over 50% not receiving their high-school diplomas.[12] Such an indicator not only demonstrates the type of students that pursue tertiary education but, more importantly, it serves to illustrate how the societal inequality that already exists is a major contributor to the disparity present in tertiary institutions. Dubet argues that the children of the parents that didn't seize their opportunity should not have to suffer from the consequences that it may entail.[13] Also, as a result of this situation, despite France being a multi-racial society, the *grandes écoles* have a remarkably well preserved Caucasian student body, apart from foreign postgraduate students.[14] In highlighting the social uniformity within these schools, Professor Dubet's study can be seen to contradict comments by the CGE's president, Mr Pierre Tapie, who defended their initial stance against government measures to increase social diversity in their universities. 'Do you think we could improve the level of our world champion handball team if we required that there were a certain percentage of people with a particular characteristic? The answer is no, of course,' he explained.[15] The irony is that Dubet's research shows that the approach of the *grandes écoles* was to produce a student group with predominantly one shared characteristic—Caucasian middle class—rather than the full talents of France.

During the year the CGE changed its stance to the government call for more diversity. By December 2010 it had published a report that recognised the role of the *grandes écoles* in realising the French republic's commitment to equal educational opportunity. Their report suggested that, while great improvements have been made in outreach, there is still considerable effort needed if the *grandes écoles* are to achieve the aim of 30% of incoming students from among the poorer social classes by 2012.[16]

Fortunately, there are innovations in the social inclusiveness of business schools arising from different corners of the globe, which the *grandes écoles* and other elite institutions could learn about. In France, one business school that has been actively trying to address social justice issues is Bordeaux Management School (BEM). A member of GRLI, BEM claims to be the first French business school to integrate civic service into its management courses, with a view to including it in all courses.[17] It has a partnership with UNIS-CITE, a non-governmental organisation dedicated to promoting the development of civil society in France, with specific goals to encourage citizen responsibility and engagement, fight against exclusion and to reinforce social cohesion and mobilise youth on social and environmental issues.[18] The partnership allows students to participate in the management of a civic project for six to nine months on territorial and social development and is an integral part of the curriculum.[19] Not only does the programme try to apply management education to social issues, it also allows students to have a more systemic view of society in working with local authorities.

BEM has also recognised that access to business schools needs to go further than scholarships for those students that show potential. As part of democratising access to the school, since 2006 it has partnerships with two local high schools whereby university undergraduates tutor socially or geographically underprivileged students in the schools. The goal is to support and provide guidance in terms of pupils' professional ambitions, and the direction necessary to access higher education courses while removing some of the socio-cultural barriers that impede such access.[20] As well as providing financial access to BEM through a solidarity fund and thus better access to opportunities, the personalised nature of the process means that it is adapted to the needs of the students in question, thus trying to address other inequality barriers that may impact upon the life of each student.

Another member of the GRLI is the Welingkar Institute of Management Development & Research in India, whose leadership programme, Project Netrutva, aims to provide social–economic empowerment to underprivileged individuals through management education. By integrating disadvantaged students that were unable to complete their school education into a management course at Welingkar, such students are encouraged to complete their higher learning, potentially enabling greater social mobility and professional development.

To facilitate the process, the school needed to think about the practical aspects of incorporating students with lower educational qualifications into the programme. A first step was to pay the selected students a stipend to replace any lost income so that they could focus on their studies. Another step was to reduce the knowledge divide between students with lower qualifications and the students that had passed through the usual entry criteria. Rather than marginalising the disadvantaged students, Welingkar inaugurated a participative approach to the programme so that peers take responsibility for the development of the students needing to catch-up.

This original approach by Welingkar is positive for several reasons. First, all disadvantaged students graduating from the programme between 2005 and 2009 succeeded in obtaining more qualified positions with better salaries. Second, the programme redefines leadership from the typical competition based management school paradigm to a values-based leadership centred on values such as goodness, courage, commitment, risk-taking and compassion. As Professor Swar Kranti explains:

> These are not just competencies but are virtues which cannot simply be learnt through books or case studies but through real life experiences and challenges. This is a challenge of the responsibility, growth and well-being of another individual. It's a challenge that has serious consequences—consequences which are far greater than examination scores and degrees.[21]

Third, Welingkar has created a conduit whereby there is a connection between education, corporations and marginalised people. As a number of companies have pledged support for the programme, not only do disadvantaged students have another chance at education, some companies also offer job placements after graduation. So by asking the question how an educational institution can address a particular social issue, Welingkar has developed a socially innovative programme for students, which inculcates the importance of a cause, not just a job.

Perhaps the leading social innovation in university education comes from South Africa. The Community Individual Development Association (CIDA) University in Johannesburg aims to provide education in business administration for the rural poor with a view to transforming its students into leaders of their communities in turn advancing the socioeconomic transformation of the country and the broader region. To do this, it focuses on four building blocks, namely: being holistically centred—that is, going beyond the technical competencies related to business; low-cost; relevant to the different segments of society including business and government; and encouraging student resourcefulness to study. The school recognises the challenging backgrounds of students including former street-kids, students from geographically isolated areas, orphans and students whose parents have criminal records, and has put in place a life skills certificate as a part of the programme.

In terms of tuition fees, all students have scholarships and according to Taddy Blecher, one of the founders of CIDA, it is 'the lowest-cost university in the world'.[22] In acknowledging the new access to opportunities that the school provides upon graduation, graduates are expected to pay the tuition fees of students that follow in their footsteps. CIDA has managed to raise large corporate support to finance the school's operations. According to Emmanuel Raufflet, associate professor of management at HEC Montréal, one of the instrumental factors in obtaining business support for the school was due to the leading role played by Lisa Kropman, head of social investment for the Investec Group, who sought political endorsement of the initiative. What this highlights is how socially innovative initiatives can unify the public and private spheres.[23]

If one is to have a lasting impact in addressing social inequalities, then it is important that students from disadvantaged backgrounds do not simply forget others from similar circumstances. François Dubet highlights the potential problem:

> Imagine that, tomorrow, 10% of the highest performing students in a marginalised area leave their school for one of the prestigious institutions: what would be good for them would be catastrophic for their neighbourhood, depriving it of the most active, the most 'intelligent' and the most open-minded people. In this case, the neighbourhood would be further impoverished and marginalised.[24]

One way that CIDA addresses this issue is by requiring students to return to their former high schools and communities of origin to teach courses such as money management, banking and insurance and entrepreneurship during their holidays.

Other approaches to this issue of transforming communities rather than removing talent from them that could be adopted by other business schools include programmes that facilitate cancellation of debts for university fees if graduates work in certain jobs. For instance, students could be encouraged to submit a proposal to organisations that are working towards social equality or perhaps sustainable development in a marginalised area. In the event that the proposal is accepted, students would be required to work a certain length of time at the organisation and the university debt owing would be cancelled. Similarly, corporations could partner with higher learning institutions so that the 'best and brightest' are working towards socially viable projects. Such a process would expand the notion of merit so that it is measured according to one's contribution to society, rather than one's place in it.

The work of CIDA highlights that business can be involved in social innovation in education. The fact that the Investec Group rallied political support for the school is an example of how the private sector can also work with government. The result was that other companies got on board to try to resolve the social issue of inequality in education in South Africa, a project of social value for the purposes of personal, professional and economic development. It illustrates that business can play a role in development, even in complex issues such as inequality in education. What will be interesting to see is how these students then go on to impact business approaches to social innovation. Perhaps it will be CIDA and BEM graduates that will shape not only issues related to inequality in education, but the business and development agenda in the future.

For more universities and business schools to act on this social agenda in a comprehensive fashion will require reconsidering some core operations and system conditions. Two key issues are school finances and school rankings. Heads of business schools have warned of the financial challenge posed by a lack of endowments and reductions in government funding due to fiscal tightening. They say this is leading them to raise fees, which will not help them in their social role.[25] However, one answer lies close to home—their own salaries. A *New York Times* article highlighted how university chancellor compensation is starting to resemble the trends in corporate executive pay. Labelled by Dr Constantine W. Curris, president emeritus of the American Association of State Colleges and Universities as an 'arms race in presidential pay', he stated that, 'What we have is a system in which presidential salaries on campus are compared to those of other CEOs.'[26] When commenting on the recent salary raise of Matthew Goldstein of the City University of New York (CUNY), which entitled him to a compensation package of just over US$600,000 per annum, Ms Barbara Bowen, president of the Professional Staff Congress, the faculty and staff union for CUNY, stated:

> Lavish salaries for top management are unfortunately standard in American higher education. . . But what's also standard is under-financing of the core activity of the university, which is instruction. The gap between the chancellor's salary [and that of lecturers], or the standard of living of many of our students and their families, is huge.[27]

A report by the *Guardian* newspaper illustrated a similar trend in the United Kingdom where some vice-chancellors had seen their annual earnings double or even triple over the last decade compared with a 45.7% rise for the same period for average higher-education teaching professionals.[28] Unless senior executives in business schools curb their pay, then expressions of commitment to social inclusion, or explanations for raising fees in the name of quality, will be seen as disingenuous.

Business school heads also need to collectively call for a change in the way rankings are produced. Currently, one of the key indicators of the success of a business school is the students' salary upon leaving the institution. If this remains, then initiatives such as encouraging graduates into social enterprise or public service, will always remain marginal. Ranking systems need to measure the social utility of projects and careers, rather than equating success with monetary worth. Although the rankings assume salary to be a key interest of prospective students, it could be that the status of the institution, i.e. its ranking, is of key interest, and thus the rankings have the opportunity to encourage, not thwart, the social purpose of business schools.

The growing profile of Aspen Institute's *Beyond Grey Pinstripes* survey is useful in this regard, but it focuses only on the social, environmental and ethical content of teaching and research, rather than the broader agenda that was beginning to be understood during 2010.[29] Although the UN Principles for Responsible Management Education (UNPRME) have played a useful role in internationalising the conversation among university staff, they do not provide a structured framework for management. It is promising, therefore, that the hosts of those principles, the United Nations Global Compact,[30] are collaborating with the World Business School Council for Sustainable Business[31] and the Globally Responsible Leadership Initiative (GRLI)[32] to prepare a high-level report on transforming business education. To help this process to produce specific guidance, we have identified 16 steps for responsible business schools to take (Box 6).[33]

Box 6: The 16 steps for responsible business schools

1. Clarify the social purpose of the institution and what it means for today's context and incorporate that into organisational mission and governance

2. Upgrade existing curricula and pedagogy to incorporate the social purpose of the institution, such as teaching on social, environmental and ethical issues

3. Create new curricula and executive courses with content and pedagogy aligned to the social purpose of the institution

4. Encourage the research projects of existing faculty and students to include more social, environmental and ethical themes

5. Encourage and fund new action-oriented rather than theory-driven research

6. Incorporate social, environmental or ethical expertise into recruitment of faculty and research students

7. Upgrade admissions procedures, fee structures, scholarships, advertising and outreach, to improve diversity of students and their ability to do progressive work upon graduating

8. Support students and alumni to organise to promote learning and action on social, environmental or ethical issues

9. Incorporate consideration of social, environmental, and ethical issues into the operations of the organisation (i.e. practices at work), including core issues such as executive compensation

10. Encourage an organisational learning environment by requiring departments put forward academics to lead compulsory internal staff training on the social, environmental or ethical dimensions of the organisational functions they are experts in

11. Host events and produce newsworthy reports or papers that stimulate public and professional discussion on social, environmental and ethical issues

12. Encourage and support staff to engage helpfully with issues affecting the local community, using their particular talents, either as volunteers or in their work for the school

13. Seek and support collaboration outside the organisation to align external factors such as institution and staff rankings, accreditations, awards, and funding, as well market demand, with these steps

14. Develop policies and procedures for private donations to be received transparently and in line with the mission of the organisation and without threatening the success of the organisation's other activities

15. Align incentives within the organisation with all these steps, including reducing perverse incentives

16. Communicate internally and externally on implementation of these steps, using (and perhaps developing) relevant benchmarks, as well as providing mechanisms for stakeholder feedback on progress

The challenge of transforming management education is at the same time highly systemic, broadly institutional and deeply personal. Prestigious universities may be able to attract millions from donors for chairs and centres in social enterprise or inclusive business, yet our brief review has found that the real innovations in education are occurring among people to whom the struggle and creativity of social change is a lived experience, not just a topic of study. Humility and exchange are the parents of new insight. Herein lies perhaps the greatest challenge for elite institutions—to overcome the pride of a high status, or the fear of losing such status. Only then will they authentically embrace a public purpose and take risks to lead, rather than just reacting to public pressure or government legislation. As Mark Drewell, Chief Executive of the GRLI Foundation, explained: 'It is about moving from being the best in the world to an era where business success is predicated on being the best for the world.'[34]

Digital sunlight

The potential impact of social media and the Internet in general on corporate responsibility moved to a new level in the last quarter of 2010. And it was timely, as November 2010 marked what some believe to be the 20th anniversary of the Internet (Tim Berners-Lee introduced his proposal for a 'WorldWideWeb' to CERN on 12 November 1990). In the same month, the social media sustainability specialists Custom Communication launched the world's first ever Social Media Sustainability Index. The index reports on how the world's largest companies communicate their CSR initiatives via social media and is an indicator of how social media will impact corporate responsibility in the near future.[35]

This also coincided with the publicity surrounding the activities of WikiLeaks, a whistle-blowing site founded in 2006 by Julian Assange, generating new debate on issues such as transparency, responsibility and the role of new media. While there are major implications in two related, but distinct areas—whistle-blowing and activism—it also raises questions about the sometimes blurry line between legality and ethics, the big-bully tactics of major corporations and the role of whistle-blowing organisations.

Whistle-blowing is the act of raising concern about alleged illegal or unethical activities by individuals or organisations. This is most often done by anonymous leaks to government, public watchdogs or the media from someone within the targeted institution. These acts are widely regarded as improving transparency and being in the public interest. Hence, most countries have legislation to protect whistle-blowers. In the US, this practice dates back to the Lloyd–La Follette Act of 1912 and was most recently reinforced and strengthened through the Sarbanes–Oxley Act of 2002.

Some argue that WikiLeaks has simply continued the honourable tradition of whistle-blowing and raised it to another level, appropriate to the open-access age of the Internet—part of what Daniel Goleman calls 'radical transparency'.[36] For instance, in September 2009, the website posted a leaked internal report from Trafigura, a commodities multinational, exposing it for dumping hazardous waste in Côte d'Ivoire.[37] The site also claimed to have damaging information linked to a major US bank, widely speculated to be the Bank of America, which some believe caused their stock price to fall by 3%.[38] In a July 2010 *TED* interview, Assange claimed to have inside information from BP as well.[39]

Not surprisingly, companies (and governments) are extremely nervous—even hostile—about the activities of WikiLeaks. The issue came to a head in the final quarter of 2010 with 'megaleaks' to various high-profile newspapers such as the *Guardian* and the *New York Times*, among others; with the release in October of 390,000 previously secret US military field reports on the Iraq war[40] and in November, over 250,000 cables from more than 250 US embassies around the world.[41] This followed a July 2010 release of over 92,000 classified documents on the War in Afghanistan.[42] When the US government declared these releases 'illegal', several companies with commercial ties to WikiLeaks, notably Mastercard and PayPal, froze their transactions, resulting in a funding crisis for the organisation.[43]

What happened next revealed the new face of activism in the 21st century. Using methods that *The Economist* called 'guerrilla transparency' and which have been dubbed by the media as 'hacktivism', there was a rapid proliferation of mirror sites and counter-attacks by hacker groups such as Anonymous in response to attempts by governments and commercial partners to shut WikiLeaks down or cut off its financial oxygen.[44] One of the tactics of these groups was to bombard the websites of organisations that were perceived to be obstructing WikiLeaks with online requests, thus causing them to crash. In the case of Mastercard, one such orchestrated DDoS (distributed denial of service) campaign by Operation Payback was successful. For a couple of weeks it appeared that online services companies were experiencing their own digital 'Brent Spar moment', as activism disrupted their business and brought new questions about their responsibilities beyond simple compliance with law.

Irrespective of the merits or demerits of these tactics, one thing is clear: WikiLeaks has blown the debate about transparency wide open, raising many more questions than it answers. For instance, what is the role of corporate social responsibility (CSR) when one leak about a corporate malpractice can destroy years of conscientious work on corporate responsibility? The research of Professors Paul Godfrey, Craig Merrill and Jared Hansen, from Brigham Young University and the University of North Carolina, is relevant to this new era of web-enabled whistle-blowing. They focused on companies experiencing negative consequences from events such as a lawsuit, new regulation, or an accident. They measured what happened to the share price of the company as a result of the event. They found that the correlation between stock price and a negative incident depended on how much of a socially responsible company it was perceived to be. Firms that rank poorly on a social responsibility index saw their share price plummet as a result of negative news, while the impact for firms with good CSR resulted in less of a drop in the stock price. The professors concluded that a socially responsible reputation acts as a form of insurance; as a result of a negative event, investors are persuaded to think that it was a one-off incident and is therefore not an indicator of something structurally wrong with the firm. However, if the company is considered socially irresponsible, then such events are understood as part of a pattern, and so the stock market reacts more strongly.[45] This is a strong argument derived from reputation management; yet the CSR rationale extends further, to encouraging organisational learning and more socially and environmentally beneficial forms of enterprise. The rewards for shifting towards such business models may only increase from more digital sunlight on the murkier areas of business practice.

Despite such evidence of the commercial sense of CSR, will this new generation of online whistle-blowing—whether by WikiLeaks or others—increase transparency, or will it simply cause governments and companies to clam up even tighter; to invest more in data security and counter-hacking measures? And if they do react defensively, will this result in what Assange called an effective 'secrecy tax', whereby those organisations with the most to hide end up being less competitive as a result of their security-related expenditures? As Assange explains:

> When an organisation acts in a more clandestine manner, its own internal efficiency decreases, because information cannot flow quickly through the organisation.[46]

This may be also interpreted as organisations not fulfilling their fiduciary duties to their shareholders, raising the question of how to measure the impact of such secrecy within a corporation.

The actions of WikiLeaks have brought into light more serious ethical and political issues that go beyond transparency and the potential impact on an organisation. If companies such as Mastercard and PayPal can use their power to impede the transactional abilities of an organisation such as WikiLeaks because it exposes government secrets, it shows that they are not apolitical. Furthermore, it also brings to light the systemic nature of the flow of information and how companies indirectly related to media organisations could affect the public's right to information. But there is also a corollary: could social media itself be a source of censorship? The latter was the theme of a December 2010 blog entitled 'Twitter is censoring the discussion of Wikileaks', which questioned some irregularities in Twitter's 'Trend' function despite the high level of discussion surrounding WikiLeaks.[47] The company rejected these claims, but it is impossible to know unless there is more transparency or, perhaps, a whistle-blower emerging from inside Twitter itself. While suspicion cannot be taken as fact, it shows that even social media organisations require levels of accountability and need to reflect more deeply on their social purpose beyond the mere distribution of information. The disturbance to the normal information order that WikiLeaks' activities has caused has helped to expose the political nature of technology hitherto assumed to simply be tools of a modern life:

credit cards, online payments, social media platforms. These tools are owned by institutions and as they become more critical to normal life, their accountability becomes more important.

Deeper questions can be asked about the future effectiveness of the WikiLeaks style of activism and other tamer campaign-based versions on social media sites. Will such activism be able to create real and sustained positive change faced with such opposition? This was the theme of an October 2010 article in *The New Yorker* entitled 'Why the revolution will not be Tweeted', by *Tipping Point* author Malcolm Gladwell. He argued that

> the drawbacks of networks scarcely matter if the network isn't interested in systemic change—if it just wants to frighten or humiliate or make a splash—or if it doesn't need to think strategically. But if you're taking on a powerful and organized establishment you have to be a hierarchy.[48]

Critics that share Gladwell's view have started to characterise the sort of online activism seen on Facebook and other social media sites as 'slacktivism', which was apparently coined by anti-scam crusader Barbara Mikkelson[49] and who defined it as 'the desire people have to do something good without getting out of their chair'.[50]

By the end of 2010, such armchair analysis already appeared a little dated. The revelations in the US cables from WikiLeaks about corruption in Tunisia fuelled protests against the regime, while Facebook, Twitter and YouTube were helping young activists in North Africa and the Middle East to organise protests. The revolutions were indeed being tweeted, and in concert with satellite TV channels, shining a digital spotlight on both injustice and a new generation of hope. If in the West Generation Y is highly individualistic and hedonistic, Generation Y in Arab regions is reminding the whole world of our ability and need to work collectively for our individual freedoms. It appears that the reason for 'slacktivism' may be found not in the technology but the mentality of those using it. The potential for massive change from new digital sunlight being shone on large institutions currently exists. The long-term implications are unclear, but it is likely that decisions that were once possible in private will need to evolve to the public domain if they are to prosper in future. Such a situation should give way to a new standard, not to mention simplified, guide for staff when confronting a business ethics dilemma: would you feel comfortable if your wider circle of friends knew you are doing what you are doing?

Those were some of the big-picture changes occurring at the end of 2010 that have implications for the future of business, and indeed society as a whole. Yet there were also a range of developments using social media within the narrower field of corporate citizenship and CSR during 2010, which give pointers to changing times ahead.

We now have companies such as GoodGuide providing sustainability ratings for over 60,000 products in the US, all accessible at the point of purchase simply by using a free iPhone barcode scanning application.[51] We have JustMeans providing a social networking platform that allows self-declared stakeholders to 'follow' a company through the site, providing not only access to their published CSR information, but also providing a conduit for feedback.[52] JustMeans and CRD Analytics have also launched an innovative platform to provide companies with the capability to verify the accuracy and completeness of their ESG data set.[53] Social media is also proving an effective platform for 'crowdsourcing', which is the act of outsourcing tasks to an undefined, large group of people through an open call. One new company, OpenEyeWorld, provides a 'crowdsourcing' tool for companies to consult with sustainability experts from around the world.[54]

However, like any new tool, social media is still a double-edged sword for companies trying to turn it their advantage in the sphere of business responsibility. An already classic case is that of Greenpeace's anti-Kit-Kat chocolate campaign, which went viral in March 2010 across the social media networks such as Facebook and Twitter. The 60-second Greenpeace video, which was at the heart of their campaign, shows a bored office worker biting into a Kit-Kat, and as he does so, it turns into the finger of an orang-utan and 'crunch!' the blood spills down his chin and over his clean white shirt. One estimate by Scott Douglas on Prezi calculated that within four days the Greenpeace report and shock-video may have reached half a million people through social media sites. This viral effect was seemingly boosted by Nestlé's attempt on its Facebook page to censor comments made by its critics (including activists who had changed their Facebook profile pictures to a defamed logo of Nestlé, which said 'Killer' instead).[55]

The fact that Nestlé took swift action by dropping the accused Indonesian supplier and that their hands are effectively tied by a lack of available sustainable palm oil did little to quell the angry reactions of online activists. Greenpeace later called off the campaign, which Nestlé Executive Vice President for Operations, José Lopez, said was achieved 'by putting on the table a very technical view of the issues we are talking about. We've demonstrated that we have a logic, a path and a process that drives continuous improvement into topics of high concern, which in this case is deforestation.'[56] Nestlé's successful resolution, however, did not take away the fact that social media is a tricky area for companies to master.

Besides the risks, however, there are also massive opportunities. For instance, in December 2010, BBC News highlighted the ways in which the Internet is empowering small traders and promoting greater equity in the supply chain. Until China Mobile's *Nongxintong*—or farming information service—became available four years ago, farmers still lacked information on commodity prices despite most farming households having mobile phones. As Liu Jing, a local manager for the service at China Mobile explained:

> Building the mobile network and covering most of the country's administrative villages, we realised that there was only a network signal. In rural areas, this is not enough. It's like having a highway and no cars![57]

As most households did not have access to the Internet, China Mobile introduced a new generation of web-enabled mobile phones, which allows 20 million farmers to stay up to date on commodity prices. Other innovations include the Geo Fair Trade research project, which is devising a geo-traceability tool for the Fair Trade sector as a way of re-personalising ethics in the Fairtrade supply chain.[58] Meanwhile, Patagonia's forsaking of GRI-style sustainability reporting in favour of their online Footprint Chronicles®, which map the impacts of their products through the supply chain, perhaps gives a glimpse into the future of transparency.[59]

Looking at the broader trends, the impact of social media has the potential to influence business management and corporate responsibility in general. Already, open-source platforms exist such as *The Management Innovation Exchange*, which aims to reinvent management for the 21st century.[60] A Harvard Business School paper argues that Web 2.0 is causing a distinct shift—from Accountability 1.0 to Accountability 2.0.[61] Accountability 1.0 is marked by one-way proclamations, campaigns and PR communications. Companies and stakeholders talk at each other more than with each other. Because it is more about speaking than listening, Accountability 1.0 processes sometimes unintentionally fuel antagonism, confrontation and mistrust between companies and stakeholders. Accountability 2.0 rests on the assumption of two-way communication, cooperation and mutual engagement. Accountability 2.0 allows actors in the accountability ecosystem to disagree over substantive issues while engaging in respectful dialogue that seeks mutual understanding and more consensus-oriented solutions. The growing recognition of a shift in approach to more interactivity on social responsibility is reflected in the increasing popularity of phrases such as 'CSR 2.0'.[62]

What this highlights is the need for companies to become networked communities of purpose. While Accountability 2.0 may facilitate the communication necessary to discuss and maybe resolve a particular social problem, what the attempted repression of WikiLeaks demonstrates is that, to be effective, such frameworks need to be measured against the power relations at play. Although the Internet provides greater access to information, the changing ecology of accountability due to social media does not mean that the existing structures that protect the interests of elites are being broken down. Corporations and indeed social media organisations still need to align their purposes with the concerns of society. For a new period of 'CSR 2.0' to be meaningful it will need not only to use new technologies but use them to become truly more open and collaborative in addressing common problems. In an age of digital sunlight, the character of our institutions, leaders, fellow citizens, and ourselves, will be clearer to see. Whether we will like what we see is up to all of us.

CSR and disaster risk reduction

One crucial area where social media is starting to have an impact is in response to natural disasters. Examples of 'crowdsourcing' through social media platforms such as Peoplefinder in the aftermath of Hurricane Katrina, and Mission 4636 following the Haiti earthquake proved to be effective tools in responding to requests for help and in locating missing persons.[63] Social media is also providing important access to information in the wake of disasters. Therefore, disaster risk reduction is one field where social media enterprise could contribute as part of its corporate social responsibility.[64] But business in general has a role to play in disaster risk reduction. As developing countries are most affected by natural disasters and many corporations have transferred their production facilities to these regions, it stands to reason that businesses start to reflect on their societal role in the event of a catastrophe.[65] How business is addressing disaster risk reduction overall is thus another part of corporate responsibility which companies need to consider.

This was highlighted by an October 2010 announcement from the Small Equity Initiative (SEI) to pilot a private-sector disaster reduction programme in Nairobi, Kenya. SEI is dedicated to education, advocacy and activism to improve the capital markets for both small business entrepreneurs and investors globally. In sponsoring the pilot, it hopes to urge private-sector innovation and investment aimed at reducing disaster risk. As Mr Philip Verges, founder of SEI, stated at the press release:

> Small businesses are an important source of disaster risk reduction support. They can build homes, commercial buildings and civil infrastructure, and provide communications as part of an emergency contingency plan.[66]

Also present at the launch was Ms Margareta Wahlström, the Special Representative of the UN Secretary-General for Disaster Risk Reduction, who called for businesses and governments to develop a new cooperative approach to reduce disaster losses. She stipulated that

> Governments, the private sector and donors need to team up to make cities and communities more resilient against disasters. We will not be able to achieve our goals without this strong partnership.[67]

According to the United Nations International Strategy for Disaster Reduction (UNISDR), disaster risk reduction is:

> The conceptual framework of elements considered with the possibilities to minimise vulnerabilities and disaster risks throughout a society, to avoid (prevention) or to limit (mitigation and preparedness) the adverse impacts of hazards, within the broad context of sustainable development.[68]

Therefore, the key to disaster reduction is to reduce the vulnerability of communities exposed to natural hazards and better be able to cope during, and recover after the event. Successful prevention activity can reduce natural disaster risks to business operations and the communities that depend on them thus improving business efficiency.

For business, two immediate applications are business continuity and sustainable development. The International Consortium for Organisational Resilience (ICOR) describes business continuity as the activity performed by an organisation to ensure that critical business functions will be available when there are disruptions.[69] While business continuity is not a new concept, its application to disasters is a natural extension to the evolving field and is starting to come to the fore. A British Standards Institution (BSi) article in October 2010 illustrated how the private equity firm Altius Associates was able to cope during the cold snap in Europe which affected people's mobility. As partner and head of client services Mr Adam Heaysman stated:

> Thanks to our business continuity plan, we had an IT infrastructure in place which allowed those members of staff to work as if they were still in the office.[70]

At the 2010 CSR Asia Summit earlier in the year, a session was dedicated to business continuity planning and the role of the private sector in disaster preparedness.[71] Rather than framing the business continuity and disaster preparedness theme in terms of business efficiency, the session looked at how core business practices and competencies could be extended to ensure the overall stability of the economic environment in the region. And it stands to reason, particularly in Asia. According to the Centre for Research on the Epidemiology of Disasters (CRED), Asia accounts for more than 40% of meteorological calamities such as typhoons.[72] In light of the many companies that have transferred their production to Asia, there is a clear business case for disaster preparedness as part of corporate responsibility.

But by broadening the scope of business continuity to one that contributes to the overall economic stability of a region, it requires companies to think about *how* their business continuity plans impact society in the event of a disaster. For instance, if business expediency is the priority, a business continuity plan could entail dropping a supplier if supplies are temporarily disrupted, effectively depriving the supplier of much-needed resources to be functional again. Such a plan would be contrary to sustainable development. If any degree of economic stability is to be achieved in developing countries, disaster preparedness needs to be understood within the context of sustainable development.

The outfall from the Eyjafjallajökull volcano eruption in Iceland at the start of 2010 was a good example. In the three days after the eruption and the subsequent grounding of aircraft, 5,000 farm workers in Kenya had been temporarily laid off due to the lack of market access.[73] While Tesco was able to organise an alternative delivery route through Spain, it raises the question of the viability of trade arrangements that create such dependencies.[74] In the case of a supermarket chain, greater corporate responsibility could involve a strategy that strengthens local markets to provide food for the local population. This would represent an investment in the supply chain rather than an opportunity to cut costs. By taking such an approach, the unpredictability of natural disasters can be tempered as there is greater supply chain capacity to respond when calamity strikes.

Furthermore, such an approach could actually avoid some disasters altogether. While a business continuity plan for fast-onset disasters such as earthquakes and volcanic eruptions can minimise the impact of a catastrophe, slow-onset disasters such as drought need not necessarily create humanitarian crises.

An Interpares study on community-based food security systems showed how poor communities in the Medak district, a semi-arid region in the Indian state of Andhra Pradesh and also part of India's 'hunger belt', were unaffected by the 2001–2002 drought.[75] By growing grain that is adapted to a low-rainfall climate and through the establishment of a community grain fund that enables food sovereignty in lean times, the communities had no need of external assistance during the emergency. What this demonstrates is that, while the drought was unavoidable, the appropriate management of resources can strengthen communities as well as reducing their vulnerability in the event of a potential disaster.

While there was no corporate involvement in the above example, companies that align their core business practices for the purposes of social development may be able to develop disaster risk reduction solutions that go beyond risk minimisation. For instance, a food services company could partner with a community to support traditional farmer methods that maintain land sovereignty and are adapted to arid climates. Rather than an emergency relief approach that is reactionary, by addressing the systemic issues that expose vulnerable communities to risk in the event of disaster, communities can be strengthened to avoid tragedy all together.

Notes

Introduction

1 publications.aomonline.org/newsletter/index. php?option=com_content&task=view&id=1187.

2 Michael E. Porter and Mark R. Kramer, 'Creating Shared Value', *Harvard Business Review: The Magazine*, January 2011; hbr.org/2011/01/the-big-idea-creating-shared-value (2011).

3 J. Bendell, *Terms for Endearment: Business, NGOs and Sustainable Development* (Sheffield, UK: Greenleaf Publishing, 2000): 97.

4 Accenture and United Nations Global Compact, *Accenture CEO Study on Sustainability 2013*; www.accenture.com/microsites/ungc-ceo-study/Pages/home.aspx.

5 J. Bendell, *Evolving Partnerships: Engaging Business for Greater Social Change* (Sheffield, UK: Greenleaf Publishing, 2011).

6 J. Bendell, *Barricades and Boardrooms: A Contemporary History of the Corporate Accountability Movement* (Geneva: UNRISD, 2004).

7 J. Vidal, 'Protect nature for world economic security, warns UN biodiversity chief', *The Guardian*, 16 August 2010; www.guardian.co.uk/environment/2010/aug/16/nature-economic-security.

8 Data recalculated from GRID-Arendal, "Vital Waste Graphics" (2004); www.grida.no/publications/vg/waste.

9 Data recalculated from United Nations Information Service, *Independent Expert on Effects of Structural Adjustment, Special Rapporteur on Right to Food Present Reports: Commission Continues General Debate On Economic, Social And Cultural Rights* (United Nations, 29 March 2004).

10 Data recalculated from news.minnesota.publicradio.org/features/2005/01/31_olsond_biodiversity and www.rain-tree.com/facts.htm.

11 Joseph L. Bower, Herman Leonard and Lynn Sharp Paine, *Capitalism at Risk: Rethinking the Role of Business* (Cambridge, MA: Harvard Business Press Books, 2011; hbr.org/product/capitalism-at-risk-rethinking-the-role-of-business/an/13297-HBK-ENG).

12 Porter and Kramer, *op. cit.*

13 Arun Maira, *Transforming Capitalism: Business Leadership to Improve the World for Everyone* (Nimby Books/Westland, 2011).

14 For instance, the economic theories of Mutualism: en.wikipedia.org/wiki/ Mutualism_(economic_theory).

15 For instance, my publication for UNRISD in 2004 was one of many from the UN agency that took a political economy perspective on corporate responsibility and accountability issues (Bendell, *op. cit.* [2004]).

16 To see the latest activity on these topics, visit the Institute for Leadership and Sustainability (IFLAS) at www.iflas.info.

17 John Ruskin, *Unto This Last* (1852); available at etext.virginia.edu/etcbin/toccer-new2?id=RusLast.xml&images=images/modeng&data=/texts/english/modeng/parsed &tag=public&part=2&division=div1.

18 K. Polanyi, *The Great Transformation* (New York: Rinehart, 1944).

19 Gilles Deleuze and Félix Guattari, *Anti Oedipus* (University of Minnesota Press, 2000).

20 This was a footnote in Ruskin's *Unto This Last* in 1852.

21 Martin Horn, *Britain, France, and the Financing of the First World War* (McGill-Queen's Press, 2002): 82.

22 Bray Hammond, 'Jackson, Biddle, and the Bank of the United States', *Journal of Economic History* 7 (1947): 1-23 (6 December 2006).

23 J. Ryan-Collins, T. Greenham, R. Werner and A. Jackson, *Where Does Money Come From? A Guide to the UK Monetary and Banking System* (London: New Economics Foundation, 2011).

24 All quotes from Ryan-Collins *et al., op. cit.*

25 N. Ferguson, *The Ascent of Money: A Financial History of the World* (London: Allen Lane, 2008): 49-50

26 All quotes from Ryan-Collins *et al., op. cit.*

27 E.C. Riegel, *Private Enterprise Money* (New York: Harbinger House, 1944); and Thomas H. Greco, Jr, *The End of Money and the Future of Civilization* (White River Junction, VT: Chelsea Green, 2009).

28 Hypothetically, if banks spent all their interest payments and also the velocity of monetary exchanges increased sufficiently, then the debts could be serviced without increasing amounts of lending. However, banks do not spend all their interest earnings; they add most of them to their capital and enable additional loans at interest.

29 Andrew Walker, 'Richest 2% own "half the wealth"', BBC, 5 December 2009; news.bbc.co.uk/1/hi/6211250.stm.

30 R. Wilkinson and K. Pickett, *The Spirit Level: Why Equality is Better for Everyone* (London: Penguin, 2009).

31 IMF, *World Economic Outlook* (Washington, DC: International Monetary Fund, 2012; www.imf.org/external/pubs/ft/weo/2012/01/pdf/text.pdf).

32 Helena Smith, 'Greek woes drive up suicide rate', *The Guardian*, 18 December 2011; www.guardian.co.uk/world/2011/dec/18/greek-woes-suicide-rate-highest.

33 Positive Money web page on the cost of housing: www.positivemoney.org.uk/2012/09/ house-prices-why-are-they-so-high-new-video, accessed 20 October 2012.

34 D. Bolchover, *The Living Dead: Switched Off, Zoned Out—The Shocking Truth about Office Life* (John Wiley & Sons, 2005).

35 B. Lietaer, C. Arnsberger, S. Goerner and S. Brunnhuber, *Money and Sustainability: The Missing Link* (Club of Rome, 2012).

36 www.beyond-gdp.eu

37 Greco, *op. cit.*

38 Lietaer *et al., op. cit.*

39 David Korten, *The Post-Corporate World: Life after Capitalism* (San Francisco: Berrett-Koehler Publishers, 1999).

40 Danielle Sacks, 'John Mackey's Whole Foods Vision to Reshape Capitalism', *Fast Company*, 1 December 2009.

41 Ted Poole, 'Conversations with North American Indians', in Ralph Osborne (ed.), *Who is the Chairman of This Meeting? A Collection of Essays* (Toronto: Neewin Publishing Company, 1972): 39ff. [43].

42 J. Ruskin, 'Essay IV: Ad Valorem', in *Unto This Last* (1860): section 77.

43 J. Bendell, *The Corporate Responsibility Movement* (Sheffield, UK: Greenleaf Publishing, 2009).

44 Elinor Ostrom, *Governing the Commons: The Evolution of Institutions for Collective Action* (Cambridge University Press, 1990).

45 E.C. Riegel, *Private Enterprise Money* (self-published, 1944; available at www.mindtrek.com/treatise/ecr-pem).

46 J. Bendell and T. Greco, 'Currencies of Transition: Transforming Money to Unleash Sustainability', in M. McIntosh (ed.), *The Necessary Transition: The Journey towards the Sustainable Enterprise Economy* (Sheffield, UK: Greenleaf Publishing, 2011): 230.

47 Z/Yen, 'Capacity Trade and Credit: Emerging Architectures for Commerce and Money', Z/Yen, UK (2011).

48 B. Lietaer, M. Kennedy and J. Rogers, *People Money: The Promise of Regional Currencies* (Triarchy Press, 2012).

49 William O. Ruddick, Morgan Richards and Jem Bendell, 'Complementary Currencies for Sustainable Development in Kenya: The Case of the Bangla-Pesa', presented at the 2nd Conference on Community and Complementary Currency Systems, The Hague, June 2013; www.iss.nl/fileadmin/ASSETS/iss/Research_and_projects/Conferences/CCS_June_2013/Papers/Will_Ruddick.pdf.

50 E.C. Riegel, *Flight from Inflation: The Monetary Alternative* (The Heather Foundation, 1978).

51 My literature review of journals of international development, human geography, business and management, sociology, environmental policy, as well as specialist journals on business ethics and corporate responsibility, found that the implications of mutual credit systems for either business or sustainable development have been neither well researched nor recognised.

52 Bendell, *op. cit.*

53 www.corrietenboom.com

54 en.wikipedia.org/wiki/Grinberg_Method

55 Susan Sontag, *Illness as Metaphor* (Farrar, Straus & Giroux, 1978).

56 www.etymonline.com/index.php?term=heal

57 Charles Eisenstein, *The Ascent of Humanity: Civilization and the Human Sense of Self* (Panenthea Productions, 2007).

58 Andrew Weil, *Spontaneous Healing* (Ballantine, 1995).

59 I. Illich, *Deschooling Society* (New York: Harper & Row, 1971).

60 Thomas Carlyle, 'A Mechanical Age', *Edinburgh Review*; www.indiana.edu/~hist104/sources/Carlyle.html.

61 Mohandas K. Gandhi, *Unto This Last: A Paraphrase* (1933; www.scribd.com/doc/18030559/Unto-This-Last-Gandhis-Paraphase-of-Ruskin): 7, 21.

62 E.C. Riegel, *The New Approach to Freedom* (self-published, 1949; available at riegelexchange.com/downloads/NewApproachToFreedom.pdf).

63 Mark Matousek, *When You're Falling, Dive: Lessons in the Art of Living* (Hay House 2009): 7.
64 Matousek, *op. cit.*: 6.
65 Matousek, *op. cit.*: 7.

2006: Introduction

1 J. Bendell, 'Business–NGO Relations and Sustainable Development', *Greener Management International* 24 (1999); www.greenleaf-publishing.com/greenleaf/journaldetail.kmod?productid=85&keycontentid=8.
2 Christian Aid. 'The Climate of Poverty: Facts, Fears and Hope', 2006; www.christianaid.org.uk/Images/climate-of-poverty.pdf.
3 AlterNet, 'Inside The Frame', 14 January 2004; www.alternet.org/story/17574.
4 R. Cialdini, *Influence: Science and Practice* (New York: HarperCollins, 1993, 3rd edn). Social proof, also known as informational social influence, is a psychological phenomenon which occurs in ambiguous social situations when people are unable to determine the appropriate mode of behaviour. Making the assumption that surrounding people possess more knowledge about the situation, they will deem the behaviour of others as appropriate or more informed. en.wikipedia.org/wiki/Social_proof.
5 J. Bendell, 'Barricades and Boardrooms: A Contemporary History of the Corporate Accountability Movement' (Technology, Business and Society Programme, Paper Number 13; Geneva: UNRISD, 2004).
6 Manage to Change, 'Blending or Balance', 2006; managetochange.typepad.com/main/2006/09/blending_or_bal.html.
7 Mira Kamdar, *Planet India: How the Fastest Growing Democracy Is Transforming America and the World* (New York: Scribner Publishing, 2007).
8 Manage to Change, *op. cit.*
9 www.oneplanetliving.org/index.html.
10 Thomas Berry, *The Great Work: Our Way into the Future* (New York: Random House, 1999).
11 Ervin Laszlo, *Science and the Akashic Field: An Integral Theory of Everything* (Rochester, VT: Inner Traditions, 2004).
12 J. Bendell, 'Debating NGO Accountability', *UN-NGLS Online*, 2006; www.un-ngls.org/site/article.php3?id_article=202.

1Q2006

1 United Nations System Standing Committee on Nutrition, 'Double Burden of Malnutrition: A Common Agenda', 2006; www.unsystem.org/scn/Publications/AnnualMeeting/SCN33/33rd_session_participants_statement.htm.
2 NewsRx, 'Global obesity epidemic putting brakes on economic development', 23 November 2004; www.newsrx.com/newsletters/Cardiovascular-Business-Week/2004-11-23/112220043331100CVW.html.
3 HHS.Govarchive, 'Overweight, obesity threaten US health gains', 13 December 2001; archive.hhs.gov/news/press/2001pres/20011213.html.
4 Ania Lichtarowicz, 'S. Africans "as fat as Americans"', *BBC News Online*, 19 October 2004; news.bbc.co.uk/2/hi/africa/3964693.stm.

5 'Obese Chinese now total 90 mln, to hit 200 mln in a decade', *China View Online*, 18 June 2005; news.xinhuanet.com/english/2005-06/18/content_3101580.htm.

6 US Food and Drug Administration, *op. cit.*

7 Anita Regmi and Mark Gehlhar, 'New Directions in Global Food Markets', *USDA/ Economic Research Department Online* (2005); www.ers.usda.gov/publications/aib794/aib794b.pdf.

8 This reference is no longer available but was originally sourced from Euromonitor, 2004.

9 'First Chr Hansen food colour plant in China opens', *FoodNaivgator.com Online*, 19 January 2005; www.foodnavigator.com/Financial-Industry/First-Chr-Hansen-food-colour-plant-in-China-opens.

10 Roger Parloff, 'Is fat the next tobacco? For Big Food, the supersizing of America is becoming a big headache', *Fortune Online*, 3 February 2003; money.cnn.com/magazines/fortune/fortune_archive/2003/02/03/336442/index.htm.

11 'WHO attacks US sugar lobby', *BBC News Online*, 22 April 2003; news.bbc.co.uk/1/hi/world/americas/2966187.stm.

12 'US pupils get obesity reports', *BBC News Online*, 12 August 2003; news.bbc.co.uk/1/hi/education/3143991.stm.

13 George Lakoff, *Don't Think of an Elephant. Know Your Values and Frame the Debate: The Essential Guide for Progressives* (White River Jct, VT: Chelsea Green, 2004).

14 'Deal will slim US school drinks', *BBC News Online*, 3 May 2006; news.bbc.co.uk/1/hi/world/americas/4970044.stm.

15 Convergence Partnership: www.convergencepartnership.org/site/c.fhLOK6PELmF/b.6136239/k.C925/About_Us.htm.

16 IBLF and WBCSD, 'The Business of Health: The Health of Business. Building the Case for Health, Safety and Wellness', 2006; www.wbcsd.ch/Plugins/DocSearch/details.asp?DocTypeId=25&ObjectId=18367&URLBack=%2Ftemplates%2FTemplateWBCSD2%2Flayout.asp%3Ftype%3Dp%26MenuId%3DODU%26doOpen%3D1%26ClickMenu%3DRightMenu%26CurPage%3D8%26SortOrder%3D.

17 Anthony Fletcher, 'Food industry not responsive to obesity, claims report', *Food Navigator Online*, 6 March 2006; www.foodnavigator.com/news/ng.asp?n=66217-kraft-cadbury-coca-cola.

18 Critics Give "Public Eye" Awards for Corporate Irresponsibility', *Accounting Web Online*, 27 January 2005; www.accountingweb.com/topic/critics-give-public-eye-awards-corporate-irresponsibility.

19 World Development Movement, 'Statement by WDM on Nestlé FAIRTRADE Partners' Blend Coffee', press release, 7 October 2005; www.wdm.org.uk/news/presrel/current/nestle.htm. This article is no longer available on the World Development Movement website but a similar article is accessible at Baby Milk Action. 'Fairtrade mark and infant health could be damaged by Nestlé application warn campaigners', 6 October 2005; www.babymilkaction.org/press/press6oct05.html.

20 Oxfam, 'Mugged: Poverty in Your Coffee Cup', September 2002; www.oxfamamerica.org/publications/mugged-poverty-in-your-coffee-cup.

21 Fairtrade Press Release, 'Launch of Nescafé partners' Blend', 7 October 2005; www.fairtrade.org.uk/press_office/press_releases_and_statements/archive_2005/oct_2005/launch_of_nescafe_partners_blend.aspx.

22 Mallen Baker, 'Nestlé: unfairly roasted over Fairtrade', *Ethical Corporation*, 7 November 2005; www.ethicalcorp.com/content.asp?ContentID=3963. This article is no longer available on the Ethical Corporation website but a commentary is accessible at Baby

Milk Action. 'Nestlé and Fairtrade: PR coup or PR disaster?', 7 November 2005; www.babymilkaction.org/action/nestlefairtrade.html.

23 Fairtrade Labelling Organisation International website: www.fairtrade.net/our_standards.html.

24 Social Rights Bulgaria, 'Fair Trade in Europe 2005: Facts and Figures on Fair Trade in 25 European Countries', 3 March 2006; www.socialniprava.info/article1400.html.

25 Fair Trade Advocacy Office, 'Towards a coherent Fair Trade Policy: Fair Trade demands to European decision makers', April 2005; www.fairtrade-advocacy.org/images/stories/publications/demands_to_eu_apr05.pdf.

26 Fairtrade Labelling Organisations International, 'Delivering Opportunities: Annual Report 2004/2005'; www.fairtrade.net/fileadmin/user_upload/content/FLO_AR_2004_05.pdf.

27 Sustain, 'Eat well and save the planet! A guide for consumers on how to eat greener, healthier and more ethical food', *BBC Online*; news.bbc.co.uk/2/shared/bsp/hi/pdfs/17_12_07_sustainguide.pdf.

28 PR News Wire, 'TransFair USA Joins Oxfam in Welcoming McDonald's Rollout of Fair Trade Certified Coffee', 31 October 2005; www.prnewswire.co.uk/news/transfair-usa.

29 David Ransom, 'Fair trade for sale', *New Internationalist* 377 (April 2005); www.newint.org/issue377/essay.htm.

30 Jeevan Vasagar, 'How Kenya is caught on the thorns of Britain's love affair with the rose: Rising demand for flowers leads to trade-off between economy and environment', *The Guardian Online*, 13 February 2006; www.guardian.co.uk/frontpage/story/0,,1708492,00.html.

31 '50 great ideas for the 21st century', *The Guardian Online*, 6 August 2006; www.independent.co.uk/news/science/50-great-ideas-for-the-21st-century-410543.html. See also Chocolate Trading Co., 'Equitably-Traded Chocolate: 100% Pure Malagasy'; www.chocolatetradingco.com/special.asp?ID=17.

32 Stan Thekaekara, 'Linking Hands', *The Guardian Online*, 8 March 2006; society.guardian.co.uk/societyguardian/story/0,,1725463,00.html.

33 Virginie Diaz Pedregal, 'Between Institutionalisation and De-institutionalisation: The Issue of Fair Trade in France', *Économie et Solidarités*, 37.2 (2006); www.ciriec.uqam.ca/pdf/numeros_parus_articles/3702/ES-3702-09.pdf.

34 Soil Association, 'Certification Equivalence', 5 December 2005; www.soilassociation.org/web/sa/saweb.nsf/848d689047cb466780256a6b00298980/289589ffa17a49ab80 2570ce005ca208!OpenDocument. The original reference is no longer available. The following document alludes to the same issue. 'Organic Market report 2007', *Soil Association Online*, 2007; www.soilassociation.org/LinkClick.aspx?fileticket=phLTvTU Yrbg=&tabid=116.

35 European Commission, 'Organic Food: New Regulation will improve clarity for consumers and farmers', online press release, 21 December 2005; europa.eu/rapid/press-release_IP-05-1679_en.htm.

36 Friends of the Earth, 'EU Commission allows GM contamination of organic farming', online press release, 22 December 2005; www.foe.co.uk/resource/press_releases/eu_commission_allows_gm_co_ 22122005.html.

37 Bernie Ward and Julie Lewis, 'Plugging the Leaks' (London: NEF, 2002; www.neweconomics.org/projects/plugging-leaks).

38 Just Change official website: www.justchangeindia.com/jci/index.php.

39 The concept of 'Globalisation 2.0' is referred to in T. Friedman, *The World Is Flat: A Brief History of the Twenty-first Century* (New York: Farrar, Straus & Giroux, 2005).

40 Fareed Zakaria, 'India Rising', *The Daily Beast Online*, 5 March 2006; www.thedailybeast.com/newsweek/2006/03/05/india-rising.html.

41 'Jack Straw acknowledges India as a global player', *Hindustan Times Online*, 29 March 2006; www.hindustantimes.com/News-Feed/NM8/Jack-Straw-acknowledges-India-as-a-global-player/Article1-80851.aspx.

42 'Bharti, Tesco plan on grocery chain', *The Economic Times Online*, 21 March 2006; economictimes.indiatimes.com/articleshow/1457629.cms.

43 UNDP, 'Human Development Index'; hdr.undp.org/reports/global/2005.

44 UNDP, 'Human Development Index. Country Sheets: India'; hdr.undp.org/statistics/data/countries.cfm?c=IND.

45 'India launches anti-poverty deal', *BBC News Online*, 2 February 2006; news.bbc.co.uk/2/hi/south_asia/ 4671328.stm.

46 'Three-Fold Increase In Central Allocation For Elimination Of Child Labour', *One India News Online*, 16 March 2006; news.oneindia.in/2006/03/16/three-fold-increase-in-allocation-for-elimination-of-child-labour-1142515537.html.

47 Official SEWA website: www.sewa.org.

48 Examples include the Modicare Foundation, www.modicarefoundation.org; and the Azim Premji Foundation, www.azimpremjifoundation.org.

49 Rang deBasanti the film, *IMDB Online*; www.imdb.com/title/tt0405508.

50 Prabhudev Konana, 'Towards corporate social responsibility', *The Hindu Online*, 9 March 2006; www.thehindu.com/2006/03/09/stories/2006030905431000.htm.

51 Coco-Cola, '2006, Corporate Responsibility Review: The Mark we Make Shapes the Future'; www.thecoca-colacompany.com/citizenship/pdf/corporate_responsibility_review2006.pdf.

52 War on Want, 'Coca-Cola: The Alternative Report', 2006; www.waronwant.org/attachments/Coca-Cola%20-%20The%20Alternative%20Report.pdf.

53 www.publiceye.ch/en/p10387.html

54 'India: police investigate death of Coca-Cola bottling plant opponent', *Environment News Service Online*, 2 February 2006; www.ens-newswire.com/ens/feb2006/2006-02-02-03.asp.

55 National Union of Students, 'Motion on Coke passed at NUS Conference in March 2006', www.nus.org.uk/PageFiles/491/CokeMotion.pdf.

56 Siddharth Srivastava, 'Indian swami takes the fizz out of Coke', *Asia Times Online*, 28 January 2006; www.atimes.com/atimes/South_Asia/HA28Df03.html.

57 Coca-Cola, 'Corporate Responsibility Review' (2005): Environment Section, page 28; citizenship.coca-cola.co.uk/pdf/cr_environment_section.pdf.

58 Official Website of the International Campaign for Justice in Bhopal: www.bhopal.net.

59 www.tata.com/0_our_commitment/corporate_governance/index.htm. This reference is no longer available on the Tata website. See 'TATA Group: A company that lives integrity', *Corporate Eye Online*, 20 May 2008; www.corporate-eye.com/blog/2008/05/tata-group-a-company-that-lives-integrity/?wpmp_switcher=mobile.

60 Mark Dummett, 'Battle over Indian steel mills', *BBC News Online*, 26 February 2006; news.bbc.co.uk/2/hi/south_asia/4686638.stm.

61 Personal communication with Shilpa Shah, 16 March 2006.

62 'China and India will shape the future of CSR', *edie.net Online*, 13 March 2006; www.edie.net/news/news_story.asp?id=11178&title=China+and+India+will+shape+the+future+of+CSR.

63 Abid Aslam, 'India's clampdown on generic drugs imperils world's poor, say advocates', *Common Dreams News Center Online*, 23 March 2005; www.commondreams.org/ headlines05/0323-04.htm.

2Q2006

1 Jennifer Bayot and Roben Farzad, 'Former WorldCom Executive Sentenced to 5 Years in Prison', *New York Times Online*, 11 August 2005; www.nytimes.com/2005/08/11/ business/11cnd-worldcom.html?ei=5094&en=79ba6dbcdeecbb25&hp=&ex=11238192 00&partner=homepage&pagewanted=all&_r=0.

2 Gretchen Hyman, 'Winnick Exits Global Crossing', *ISP News*, 2 January 2003; web.archive.org/web/20030109064408/isp-planet.com/news/2003/global_ crossing_030102.html.

3 Dean Starkman, 'Rigases Given Prison Terms: Former Adelphia Executives Sentenced for Conspiracy, Fraud', *Washington Post*, 21 June 2005; www.highbeam.com/doc/1P2-34062.html upon subscription.

4 Gregory Crouch, 'Ahold to Pay $1.1 Billion to Settle Fraud Suits', *New York Times Online*, 29 November 2005; www.nytimes.com/2005/11/29/business/worldbusiness/29ahold. html.

5 Securities and Exchange Commission, 'AIG to Pay $800 Million to Settle Securities Fraud Charges by SEC: Over $1.6 Billion to be Paid to Resolve Federal and New York State Actions', press release, 9 February 2006; www.sec.gov/news/press/2006-19.htm.

6 'Accounting Scandal'; en.wikipedia.org/wiki/HealthSouth.

7 Matthew Borghese, 'Report on Fannie Mae's Accounting Problems Ready for Release', *All Headline News*, 16 May 2006; web.archive.org/web/20060615183925/www. allheadlinenews.com/articles/7003599932.

8 Carolyn Said, 'The Enron Verdict: From White Collars to Prison Blues', *San Francisco Chronicle Online*, 26 May 2006; www.sfgate.com/cgi-bin/article.cgi?f=/c/ a/2006/05/26/BUGL3J2D3B33.DTL.

9 Brooke A. Masters, 'Shareholders Flex Muscles: Proxy Measures Pushing Corporate Accountability Gain Support', *Washington Post Online*, 17 June 2006; www. washingtonpost.com/wp-dyn/content/article/2006/06/16/AR2006061601860.html.

10 We use the term 'extra-financial' rather than 'non-financial' to refer to social, environmental and governance issues as this better reflects the potential financial materiality of these issues, despite not being included in normal financial accounts and reports.

11 Covalence official website: www.covalence.ch.

12 Frank Dixon, 'Strategic Thinking', *GreenBiz*, January 2005; www.greenbiz.com/news/ columns_third.cfm?NewsID=27578. This link is no longer available.

13 John Ruggie, 'Interim Report of the Special Representative of the Secretary-General on the Issue of Human Rights and Transnational Corporations and Other Business Enterprises', UN Doc. E/CN.4/2006/97 (2006); www1.umn.edu/humanrts/business/ RuggieReport2006.html.

14 Global Compact, 'New Human Rights Guide for Business', 6 June 2006; www. unglobalcompact.org/NewsAndEvents/news_archives/2006_06_06.html.

15 Amnesty International US, 'UN Norms for Business: Taking Corporate Responsibility for Human Rights to the Next Level!', 16 September 2005; web.archive.org/ web/20110218210058/www.amnestyusa.org/business-and-human-rights/promoting-legal-accountability/un-norms-for-business/page.do?id=1101637. See also letter

to John Ruggie from Guy Sebban, Secretary-General, ICC, and Antonio Peñalosa, Secretary-General, IOE, 14 October 2005; www.google.com/search?q=letter+to+Joh n+Ruggie+from+Guy+Sebban%2C+Secretary-General%2C+ICC%2C+and+Antonio +Pe%C3%B1alosa%2C+Secretary-General%2C+IOE%2C+14+October+2005&ie=utf-8&oe=utf-8&aq=t&rls=org.mozilla:fr:official&client=firefox-a.

16 *Ibid.*

17 Ruggie, *op. cit.*

18 Letter to John Ruggie from Amnesty International *et al.*, 18 May 2006; web. archive.org/web/20110219145200/www.amnestyusa.org/document. php?lang=e&id=engior500032006.

19 Ruggie, *op. cit.*

20 'Norms on the Responsibilities of Transnational Corporations and Other Business Enterprises with Regard to Human Rights', UN Doc. E/CN.4/Sub.2/2003/12/Rev.2 (2003); www1.umn.edu/humanrts/links/norms-Aug2003.html.

21 Ruggie, *op. cit.*

22 D. Weissbrodt, 'UN Perspectives on "Business and Humanitarian and Human Rights Obligations"', presentation at panel of the American Society of International Law, 30 March 2006.

23 Letter from John Ruggie to Amnesty International *et al.*, 22 May 2006; www.reports-and-materials.org/Ruggie-response-to-joint-NGO-letter-22-May-2006.pdf.

24 Ruggie, *op. cit.*

25 Hilary Putnam, *Pragmatism: An Open Question* (Oxford, UK: Blackwell Publishers, 1995).

26 Jeremy Waldron (ed.), *Theories of Rights* (Oxford, UK: Oxford University Press, 1984).

27 Letter from Irene Khan, Secretary-General, Amnesty International, to John Ruggie, 27 April 2006; web.archive.org/web/20110219145158/www.amnestyusa.org/document. php?lang=e&id=engior500022006.

28 Aron Cramer, 'Business for Social Responsibility Commentary: Interim Report of the Special Representative on Business and Human Rights', March 2006; www.coc-runder-tisch.de/news/news_april2006/BSR_Ruggie-Interim-Report_BSR-Comments_200603. pdf.

29 United Nations, 'New Human Rights Council Convenes First Session in Geneva, 19 June', press release, 15 June 2006; www.un.org/News/Press/docs/2006/hrc2.doc.htm.

30 World Bank, 'World Bank Announces Strategy to Combat Corruption', Press Release No. 2006/358/EXC, 11 April 2006; web.worldbank.org/WBSITE/EXTERNAL/NEWS/0,,c ontentMDK:20884956~menuPK:34463~pagePK:34370~piPK:34424~theSitePK:4607,00. html.

31 World Bank, 'Anticorruption'; web.archive.org/web/20110708131157/web.worldbank. org/WBSITE/EXTERNAL/TOPICS/EXTPUBLICSECTORANDGOVERNANCE/EXTANT ICORRUPTION/0,,contentMDK:21540659~menuPK:384461~pagePK:148956~piPK:2 16618~theSitePK:384455,00.html. See also, web.worldbank.org/WBSITE/EXTERNAL/ EXTABOUTUS/ORGANIZATION/EXTPRESIDENT/EXTPASTPRESIDENTS/EXTOFFICE PRESIDENT/0,,enableDHL:TRUE~menuPK:51175739~pagePK:64260331~piPK:511742 19~theSitePK:1014541,00.html.

32 Paul Blustein, 'World Bank Strategy Targets Corruption: Plan Aims to Clean Up Bribe-Taking Countries', *Washington Post Online*, 12 April 2006; www.washingtonpost.com/ wp-dyn/content/article/2006/04/11/AR2006041101403.html.

33 Ruggie, *op. cit.*

34 F. Leautier, D. Petkoski and M. Jarvis, 'Development Outreach', Editorial, World Bank Institute, Embargoed Copy, 17 September 2006.

35 EITI official website: eiti.org.
36 F. Leautier *et al.*, *op. cit.*
37 CEE Bankwatch Network, Friends of the Earth International, Center for Environment and Development and Environmental Defense, 'Banks and Exxon Celebrate Chad–Cameroon Pipeline: International Organisations Support Chadian Day of Mourning', press release, 9 October 2003; web.archive.org/web/20070312225550/www.foei.org/media/2003/1009.html.
38 World Bank, 'Questions and Answers'; web.worldbank.org/WBSITE/EXTERNAL/COUNTRIES/AFRICAEXT/EXTREGINI/EXTCHADCAMPIPELINE/0,,contentMDK:20531903~menuPK:1104029~pagePK:64168445~piPK:64168309~theSitePK:843238,00.html.
39 *Ibid.*
40 CEE Bankwatch Network *et al.*, *op. cit.*
41 World Bank, 'World Bank, Govt of Chad Sign Memorandum of Understanding on Poverty Reduction', News Release No. 2007/19/EXC, 14 July 2006; web.worldbank.org/WBSITE/EXTERNAL/COUNTRIES/AFRICAEXT/CHADEXTN/0,,contentMDK:20994138~menuPK:349881~pagePK:141137~piPK:141127~theSitePK:349862,00.html.
42 World Bank, 'World Bank, Chad Reach Interim Agreement on Funding, Oil Revenue Management', Press Release No. 2006/383/AFR, 26 April 2006; web.worldbank.org/WBSITE/EXTERNAL/NEWS/0,,contentMDK:20903775~pagePK:34370~piPK:34424~theSitePK:4607,00.html.
43 *Ibid.*
44 World Economic Forum, 'Key Coalition Formed to Fight Private Sector Corruption on Anti-corruption Day', 9 December 2005; web.archive.org/web/20100703064006/www.weforum.org/en/media/Latest%20Press%20Releases/PRESSRELEASES88.
45 Transparency International, 'Business Principles for Countering Bribery'; www.transparency.org/global_priorities/private_sector/business_principles.
46 'Google "Compromised Principles" in China, Founder Admits', *South China Morning Post*, 7 June 2006, as reprinted at asiamedia.ucla.edu/article.asp?parentid=47255.
47 Jeffry Bartash, 'Internet-freedom backers struggle on', *MarketWatch*, 14 June 2006; articles.marketwatch.com/2006-06-14/news/30702743_1_net-neutrality-supporters-net-neutrality-net-neutrality.
48 Electronic Frontier Foundation, 'AOL Starts Pay-to-Send Email Shakedown', 9 May 2006; https://www.eff.org/press/archives/2006/05/09.
49 The official DearAOL website is no longer accessible. See also www.spamresource.com/2007_02_07_archive.html.
50 Amnesty International USA, 'Censorship in China: Overview'; web.archive.org/web/20110220032939/www.amnestyusa.org/business/censorship.html.
51 Reporters Without Borders, 'Test of Filtering by Sohu and Sina Search Engines Following Upgrade', 22 June 2006; en.rsf.org/china-test-of-filtering-by-sohu-and-sina-22-06-2006,18015.html.
52 Amnesty International USA, 'Censorship in China: Business Standards in China'; web.archive.org/web/20110220042532/www.amnestyusa.org/business/standards.html.
53 'Response to Business and Human Rights Resource Centre Regarding Amnesty International Item: "Fighting for Human Rights in Cyberspace"', 16 May 2006; www.reports-and-materials.org/Microsoft-response-re-Amnesty-action-on-China-censorship-16-May-2006.doc.

3Q2006

1 The China CSR Map official website: www.chinacsrmap.org/index_EN.asp.

2 UNDP China Human Development Report 2005; www.undp.org.cn/modules.php?op= modload&name=News&file=article&catid=18&topic=8&sid=242&mode=thread&order =0&thold=0.

3 'Switzerland, Finland and Sweden take the lead in the rankings of the World Economic Forum's Global Competitiveness Index, but US drops', World Economic Forum; web. archive.org/web/20101022021137/www.weforum.org/en/media/Latest%20Press%20 Releases/GCRpressrelease06.

4 'Top China leader fired for graft', *BBC News Online*, 25 September 2006; news.bbc. co.uk/2/hi/asia-pacific/5376858.stm.

5 Minxin Pei, 'The Tide of Corruption Threatening China's Prosperity', *Financial Times Online*, 27 September 2006; www.ft.com/intl/cms/s/1/f8c5f0a8-4d82-11db-8704-0000779e2340.html.

6 Zijun Li, 'Lack of Corporate Social Responsibility behind Recent China Accidents', Worldwatch, 12 December 2005; www.worldwatch.org/node/3859.

7 Simon Zadek, 'China's Route to Business Responsibility', openDemocracy, 30 November 2005; www.opendemocracy.net/democracy-china/china_business_3076. jsp.

8 Tom Miller, 'Working Up the Value Chain', *Asia Times Online*, 23 November 2006; www. atimes.com/atimes/China_Business/HK23Cb01.html.

9 Zadek, *op. cit.*

10 Shobhana Chandra and Matthew Benjamin, 'Global trade no longer hostage to US consumers', *New Zealand Herald Online*, 27 September 2006; www.nzherald.co.nz/ business/news/article.cfm?c_id=3&objectid=10403054.

11 Ben Schiller, 'The China Model', openDemocracy, 20 December 2005; www. opendemocracy.net/democracy-china/china_development_3136.jsp.

12 Joseph Kahn. 'China Puts Stricter Limits on Distribution of Foreign News', *The New York Times Online*, 11 September 2006; www.nytimes.com/2006/09/11/world/ asia/11china.html.

13 *CSR Asia Weekly*, Vol. 1 Week 49 (7 December 2005): 7; www.csr-asia.com/pastissue. php?year=2005 upon subscription.

14 *Ibid.*

15 'Green group moving into Wal-Mart's backyard', *NBCNews.com*, 12 July 2006; msnbc. msn.com/id/13828326/ from/ET.

16 Conversation with Jem Bendell, August 2006.

17 US Department of Labor Occupational Safety and Health Administration, 'OSHA fines BP Products North America more than $21 million following Texas City explosion', 22 September 2005; www.osha.gov/pls/oshaweb/owadisp. show_document?p_table=NEWS_RELEASES&p_id=11589.

18 Daren Fonda, 'Is BP really that green?', *Time Online*, 29 June 2006; www.time.com/ time/business/article/0,8599,1209454,00.html.

19 *Ibid.*

20 *Ibid.*

21 Steven Mufson, 'Pipeline closure sends oil higher', *Washington Post Online*, 8 August 2006; www.washingtonpost.com/wp-dyn/content/article/2006/08/07/ AR2006080700131.html.

22 Steven Mufson, 'BP executives rebuked in Hill appearance', *Washington Post Online*, 8 September 2006; www.washingtonpost.com/wp-dyn/content/article/2006/09/07/AR2006090700524.html?sub=AR.

23 'Short- to Long-Term: Who Cares? Institutional Investors, Beneficiaries and Investees in Dialogue', *The Sustainability Forum*. August/September 2006; www.sustainability-zurich.org/cm_data/Report_From_Short_to_Long_Term.pdf.

24 Mike Scott, 'Investors start to appreciate the value of a long-term view', *Financial Times*, 9 May 2006.

25 The Marathon Club official website: www.marathonclub.co.uk.

26 'Marathon club reports on industry response to long term, long only investing consultation paper', press release, 2 August 2006; www.uss.co.uk/Marathonclubpressrelease/MC%20PR%20on%20industry%20response%20to%20Long%20Term%20Long%20Only%20Consultation%20Aug%202006.pdf.

27 Scott, *op. cit.*

28 *Ibid.*

29 Adam Lerrick, 'Good Intentions at the Expense of the Poor', *Financial Times Online*, 1 August 2006; www.ft.com/intl/cms/s/1/3d4638b2-2184-11db-b650-0000779e2340.html.

30 The New Ventures and Vantage Points official websites: www.new-ventures.org and www.vantagep.org.

31 George Lakoff, *Don't Think of an Elephant. Know Your Values and Frame the Debate: The Essential Guide for Progressives* (White River Junction, VT: Chelsea Green, 2004).

32 The European Transparency Initiative: ec.europa.eu/comm/eti/index.htm.

33 J. Bendell *et al.*, *The Corporate Responsibility Movement: Five Years of Global Corporate Responsibility Analysis from Lifeworth, 2001–2005* (Sheffield, UK: Greenleaf Publishing, 2009).

34 Richard Berman, 'Deep-Fried Hysteria', *Center for Consumer Freedom*, 29 September 2006; web.archive.org/web/20100927082211/consumerfreedom.com/oped_detail.cfm/o/407-deep-fried-hysteria.

35 The SCORE and CSCP official websites: www.score-network.org and www.scp-centre.org.

36 J. Manoochehri, *Consumption Opportunities. Strategies for Change: A Report for Decision-makers* (Geneva: UNEP, 2001; www.unep.org/publications/search/pub_details_s.asp?ID=350).

37 The Sustainable Consumption Opportunities for Europe Project: www.unep.ch/scoe.

38 'Journalists sued over iPod story', *China Economic Net*, 29 August 2006; en.ce.cn/Business/Enterprise/200608/29/t20060829_8338445.shtml.

39 'iPod City: Inside Apple's iPod factories', *Appleinsider*, 12 June 2006; appleinsider.com/articles/06/06/12/ipod_city_inside_apples_ipod_factories.html.

40 'Taiwan firm drops China iPod libel case', *Reuters*, 3 September 2006; chinadigitaltimes.net/2006/09/taiwan-firm-drops-china-ipod-libel-case-reuters.

41 'Amnesty International alarmed over Philippine killings', *South China Morning Post Online*, 26 July 2006; web.archive.org/web/20070219215643/www.asiamedia.ucla.edu/article.asp?parentid=49849.

42 '47th journalist killed under Arroyo government', *Pacific Media Watch*, 11 December 2006; www.pmw.c2o.org/2006/phil5079.html.

43 Raissa Robles, 'Arroyo under new media challenge', *South China Morning Post Online*, 18 November 2006; www.ellentordesillas.com/2006/11/18/arroyo-under-new-media-challenge.

44 Discussions with *Newsbreak* editors.

45 Hugo Restall. 'Singapore's Martyr, Chee Soon Juan'; *Far Eastern Economic Review*, July/August 2006; www.feer.com/articles1/2006/0607/free/p024.html.

46 Sara Webb, 'Singapore's media controls jar with regional aims', *Reuters*, 30 August 2006; www.singapore-window.org/sw06/060830R1.HTM; and 'Singapore tightens rules on some foreign media', *Agence France Presse*, 4 August 2006; www.singapore-window.org/sw06/060804AF.HTM.

47 *Ibid.*

48 World Bank, *Free and Independent Media Empower the Poor and Spur Development* (Washington, DC: World Bank, 2002).

49 Webb, *op. cit.*

50 'Petron slips', *Newsbreak*, 25 September 2006; sludge.wordpress.com/2006/09/12.

51 *CSR Asia Weekly* Vol. 2 Week 39; www.csr-asia.com/pastissue.php?year=2006 upon subscription.

52 'Beijing keen to unlock ASEAN investment doors', *Asia Times Online*, 2 November 2006; www.atimes.com/atimes/China_Business/HK02Cb01.html.

4Q2006

1 Karl D. John, 'The new Vietnam welcomes the world', *Asia Times Online, 16 November 2006;* www.atimes.com/atimes/Southeast_Asia/HK16Ae02.html.

2 Extracts from the presentation of Dr Vu Tien Loc, President of Vietnam Chamber of Commerce and Industry, 'A Glimpse of Business Environment of Vietnam in 2006', *VCCI News Online*, 20 December 2006; vccinews.com/news_detail.asp?news_id=8533.

3 Clay Chandler, 'Vietnam is Surging Ahead', *Fortune Magazine Online*, 11 December 2006; money.cnn.com/magazines/fortune/fortune_archive/2006/12/11/8395481/index.htm.

4 William Pesek, 'Booms, Busts and Bombs that Colored Asia's 2006', *Bloomberg, 18 December 2006;* www.bloomberg.com/apps/news?pid=newsarchive&sid=aHPTluJX3nMc.

5 Quote from Chandler, *op. cit.*

6 Freshfields Bruckhaus Deringer, 'Briefing. Vietnam: New Investment Law', March 2006; www.mekongresearch.com/doc/New%20Investment%20Law%20Sector%20Update.pdf.

7 UNCTAD, *World Investment Report 2006. FDI from Developing and Transition Economies: Implications for Development* (Geneva: UN, 2006; unctad.org/en/Docs/wir2006_en.pdf).

8 Hisane Masaki, 'Japan Inc. Smitten by Vietnam', *Asia Times Online, 15 June 2006;* www.atimes.com/atimes/Japan/HF15Dh01.html.

9 Frederik Balfour, 'Good Morning, Vietnam: Intel's deal to build a factory is likely to spur more Western investment', *BusinessWeek, 13 March 2006;* www.businessweek.com/magazine/content/06_11/b3975068.htm.

10 Bill Heyton, 'ABN Amro makes Vietnam settlement', *BBC News Online*, 27 November 2006; news.bbc.co.uk/2/hi/business/6188646.stm.

11 A proposed 2003 project to be administered by a World Bank team, which includes Nigel Twose, Amy Luinstra and Ziba Cranmer, 'Corporate Social Responsibility in Vietnam: The athletic shoe industry and labor issues', *Global Standards*, 15 July 2002; www.google.com/search?q=Nigel+Twose%2C+Amy+Luinstra%2C%2C+Ziba+Cranmer+vietnam&ie=utf-8&oe=utf-8&aq=t&rls=org.mozilla:fr:official&client=firefox-a.

12 Mark Manyin, 'Vietnam's Labor Rights Regime: An Assessment, for the US Congress', updated 14 March 2002; digital.library.unt.edu/govdocs/crs//data/2002/upl-meta-crs-3540/RL30896_2002Mar14.pdf?PHPSESSID=25a9753dad36b5962c9469f7043f2d8e.

13 *Ibid.*

14 *Ibid.*

15 *Ibid.*

16 Amy Kazmin, 'Vietnam boosted by Intel's $1bn plan for plant', *Financial Times Online, 13 November 2006;* www.ft.com/intl/cms/s/0/472766ac-72bb-11db-a5f5-0000779e2340.html#axzz2CdUMxtMy.

17 Clay Chandler, 'Quote from Vietnam Vrooooom . . .', *Fortune Online,* 13 November 2006; money.cnn.com/magazines/fortune/fortune_archive/2006/12/11/8395481/index.htm.

18 Robert Buderi and Gregory Huang, Guanxi, *The Art of Relationships: Microsoft, China, and Bill Gates's Plan to Win the Road Ahead* (New York: Simon & Schuster, 2006).

19 Shawn Donnan, 'Investors increasingly enthusiastic for Vietnam's growth story', *Financial Times Online,* 3 May 2006; www.ft.com/intl/cms/s/0/3bb413fa-da41-11da-b7de-0000779e2340.html.

20 Amy Kazmin, 'In Beijing's footsteps', *Financial Times Online,* 7 January 2006; www.ft.com/intl/cms/s/1/1f1c517e-9e79-11db-ac03-0000779e2340.html#axzz2CdUMxtMy.

21 'Vietnam's stock market overly hot: HSTC', *VietNamNet Bridge,* 21 December 2006; web.archive.org/web/20071224112020/english.vietnamnet.vn/biz/2006/12/646427.

22 George Lakoff, *Don't Think of an Elephant. Know Your Values and Frame the Debate: The Essential Guide for Progressives* (White River Junction, VT: Chelsea Green, 2004).

23 Shawn Crispin, 'In capitalist Vietnam, it's "repression as usual"', *Asia Times Online,* 6 July 2007; www.atimes.com/atimes/Southeast_Asia/HG06Ae03.html.

24 Lakoff, *op. cit.*

25 Crispin, *op. cit.*

26 *Ibid.*

27 World Bank: Vietnam Environment; web.worldbank.org/WBSITE/EXTERNAL/COUNTRIES/EASTASIAPACIFICEXT/EXTEAPREGTOPENVIRONMENT/0,,contentMDK:20266331~pagePK:34004173~piPK:34003707~theSitePK:502886,00.html.

28 Tinh Dang Nguyen, 'Coping with drought in the central highlands: Vietnam', Institute of Environment & Resources Technical University of Denmark, October 2006; www.fiva.dk/doc/thesis/nguyen.pdf.

29 ThanhNien News, 'Vietnam "highly vulnerable" to climate change: report', 5 February 2007; www.thanhniennews.com/society/?catid=3&newsid=25006. The original weblink reference is longer available. For an alternative, see Jeremy Carew-Reid, 'Rapid Assessment of the Extent and Impact of Sea Level Rise in VietNam', February 2008; www.icem.com.au/documents/climatechange/icem_slr/ICEM_SLR_final_report.pdf or World Bank, 'Economics of Adaptation to Climate Change: Vietnam', 2010; climatechange.worldbank.org/sites/default/files/documents/EACC_Vietnam.pdf.

30 2007 Report of the UN Intergovernmental Panel on Climate Change: www.ipcc.ch.

31 Stern Review on the Economics of Climate Change, 2007; www.hm-treasury.gov.uk/independent_reviews/stern_review_economics_climate_change/sternreview_index.cfm.

32 World Health Organisation Climate Change Programme; www.who.int/globalchange/climate/en.

33 Kalpana Sharma, 'Should we care about global warming?', *The Hindu Online,* 28 November 2006; www.hindu.com/2006/11/28/stories/2006112803331000.htm.

34 Mohammed Saqib, Rajesh Sehgal and Dennis Pamlin, 'Indian Companies in the 21st Century: An Opportunity for Innovation that can Save the Planet', WWF, December 2006; www.wwfindia.org/about_wwf/what_we_do/cel/trade/newpusb.cfm.

35 Global Witness, 'Combating Conflict Diamonds: Global Witness and Amnesty International launch new survey'; www.globalwitness.org/pages/en/conflict_diamonds.html.

36 John Bowe, 'NOBODIES: Does slavery exist in America?', *The New Yorker Online*, 21 April 2003; www.sfalliance.org/media/New-Yorker-4-03.pdf.

37 Felicity Lawrence, 'Migrants in bonded labour trap', *The Guardian Online*, 29 March 2004; www.guardian.co.uk/immigration/story/0,,1422657,00.html.

38 'In depth: slavery in the 21st century', *BBC News Online*, 6 June 2006; news.bbc.co.uk/2/hi/in_depth/world/slavery/default.stm.

39 Harsh Mander, 'In bonded servitude', *Frontline Online*, 18–23 January 2003; www.frontlineonnet.com/fl2002/stories/20030131006710600.htm.

40 Michael Smith and David Voreacos, 'The Secret World of Modern Slavery', *Bloomberg Markets*, 17 November 2006; www.bloomberg.com/apps/news?pid=newsarchive&sid=aul9sXScm.QE.

41 *Ibid.*

42 Patrick Belser, *Forced Labour and Human Trafficking: Estimating the Profits* (Geneva: ILO, 2005; www.ilo.org/sapfl/Informationresources/ILOPublications/WCMS_081971/lang--en/index.htm).

43 UNODC definition of trafficking persons: www.unodc.org/eastasiaandpacific/en/topics/illicit-trafficking/human-trafficking-definition.html.

44 Belser, *op. cit.*

45 Smith and Voreacos, *op. cit.*

46 David Voreacos and Michael Smith, 'Automakers Pledge Joint Effort With Suppliers to Fight Slavery', *Bloomberg Markets*, 11 December 2006; www.bloomberg.com/apps/news?pid=20601086&sid=aqs8kA0Qrpzw.

2007: Introduction

1 Reckitt Benckiser, 'Reckitt Benckiser targets a new standard in carbon reduction', press release, 1 November 2007; www.rb.com/site/RKBR/Templates/MediaInvestorsGeneral2.aspx?pageid=259&cc=GB.

2 'Cisco To Implement Department-Level Carbon Quotas', *Environmental Leader*, 19 December 2007; www.environmentalleader.com/2007/12/19/cisco-to-implement-department-level-carbon-quotas-.

3 Jonathan Birchall, 'P&G sets "greener" products targets', *Financial Times Online*, 28 October 2007; www.ft.com/cms/s/0/d27db95a-8597-11dc-8170-0000779fd2ac.html?nclick_check=1 (upon registration).

4 WWF, 'Climate Solutions: WWF's Vision for 2050', 2007; awsassets.panda.org/downloads/climatesolutionweb.pdf.

5 'Net Impact announces first Europe Conference', *CSRWire*, 11 December 2007; www.csrwire.com/press_releases/17188-Net-Impact-announces-first-Europe-Conference.

1Q2007

1 EasyJet official website, 'Environment'; web.archive.org/web/20100206010920/www.easyjet.com/EN/About/Information/infopack_environmentalpolicy.html.

2 The Great Global Warming Swindle official website: www.greatglobalwarmingswindle. co.uk.

3 Gavin Schmidt, 'The Lure of Solar Forcing', *RealClimate*, 15 July 2005; www.realclimate. org/index.php/archives/2005/07/the-lure-of-solar-forcing.

4 David Adam, 'Oil firms fund climate change "denial"', *The Guardian Online*, 27 January 2005; www.guardian.co.uk/world/2005/jan/27/environment.science.

5 Environmental News Service, 'UN Climate Change Impact Report: Poor Will Suffer Most', 6 April 2007; www.ens-newswire.com/ens/apr2007/2007-04-06-01.asp.

6 Christian Aid, 'Government failing to act on UK's missing carbon millions'; www. christianaid.org.uk/news/media/pressrel/070219p.htm, 19 February 2007.

7 Warren Evans, 'The Impact of Climate Change on the Poor', Private Sector Development Blog, 19 May 2006; blogs.worldbank.org/psd/node/12213. See also, UN News Centre, 'Poor will feel greatest impact of climate change, scientist tells UN commission', 4 May 2006; www.un.org/apps/news/story.asp?NewsID=18360&Cr=clim ate&Cr1=change.

8 World Business Council for Sustainable Development (WBCSD), 'WEF warns of increased climate change risk', 11 January 2007; www.wbcsd.ch/plugins/ DOCSEARCH/details.asp?DocTypeId=-1&ObjectId=MjIzNzc&URLBack=result. asp%3FDocTypeId=-1%26SortOrder=doctitle+asc%26CurPage=888.

9 'The Race against Climate Change', *BloombergBusinessWeek Online*, 11 December 2005; www.businessweek.com/stories/2005-12-11/the-race-against-climate-change.

10 World Business Council for Sustainable Development, 'GHG Corporate Accounting and Reporting Standard (Corporate Standard)'; web.archive.org/ web/20070708160003/www.ghgprotocol.org/templates/GHG5/layout.asp?type=p&Me nuId=ODk2&doOpen=1&ClickMenu=Corporate%20Module.

11 At the time of access, the Unilever website stated: 'For example, many of our laundry detergent brands, such as Omo, Surf and Persil, can now be used at temperatures as low as 30 degrees centigrade. We intend to incorporate a "greenhouse gas index" into our product development process, to assess, and where possible reduce, impacts during product use'; unilever.com/ourvalues/environment-society/sus-dev-report/ wider-environmental-footprint. For updated information, see https://www.unilever. com/sustainability/environment/climate/CleanerPlanetPlan/index.aspx.

12 David Suzuki Foundation, 'What is a carbon offset?'; www.davidsuzuki.org/issues/ climate-change/science/climate-change-basics/carbon-offsets.

13 Fiona Harvey, 'Beware the carbon offsetting cowboys', *Financial Times Online*, 26 April 2007; www.ft.com/cms/s/0/dcdefef6-f350-11db-9845-000b5df10621. html#axzz2Bbe1ZqAV.

14 The Gold Standard Foundation, 'About Us', www.cdmgoldstandard.org/about-us.

15 World Development Movement (WDM), *The Voluntary Carbon Offset Market: Memorandum to the EAC by the World Development Movement* (WDM, January 2007).

16 GLOBE-Net, 'The Debate over Biofuels', World Business Council for Sustainable Development, 2 May 2007; www.wbcsd.ch/plugins/DOCSEARCH/ details.asp?DocTypeId=-1&ObjectId=MjQ0Njc&URLBack=result. asp%3FDocTypeId%3D-1%26SortOrder%3Ddoctitle+asc%26CurPage%3D765.

17 Nitrogen runoffs have already caused a 'dead zone' in the Gulf of Mexico, a body of water with so little oxygen that it can barely support life. See C. Ford Runge and Benjamin Senauer, 'How biofuels could starve the poor', *Foreign Affairs*, May/June 2007; www.foreignaffairs.org/20070501faessay86305-p10/c-ford-runge-benjamin-senauer/how-biofuels-could-starve-the-poor.html.

18 Bruno Waterfield, 'EU green targets will damage rainforests', *The Telegraph Online*. 27 April 2007; www.telegraph.co.uk/earth/earthnews/3291567/EU-green-targets-will-damage-rainforests.html.

19 Runge and Senauer, *op. cit.*

20 Noam Chomsky, 'Starving the Poor', 15 May 2007; www.chomsky.info/articles/20070515.htm.

21 Michael Bradshaw, 'The Sakhalin End Game: Two Wrongs Don't Make a Right' (Pacific Russia Oil and Gas Report; Pacific Russia Information Group LLC, 2007; www.geog.le.ac.uk/staff/mjb41/articles/sakhalinarticles.html).

22 *Ibid.*

23 *Ibid.*

24 'The Business of Climate Change', *BBC World Service Online Audio*, 7 April 2007; www.bbc.co.uk/worldservice/specials/1512_debates/page13.shtml.

25 The Future Laboratory, 'Mobile Work Futures for Microsoft', January 2007: 21.

26 Let us note that, though this concept is relatively new, certain professions have already incorporated these aspects: some journalists, for instance, are known to work odd hours and from odd places, while having deep personal investment in their work.

27 Future Laboratory, *op. cit.*

28 Ryan Healy, 'Twentysomething: Why I don't want work/life balance', 2 April 2007, and subsequent comments; blog.penelopetrunk.com/2007/04/02/twentysomething-why-i-dont-want-worklife-balance.

29 *Ibid.*

30 There are also cultural variations: recent fathers employed in countries that afford paternity leave, and in which men are expected to take it, might have an easier time blending than in places where a more traditional distribution of tasks is commonplace.

31 Jacqui Cheng, 'Survey: BlackBerry owners chained to work', *Ars Technica*,15 February 2007; arstechnica.com/news.ars/post/20070215-8858.html.

32 *Ibid.*

33 Tuck School of Business at Dartmouth, 'Work–Life Symposium: Defining Your Boundaries', 2005; www.tuck.dartmouth.edu/news/features/worklife_2005.html. This link is no longer available.

34 Cheng, *op cit.*

35 Ryan Healy, 'Shedding some light on the blended life', 5 April 2007; www.employeeevolution.com/archives/2007/04/05/shedding-some-light-on-the-blended-life.

36 Department for International Development, 'Buy African flowers on Valentine's day to help make poverty history', 13 February 2007; www.dfid.gov.uk/news/files/speeches/trade/hilary-roses-feb07.asp.

37 Ochieng' Ogodo, 'The Hidden Costs of Valentine's Day', *Islam Online*, February 2007; cmsdata.iucn.org/downloads/the_hidden_costs_of_valentine_s_day.pdf.

38 *Ibid.*

39 *Ibid.*

40 *Ibid.*

2Q2007

1 Danny Fortson, 'G8 Summit: Unions in international attack on private equity and hedge funds', *The Independent Online*, 3 June 2007; web.archive.org/web/20080706144005/news.independent.co.uk/business/news/article2607324.ece.

2 Ben Schiller, 'Special Report: Finance. Hedge Funds and Private Equity: Trading Down Corporate Responsibility', *Ethical Corporation*, 14 November 2006; www.ethicalcorp.com/content/special-report-finance-hedge-funds-and-private-equity-trading-down-corporate-responsibility.

3 Steven Cohen: en.wikipedia.org/wiki/Steven_A._Cohen.

4 'On the Hedge', *BBC Radio Online*, 26 October 2006; www.bbc.co.uk/radio4/news/inbusiness/inbusiness_20061026.shtml.

5 Man Group plc, *2006 Corporate Responsibility Report*.

6 Simon Kennedy, 'Man Group expects to beat market expectations: Hedge fund manager sees earnings up 35% due to strong sales', *MarketWatch*, 29 September 2006; www.marketwatch.com/news/story/story.aspx?guid=%7B4A3FF8AC-3A68-477E-B430-5CFCB5071D85%7D.

7 Marcia Vickers, 'Start your own hedge fund: How hard could it be?', *Fortune*, 31 July 2006; money.cnn.com/magazines/fortune/fortune_archive/2006/08/07/8382584/index.htm.

8 Joseph A. Giannone, 'Unions vow to crank up the heat on buyout firms', *Reuters*, 27 June 2007; www.reuters.com/article/bondsNews/idUSN2742886220070627.

9 Schiller, *op. cit.*

10 John Russell, 'Private Equity: Humbling the Barbarians', *Ethical Corporation*, 1 April 2007; www.ethicalcorp.com/content/private-equity-%E2%80%93-humbling-barbarians.

11 *Ibid.*

12 Andrew Taylor and Chris Bryant, 'Buy-out firms defy job-cutting reputation', *Financial Times Online*, 1 April 2007; www.ft.com/intl/cms/s/0/61359db8-e08c-11db-8b48-000b5df10621.html.

13 Schiller, *op. cit.*

14 Mallen Baker, 'Private Equity: Agents or Destroyers of Responsible Business?', *MallenBaker.net*, 13 May 2007; www.mallenbaker.net/csr/CSRfiles/page.php?Story_ID=1856.

15 Taylor and Bryant, *op. cit*

16 Russell, *op. cit.*

17 John Russell, 'Blog: Private equity bosses slam corporate responsibility', *Ethical Corporation*, 4 July 2007; www.ethicalcorp.com/content/private-equity-bosses-slam-corporate-responsibility.

18 Baker, *op. cit.*

19 For a report on the summit see: adcforum.org/wp-content/uploads/2012/02/FutureSummitReport2007.pdf.

20 Michael Wolff, 'Serious Money', *Vanity Fair*, May 2007: 74-82.

21 Russell, *op. cit.*

22 Bill Stein, 'The Hedge Fund Class and the French Revolution', *New York Times Online*, 29 July 2007; www.nytimes.com/2007/07/29/business/yourmoney/29every.html?em&ex=1185940800&en=3242cc881e9ecb09&ei=5087.

23 Fortson, *op. cit.*

24 Jem Bendell, *Barricades and Boardrooms: A Contemporary History of the Corporate Accountability Movement* (Programme Paper 13; Geneva: UNRISD, 2004).

25 Banktrack official website: www.banktrack.org.
26 Dunstan Prial, 'Cranberries go to the dogs . . . and cats', *The Standard Times Online*, 21 April 2005; web.archive.org/web/20090129230022/archive.southcoasttoday.com/daily/04-05/04-21-05/a01lo774.htm.
27 'More dry pet food recalled, human food supply at risk', *North Country Gazette Online*, 20 April 2007; www.northcountrygazette.org/articles/2007/042007HumanRisk.html.
28 'Tainted Pet Food Linked to Indiana Chickens', *Undemocratic Underground. com*. 30 April 2007; www.democraticunderground.com/discuss/duboard. php?az=view_all&address=102x2829233.
29 Lisa Wade McCormick, 'Pet food contamination scandal spreads to pork, FDA opens criminal investigation: California hogs were fed contaminated feed', *ConsumerAffairs. Com*, 21 April 2007; www.consumeraffairs.com/news04/2007/04/pet_food_recall33. html.
30 US Food and Drug Administration, 'FDA detains imports of farm-raised Chinese seafood: products have repeatedly contained potentially harmful residues', press release, 28 June 2007; web.archive.org/web/20110624095440/www.fda.gov/NewsEvents/Newsroom/PressAnnouncements/2007/ucm108941.htm.
31 'Pet food officer sold stock before recall', *Washington Post Online*, 11 April 2007; www.washingtonpost.com/wp-dyn/content/article/2007/04/10/AR2007041001691.html.
32 European Commission, 'Commission pushes forward co-operation with China on food and product safety', Press Release IP/06/1210, 19 September 2006; europa.eu/rapid/press-release_IP-06-1210_en.htm.
33 Alexei Barrionuevo, 'Globalization in Every Loaf', *New York Times Online*, 16 June 2007; www.nytimes.com/2007/06/16/business/worldbusiness/16food. html?pagewanted=all.
34 'The Stages of Grief', Greenville Hospital System; www.ghs.org/stagesofgrief.
35 Edward Cody, 'China says food export inspections are effective', *Washington Post Online*, 1 June 2007; www.washingtonpost.com/wp-dyn/content/article/2007/05/31/AR2007053100901.html.
36 'China's top drug regulator gets death sentence: Zheng convicted of accepting bribes, dereliction of duty', *Associated Press*, 29 May 2007; www.msnbc.msn.com/id/18911849.
37 'China rejects two US food products containing excessive bacteria, chemicals', *7News wsvn.com*, 26 June 2007; www.wsvn.com/news/articles/world/MI52778.
38 'China to establish food recall system', *China.org.cn*, 29 May 2007; www.china.org.cn/english/government/212231.htm.
39 'China shuts 180 food plants for tainted ingredients', *USA TODAY Online*, 27 June 2007; usatoday30.usatoday.com/money/world/2007-06-27-china-food_N.htm.
40 'China's 2006 trade surplus jumps 74 percent', *New York Times Online*, 10 January 2007; www.nytimes.com/2007/01/10/business/worldbusiness/10iht-yuan.4159584.html.
41 Richard McCormack, 'China replaces US as world's largest exporter: Trade imbalances could cause financial upheaval; MAPI analyst implores US, IMF to act now on China's yuan', *Manufacturing and Technology News* 13.6 (5 September 2006); www.manufacturingnews.com/news/06/0905/art1.html.
42 *Time Magazine*, 'The Global Warming Survival Guide', 9 April 2007; www.time.com/time/magazine/0,9263,7601070409,00.html.
43 Lisa Takeuchi Cullen, 'Going Green at the Office', *Time Online*, 7 June 2007; www.time.com/time/magazine/article/0,9171,1630552,00.html.
44 Vanity Fair. 'The 2007 Green Issue', 4 April 2007; www.vanityfair.com/politics/features/2007/05/greenlinks200705.

45 'Discovery communications to dedicate 24-hour television network exclusively for the environmentally conscious lifestyle', *PRNewswire*, 5 April 2007; www.prnewswire.com/cgi-bin/stories.pl?ACCT=104&STORY=/www/story/04-05-2007/0004560432&EDATE=.

46 'Sundance Channel Creates Advisory Committee for THE GREEN(TM) Presented by Robert Redford', *PRNewswire*. 17 April 2007; www.prnewswire.com/news-releases/sundance-channel-creates-advisory-committee-for-the-greentm-presented-by-robert-redford-57938242.html.

47 Steven Mufson, 'ExxonMobil warming up to global climate issue', *Washington Post Online*, 10 February 2007; www.washingtonpost.com/wp-dyn/content/article/2007/02/09/AR2007020902081.html.

48 'Washington radio station goes "green"', *Southgate Amateur Radio News*; www.southgatearc.org/news/february2007/green_radio_station.htm.

49 Jura Koncius, 'Wedded to Green: Planning Celebrations with an Eco-Friendly Ring', *Washington Post Online*, 21 June 2007; www.washingtonpost.com/wp-dyn/content/article/2007/06/20/AR2007062000519.html.

50 Wine Spectator, 'The Green Issue', June 2007; www.winespectator.com/issue/show/date/2007-06-30.

51 Gary Stix, 'Beyond petroleum with Vivoleum', *Scientific American.com Online*, 19 June 2007; web.archive.org/web/20070804033431/blog.sciam.com/index.php?title=beyond_petroleum_with_vivoleum&more=1&c=1&tb=1&pb=1.

52 Mataliandy, 'Vivoleum, solves global warming and peak oil', *Daily Kos*, 14 June 2007; www.dailykos.com/story/2007/6/14/214445/536.

53 The Yes Men official website: theyesmen.org/hijinks/vivoleum.

54 See the trailer at www.youtube.com/watch?v=SVpN312hYgU.

55 Benjamin R. Barber, *Consumed: How Markets Corrupt Children, Infantilize Adults, and Swallow Citizens Whole* (New York: W.W. Norton, 2007).

3Q2007

1 'New graduation skills', *The Economist Online*, 12 May 2007: 75-76; www.economist.com/printedition/displayStory.cfm?story_id=9149115&fsrc=RSS.

2 Sumantra Ghoshal, 'Bad management theories are destroying good management practices', *Academy of Management Learning and Education* 4.1: 75-91.

3 World Health Organisation, 'F84. Pervasive developmental disorders', *International Statistical Classification of Diseases and Related Health Problems* (10th edn [ICD-10], 2006); and also F. Happé, 'Understanding Assets and Deficits in Autism: Why success is more interesting than failure', *The Psychologist* 12.11 (1999): 540-46.

4 D.A. Treffert, 'Savant Syndrome: An Extraordinary Condition. A Synopsis: Past, Present, Future', Wisconsin Medical Society (2007); www.wisconsinmedicalsociety.org/savant_syndrome/overview_of_savant_syndrome/synopsis.

5 Zoe Smith. 'Autisic Academics', *New Scientist*, 17 March 2001, Issue 2282: 61.

6 As political economy has been undermined within the broad economics discipline, so economics has been further reduced in its ability to study the making of a good society. Louis Uchitelle. 'Students are Leaving the Politics Out of Economics?', *New York Times Online*, 27 January 2006; www.nytimes.com/2006/01/27/business/27econ.html?pagewanted=all&_r=0.

7 J. Bendell, 'Psychos in Suits: Corporate CEOs in Need of (an) Asylum', *openDemocracy*, 23 July 2002; opendemocracy.net/globalization-corporations/article_260.jsp?1.

8 'New graduation skills', *The Economist Online*, 12 May 2007: 75-76; www.economist. com/printedition/displayStory.cfm?story_id=9149115&fsrc=RSS.

9 UN Global Compact official website: www.unglobalcompact.com/HowToParticipate/ academic_network/index.html#bus_ed.

10 American College and University Presidents Climate Commitment: www. presidentsclimatecommitment.org.

11 'The Greening of America's Campuses', *Bloomberg Business Week*, 9 April 2007; www. businessweek.com/stories/2007-04-08/the-greening-of-americas-campuses.

12 AASHE, 'AASHE Digest: Annual Review of Sustainability in Higher Education', press release, 12 April 2007; www.aashe.org/highlights/digest06.php.

13 UNDP, 'Accelerating CSR Practices in the new EU Member States and candidate countries as a vehicle for harmonization, competitiveness, and social cohesion in the EU', 2007; www.undp.hr/upload/file/205/102972/FILENAME/DOP_english.pdf.

14 For information on this case, see: www.culture.lt/petition; Neil Harrison, 'The end of Lietuva cinema, the death of community culture', *The Baltic Times Online*, 8 June 2005; www.baltictimes.com/news/articles/12887; Geert Lovink, 'Hacking Public Spaces in Vilnius', Institute on Network Cultures, 22 June 2005; www.networkcultures.org/ weblog/archives/2005/06/hacking_public.html.

15 G. Kadziauskas, '"Lietuva": viesojo intereso falsifikacija', 2006; www.delfi.lt/news/daily/ comments/article.php?id=10402618 (in Lithuanian).

16 Madara official website: www.madara-cosmetics.lv.

17 Naomi Klein, *Fences and Windows: Dispatches from the Front Lines of the Globalization Debate* (London: Flamingo, 2002): 34.

18 Lyndall Herman and Michael Hammer, 'Peacebuilding without the Cherry Picking', *One World Trust*, 19 July 2007; oneworldtrust.org/component/search/ peacebuilding%20without%20the%20cherry%20picking?ordering=newest&searchphr ase=all#content.

19 Joel Fleishman, *The Foundation: A Great American Secret* (New York: Public Affairs, 2007).

20 Jem Bendell, *Debating NGO Accountability* (Geneva: UN-NGLS, 2006; www.un-ngls. org/pdf/NGO_Accountability.pdf).

21 Jem Bendell and Phyllida Cox, 'The Donor Accountability Agenda', in Lisa Jordan and Peter van Tuijl, *NGO Accountability* (London: Earthscan, 2006): 109-28.

22 Charles Piller, Edmund Sanders and Robyn Dixon, 'Dark Cloud over Good Works of Gates Foundation', *LA Times Online*, 7 January 2007; www.latimes.com/news/ nationworld/nation/la-na-gatesx07jan07,0,6827615.story.

23 Kristi Heim, 'Gates Foundation to review investments', *The Seattle Times Online*, 10 January 2007; seattletimes.nwsource.com/html/localnews/2003517601_gatesinvest10. html.

24 'Gates Foundation to maintain its investment plan', *The Austin Statesman*, 14 January 2007.

25 Charles Piller, 'Berkshire wealth clashes with Gates mission in Sudan', *LA Times Online*, 4 May 2007; www.latimes.com/news/nationworld/nation/la-na-berkshire4may04,0,6075683.story?coll=la-home-headlines.

26 'Gates Foundation Backing off from Its Pledge to Review Investments', *Ideolog*, 11 January 2007; www.idealog.us/2007/01/gates_foundatio.html.

27 Michael Connor, 'Rates of Return: How best to accomplish a foundation's mission? Passive investment vs. shareholder activism', *Corporate Responsibility Magazine Online*; www.thecro.com/node/359.

28 Nathan Cummings Foundation official website: www.nathancummings.org.
29 Charity SRI official website: www.charitysri.org.
30 UNEPFI, 'UNEPFI and WWF Workshop on Innovative Financing for Sustainable SMEs in Africa', 26 September 2007; www.unepfi.org/events/2007/geneva/index.html.
31 www.karmabanque.com

4Q2007

1 'Ethical leaders: Best of the best: 15 leaders who made a difference in 2007', *Being Sustainable*, 2007; being-sustainable.com/site/2007-ethical-leaders-a-10.html.
2 Catherine Cornet, 'Gomarra and Camorra', *Babel Med*, 2007; www.babelmed.net/dossier/2421-gomarra-et-camorra.html [in French].
3 Imran Amed, 'Made in Italy: Time for accountability', *The Business of Fashion*, 4 December 2007; www.businessoffashion.com/2007/12/made-in-italy-time-for-accountability.html.
4 Alessandra Ilari and Luisa Zargani, 'Italian Television Program Alleges Fashion Misconduct', *Women's Wear Daily*, 4 December 2007; www.wwd.com/media-news/film-tv/italian-television-program-alleges-fashion-misconduct-474654?navSection=issues upon subscription.
5 Jem Bendell and Anthony Kleanthous, 'Deeper Luxury: Quality and style when the world matters', WWF, 2007; www.wwf.org.uk/deeperluxury.
6 The Business of Fashion, 'Made in Italy: Time for Accountability', 4 December 2007; www.businessoffashion.net/2007/12/made-in-italy-p.html.
7 lifeworth.com/2007review/qtr41-2007.htm.
8 Bendell and Kleanthous, *op. cit.*
9 Vanessa Friedman, 'Luxury brands fail to make ethical grade', *Financial Times Online*, 29 November 2007; www.ft.com/intl/cms/s/0/dbe49fbc-9dda-11dc-9f68-0000779fd2ac.html#axzz2Bbe1ZqAV.
10 'Media Response to WWF-UK Report on Luxury Brands Could Be Tipping Point for the Industry', Lifeworth Press Release, 6 December 2007; www.csrwire.com/News/10355.html.
11 Marian Buckley, 'WWF's Deeper Luxury Report', fuk.co.uk; 29 November 2007; fuk.co.uk/news/wwf_deeper_luxury_report.
12 'At IHT luxury conference, ethics are in vogue', Alison Smale, *International Herald Tribune Online*, 28 November 2007; www.iht.com/articles/2007/11/28/style/rlive.php.
13 www.portfolio.com/views/blogs/fashion-inc/2007/11/29/luxury-and-ethics-the-words-v-the-reality.
14 Joe Ayling, 'FRANCE: PPR Group commits to improving sustainability', *Just-Style.com*, 5 December 2007; www.just-style.com/article.aspx?id=99314.
15 Jeff Miller, 'CRJP Asks WWF-UK to Withdraw 'Deeper Luxury' Report', *Diamonds.net*, 7 December 2007; www.diamonds.net/news/NewsItem.aspx?ArticleID=19927.
16 Anthony Kleanthous, 'Brand Awareness', *The Guardian Online*, 1 December 2007; commentisfree.guardian.co.uk/anthony_kleanthous/2007/12/brand_awareness.html.
17 The Authentic Luxury official website: www.authenticluxury.net.
18 Bonnie Alter, 'Ecostyle Malaysia', *Tree Hugger*, 14 January 2008; www.treehugger.com/style/ecostyle-malaysia.html.
19 Julia Kirby, 'Mad about Plaid', *Harvard Business Review Magazine Online*, November 2007; hbr.org/2007/11/mad-about-plaid/ar/1.

20 'Keep Burberry British', *Wenling-Jomec*, 13 December 2006; braveman.wordpress. com/2006/12/13/keep-burberry-british.

21 *Monocle* 4 (2007): 121.

22 'Tata's Orient-Express bid hits hurdle', *The Business Standard Online*, 12 December 2007; www.business-standard.com/india/news/tatas-orient-express-bid-hits-hurdle/307269.

23 'Tata wants US hotel chain to apologise', *India eNews*, 20 December 2007; www. indiaenews.com/business/20071220/87348.htm.

24 Wayne Visser, Dirk Matten, Manfred Pohl and Nick Tolhurst (eds.), *The A to Z of Corporate Social Responsibility: The Complete Reference of Concepts, Codes and Organisations* (London: John Wiley, 2007).

25 *Together for a Better Tomorrow: Sustainable Enterprise Conference 2007*, 4–5 May 2007, Sonoma Mountain Village, Sonoma County, California; www.sec2007.com.

26 Stuart School of Business: Centre for Sustainable Enterprise: www.stuart.iit.edu/cse.

27 Johnson Cornell University: Center for Sustainable Global Enterprise; www.johnson. cornell.edu/sge/Www.gbs.edu.au.

28 www.ethicalcorp.com/content.asp?ContentID=4938. This link is no longer available but a similar discussion can be found at Malcolm McIntosh and Sandra Waddock, 'A Global Conversation on the Emerging Sustainable Enterprise Economy', June 2010; www.griffith.edu.au/__data/assets/pdf_file/0005/220766/McIntosh-and-_Waddock_ The_Sustainable_Enterprise_Economy.pdf.

29 11th Impact Conference, 'Ideas into Action: Leadership for Sustainable Enterprise', *EconBiz*, 17–19 June 2008; www.econbiz.de/index. php?id=detailed_view&itemId=10005874650&L=2.

30 For an early popular proponent of this usage, see M. McIntosh, D. Leipziger, K. Jones and G. Coleman, *Corporate Citizenship: Successful. Strategies for Responsible Companies* (London: Financial Times Pitman, 1998).

31 For an early introduction of the notion of corporate citizenship implying submission to a new global governance framework in return for current and growing economic freedoms, see the conclusion of J. Bendell (ed.), *Terms for Endearment: Business, NGOs and Sustainable Development* (Sheffield, UK: Greenleaf Publishing, 2000): 239-54.

32 For the latest on these intellectual discussions, see A. Crane, D. Matten and J. Moon, *Corporations and Citizenship* (Cambridge, UK: Cambridge University Press, 2008).

33 The History of Painters: www.georgesbraque.org/georges-braque-quotes.jsp.

34 'RESPONSE Project: Understanding and Responding to Societal Demands on Corporate Responsibility', *Cordis*, 14 April 2011; cordis.europa.eu/search/index. cfm?fuseaction=lib.document&DOC_LANG_ID=EN&DOC_ID=127976221&q.

2008: Introduction

1 It may help resolve social problems or promote sustainable development but the foremost purpose is commercial.

2 'Top companies: Biggest employers', *CNN Money Online*, 21 July 2008; money.cnn. com/magazines/fortune/global500/2008/performers/companies/biggest

3 *Ibid.*
By the end of 2008, the IMF estimated that global foreign currency reserves stood at $6.71 trillion. Source: 'Global reserves fall for second straight period in Q4-IMF', *Reuters*, 31 March 2009; www.forexpros.com/news/forex-news/global-reserves-fall-for-second-straight-period-in-q4-imf-41025.

4 This is an extrapolation based on figures from the WTO that show in 1990 intra-trade was 42 % and extra-trade was 58%, whereas in 2007, intra and extra-trade were both at 50%. Source: International Trade Statistics 2008 (WTO: Geneva; www.wto.org/english/res_e/statis_e/its2008_e/its08_toc_e.htm).

5 John Parker, 'Special report: Burgeoning bourgeoisie', *The Economist Online*, 12 February 2009; www.economist.com/specialreports/displayStory.cfm?story_id=13063 298&source=hptextfeature.

6 Sean O'Grady, 'The Big Question: As Jaguar/Land Rover is bought by Tata, is the UK car industry finished?', *The Independent Online*, 27 March 2008; www.independent. co.uk/news/business/analysis-and-features/the-big-question-as-jaguarland-rover-is-bought-by-tata-is-the-uk-car-industry-finished-801176.html.

7 'Football Crazy', *The Economist Online*, 2 September 2008; www.economist.com/daily/chartgallery/displayStory.cfm?story_id=12032408.

8 Bobbie Johnson, 'US role as internet hub starts to slip' *The Guardian Online*, 8 December 2008; www.guardian.co.uk/technology/2008/dec/08/internet-usa.

9 Robert Peston. 'New World Order'. *BBC News Online*, 18 September 2008; www.bbc. co.uk/blogs/thereporters/robertpeston/2008/09/new_world_order.html.

10 John Gray, 'A shattering moment in America's fall from power', *The Guardian Online*, 28 September 2008; www.guardian.co.uk/commentisfree/2008/sep/28/usforeignpolicy. useconomicgrowth.

11 'India launches first Moon mission', *BBC Online*, 22 October 2008; news.bbc.co.uk/2/hi/science/nature/7679818.stm.

12 Aida Edemariam, 'The big meltdown', *The Guardian Online*, 25 June 2008; www.guardian.co.uk/world/2008/jun/25/china.commodities/print.

13 Kishore Mahbubani, *The New Asian Hemisphere: The Irresistible Shift of Global Power to the East* (New York: PublicAffairs, 2008).

14 Refer to the UK debate about the future of their overseas aid: 'Tories refuse to give China aid', *BBC Online*, 29 September 2008; news.bbc.co.uk/2/hi/uk_news/politics/7643214.stm.

15 A. Ibrahim, *The Asian Renaissance* (Singapore: Marshall Cavendish Editions, 2008): 18.

16 Jonathan Watts. 'Buy! Buy! Buy!', *The Guardian Online*, 13 March 2008; www.guardian. co.uk/artanddesign/2008/mar/13/art.chinaarts2008.

17 Ibrahim, *op. cit.*: 13.

18 Roger Scruton, 'The West and the Rest: Globalisation and the terrorist threat' (Intercollegiate Studies Institute, 2003).

19 Ibrahim, *op. cit.*: 27.

20 Eva Alessi and Patrizia Zaratti, 'The Asian giant's unsustainable footprint', *Vita. it Online*, 8 August 2008; www.vita.it/ambiente/sostenibilita/the-asian-giant-s-unsustainable-footprint.html.

21 Andrew Jacobs, 'UN Reports Pollution Threat in Asia', *The New York Times Online*, 13 November 2008; www.nytimes.com/2008/11/14/world/14cloud.html?_r=0.

22 See for instance: Ricky Y.K. Chan, Y.H. Wong and T.K.P. Leung, 'Applying Ethical Concepts to the Study of "Green" Consumer Behavior: An Analysis of Chinese Consumers' Intentions to Bring their Own Shopping Bag', *Journal of Business Ethics* 79.4 (June 2008): 469.

23 Robin Wigglesworth, 'Wealth brings weighty problem for the Gulf', *The Financial Times Online*, 30 August 2008, www.ft.com/intl/cms/s/0/fce0a2b8-762b-11dd-99ce-0000779fd18c.html.

24 Parker, *op. cit.*

25 Teh Shi Ning, 'Altruism still very much alive and kicking', *The Business Times Online*, 18 October 2008; www.asiaone.com/Business/My%2BMoney/Starting%2BOut/ Investments%2BAnd%2BSavings/Story/A1Story20081016-94195.html.

26 Stephen Frost and Mary Ho, '"Going out": the growth of Chinese foreign direct investment in Southeast Asia and its implications for corporate social responsibility', *Corporate Social Responsibility and Environmental Management* 12.3 (September 2005): 157.

27 '2008 Review of the corporate responsibility performance of large emerging market enterprises', UNCTAD and EIRIS, 2008; www.unctad.org/en/docs/c2isarcrp3_en.pdf.

28 'Environment Tax to be Levied in 2009', *China CSR*, 31 December 2008; www.chinacsr. com/en/2008/12/31/4016-chinese-environment-tax-to-be-levied-in-2009.

29 'Government to launch product label as guarantee over child labour'; www. mallenbaker.net/csr/CSRfiles/page.php?Story_ID=2341.

30 All data from ISO. 'The ISO Survey: 2007' (Geneva: ISO, 2008; www.iso.org/iso/ survey2007.pdf): 27.

31 The Asean Foundation official website: www.aseanfoundation.org/csr/index.php.

32 The UNPRI official website: www.unpri.org.

33 The ASES official website: www.asiases.org.

34 The Social Innovators Forum official website: www.socialinnovatorsforum.org.

35 The Ashoka official website: www.ashoka.org.

36 'Credit delivery system', *Grameen Communications*; www.gdrc.org/icm/grameen-feature.html.

37 'Grameen Bank at a Glance', *Grameen Communications*, April 2008; web01.grameen. com/bank/atagrlance/GBGlance.htm.

38 Sharmila Devi, 'Little loans earn banker a whole lot of credit', *The National Online*, 25 April 2008; muhammadyunus.org/index2.php?option=com_content&task=view&id=8 8&pop=1&page=0&Itemid=128.

39 George Wehrfritz, 'In The Slow Lane: Plug-and-play electric cars for urban drivers are pushing the envelope on green. Just don't try gunning them—yet', *Newsweek Online*, 16 February 2008; www.newsweek.com/id/112730/output/print.

40 The BYD official website: www.byd.com.

41 'Plug-In Hybrid Goes On Sale, In China Only', *Hybrid Cars*, 3 November 2008; www. hybridcars.com/news/plug-hybrid-goes-sale-china-only-25222.html.

42 The Better Place official website: www.betterplace.com.

43 World Bank. 'Philippines: Beach Town Hums with Progress', *Online*, 4 February 2009; web.worldbank.org/WBSITE/EXTERNAL/NEWS/0,,contentMDK:22052230~page PK:34370~piPK:34424~theSitePK:4607,00.html. See also wikimapia.org/9157545/ Bangui-Windmills.

44 From 2000 to 2007 there were a total of 291 relevant academic articles in these journals, giving an average of 36.375 a year. Given the *Journal of Corporate Citizenship* did not publish in 2001, this can be rounded up to 40 articles (i.e. *JCC* published an average of four articles on Asia prior to 2008).

45 Gabriel D Donleavy, Kit-Chun Joanna Lam and Simon S.M. Ho, 'Does East Meet West in Business Ethics? An Introduction to the Special Issue', *Journal of Business Ethics* 79.1–2 (April 2008): 1.

46 EIRIS, 'A Review of ESG Practices in Large Emerging Market Companies', March 2009; www.eiris.org/files/research%20publications/emergingmarketsmar09.pdf.

47 See for instance: Wendy Chapple and Jeremy Moon, 'Corporate Social Responsibility (CSR) in Asia: A Seven-Country Study of CSR Web Site Reporting', *Business and Society*

44.4 (December 2005): 415; David Kimber and Phillip Lipton, 'Corporate Governance and Business Ethics in the Asia-Pacific Region', *Business and Society* 44.2 (June 2005): 178.

48 See for instance: Daryl Koehn and Alicia Leung, 'Dignity in Western Versus in Chinese Cultures: Theoretical Overview and Practical Illustrations', *Business and Society Review* 113.4 (Winter 2008): 477; Scott J. Vitell and Abhijit Patwardhan, 'The Role of Moral Intensity and Moral Philosophy in Ethical Decision Making: A Cross-Cultural Comparison of China and the European Union', *Business Ethics: A European Review* 17.2 (April 2008): 196-209; Lorne S. Cummings, 'Managerial Attitudes toward Environmental Management within Australia, the People's Republic of China and Indonesia', *Business Strategy and the Environment* 17.1 (January 2008): 16; Gregory Jackson and Andreas Moerke, 'Continuity and Change in Corporate Governance: Comparing Germany and Japan', *Corporate Governance: An International Review* 13.3 (May 2005): 351.

49 See, for instance, Audun Ruud, 'Environmental management of transnational corporations in India: Are TNCs creating islands of environmental excellence in a sea of dirt?', *Business Strategy and the Environment*, 1.2 (March/April 2002): 103; Aris Solomon, Jill Solomon and Megumi Suto, 'Can the UK Experience Provide Lessons for the Evolution of SRI in Japan?', *Corporate Governance: An International Review* 12.4 (October 2004): 552; Mooweon Rhee and Ji-Hwan Lee, 'The Signals Outside Directors Send to Foreign Investors: Evidence from Korea', *Corporate Governance: An International Review* 16.1 (January 2008): 41.

50 Ibrahim, *op. cit.*: 20.

51 Yahya Wijaya, 'The Prospect of Familism in the Global Era: A Study on the Recent Development of the Ethnic-Chinese Business, with Particular Attention to the Indonesian Context', *Journal of Business Ethics* 79.3 (May 2008): 311.

52 Po-Keung Ip, 'Corporate Social Responsibility and Crony Capitalism in Taiwan', *Journal of Business Ethics* 79.1–2 (April 2008): 167.

53 For instance, in reverse chronological order, some of the articles in that journal include: Chris Provis, 'Guanxi and Conflicts of Interest', *Journal of Business Ethics* 79.1–2 (April 2008): 57; Danielle E. Warren, Thomas W. Dunfee and Naihe Li, 'Social Exchange in China: The Double-Edged Sword of Guanxi', *Journal of Business Ethics* 55.4 (December 2004): 353; Chenting Su, M Joseph Sirgy and James E. Littlefield, 'Is Guanxi Orientation Bad, Ethically Speaking? A Study of Chinese Enterprises', *Journal of Business Ethics* 44.4 (June 2003): 303; Doreen Tan,and Robin Stanley Snell, 'The Third Eye: Exploring Guanxi and Relational Morality in the Workplace', *Journal of Business Ethics* 41.4 (December 2002): 361; Ricky Y.K. Chan, Louis T.W. Cheng and Ricky W.F. Szeto, 'The Dynamics of Guanxi and Ethics for Chinese Executives', *Journal of Business Ethics* 41.4 (December 2002): 327; Ying Fan, 'Guanxi's Consequences: Personal Gains at Social Cost', *Journal of Business Ethics* 38.4 (July 2002): 371; Chenting Su and James E. Littlefield, 'Entering Guanxi: A Business Ethical Dilemma in Mainland China?', *Journal of Business Ethics* 33.3 (October 2001): 199; Thomas W. Dunfee, Danielle E. Warren, 'Is Guanxi Ethical? A Normative Analysis of Doing Business in China', *Journal of Business Ethics* 32.3 (August 2001): 191; Alan K.M. Au, and Danny S.N. Wong, 'The Impact of Guanxi on the Ethical Decision-Making Process of Auditors: An Exploratory Study on Chinese CPAs in Hong Kong', *Journal of Business Ethics* 28.1 (November 2000): 87.

54 Po–Keung Ip, 'Business Ethics and a State-Owned Enterprise in China', *Business Ethics: A European Review* 12.1 (January 2003): 64-77.

55 Personal communication with Jem Bendell, January 2009.

56 Linfen Jennifer Huang and Robin Stanley Snell, 'Turnaround, Corruption and Mediocrity: Leadership and Governance in Three State Owned Enterprises in Mainland China', *Journal of Business Ethics* 43.1–2 (March 2003): 111.

57 He Shan, 'More firms pay attention to social responsibility', *China.org.cn*, 10 December 2008; www.china.org.cn/business/news/2008-12/10/content_16928942.htm.

58 Bendell *et al.*, *The Corporate Responsibility Movement.*

59 Richard Welford, Clifford Chan and Michelle Man, 'Priorities for Corporate Social Responsibility: A Survey of Businesses and their Stakeholders', *Corporate Social Responsibility and Environmental Management* 15.1 (January/February 2008): 52.

60 EIRIS, 'The State of Responsible Business: Implications for PRI Signatories', October 2008; www.eiris.org/files/research%20publications/stateofrespbusinesssep08.pdf.

61 Sarah Parsons, 'The Problem with Palm: Using palm oil to make biodiesel may cause more trouble than it prevents', *Mother Nature Network*, 21 April 2008; www.mnn.com/the-home/household-products/stories/the-problem-with-palm.

62 Ibrahim, *op. cit.*: 18.

63 For some discussion of the role of religion in business in Asia see: Mohammed Y.A. Rawwas, Ziad Swaidan and Jamal Al-Khatib, 'Does Religion Matter? A Comparison Study of the Ethical Beliefs of Marketing Students of Religious and Secular Universities in Japan', *Journal of Business Ethics* 65.1 (April 2006): 69; Chau-kiu Cheung and Andrew Chi-fai Chan, 'Philosophical Foundations of Eminent Hong Kong Chinese CEO's Leadership', *Journal of Business Ethics* 60.1 (August 2005): 47; Heungsik Park, Michael T. Rehg and Donggi Lee, 'The Influence of Confucian Ethics and Collectivism on Whistleblowing Intentions: A Study of South Korean Public Employees', *Journal of Business Ethics* 58.4 (June 2005): 387; Tak Sing Cheung and Ambrose Yeo-chi king, 'Righteousness and Profitableness: The Moral Choices of Contemporary Confucian Entrepreneurs', *Journal of Business Ethic* 54.3 (October 2004): 243; Calvin M Boardman and Hideaki Kiyoshi Kato, 'The Confucian Roots of Business Kyosei', *Journal of Business Ethics* 48.4 (December 2003): 317; Kam-hon Lee, Dennis P. McCann and Mary Ann Ching, 'Christ and Business Culture: A Study of Christian Executives in Hong Kong', *Journal of Business Ethics* 43.1–2 (March 2003): 103; Juliet Roper and Ed Weymes, 'Reinstating the Collective: A Confucian Approach to Well-being and Social Capital Development in a Globalised Economy', *Journal of Corporate Citizenship* 26 (Summer 2007): 135;

64 Skip Worden, 'The Role of Religious and Nationalist Ethics in Strategic Leadership: The Case of J.N. Tata', *Journal of Business Ethics* 47.2 (October 2003): 147.

65 Ibrahim, *op. cit.*: 128.

66 Mahbubani, *op. cit.*

67 M. Kline, *Mathematical Thought from Ancient to Modern Times* (Oxford University Press, 1972): Vol. 1, 193-95.

68 N.M. Mathew, *Malankara Marthoma Sabha Charitram* (*History of the Marthoma Church*) (2006): Vol. 1. See also www.marthomasyrianchurch.org.

69 Ibrahim, *op. cit.*: 25.

70 Regino P. Paular (ed.), *Rizal as an Internationalist* (Manila: National Historical Institute, 1992): 59.

71 Ibrahim, *op. cit.*: 28.

72 Tu Wei Ming, Way, *Learning and Politics: Essays on the Confucian Intellectual* (State University of New York Press, 1993).

73 For more on academic explorations of this dialogue of values, see the April 2008 Special Issue of the *Journal of Business Ethics*. See also Katharina J. Srnka, A. Ercan

Gegez and S. Burak Arzova, 'Why Is It (Un-)ethical? Comparing Potential European Partners: A Western Christian and An Eastern Islamic Country—On Arguments Used in Explaining Ethical Judgments', *Journal of Business Ethics* 74.2 (August 2007): 101.

74 Muthiah Alagappa (ed.), *Civil Society and Political Change in Asia: Expanding and Contracting Democratic Space* (Stanford University Press, 2004).

75 EIRIS, 'A Review of ESG Practices in Large Emerging Market Companies', March 2009; www.eiris.org/files/research%20publications/emergingmarketsmar09.pdf.

76 Krishna Dutta and Andrew Robinson, *Rabidranath Tagore: The Myriad Minded Man* (New York: St Martin's Press, 1995): 137.

77 Robert Kagan, *The Return of History and the End of Dreams* (New York: Knopf, 2008).

78 Ibrahim, *op. cit.*: 41.

79 Bendell *et al.*, *The Corporate Responsibility Movement*: 24-34.

80 'Writing in Young India', 26 November 1931: 369; www.mkgandhi.org/momgandhi/chap53.htm.

81 Prof. M.L. Dantwala writing Gandhi's views in *Harijan*, 25 October 1952: 301; www.mkgandhi.org/momgandhi/chap53.htm.

82 Writing in *Harijan*, 31 March 1946: 63-64; www.mkgandhi.org/momgandhi/chap53.htm.

83 R.C. Sekhar, 'Trends in Ethics and Styles of Leadership in India', *Business Ethics: A European Review* 10.4 (October 2001): 360-63.

84 Bendell *et al.*, *The Corporate Responsibility Movement*: 24-34.

1Q2008

1 'Notable cases of Attorney General Eliot Spitzer', Wikipedia; en.wikipedia.org/wiki/Notable_cases_of_Attorney_General_Eliot_Spitzer.

2 'Spitzer's Resignation Speech: Transcript', *The Huffington Post*, 12 March 2008; www.huffingtonpost.com/2008/03/12/spitzers-resignation-spe_n_91157.html.

3 Greg Palast, 'Eliot's Mess: The $200 billion bail-out for predator banks and Spitzer charges are intimately linked', Reporting for Air America Radio's *Clout*, 14 March 2008; archive.org/details/sglGregPalastreportsEliot_sMess.

4 'Prison term in VW corruption case', *BBC News Online*, 22 February 2008; news.bbc.co.uk/2/hi/business/7258438.stm.

5 Kate Connolly, 'Bribery, brothels, free Viagra: VW trial scandalises Germany', *The Observer Online*, 13 January 2008; www.guardian.co.uk/world/2008/jan/13/germany.automotive.

6 David Sapsted, 'Oil chief gave his favourite prostitute a contract with the company', *The Telegraph Online*, 2 February 2005; www.telegraph.co.uk/news/worldnews/northamerica/usa/1482557/Oil-chief-gave-his-favourite-prostitute-a-contract-with-the-company.html.

7 'China arrests 38 for graft related to the Olympics', *The Star Online*, 31 January 2008; thestar.com.my/sports/story.asp?file=/2008/1/31/sports/20182215&sec=sports.

8 Richard McGregor, 'Corruption poses "lethal threat" to China', *The Financial Times Online*, 10 October 2007; www.ft.com/cms/s/0/3dbe4178-774a-11dc-9de8-0000779fd2ac.html?nclick_check=1; upon registration.

9 Minxin Pei, 'Corruption Threatens China's Future', Carnegie Endowment, October 2007; www.carnegieendowment.org/publications/index.cfm?fa=view&id=19628&prog=zch.

10 Ram Gorni, 'China: Rule of law, Sometimes', *Asia Times Online, 3 July 2003;* www. atimes.com/atimes/China/EG03Ad03.html.

11 Pei, *op. cit.*

12 *Ibid.*

13 Luo Bing, 'Chinese leader states corruption will destroy the Chinese Communist Party', *Chengming Magazine*, 29 February 2008.

14 'China to step up anti-corruption crackdown (Xinhua)', *China Daily Online*, 21 February 2008; www.chinadaily.com.cn/china/2008-02/21/content_6471821.htm.

15 'China's new anti-corruption website breakdown as masses log on', *China View Online*, 19 December 2007; news.xinhuanet.com/english/2007-12/19/content_7281144.htm.

16 *Ibid.*

17 Lala Rimando, 'Lozada: Benjamin Abalos and Mike Arroyo behind broadband deal overprice', *Newsbreak Archives Online*, 7 February 2008; archives.newsbreak-knowledge.ph/2008/02/07/lozada-benjamin-abalos-and-mike-arroyo-behind-broadband-deal-overprice.

18 Lala Rimando, 'NBN witness: US$65-M overprice acceptable', *Newsbreak Archives Online*, 8 February 2008; archives.newsbreak-knowledge.ph/2008/02/08/nbn-witness-us65-m-overprice-acceptable.

19 Greg Mills and Chris Thompson, 'China: Partner or predator in Africa?', *Asia Times Online, 25 January 2008;* www.atimes.com/atimes/China_Business/JA25Cb02.html.

20 Tom Leander, 'National Champion: How ZTE is taking China's economic ambitions to the developing world', *CFO Asia*, 16 May 2007; web.archive.org/web/20081202062655/www.cfoasia.com/archives/200705-01.htm.

21 Huawei, 'Milestones'; www.huawei.com/en/about-huawei/corporate-info/milestone/index.htm.

22 Leander, *op. cit.*

23 Huawei, 'Corporate Citizenship'; www.huawei.com/en/about-huawei/corporate-citizenship/index.htm.

24 ZTE, 'Corporate Citizenship'; wwwen.zte.com.cn/en/about/corporate_citizenship.

25 Stephen Frost, 'Alcatel-Lucent inks deal in Burma', CSR-Asia, 13 September 2007; www.csr-asia.com/index.php?id=10616.

26 'CSR Guideline for State-Owned Enterprises (SOE)', Syntao.com, 1 January 2008; syntao.com/E_Page_Show.asp?Page_ID=6407.

27 'China to step up anti-corruption crackdown (Xinhua)', *China Daily Online*, 21 February 2008; www.chinadaily.com.cn/china/2008-02/21/content_6471821.htm.

28 Juliet Roper and Ed Weymes, 'Reinstating the Collective: A Confucian Approach to Well-being and Social Capital Development in a Globalised Economy', *Journal of Corporate Citizenship* 26 (2007): 135-44.

29 Jem Bendell *et al.*, Foreword to *The Global Step Change: Lifeworth Annual Review of Corporate Responsibility in 2007*. lifeworth.com/2007review/default.htm.

30 '19 Feb London On Tap: The Clear Choice', Thames Water press release; www.thameswater.co.uk/media/press-releases/4347.htm.

31 Official website of the London on Tap campaign: www.thameswater.co.uk/your-water/8316.htm.

32 Janet Larsen, 'Bottled water backlash is growing', 7 December 2007; peopleandplanet.net/doc.php?id=3156 (please note that this link is no longer available).

33 New York City Department of Environmental Protection, 'NYC 2006 Drinking Water Supply and Quality Report'; www.nyc.gov/html/dep/html/drinking_water/wsstate.shtml.

34 London On Tap, 'Facts and Figures'; www.thameswater.co.uk/media/806.htm.
35 *Ibid.*
36 'Coca-Cola Enterprises forms Coca-Cola Recycling LLC to help lead recycling efforts', Coca-Cola Enterprises news release, 5 September 2007; ir.cokecce.com/phoenix. zhtml?c=117435&p=irol-newsArticle&ID=1305876&highlight=.
37 Nestlé official website. 'Creating Shared Value'; www.nestle.com/CSV/Pages/ Homepage.aspx.

2Q2008

1   '18th Global Summit of Women opens in Hanoi, Vietnam', *People's Daily Online*, 5 June 2008; english.people.com.cn/90001/90777/90851/6425364.html.
2   'Global Summit of Women 2008: Irene Natividad Opening Statement', *Globewomen*, 5 June 2008; globewomen.org/summit/2008/Speeches/Text/Natividad_Opening.htm.
3   Anna Murphy, 'Pregnant pause: Why so many working mothers still get passed over for promotion', *The Independent Online*, 16 May 2008; www.independent.ie/business/ pregnant-pause-1376461.html.
4   Louis Uchitelle, 'Women are now equal as victims of poor economy', *New York Times Online*, 22 July 2008; www.nytimes.com/2008/07/22/business/22jobs.html?_r=2&page wanted=1&hp&oref=slogin.
5   K. Grosser and J. Moon, 'Developments in Company Reporting on Workplace Gender Equality? A Corporate Social Responsibility Perspective', *Accounting Forum* 32.3 (September 2008): 179-98.
6   Institute for Social-Ecological Research, *Rhetoric and Realities: Analysing Corporate Social Responsibility in Europe (RARE)*; www.isoe.de/ftp/RARE_Flyer_Gender.pdf.
7   For more information about the aims of the MDG3 Global Call to Action campaign, visit um.dk/en/danida-en/activities/strategic/human-right-demo/gender/mdg3.
8   *Ibid.*
9   The OECD Development Centre website on gender can be accessed at www.oecd.org/ document/23/0,3343,en_2649_33935_36225815_1_1_1,00.html.
10 The survey is available at www.masterintelligence.com/ViewRegion.jsp?hidReportTyp eId=4&hidUserId=null.
11 ILO, 'Global Employment Trends for Women 2008', 2008; www.ilo.org/wcmsp5/groups/ public/---dgreports/---dcomm/documents/publication/wcms_091225.pdf.
12 'Are men and women equal in Hong Kong today?', *CSR Asia* monthly briefing: CSR Wednesday, Equal Opportunities Commission, Hong Kong, 4 June 2008.
13 Andrea Rossi and Yianna Lambrou, *Gender and Equity Issues in Liquid Biofuels Production: Minimizing the Risks to Maximize the Opportunities* (Rome: FAO; www.fao. org/docrep/010/ai503e/ai503e00.htm).
14 Irmgard Schultz, *Background Paper on EU Policies on Gender Equality in the Private Sector* (Rhetoric and Realities: Analysing Corporate Social Responsibility in Europe [RARE], Deliverable 17: Policy Paper Gender Equality, 2007; www.isoe.de/ftp/rare/ rare17casestudy.pdf).
15 www.ibm.com/ibm/ideasfromibm/us/ceo/20080505/index.shtml
16 Grosser and Moon, *op. cit.*
17 Judi Marshall, 'The Gendering of Leadership in Corporate Social Responsibility', *Journal of Organizational Change Management* 20.2 (2007): 165-81.
18 Schultz, *op. cit.*
19 Marshall, *op. cit.*

20 John Carvel, 'Harman delivers diluted version of equality bill', *The Guardian Online*, 27 June 2008; www.guardian.co.uk/society/2008/jun/27/equality.constitution.

21 Marie-Victoire Louis, 'Tell me, what does "gender" really mean?' (October 2005; www.marievictoirelouis.net/document.php?id=737&themeid=740).

22 *Ibid.*

23 *Op. cit.*

24 *Catalyst*, 'The Bottom Line: Connecting Corporate Performance and Gender Diversity', January 2004; www.catalyst.org/publication/82/the-bottom-line-connecting-corporate-performance-and-gender-diversity; and 'Advancing Women Leaders: The Connection between Women Board Directors and Women Corporate Officers', July 2008; www.catalyst.org/publication/273/advancing-women-leaders-the-connection-between-women-board-directors-and-women-corporate-officers.

25 Calvert Investments official website, 'Special Report: Calvert Women's Principles'; www.calvert.com/womensPrinciples.html.

26 *Op. cit.*

27 Audience member at Net Impact Europe conference, Geneva, June 2008. See also (Red) Fact Sheet; www.joinred.com/wp-content/uploads/2012/pdf/%28RED%29%20Fact%20Sheet.pdf.

28 Ron Nixon, 'Bottom Line for (Red)', *New York Times Online*, 6 February 2008; www.nytimes.com/2008/02/06/business/06red.html?pagewanted=all.

29 J. Bendell, *Waking Up to Risk? Corporate Responses to HIV/AIDS in the Workplace* (Geneva: UNRISD, 2003).

30 *Ibid.*

31 The report can be accessed by searching 'Motorola Corporate Responsibility Report 2007'.

32 Joachim Melchers, 'Cooperation with Giorgio Armani: Owusu-Ankomah supports the fight against AIDS', Owusu-Ankomah website: www.owusu-ankomah.de/review.html.

33 'Taking Steps Towards Hope', 8 September 2006; web.archive.org/web/20071031223440/www.gapinc.com/red/progress_article_2.html.

34 reinspired.blogspot.com/2006/11/frequently-asked-questions.html. Please note that this link is no longer available.

35 Audience member at Net Impact Europe conference, Geneva, June 2008.

36 Bobby Shriver, 'Point/Counter-point', 20 June 2006; web.archive.org/web/20070620125316/www.joinred.com/archive/adage/pcp.asp.

37 Sam Bond, 'China and India will shape the future of CSR', *edie.net*, 13 March 2006; www.edie.net/news/news_story.asp?id=11178&channel=0.

38 Eddie Rich, '10 Developments that EITI will Face in 2008', Extractive Industries Transparency Initiative, 2008; eiti.org/blog/10-developments-eiti-will-face-2008#.

39 J. Bendell, 'Broader and Deeper: The Future of CSR Research' (Occasional Paper; Geneva: Lifeworth, 2008; www.lifeworth.com/BroaderAndDeeper.pdf).

40 In July 2008.

41 J. Bendell *et al.*, *The Corporate Responsibility Movement: Five Years of Global Corporate Responsibility Analysis from Lifeworth, 2001–2005* (Sheffield, UK: Greenleaf Publishing 2009).

3Q2008

1 G. Jeffrey MacDonald, 'How can investors help the hungry?', *Christian Science Monitor*, 25 August 2008; www.csmonitor.com/2008/0825/p13s01-wmgn.html.

2 Sarah Griffiths, 'How to invest ethically in commodities', *Investment Week*; www.investmentweek.co.uk/public/showPage.html?page=797742. Upon registration.

3 MacDonald, *op. cit.*

4 'Chris Martenson on Economic, Environmental, and Energy "Hockey Sticks"', Sea Change Radio, 9 April 2008; www.cchange.net/2008/04/09/chris-martenson-on-economic-environmental-and-energy-hockey-sticks.

5 David M. Herszenhorn, 'Administration is seeking $700 billion for Wall Street', *New York Times Online*, 20 September 2008; www.nytimes.com/2008/09/21/business/21cong.html.

6 Robert Borosage *et al.*, 'The Bailout: A Call for Common Sense', Campaign for America's Future; www.ourfuture.org/page/2008093923/bailout-call-common-sense.

7 Stephen Foley, 'How Goldman Sachs took over the world', *The Independent Online*, 22 July 2008; www.independent.co.uk/news/business/analysis-and-features/how-goldman-sachs-took-over-the-world-873869.html; and Dean Baker, 'Wall Street's Infinite Sleaze: Goldman and AIG', *Huffington Post Online*, 28 September 2008; www.huffingtonpost.com/dean-baker/hi-dean-baker-your-profil_b_129954.html.

8 Jenny Anderson, Vikas Bajaj and Leslie Wayne, 'Big financiers start lobbying for wider aid', *New York Times Online*, 21 September 2008; www.nytimes.com/2008/09/22/business/22lobby.html.

9 'Brokering the Bail-out', *The Guardian Online*, 26 September 2008; www.guardian.co.uk/commentisfree/2008/sep/26/wallstreet.useconomy.

10 UNI Global Union, 'UNI-Europa Finance demands the preservation of the diversity of the European financial services markets', 24 September 2007; mail.uniglobalunion.org/UNIFinance.nsf/$webDocuments/D76C76A9B12FF6DBC12573620046EA8F?OpenDocument.

11 Lina Saigol, 'Bigger may not be better', *Financial Times Online*, 21 September 2008; www.ft.com/cms/s/0/5cf3e746-87f7-11dd-b114-0000779fd18c.html. Upon registration.

12 John Gapper, 'This greed was beyond irresponsible', *Financial Times Online*, 17 September 2008; www.ft.com/cms/s/0/9c0e75cc-84e1-11dd-b148-0000779fd18c.html. Upon registration.

13 Robert L. Borosage, 'Wall Street Socialism', *Huffington Post Online*, 15 July 2008; www.huffingtonpost.com/robert-l-borosage/wall-street-socialism_b_112940.html.

14 John Plender, 'Capitalism in Convulsion: Toxic assets head towards the public balance sheet', *Financial Times Online*, 19 September 2008; www.ft.com/cms/s/0/b210deec-8675-11dd-959e-0000779fd18c.html. Upon registration.

15 Borosage, *op. cit.*

16 Nick Leeson, 'Escape of the Bankrupt', *The Guardian Online*, 19 September 2008; www.guardian.co.uk/commentisfree/2008/sep/19/banking.creditcrunch.

17 Joanna Chung, 'Lehman Brothers: Mortgage collapse inquiry widened', *Financial Times Online*, 24 September 2008; www.ft.com/cms/s/0/cd58087e-8a62-11dd-a76a-0000779fd18c.html. Upon registration.

18 'Shareholder lawsuits certain to follow financial crisis', *PRNewswire*, 24 September 2008; biz.yahoo.com/prnews/080924/law081.html. This weblink is no longer available but a Habib Al Mulla Company report entitled *Financial Crisis and its Impact on International Litigation* highlights this issue.

19 Sean O'Grady, Sean Farrell and Stephen Foley, 'Credit Crunch One Year On', *The Independent Online*, 5 August 2008; www.independent.co.uk/news/business/analysis-and-features/credit-crunch-one-year-on-885315.html.

20 *Ibid.*
21 Interfaith Center on Corporate Responsibility, 'Faith-Based Early Warning System for Investors: "Prophetic": religious groups sounded sub-prime loan alarm 15 years ago', 10 September 2008; www.iccr.org/news/press_releases/2008/pr_subprime091008. htm.
22 Common Cause Education Fund, 'Ask yourself why . . . mortgage foreclosure rates are so high', May 2007; www.commoncause.org/atf/cf/%7BFB3C17E2-CDD1-4DF6-92BE-BD4429893665%7D/SUBPRIME%20LENDING%20REPORT%20FINAL.PDF.
23 Ellen Schloemer, Wei Li, Keith Ernst and Kathleen Keest, Center for Responsible Lending, 'Losing Ground: Foreclosures in the Subprime Market and their Cost to Homeowners', December 2006; www.responsiblelending.org/mortgage-lending/research-analysis/foreclosure-paper-report-2-17.pdf.
24 Edmund L. Andrews, 'Fed shrugged as subprime crisis spread', *New York Times Online*, 18 December 2007; www.nytimes.com/2007/12/18/business/18subprime. html?pagewanted=3&_r=2&ref=business.
25 Huw Jones, 'Market "ignored" pre-subprime warnings: BIS' Knight', *Reuters*, 29 May 2008; www.reuters.com/article/gc06/idUSL2931263120080529?pageNumber=1&virtua lBrandChannel=0.
26 Kenneth Rogoff, 'End of Financial Triumphalism?', *The Guardian Online*, 4 August 2008; www.guardian.co.uk/commentisfree/2008/aug/04/economicgrowth.useconomi cgrowth?gusrc=rss&feed=worldnews..
27 International Labour Organisation, *Newsletter* No. 10/2007; web.archive.org/web/20090109035143/www.ilo.org/public/english/region/eurpro/brussels/news/archives/oct2007/news.htm.
28 Jonathan Porritt, *Capitalism as if the World Matters* (London: Earthscan, 2005).
29 Niall Ferguson, *The Ascent of Money: A Financial History of the World* (London: Allen Lane, 2008).
30 Jem Bendell and Kate Kearins, 'The "Political Bottom Line": The Emerging Dimension to Corporate Responsibility for Sustainable Development', *Business Strategy and the Environment* 14.6 (2005): 372-83.
31 Common Cause Education Fund, *op. cit.*
32 Robert Kuttner, 'The Bubble Economy', *The American Prospect*, 24 September 2007; www.prospect.org/cs/articles?article=the_bubble_economy.
33 Jonathan Larsen, 'McCain economic policy shaped by lobbyist', mnsnbc.com, 27 May 2008; www.msnbc.msn.com/id/24844889.
34 Marjorie Kelly, *The Divine Right of Capital* (San Francisco, Berrett-Koehler, 2001).
35 Jem Bendell *et al.*, *The Corporate Responsibility Movement: Five Years of Global Corporate Responsibility Analysis from Lifeworth, 2001–2005* (Sheffield, UK: Greenleaf Publishing, 2009).
36 United Nations Principles on Responsible Investment, 'Rapid growth in responsible investment despite credit crisis', press release, 7 August 2008; www.unpri.org/files/credit%20crunch%20_final.pdf.
37 Elitsa Vucheva, 'France: Laissez-Faire Capitalism is Over', *Bloomberg BusinessWeek*, 29 September 2008; www.businessweek.com/stories/2008-09-29/france-laissez-faire-capitalism-is-overbusinessweek-business-news-stock-market-and-financial-advice.
38 TUAC, 'Statement by the TUAC Secretariat', 19 September 2008; www.tuac.org/en/public/e-docs/00/00/03/13/document_news.phtml.

39 UNI Global Union, 'Financial Crisis: The Price Tag on Intervention', 21 September 2008; web.archive.org/web/20090310143435/www.uniglobalunion.org/UNIFinance. nsf/$webDocuments/E1026A334DA9734FC12574CB002EAC1C.

40 UNI Global Union, 'Demands on Regulation of Financial Markets (Statement)', 16 June 2008; www.uniglobalunion.org/UNIFinance.nsf/By+Date/036A280F58FB4DEAC 12574670051635B. This link is no longer available but the following link has the same demands: www.uniglobalunion.org/Apps/UNINews.nsf/7a1fe394b29b0003c12574c 6004d8645/6570150c6eb28966c125756a0046060f/$FILE/financial%20regulation%20 assessment-1e-28-01-09.pdf.

41 This concept is developed as 'capital accountability' in Jem Bendell, 'Barricades and Boardrooms' (UNRISD, 2004).

42 Personal communication with Jem Bendell, September 2008.

43 Network for Sustainable Financial Markets official website: www. sustainablefinancialmarkets.net.

44 Robert Peston. 'New World Order'. *BBC News Online*. 18 September 2008; www.bbc. co.uk/blogs/thereporters/robertpeston/2008/09/new_world_order.html.

45 Aida Edemariam, 'The Big Meltdown', *The Guardian Online*, 25 June 2008: G2, 7; www. guardian.co.uk/world/2008/jun/25/china.commodities/print.

46 Sue Asci, 'Congressional caucus asks funds to divest in Sudan', *Investment News*, 22 September 2008; www.investmentnews.com/apps/pbcs.dll/article?AID=/20080922/ REG/309229968/1030/MUTUALFUNDS. Upon registration.

47 Brendan O'Neill, 'The Farce of Bashing China's Human Rights Record', *The Times Online*, 14 July 2008; www.timesonline.co.uk/tol/comment/specials/article4329902. ece.

48 Janine Erasmus, 'Dragon in the Dark', iafrica.com, 15 September 2008; business.iafrica. com/features/1142660.htm.

49 'China starts building infrastructure in the DRC', Zonafri, 19 September 2008; www. zonafri.com/index.asp?ItemID=3613. This weblink is no longer available but a 2010 OECD report entitled *How China is Influencing Africa's Development* confirms this number; www.oecd.org/dev/perspectivesonglobaldevelopment/45068325.pdf.

50 *Ibid.*

51 'Investment: Africa finance chiefs pledge transparency', *This Day*, 4 August 2008; www. thisdayonline.com/nview.php?id=118702. This link is no longer available.

52 Daniel Magnowski and Vincent Fertey, 'Africa finance chiefs eye consensus on China funds', *Reuters*, 1 August 2008; www.reuters.com/article/latestCrisis/idUSL1577330.

53 Vivien Foster, William Butterfield, Chuan Chen and Nataliya Pushak, 'Building Bridges: China's Growing Role as Infrastructure Financier for Sub-Saharan Africa', World Bank, 10 July 2008; web.archive.org/web/20080829110943/allafrica.com/sustainable/ resources/00011582.html.

54 Erasmus, *op. cit.*

55 Rosalind McLymont, 'The Great Chinese Takeout: Beijing aggressively pursues Africa's natural resources and consumer markets', *Shipping Digest*, 8 September 2008; www. freerepublic.com/focus/f-news/2078491/posts.

56 David Connett, 'Standard Chartered at centre of Zimbabwe sanctions inquiry', *The Independent Online*, 15 June 2008; www.independent.co.uk/news/business/news/ standard-chartered-at-centre-of-zimbabwe-sanctions-inquiry-847312.html.

57 Paul Lewis and David Pallister, 'Shell ready to quit Zimbabwe as Mugabe cronies hoard fuel', *The Observer Online*, 6 July 2008; www.guardian.co.uk/world/2008/jul/06/ zimbabwe.southafrica1.

58 Dominic White, 'WPP sells Mugabe agency', *The Telegraph Online*, 23 August 2008; www.telegraph.co.uk/finance/newsbysector/mediatechnologyandtelecoms/2795242/ WPP-sells-Mugabe-agency.html.

59 The Burma Campaign UK, 'New report exposes insurance industry Burma Links', 29 July 2008; www.burmacampaign.org.uk/pm/weblog.php?id=P376.

60 Mark Jewell, 'Pax fined for failure to screen investment funds', *USA TODAY Online*, 30 July 2008; usatoday30.usatoday.com/money/economy/2008-07-30-1549841276_x.htm.

61 Robert D. Feinman, 'Economists: Intellectual Whores', 2006; robertdfeinman.com/society/whores.html.

62 A. Craig Copetas, '"Out of Control": CEOs spurned Davos warnings on risk', Bloomberg, 24 October 2008; www.bloomberg.com/apps/news?pid=20601109&sid=a9 wVqOPk.T_4&refer=home.

63 *Ibid.*

64 *Ibid.*

4Q2008

1 Chelsea Schilling, 'US Treasury teaches "Islamic Finance 101": advisers, scholars to promote controversial Shariah funding', *World Net Daily*, 5 November 2008; www.wnd.com/2008/11/80003.

2 *Ibid.*

3 See M. Iqbal and D.T. Llewellyn, *Islamic Banking and Finance: New Perspectives on Profit-sharing and Risk* (Cheltenham, UK: Edward Elgar, 2002).

4 Islamic Financial Services Board official website: www.ifsb.org.

5 Ciarán Hancock, '$25m funding for Blue Ocean', *Irish Times*, 25 September 2008; www.irishtimes.com/newspaper/finance/2008/0925/1222207743548.html.

6 FSA white paper *Islamic Finance in the UK: Regulation and Challenges*. November 2007; www.fsa.gov.uk/pubs/other/islamic_finance.pdf.

7 Emma Vandore, 'Crisis widens appeal of Islamic finance', *The Jakarta Post*. 24 December 2008; www.thejakartapost.com/news/2008/12/25/crisis-widens-appeal-islamic-finance.html.

8 S.J. Liebowitz, 'Anatomy of a Train Wreck: Causes of the Mortgage Meltdown', Independent Institute, 2008; www.independent.org/publications/policy_reports/detail.asp?type=full&id=30.

9 Hersh Shefrin and Meir Statman, *Beyond Greed and Fear: Understanding Behavioral Finance and the Psychology of Investing* (Boston, MA: Harvard Business School Press, 2002).

10 See Vandore, *op. cit.*

11 Mohammad Awan, 'Islamic finance could have avoided subprime crisis', Islamic Finance Resource Blog, 14 May 2008; islamicfinancenews.wordpress.com/2008/05/14/islamic-finance-could-have-prevented-subprime-crisis.

12 'Sukuk strikes the right chord', Islamic Finance Asia, August/September 2008; www.islamicfinanceasia.com/cover.php.

13 *Islamic Finance News Guide 2008*; www.islamicfinancenews.com/pdf/guide08.pdf.

14 See Vandore, *op. cit.*

15 Anwar, Zarinah, 'Coping with the Global Financial Turmoil, Restoring Investor Confidence', 13th Malaysian Capital Market Summit 2008, Kuala Lumpur, 4 December 2008; www.sc.com.my/main.asp?pageid=375&linkid=2000&yearno=2008&mod=paper.

16 B.A. Lietaer, *The Future of Money: Creating New Wealth, Work and a Wiser World* (Century, 2001).

17 Haris Anwar, 'Islamic bond decree cripples sukuk, imperils projects (Update 2)', Bloomberg.com, 3 September 2008; www.bloomberg.com/apps/news?pid=20601109&sid=a_Zh0q70aPxY&refer=home.

18 'IMF deal on foreign wealth funds', *BBC News*, 3 September 2008; news.bbc.co.uk/1/hi/business/7595672.stm.

19 Patrick Hosking, 'Co-op boycotts funds over human rights', *The Times Online*, 21 May 2008; web.archive.org/web/20080718182702/business.timesonline.co.uk/tol/business/industry_sectors/banking_and_finance/article3972375.ece.

20 Kevin Lim, 'IMF says voluntary code for sovereign funds by October', ArabianBusiness.com, 10 July 2008; www.arabianbusiness.com/524417-imf-says-voluntary-code-for-sovereign-funds-by-oct.

21 'OECD countries commit to open climate for Sovereign Wealth Funds', Paris, 6 June 2008; trade.ec.europa.eu/doclib/docs/2008/june/tradoc_139096.pdf.

22 Diana Farrell, 'The New Power Brokers', *BusinessWeek*, 15 July 2008; www.mckinsey.com/mgi/mginews/new_power_brokers.asp.

23 'IMF deal on foreign wealth funds' (*op. cit.*).

24 Kevin Lim and Saeed Azhar, 'GIC has large cash pile, sees opportunities in US', *Reuters*, 23 September 2008; www.reuters.com/article/ousiv/idUSTRE48M3RT20080923.

25 Lim, *op. cit.*

26 Terry Macalister, 'Investment: Norway offloads £500m of Rio Tinto shares over "unethical" mine stake', *The Guardian Online*, 10 September 2008; www.guardian.co.uk/business/2008/sep/10/riotinto.mining.

27 *Ibid.*

28 *Ibid.*

29 *Ibid.*; and Tarjei Kidd Olsen, 'Norway: oil fund finds ethical success', *Interpress Service*, 31 July 2008; www.ipsnews.net/2008/07/norway-oil-fund-finds-ethical-success.

30 Asia Pacific Academy of Business In Society official website: www.apabis.org.

31 Asian Forum on Corporate Social Responsibility official website: www.asianforumcsr.com.

32 Global Social innovators Forum official website: www.socialinnovatorsforum.org.

33 CSR Asia Summit 2008 official website: www.csr-asia.com/summit08.

34 Rikke Netterstrom, 'Sustainability reporting: it is painful, but gets easier', *CSR Asia Weekly*, Vol. 4 Week 47 (19 November 2008); www.csr-asia.com/upload/cover/703885681578.pdf.

35 'CSR Asia Business Barometer 2008: The State of CSR Disclosure in Asia'; www.csr-asia.com/upload/Barometer_Research_Brochure_2008.pdf.

36 Catherine Walter, 'Welcoming Remarks and Keynote Speeches', *CSR Asia Weekly* Vol. 4 Week 46 (12 November 2008); www.csr-asia.com/upload/cover/888330905168.pdf.

37 Mabel Wong, 'CSR Reporting through Project Partnerships: The Case of imPACT', *CSR Asia Weekly*, Vol. 4 Week 47 (19 November 2008); www.csr-asia.com/upload/cover/703885681578.pdf.

38 'Wanchoo gets SIP Fellow Award', *Rising Kashmir News*, 2008; www.risingkashmir.com/index.php?option=com_content&task=view&id=9133. Global Social Innovators Forum. 'SIP Fellow Award'; www.socialinnovatorsforum.org/fellows/sipfellow.

39 *Ibid.*

2009: Introduction

1 J. Bendell, N. Alam, S. Lin, C. Ng, L. Rimando, C. Veuthey and B. Wettstein, *The Eastern Turn in Responsible Enterprise: A Yearly Review of Corporate Responsibility from Lifeworth* (Manila, Philippines: Lifeworth, 2009; lifeworth.com/lifeworth2008/2009/05/the-eastern-turn-in-academe).

2 J. Bendell, *The Global Step Change: Lifeworth Annual Review of Corporate Responsibility in 2007* (Manila, Philippines: Lifeworth, 2008; lifeworth.com/2007review/intro-2007.htm).

3 John Arlidge, 'I'm doing "God's work": Meet Mr Goldman Sachs', *The Sunday Times Online*, 8 November 2009; www.thesundaytimes.co.uk/sto/news/world_news/article189615.ece (upon subscription).

4 *Ibid.*

5 Matt Taibbi, 'The Great American Bubble Machine', *Rolling Stone*, 9 July 2009; www.rollingstone.com/politics/news/the-great-american-bubble-machine-20100405.

6 John Arlidge, *op. cit.*

7 www.michaelmoore.com/books-films/capitalism-love-story

8 'French, German Leaders Call for "Moralization" of Capitalism', *Deutcshe Welle Online*, 8 January 2009; www.dw-world.de/dw/article/0,,3930542,00.html.

9 Quoted in Peter Whitelegg, 'The Last Resort' *L&TUR* 195 (2009); www.ltureview.com/user/story.php?id=437.

10 Noah Berger, 'Kyocera founder Kazuo Inamori criticizes US CEO excesses,' *USA TODAY Online*, 21 April 2009; usatoday30.usatoday.com/money/companies/management/advice/2009-04-19-advice-inamori_N.htm.

11 Irene Finel-Honigman, *A Cultural History of Finance* (Routledge Explorations in Economic History, 2009).

12 Bob Hancké, *Debating Varieties of Capitalism* (USA: Oxford University Press, 2009).

13 Richard W. Carney, *Contested Capitalism: The Political Origins of Financial Institutions* (Routledge Advances in International Political Economy, 2009).

14 John Perkins, *Hoodwinked: An Economic Hit Man Reveals Why the World Financial Markets Imploded—and What We Need to Do to Remake Them* (New York: Crown Business, 2009).

15 Martin Lowy, *Debt Spiral: How Credit Failed Capitalism* (Public Policy Press, 2009).

16 Robert J. Barbera, *The Cost of Capitalism: Understanding Market Mayhem and Stabilizing our Economic Future* (Colombus, OH: McGraw-Hill, 2009)

17 R.P. Bootle, *The Trouble with Markets: Saving Capitalism from Itself* (London: Nicholas Brealey Publishing, 2009).

18 Arlidge, *op. cit.*

19 Barry C. Lynn, *Cornered: The New Monopoly Capitalism and the Economics of Destruction* (UK: John Wiley, 2010).

20 Janine R. Wedel, *Shadow Elite: How the World's New Power Brokers Undermine Democracy, Government, and the Free Market* (New York: Basic Books, 2009).

21 Steve Forbes and Elizabeth Ames, *How Capitalism Will Save Us: Why Free People and Free Markets Are the Best Answer in Today's Economy* (New York: Crown Business, 2009).

22 Yale Hirsch and William J. O'Neil, *The Capitalist Spirit: How Each and Every One of Us Can Make A Giant Difference in Our Fast-Changing World* (UK: John Wiley 2010).

23 Brian S. Wesbury and Amity Shlaes, *It's Not as Bad as You Think: Why Capitalism Trumps Fear and the Economy Will Thrive* (UK: John Wiley, 2009).

24 Howard K. Bloom, *The Genius of the Beast* (New York: Prometheus Books, 2009).

25 Michael Kinsley and Conor Clarke, *Creative Capitalism: A Conversation with Bill Gates, Warren Buffett, and Other Economic Leaders* (New York: Simon & Schuster, 2009).

26 John Mackey, *Be the Solution: How Entrepreneurs and Conscious Capitalists Can Solve All the World's Problems* (UK: John Wiley, 2009).

27 Danielle Sacks, 'John Mackey's Whole Foods Vision to Reshape Capitalism', *Fast CompanyOnline*, 1 December 2009.

28 Bill Baue, '2009 CSR Year in Review: Corporate Social Responsibility Solidifies Into a Movement', *CSRwire*, 20 January 2010.

29 J. Porritt, *Capitalism as if the World Matters* (New York: Routledge, 2005): 182.

30 Marjorie Kelly, *The Divine Right of Capital* (San Francisco: Berrett-Koehler Publishers, 2003).

31 David Korten, 'Money Versus Wealth', *Yes Online*, 30 June 1997; www.yesmagazine.org/issues/money-print-your-own/money-versus-wealth.

32 Korten, *When Corporations Rule the World*: 307.

33 Henry Mintzberg, *Mintzberg on Management: Inside Our Strange World of Organizations*, (UK: John Wiley, 1989): 328.

34 Kelly, *op. cit.*

35 Richard Whitley, *Divergent Capitalisms: The Social Structuring and Change of Business Systems* (Oxford, UK: Oxford University Press, 2000).

36 en.wikipedia.org/wiki/Capitalism, accessed January 2010.

37 Porritt, *op. cit.*

38 Whitley, *op. cit.*

39 J. Bendell, *Barricades and Boardrooms: A Contemporary History of the Corporate Accountability Movement* (Geneva: UNRISD, 2004).

40 M.K. Gandhi, 'Gandhi's Philosophy on Trusteeship', 'Mahatma Gandhi's One Spot Information Website Online', *Harijan*, 31 March 1946: 63-64; www.gandhi-manibhavan.org/gandhiphilosophy/philosophy_trusteeship.htm.

41 Gandhi, *op. cit.*

42 Jeff Gates, *The Ownership Solution*, (Portland, OR: Perseus Press, 1998).

43 The term 'economic democracy' is already used to describe some other concepts and approaches, and is often used to speak in unspecific terms about economic reform.

44 Baue, *op. cit.*

45 Berger, *op. cit.*

46 J. Bendell and K. Kearins, '"The Political Bottom Line": The Emerging Dimension to Corporate Responsibility for Sustainable Development', *Business Strategy and the Environment* 14.6 (2005): 372-83.

47 For more information see www.thefinancelab.org, www.corporation2020.org and www.presencing.com.

48 David F. Murphy and Jem Bendell, *In the Company of Partners: Business, Environmental Groups and Sustainable Development Post-Rio* (Bristol, UK: Policy Press, 1997): 245.

1Q2009

1 Mauricio Cárdenas and Julia Guerreiro, 'The Limits to Fiscal Stimulus in Latin America and the Caribbean', Brookings Institution, 20 March 2009; www.brookings.edu/articles/2009/0323_latin_america_cardenas.aspx.

2 HSBC, 'Climate for Recovery: The colour of stimulus goes green', 25 February 2009; globaldashboard.org/wp-content/uploads/2009/HSBC_Green_New_Deal.pdf.

3 Erik de la Cruz, 'RP will benefit the most from fiscal stimulus—UOB', *ABS-CBNnews. com Online*, 24 March 2009; https://abs-cbnnews.com/business/03/23/09/rp-will-benefit-most-fiscal-stimulus-uob.

4 The EU number included public spending on welfare which automatically starts to increase during an economic downturn because of higher unemployment and social benefits, or what are called automatic stabilisers.

5 Cárdenas and Guerreiro, *op. cit.*

6 'China stimulus package under scrutiny', *The Hindu Online*, 25 November 2008; www. hindu.com/2008/11/25/stories/2008112559631300.htm.

7 Committee on Appropriations, 'Summary: American Recovery and Reinvestment. Conference Agreement', 13 February 2009; appropriations.house.gov/pdf/ PressSummary02-13-09.pdf.

8 US Department of the Treasury, 'Treasury Secretary Tim Geithner Written Testimony House Financial Services Committee Hearing', press release, 24 March 2009; www. treasury.gov/press-center/press-releases/Pages/tg67.aspx.

9 Personal communication with the Aron Cramer.

10 Interview with Jonathan Cohen, 18 March 2009.

11 'UK needs "Green New Deal" to tackle "triple crunch" of credit, oil price and climate crises', New Economics Foundation, 21 July 2008; www.neweconomics. org/press-releases/uk-needs-%E2%80%98green-new-deal%E2%80%99-tackle-%E2%80%98triple-crunch%E2%80%99-credit-oil-price-and-climate-crises.

12 HSBC, Climate for Recovery, *Op. cit.* This issue of *JCC* covered the first quarter and does not reflect any monies committed by the G20 after that date.

13 UN Environment Programme, 'A Global Green New Deal', February 2009; www.unep. ch/etb/publications/Green%20Economy/UNEP%20Policy%20Brief%20Eng.pdf.

14 Peterson Institute for International Economics and World Resources Institute, 'Green Economic Stimulus Creates Jobs, Saves Taxpayers Money', 10 February 2009; www.wri. org/press/2009/02/green-economic-stimulus-creates-jobs-saves-taxpayers-money.

15 Robert Pollin, Heidi Garrett-Peltier, James Heintz and Helen Scharber, 'Green Recovery: A Program to Create Good Jobs and Start Building a Low-Carbon Economy', Center for American Progress, 2008; www.americanprogress.org/issues/2008/09/pdf/ green_recovery.pdf.

16 UN Environment Programme, *op. cit.*

17 'Chinese government to start buying green', *GreenBiz.com Online*, 4 December 2006; www.greenbiz.com/news/2006/12/02/chinese-government-start-buying-green.

18 'Examples of Sustainable Procurement Strategies and Policies'; www.iclei-europe.org/ index.php?id=5556.

19 Christoph Erdmenger (ed.), *Buying into the Environment: Experiences, Opportunities and Potential for Eco-procurement* (Sheffield, UK: Greenleaf Publishing, 2003).

20 'Law Concerning the Promotion of Procurement of Eco-friendly Goods and Services by the State and Other Entities'; www.env.go.jp/en/laws/policy/green/1.pdf.

21 ICLEI. 'EcoProcura Call for Action: Moving the Market', 8 May 2007; www.iclei. org/index.php?id=1487&tx_ttnews[pointer]=87&tx_ttnews[pS]=1250113521&tx_ ttnews[tt_news]=1031&tx_ttnews[backPid]=1556&cHash=9e0687c aef.

22 Liam Tung, 'Qld govt sets lean, green PC shopping policy', *ZDNet Australia Online*, 27 August 2007; www.zdnet.com.au/news/hardware/soa/Qld-govt-sets-lean-green-PC-shopping-policy/0,130061702,339281538,00.htm?feed=pt_government.

23 Eliza Barclay, 'Mexican government establishes green procurement standards', 12 April 2007; www.treehugger.com/files/2007/12/mexico_to_boost.php.

24 Jonathan Cohen, 'The United Nations and the Globalisation of Corporate Citizenship', in J. Andriof and M. McIntosh (eds), *Perspectives on Corporate Citizenship* (Sheffield, UK: Greenleaf Publishing, 2001).

25 UNOPS Procurement Manual, Rev. 2, December 2007, www.unops.org/ SiteCollectionDocuments/Procurement%20docs/UNOPS%20procurement%20 manual%20EN.pdf; UNOPS General Conditions for Goods, August 2005, www.unops. org/SiteCollectionDocuments/Procurement%20docs/UNOPS%20General%20 Conditions%20for%20Goods.pdf.

26 UNPRI, 'Global pension fund leaders call for more active, collaborative owners in response to crisis', 23 February 2009; www.unpri.org/files/PR_statement_final.pdf.

27 Deborah Seligsohn, 'A "Green Lining" in China's Economic Stimulus Plan', World Resources Institute, 26 November 2008; www.wri.org/stories/2008/11/green-lining-chinas-economic-stimulus-plan.

28 NRDC, 'Summary of Energy and Transportation Provisions of the Economic Recovery Bill', 19 February 2009; switchboard.nrdc.org/blogs/paltman/media/Econ%20Rec%20 Bill%20Summary%20(Final)%202-19-09.doc.

29 HSBC, Climate for Recovery, *op. cit.*

30 Seligsohn, *op. cit.*

31 NRDC, *op. cit.*

32 HSBC, Climate for Recovery, *op. cit.*

33 Cárdenas and Guerreiro, *op. cit.*

34 HSBC, Climate for Recovery, *op. cit.*

35 *Ibid.*

36 Dave Burdick, 'Project Movele: Spain's Electric Car Plan', *Huffington Post Online*, 19 March 2009; www.huffingtonpost.com/2009/03/19/project-movele-spains-ele_n_176779.html.

37 HSBC, Climate for Recovery, *op. cit.*

38 NRDC, *op. cit.*

39 HSBC, Climate for Recovery, *op. cit.*

40 *Ibid.*

41 Cárdenas and Guerreiro, *op. cit.*

42 'Factbox: Europe's fiscal stimulus plans', *Reuters Online*, 16 February 2009; www. reuters.com/article/economicNews/idUSLG71844920090216.

43 Burdick, *op. cit.*

44 NRDC, *op. cit.*

45 HSBC, Climate for Recovery, *op. cit.*

46 *Reuters, op. cit.*

47 'Environmental Audit Committee, Third Report. Pre-Budget Report 2008: Green Fiscal Policy in a Recession', House of Commons, 10 March 2009; www.publications. parliament.uk/pa/cm200809/cmselect/cmenvaud/202/20202.htm.

48 Peterson Institute for International Economics and World Resources Institute, *op. cit.*

49 UK Sustainable Development Commission, 'Prosperity without Growth? The Transition to a Sustainable Economy', 30 March 2009; www.sd-commission.org.uk/ publications/downloads/prosperity_without_growth_report.pdf.

50 *Ibid.*

51 John Attarian, 'The Steady State Economy: What It Is, Why We Need It', 2005; www.npg. org/forum_series/TheSteadyStateEconomy001.pdf.

52 Herman E. Daly, *Beyond Growth: The Economics of Sustainable Development* (Boston, MA: Beacon Press, 1996).

53 'Prosperity without Growth? Victor Anderson interviews Professor Tim Jackson, SDC Commissioner for Economics'; www.sd-commission.org.uk/publications/downloads/Prosperity%20without%20Growth_transcript.pdf.

54 UK Sustainable Development Commission, *op. cit.*

55 *Ibid.*

56 C.D. Butler, 'Inequality, Global Change and the Sustainability of Civilisation', *Global Change and Human Health* 1.2 (2000): 156-72.

57 World Health Organisation, 'Closing the Gap in a Generation: Health Equity through Action on the Social Determinants of Health. Final Report of the Commission on Social Determinants of Health', 2008.

58 UK Sustainable Development Commission, *op. cit.*

59 Herman E. Daly, *Steady-State Economics* (Washington, DC: Island Press, 2nd edn 1991).

60 *Ibid.*

61 'Berlin Address by Federal President Horst Köhler 24 March 2009'; www.bundespraesident.de/SharedDocs/Reden/EN/HorstKoehler/Reden/2009/03/20090324_Rede.html.

62 'France to ban bonuses for bailed out firms', *CNN.com/Europe Online*, 26 March 2009; edition.cnn.com/2009/WORLD/europe/03/26/france.bonuses.banks/index.html?eref=edition.

63 'Banks agree to cap trader bonuses', *France 24 Online*. 7 February 2009; www.france24.com/en/20090207-banks-agree-cap-trader-bonuses-.

64 Jem Bendell *et al.*, *The Corporate Responsibility Movement: Five Years of Global Corporate Responsibility Analysis from Lifeworth, 2001–2005* (Sheffield, UK: Greenleaf Publishing, 2009).

65 Jem Bendell *et al.*, *The Eastern Turn in Responsible Enterprise* (Manila, Philippines: Lifeworth, 2009; lifeworth.com/lifeworth2008/2009/05/the-eastern-turn-in-academe).

66 'Plug-in hybrid goes on sale, in China only', Hybrid Cars, 3 November 2008; www.hybridcars.com/news/plug-hybrid-goes-sale-china-only-25222.html.

67 Jerry Garrett, 'Chinese cars inch closer to US', *New York Times Online*, 18 January 2009; www.nytimes.com/2009/01/18/automobiles/autoshow/18CHINA.html?fta=y.

68 Marc Gunther, 'Warren Buffett takes charge', *Fortune Online*, 13 April 2009; money.cnn.com/2009/04/13/technology/gunther_electric.fortune/index.htm.

69 'China's BYD Auto launches S6 Lexus RX clone, holds European patent for design copyrights . . .', *Carscoop*, 25 March 2009; carscoop.blogspot.com/2009/03/china-byd-auto-launches-s6-lexus-rx.html.

70 Information from www.betterplace.com/faq.

71 Amy Rolph, 'City offering Zipcar access to employees', *Seattle Post-Intelligencer Online*, 5 February 2009; www.seattlepi.com/local/398981_zip06.html.

72 'Zipcar, San Francisco launch plug-in hybrid pilot program', SustainableBusiness.com, 19 February 2009; www.sustainablebusiness.com/index.cfm/go/news.display/id/17703.

73 Volans, *The Phoenix Economy: 50 Pioneers in the Business of Social Innovation* (London: Volans, 2009).

74 Adam Smith, 'Germany's Auto-Woes Fix: Scrap That Clunker!', *Time Online*, 12 March 2009; www.time.com/time/business/article/0,8599,1884711,00.html.

75 Simon Zadek, 'All the King's Horses', *AccountAbility*, 31 December 2008; previously available at www.accountability21.net.
76 Lucy Kellaway, 'The year of the CFO', *The Economist Online*, 19 November 2008; www.economist.com/theworldin/displaystory.cfm?story_id=12494665.
77 Volans, *op. cit.*
78 SustainAbility, 'Director: Phoenix will rise again', 30 January 2009; www.sustainability.com/library/phoenix-will-rise-again-director#.UJDADlL_KZc upon subscription.

2Q2009

1 The London Summit 2009, 'Global Plan for Recovery and Reform', 2 April 2009; www.treasury.gov/resource-center/international/g7-g20/Documents/London%20April%20 2009%20Leaders%20final-communique.pdf.
2 Katinka Barysch, 'The Real G20 Agenda: From Technics to Politics', *Open Democracy* 16 March 2009; www.opendemocracy.net/article/the-real-g20-agenda-from-technics-to-politics; and *idem.*, 'The Real G20 Agenda', 13 March 2009; www.centreforeuropeanreform.blogspot.com/2009/03/real-g20-agenda.html.
3 'Fraude Fiscale au Liechtenstein: la Justice Française Lance une Enquête', *Le Parisien Online*, 1 April 2009; www.leparisien.fr/liveafp-economie/fraude-fiscale-au-liechtenstein-la-justice-francaise-lance-une-enquete-01-04-2009-462399.php [in French]; John Lichfield, 'Adidas and Michelin in Tax Haven Fraud Inquiry', *The Independent Online*, 1 April 2009; www.independent.co.uk/news/world/europe/adidas-and-michelin-in-taxhaven-fraud-inquiry-1658974.html [in English].
4 'Total CEO says its tax haven accounts are known', *Reuters.com Online*, 3 April, 2009; www.reuters.com/article/rbssEnergyNews/idUSL338331120090403.
5 John Christensen and Sony Kapoor, 'Tax Avoidance, Tax Competition and Globalisation: Making Tax Justice a Focus for Global Activism', *Global Activism, Accountancy Business and the Public Interest* 3.2 (2004).
6 J. Bendell *et al.*, *The Corporate Responsibility Movement: Five Years of Global Corporate Responsibility Analysis from Lifeworth, 2001–2005* (Sheffield, UK: Greenleaf Publishing, 2009).
7 David F. Williams, 'Tax and Corporate Social Responsibility: A Discussion Paper', September 2007; www.kpmg.co.uk/pubs/Tax_and_CSR_Final.pdf: 4.
8 Organisation for Economic Cooperation and Development, 'Tax Haven Criteria'; www.oecd.org/document/63/0,3343,en_2649_33745_30575447_1_1_1_37427,00.html.
9 Tax Justice Network, 'Identifying Tax Havens and Offshore Finance Centres'; www.taxjustice.net/cms/upload/pdf/Identifying_Tax_Havens_Jul_07.pdf: 1, 7.
10 Nick Mathiason, 'Tax Savings: Only the Rich Need Apply', *The Guardian Online*, 22 April 2007; www.guardian.co.uk/business/2007/apr/22/theobserver.observerbusiness1.
11 Richard Murphy, 'The UK is an Offshore Finance Centre—According to an IMF Study', Tax Research UK, 19 April 2007; www.taxresearch.org.uk/Blog/2007/04/19/the-uk-is-an-offshore-finance-centre-according-to-an-imf-study; Ahmed Zoromé, 'Concept of Offshore Financial Centers: In Search of an Operational Definition', April 2007; www.imf.org/external/pubs/ft/wp/2007/wp0787.pdf: 26.
12 Nick Mathiason, 'Welcome to London, the Onshore Tax Haven', *The Guardian Online*, 8 July 2007; www.guardian.co.uk/money/2007/jul/08/tax.business1.

13 Tax Justice Network, 'The City of London Corporation: The State within a State', 7 February 2009; taxjustice.blogspot.com/2009/02/corporation-of-london-state-within. html.

14 The City of London official website, 'What we do'; www.cityoflondon.gov.uk/about-the-city/what-we-do/Pages/default.aspx.

15 The City of London official website, 'Sustainability'; www.cityoflondon.gov.uk/services/environment-and-planning/sustainability/Pages/default.aspx.

16 Financing the Future: The London Principles, 'The Role of UK Financial Services in Sustainable Development', Department for Environment, Food and Rural Affairs; www.responsible-credit.net/media.php?t=media&f=file&id=3478: 48-49.

17 One author's personal correspondence with the City of London Corporation's CSR Team, 25 June 2009.

18 Alternatives Economiques: www.alternatives-economiques.fr/fic_bdd/article_pdf_fichier/1236789681_Entreprises_francaises_et_paradis_fiscaux.xls [in French].

19 Tax Justice Network, 'The OECD Global Forum: The List', 3 April 2009; taxjustice.blogspot.com/2009/04/oecd-global-forum-list.html.

20 Letter addressed to Mr Luc Frieden from Angel Gurría, Organisation for Economic Cooperation and Development, 13 March 2009; www.gouvernement.lu/salle_presse/communiques/2009/04-avril/03-frieden-ocde/lettre.pdf.

21 OECD, 'Overview of the OECD's Work on Countering International Tax Evasion: A Background Information Brief', 13 November 2009; www.oecd.org/dataoecd/32/45/43757434.pdf.

22 OECD, 'Tax Information Exchange Agreements (TIEAS)', 2009; www.oecd.org/document/7/0,3343,en_2649_33745_38312839_1_1_1_1,00.htm.

23 Raymond Baker, 'India's Curse of "Black Money"', *Financial Times*, 23 April 2009; www.ft.com/cms/s/1fdc10ac-303c-11de-88e3-00144feabdc0,Authorised=false. html?_i_location=http%3A%2F%2Fwww.ft.com%2Fcms%2Fs%2F0%2F1fdc10ac-303c-11de-88e3-00144feabdc0.html&_i_referer=http%3A%2F%2Ftaxjustice.blogspot. com%2F2009%2F04%2Fraymond-baker-of-global-financial.html [upon subscription]; *idem.*, 'Global Financial Integrity in the FT', Tax Justice Network, 24 April 2009; taxjustice.blogspot.com/2009/04/raymond-baker-of-global-financial.html.

24 Martin A. Sullivan, 'Lessons from the Last War on Tax Havens', Tax Analysts, 30 July 2007; www.taxanalysts.com/www/features.nsf/Articles/F3AA18739F0EFF008525744B0 066459B?OpenDocument.

25 Tax Justice Network, 'Tax Information Exchange Arrangements', April 2009; www. taxjustice.net/cms/upload/pdf/TJN_0903_Exchange_of_Info_Briefing_draft.pdf [in English]; Anne-Catherine Husson-Traore, 'G20: Réactions Mitigées sur la Nouvelle Donne', *Novethic*, 4 March 2009; www.novethic.fr/novethic/planete/institution/institutions_internationales/g_20_reactions_mitigees_nouvelle_donne/119898.jsp [in French].

26 'The G20 and Tax Haven Hypocrisy', *The Economist Online*, 26 March 2009; www. economist.com/displaystory.cfm?story_id=13382279; Richard Murphy, 'Britain and the US may be the dirtiest tax havens', Tax Research UK, 27 March 2009; www.taxresearch. org.uk/Blog/2009/03/27/new-study-britain-and-the-us-may-be-the-dirtiest-tax havens.

27 Sullivan, *op. cit.*

28 Baker, *op. cit.*

29 Sullivan, *op. cit.*

30 *Ibid.*

31 Michael Meacher, 'Is the government serious about stopping tax avoidance?', 9 May 2009; www.michaelmeacher.info/weblog/2009/05/is-the-government-serious-about-stopping-tax-avoidance.

32 Christensen and Kapoor, *op. cit.*

33 Attac France, 'G20: Analyse du Rapport Larosière: La Politique du Renard Libre dans un Poulailler Libre: Pour Regler la Crise, l'Union Européenne s'en Remet aux Banquiers', 3 April 2009; www.france.attac.org/spip.php?article9627 [in French]; Kenneth Haar, Andy Rowell and Yiorgos Vassalos, 'Would you bank on them? Why we shouldn't trust the EU's financial "wise men"', February 2009; www.scribd.com/doc/13317915/EUs-wise-men-on-financial-system-reform [in English].

34 BNP Paribas, 'Rapport sur la Responsabilité Sociale et Environnementale 2008'; media-cms.bnpparibas.com/file/66/6/bnp_rse_complet.6666.pdf: 153-54 [in French]; *idem.*, 'Report on Environmental and Social Responsibility 07'; media-cms.bnpparibas.com/file/88/5/5885.pdf: 84 [in English].

35 Novethic, 'Chercher un Fonds ISR'; www.novethic.fr/novethic/developpement-durable/liste-fonds-investissement-socialement-responsable-isr/?societe=23214 [in French].

36 One author's personal correspondence, 26 July 2009.

37 Henderson Global Investors, 'Task, Risk and Corporate Governance: Findings from a Survey of the FTSE350', February 2005; www.henderson.com/content/sri/publications/reports/taxriskcorporategovernance.pdf: 11.

38 Jem Bendell and Rupesh Shah, 'World Review', *Journal of Corporate Citizenship* 6 (Summer 2002).

39 PricewaterhouseCoopers, 'Total Tax Contribution: What are your true tax costs?', 2009; www.pwc.com/ca/en/tax/total-contribution.jhtml.

40 Richard Murphy, 'PwC's Total Tax Contribution', Tax Research UK, 24 August 2006; www.taxresearch.org.uk/Blog/2006/08/24/pwcs-total-tax-contribution.

41 'See What You are Buying Into: Social, Environmental, Ethical', 2003–2009; www.seewhatyouarebuyinginto.com. SEE has been rebranded as Profit through Ethics: www.profitthroughethics.com.

42 Novethic, 'Chiffres 2008 et Analyse du Marche Français de l'ISR', 2009; www.novethic.fr/novethic/upload/etudes/Etude_Marche_ISR_2009.pdf [in French]; Hugh Wheelan, 'RI Round up June 22: RI's Regular Round-up of the Most Important RI News Stories', *Responsible Investor*, 22 June 2009; www.responsible-investor.com/home/article/ri_round_up_june_22/P1 [upon subscription] [in English].

43 OECD, 'OECD in Figures 2009'; www.oecd-ilibrary.org/economics/oecd-in-figures-2009_oif-2009-en.

44 J.B. Nadeau and J. Barlow, *Sixty Million Frenchmen Can't Be Wrong: What Makes the French so French?* (London: Robson Books, 2004): 283.

45 'Répertoire des Producteurs de Terminologie', *Le Grand Dictionnaire: Terminologique*; www.granddictionaire.com/btml/fra/r_motclef/index800_1.asp [in French]; www.granddictionaire.com/btml/fra/r_motclef/index800_1.asp [in English].

46 One author's conversation with Jean-François Jenni, Chief Certification Officer of Ethics SA, 25 March 2009.

47 One author's personal observations.

48 'Pour Sortir de la Crise: Dépasser le Capitalisme?', Manifeste de Québec Solidaire, May 2009; www.quebecsolidaire.net/manifeste-sortir-de-la-crise-1er-mai-2009 [in French].

49 J. Bendell *et al.*, 'World Review', *Journal of Corporate Citizenship* 32 (Winter 2008).

50 Actu-Environnement, 'Responsabilité Sociétale des Entrepreneurs: Comment se Distinguer?', 6 September 2009; www.actu-environnement.com/ae/news/parlement_ entrepreneurs_avenir_7550.php4 [in French].

51 'Rapport de Mission Remis au Gouvernement: Bilan Critique de l'Application par les Enterprises de l'Article 116 de la loi NRE', April 2004; www.oree.org/docs/grenelle/ rapport-nre.pdf: 17, 65 [in French].

52 A. Antal and A. Sobczak, 'Business and Society', *Corporate Social Responsibility in France: A Mix of National Traditions and International Influences* 46.1 (2007): 9-32.

53 'Le Projet de Loi Grenelle 1 Revient Devant les Députés', *Liberation.fr Online*, 6 September 2009; www.liberation.fr/terre/0101572422-le-projet-de-loi-grenelle-1-revient-devant-les-deputes [in French].

54 'Regard sur le Grenelle 2: Projet de loi Engagement National pour l'Environnement', May 2009; www2.ademe.fr/servlet/getBin?name=D43B973704BB7A8F2806A1FCA249 5CD11244122407037.pdf: 47-49 [in French].

55 ISO, 'The ISO Survey', 2007; www.iso.org/iso/survey2007.pdf: 26.

56 Actu-Environnement, 'ISO 26 000, une Révolution Silencieuse ?', 10 August 2008; www.actu-environnement.com/ae/news/ISO_26000_5908.php4 [in French]; Sarah le Quere, 'Responsabilité Sociétale des Organisations: Guide d'Application de l'ISO 26 000 aux Départements'; www.afqho.com/Images/GUIDE%20ISO%2026%20000. pdf [in French]; ACI (Action Catholique des Milieux Indépendants), 'La Responsabilité Sociale des Entreprises, La Responsabilité Sociétale des Entreprises (Corporate Social Responsibility)', 20 February 2009; rse-et-ped.info/IMG/pdf/RSE-Definitions-Projet_ de_norme.pdf: 7 [in French].

57 Valérie Froger, 'Le Poste de Responsable du Développement Durable est-il . . . Durable?', *Cadremploi.fr*, 26 March 2009; www.cadremploi.fr/edito/actu-et-conseils/vie-professionnelle/coaching-carriere/d/1/le-poste-de-responsable-du-developpement-durable-est-il-durable?xtor=EPR-375 [in French]. This link is no longer accessible.

58 Sustainable Luxury Fair, '1.618: The Concept', 2009; www.businessmanconfidential. com/bmc13/menusalon.html.

59 'Indicateurs d'Evaluation de la Responsabilité Sociale et Environnementale (RSE) des Entreprises', *iaelyon*, 10 June 2009; iae.univ-lyon3.fr/1227194956090/0/fiche_04__ actualite [in French].

60 Della Bradshaw, 'Name Change for Rouen Business School', *FT.com Online*, 11 June 2009; www.ft.com/cms/s/0/2af74156-5674-11de-9a1c-00144feabdc0,dwp_ uuid=02e16f4a-46f9-11da-b8e5-00000e2511c8.html.

61 Ann Graham, 'Out in Front: Top Ranking French Business Schools', in 'Top Grad School Guide 2009', *issuu*, 2009; issuu.com/jamesiandonald/docs/qstgsg2009/50: 49-50; Doreen Carvajal, 'In Many Business Schools, the Bottom Line is in English', *New York Times Online*, 10 April 2007; www.nytimes.com/2007/04/10/world/europe/10iht-engbiz.2.5212499.html?_r=1&scp=1&sq=in%20many%20business%20schools&st=cse.

62 Antal and Sobczak, *op. cit.*

63 *Ibid.*; Nadeau and Barlow, *op. cit.*

64 Company and Sustainable Development Forum', Ministère du Développement Durable, 24 January 2007 [in French].

65 J. Fairbrass, 'University of Bradford Working Paper Series', *EU, UK and French CSR Policy: What is the Evidence for Policy Transfer and Convergence?* 8/20 (October 2008): 9-10.

66 *Ibid.*

67 'French National Sustainable Development Strategy 2003–2008', Ministère du Développement Durable, 13 November 2006 [in French].

68 Antal and Sobczak, *op. cit.*

69 International Event about ISO 26000 Social Responsibility for Organization, 'Québec: About ISO 26000', 14 May 2009; www.scc.ca/en/news-events/events/events-quebec-2009-7th-iso-social-responsibility-plenary-meeting.

70 SIFCA, 'A Regional Agribusiness Stakeholder in West Africa', 2009; www.groupesifca.com.

71 Melanie Zimmer and Lothar Rieth, 'Impact of Voluntary CSR Initiatives: The Global Compact and its regional learning platform in Sub-Sharan-Africa' (GTZ, November 2007): 9.

72 SIFCA, 'Développement Durable: Rapport 2008', 2008; www.groupesifca.com/pdf/rapport_dd_08.pdf [in French].

73 One author's personal correspondence with Cap Conseil, 13 July 2009.

74 Marie d'Huart, 'Afrique-Chine: Une Vision Sud-Nord de la Chaine d'Approvisionnement', Québec: About ISO 26000, 14 May 2009; www.bnq.qc.ca/documents/iso-26000_marie-dHuard.pdf [in French].

75 Zimmer and Rieth, *op. cit.*

76 Wayne Visser, *Business Frontiers: Social Responsibility, Sustainable Development and Economic Justice* (Hyderabad: ICFAI University Press, 2005): 116-17, 120.

77 One author's personal correspondence with Dr Richter, 23 April 2009.

78 ISO, 'The ISO Survey', 2007; www.iso.org/iso/home/news_index/news_archive/news.htm?refid=Ref117: 26.

79 Global Reporting Initiative official website: https://www.globalreporting.org/resourcelibrary/GRI-Reporting-Stats-2010.pdf.

80 V. Commene, *Responsabilité Sociale et Environnementale: L'engagement des acteurs économiques* (Paris: Editions Charles Léopold Mayer, 2006): 64, 229.

81 Carrie Hall, 'United Nations Global Compact 2008 Annual Review', March 2009; www.unglobalcompact.org/docs/news_events/9.1_news_archives/2009_04_08/GC_2008AR_FINAL.pdf.

3Q2009

1 Ethical Corporation, 'The Guide to Industry Initiatives in CSR', 2009; reports.ethicalcorp.com/reports/voluntaryinitiatives.

2 C. O'Faircheallaigh and S. Ali (eds.), *Earth Matters: Indigenous Peoples, the Extractive Industries and Corporate Social Responsibility* (Sheffield, UK: Greenleaf Publishing, 2008).

3 Wal-Mart, 'Love, Earth' Initiative, 2009; www.loveearthinfo.com.

4 Letter addressed to RJC from the Civil Society Coalition, 6 August 2009; www.earthworksaction.org/library/detail/ngo_letter_to_the_responsible_jewellery_council_august_2009.

5 Michael Rae. 'CRJP condemns WWF-UK "Deeper Luxury" report', Responsible Jewellery Council, 7 December 2007; www.responsiblejewellery.com/files/CRJP%20WWF-UK%20Deeper%20Luxury.pdf.

6 Responsible Jewellery Council, official website: www.responsiblejewellery.com.

7 Letter addressed to RJC from the Civil Society Coalition, 6 August 2009; www.earthworksaction.org/library/detail/ngo_letter_to_the_responsible_jewellery_council_august_2009.

8 'Greg Valerio Interviews Michael Rae, CEO of the Responsible Jewellery Council', Marc Choyt, Fair Trade Jewelry, 29 June 2009; www.fairjewelry.org/greg-valerio-interviews-michael-rae-ceo-of-the-responsible-jewellery-council.

9 Letter addressed to RJC, Rae, Solomon and CRJP members from Sampat (Earthworks NGO) and comments on first Mining Supplement draft, 17 October 2008; www.earthworksaction.org/files/publications/CRJP_Mining_Supplement_public_review_draft_v1-Earthworks%20comments.pdf.

10 Letter addressed to Maldar (CAFOD), Sampat (Earthworks), Chambers (Center for Science in Public Participation), Hill (Oxfam Australia) and Hadder (Great Basin Resource Watch) from RJC, 17 September 2009; www.responsiblejewellery.com/files/RJC_CEO_response_NGOs_Sept_2009.pdf; and 'The RJC System: Credible Performance Standards Backed by Independent, Third Party Certification', Responsible Jewellery Council, September 2009; www.responsiblejewellery.com/files/RJC_SystemCrediblePerf_Stand_Indep_3rdparty_cert.pdf.

11 Personal communication with Jem Bendell, July 2009.

12 Letter addressed to RJC from the Civil Society Coalition, 6 August 2009; www.earthworksaction.org/library/detail/ngo_letter_to_the_responsible_jewellery_council_august_2009.

13 CASM (Communities and Small-Scale Mining) official website: www.artisanalmining.org.

14 'Government of Mozambique 9th Annual CASM Conference (ACC): "ASM: An Opportunity for Rural Development"', CASM, Maputo 8–10 September 2009 and Chimoio, 11–14 September 2009; www.artisanalmining.org/casm/sites/artisanalmining.org/files/files/9thACC_Brochure_8_20.pdf.

15 World Bank, 'World Bank's CASM Initiative and Mozambique Aim to Tap on Small-Scale Mining Opportunities to Reduce Rural Poverty', press release, 3 September 2009; web.worldbank.org/WBSITE/EXTERNAL/NEWS/0,,contentMDK:22300250~pagePK:34370~piPK:34424~theSitePK:4607,00.html.

16 Mpho Lakaje, 'Horror of South African Miners' Deaths', *BBC News Online*, 6 June 2009; news.bbc.co.uk/1/hi/world/africa/8085258.stm; 'Anglogold confirms death of illegal miner', *Ghana Broadcasting Corporation News Online*, 6 September 2009; www.modernghana.com/news/236215/1/anglogold-confirms-death-of-illegal-miner.html; 'Deadly Game of Kenya's Gem Trade', *BBC News Online*, 14 August 2009; news.bbc.co.uk/1/hi/world/africa/8200465.stm; and Barney Jopson, 'Congo Miners Suffer as Boom Turns to Bitter Bust', *Financial Times Online*, 10 March 2009; www.ft.com/cms/s/0/36fffe70-0d13-11de-a555-0000779fd2ac.html [upon sign-in].

17 CASM. 'Small Stories: 12 Stories About Small-Scale Mining', 2009; www.artisanalmining.org/casm/sites/artisanalmining.org/files/publication/CASMshortstoriesBooklet_FINAL_low.pdf.

18 Child labour in mining has been classified by the ILO's International Programme for the Elimination of Child Labour (IPEC) as one of the 'Worst Forms of Child Labour': Mottaz, 'Child Labour in Gold Mining: The Problem', June 2006; www.ilo.org/ipecinfo/product/download.do?type=document&id=4146.

19 CommDev, 'Mining Together: Large-scale Mining Meeting Artisanal Mining: A Framework for Action', January 2008; commdev.org/content/document/detail/2018: 5; and Goldlake Group official website, 'Eurocantera'; www.goldlake.co.uk/The_projects/Eurocantera.aspx.

20 'Communities and Artisanal and Small-Scale Mining: A Global Partnership for Action', brochure, CASM, 2009; www.artisanalmining.org/UserFiles/file/CASMbrochure_ Updated.pdf.

21 This shift from risk to opportunity is not new and has already been the subject of debate in the wider CSR arena for several years: David Grayson and Adrian Hodges, *Corporate Social Opportunity! Seven Steps to Make Corporate Social Responsibility Work for your Business* (Sheffield, UK: Greenleaf Publishing, 2004; www.greenleaf-publishing.com/productdetail.kmod?productid=63).

22 United Nations, 'UN to Review Progress on the Millennium Development Goals at High-level Meeting in September 2010', 2009; www.un.org/millenniumgoals/ sept_2010_more.shtml.

23 Nancy J. White, 'Barrick Gold Brings Artisanal Miners into the Fold', Republic of Mining, 27 October 2008; www.republicofmining.com/2008/10/27/barrick-gold-brings-artisanal-miners-into-the-fold-by-nancy-j-white; AngloGold Ashanti, 'Report to Society 2008'; www.anglogold.com/subwebs/informationforinvestors/reports08/ reporttosociety08/f/community.pdf: 12.

24 In this respect, CASM and CommDev are collaborating on a responsible business practice and ASM initiative: 'mining together' (when large-scale mining meets small-scale mining). A paper has been produced and an LSM–ASM 'toolkit' is currently being 'draft road-tested' and is due to be published by the end of 2009 or early 2010. 'Mining Together: Large-scale Mining Meeting Artisanal Mining: A Framework for Action', CommDev, January 2008; commdev.org/content/document/detail/2018: 5.

25 Personal communication between Veerle van Wauwe of Transparence and Jem Bendell, July 2009

26 Cartier official website, 'Cartier and Goldlake'; www.cartier.com/en/CSR#/tell-me/ excellence/commitment:/tell-me/excellence/commitment/cartier-responsible-jeweler/cartier-and-goldlake; Nicola Copping, 'Cartier Provides a New Gold Standard', *Financial Times Online*, 12 September 2009; www.goldlake.co.uk/public/file/ Goldlake/rassegna%20nuovo%20sito/ft%20120909.pdf; Goldlake Group official website, 'Eurocantera'; www.goldlake.co.uk/The_projects/Eurocantera.aspx.

27 Cartier official website, 'Our Gold Sourcing'; www.cartier.com/en/CSR#/tell-me/ excellence/commitment:/tell-me/excellence/commitment/cartier-responsible-jeweler/our-gold-sourcing.

28 PACT World, 'Cartier Signs Sourcing Agreement with an Innovative Italian Gold Mining Venture Operating in Honduras', Cartier, September 2009; pactworld.org/galleries/ default-file/CCE_Cartier_Announcement.pdf.

29 Corporacion Oro Verde official website, 'Certified Green Gold Program'; www. greengold-oroverde.org/ingles/oroverde_ing.html.

30 Alliance for Responsible Mining (ARM), October 2009; communitymining.org; Cristina Echavarria, 'Getting to Fair Trade Gold . . . and Jewellery', ARM, The Madison Dialogue, 2007; www.madisondialogue.org/ARM_MadisonDialogue.pdf.

31 Alliance for Responsible Mining, 'The Golden Vein: A Guide to Responsible Artisanal and Small-Scale Gold Mining', 2006–2007; communitymining.org/attachments/081_ THE%20GOLDEN%20VEIN%20WEB_4_Parte2.pdf.

32 Rahilla Zafar, 'Gold lures small-scale miners into global market', INSEAD, *Knowledge*, January 2009; knowledge.insead.edu/csr/social-entrepreneurship/gold-lures-small-scale-miners-into-global-market-1740.

33 Letter addressed to RJC, Rae, Solomon and CRJP members from Sampat (Earthworks NGO) and comments on first Mining Supplement draft, 17 October 2008; www.

earthworksaction.org/files/publications/CRJP_Mining_Supplement_public_review_draft_v1-Earthworks%20comments.pdf.

34 D.F. Murphy and J. Bendell, 'Partners in Time?' (UNRISD Discussion Paper 109; Geneva: UNRISD, 1999).

35 J. Bendell, 'In Whose Name? The Accountability of Corporate Social Responsibility', *Development in Practice* 15.3–4 (June 2005): 362-74.

36 See J. Bendell, 'Civilizing Markets', *The UN Chronicle* 37.2 (New York: UN Department of Public Information, 2000) for a discussion of how the UN needs to play a role in establishing guidelines for credible accountable multi-stakeholder private standards and their application, and that the Global Compact could input into that.

37 Leah Armstrong, 'Trend for natural and organic cosmetics set to rocket, according to new report', *Cosmetics Design-Europe.com*, 29 July 2009; www.cosmeticsdesign-europe.com/Products-Markets/Trend-for-natural-and-organic-cosmetics-set-to-rocket-according-to-new-report.

38 'Prélude: Quoi de neuf en 2009?', Quelle Santé Hors série, Quelle Santé, September 2009: 8 [in French].

39 Leah Armstrong, 'Cosmeeting Beyond Beauty Paris 2009 Awards: A Triumph for Natural Cosmetics', *Cosmetics Design-Europe.com*, 16 September 2009; www.cosmeticsdesign-europe.com/Products-Markets/Cosmeeting-Beyond-Beauty-Paris-2009-awards-A-triumph-for-natural-cosmetics.

40 *Ibid.*

41 Aïny official website: en.ainy.fr.

42 A.M. Todd, 'The Aesthetic Turn in Green Marketing: Environmental Consumer Ethics of Natural Personal Care Products', *Ethics and the Environment* 9.2: 88-102.

43 J. Bendell and A. Kleanthous, 'Deeper Luxury: Quality and Style when the World Matters', WWF-UK, November 2007; www.wwf.org.uk/deeperluxury/report.html: 48.

44 'Cosmetics, Emotions and Self Image', LNMH Recherche: Parfums & Cosmétiques, 2009.

45 For reference details, please contact Madame Germaine Gazano, Director of Marketing and Consumer Intelligence at LVMH Research, who presented the findings.

46 N. Etcoff *et al.*, 'The Real Truth About Beauty: A Global report. Findings of the Global Study on Women, Beauty and Well-Being', September 2004; www.clubofamsterdam.com/contentarticles/52%20Beauty/dove_white_paper_final.pdf: 13.

47 See also Todd, *op. cit.*: 89.

48 Ms Polla authorised the use of this citation. In one author's personal conversation, she cautioned that women's beauty is heavily linked to their biology, while in the case of men it is linked to their social function.

49 Etcoff *et al.*, *op. cit.*: 25-27.

50 S. Malkan, *Not Just a Pretty Face: The Ugly Side of the Beauty Industry* (Canada: New Society Publishers, 2007): 66-68.

51 A. Kleanthous and J. Peck, 'Let Them Eat Cake: Satisfying he New Consumer Appetite for Responsible Brands: Abridged Version', WWF-UK, September 2005; www.wwf.org.uk/filelibrary/pdf/let_them_eat_cake_abridged.pdf: 11.

52 Graham Menzies Foundation, 'The Globalization of Eating Disorders', Graham Menzies Foundation, 24 February 2008; grahammenziesfoundation.wordpress.com/2008/02/24/the-globalization-of-eating-disorders.

53 Etcoff *et al.*, *op. cit.*: 38.

54 Malkan, *op. cit.*: 68-69. See also the documentary *Wet Dreams and False Images*.

55 Kleanthous and Peck, *op. cit.*: 11.

56 One author's notes during the symposium.

57 Bendell and Kleanthous, *op. cit.*: 48.
58 Mark Simpson, 'MetroDaddy speaks!', 5 January 2004; www.marksimpson.com/metrodaddy-speaks.
59 Helen Pidd, 'Men seeking Beckham effect go wild for Boyzilians: Intimate waxing is gaining popularity among males gay and straight, salons say', *The Guardian Online*, 26 January 2008; www.guardian.co.uk/uk/2008/jan/26/fashion.lifeandhealth.
60 Kirsten Hansen, 'Hair or Bare? The History of American Women and Hair Removal, 1914–1934', 18 April 2007; history.barnard.edu/sites/default/files/inline/kirstenhansenthesis.pdf; 'Who Decided Women Should Shave Their Legs and Underarms?', *The Straight Dope*, 6 February 1991; www.straightdope.com/columns/read/625/who-decided-women-should-shave-their-legs-and-underarms.
61 Todd, *op. cit.*: 88-102.

4Q2009

1 'Copenhagen deal reaction in quotes', *BBC Online*, 19 December 2009; news.bbc.co.uk/2/hi/8421910.stm.
2 M. Lynas, 'How do I know China wrecked the Copenhagen deal? I was in the room', *The Guardian Online*, 22 December 2009; www.guardian.co.uk/environment/2009/dec/22/copenhagen-climate-change-mark-lynas.
3 P. Romero, 'Copenhagen talks: RP negotiator out, Arroyo party in', *abs-cbnNEWS.com Online*, December 2009; www.abs-cbnnews.com/nation/12/04/09/rp-dumps-climate-change-negotiator-copenhagen-talks.
4 Avaaz, 'People vs Polluters'; https://secure.avaaz.org/en/people_vs_polluters.
5 Christopher Booker, 'Copenhagen accord keeps Big Carbon in business', *The Telegraph Online*, 19 December 2009; www.telegraph.co.uk/comment/columnists/christopherbooker/6845686/Copenhagen-accord-keeps-Big-Carbon-in-business.html.
6 Paul Toni interview with Jem Bendell, Brisbane, 4 November 2009; www.griffith.edu.au/__data/assets/pdf_file/0011/239429/Paul-Toni.pdf.
7 John Vidal, Allegra Stratton and Suzanne Goldenberg, 'Low targets, goals dropped: Copenhagen ends in failure', *The Guardian Online*, 19 December 2009; www.guardian.co.uk/environment/2009/dec/18/copenhagen-deal.
8 Alan AtKisson, 'The Earthquake in Copenhagen: Reflections on CoP-15 and its Aftermath', 21 December 2009; alanatkisson.wordpress.com/2009/12/21/the-earthquake-in-copenhagen-reflections-on-cop-15-and-its-aftermath/.
9 AccountAbility, 'Responsible Competitiveness in China 2009: Seizing the low carbon opportunity for green development', November 2009; www.csr-china.net/ind/nationalcsr/files/%E5%9B%BD%E5%AE%B6%E8%B4%A3%E4%BB%BB%E7%AB%9E%E4%BA%89%E5%8A%9B%EF%BC%882009%EF%BC%89%E7%A0%94%E7%A9%B6%E6%8A%A5%E5%91%8A%EF%BC%88%E8%8B%B1-%E6%96%87%E7%89%88%EF%BC%89.pdf.
10 J. Bendell, 'What's an NGO to do?', 2007; jembendell.wordpress.com/2007/07/17/whats-an-ngo-to-do.
11 Oscar Reyes, 'Taking Care of Business', *The New Internationalist Online*, December 2009; www.newint.org/features/2009/12/01/corporate-influence.
12 The position of the USCC was critiqued in the *New York Times* and *Washington Post*: 'Way Behind the Curve', *New York Times Online*, 29 September 2009; www.nytimes.com/2009/09/30/opinion/30wed3.html and 'The U.S. Chamber vs. honesty', *The*

Washington Post Online, 27 October 2009; www.washingtonpost.com/wp-dyn/content/article/2009/10/26/AR2009102602714.html.

13 Marianne Lavelle, 'Gore business: 2340 climate lobbyists', *Politico*, 25 February 2009; www.politico.com/news/stories/0209/19255.html.

14 Suzanne Goldenberg, 'Apple joins Chamber of Commerce exodus over climate change scepticism: Technology firm becomes latest in line of high-profile departures after federation opposes efforts to reduce emissions', *The Guardian Online*, 6 October 2009; www.guardian.co.uk/environment/2009/oct/06/chamber-commerce-apple-climate-change.

15 Nick Robins, Robert Clover and Charanjit Singh, 'Climate for Recovery: The colour of stimulus goes green' (London: HSBC, 2009; www.globaldashboard.org/wp-content/uploads/2009/HSBC_Green_New_Deal.pdf).

16 Reyes, *op. cit.*

17 D. Pearce, 'The United Kingdom Climate Change Levy: A study in political economy', OECD Environment Directorate, Centre for Tax Policy and Administration, 20 January 2005; search.oecd.org/officialdocuments/displaydocumentpdf/?doclanguage=en&cote=com/env/epoc/ctpa/cfa%282004%2966/final.

18 Johann Hari, 'Leaders of the rich world are enacting a giant fraud: Corporate lobbyists can pressure or bribe governments to rig the system in their favour', *The Independent Online*, 11 December 2009; www.independent.co.uk/opinion/commentators/johann-hari/johann-hari-leaders-of-the-rich-world-are-enacting-a-giant-fraud-1837963.html.

19 M.W. Wara and D.G. Victor, 'A Realistic Policy on International Carbon Offsets' (Stanford University PESD Working Paper No. 74, April 2008; fsi.stanford.edu/publications/a_realistic_policy_on_international_carbon_offsets/).

20 Democracy Now, 'James Hansen interviewed by Amy Goodman', 22 December 2009; www.democracynow.org/2009/12/22/leading_climate_scientist_james_hansen_on.

21 Phil Izzo, 'Is It Time for a New Tax on Energy?', *Wall Street Journal Online*, 9 February 2007; online.wsj.com/public/article/SB117086898234001121.html. =

22 Patrick O'Connor and Alex Safari, 'Climate change, Kyoto, and carbon trading', *Socialist Equality Party*, 7 November 2007; www.sep.org.au/articles07/clim-071107.html.

23 Christopher Booker, 'What links the Copenhagen conference with the steelworks closing in Redcar?', *Climate Realists*, 12 December 2012; climaterealists.com/index.php?id=4636.

24 Reyes, *op. cit.*

25 'The deal we need from Copenhagen', *FT Online*, 2 November 2009; www.ft.com/intl/cms/s/0/97c3e570-c7e7-11de-8ba8-00144feab49a.html#axzz2AtJ634Ci.

26 Lisa Kassenaar, 'Carbon Capitalists Warming to Climate Market Using Derivatives', *Bloomberg*, 4 December 2009; www.bloomberg.com/apps/news?pid=20601086&sid=aXRBOxU5KT5M.

27 *Ibid.*

28 *Ibid.*

29 Chris Lang, '"Subprime Carbon?": New Friends of the Earth report', *redd-monitor.org*, 10 April 2009; www.redd-monitor.org/2009/04/10/subprime-carbon-new-friends-of-the-earth-report/.

30 Matt Taibbi, 'The Great American Bubble Machine: From tech stocks to high gas prices, Goldman Sachs has engineered every major market manipulation since the Great Depression—and they're about to do it again', *Rolling Stone Online*, 5 April 2010; www.rollingstone.com/politics/story/29127316/the_great_american_bubble_machine.

31 William Tate, 'Will Dems allow Goldman to manipulate a cap-and-trade market?', *American Thinker*, 14 July 2009; www.americanthinker.com/2009/07/will_dems_allow_goldman_to_man.html.

32 Fiona Harvey, 'Industries tread a green line', *FT Online*, 11 December 2009; www.ft.com/intl/cms/s/0/cbea126e-e5ad-11de-b5d7-00144feab49a.html#axzz2AtJ634Ci.

33 Joshua Rhett Miller, 'Fraud in Europe's Cap and Trade System a "Red Flag," Critics Say', *FoxNews.com*, 19 December 2009; politics.foxnews.mobi/quickPage.html?page=21292&content=28795207&pageNum=-1.

34 Carbon Me official website: www.carbonme.org/terms.php.

35 Dirk Fleischmann, 'The Carbon Me Story Part (1)', *Myforestfarm.com*, 16 March 2008; www.myforestfarm.com/blog.html.

36 'The deal we need from Copenhagen', *FT Online, op. cit.*

37 Tim Harford, 'Political ill wind blows a hole in the climate change debate', 28 November 2009; timharford.com/2009/11/political-ill-wind-blows-a-hole-in-the-climate-change-debate.

38 John M. Broder, 'Gore's Dual Role: Advocate and Investor', *New York Times Online*, 2 November 2009; www.nytimes.com/2009/11/03/business/energy-environment/03gore.html?_r=2&em.

39 Christopher Booker and Richard North, 'Questions over business deals of UN climate change guru Dr Rajendra Pachauri', *The Heartland Institute*, 20 December 2009; heartland.org/policy-documents/questions-over-business-deals-un-climate-change-guru-dr-rajendra-pachauri.

40 Evo Morales, 'Bolivia stuns climate summit with target', *The Hindu Online*, 18 December 2009; www.hindu.com/2009/12/18/stories/2009121855951500.htm.

41 Democracy Now, 'James Hansen interviewed by Amy Goodman', 22 December 2009; www.democracynow.org/2009/12/22/leading_climate_scientist_james_hansen_on.

42 'The deal we need from Copenhagen', *FT Online, op. cit.*

43 Democracy Now, *op. cit.*

44 Nadeje Puliak, 'Sarkozy unveils new French carbon tax', *Sydney Morning Herald Online*, 10 September 2009; news.smh.com.au/breaking-news-world/sarkozy-unveils-new-french-carbon-tax-20090910-fjhw.html.

45 'Carbon tax of €15 a tonne announced', *Inside Ireland Online*, 9 December 2009; insideireland.ie/2009/12/09/archive2313-2373/.

46 'Government "to impose Carbon Tax", says official', *China.org.cn*, 22 April 2009; www.china.org.cn/environment/policies_announcements/2009-04/22/content_17652059.htm.

47 'Sarkozy insists on carbon tariff on EU borders', *China View.cn*, 7 January 2010; news.xinhuanet.com/english/2010-01/07/content_12770447.htm.

48 Susan Kraemer, 'First Carbon Tariff Will Tax CO_2 at the Border', *Scientific American Online*, 1 January 2010; www.scientificamerican.com/article.cfm?id=first-carbon-tariff-will-tax-co2-at-2010-01.

49 Simon Zadek, 'Revising Plan A', 16 December 2009; zadek.wordpress.com/2009/12/16/revising-plan-a.

50 For more on carbon charges see the following websites (not that I necessarily endorse their content or approach): www.carbontax.org/; http://en.wikipedia.org/wiki/Carbon_tax; http://www.carbonfees.org.

51 WWF, 'Business: The Real Deal', 4 November 2009; assets.panda.org/downloads/action_bybusiness_onclimate_paper_corrected.pdf.

52 The University of Cambridge Programme for Sustainable Leadership official website: www.cpsl.cam.ac.uk.

53 Taibbi, *op. cit.*

54 Intergovernmental Panel on Climate Change, 'Proposals for Climate Change Agreements'; www.ipcc.ch/publications_and_data/ar4/wg3/en/ch13-ens13-3-3.html.

55 'Gore in Copenhagen: Favors Carbon Tax; Calls Deniers "Reckless Fools"', *Common Dreams*, 16 December 2009; www.commondreams.org/headline/2009/12/16-4.

56 Daniel Whitten, 'Caterpillar, FedEx Favor Carbon Tax Over Cap-and-Trade Measure', *Bloomberg*, 23 September 2009; www.bloomberg.com/apps/news?pid=newsarchive&s id=af7xdAInGuOQ.

57 Angelique Van Engelen, 'Carbon Tax Versus Cap-and-Trade', *TriplePundit*, 28 January 2009; www.triplepundit.com/2009/01/carbon-tax-versus-cap-and-trade.

58 Jem Bendell and Annekathrin Ellersiek, *Noble networks? Advocacy for Global Justice and the 'Network Effect'* (Geneva: United Nations Research Institute for Social Development, 2009; www.unrisd.org/80256B3C005BCCF9/search/A93CF6EAA4EDAD 27C125757D002931BA?OpenDocument).

59 J. Bendell *et al.*, *The Corporate Responsibility Movement: Five Years of Global Corporate Responsibility Analysis from Lifeworth, 2001–2005* (Sheffield, UK: Greenleaf Publishing, 2009).

60 Kyle Peterson and Marc Pfitzer, 'Lobbying for Good', *Stanford Social Innovation Review*, Winter 2009; www.ssireview.org/pdf/LobbyingForGood.pdf.

61 J. Bendell and K. Kearins, 'The "Political Bottom Line": The Emerging Dimension to Corporate Responsibility for Sustainable Development', *Business Strategy and the Environment* 14.6 (2005): 372-83.

62 AccountAbility, 'Responsible Competitiveness in China 2009: Seizing the low carbon opportunity for green development', November 2009; www.csr-china. net/ind/nationalcsr/files/%E5%9B%BD%E5%AE%B6%E8%B4%A3%E4%BB% BB%E7%AB%9E%E4%BA%89%E5%8A%9B%EF%BC%882009%EF%BC%89% E7%A0%94%E7%A9%B6%E6%8A%A5%E5%91%8A%EF%BC%88%E8%8B%B1- %E6%96%87%E7%89%88%EF%BC%89.pdf.

63 Bendell *et al.*, *op. cit.*

64 Naomi Klein, 'Better to have no deal at Copenhagen than one that spells catastrophe', *The Guardian Online*, 17 December 2009; www.guardian.co.uk/commentisfree/ cif-green/2009/dec/17/copenhagen-no-deal-better-catastrophe.

65 *An Inconvenient Truth*: the film (2006); www.imdb.com/title/tt0497116/quotes.

66 Hari, *op. cit.*

67 Democracy Now, *op. cit.*

68 If you are leading an initiative to gain cross-sector international support for a global carbon charge, that is effective, efficient and fair, please leave a comment on the online posting that introduces a version of this section: www.lifeworth.com/ consult/2010/01/climateleadership.

69 Social Innovation Park official website: www.socialinnovationpark.org.

70 Syinc official website: www.syinc.org.

71 Centre for Social Innovation, 'Thought Leaders' 2009; www.lcsi.smu.edu.sg/Social_ icon/2009/speakers.asp.

72 CSR Asia official website, 'CSR Asia Summit 2009', www.csr-asia.com/summit09.

73 Shokay official website: www.shokay.com.

74 In a Planet of Our Own, 'A Vision of Sustainability from Across Six Continents', 3–7 November 2009; www.inaplanetofourown.net/conference.html.

75 DMI official website, 'Design Complexity and Change', 18–20 October 2009; www.dmi. org/dmi/html/conference/annual09/annual.htm.

76 www.businessdictionary.com/definition/innovation.html.

77 T. Golsby-Smith *et al.*, *High Performance Thinking: Methods to Shape Strategic Thinking* (workbook; Sydney: Second Road, 2007).

78 P. Toni, WWF Australia, 'Innovation and the Emerging Sustainable Enterprise Economy in Asia-Pacific', presentation at APABIS Conference, Brisbane, 6 November 2009.

79 *Ibid.*

80 M. Berns, A. Townend, Z. Khayat B. Balagopal, M. Reeves, M. Hopkins and N. Kruschwitz, *The Business of Sustainability: What it Means to Managers Now* (Boston Consulting Group, October 2009; www.bcg.com/expertise_impact/publications/ PublicationDetails.aspx?id=tcm:12-32196).

81 *Ibid.*: 17.

82 L. Tischler, 'What's thwarting American innovation? Too much science, says Roger Martin', *Fast Company Online*, 4 November 2009; www.fastcompany.com/blog/linda-tischler/design-times/ whats-thwarting-american-innovation-too-much-science-says-roger-mar.

83 *Ibid.*

84 V. Wong, 'How business is adopting design thinking', *Bloomberg*, 3 November 2009; www.businessweek.com/innovate/content/sep2009/id20090930_853305. htm?chan=innovation_design+index+page_special+report+---+design+thinking.

85 D. Patnaik, 'Forget design thinking and try hybrid thinking', *Fast Company Online*, 25 August 2009; www.fastcompany.com/blog/dev-patnaik/innovation/ forget-design-thinking-and-try-hybrid-thinking.

86 Wong, *op. cit.*

87 Berns *et al.*, *op. cit.*: 14.

88 UNEP, *Consumption Opportunities: Strategies for Change. A Report for Decision-makers* (Geneva: UNEP, 2001; www.unep.org/publications/search/pub_details_s.asp?ID=350).

89 Environmental Working Group's 'Skin Deep Cosmetic Safety Database', 2009; www. cosmeticsdatabase.com/wordsearch_free.php?hq=Procter+%26+Gamble&go=go.

90 P&G official website, 'Sustainability: Strategy, Goals and Progress'; www.pg.com/ en_US/sustainability/strategy_goals_progress.shtml.

91 P. Merholz, 'Why Design Thinking Won't Save You', *Harvard Business Publishing Online*, 9 October 2009; blogs.harvardbusiness.org/merholz/2009/10/why-design-thinking- wont-save.html.

92 Patnaik, *op. cit.*

93 R. Martin, *The Design of Business: Why Design Thinking Is the Next Competitive Advantage* (Boston: Harvard University Press, 2009): 40-41.

94 *Ibid.*: 48.

95 One author's personal correspondence with Alessandro Rancati, founder and owner of Direccion Creativa, an innovation and design consulting firm based in Barcelona.

96 Martin, *op. cit.*: 33-56. See also T. Golsby-Smith, *Pursuing the Art of Strategic Conversations: An Investigation of the Role of the Liberal Arts of Rhetoric and Poetry in the Business World* (PhD; University of Western Sydney, 2001): 191-220.

97 The effectiveness of stakeholder dialogues is discussed as part of our reflection for the 2007 year.

1Q2010

1 WBCSD, 'Vision 2050 Lays a Pathway to Sustainable Living Within Planet', 2010; www. wbcsd.org/pages/edocument/edocumentdetails.aspx?id=219&nosearchcontextkey=t rue.

2 J. Bendell, *The Corporate Responsibility Movement: Five Years of Global Corporate Responsibility Analysis from Lifeworth, 2001–2005* (Sheffield, UK: Greenleaf Publishing, 2009).

3 WBCSD, *op. cit.*

4 J. Bendell, *Debating NGO Accountability* (Geneva: UN Non-governmental Liaison Service, 2006; www.un-ngls.org/spip.php?article945).

5 UNEP, 'Green Jobs: Towards Decent Work in a Sustainable, Low-Carbon World'; www. unep.org/labour_environment/PDFs/Greenjobs/UNEPGreenJobs-E-Bookp275-293-Part3section1.pdf.

6 WBCSD, 'Vision 2050: The New Agenda for Business' (WBCSD, 2010). Only in graph 3.4 'Reconsidering success and progress', p. 18, is inequality mentioned as having a potential negative impact on living conditions.

7 Justin Frewen, 'The "Old" Evils of Poverty, Hunger and Inequality', Share The World's Resources, 12 February 2010; www.stwr.org/poverty-inequality/the-old-evils-of-poverty-hunger-and-inequality.html.

8 W. Salverda, B. Nolvan and T.M. Smeeding, *Economic Inequality* (New York: Oxford University Press, 2009; books.google.fr/books?hl=fr&lr=&id=dFQ4puHrXM4C&oi=fnd &pg=PT12&dq=The+Oxford+Handbook+of+Economic+Inequality&ots=7wNsqHGXrJ &sig=6Bwstn93wPawYsYw6OZf9FSt7GE#v=onepage&q&f=false): 3-9.

9 The Equality Trust, 'The Spirit Level Slides'; www.slideshare.net/equalitytrust/the-spirit-level-slides-from-the-equality-trust. See also: Tom Clark, 'Inequality: Mother of All Evils', *The Guardian*, 13 March 2009; image.guardian.co.uk/sys-files/Guardian/documents/2009/03/13/inequality.pdf.

10 Inequality.org, 'By the Numbers'; inequality.org/wp-content/uploads/2011/01/wealth-inequality-charts.pdf.

11 Robert Frank, 'U.S. Millionaire Tally Soared 16% in '09', *WSJ Online*. 09 March 2010; blogs.wsj.com/wealth/2010/03/09/us-millionaire-population-soared-16-in-2009/?mod=rss_WSJBlog.

12 National Equality Panel, 'An Anatomy of Inequality in the UK' (2010).

13 Michael Bristow, 'China "must reduce rich–poor gap"—Premier Wen', BBC News, 5 March 2010; news.bbc.co.uk/2/hi/asia-pacific/8550930.stm.

14 Colin David Butler, 'Inequality and Sustainability,' 2002, PhD, The Australian National University; https://digitalcollections.anu.edu.au/bitstream/1885/46233/5/01front. pdf.

15 Lifeworth Consulting, 'Capitalism in Question', January 2010; www.lifeworth.com/capitalisminquestion.pdf.

16 P. Utting and J.C. Marques (eds.), *Corporate Social Responsibility and Regulatory Governance: Towards Inclusive Development?* (Palgrave, 2009).

17 J. Bendell, 'Making Business Work for Development' (Insights 54; ID21; UK: Institute of Development Studies, 2005).

18 See footnote 9.

19 International Labour Organisation, 'The Inequality Predicament: Report on the World Social Situation 2005—United Nations' (ILO, 2005; www.ilo.org/public/english/region/ampro/cinterfor/news/inf_05.htm). See also R. Wilkinson and K. Pickett, *The Spirit*

Level: Why Greater Equality Makes Societies Stronger (London: Bloomsbury Press, 2009).

20 R. Foroohar, 'The Recession Generation', *Newsweek*, 9 January 2010; www.newsweek. com/id/229959. See also B. Judson, 'New Income Inequality Data: Surprising and Frightening', 29 September 2009; bx.businessweek.com/income-inequality/view?url= http%3A%2F%2Fitcouldhappenhere.com%2Fblog%2Ffrightening%2F.

21 James K. Boyce, 'Inequality as a Cause of Environmental Degradation', *Ecological Economics* 11 (1994); also available at: www.peri.umass.edu/fileadmin/pdf/published_ study/PS1.pdf.

22 This is discussed in some depth in the climate policy section of 'Capitalism in Question' (see footnote 15).

23 E. Perotti and E.L. von Thadden, 'Corporate Governance and the Distribution of Wealth: A Political Economy Perspective', *Journal of Institutional and Theoretical Economics* 162.1 (2006): 217.

24 Lifeworth Consulting, *op. cit.*

25 The search terms were: *equality, inequality, ungleichheit, igualdad, desigualdad, imparidad, disparit, igualdade, desigualdade, uguaglianza, disuguaglianza, ineguaglianza* and the Hebrew for 'equality' and 'inequality'.

26 Banco Bradesco, 'Banco Bradesco 2008 Sustainability Report'; www.unglobalcompact. org/COPs/detail/4079.

27 Otto Group, 'Sustainability Report 2009'; www.ottogroup.com/media/docs/en/ Nachhaltigkeitsbericht/1-Otto_Group_Sustainability_Report_2009.pdf.

28 Caja da Burgos, 'Informe anual: Economico, Social y Ambiental 2008'; www. cajadeburgos.com/imgfiles/institucional/memRSC2008.pdf; Larsen & Toubro, 'Sustainability Report 2009'; www.larsentoubro.com/lntcorporate/LnT_NWS/PDF/ LnTCSR2009report_7Dec09y2.pdf.

29 Larsen & Toubro, *op. cit.*: 4.

30 The Co-operative Group, 'Sustainability Report 2008/2009'; www.cfs.co.uk/corp/pdf/ Sustainability_Report_2008-09.pdf: 46.

31 Téléfonica S.A., 'Annual Corporate Responsibility Report Telefonica S.A.'; www. telefonica.com/en/annual_report/pdf/Telefonica_RC09.pdf.

32 John Lewis Partnership, www.johnlewispartnership.co.uk/about.html.

33 Julia Kollewe and Zoe Wood, 'John Lewis Staff to Share £151m in bonuses', *The Guardian Online*, 11 March 2010; www.guardian.co.uk/business/2010/mar/11/john-lewis-staff-share-151m-in-bonuses.

34 *Ibid.*

35 Daniel Brooksbank, 'Swedish govt fund vows to vote down short-term excessive bonuses', *Responsible Investor*, 16 March 2010; *Sustainable Investment Research Platform Online*, 16 March 2010; www.sirp.se/web/page.aspx?refid=62&newsid=61944 &page=72.

36 There are two models of employer ownership: indirect ownership, where shares are held in a trust for the benefit of employees; and direct ownership, where the business is directly owned by shareholders who are employees. The latter might be difficult to sustain since shareholders might want to sell their shares. Therefore, many companies opt for a mixture of trust and direct ownership.

37 Jeff Gates, *The Ownership Solution: Toward a Shared Capitalism for the 21st Century* (Perseus Books, 1999).

38 M. Goyder, 'Tomorrow's Owners: Stewardship of Tomorrow's Company' (Corporation 20/20 Paper Series on Restoring the Primacy of the Real Company; www. corporation2020.org/corporation2020/documents/Papers/2nd-Summit-Paper-Series.

pdf): 16-25. See also Marjorie Kelly, 'Not Just for Profit: Emerging Alternatives to the Shareholder Centric Model' (Corporation 20/20 Paper Series on Restoring the Primacy of the Real Company; www.corporation2020.org/corporation2020/documents/Papers/2nd-Summit-Paper-Series.pdf): 34-41.

39 *Ibid.*
40 Marjorie Kelly and Allen White, 'Corporate Design: The Missing Business and Policy Link of Our Time'; www.jussemper.org/Resources/CorporateDesign.pdf.
41 Cecile G. Betit, 'The Carris Companies: Doing the Next Right Thing', *Journal of Corporate Citizenship* 30 (Summer 2008): 107-22; www.greenleaf-publishing.com/jcc30. See also Cecile G. Betit, 'Carris Companies' Practice of Employee Governance', *Journal of Corporate Citizenship* 6 (Summer 2002): 87-109; www.greenleaf-publishing.com/productdetail.kmod?productid=104.
42 Véronique Smée. 'Coopaname, or how to reconcile the company and the employee', *Novethic Online*, 2 April 2010; www.novethic.fr/novethic/entreprise/ressources_humaines/conditions_de_travail/coopaname_ou_comment_reconcilier_entreprise_et_salarie/128637.jsp?utm_source=newsletter&utm_medium=Email&utm_content=novethicInfo&newsletter=ok.
43 SouthAfrica.info, 'Sappi unveils R800m empowerment deal', 25 March 2010; www.southafrica.info/business/trends/empowerment/sappi-250310.htm.
44 SouthAfrica.info, 'Rezidor expands SA Partnership', 5 February 2010; www.southafrica.info/business/trends/empowerment/rezidor-050210.htm.
45 SouthAfrica.info, 'Black economic empowerment'; www.southafrica.info/business/trends/empowerment/bee.htm.
46 Samantha Enslin-Payne, 'Mining sets pace in BEE transactions', *BusinessReport Online*, 6 January 2010; solidariteitinstituut.co.za/rabib/index.php?title=Mining_sets_pace_in_BEE_transactions.
47 Murray Leibbrandt *et al.*, 'Trends in South African Income Distribution and Poverty since the Fall of Apartheid', OECD, 20 January 2010; www.oecd.org/LongAbstract/0,3425,en_33873108_39418625_44446163_1_1_1_1,00.html. See also 'Black Economic Empowerment: Sasol's Smart Move', Ethical Corporation; www.ethicalcorp.com/content.asp?ContentID=5912.
48 Personal conversation with the author.
49 M. Savage, 'Culture, Class and Classification', in T. Bennett and J. Frow (eds.), *A Handbook of Cultural Analysis* (Sage Publications, 2007).
50 Jem Bendell thanks Dr Mark Bendell, University of Chester, for discussions that led him to articulate this concept as 'glass corridors'.
51 Human Rights Watch, 'World Report 2010'; www.hrw.org/world-report-2010.
52 Migrant Rights, 'New HRW Report Slams Gulf States for Migrant Abuses', 26 January 2010; www.migrant-rights.org/2010/01/26/new-hrw-report-slams-gulf-states-for-migrant-abuses.
53 Migrant Rights, 'Every two days a migrant worker attempts or commits suicide in Kuwait', 28 March 2010; www.migrant-rights.org/2010/03/28/every-two-days-a-migrant-worker-attempts-or-commits-suicide-in-kuwait.
54 Migrant Rights, 'Top 5 Migrants' Rights Stories in the Middle East for 2009', 2 January 2010; www.migrant-rights.org/2010/01/02/top-5-migrants-rights-stories-in-the-middle-east-for-2009.
55 Human Rights Watch, 'The Island of Happiness: Exploitation of Migrant Workers on Saadiyat Island, Abu Dhabi', 19 May 2009; www.hrw.org/node/83111.
56 The Government of UAE put forward a draft labour law attempting to rectify some of these abuses in 2007; however, this was later withdrawn. For the 2006 report

see Human Rights Watch, 'Building Towers, Cheating Workers: Exploitation of Migrant Construction Workers in the United Arab Emirates', 2006; www.hrw.org/en/ reports/2006/11/11/building-towers-cheating-workers.

57 John Zinkin and Geoffrey Williams, 'Islam and CSR: A Study of the Compatibility between the Tenets of Islam and the UN Global Compact', *Journal of Business Ethics* 91.4 (2010): 519-33.

58 Al Haqq Society, 'Sustainability Advisory Group': Middle East CSR Executive Survey', 13 January 2010; alhaqqsociety.wordpress.com/2010/01/13/sustainability-advisory-group-middle-east-csr-executive-survey.

59 Marios I. Katsioloudes and Tor Brodtkorb, 'Corporate Social Responsibility: An Exploratory Study in the United Arab Emirates', *SAM Advanced Management Journal* 72.4 (2007).

60 Djordjija Petkoski, Michael Jarvis and Cecilia Brady, 'From Corporate Philanthropy to Strategic Partnerships: The Potential of Inclusive and Sustainable Business Models in MENA', Arab Planning Institute; www.arab-api.org/conf_0309/p21.pdf.

61 Hawkawah: The Institute for Corporate Governance, 'Report from Hawkamah and IFC Outlines Scope for Improvement in MENA Corporate Governance', 2008; www. hawkamah.org/news_and_publications/publications/IFC/index.html.

62 FDIH, 'Algérie: les multinationales violent le droit du travail en toute impunité', 22 February 2010; www.fidh.org/Algerie-les-multinationales [in French].

63 German Embassy, Algiers, via CSR WeltWeit, 'Algeria: The Role of CSR'; www.csr-weltweit.de/en/laenderprofile/profil/algerien/index.nc.html.

64 Human Rights Watch, 'Building Towers, Cheating Workers: Exploitation of Migrant Construction Workers in the United Arab Emirates' 12 November 2006, www.hrw.org/ en/reports/2006/11/11/building-towers-cheating-workers.

65 Melsa Ararat, 'Corporate Social Responsibility: Across Middle East and North Africa', 1 April 2006; https://research.sabanciuniv.edu/802/1/stvkaf07a66.pdf.

66 Figure calculated from listings of signatories at www.unglobalcompact.org and www. unpri.org/signatories as of 1 April 2010. The countries chosen were based on The Pew Forum on Religion & Public Life 2009 survey, 'Mapping the Global Muslim Population'; pewforum.org/docs/?DocID=450. The countries are Morocco, Algeria, Nigeria, Egypt, Turkey, Iran, Pakistan, India, Bangladesh and Indonesia.

67 Voluntary Principles on Human Rights and Security, 'Participants', www. voluntaryprinciples.org/participants.

68 Zinkin and Williams, *op. cit.*

69 Johan Graafland, Corrie Mazereeuw and Aziza Yahia, 'Islam and Socially Responsible Business Conduct: An Empirical Study of Dutch Entrepreneurs', *Business Ethics: A European Review* 15.4 (October 2006).

70 Al Haqq Society, *op. cit.*

71 Lifeworth Consulting, *The Eastern Turn In Responsible Enterprise*; lifeworth.com/ lifeworth2008/2009/05/the-eastern-turn-in-academe.

72 2nd World Congress of Muslim Philanthropists, 'Conventional to Strategic: A New Paradigm in Giving', March 2009: www.thewcmp.org/img/downloads/pdf/ WCMP_2009_summary0.pdf.

73 Tamkeen Development and Management Consulting. 'Saudi companies and corporate responsibility: Challenges and ways forward'. February 2007; www.tamkeenconsult. com/pdf/study.pdf.

74 Marios I. Katsioloudes and Tor Brodtkorb, 'Corporate Social Responsibility: An Exploratory Study in the United Arab Emirates', *SAM Advanced Management Journal* 72.4 (2007).

75 Migrants Rights, 'Lebanon's Minister of Interior makes promises to improve migrant rights', 3 December 2009; www.migrant-rights.org/2009/12/03/lebanon%E2%80%99s-minister-of-interior-makes-promises-to-improve-migrant-rights.

76 Ararat, *op. cit.*

77 German Embassy, Jakarta, via CSR WeltWeit, 'Indonesia: The Role of CSR'; www.csr-weltweit.de/en/laenderprofile/profil/indonesien/index.nc.html.

78 Petkoski, Jarvis and Brady, *op. cit.* See also 'Statement of Mr James W. Rawley, UNDP Resident Representative, Opening & Welcoming Remarks, National Corporate Social Responsibility Conference', 24 March 2008; www.undp.org.eg/Portals/0/Links%20Poverty/080324_SP_CSR%20Conference_JR%20Eng.doc.

79 Daromir Rudnyckyj, 'Market Islam in Indonesia', *Journal of the Royal Anthropological Institute*. 15 (special issue): 183-201.

80 *Ibid.*

81 *Ibid.*

82 Philippe D'Iribarne, 'Motivating Workers in Emerging Countries: Universal Tools and Local Adaptations', *Journal of Organizational Behavior* 23.3 (May 2002): 243-56; www.jstor.org/stable/4093802.

83 Tareq Emtairah, Asya Al-Ashaikh and Abdulmohsen Al-Badr, 'Contexts and Corporate Social Responsibility: The Case of Saudi Arabia International', *International Journal of Sustainable Society* 1.4 (2009): 325-46.

84 Heidi Ryan, 'What do Middle Eastern leaders think of CSR? Positioning business for post-crisis growth', *The Sustainability Advisory Group Online*, November 2009, www.sustainabilityadvisory.net/cms/media/CSR%20survey.pdf.

85 *Ibid.*

86 An Islamic international autonomous non-profit corporate body that prepares accounting, auditing, governance, ethics and Shari'ah standards for Islamic financial institutions and the industry.

87 AAOIFI, 'Corporate Social Responsibility Conduct and Disclosure for Islamic Financial Institutions: Exposure Draft on Governance Standard for Islamic Financial Institutions'; www.dinarstandard.com/maqasid/CSR%20Exposure%20Draft.pdf

88 *Ibid.*

89 'IEMA Workshop: An Accredited CSR Practitioners Workshop held by CSE in Dubai', *The CSR Digest Online*, 28 January 2010; www.csrdigest.com/tag/middle-east.

90 AccountAbility, 'The Saudi Responsible Competitiveness Index Report', 25 January 2009; www.accountability.org/about-us/publications/the-saudi.html.

91 Petkoski, Jarvis and Brady, *op. cit.*

92 Zainab Mansoor, 'GCC companies honored for good corporate citizenship', *Dinar Standard Online*, 13 July 2008; www.dinarstandard.com/current/5thCSR071308.htm.

93 Kim T. Saether and Ruth V. Aguilera, 'Corporate Social Responsibility in a Comparative Perspective', in A. Crane *et al.*, *The Oxford Handbook of Corporate Social Responsibility* (Oxford, UK: Oxford University Press 2005).

94 Michael Hopkins, 'Corporate Social Responsibility: An Issues Paper' (ILO Working Paper No. 27; Policy Integration Department, World Commission on the Social Dimension of Globalization; Geneva: International Labour Office, 2004).

95 Heidi Ryan, 'What do Middle Eastern leaders think of CSR? Positioning business for post-crisis growth', *The Sustainability Advisory Group Online*, November 2009; www.sustainabilityadvisory.net/cms/media/CSR%20survey.pdf.

96 Mahmood Ayub, UNDP, 'Turkey Corporate Social Responsibility Baseline Report', UNDP 2008; www.undp.org.tr/publicationsDocuments/CSR_Report_en.pdf.

97 Alexander Schieffer, Ronnie Lessem and Odeh Al-Jayyousi, 'Corporate Governance: Impulses from the Middle East', *Transition Studies Review* (Springer Mediterranean and Middle East Papers) 1.2 (September 2008): 335-42.

98 Asyraf Wajdi Dusuki, 'What does Islam say about Corporate Social Responsibility (CSR)?', *Review of Islamic Economics* 12.1 (International Association for Islamic Economics, May 2008): 5-28.

99 Jem Bendell, Chew Ng and Niaz Alam, 'World Review', *Journal of Corporate Citizenship* 33 (Spring 2009): 11-22; www.greenleaf-publishing.com/jcc33.

100 Geoffrey Williams and John Zinkin, 'Doing Business with Islam: Can Corporate Social Responsibility Be a Bridge between Civilizations?', October 2005; available at SSRN: ssrn.com/abstract=905184 or dx.doi.org/10.2139/ssrn.905184.

101 Lifeworth Consulting, 'The Eastern Turn', 2009; lifeworth.com/lifeworth2008/2009/05/the-eastern-turn-in-academe.

2Q2010

1 J. Bendell, 'What if we are Failing? Towards a Post-crisis Compact for Systemic Change', in *Journal of Corporate Citizenship* 38 (2010); globalcompactcritics.blogspot.com/2010/06/what-if-we-are-failing-towards-post.html.

2 See for instance the series of reflections published by Griffith Business School at: www.griffith.edu.au/__data/assets/pdf_file/0003/287706/The-UN-Global-Compact.pdf.

3 'Chief executives believe overwhelmingly that sustainability has become critical to their success, and could be fully embedded into core business within ten years: UN Global Compact and Accenture release findings of largest CEO research study on corporate sustainability', Accenture, 22 June 2010; newsroom.accenture.com/article_display.cfm?article_id=5018.

4 These reviews are available in J. Bendell; *et al.*, *The Corporate Responsibility Movement: Five Years of Global Corporate Responsibility Analysis from Lifeworth, 2001–2005* (Greenleaf Publishing, 2009; www.greenleaf-publishing.com/productdetail.kmod?productid=2767).

5 'Wrapped in the flag', *The Economist* online, 22 June 2010; www.economist.com/blogs/newsbook/2010/06/corporate_ethics.

6 D. Scheffer, 'BP shows the need for a rethink of regulation', *Financial Times*, 27 May 2010; www.ft.com/intl/cms/s/0/919f37fe-69c1-11df-8432-00144feab49a.html#axzz2Af10xGF1.

7 Professor McIntosh called for a focus on creating a sustainable economy; the video can be seen at: www.un.org/webcast/globalcompact/leaderssummit2010/?mediaID=ls100625-8.

8 'Global CEOs want investors to act to create sustainability tipping point', UNGC press release, 24 June 2010; www.unglobalcompact.org/news/49-06-24-2010.

9 UN Global Compact, *Blueprint for Corporate Sustainability Leadership* (2010); www.unglobalcompact.org/docs/news_events/8.1/Blueprint.pdf.

10 See Bendell *et al.*, *The Corporate Responsibility Movement* (see footnote 4).

11 Jem Bendell and Annekathrin Ellersiek, *Noble Networks? Advocacy for Global Justice and the 'Network Effect'* (Geneva: United Nations Research Institute for Social Development [UNRISD], 2009).

12 John Elkington, 'A New Paradigm for Change', McKinsey & Company: What Matters, 6 April 2010; whatmatters.mckinseydigital.com/social_entrepreneurs/a-new-paradigm-for-change.

13 Ken Wilber, *A Theory of Everything: An Integral Vision for Business, Politics, Science and Spirituality* (Boston, MA: Shambhala, 2000). (Note that this is not an actual model of change, but a tool for helping people to think outside and inside their existing focus for the object of their change intention.)

14 'The Elephant in the Room', Crane and Matten blog, 25 June 2010; craneandmatten. blogspot.com/2010/06/elephant-in-room.html.

15 For a discussion of this issue, see J. Bendell, 'In Whose Name? The Accountability of Corporate Social Responsibility', *Development in Practice* 15.3–4 (June 2005): 362-74.

16 José Carlos Marques and Peter Utting, *Business, Politics and Public Policy: Implications for Inclusive Development* (Basingstoke, UK: Palgrave, 2010).

17 See footnote 1.

18 The Role of Governments in Promoting Corporate Responsibility and Private Sector Engagement in Development (2010) UNGC and Bertelsmann Stiftung.

19 UNGC and UNPRI (UN Principles for Responsible Investment), *Guide on Responsible Business in Conflict-Affected and High-Risk Areas: A Resource for Companies and Investors* (2010); unglobalcompact.org/AboutTheGC/tools_resources/business_and_peace.html.

20 Ewen MacAskill, 'Disquiet grows over performance of Ban Ki-moon, UN's "invisible man"', *The Guardian Online*, 22 July 2010; www.guardian.co.uk/world/2010/jul/22/ban-ki-moon-secretary-general-un.

21 World Business Council for Sustainable Development, 'WBCSD launches "Inclusive Business Challenge"', 22 April 2010; www.inclusivebusiness.org/2010/04/wbcsd-inclusive-business-challenge.html.

22 Bimtech, 'Corporate Social Responsibility: A Strategy for Inclusive Development'; DevelopmentCrossing.com, 9 April 2010; www.developmentcrossing.com/events/international-summit-on-csr.

23 Business Civic Leadership Center and United Nations Office for Partnerships, *Investing in the Millennium Development Goals* conference, 8 April 2010; www.un.org/partnerships/Docs/BCLC_Agenda.pdf.

24 UNDP, '2010 World Business and Development Awards Launched', 20 May 2010; www.undp.org/content/india/en/home/presscenter/pressreleases/2010/05/19/2010-world-business-and-development-awards-launched.

25 National Committee for International Cooperation and Sustainable Development, *Business Impact Report 2010: Scanning the Contribution of 20 Multinationals to the Millennium Development Goals* (2010); www.sustainalytics.com/sites/default/files/BusinessImpactReport2010.pdf.

26 United Nations Global Compact, 'Innovating for a Brighter Future: The Role of Business in Achieving the MDGs', (2010); unglobalcompact.org/docs/issues_doc/development/Innovating_for_Brighter_Future.pdf.

27 J. Bendell, *Barricades and Boardrooms: A Contemporary History of the Corporate Accountability Movement* (Geneva: UNRISD, 2004).

28 J. Bendell and W. Visser, 'World Review', *Journal of Corporate Citizenship* 17 (2005); www.greenleaf-publishing.com/greenleaf/journaldetail.kmod?productid=140&keycontentid=7.

29 Stefan Stern, 'Manifesto writer for business survival', *Financial Times Online*, 18 April 2010; www.ft.com/intl/cms/s/0/77f4abf4-4b49-11df-a7ff-00144feab49a.html#axzz2Af10xGF1.

30 Anand Kumar Jaiswal, 'The Fortune at the Bottom or the Middle of the Pyramid?', *Innovations: Technology, Governance and Globalization* 3.1 (2008): 85-100.

31 J. Bendell, 'From Responsibility to Opportunity: CSR and the Future of Corporate Contributions to World Development', *MHCi Monthly Feature*, February 2005; mhcinternational.com/monthly-features/articles/127-from-responsibility-to-opportunity-csr-and-the-future-of-corporate-contributions-to-world-development.

32 J. Bendell, 'Making Business Work for Development: Rethinking Corporate Social Responsibility', *id21 insights* 54.4 (2005): 1.

33 Andrew Crabtree, 'Evaluating the Bottom of the Pyramid from a Fundamental Capabilities Perspective' (Copenhagen Business School, 2007; www.globalcitizen.net/data/topic/knowledge/uploads/2011032510536705.pdf).

34 Aneel Karnani, 'The Mirage of Marketing to the Bottom of the Pyramid: How the Private Sector Can Help Alleviate Poverty', *California Management Review* 47.4 (Summer 2007): 90.

35 Suparna Chatterjee, 'Selling to the Poor: Reflection, Critique and Dialogue' (23 August 2009); warrington.ufl.edu/graduate/academics/pdb/docs/proposals/2009_SuparnaChatterjee.pdf.

36 Jem Bendell, Lala Rimando and Claire Veuthey, 'World Review', *Journal of Corporate Citizenship* 30 (2008): 10-22.

37 Schwab Foundation, 'Rajiv Khandelwal and Krishnavtar Sharma Awarded Social Entrepreneurs of the Year 2010 for India'. 16 November 2010; www.schwabfound.org/sf/Events/WorldEconomicForumEvents/2010/index.htm.

38 Nobel Foundation, 'The Nobel Peace Prize 2006'; nobelprize.org/nobel_prizes/peace/laureates/2006. See also Bendell and Visser 2005 (see footnote 28) for other discussions on the Grameen group of businesses.

39 Grameen Shakti, 'Bringing Green Energy, Health, Income and Green Jobs to Rural Bangladesh' (October 2009); www.worldfuturecouncil.org/fileadmin/user_upload/Presentations/Grameen_Shakti_Bangladesh_Part_1.pdf.

40 *Ibid.*

41 *Ibid.*

42 Telenor Group official website: telenor.com/global-presence/bangladesh.

43 *Ibid.*

44 *Ibid.*

45 Caroline Ashley, 'Harnessing Core Business for Development Impact: Evolving Ideas and Issues for Action', Overseas Development Institute, Background Note, February 2009; www.odi.org.uk/resources/download/2714.pdf.

46 UNDP, 'Creating Value for All: Growing Inclusive Markets' (2008); www.undp.org/content/undp/en/home/ourwork/partners/private_sector/GIM.html.

47 Beth Jenkins, Eriko Ishikawa, Alexis Geaneotes and John H. Paul, *Scaling Up Inclusive Business: Advancing the Knowledge and Action Agenda* (Washington, DC: International Finance Corporation and the CSR Initiative at the Harvard Kennedy School, 2010); www.ifc.org/ifcext/advisoryservices.nsf/AttachmentsByTitle/BOP_Scaling_Up_Inclusive_Business/$FILE/BOP_Scaling_Up_Inclusive_Business.pdf: 36.

48 *Ibid.*

49 *Ibid.*

50 Ximena Mora Lopez, 'Promoting Inclusive Business: Seeking Opportunity in crisis' (Asian Development Bank/Alliance WBCSD-SNV, 2009; www.docstoc.com/docs/56725108/Promoting-Inclusive-Business-See).

51 Jenkins *et al.*, *op. cit.*

52 IFC funded 1,579 companies in 2009. IFC, 'Annual Portfolio Performance Review—FY09' (IFC/R2009-0227; 25 August 2009): 14; publicintelligence.net/international-finance-corporation-annual-portfolio-performance-review-fy09.

53 HKS, 'Starting and Scaling Inclusive Business Models: Summary of a Dialogue' (co-hosted by IFC and the CSR Initiative at the Harvard Kennedy School, Washington, DC, 9 April 2010): 3; ifcext.ifc.org/ifcext/advisoryservices.nsf/AttachmentsByTitle/BOP_April_9_Dialogue_Summary/$FILE/BOP_April_9_Dialogue_Summary.pdf.

54 *Ibid.*

55 Amnesty International, 'States must not ignore human rights in efforts to end poverty', 9 June 2010; www.amnesty.org/en/news-and-updates/report/states-must-not-ignore-human-rights-efforts-end-poverty-2010-06-09.

56 UN-NGLS, *Decent Work and Fair Globalisation: A Key to Meeting Development Goals and Eradicating Poverty*, 16 June 2010; www.un-ngls.org/spip.php?article2647.

57 Peter Utting and Ann Zammit, *Beyond Pragmatism: Appraising UN–Business Partnerships* (Markets, Business and Regulation Programme Paper Number 1; Geneva: United Nations Research Institute for Social Development, October 2006; www.unrisd.org/80256B3C005BCCF9/%28httpAuxPages%29/225508544695E8F3C12572300038ED22/$file/uttzam.pdf): 47.

3Q2010

1 Anthony Miller and Jem Bendell (eds.), *Investment and Enterprise Responsibility Review* (Geneva: UNCTAD, 6 September 2010; unctad.org/en/Docs/diaeed20101_en.pdf).

2 *Factsheet: FTSE4Good Environmental Leaders Europe 40 Index* (FTSE International and EIRIS, 2007; www.ftse.com/Indices/FTSE4Good_Environmental_Leaders_Europe_40_Index/Downloads/FTSE4Good_Environmental_Leaders_Europe_40_Index_Factsheet.pdf).

3 Adrienne Hill, 'Investing in Oil: Socially Responsible?', *American Public Media Online*, 10 August 2010; www.marketplace.org/topics/your-money/bp-spill-ripples/investing-oil-socially-responsible.

4 Hugh Wheelan, '42 per cent of French want SRI info on savings: Friends of the Earth slams "illegitimate" SRI funds', *Responsible Investor Online*, 5 October 2010; www.responsible-investor.com/home/article/france_sri_retail. Requires subscription.

5 SustainAbility, 'Rate the Raters, Phase Two: Taking Inventory of the Ratings Universe', SustainAbility, 5 October 2010; www.sustainability.com/library/rate-the-raters-phase-two.

6 Michael Sadowski, 'Now Is the Time to Get Ratings Right', SustainAbility, 1 October 2010; www.sustainability.com/blog/now-is-the-time-to-get-ratings-right.

7 Anthony Miller and Jem Bendell (eds.), *Investment and Enterprise Responsibility Review* (Geneva: UNCTAD, 6 September 2010; unctad.org/en/Docs/diaeed20101_en.pdf).

8 *Principles for Responsible Investment: Report on Progress 2010* (UNEP Finance Initiative and United Nations Global Impact, 2010; www.unpri.org/files/2010_Report-on-Progress.pdf).

9 Eurosif, *European SRI Study 2010* (Eurosif, 13 October 2010; www.eurosif.org/research/eurosif-sri-study/2010).

10 SustainAbility, 'Rate the Raters, Phase Two', *op. cit.*

11 MSCI, 'Press Release: MSCI Completes Acquisition of Riskmetrics' (New York: MSCI, 1 June 2010; www.mscibarra.com/news/pressreleases/archive/MSCI_Completes_RiskMetrics_Acquisition.pdf).

12 Daniel Brooksbank, 'Thomson Reuters Buys ASSET4', *Responsible Investor Online*, 30 November 2009; www.responsible-investor.com/home/article/thomson_reuters_buys_asset4 [requires subscription]. See also Daniel Brooksbank, 'Bloomberg Chief Outlines ESG Data Strategy', *Responsible Investor Online*, 24 June 2010; www.responsible-investor.com/home/article/bloomberg_chief_outlines_esg [requires subscription].

13 Brooksbank, *op. cit.*

14 Jem Bendell thanks Anthony Miller, James Gifford, Tom Rotheram, Lucy Carmody, Antoine Mach, Allen White, Claire Veuthey, Stephen Hines, and Richard Welford for responses to various questions during preparation of this section.

15 SustainAbility, 'Rate the Raters, Phase Two', *op. cit.*

16 Karen Reiner, 'BP calls into question existing ESG research and shows the need for third-party information: The oil major was a high risk, reputation concern before the Gulf of Mexico spill', Responsible Investor, 8 September 2010; www.responsible-investor.com/home/article/rep_risk [requires subscription].

17 Swartz, *op. cit.*

18 Tom Stabile, 'Architects of a "Social Investment Data Engine"', *Financial Times Online*, 11 April 2010; www.ft.com/cms/s/0/e297b7de-440b-11df-9235-00144feab49a.html [requires subscription]. Also available at www.globalimpactinvestingnetwork.org/cgi-bin/iowa/resources/clipping/83.html.

19 *Ibid.*

20 SustainAbility, 'Influencing Power', SustainAbility and WWF-UK, 19 July 2005; www.sustainability.com/library/influencing-power. See also SustainAbility, 'Coming in from the Cold', SustainAbility and WWF-UK, 20 June 2007; www.sustainability.com/library/coming-in-from-the-cold; Jem Bendell and Kate Kearins, 'The "Political Bottom Line": The Emerging Dimension to Corporate Responsibility for Sustainable Development', *Business Strategy and the Environment* 14.6 (November/December 2005): 372-83; and finally United Nations Global Compact, *Blue Print for Sustainability Leadership* (UN Global Compact, 2010; www.unglobalcompact.org/docs/news_events/8.1/Blueprint.pdf).

21 Daniel Brooksbank, 'European Analysts Call for ESG Reporting Link to IFRS', *Responsible Investor Online*, 14 May 2010; www.responsible-investor.com/home/article/european_analysts_call_for_esg. Requires Subscription.

22 Matthew J. Kiernan, 'Around the World in 75 Minutes: What's New with ESG?', *SRI in the Rockies 2010*, Tucson, CD, 27 October 2009; www.sriconference.com/2009/agendaDetail.jsp?eventId=292.

23 Bethany McLean and Peter Elkind, *The Smartest Guys in the Room: The Amazing Rise and Scandalous Fall of Enron* (New York: Array, 2003).

24 Jem Bendell, Ian Doyle and Nicky Black, 'World Review', *Journal of Corporate Citizenship* 37 (May 2010; www.greenleaf-publishing.com/jcc37).

25 Jem Bendell, *Barricades and Boardrooms: A Contemporary History of the Corporate Accountability Movement* (Programme Paper 13; Geneva: UNRISD, 2004).

26 R.P. Siegel, 'When Pigs Fly: Halliburton Makes the Dow Jones Sustainability Index', Triple Pundit, 2010; www.triplepundit.com/2010/09/when-pigs-fly-halliburton-makes-the-dow-jones-sustainability-index.

27 Jeff Swartz, 'How to Make Socially Responsible Investments Pay Off', *Halalfocus.com*, 31 August 2009; halalfocus.net/2009/08/31/how-to-make-socially-responsible-investments-pay-off.

28 Gill Wadsworth, 'Investors must do more to drive sustainability, CEOs say', Investment and Pensions Europe, 25 June 2010; www.ipe.com/news/investors-must-do-more-to-drive-sustainability-ceos-say_35850.php [with login]. Also available at www.ipe.com/articles/print.php?id=35850.

29 Paul Hawken, 'The Truth About Ethical Investing', *AlterNet*, 29 April 2005; www.alternet.org/story/21888. This reference is no longer accessible but the same article can be found at www.organicconsumers.org/BTC/hawken051205.cfm.

30 Taylor Gray, 'Investing for the Environment? The Limits of the UN Principles of Responsible Investment', Social Science Research Network, 8 June 2009; papers.ssrn.com/sol3/papers.cfm?abstract_id=1416123.

31 Lachlan Colquhoun, 'Australia Acts on Responsible Investment', *Financial Times Online*, 13 December 2009; www.ft.com/intl/cms/s/0/feef919a-e687-11de-98b1-00144feab49a.html.

32 Raj Thamotheram, 'Changing the System: Why Sell Side Research Must Improve', *Responsible Investor Online*, 1 May 2008; www.responsible-investor.com/home/article/raj1/P0 [requires subscription].

33 Reiner, *op. cit.*

34 Daniel Brooksbank, 'Norwegian Global Fun Takes €1.1bn Hit on BP', *Responsible Investor Online*, 13 August 2010; www.responsible-investor.com/home/article/norwegian_global_fund_takes_11bn_hit_on_bp [requires subscription].

35 Daniel Brooksbank, 'New Global Sustainability Ratings Set to Launch', *Responsible Investor Online*, 12 April 2010; www.responsible-investor.com/home/article/new_global_sustainability_ratings_initiative_launch [requires subscription].

36 *Ibid.*

37 To see a development of this idea and implications for the goals of CSR, see Jem Bendell, *The Corporate Responsibility Movement: Five Years of Global Corporate Responsibility Analysis from Lifeworth, 2001–2005* (Sheffield, UK; Greenleaf Publishing, 2009; www.greenleaf-publishing.com/crmovement).

4Q2010

1 Rakesh Khurana, *From Higher Aims to Hired Hands: The Social Transformation of American Business Schools and the Unfulfilled Promise of Management as a Profession* (Princeton, NJ: Princeton University Press, 2007).

2 UNDP, 'The Real Wealth of Nations: Pathways to Human Development', *Human Development Report* 2010—20th Anniversary Edition; hdr.undp.org/en/reports/global/hdr2010.

3 Inequality-adjusted Human Development Index (IHDI): hdr.undp.org/en/statistics/ihdi.

4 Jem Bendell, Hanniah Tariq, Ian Doyle and Janna Greve, 'World Review', *Journal of Corporate Citizenship* 38 (2010); www.greenleaf-publishing.com/jcc38.

5 'Inequality and Crisis', *The Economist Online*, 14 December 2010; www.economist.com/blogs/freeexchange/2010/12/income_inequality.

6 Michael Kumhof and Romain Ranciere, 'Inequality, Leverage and Crises' (International Monetary Fund Working Paper; WP/10/268, 2010; www.imf.org/external/pubs/ft/wp/2010/wp10268.pdf).

7 Drake Bennett, 'The Inequality Delusion: Americans think the US has far more income equality than it has. They want it to be even fairer. Yet they hate the policies that would make it so', *Bloomberg Business Week Online*, 21 October 2010; www.businessweek. com/magazine/content/10_44/b4201008238184.htm.

8 (One author's translation.) Marc Thibodeau, 'Controverse en France: élitistes, les grandes écoles?', *La Presse Online*, 9 Janvier 2010; www.cyberpresse.ca/international/ europe/201001/08/01-937530-controverse-en-france-elitistes-les-grandes-ecoles-. php [in French]. Angela Charlton, 'French schools at odds over putting poor into top schools', *Associated Press*, 6 January 2010; abcnews.go.com/International/ wireStory?id=9490927 [in English].

9 'Sabeg furieux contre les grandes écoles', *Figaro Online*, 4 January 2010; www.lefigaro. fr/flash-actu/2010/01/04/01011-20100104FILWWW00583-sabeg-furieux-contre-les- grandes-ecoles.php [in French].

10 Charlton, *op. cit.*

11 Maryline Baumard, 'Ecole: l'échec du modèle français d'égalité des chances', *LeMonde. fr*, 7 January 2010; www.lemonde.fr/societe/article/2010/02/11/ecole-l-echec-du- modele-francais-d-egalite-des-chances_1304257_3224.html [in French].

12 The word *cadres* to which this study refers has no direct translation in English. The term 'professional' has been used to designate professions such as management, lawyers, engineers, doctors, economists, teachers, academics, etc. More precisely, 'professional' refers to non-manual work.

13 François Dubet, 'Les Paradoxes de l'égalité des chances', *Observatoire des inégalités*, 7 January 2010; www.lemonde.fr/societe/article/2010/02/11/ecole-l-echec-du-modele- francais-d-egalite-des-chances_1304257_3224.html [in French].

14 Charlton, *op. cit.*

15 *Ibid.*

16 'Work Remains to Ensure Equality in Grandes Écoles', *International Herald Tribune*, 19 December 2010; www.nytimes.com/2010/12/20/world/europe/20iht-educBrief.html.

17 One author's communication with Philip McLaughlin, Dean at BEM, 26 May 2010.

18 Unis-Cité, 'Qui Sommes Nous?'; www.uniscite.fr/qui-sommes-nous-notre-mission. php [in French].

19 E-tud.com, 'BEM intègre le service civil volontaire au sein de son programme ESC Grande Ecole', January 2010; actualite.e-tud.com/1221-bem-integre-le-service-civil- volontaire-au-sein-de-son-programme-esc-grande-ecol [in French].

20 One author's communication with Philip McLaughlin, Dean at BEM, 26 May 2010.

21 Personal correspondence with Professor Swar Kranti at Welingkar, 27 April 2010.

22 Emmanuel Raufflet, 'Mobilizing Business for Post-Secondary Education: CIDA University, South Africa', *Journal of Business Ethics* 89 (2010): 191-202.

23 *Ibid.*

24 (Author's translation.) François Dubet, 'Les Paradoxes de l'égalité des chances', *Observatoire des inégalités*, 7 January 2010; www.inegalites.fr/spip.php?article1170&id_ mot=31 [in French].

25 FDC and EFMD, *Strategic Movements in Business Education* (Brazil: Fundação Dom Cabral—FDC, in partnership with the European Foundation for Management Development, 2010; www.fdc.org.br/efmdconference/Pages/default.aspx. This reference is no longer available. For a similar reflection on this theme, see 'University fee rise has an impact—but is the issue as simple as it seems?', *The Guardian Online*, 9 August 2012; www.google.com/search?q=rising+university+fees+spcial+role&ie=utf- 8&oe=utf-8&aq=t&rls=org.mozilla:fr:official&client=firefox-a.

26 Lisa Foderaro, 'Growth in CUNY Chancellor's salary outpaces rise in faculty's pay', *New York Times Online*, 13 May 2010; www.nytimes.com/2010/05/14/nyregion/14cunypay. html.

27 *Ibid.*

28 David Leigh and Rob Evans, 'Salaries soar for heads of British universities', *The Guardian Online*, 14 March 2010; www.guardian.co.uk/education/2010/mar/14/ university-heads-vice-chancellor-salaries.

29 Aspen Institute official website: www.beyondgreypinstripes.org.

30 UN Global Compact official website: www.unglobalcompact.org.

31 World Business School Council for Sustainable Business official website: www.wbscsb. com.

32 The Globally Responsible Leadership Initiative official website: www.GRLI.org.

33 These steps were identified by Jem Bendell through his work in advising Griffith Business School on implementing the mission it adopted in 2006 to be a responsible business school committed to sustainability and community.

34 GRLI, '50+20 report on the future of business education to be presented at Rio+20 Earth Summit'; www.grli.org/index.php/component/content/article/53-latest-news- /248-5020-report-on-the-future-of-business-education-.

35 'The Social Media Sustainability Index', *Social Media Influence Online*, 16 November 2010; socialmediainfluence.com/2010/11/16/the-social-media-sustainability-index.

36 D. Goleman, *Ecological Intelligence: How knowing the hidden impacts of what we buy can change everything* (New York: Random House, 2009).

37 'Be afraid: Companies must adapt to a world where no secret is safe', *The Economist Online*, 10 December 2010; www.economist.com/node/17680643#footnote1.

38 N.D. Schwartz, 'Facing threat from WikiLeaks, bank plays defense', *New York Times Online*, 2 January 2011; www.nytimes.com/2011/01/03/business/03wikileaks-bank. html.

39 J. Assange, 'Why the world needs WikiLeaks', *TED*, July 2010; www.ted.com/talks/ julian_assange_why_the_world_needs_wikileaks.html.

40 'The Iraq Archive: The Strands of a War', The War Logs, *New York Times Online*, 22 October 2010; www.nytimes.com/2010/10/23/world/middleast/23intro.html. See also Nick Davies, Jonathan Steele and David Leigh, 'Iraq war logs: Secret files show how US ignored torture', *The Guardian Online*, 22 October 2010; www.guardian.co.uk/ world/2010/oct/22/iraq-war-logs-military-leaks.

41 Scott Shane and Andrew Lehren, 'Leaked cables offer raw look at US diplomacy', *New York Times Online*, 28 November 2010; www.nytimes.com/2010/11/29/ world/29cables.html?_r=1. See also David Leigh, 'The US embassy cables leak sparks global diplomatic crisis', *The Guardian Online*, 22 November 2010; www.guardian. co.uk/world/2010/nov/28/us-embassy-cable-leak-diplomacy-crisis.

42 Nick Davies and David Leigh, 'Afghanistan War Logs: Massive leak of secret files exposes truth of occupation', *The Guardian Online*, 25 July 2010; www.guardian.co.uk/ world/2010/jul/25/afghanistan-war-logs-military-leaks.

43 M. Hickman, 'WikiLeaks vs The Machine', *The Independent*, 9 December 2010; www. independent.co.uk/news/world/americas/wikileaks-vs-the-machine-2155031.html.

44 'Wikileaks and the creed of guerrilla transparency', *The Economist Online*, 13 December 2010; www.economist.com/blogs/democracyinamerica/2010/12/ future_wikileaks.

45 Paul C. Godfrey, Craig B. Merrill and Jared M. Hansen, 'The Relationship between Corporate Social Responsibility and Shareholder Value: An Empirical Test of the Risk Management Hypothesis', *Strategic Management Journal* 30 (2009): 425-45.

46 Ed Vulliamy, 'Julian Assange: "How do you attack an organisation? You attack its leadership"', *The Guardian Online*, 30 January 2011; www.guardian.co.uk/media/2011/jan/30/julian-assange-interview.

47 'Twitter is censoring the discussion of #Wikileaks', *Safety First*, 5 December 2010; bubbloy.wordpress.com/2010/12/05/twitter-is-censoring-the-discussion-of-wikileaks.

48 M. Gladwell, 'Small Change: Why the revolution will not be Tweeted', *New Yorker Online*, 4 October 2010; www.newyorker.com/reporting/2010/10/04/101004fa_fact_gladwell.

49 B. Feder, 'They weren't careful what they hoped for', *New York Times Online*, 29 May 2002; www.nytimes.com/2002/05/29/nyregion/they-weren-t-careful-what-they-hoped-for.html.

50 *Wikipedia* defines *slacktivism* as 'a pejorative term that describes "feel-good" measures, in support of an issue or social cause, that have little or no practical effect other than to make the person doing it feel satisfaction' (4 January 2011).

51 *Good Guide* official website: www.goodguide.com/about/mobile.

52 *JustMeans* official website: www.justmeans.com.

53 *JustMeans* official website: www.justmeans.com/companies/crd-analytics/214662.html.

54 *OpenEyeWorld* official website: openeyeworld.com.

55 Scott Douglas, 'The astonishing numbers in the Kit Kat social media case and why business should take notice', *Holyroodpr Online*, 22 March 2010; www.holyroodpr.co.uk/blog/entry/the_astonishing_numbers_in_the_kit_kat_social_media_case_and_why_business_s.

56 P. Courtice, 'Interview of José Lopez by Polly Courtice, Director of the Cambridge Programme for Sustainability Leadership', 17 June 2010.

57 Nick Mackie, 'Facebook for farmers: Technology empowers China's rural workers', *BBC Online*, 19 December 2010; www.bbc.co.uk/news/business-12010549.

58 Jérôme Ballet and Aurélie Carimentrand, 'Fair Trade and the Depersonalization of Ethics', *Journal of Business Ethics* 92.2 (April 2010): 317-30.

59 *Patagonia: The Footprint Chronicles*; www.patagonia.com/us/footprint.

60 Innovation Exchange; www.managementexchange.com/about-the-mix.

61 B. Baue and M. Murninghan, 'The Accountability Web: Weaving Corporate Accountability and Interactive Technology', *Harvard Business School Working Paper* 58 (May 2010).

62 W. Visser, *The Age of Responsibility: CSR 2.0 and the New DNA of Business* (London: Wiley, 2011). See also a paper of the same title in *Journal of Business Systems, Governance and Ethics* 5.3 (Special Issue on Responsibility for Social and Environmental Issues, November 2010): 7-22.

63 Visser, *The Age of Responsibility*.

64 Imogen Wall, 'After Disaster: Information for Life', *Open Democracy Online*, 26 October 2008; www.opendemocracy.net/article/after-disaster-information-for-life.

65 Alyson Warhurst, 'Disaster Prevention: A Role for Business', *Prevention Consortium Online*, August 2006; reliefweb.int/sites/reliefweb.int/files/resources/A146217732AA5FE0C12572DE00484B85-Full_Report.pdf.

66 'Small Equity Initiative to Pilot Private Sector Disaster Reduction', *Marketwire Online*, 14 October 2010; www.marketwire.com/press-release/Small-Equity-Initiative-to-Pilot-Private-Sector-Disaster-Reduction-Program-OTCQB-NVAE-1335196.htm.

67 'Governments and private sector urged to reduce disaster losses together', UNISDR, 13 October 2010; www.unisdr.org/news/v.php?id=15869.

68 UNISDR, *Living with Risk: A Global Review of Disaster Reduction Initiatives* (UNISDR, 2004): 17; www.unisdr.org/we/inform/publications/657.

69 ICOR: Business Continuity Management; www.theicor.org/disc/bcm.html. See also David Honour, 'Defining Business Continuity', *Continuity Central Online*, 29 September 2006; www.continuitycentral.com/feature0398.htm.

70 Talking Business Continuity, 'When disaster strikes, it's time to implement business continuity plans', *BSi Online*, 24 November 2010; www.talkingbusinesscontinuity.com/bcm-news-and-events/news/when-disaster-strikes-its-time-to-implement-business-continuity-plans.aspx.

71 CSR Asia Summit 2010; www.csr-asia.com/summit2010/issue.php#2b.

72 Sophie Fabrégat. 'Catastrophes naturelles: Des phénomènes en augmentation et amplifiés par l'homme', *Actu-Environnement Online* 11 August 2010; www.actu-environnement.com/ae/news/inondations-coulees-boue-10827.php4#xtor=EPR-1 [in French].

73 Nick Wadhams 'Iceland volcano: Kenya's farmers losing $1.3m a day in flights chaos', *Guardian Online*, 18 April 2010; www.guardian.co.uk/world/2010/apr/18/iceland-volcano-kenya-farmers.

74 'Volcanic ash: Tesco delivers Kenyan produce via Spain', *BBC News Online*, 20 April 2010; news.bbc.co.uk/2/hi/business/8631286.stm.

75 'Community-Based Food Security Systems: Local Solutions for Ending Chronic Hunger and Promoting Rural Development', *Interpares Online*; www.interpares.ca/en/publications/pdf/food_security_brief.pdf.

Thematic index*

This is an index of industry *sectors*, corporate responsibility *topics*, organisational *functions*, featured *persons* and *organisations*, to help you navigate this volume. The industry *sectors* are based on the international classification benchmark, with some combinations and additions to include non-commercial sectors. The organisational *functions* are those most typically identified by management schools. The corporate responsibility *topics* are adapted from the topic headings identified in the ISO 26000 standard. Some of those headings are combined and some are added, such as 'fair taxation', 'fair supplier relations' and 'employee ethics'. The topics are identified in the way they present themselves to management. Often the reviews discussed economy-wide issues, such as trade regulation and global governance, and the way those issues relate to a company is through the management's 'political involvement'. Definitions for the specific terms used in this index can be found online in a 'glossary of terms' at www.lifeworth.com.

Key

---

* This thematic index was prepared with the help of Lifeworth Senior Associate, Ian Doyle.

Functions

Accounting, Auditing, Verification	6, 25, 56, 68, 69, 71, 72, 87
Administration and Operations	25, 28, 43, 71, 83, 102
Communications	2, 9, 74
Direction, Strategy or Planning	2, 6, 7, 18, 23, 27, 41, 42, 68, 73, 80, 82, 83, 85, 86, 87, 88, 89, 90, 91
Evaluation or Review	71
Finance	12, 13, 18, 20, 27, 30, 31, 32, 40, 46, 51, 54, 55, 56, 61, 62, 68, 83, 88, 89
Human Resources	28, 83, 86, 87
Innovation or Design	3, 73, 82, 83, 90, 91
IT	9, 101
Legal	6, 87
Programme, Project or Account Management	
Purchasing or Supply	2, 3, 19, 23, 43, 65, 71, 72, 73, 82, 102
Research (Corporate)	83
Sales	

Organisational functions not discussed in this volume are 'Specialist Practice', such as a medical professional, and 'Public Service', such as diplomacy, military or law enforcement. General staff within other specialist sectors, such as the clergy, have been categorised as either 'Operations' or 'Communications'.

Sectors

Aerospace, Defence or Security	
Agriculture or Fishing	2, 3, 26, 29, 54
Alternative or Renewable Energy	26, 27, 64, 65, 83
Automobiles	23, 26, 27, 66
Banking, Finance or Insurance	12, 13, 18, 20, 27, 30, 31, 32, 40, 46, 51, 54, 55, 56, 58, 60, 61, 62, 68, 78, 79, 80, 88, 89, 92-99
Business Services or Consulting	68, 89
Chemicals	73
Clothing, Footwear or Accessories	19, 41, 42, 43, 82
Construction or Materials	10, 23, 86

Key sectors not discussed in this volume are 'Biotechnology', 'Utilities', 'Specialised Consumer Services', 'Real Estate', 'Recycling or Disposal', 'Household or Leisure Goods', and 'Forestry or Paper'. All of these are discussed in 'World Reviews' in the *Journal of Corporate Citizenship* subsequent to 2005.

Topics

Capacity-Building	2, 3, 13, 52, 73, 90, 91, 102
Clean Technology	26, 65, 66,
Climate Change	2, 11, 15, 24, 26, 27, 66, 76, 77, 78, 79, 80, 81
Community Involvement and Philanthropy	4, 40, 70, 73, 87
Consumer Issues	1, 2, 5, 9, 41, 42, 50, 52
Corporate Governance and Risk	6, 7, 8, 46, 47, 48, 62, 68, 70, 85, 86, 87, 88, 89
Corruption/Anti-Corruption	6, 8, 10, 41, 46, 47, 48
Economic Inequality	66, 84, 100
Education or Culture	36, 37, 38, 45, 100
Employment Creation	52, 73, 82, 90, 91
Employee Ethics	46
Fair Competition	2, 3, 71, 73, 78
Fair Marketing	1, 35, 50, 74
Fair Supplier Relations	2, 3, 41, 82, 72, 73
Fair Taxation	68
Gender, Diversity and Non-Discrimination	46, 51, 100
General Environment	2, 4, 5, 21, 22, 25, 26, 27, 29, 38, 50
Health or Safety at work	5
Human Development	3, 4, 71, 72, 73, 82, 90, 91, 102
Human Rights and Security	4, 5, 7, 46, 86, 87, 102
Intellectual Property and Access to Technology	5, 73
Labour Practices	3, 16, 19, 23, 28, 39, 41, 43, 52, 46, 73, 82, 86, 87
Political Involvement	1, 2, 6, 54, 55, 56, 67, 76, 77, 78, 80, 89, 94
Pollution Prevention	24, 25, 50, 65
Public Health	1, 4, 5
Responsible Consumption	15, 22, 35, 50, 52
Responsible Investment	6, 12, 13, 20, 30, 31, 32, 40, 51, 54, 55, 56, 58, 61, 62, 65, 68, 69, 85, 88, 92-99
Responsible Procurement	48, 65
Social Development	2, 3, 4, 48, 71, 72, 73, 82, 84, 100, 102
Social Dialogue	71, 72
Social Enterprise	3, 39, 44, 63, 73, 82, 85, 90

Stakeholder Engagement	6, 8, 45, 46, 71, 72
Sustainable Enterprise	44
Sustainable Mobility	66
Sustainable Resource Use	5, 50, 66, 74, 82
Sustainability Reporting	6, 48, 49, 53, 63, 71, 87

Key sectors not discussed in this volume are 'Humanitarian Support', 'Nutrition', 'Consumer Awareness', and 'Conservation'. All of these are discussed in 'World Reviews' in the *Journal of Corporate Citizenship* subsequent to 2005.

Persons

Organisations

For Product Safety Concerns and Information please contact our EU
representative GPSR@taylorandfrancis.com Taylor & Francis Verlag GmbH,
Kaufingerstraße 24, 80331 München, Germany

Printed and bound by CPI Group (UK) Ltd, Croydon, CR0 4YY
08/05/2025
01864417-0001